**Gary Cambers and Steve Sibley**

Cambridge IGCSE®

# Geography
## Coursebook

CAMBRIDGE UNIVERSITY PRESS

## CAMBRIDGE
### UNIVERSITY PRESS

University Printing House, Cambridge CB2 8BS, United Kingdom

One Liberty Plaza, 20th Floor, New York, NY 10006, USA

477 Williamstown Road, Port Melbourne, VIC 3207, Australia

4843/24, 2nd Floor, Ansari Road, Daryaganj, Delhi – 110002, India

79 Anson Road, #06–04/06, Singapore 079906

Cambridge University Press is part of the University of Cambridge.

It furthers the University's mission by disseminating knowledge in the pursuit of education, learning and research at the highest international levels of excellence.

Information on this title: education.cambridge.org

© Cambridge University Press 2015

This publication is in copyright. Subject to statutory exception
and to the provisions of relevant collective licensing agreements,
no reproduction of any part may take place without the written
permission of Cambridge University Press.

First published 2010
Second edition 2015
20 19 18 17 16 15 14 13 12 11 10 9 8 7

Printed in Spain by GraphyCems

*A catalogue record for this publication is available from the British Library*

ISBN 978-1-107-45894-9 Paperback

Cambridge University Press has no responsibility for the persistence or accuracy of URLs for external or third-party internet websites referred to in this publication, and does not guarantee that any content on such websites is, or will remain, accurate or appropriate.

..................................................................................................

NOTICE TO TEACHERS IN THE UK
It is illegal to reproduce any part of this work in material form (including photocopying and electronic storage) except under the following circumstances:
(i) where you are abiding by a licence granted to your school or institution by the Copyright Licensing Agency;
(ii) where no such licence exists, or where you wish to exceed the terms of a licence, and you have gained the written permission of Cambridge University Press;
(iii) where you are allowed to reproduce without permission under the provisions of Chapter 3 of the Copyright, Designs and Patents Act 1988, which covers, for example, the reproduction of short passages within certain types of educational anthology and reproduction for the purposes of setting examination questions.

..................................................................................................

IGCSE© is the registered trademark of Cambridge International Examinations.

..................................................................................................

The past paper questions on pages 267–282 are reproduced with the permission of Cambridge International Examinations.

..................................................................................................

DISCLAIMER
Cambridge International Examinations bears no responsibility for the example answers to questions taken from its past papers which are contained in this publication. In examination, the way the marks are awarded may be different.

..................................................................................................

The questions on pages 58–61, 128–131, 230–237, 254–264, and example answers, marks awarded and or comments that appear on pages 267–282 were written by the authors and are not the responsibility of Cambridge University Press.
In examination, the way the marks are awarded may be different.

# Contents

| | | |
|---|---|---:|
| **Introduction** | | vii |

## Part A
## Geographical Themes   1
World map – Location of Case Studies   2

## Theme 1 Population and Settlement   3

| | | |
|---|---|---:|
| Topic 1 | World population increase | 4 |
| Topic 2 | Over-population and under-population | 6 |
| | Case Study: Over-population – Nigeria | 8 |
| | Case Study: Under-population – Australia | 10 |
| Topic 3 | Causes of a change in population size | 12 |
| Topic 4 | Population change | 14 |
| | Case Study: High rate of natural population growth – Niger | 16 |
| | Case Study: Population decline – Russia | 18 |
| Topic 5 | Population policies | 20 |
| Topic 6 | Population migration | 22 |
| Topic 7 | The impacts of migration | 24 |
| | Case Study: An international migration – Qatar | 26 |
| Topic 8 | Finding out about the population | 28 |
| | Case Study: A country with high dependency – Italy | 30 |
| Topic 9 | Factors influencing population density | 32 |
| | Case Study: High population density – Japan | 34 |
| | Case Study: Low population density – Namibia | 36 |
| Topic 10 | Settlement patterns | 38 |
| Topic 11 | Settlement sites, growth and functions | 40 |
| Topic 12 | Settlement hierarchies | 42 |
| | Case Study: Settlement and service provision in Sardinia | 44 |
| Topic 13 | Urban land use | 46 |
| Topic 14 | Urban problems and solutions | 48 |
| | Case Study: An urban area – Atlanta, USA | 50 |
| Topic 15 | Rapid urban growth | 52 |
| Topic 16 | Impacts of urban growth | 54 |
| | Case Study: Urbanisation in Peru – Lima | 56 |
| **Exam-Style Questions** | | **58** |
| **Global Theme 1 – HIV/AIDS** | | **62** |

# Cambridge IGCSE Geography

## Theme 2 The Natural Environment — 63

| | | |
|---|---|---|
| Topic 17 | Types and features of earthquakes and volcanoes | 64 |
| Topic 18 | Plate tectonics | 66 |
| Topic 19 | Causes and effects of earthquakes and volcanoes | 68 |
| Topic 20 | Volcanoes present hazards and opportunities | 70 |
| Topic 21 | Reducing the impacts | 72 |
| | Case Study: An earthquake – Haiti | 74 |
| | Case Study: A volcano – Mount Sinabung, Indonesia | 76 |
| Topic 22 | Rivers and drainage basins | 78 |
| Topic 23 | The work of rivers | 80 |
| Topic 24 | River landforms – 1 | 82 |
| Topic 25 | River landforms – 2 | 84 |
| Topic 26 | Rivers – hazards and opportunities | 86 |
| Topic 27 | Managing river flooding | 88 |
| | Case Study: The Elbe river | 90 |
| Topic 28 | The work of the sea | 92 |
| Topic 29 | Coastal landforms created by erosion | 94 |
| Topic 30 | Coastal landforms created by deposition | 96 |
| Topic 31 | Coral reefs and mangrove swamps | 98 |
| Topic 32 | Hazards and opportunities | 100 |
| Topic 33 | Managing coastal erosion | 102 |
| | Case Study: An area of coastline – Mauritius | 104 |
| Topic 34 | Collecting weather data – 1 | 106 |
| Topic 35 | Collecting weather data – 2 | 108 |
| Topic 36 | Using weather data | 110 |
| Topic 37 | Using weather and climate data | 112 |
| Topic 38 | The equatorial climate | 114 |
| Topic 39 | Tropical rainforest ecosystems | 116 |
| Topic 40 | Rainforest deforestation | 118 |
| | Case Study: The tropical rainforest – Ecuador | 120 |
| Topic 41 | Hot desert climates | 122 |
| Topic 42 | Hot desert ecosystems | 124 |
| | Case Study: A hot desert – the Sahara and Mali | 126 |

**Exam-Style Questions** — 128

**Global Theme 2 – Reducing Carbon Emissions** — 132

## Theme 3 Economic Development — 133

| | | |
|---|---|---|
| Topic 43 | Indicators of development | 134 |
| Topic 44 | Identifying inequalities | 136 |

| | | |
|---|---|---|
| Topic 45 | Classifying production | 138 |
| Topic 46 | Employment structure varies | 140 |
| Topic 47 | Globalisation | 142 |
| | Case Study: A transnational corporation – Nokia, Finland | 144 |
| Topic 48 | Agricultural systems | 146 |
| | Case Study: An arable farm in Lincolnshire, UK | 148 |
| Topic 49 | Food shortages | 150 |
| | Case Study: Food shortages in Darfur, Sudan | 152 |
| Topic 50 | Industrial systems | 154 |
| Topic 51 | Industrial location | 156 |
| | Case Study: The Pakistan steel complex at Pipri, near Karachi | 158 |
| Topic 52 | The growth of tourism | 160 |
| Topic 53 | The benefits and disadvantages of tourism | 162 |
| Topic 54 | Managing tourism for sustainability | 164 |
| | Case Study: An area where tourism is important – Dubai, UAE | 166 |
| Topic 55 | Energy use varies | 168 |
| Topic 56 | Nuclear power or renewables | 170 |
| | Case Study: Energy supply in Iceland | 172 |
| Topic 57 | Using water | 174 |
| Topic 58 | Managing water | 176 |
| | Case Study: Water supply in Lesotho | 178 |
| Topic 59 | Economic activities pose threats | 180 |
| Topic 60 | Managing for sustainable development | 182 |
| Topic 61 | Conserving natural resources | 184 |
| | Case Study: Fracking in California, USA | 186 |

**Exam-Style Questions** — **188**

**Global Theme 3 – Reduce, reuse, recycle** — **192**

# Part B
## Geographical Skills — 193

1. 1:50 000 Monsefu, Peru — 194
2. 1:50 000 Harare, Zimbabwe — 200
3. 1:25 000 North York Moors, UK — 206
4. 1:25 000 Montego Bay, Jamaica — 212
5. 1:25 000 Negara, Indonesia — 218
6. 1:50 000 Leicester, UK — 224

**Exam-Style Questions** — **230**

**Map skills checklist** — **238**

## Part C
## Geographical Enquiry 239
The Coursework Assignment 240
Topic 1 Investigating the CBD 242
Topic 2 Investigating rivers 244
Topic 3 Investigating tourism 246
Topic 4 Investigating weather 248
Fieldwork checklist 250

**The Alternative to Coursework** **253**

**Exam-Style Question 1** **254**

**Exam-Style Question 2** **260**

## Part D
## Preparing for examinations 265
Geographical Themes: Case Studies 266
Geographical Skills 270
The Alternative to Coursework 273

## Resources 283
### World map 284
### Glossary 286
### Index 290
### Acknowledgements 295

# Introduction

The IGCSE Geography textbook and CD have been extensively revised to prepare students for Cambridge IGCSE® Geography.

## Part A: Geographical Themes

Part A deals with the Cambridge syllabus Themes in the order in which they appear in the Cambridge syllabus. As the contents page shows, there is a close and deliberate link in Part A to the Cambridge syllabus. The following three themes are covered:

*Theme 1: Population and Settlement*
*Theme 2: The Natural Environment*
*Theme 3: Economic Development*

The authors have closely matched the content of this book to the Cambridge syllabus topics and to the bullet points within each topic which provide further guidance on what students should be able to do as part of their course. Teachers requested more specific guidance on case studies and in the Cambridge syllabus, specific case studies are listed at the end of each of the 19 topics. It is important for teachers to be aware that all of the listed content in each topic should be incorporated into the case studies that they use.

The case studies come from 25 different countries, most of which have CIE Centres where the IGCSE Geography syllabus is studied. Centres that have been requesting resources to prepare students more effectively for this important part of the syllabus will find a wide range of examples to use. All are resource-based and involve problem-solving and free-response writing as required.

At the end of each Theme there are four full examples of exam-style questions. Each question has a part (a) and (b) with resources to respond to, followed by the case study. The students can use the examples provided in the Themes in the book or others they have been taught. Three global issues are also studied at the end of each Theme and a world map showing countries is provided for reference along with time zones, which are relevant to examining in an international context.

## Part B: Geographical Skills

Paper 2 is mainly skills-based and tests a student's ability to handle geographical information, without requiring knowledge as in Paper 1. As the first question will always be based on a large-scale (1:25 000 or 1:50 000) topographical map of any area in the world, Part B of the textbook provides six examples of these maps from the UK (2), Peru, Zimbabwe, Jamaica and Indonesia. The new Cambridge syllabus allows for maps to be selected from anywhere in the world. For each example an extract of a map is provided with appropriate map skills questions. Further work continues to develop map skills, as well as dealing with topics of relevance which relate to the map extract.

Examples of exam-style questions, incorporating questions based on a topographical map of Ireland, are provided for practice at the end of Part B.

## Part C: Geographical Enquiry

For a variety of reasons, many Centres do not choose – or cannot carry out – coursework; however, some guidance is given in this book for those that may be considering it. Examples of coursework topics that may be undertaken in different countries are provided.

These suggest the type of fieldwork or coursework that teachers might consider introducing. The 'Route to Geographical Enquiry' that is used in the Cambridge syllabus has been adapted for use in the classroom and a world map illustrates 16 different coursework titles that could be used in schools in different countries of the world. Guidance is also given with ideas on how to carry out coursework in four topics – the CBD, Rivers, Tourism and the Weather. A fieldwork checklist is provided for teachers and students to ensure that complete coverage prepares students for coursework. With Health and Safety such an important part of planning and carrying out coursework, a page is devoted to different topics and safety issues in each that should be considered.

Paper 4 is taken by students as a written examination instead of carrying out coursework and/or fieldwork. Although the majority of Centres do choose Paper 4 as an alternative to coursework, it is important that teachers try to carry out some local fieldwork and Part C encourages this.

Two examples of exam-style questions are provided; these are repeated on the Student CD with lines for writing.

## Part D: Preparing for Examinations

This part of the book looks at sample questions taken from previous examination papers along with possible answers and illustrations of how they might be marked.

For Paper 1 the focus is on marking case studies as these count for 21 out of 75 marks on this paper. For each of the three Themes, one example question is provided. Each question is followed by three answers of different quality with a commentary on how they might be marked.

For Paper 2 a few selected questions that cover a range of skills are provided with various answers of different quality. A commentary on the possible marking follows.

For Paper 4 one whole question is provided and, again, a range of sample answers are followed by a commentary on their strengths and limitations.

## The Student CD

This is provided with the textbook and includes the following:

**Outline maps:** These are always useful for teachers to use with several tasks. Eleven outline maps are provided covering the major regions of the world. In addition a sheet of triangular graph paper is provided as this is difficult to obtain in many countries.

**Student sheets:** Photocopiable extension and support sheets are provided.

**Examples of exam-style questions**: all the sample questions from Parts A, B and C are provided with lines to write on so that students can practise answering them as they would in an examination situation.

**Glossary:** The glossary used in the textbook is repeated here for reference.

## The Teacher CD

This can be purchased separately from the textbook and Student CD. It contains answers to all the Tasks and exam-style questions in parts A, B and C.
It also contains advice on teaching the syllabus, including sample schemes of work and lesson plans.

# Part A

# Geographical Themes

Part A of this coursebook covers the three Geographical Themes set out in the Cambridge syllabus: Population and Settlement; The Natural Environment; and Economic Development. At the end of each theme there are four exam-style questions, written by the authors.

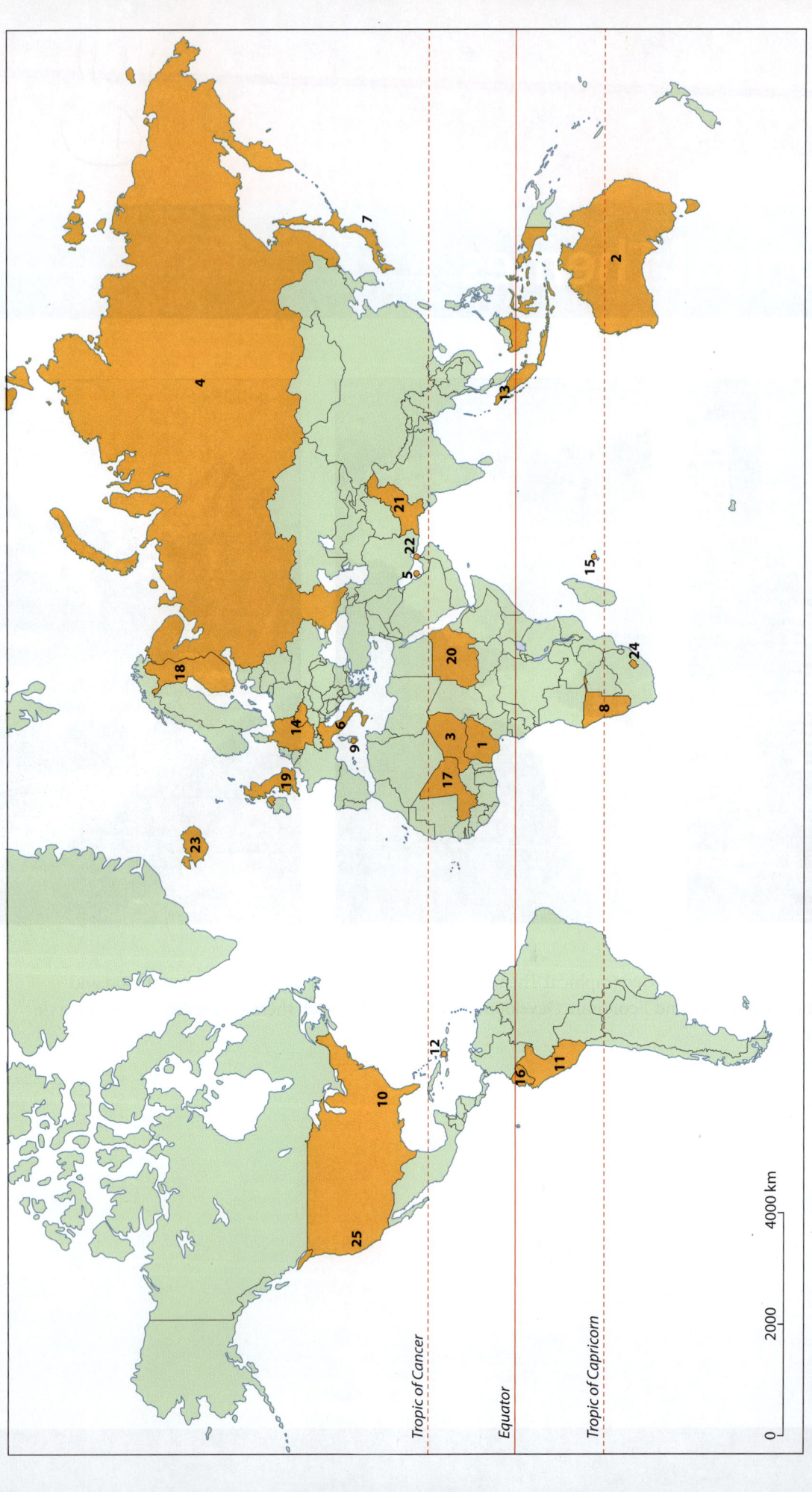

## The location of case studies used in PART A: GEOGRAPHICAL THEMES

1 Over-population: Nigeria (p.8)
2 Under-population: Australia (p.10)
3 Population growth: Niger (p.16)
4 Population decline: Russia (p.18)
5 International migration: Qatar (p.26)
6 High population dependency: Italy (p.30)
7 High population density: Japan (p.34)
8 Low population density: Namibia (p.36)
9 Settlement and services: Sardinia (p.44)
10 An urban area: Atlanta, USA (p.50)
11 Urbanisation: Peru, Lima (p.56)
12 An earthquake: Haiti (p.74)
13 A volcano: Mt Sinabung, Indonesia (p.76)
14 The Elbe river: Germany and Czech Republic (p.90)
15 A coastline: Mauritius (p.104)
16 Tropical rainforest: Ecuador (p.120)
17 A hot desert: Sahara and Mali (p.126)
18 Transnational corporation: Nokia, Finland (p.144)
19 An arable farm: Lincolnshire, UK (p.148)
20 Food shortages: Darfur, Sudan (p.152)
21 Pakistan steel at Pipri, Karachi (p.158)
22 Tourism: Dubai, UAE (p.166)
23 Energy supply in Iceland (p.172)
24 Water supply in Lesotho (p.178)
25 Fracking in California, USA (p.186)

# Theme 1:
# Population and Settlement

**Cambridge IGCSE Geography** — **Population Dynamics**

# 1 World population increase

## Population explosion

The population of the world is 'exploding'. It is growing by 78 million people every year, which means an extra 215 060 people every day. There are 150 more people now than there were one minute ago! If there are 30 people in your class, the world's population increases by this amount every 12 seconds.

Recently the United Nations (UN) released a report which said that the world's population was likely to be more than 10 billion people by 2100, over 3 billion more than live in the world today. It took until 1804 for the world to reach its first billion people, and a century more until it hit 2 billion in 1927. However, due to reductions in the death rates in many countries during the 20th century the population had risen to 6 billion in 1999 and by 2011 it had reached 7 billion.

The UN is forecasting that the world's population will reach 8 billion by 2025 and 10 billion by 2083, but these numbers are estimates. The size of the increase during the rest of the 21st century will depend on whether the number of deaths continues to fall and whether the number of births can be reduced in those parts of the world where they still remain much higher than death rates.

All of those extra people mean more living space will be needed, and many parts of our planet are already becoming more and more crowded. There will be a lot more mouths to feed and more water will be needed. More energy will be required and there will also be a lot more waste to dispose of. More people will mean that more transport is needed and more roads, railway lines and airports will need to be built.

**A** From 1 to 7 billion

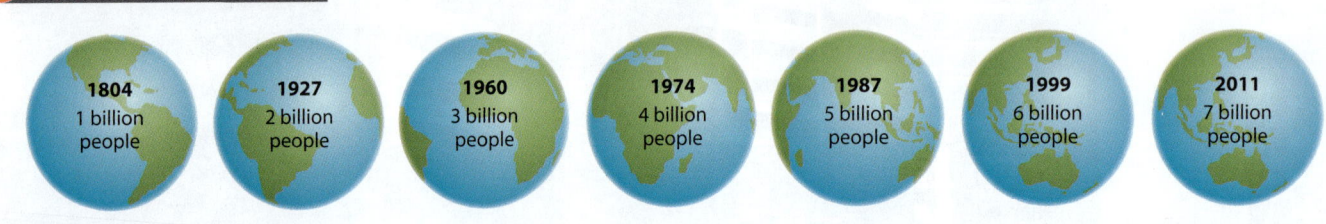

| 1804 | 1927 | 1960 | 1974 | 1987 | 1999 | 2011 |
|---|---|---|---|---|---|---|
| 1 billion people | 2 billion people | 3 billion people | 4 billion people | 5 billion people | 6 billion people | 7 billion people |

**B** World population growth

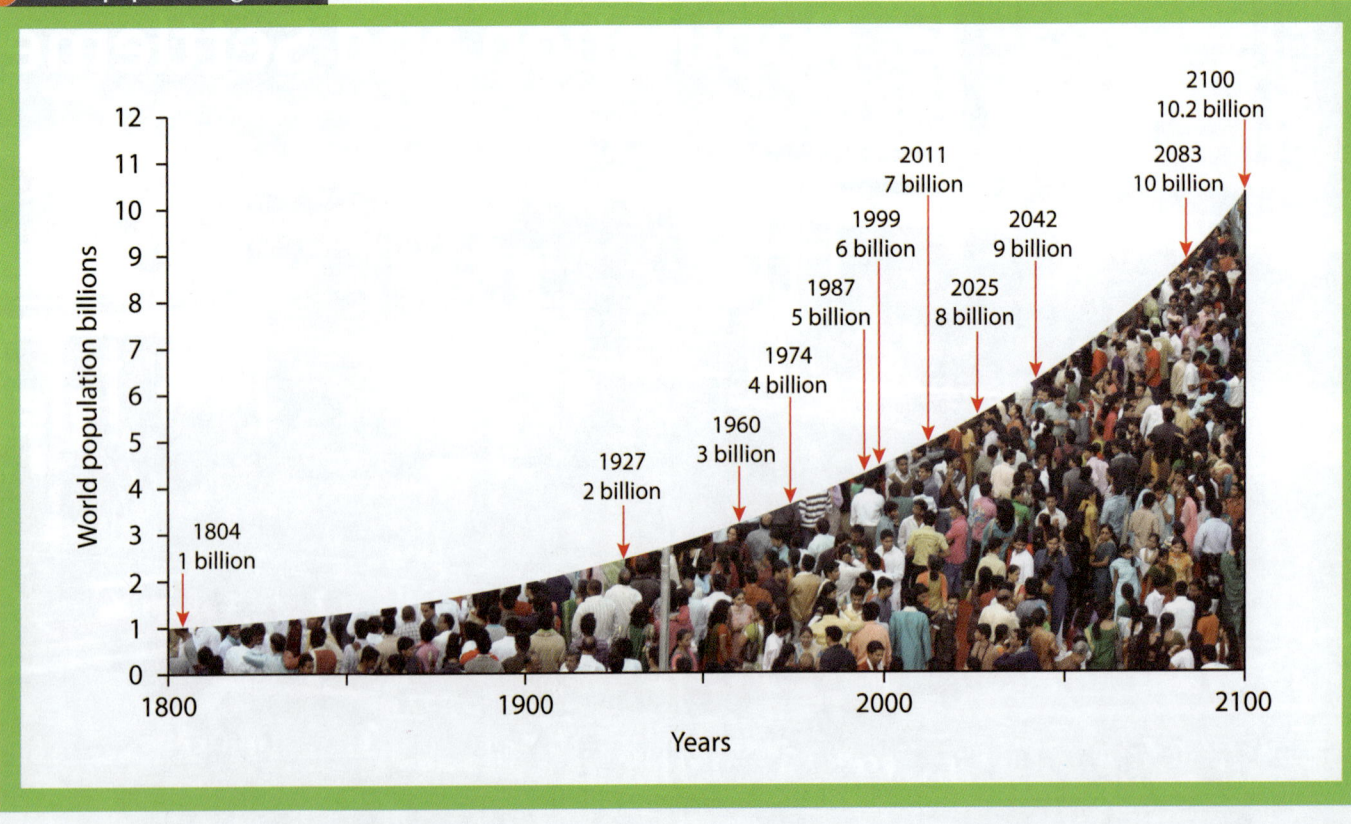

- 1804 – 1 billion
- 1927 – 2 billion
- 1960 – 3 billion
- 1974 – 4 billion
- 1987 – 5 billion
- 1999 – 6 billion
- 2011 – 7 billion
- 2025 – 8 billion
- 2042 – 9 billion
- 2083 – 10 billion
- 2100 – 10.2 billion

Theme 1: Topic 1

### C The world's 7 billionth baby

## POPULATION REACHES 7 BILLION

Countries around the globe marked the world's population reaching 7 billion on Monday, with lavish ceremonies for newborn infants symbolising the milestone and warnings that there may be too many humans for the planet's resources.

Festivities are being held worldwide, with a series of symbolic seven-billionth babies being born. The celebrations began in the Philippines, where baby Danica May Camacho was greeted with cheers at Manila's Jose Fabella Memorial Hospital.

'She looks so lovely,' the mother, Camille Galura, whispered as she cradled the baby, who was born about a month premature.

The baby was the second for Galura and her partner, Florante Camacho, a struggling driver who supports the family on a tiny salary.

Dr Eric Tayag of the Philippines' Department of Health said later that the birth came with a warning.

'Seven billion is a number we should think about deeply,' he said.

'We should really focus on the question of whether there will be food, clean water, shelter, education and a decent life for every child,' he said. 'If the answer is no, it would be better for people to look at easing the population explosion.'

*Adapted from NBC World News, 31 October 2011*

### TASK 1: Study Sources A and B

a How many years did it take the world's population to increase from:
- 1 to 2 billion?
- 6 to 7 billion?

b By 2100 there are likely to be over 3 billion more people living in the world than today. Choose **two** problems which you think will be caused by this. Explain why you think each of these problems will be difficult to solve.

c The figures for 2100 are estimates. Explain why it is difficult to predict exact population numbers for the future.

### TASK 2

World population growth is worked out by subtracting the number of people who die from the number who are born (births minus deaths).

With a partner, use the Internet to find information to explain the following facts.

- People lived longer on average at the end of the 20th century than at the start of it.
- In some parts of the world there has been no reduction in the numbers of children being born.

When you have found out the answers, write a paragraph in your own words to explain why world population grew so much in the 20th century.

### TASK 3: Study Sources C and D

a Do you agree with the warning given by Dr Eric Tayag? Explain your view.

b Suggest **three** things that could be done to 'ease the population explosion'.

c What message do you think the cartoon in Source D is giving about the world's 7 billionth baby?

### D Look what the stork has brought!

# Cambridge IGCSE Geography — Population Dynamics

## 2 Over-population and under-population

### Too many or too few?

**Source A** shows part of Jakarta, a city on the Indonesian island of Java, which is **over-populated**. **Source B** shows part of Australia, an **under-populated** country.

If the number of people living in an area is greater than the resources and technology available to maintain an adequate standard of living for the population, it is over-populated. A large population in a country does not mean that it is over-populated. For example, there are many people living in Germany but it has enough resources to support its population. However, some rural communities in parts of Africa are over-populated. This isn't because they are crowded with people but because there are not enough resources to support the population living there.

If the number of people living in an area is less than is needed to make full use of the resources available, then the area can be described as under-populated. For example, Australia has many resources but it is not using them fully. The country could support a higher population, which means that it is under-populated.

**A** Over-populated or …

**B** … under-populated?

**C** Population and resources

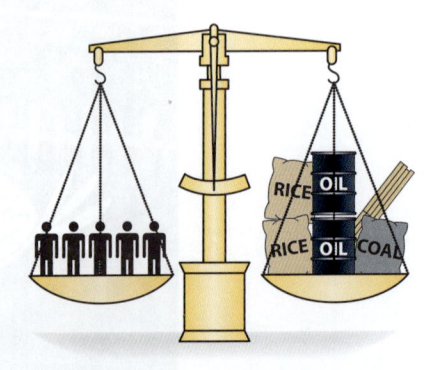

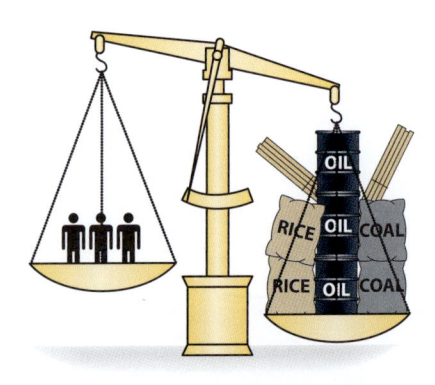

Over-population | Optimum population | Under-population

Theme 1: Topic 2

### D New index highlights most over-populated countries

Singapore is the world's most over-populated country, followed by Israel and Kuwait, according to a new league table ranking countries by their degree of over-population. The Overpopulation Index, published by the Optimum Population Trust to mark World Population Day, is thought to be the first international 'league table' to rank countries according to the sustainability of their populations. It examines data for over 130 individual countries and concludes that 77 of them are over-populated – they are consuming more resources than they are producing and are dependent on other countries. These include China and India, along with many Middle Eastern and European countries.

**Adapted from** *Population Matters*

### E Consequences of over-population and under-population

| Over-population | Under-population |
| --- | --- |
| not enough housing | shortage of workers |
| water and air pollution | low level of production |
| shortage of food and water | resources underused |
| high crime rates | high taxes |
| not enough health care and education | lack of government income |
| lack of employment | small market for goods and services |
| poverty | low value of exports |

### F Different causes of over-population

**TASK 1:** Study Sources A and B
Use the evidence in the photographs to help you write definitions for over-population and under-population.

**TASK 2:** Study Source C
a Use the diagrams to explain what is meant by optimum population.
b Explain why a country with a large population may not be over-populated.
c Explain why a country with a small population may be over-populated.

**TASK 3:** Study Source D
a Name the **three** most over-populated countries according to the Optimum Population Trust.
b Choose **one** of the countries named in Source D. Use the Internet to find out why your chosen country is over-populated.

**TASK 4:** Study Source E
Describe the problems caused by over-population and under-population. For each problem you should add extra detail to the simple ideas listed in Source E.

**TASK 5:** Study Source F
Explain how the two types of over-population shown have different causes.

7

# Cambridge IGCSE Geography | Population Dynamics

## Case Study
### Over-population – Nigeria

#### Nigeria's population – a silent killer

In 2013 Nigeria had a population of 175 million people with over 60% living on less than one dollar a day. It occupies only 3% of Africa but is home to over 15% of its people. Over-population means pressure on natural resources, high levels of air and water pollution, and a lack of essential services such as health care and education. Overcrowding and lack of accommodation have resulted in increased disease levels, inadequate sanitation and scarcity of resources for medical care and education. Lack of employment and poverty, and the desperation to survive have increased the crime rate and the country now experiences serious over-congestion of public transport, roads and bridges.

**B** Lagos according to *Lonely Planet*

Lagos is the largest city in Africa, it has wall-to-wall people, bumper-to-bumper cars, noise and pollution beyond belief, an intimidating crime rate, and the public utilities cannot cope with the number of people who need to use them. Elevated motorways ringing the city are jammed with speed freaks and absurd traffic jams ('go-slows') on top, and tin-and-cardboard shacks underneath.

Named after the Portuguese word for lagoon, Lagos, the economic and cultural powerhouse of the country, has been a major port, a British political centre and, until 1991, Nigeria's capital.

**Adapted from *Lonely Planet***

**A** Some problems caused in Nigeria by over-population

- Not enough housing in Kano
- Pollution of air and water in Port Harcourt
- Shortage of food and water in Yola
- High crime rates in Jos
- Not enough health care and schools in Ibadan
- Congested roads in Lagos

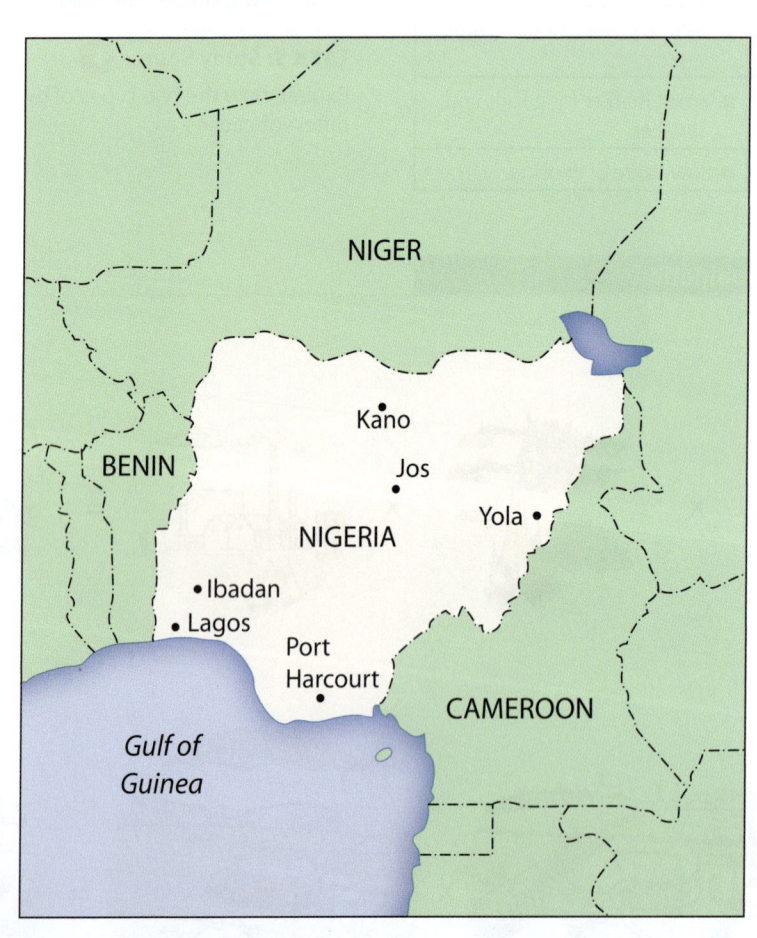

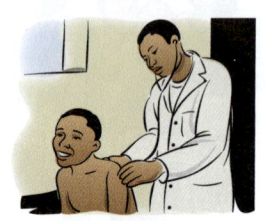

# Case Study: Over-population – Nigeria

## C Problems in Lagos

Lagos, Nigeria: The maze of shacks on stilts stretch out across the filthy water's surface, canoes colliding as they hustle between them in Makoko, a slum that serves as a warning for the world's fastest growing continent.

Tens of thousands of people live in unhygienic conditions with no public services in this water-top neighbourhood in Lagos, the largest city in Africa.

'I'm just like the other people. I don't have shelter anywhere else,' Friday Gezo, a 25-year-old teacher at a school started through donations, said from his wood-frame classroom when asked why he lived in the slum.

**Adapted from** *Gulf News*, 30 October 2011

---

Nnamdi Elendu, an electronics trader has just moved into an apartment in Ijesha, a Lagos suburb. The gutter that runs in front of his entrance gate is constantly filled with rubbish made up of soggy paper, bulging black nylon bags, and empty water bottles. A plastic pipe sticks out of a hole in his neighbour's fence. 'Four different families live in that house, and all of them wash their plates and pots and clothes and empty the water and mess through this pipe.'

'When I was a kid, only two families lived here, but now we have six different tenants sharing the facilities,' said Shalewa Omoluabi, a retired teacher who lives in Surulere.

**Adapted from** *Osun Defender*

## TASK 1
a  Using your own words, write **two** sentences using Nigeria's population statistics to show that the country is over-populated.

b  Define the following terms:
- pressure on natural resources
- lack of essential services
- inadequate sanitation.

## TASK 2: Study Source A
Look at the six problems shown on the spider diagram.

a  For each problem explain how it can be caused by over-population.

b  Choose **one** of the problems. Use the Internet to write a paragraph about your chosen problem in any named town or city in Nigeria.

## TASK 3: Study Sources B, C and D
Quality of life is a measure of the happiness, well-being and satisfaction of a person. It is affected by many factors – for example family, income and access to services.

Use the evidence in the photographs and extracts to write a short newspaper article about how over-population in Lagos affects the quality of life of its people.

## D Life in Lagos

# Cambridge IGCSE Geography
## Population Dynamics

# Case Study
## Under-population – Australia

### Under-populated Australia

The United States of America and Australia are not very different in size, but the USA has over 300 million people and Australia fewer than 25 million. Many areas of Australia are empty and the resources are not being used fully, so the country could support a higher population. This means that Australia is under-populated. Indeed, successive Australian governments have tried to increase its population, to develop the country economically, by attracting migrants from other countries. From only 3.7 million in 1901, the population has increased to its current 23 million.

**A** Australia

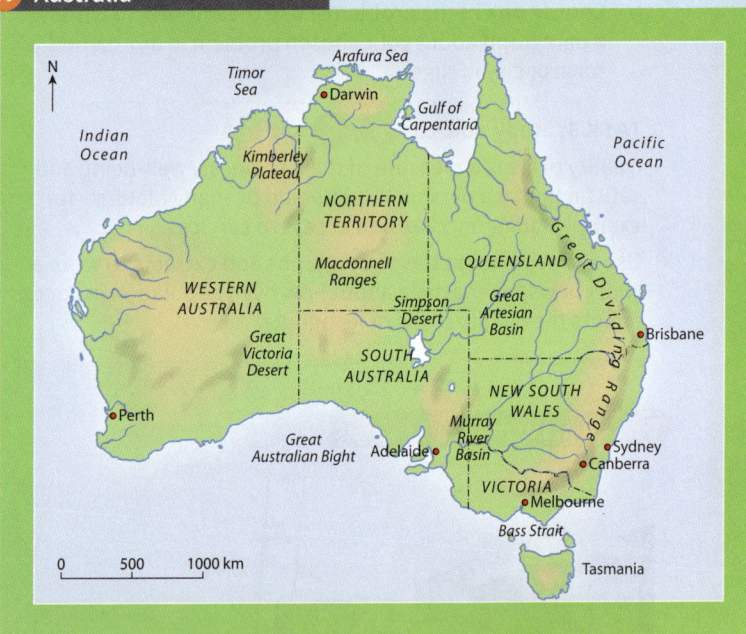

### FACTFILE AUSTRALIA

- Area: 7 686 850 km$^2$
- Population: 23 344 735 (2013)
- Main agricultural products: wheat, barley, sugarcane, fruits; cattle, sheep, poultry
- Main industries: mining, industrial and transportation equipment, food processing, chemicals, steel
- Oil production: 482 500 billion barrels/day
- Natural gas production: 44.99 billion m$^3$
- Value of exports: US$258.8 billion
- Cost of imports: US$239.7 billion

**B** USA

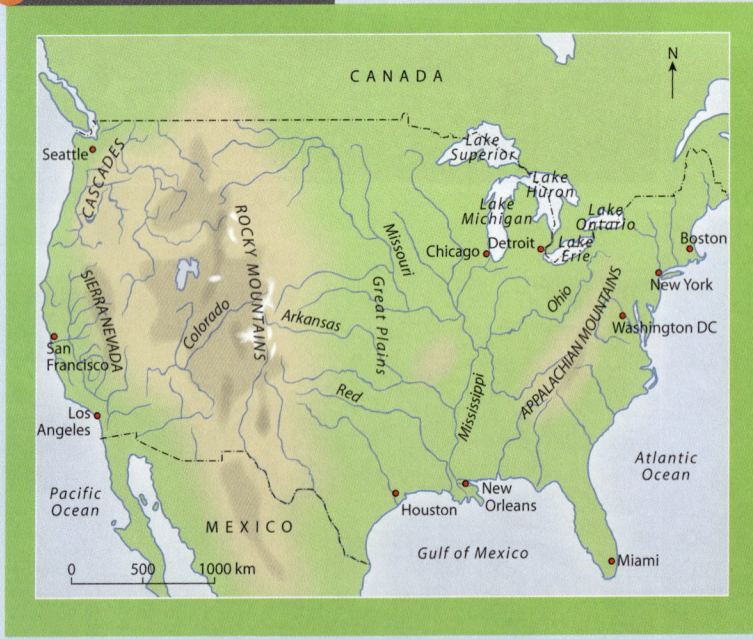

### FACTFILE USA

- Area: 9 826 630 km$^2$
- Population: 316 668 567 (2013)
- Main agricultural products: wheat, corn, other grains, fruits, vegetables, cotton; beef, pork poultry, dairy products; fish; forest products
- Main industries: petroleum, steel, motor vehicles, aerospace, telecommunications, chemicals, electronics, food processing, consumer goods, timber, mining
- Oil production: 9.023 billion barrels/day
- Natural gas production: 561.3 billion m$^3$
- Value of exports: US$1.564 trillion
- Cost of imports: US$2.299 trillion

# Case Study: Under-population – Australia

## C Under-populated Australia?

> We're in a drought, so to invite more people to share in the limited water supply on the driest continent on Earth doesn't make much sense.

> Give benefits to people having children and the benefits should increase depending on the number of children.

> Who says Australia is under-populated? Sure, it's a whole continent but most of it's desert where no one wants to live. And there's not all that much land for farming.

> Australia is a beautiful country, and one of its great attractions is that there are so many wide open spaces, and so few people in them. I would hate Australia to become like China or the USA! We already have heaps of people here from other countries who can't speak English, and this causes problems in many areas.

> How should Australia solve its under-population problem? By relaxing the visa rules so that more immigrants can get citizenship, and by expanding the economy. If the economy is prosperous more people will move here for job opportunities.

## D Migration to Australia

The face of Australia is changing – and it starts at our borders. Whereas Australia's migrant population once came mainly from Europe, now many come from countries in Asia to fill skills gaps in the workforce. In 2011–12, India (29 018) and China (25 509) were ahead of Australia's traditional source country for permanent migrants, the United Kingdom, which dropped to fourth on the list with 25 274 migrants.

*The Conversation, 8 June 2013*

The Australian Industry Group wants the government to increase the number of immigrants from 190 000 this financial year to 220 000 in 2014–15, especially skilled migrants. Chief Executive Innes Willox says 'now is the right time to increase skilled migration given Australia's ageing workforce and skills shortages in industries including mining, construction, engineering and health care. The Australian Workplace Productivity Agency has calculated that Australia will need an increase of about 2.8 million people with quite specific skills over the next decade to fill some of those gaps.'

*ABC, 13 January 2014*

---

**TASK 1:** Study Sources **A** and **B**

Use the evidence in the maps and factfiles to explain why Australia can be considered to be under-populated compared with the USA.

**TASK 2:** Study Sources **C** and **D**

a Identify **three** methods which could be used to solve the under-population problem in Australia.

b Identify **three** problems which may be caused if more people are encouraged to migrate to Australia.

c Explain why some people think that Australia is not under-populated.

# Cambridge IGCSE Geography — Population Dynamics

## 3 Causes of a change in population size

### Calculating population change

Natural population change is calculated by subtracting the **death rate** from the **birth rate**. Malta's birth rate in 2013 was 10.3 per 1000 and its death rate was 8.8 per 1000. So its natural population change in 2013 was:

10.3 − 8.8 = 1.5 per 1000 people (i.e. 0.15%).

To calculate the overall population change, the **net migration** must be considered. If more people per 1000 move into the country than move out of it, this is added. If more move out of the country than into it, this is subtracted. Malta's net migration in 2013 was 2.4 per 1000. So its overall population change was:

10.3 − 8.8 + 2.4 = 3.9 per 1000 people (i.e. 0.39%).

If the answer is positive the population is growing, if it is negative it is getting smaller.

### A  Birth rate, death rate and migration

Birth rate is the average number of births per 1000 people per year.

Death rate is the average number of deaths per 1000 people per year.

Net migration is the average number of people moving into a country minus those moving out of it per 1000 people per year.

### B  Population change

| Country | Birth rate (per 1000 people) | Death rate (per 1000 people) | Net migration (per 1000 people) |
| --- | --- | --- | --- |
| Belgium | 10.0 | 10.7 | +1.2 |
| Greece | 8.9 | 10.9 | +2.3 |
| India | 20.2 | 7.3 | −0.1 |
| Morocco | 18.7 | 4.8 | −3.7 |
| Poland | 9.9 | 10.3 | −0.5 |

# The Demographic Transition Model

The Demographic Transition Model is a model of the way that population growth can be divided into four stages as birth and death rates change over time. It is based on what has happened in Europe and North America.

The part of the graph representing population growth is the area between the lines, where birth rate is higher than death rate.

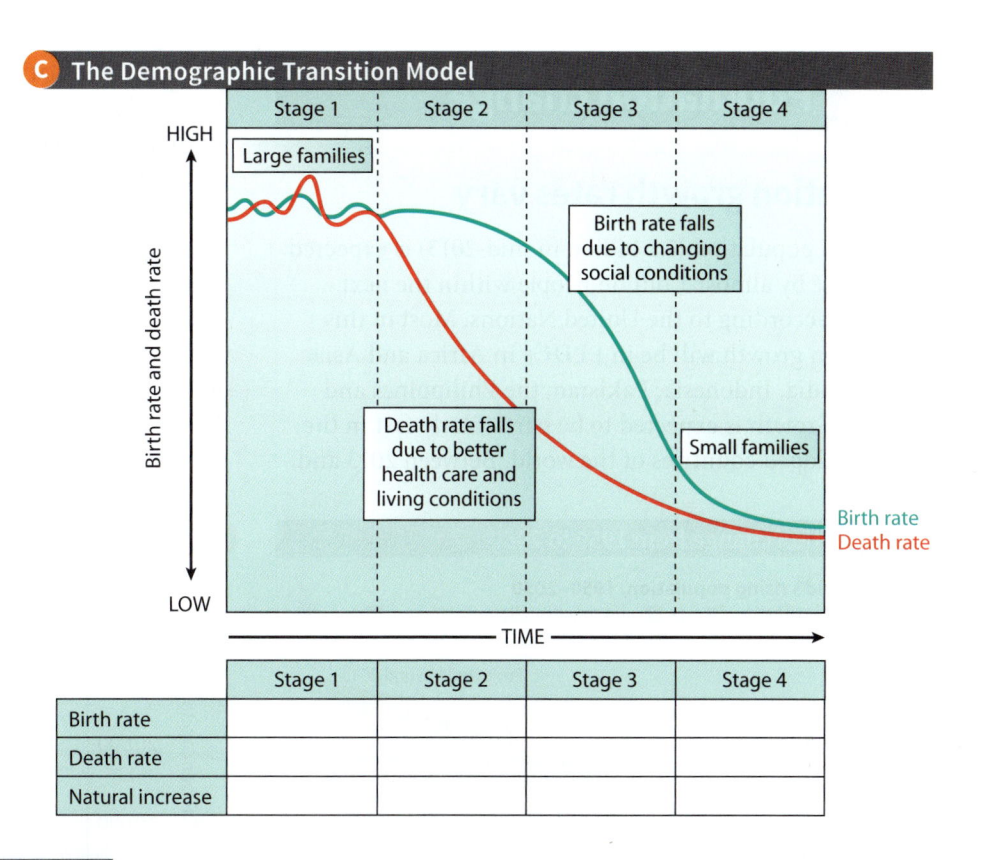

**C** The Demographic Transition Model

*Graph showing Stages 1-4 with birth rate and death rate curves over time. Labels: "Large families" (Stage 1), "Death rate falls due to better health care and living conditions" (Stage 2), "Birth rate falls due to changing social conditions" (Stage 3), "Small families" (Stage 4).*

|  | Stage 1 | Stage 2 | Stage 3 | Stage 4 |
|---|---|---|---|---|
| Birth rate |  |  |  |  |
| Death rate |  |  |  |  |
| Natural increase |  |  |  |  |

**D** Reasons for falling birth rates and death rates

| Falling birth rates are caused by: | Falling death rates are caused by: |
|---|---|
| ■ availability of contraception | ■ improvement in health care facilities |
| ■ more women go out to work | ■ increased availability of medicines and doctors |
| ■ girls are educated and marry later | ■ more and better quality food available |
| ■ reduction of infant mortality | ■ improvement in water supplies |
| ■ more family planning education | ■ improvement in sanitation and hygiene |
| ■ less need for children as a labour source | ■ reduction in wars and conflicts |

**TASK 1: Study Source A**
a What is meant by birth rate, death rate and net migration?
b What is the difference between natural population change and overall population change?
c Explain how a country with a high birth rate could experience population decline.
d Explain how a country with a low birth rate could have a high rate of population growth.

**TASK 2: Study Source B**
a Calculate the natural population change of Morocco per 1000 people.
b Calculate the overall population change of Poland per 1000 people.
c Draw a bar graph to show the overall population change for all five countries listed in Source B.
d Calculate the overall rate of population change of the country in which you live, as a percentage. You will need to find out the birth rate, death rate and net migration. For any country this information can be found at: www.indexmundi.com/factbook/countries

**TASK 3: Study Source C**
a Make a copy of the Demographic Transition Model in Source C. Shade in the natural increase.
b Make a copy of the table under the graph. Complete the first two rows of the table using the words *high, low* or *decreasing*. Complete the third row using the phrases *small increase, large increase, slower increase* and *fluctuating*.
c Explain why a large population increase occurs when a country is in Stage 2.
d Explain why there is only a small population increase when a country is in Stage 4.
e Today some countries have birth rates that are lower than death rates, so their population is declining. On your copy of the Demographic Transition Model, add an extra stage to show this and label it 'Stage 5'.

# Cambridge IGCSE Geography — Population Dynamics

## 4 Population change

### Population growth rates vary

The world population (7.2 billion in mid-2013) is expected to increase by almost 1 billion people within the next 12 years, according to the United Nations. Most of this population growth will be in **LEDCs** in Africa and Asia, such as India, Indonesia, Pakistan, the Philippines and Nigeria. Growth is expected to be particularly fast in the least developed countries of the world. Between 2013 and 2100, the populations of 35 countries could more than triple. Among them, the populations of Burundi, Malawi, Mali, Niger, Nigeria, Somalia, Uganda, Tanzania and Zambia are projected to increase at least fivefold by 2100.

In contrast, the population of the **MEDCs** is not expected to change much and most of the net increase will be due to migration from LEDCs to MEDCs. The populations of 40 countries are expected to decrease between 2013 and 2100. The population of some countries is expected to decline by more than 15 per cent by 2050, including Bulgaria, Croatia, Cuba, Georgia, Latvia, Lithuania, Romania, Russia and Ukraine.

**A Population change from 1950 to 2050**

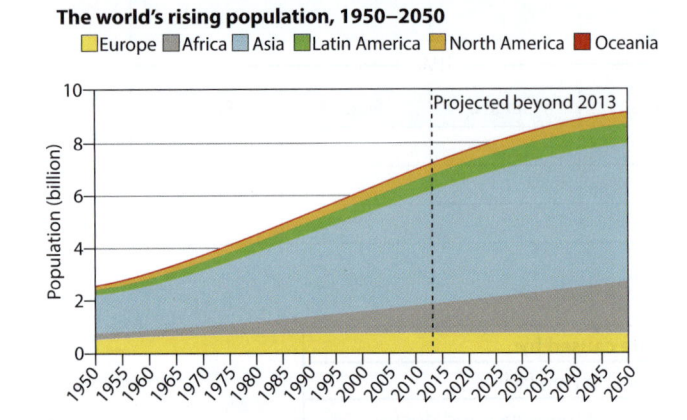

The world's rising population, 1950–2050
(Europe, Africa, Asia, Latin America, North America, Oceania)

**B Population growth rates**

Population increase %:
- 4+
- 3.5–4
- 3–3.5
- 2.5–3
- 2–2.5
- 1.5–2
- 1–1.5
- 0.5–1
- 0–0.5
- <0

**C Gross Domestic Product (GDP) and population growth**

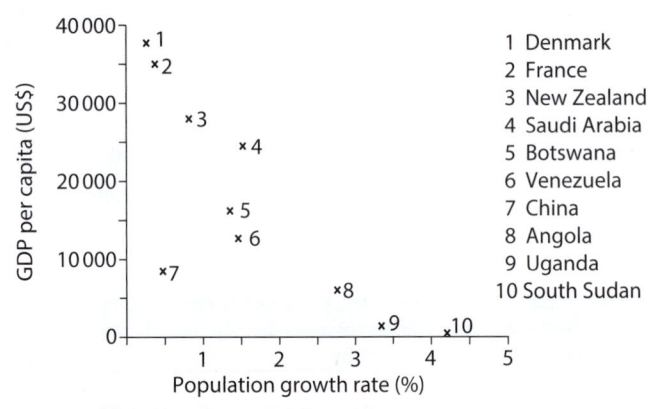

1. Denmark
2. France
3. New Zealand
4. Saudi Arabia
5. Botswana
6. Venezuela
7. China
8. Angola
9. Uganda
10. South Sudan

GDP per capita is a measure of wealth.

---

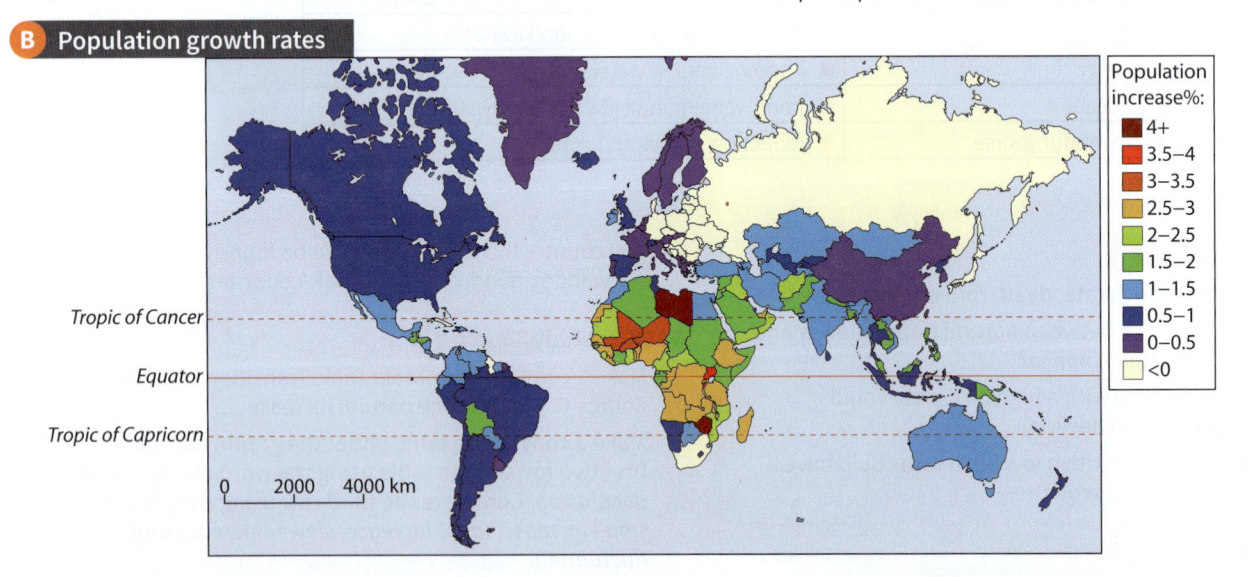

**TASK 1:** Study Source A

a Copy out the sentences below, adding the correct names of the continents.

_____ had around a quarter of the world's population in 1950 but by 2050 it will have less than a tenth.

_____ had more than half of the world's population in 1950 and its share has continued to increase.

From 2013 _____'s share of the world's population is increasing faster than any other continent.

b Estimate the figures (in billions) for the population in each continent in 1950 and 2050. Write a paragraph describing the main differences that are expected.

### D Population growth in four countries

> Here, most couples use contraception and plan their families as most women are educated and want to continue their careers rather than staying at home and looking after children. Many couples now wait until they are at least 30 to have a family and have only one or two children. It is so expensive here to bring up children as they all attend school and many go on to university, and many live at home and need supporting for many years. Even though families are small, our country's population is still growing because most people live until they are 80 and we have immigrants coming here from other countries.
>
> Margrethe (Denmark)

> I am very proud of my family of seven children, which is not unusual in this village. The three oldest children are girls and we wanted to make sure that we had some boys too. Even if I could afford it I wouldn't use contraception as children are a gift from God. I cannot afford to send all of the children to school; the girls work hard helping in and around the house and they help me to fetch water and firewood. The boys work in the fields and when they are older they are hoping to go to the towns and earn money for our family.
>
> Nabulungi (Uganda)

> I have had four babies but only one of them is still alive. The others died before they were one year old because they became sick and I could not afford to take them to the clinic in the town. HIV/AIDS is a big problem in this country and so many people are dying that now it is unusual for anyone to live longer than 50 years. I hope I will have more babies because I need to make sure that I have someone to look after me when I get old or if I become ill.
>
> Precious (Botswana)

> I have only been able to have one daughter as the laws of the country make it almost impossible to have more than one child. I cannot afford to pay the fines to the government officials, who watch us so closely and give out fines and other punishments if we break the rules. I read last month that the government is going to change this policy and allow two or more children per family, as there are so few children being born that there will not be enough people to do all the jobs in the country in the future.
>
> Jiahui (China)

### E Afghanistan: large families encouraged by culture as well as religion

Sadia from Fazelbeg in the Qarabagh district of Kabul, is 37 and has 10 children. Like most Afghan women, she has little say in the decision-making about the size of her family. Asked why she chose to have so many children, Sadia said 'This is according to whatever Allah has given us. I would like to have more children.'

Sadia had her first child, a daughter, at the age of 13. Ever since then her life has revolved around her household, her husband and her children. She rarely goes out in public and then only with the permission of her husband. As in many Afghan households, it is the older daughters who help their mother with the daily tasks. They are considered too old to go to school, although the secondary school is nearby.

'No one in my husband's family educated their daughters beyond the primary class and he did not want to get a bad name in the family.'

**Adapted from** *Women's News Network, 2012*

---

**TASK 2:** Study Source **B**

a Use an atlas to put the following countries into rank order from the highest to the lowest rate of population growth.
- Brazil
- Germany
- Pakistan
- Libya
- Madagascar

b Write a paragraph to compare rates of population growth in African countries with those in Europe. Give examples of countries and growth rates to back up the points you are making.

**TASK 3:** Study Source **C**

a Which countries are being described?
- The GDP per capita is US$28 000 and the population growth rate is 0.85%.
- The GDP per capita is US$6000 and the population growth rate is 2.78%.

b What general relationship is shown on the graph between the GDP per capita and the population growth rate? Name countries and use statistics to support your answer.

c What do the statistics on the graph tell you about China's GDP per capita and its population growth compared with the other nine countries?

**TASK 4:** Study Sources **D** and **E**

a Explain in detail why birth rates are high in some countries but low in others. Give examples for each.

b It is not just birth rate which determines population growth rates. Explain how death rates and migration influence rates of population growth.

# Cambridge IGCSE Geography — Population Dynamics

## Case Study
## High rate of natural population growth – Niger

### Niger – a country in West Africa

The Republic of Niger is a **land-locked** country in West Africa, named after the Niger river which flows through the south-west. Its climate is mainly very hot and dry, with many desert areas. It is one of the poorest countries in the world.

The largest ethnic groups in Niger are the Hausa and Djerma-Songhai, **sedentary** farmers who live in the southern part of the country. The rest are **nomadic** or semi-nomadic livestock-raising peoples – Fulani, Tuareg, Kanuri, Arabs and Toubou.

The population of Niger grew from 1.7 million in 1960 to almost 17 million in 2013, with almost half of the country under 15 years old. With a high population growth rate of 3.4% it is expected to reach 56 million by 2050. With an average of just over seven births per woman, Niger has one of the highest **fertility rates** in the world.

### Falling death rates in Niger

During the last 50 years death rates have been falling in many parts of Africa, especially in the poorer countries such as Niger.

There are now lower death rates because health care, food supply, water supply and sanitation have improved, particularly in the capital city, Niamey, and other urban areas such as Zinder, Maradi, Agadez, Arlit, Dosso, Tessaoua and Dogondoutchi. During most years death rates continue to fall because:

- babies are inoculated against diseases and treated when ill
- there are improved supplies of clean water so there are less water-borne diseases
- people eat more food and a more varied diet
- there are more clinics and hospitals with trained doctors and nurses
- there is better education about health and hygiene.

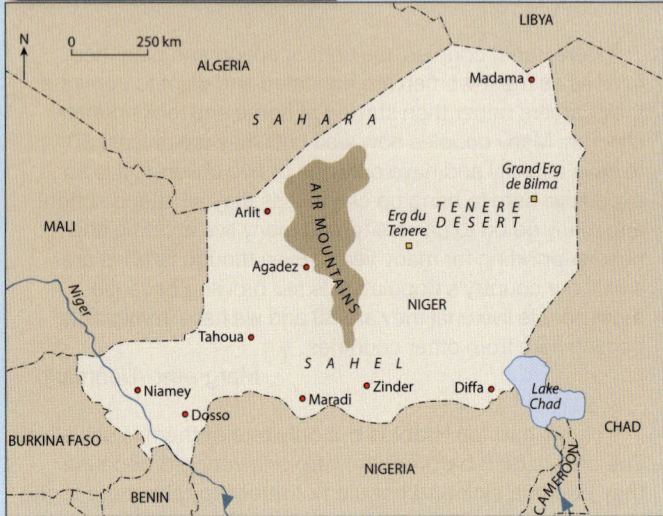

### A  Where is Niger?

### B  Niger factfile

- Total population 16.9 million
- Population growth rate 3.4%
- Life expectancy 54.3 years
- Literacy 28.7%
- GDP per capita US$800
- Population below poverty line 63%
- Workforce
  - Agriculture 90%
  - Industry 6%
  - Services 4%

### C  Birth and death rates in Niger

| Year | Birth rate (per 1000 people) | Death rate (per 1000 people) |
|---|---|---|
| 2000 | 53.1 | 16.8 |
| 2001 | 52.7 | 16.2 |
| 2002 | 52.3 | 15.6 |
| 2003 | 51.9 | 15.0 |
| 2004 | 51.5 | 14.5 |
| 2005 | 51.2 | 13.9 |
| 2006 | 50.9 | 13.4 |
| 2007 | 50.6 | 13.0 |
| 2008 | 50.4 | 12.6 |
| 2009 | 50.2 | 12.2 |
| 2010 | 50.1 | 11.8 |
| 2011 | 49.9 | 11.5 |
| 2012 | 47.6 | 13.4 |
| 2013 | 46.8 | 13.1 |

# Case Study: High rate of natural population growth – Niger

## D Population explosion threatens development gains in Niger

### NIGER: POPULATION EXPLOSION THREATENS DEVELOPMENT GAINS

If the people of Niger remain uninformed about family planning and keep reproducing at the current rate, the country's population will more than quadruple by 2050, according to research by Niger's national statistics agency. Niger's population will make it impossible for the government to provide adequate health, education, jobs and water – tasks that it is already finding difficult, with a fraction of the population.

'We surveyed the country and found that the average number of children per mother is 7.1. However, we also asked them how many they would like to have – women said 9 and men said 12, but some families said they would like 40 or 50 children,' said Adamou Soumana. For poor families children are a source of wealth. They work on the land, go into the towns to earn money and look after their parents when they are old.

Just 5% of the people of Niger use family planning and contraception. 'People aren't informed enough about the negative consequences of having so many children,' Soumana added.

**Adapted from** *Population explosion* (2007)

## E An action plan

### GOVERNMENT ACTION PLAN

Niger's government has put in place a plan to slow down population growth.

The government wants the number using family planning to increase from 5 to 20% by 2015. The plan also calls for information campaigns to educate religious leaders and especially women about the availability and importance of family planning. It proposes that the number of early marriages be cut. Many girls in Niger marry before the age of 15. Raising the marriage age to 18 would take up to four years off a woman's reproductive life.

---

**TASK 1:** Study Source **A** and an atlas

Describe the size and location of Niger. Refer to distance and direction.

**TASK 2:** Study Source **B**

a Make a copy of Source B. Draw an extra column and fill this in with information about the country in which you are living. For any country this information can be found at: www.indexmundi.com/factbook/countries

b Use the information about Niger and your own country to write a paragraph to show that Niger is one of the poorest countries in the world.

**TASK 3:** Study Source **C**

a Draw a graph to show the birth and death rates of Niger between 2000 and 2013. Use different coloured lines for each of the birth and death rates and shade in the area in between them that represents the natural population growth.

b Choose the correct words or phrases to complete the **four** sentences below about Niger:
- Birth rates and death rates generally *increased/ decreased* between 2000 and 2013.
- Birth rates between 2000 and 2013 were always *higher/ lower* than death rates.
- Natural population growth in 2013 was *20.2/28.4/33.7* per 1000 people.
- This was *higher/lower* in 2013 than it was in 2000.

c What stage of the Demographic Transition Model do you think Niger is in? Justify your answer. Refer to page 13.

**TASK 4**

Working in groups, discuss the reasons why death rates have been reduced in Niger. Put the reasons in order of importance and explain your group's order to the rest of the class.

**TASK 5:** Study Source **D**

Draw a spider diagram to show reasons why birth rates are still high in Niger. Follow these instructions:

a Draw a circle in the middle of your page. Write in it 'Why birth rates are high in Niger'.

b Draw lines radiating from the circle.

c Write a reason at the end of each line.

**TASK 6:** Study Source **E**

a The government of Niger has an action plan to slow down population growth. Design a poster that shows how it is attempting to do this.

b Explain why it will be difficult to persuade people in Niger to have smaller families.

# Cambridge IGCSE Geography — Population Dynamics

# Case Study
## Population decline – Russia

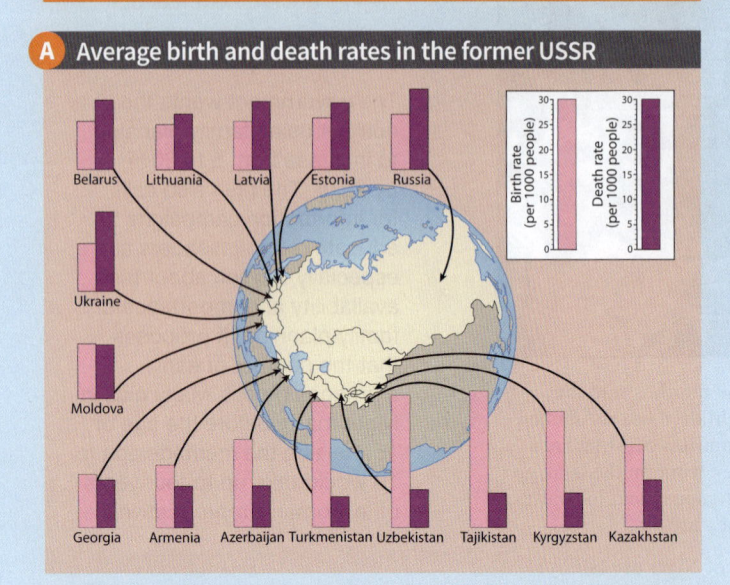

**A** Average birth and death rates in the former USSR

## What is happening to Russia's population?

**Source A** shows Russia and the other countries which, up to 1991, formed the Union of Soviet Socialist Republics (USSR). The population of Russia in 2013 was 143 million. In 1991 the population was at its highest but it has decreased mainly because of a higher death rate than birth rate. Despite some recent increases in the birth rate, the population is predicted to continue to decrease throughout the rest of the century. Alcohol-related deaths in Russia are very high, levels of HIV/AIDS, heart disease and tuberculosis are high, and male life expectancy is relatively low at 64 years. Russian women, who are highly educated, do not want large numbers of children. Immigration into Russia is low, and many emigrants are moving away from Russia, particularly to Western Europe to look for a better lifestyle.

**B** Russia's population 1960 to 2100

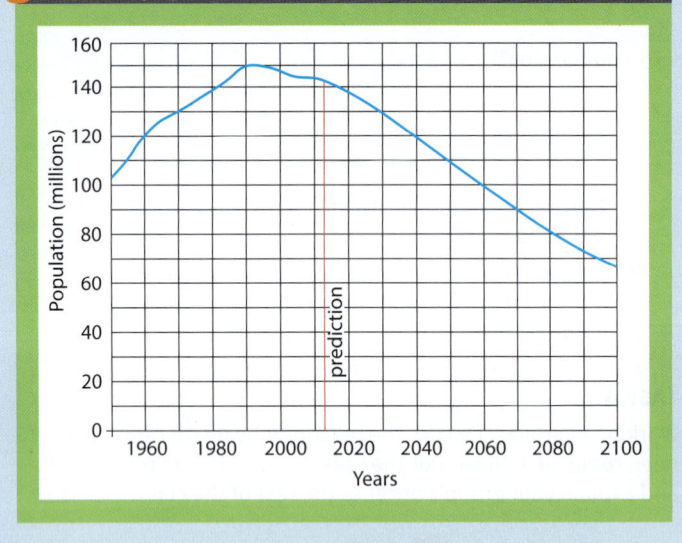

**C** Russia's birth and death rates 1950 to 2014

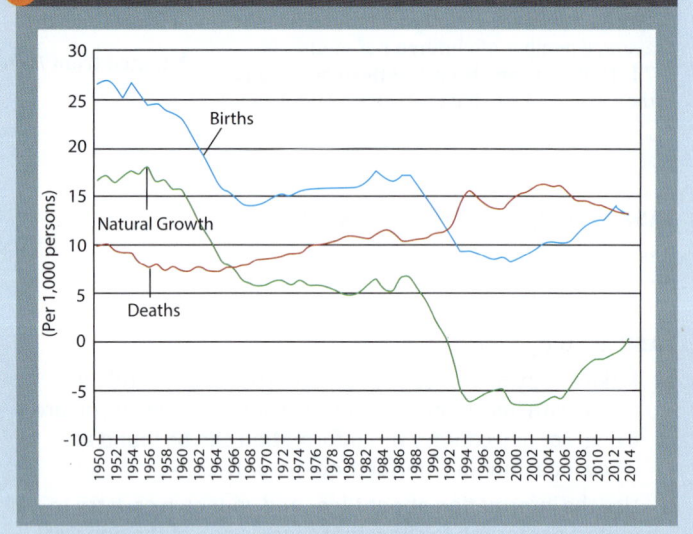

---

**TASK 1:** Study **Source A**

a  Name the country shown on the map with the highest rate of natural population growth.

b  Work out the average natural population decline of Russia per 1000 people.

c  Name **three** other countries shown on the map that have experienced natural population decline.

**TASK 2:** Study **Source B**

a  Describe how the total population of Russia changed between 1960 and 2013 and is predicted to change up to 2100. Use statistics and years in your answer.

b  Match the following beginnings and endings of sentences to complete three sentences which explain why Russia's population is now declining.

Death rates are high … … because Russian women prefer to have careers rather than large numbers of children.

Birth rates are low … … as more people move out of Russia than into the country.

Population is lost through migration … because of high levels of alcoholism, heart disease and accidents.

# Case Study: Population decline – Russia

## D Population graphs for the G8 countries

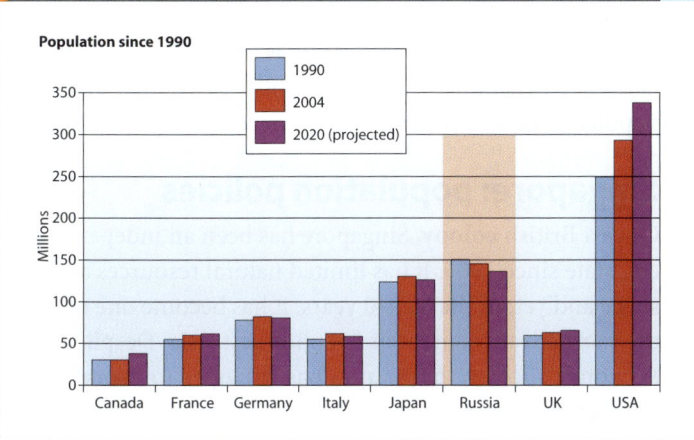

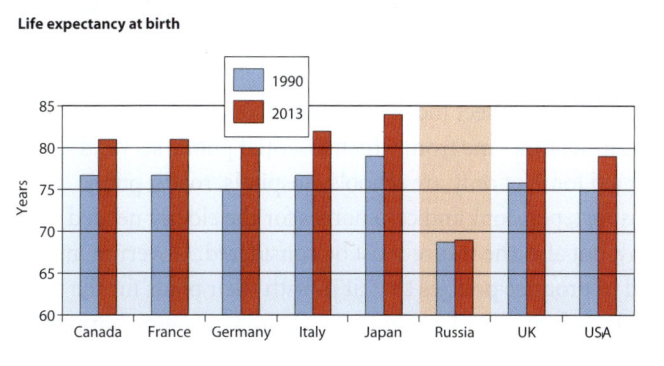

**Population since 1990** (1990, 2004, 2020 projected, in Millions) – Canada, France, Germany, Italy, Japan, Russia, UK, USA

**Life expectancy at birth** (1990, 2013, in Years) – Canada, France, Germany, Italy, Japan, Russia, UK, USA

Russia is one of the G8 countries – one of the world's most powerful nations

## E Cash for more babies (2006)

### A second baby? Russia's mothers aren't persuaded

President Vladimir Putin last week promised to spend some of the country's oil profits on efforts to solve the population problem. He ordered parliament to more than double monthly child support payments to 1500 roubles (about US$55) and added that women who choose to have a second baby will receive 250,000 roubles (US$9200); a very large amount in a country where average monthly incomes are close to US$330.

On Monday, young women at the Family Planning Youth Centre in Moscow said they liked the sound of more money, but suggested that Mr Putin has no idea about their lives. 'A child is not an easy project, and in this world a woman is expected to get an education, find a job, and make a career,' says Svetlana Romanicheva, a student who says she won't consider having a baby for at least five years.

Others say Putin is right. 'Russian women typically have one child ... but many of my patients would like a second if they felt they had enough support,' says Galina Dedova, a doctor at Happy Families, a private Moscow clinic. 'Most of my patients count their roubles ... If they could get more money, some might have more children.'

*The Christian Science Monitor*, 19 May 2006

## F Putin hails Russian birth rate rise (2012)

Vladimir Putin paused last week, in the midst of his most important speech of the year, to outline Russia's new strategy for population growth. In 2012, for the first time since the fall of the Soviet Union, there were slightly more births than deaths in Russia. 'The population had grown more than 200 000 from January to September; the population policies of the last decade are working,' he said.

Throughout more than a decade of his rule, Mr Putin followed a policy, known as 'mother capital', of paying women up to $10 000 to have second children.

In a speech last week, he proposed additional incentives in 50 low-birth regions for women to have three children. 'The three-child family should become the norm in Russia,' he said.

Mr Krupnov, director of the Moscow-based Institute for Demography, Migration and Regional Development, estimates that soon the downward trend will resume, as the 'tiny generation' of the 1990s, when birth rates fell drastically, begin to reproduce.

The last available long-term prediction by Goskomstat, the state statistics agency, shows Russia could soon be losing population at the rate of up to a million a year. Even under the most optimistic forecasts, the 'natural' rate of decline will be about 400 000 a year, though it will be made up for by immigration.

*Financial Times*, 21 December 2012

---

**TASK 3:** Study Source **C**

a Describe how birth rates and death rates changed in Russia between 1950 and 2014.

b Identify the years when the total population:
- increased
- remained the same
- decreased.

**TASK 4:** Study Source **D**

a Identify the main differences between Russia and the other G8 countries. Use figures and examples in your answer.

b Suggest reasons for these differences.

**TASK 5:** Study Sources **E** and **F**

a A Russian couple are trying to decide whether to have a second child. Write a conversation between them which includes information about the advantages and problems of having another child.

b Suggest reasons why Vladimir Putin considers it important to increase birth rates in Russia.

# 5 Population policies

## The role of government

Governments collect money through taxes. These taxes form government income from which essential public services are paid for. Not only are schools, hospitals, roads, public transport, pensions and care homes for the elderly needed today, but also the future must be considered. Governments need to produce policies that fit in with their plans for the country's future. Perhaps too many babies are being born and the birth rate needs reducing; or maybe there are not going to be enough workers – so one answer may be to encourage immigration. If there are going to be many old people in ten years' time, their care needs to be planned for. The government can try to solve these problems by influencing the natural population growth by bringing in policies that affect birth and death rates. Another way is to influence migration patterns by encouraging people to move in to add to the population or force people out to reduce it.

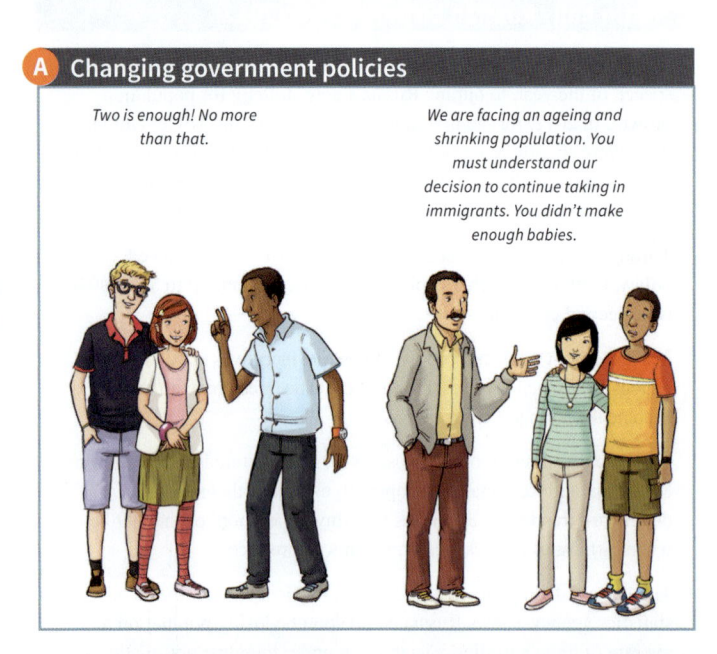

## Singapore: population policies

Once a British **colony**, Singapore has been an independent city state since 1965. It has limited natural resources and space and yet, in the last 40 years, it has become one of the most advanced nations in south-east Asia. Despite this economic success, the country has struggled to manage its population numbers.

Since independence it has introduced population control policies. For example, in 1970 abortion and voluntary sterilisation were made legal. The 'Stop at Two' campaign introduced:

- extra taxes for a third child
- no paid maternity leave for third child
- parents with more than two children could not enrol at the best schools.

These policies reduced the average number of births per woman (fertility rate) to less than two by the 1980s. Population growth had become too low to provide a young, vibrant workforce to develop the economy of the future. In a reversal of policy the government decided to encourage rapid population growth.

## Reducing population in China

Since 1949 the Communist Party has ruled China. Although there was no government control on population growth, it did encourage large families to make China strong. In 1970 the 'Later, Longer, Fewer' policy emerged where parents were encouraged to delay their first child,

**A** Changing government policies

*Two is enough! No more than that.*

*We are facing an ageing and shrinking population. You must understand our decision to continue taking in immigrants. You didn't make enough babies.*

**B** Singapore – population too low

### HAVE THREE OR MORE, IF YOU CAN AFFORD IT

If you have three or more babies, look what you can get.

- Tax rebates for the third child.
- Subsidies for day-care.
- Priority in enrolling at the best schools.
- Priority in gaining housing for large families.
- Extended sick leave.
- Up to 4 years' maternity leave for civil servants.

*Contact our counselling service if you are considering abortion or sterilisation.*

**DON'T PASSIVELY WATCH OURSELVES GO EXTINCT!**

| Year | Children per woman |
|------|--------------------|
| 1957 | 6.4 |
| 1965 | 4.8 |
| 1975 | 2.0 |
| 1985 | 1.6 |
| 1995 | 1.7 |
| 2005 | 1.4 |
| 2012 | 1.2 |

"Unfortunately, despite all the incentives, the birth rate stayed at its lowest level of 1.4 children per woman in 1987 – far less than needed to maintain the population. Working people wanted more material assets and men and women were keen to pursue careers. Marriages were later too. The government tried other means such as a campaign to promote the joys of marriage and parenthood and a matchmaking agency for those with A levels. It also offered a 20 000 Singapore dollars tax rebate for the fourth child. But the birth rate remained low. However, 20 000 people enter Singapore each year to work. The problems facing the government will be a larger elderly population to be housed on limited land as well as a small working population supporting a large number of old people."

Demographer at the University of Singapore

allow a longer interval between births and have fewer children in total. By 1979 it was clear that there would still not be enough food, jobs or services to cope with the rapidly growing population. In 1979 the first 'one family, one child' policy was introduced as rapid growth was seen as a barrier to development. Since then various incentives, such as free education and health care, have been offered to those families with one child, along with punishments, such as fines, for those who had more children.

## Consequences of the 'One family, one child' policy

Various forms of the one-child policy were implemented between 1979 and 2014. The fertility rate was reduced in this time from 5.8 to 1.7, meaning that China did not have to cope with an estimated 400 million extra births. But by 2014, with an increasing amount of old people and a shrinking workforce, the government realised that the policy needed to be changed.

**TASK 1:** Study Source A
a  Give **two** reasons why governments may want to use population policies.
b  Most government policies that are in place to control growth are designed to influence birth rates. Suggest why government policies, in general:
  - do not propose to increase or decrease death rates
  - do not propose mass emigration or immigration.
c  Give **two** examples of policies used by the government of Singapore in the 'Stop at Two' campaign.

**TASK 2:** Study Source B
a  How can you tell that policies to reduce the birth rate were in operation after 1965?
b  Explain why the government reversed its policies and encouraged population growth from the mid-1980s.
c  List **three** incentives of the 'Have Three or More' scheme.
d  Explain why the scheme did not increase birth rates.

### C  China's population by age group (millions)

| Age | 1950 | 1995 | 2010 | 2025 (estimated) | 2050 (estimated) |
|---|---|---|---|---|---|
| 50+ | 87 | 209 | 332 | 526 | 631 |
| 20–49 | 228 | 594 | 665 | 597 | 529 |
| 5–19 | 165 | 320 | 290 | 278 | 247 |
| 0–4 | 76 | 103 | 93 | 86 | 78 |
| Total | 556 | 1226 | 1380 | 1487 | 1485 |

### D  Increasing population in China

**CHINA'S ONE-CHILD POLICY TO CHANGE IN 2014**

The Chinese government has ended the country's family planning laws to allow some families to have two children. These laws will come into effect in early 2014 and will apply to couples where one parent is an only child. The 1979 one-child policy has seen Chinese families prefer to have male children. This led to selective abortions and infanticide of females. The changes are because of a falling working population in China. People over 65 will make up a quarter of the population by 2030; currently this is 1 in 7. Meanwhile the state predicts the working population will decrease by 8 million people each year from 2023. The new laws should add an extra 2 million babies per year to the population's young people. It will take more than a decade though for these extra births to work through into the potential working population.

Adapted from *the Independent*, 29 December 2013

**TASK 3:** Study Source C
a  Draw a graph to represent this data.
b  By how much is it estimated that population will grow between 1950 and 2050? Is there any evidence that stability might be achieved?
c  What is expected to happen to the 0–4 and 50+ age groups over this period?
d  Suggest problems that China's government will face in 2050 if these estimates are correct. How could these be overcome?

**TASK 4:** Study Source D
a  Why has the Chinese government relaxed the one-child policy?
b  Explain why this revised policy will not have any great impact until around 2030.
c  Suggest why some companies and organisations may benefit from this change but others may not.

# 6 Population migration

## Types of migration

Migrants are people who move from one place to another in order to live or work. Unless they are forced to move, many groups of people and individuals choose to migrate to new destinations. These movements are usually voluntary and often involve looking, and hoping for, a better **quality of life** and **standard of living** at the new destination.

Some groups of people and individuals are forced to migrate; their movement is involuntary. They often do not know where their destination will be or what their quality of life and standard of living will be like. It is usually worse than they experienced where they used to live.

Migrants who move out of a country are called **emigrants**. Migrants who move into a country are called **immigrants**.

### A  Important definitions

| Type of migrant | Definition |
| --- | --- |
| Asylum seeker | A person who leaves their country of origin for fear of persecution. They have asked for permission to stay in another country and are waiting for a decision on this. |
| Refugee | A person who leaves their country of origin in fear of their lives. They run away often with no idea where they will end up and with no permission to stay in another country. |
| Illegal immigrant | A person who enters a country to live and work there without permission. |
| Economic migrant | A person who moves to live and work in a different country for at least a year. |
| Internal migrant | A person who moves to live or work in a different place within the same country. |

*A Mexican navy fast boat escorts a Mexican patrol boat carrying illegal Cuban immigrants to a navy base before sending them back to Cuba.*

### B  Migration in the news ...

**Syrian refugees left to fend for themselves in freezing cold**

For more than a year, a group of 200 refugees who fled from the civil war in northern Syria have survived in huts and derelict buildings at the foot of the mountains of the Bakaa Valley in neighbouring Lebanon. Now they face torrential rain, deep snow and sub-zero temperatures in huts made of scrap wood and plastic sheeting.

**Adapted from** *The Times*, 13 December 2013

**Rudd will send boat people to 'harsh' Papua New Guinea centre**

Asylum seekers arriving in Australia by fishing boat from Indonesia will be sent to a detention centre in Papua New Guinea, the Australian prime minister has said. The new policy was unveiled after violence broke out between 150 detainees and prison security and police on the South Pacific island of Nauru which is used to detain asylum seekers.

**Adapted from** *The Times*, 20 July 2013

**South Africa: a long-awaited policy on economic migrants**

After a decade of uncertainty and mass deportations of migrants, South Africa is to introduce a permit that will grant thousands of Zimbabweans the right to live and work in South Africa and access health care and education for an initial period of six months. Zimbabwe's economic collapse and political crisis is a decade old now, during which immigrants travelled over the northern borders of South Africa but could only stay if granted asylum. Most were deported back or worked illegally in large cities such as Johannesburg. Now their importance to the economy will be legally recognised.

**Adapted from** *IRIN*, 20 January 2014

**Cubans still illegally entering USA through Mexico**

Since 1959, when Castro led his communist army into the capital, Havana, causing the end of cordial relations and open migration between the USA and Cuba, many people have wanted to emigrate out of the country. The two sea routes favoured by illegal migrants are hazardous and involve crossing the 250km Straits of Florida to Miami or travelling 200km west by boat across the Caribbean Sea to Mexico to illegally cross the Mexico-USA border by land. Cuba eased its migration controls in 2013 allowing more people who met certain conditions to leave; despite this, there were still 994 illegal migrants caught in 2013 compared to 2300 in 2012. The Mexico-USA border is over 3000 km long and difficult to police; it is estimated that 15000 migrants illegally enter the USA each year.

**Adapted from** *Miami Mercury*, 23rd March 2014

# The push-pull model of migration

Voluntary population movements or migrations usually take place because of inequalities in resources and opportunities. Unless forced, people do not usually move to another place unless:

- there are **push** factors – these are features of their home area that make them want to move away.
- there are **pull** factors – these are features of their new destination that make them want to move there.

The main pull factor that makes people volunteer to move from one place to another is economic – the promise of work for better wages. This is true of internal and international migrations. This is not true, however, of most forced migrations where people have no choice but to move – job or no job.

### C Push-pull factors

| Push factors from rural areas | Pull factors to urban areas |
| --- | --- |
| Unemployment | Work |
| Low-paid jobs | Better paid jobs |
| Farm too small | Higher education |
| Poor housing/shelter | Join family |
| No electricity | Better housing/shelter |
| Poor water supply | Electricity supply |
| Few schools | Water supply |
| Natural disaster | More reliable transport |
| Harsh climate | More doctors/hospitals |
| Few doctors/clinics | Better entertainment |
| Crop failure | Safer |
| Civil war | More reliable food supply |
| Persecution | Chance to improve |
| Poor transport | Freedom of speech |
| Safety | Bright lights/word of mouth |

### D Intervening obstacles

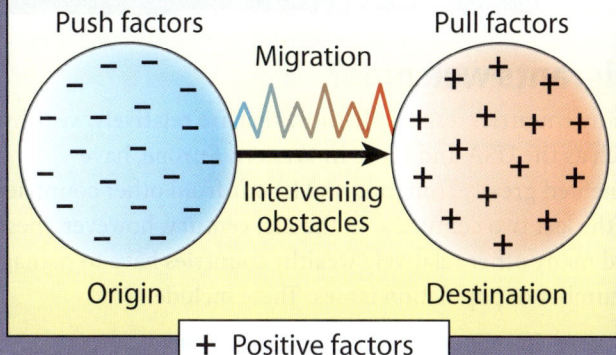

*Intervening obstacles may be many, e.g. cost of moving, physical obstacles, passport/visa issues.*

*Migrants from north Africa arrive on the island of Lampedusa, near Malta, after a perilous sea crossing. Between January and June 2015 more than 165,000 migrants arrived by sea at Lampedusa, the south coasts of Italy, Spain and France or on the Greek island of Lesvos. But over 1800 are believed to have drowned in the Mediterranean Sea because their boats sank as they were carrying too many people desperate to find a better life in Europe.*

### TASK 1
a What is meant by *migration*?
b What is the difference between:
- involuntary and voluntary migration?
- an internal and an international migrant?

c How is an *immigrant* different from an *emigrant*?

### TASK 2: Study Sources A and B
a Copy Source A and add a third column titled *Examples*.
b Source B illustrates four examples of different types of *international migrants*. Match each example to the four types of *international migration* listed in Source A.
c Use an atlas and an outline map of the world to locate, label and annotate these *international migrations*.
d Describe **one** example of *internal migration* that has taken place in the country where you live. Add your example to your copy of Source A.

### TASK 3: Study Source C
Look at the push-pull factors shown in Source C. Create a two-column table headed **Push** and **Pull** factors. Sort out the factors into four groups within each column as follows:
- physical factors
- economic factors
- social factors
- political factors

### TASK 4: Study Source D
a How might 'intervening obstacles' be different for internal and international migration?
b What was the main 'intervening obstacle' between north Africa and Italy?
c Why do so many migrants not survive the journey from north Africa?

# Cambridge IGCSE Geography — Migration

## 7 The impacts of migration

### Migrants welcome?

Many countries, especially those that are relatively wealthy such as the USA and those in Western Europe, have benefited greatly from migrant labour from other countries in the last two centuries. In the 21st century, however, these and many other relatively wealthy countries have to manage a number of population issues. These include:

- an ageing population with people living longer
- a diminishing workforce
- a reduced birth rate
- a workforce that does not wish to work long hours and carry out low-paid work
- a workforce that lacks the skills that the country needs.

To solve these problems, some countries are encouraging people to emigrate from other countries to carry out these jobs. This has had both positive and negative impacts on:

- the migrants, their families and the places they have left
- the indigenous people already living at the migrant's destination.

### A International migrants work

*A migrant in Cairo can work for himself as a shoe-shiner.*

**OVERSEAS NURSES ARRIVE IN CITY**
A group of 49 nurses have joined staff at Leicester's hospitals. They have been recruited from Ireland, Spain and Portugal. Fifty-five more staff will arrive in February. 'We are looking to recruit 200 international staff in 2014,' said a spokesman.

Adapted from *Leicester Mercury*, 22 January 2014

### B International migration has positive and negative impacts

| | Positive impacts | Negative impacts |
|---|---|---|
| **Origin** | Can send money home to family. More resources for people left behind. Learn new skills which may be used if the migrant returns home. | Loss of contact with family and friends. Away from home for long period of time. |
| **Destination** | Chance to obtain regular work. Chance to save some money. Chance of better quality of life. Chance of better standard of living. | May be low-paid work. May be exploited by long hours and poor working conditions. May be racial and cultural problems. May struggle with language. Hard to get housing. |

### C International migrants are not always welcome

**Singaporeans turn on migrants after riots**
The worst riots in more than 40 years in the Racecourse Road area of Little India sparked an angry backlash against migrant workers accused of causing the trouble. Residents have asked for a crackdown on immigration. South Asian men were filmed destroying buses with rubbish bins while vehicles were set alight. Singapore's 5.4 million citizens were asked to stay calm. About ¾ of the country is ethnically Chinese but it also has a large South Asian community with about 1.3 million foreign workers, many of whom work in the booming construction and service industries for salaries of between £225 and £340 compared with Singapore's average monthly wage of £2165. Many endure poor working conditions and discrimination.

Adapted from *The Times*, 11 December 2013

**Migrant workers poorly treated in Canada**
Following the death of 10 migrant workers in a road accident, questions are being asked about Canada's treatment of migrants. A spokesperson for the Justice for Migrants Office said 'Where they are reliant on one employer for their status, they are not allowed to be on the free market and have no labour mobility. They are here to do work that Canadians are too lazy or not prepared to do. They work for the minimum wage and rarely earn enough to send any money home. Remember, most have paid $15 000 to get here.' Migrants still live in trailers or bunk houses where sanitation, overcrowding and heat can be health and safety hazards.

Adapted from the *Toronto Sun*, 23 February 2014

**Bulgaria puts up razor-wire fence to keep out migrants**
Bulgaria has completed the first phase of a 20-mile border fence to hold back a flood of Syrian refugees that has overwhelmed the country. More than 11 000 people have illegally crossed Bulgaria's frontier with Turkey this year, forcing the government to turn former schools and army camps into makeshift detention centres.

Adapted from *The Times*, 30 November 2013

## Internal migration has impacts

The largest internal migration in the world is taking place in China. In the last 30 years over 120 million people have moved to the cities – mostly Beijing and Shanghai – and another 80 million have moved to small towns seeking work.

Until 1978, less than 20 per cent of its population lived in cities. Three decades of staggering economic growth mean that, since 2000, almost 1 million villages have been abandoned or destroyed due to urban sprawl. Many villages close to towns have been taken over by construction of urban housing, motorways or rail links. Others have been left derelict and overgrown as residents migrated to cities. Many people have left villages to work on huge construction projects in cities, including the Beijing Olympics in 2008 and the Shanghai International Exposition in 2010.

More and more subsistence farmers are being resettled by the government into identical housing estates close to the expanding towns and cities. Between 2010 and 2025, 300 million people are expected to move to urban areas. By 2034 the Chinese government aims to have 75% of its population living in cities.

### D  Newspaper extract

#### History's greatest migration and the death of the Chinese village

Five generations of the Qiao family have lived in the isolated, mountain-top village of Maijieping in Hunan province. They watched as civil war, revolution, hunger and finally massive economic change swept the nation. Now the family's days there are over as thousands of Chinese villages are deserted as young people move away. 'The young generation find life too hard here,' sighs 58-year-old Qiao Jinchao, who is one of only four residents left in a village that was once home to 140. 'The young people have left and feel no loyalty to the land. They are not coming back. Transport is bad and they don't want to farm. It's hard work and the money is not good. If you work in cities you can earn 2000 yuan (£202) a month. The living conditions are better there too.'

The damage began for Maijieping in the mid-1980s as China became the 'factory of the world'. Some residents moved or married into villages that were less remote while others left to work in the nearby cities. The effects on the village are clear to see. The four residents are kept company by a few chickens, cows, dogs and cats. A local primary school has been converted into a barn. Mud-brick homes are now chicken barns, or cowsheds. There can be little social life or sense of community with just four residents.

Qiao Jinchao and the other three residents have been asked to sign up for a new village being built near the city of Yanshi. 'Enjoy the city life: build a new rural community,' says one poster. 'In another ten years we will have to move down the mountain too,' he says. 'We won't be able to walk so we will have to go where our children are.'

**Adapted from** *The Sunday Telegraph,* 24 November 2013

### TASK 1: Study Source A
a  Suggest ways in which the two jobs are different in terms of:
   - skills required
   - working hours
   - amount of pay and taxes paid
   - job satisfaction.
b  Decide whether each job is formal or informal work. Explain your choice.
c  Suggest why each of these jobs is more likely to be carried out by migrant workers than the indigenous population. Explain your views.

### TASK 2: Study Source B
Describe **two** positive and **two** negative impacts of migration for:
- the migrant
- the origin of the migrant
- the migrant's destination.

### TASK 3: Study Source C
a  Suggest why migrants in some countries are:
   - not wanted
   - not liked
   - not treated or paid well.
b  Suggest how governments can ensure that migrants are treated fairly once they are allowed into a country to work.

### TASK 4: Study Source D
a  Identify:
   - **three** push factors that explain why people have left Maijieping
   - **three** pull factors that explain why people have left Maijieping.
b  Describe the impacts on the village, its environment and the remaining residents of the migration away from the village.
c  Which of the migrations mentioned is *voluntary* and which *involuntary*? Explain your decisions.

### TASK 5
Discuss with a partner your view on two policies of the Chinese government:
- To have 75% of the population living in cities by 2034.
- To introduce a law that makes people return home to visit their ageing parents at least twice a year.

# Cambridge IGCSE Geography — Migration

## Case Study
## An international migration – Qatar

### From pearl fishing to prosperity

Life in Qatar before 1930 involved widespread poverty, malnutrition and disease. Most people worked in the pearl fishing industry but that collapsed when the Japanese began to make artificial pearls. In 1935 the arrival of oil prospectors signalled a new future for the state. The Second World War of 1939–45 delayed oil production for ten years but, once production began, the oil income changed this tiny, impoverished nation into one with the second highest per capita income in the world.

Progress was rapid. Qatar's first school opened in 1952; its first hospital in 1959. In 1971 it became an independent state and began to use oil revenue to develop the country. Since 1995, increasing oil prices and political stability have helped to create one of the fastest-growing economies in the world. This has been helped by having 6 per cent of the world's natural gas reserves.

Gaining such enormous wealth in a short time span has meant that the development of the country has relied on using overseas companies who employ foreign migrants to construct houses, hotels, offices, and infrastructure such as schools and roads. Because of the rapid increase in wealth (GDP per capita is US$92 501), most of the indigenous population either do not have the necessary skills or do not need to work, so it is difficult to find local people to do many jobs, especially if they are low-paid service jobs such as waitresses and taxi drivers.

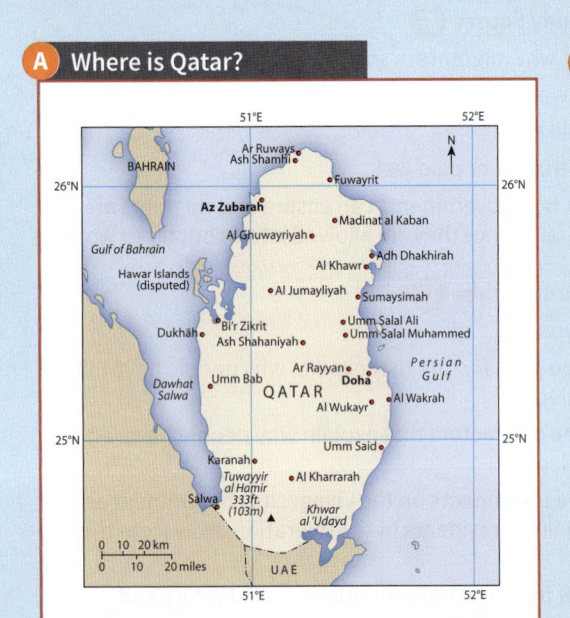

### A  Where is Qatar?

### B  Population growth

| Year | Population |
|---|---|
| 1965 | 75 000 |
| 1970 | 140 000 |
| 1975 | 200 000 |
| 1980 | 225 000 |
| 1985 | 375 000 |
| 1990 | 440 000 |
| 1995 | 525 000 |
| 2000 | 650 000 |
| 2005 | 775 000 |
| 2010 | 1 700 000 |
| 2015 (est.) | 2 500 000 |

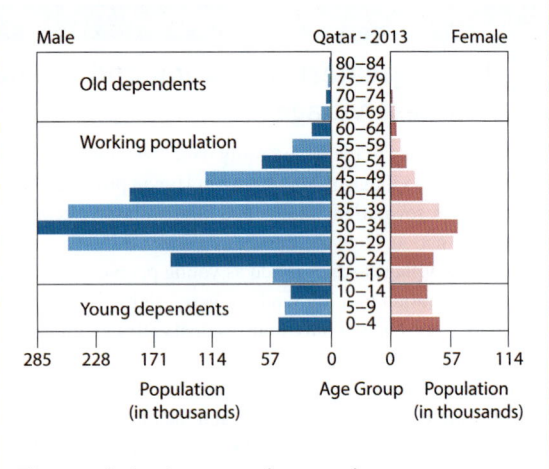

The population is expected to grow by another 15% during 2015.

---

**TASK 1:** Study Source **A** and the information above.

a  Use an atlas and this map to describe the location of Qatar in relation to your own country. Refer to distance and direction.

b  Describe the location of Qatar in relation to lines of latitude and longitude, neighbouring countries and sea areas.

c  Draw a time-line to illustrate Qatar's growth in the last 90 years.

**TASK 2:** Study Source **B**

a  Draw a line graph to show how the population changed between 1965 and 2015.

b  Describe the graph using data and referring to at least **two** trends on the graph.

c  In 2010, 80% of the population was made up of migrants. Indicate this on your line graph.

d  Describe and explain:
   - the shape of Qatar's population structure
   - the gender balance.

e  Suggest **three** population problems that the Qatari government might need to address in the next few years.

# Case Study: An international migration – Qatar

## C Doha: the capital of Qatar

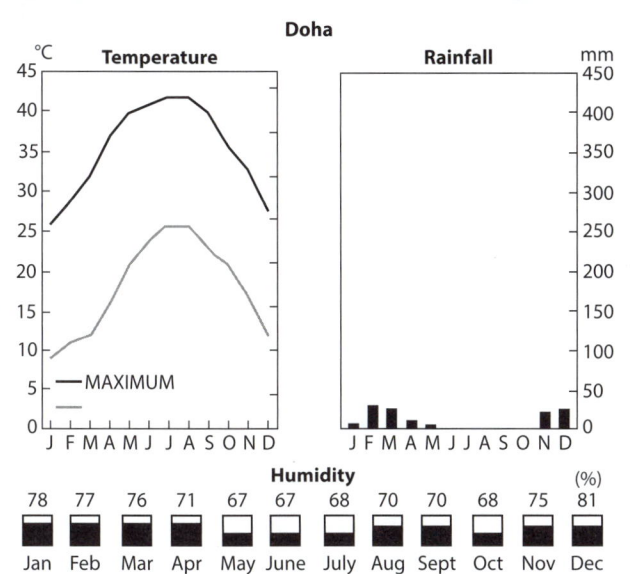

Doha Temperature (°C) – Maximum line rising from ~26 in Jan to ~42 in Jul/Aug, falling to ~28 in Dec. Minimum line from ~10 in Jan rising to ~26 in Jul/Aug, falling to ~12 in Dec.

Rainfall (mm): small bars in Jan, Feb, Mar, and Nov, Dec; negligible rainfall Apr–Oct.

Humidity (%):
| Jan | Feb | Mar | Apr | May | June | July | Aug | Sept | Oct | Nov | Dec |
|---|---|---|---|---|---|---|---|---|---|---|---|
| 78 | 77 | 76 | 71 | 67 | 67 | 68 | 70 | 70 | 68 | 75 | 81 |

## D Where are the migrants from?

**The origin of migrants: the top 14 (2013)**

| Country of origin | Number of migrants |
|---|---|
| India | 545 000 |
| Nepal | 341 000 |
| Philippines | 185 000 |
| Bangladesh | 137 000 |
| Sri Lanka | 100 000 |
| Pakistan | 90 000 |
| Sudan | 42 000 |
| Indonesia | 38 000 |
| Jordan | 34 000 |
| Iran | 30 000 |
| Lebanon | 25 000 |
| Palestine | 20 500 |
| UK | 20 000 |
| USA | 15 000 |

## E What are they doing there?

Visitors arriving at Qatar Airport will have their passport stamped by a Qatari. After that they will feel they are in several other countries! There are car-hire attendants from Pakistan, taxi-drivers from Bangladesh, hotel porters from India, waitresses from the Philippines, shopkeepers from India, building labourers from Nepal, teachers from the UK and Americans turning pink on their day off from the oil and gas industries. If you commit a crime you may find yourself before a judge from Egypt.

The kafala system: Foreign workers must be sponsored by companies based in Qatar. They become responsible for their visa, legal status and working conditions. The workers must hand in their passports to their employers. They cannot change jobs or leave the country at will. They need an exit permit to get out of Qatar and that has to be approved by the employer.

### TASK 3: Study Source C

a Describe the climate of Qatar throughout the year. Refer to:
- minimum and maximum average temperatures
- rainfall
- humidity.

b How does this compare with the climate where you live?

c Suggest the physical problems migrants have to cope with in Qatar. How might they be solved?

### TASK 4: Study Source D

a There were 278 000 Qataris living in Qatar in 2013. Which **two** countries had most migrant workers in the country?

b Using a world outline map, draw a flow-diagram to show the origin of the top 14 countries supplying migrants in 2013. Use a scale of 1 mm = 30 000 migrants.

c Describe and explain the pattern you have drawn.

### TASK 5: Study Source E

a Divide the different jobs that migrant workers can do in Qatar into two lists:
- jobs requiring high skills and qualifications
- jobs requiring low skills and no qualifications.

b What evidence is there in the photograph of:
- building work taking place?
- workers protecting themselves against the climate?

c What is your view of the *kafala* system and how it affects migrants in Qatar?

### TASK 6:

Many migrants are helping to build stadiums and infrastructure for the World Cup in 2022. Research the current situation in Qatar regarding this event.

# Cambridge IGCSE Geography | Population structure

## 8 Finding out about the population

### Collecting population data

Nobody knows how many people there are in the world. Many governments carry out a **census**, or count, every few years to get an idea of the structure of their population. But some countries cannot afford a census; others choose not to have one.

### Features of a population pyramid

Population pyramids can give you information about three different groups of people.

- The youngest age group of 0–14 are dependants as they are usually of school age and depend on others for resources.
- The 15–64 age group are usually working, and young and elderly groups are dependent on them. They provide resources that the other groups depend on.
- The elderly group from 65 upwards are dependants as they are not usually in work.

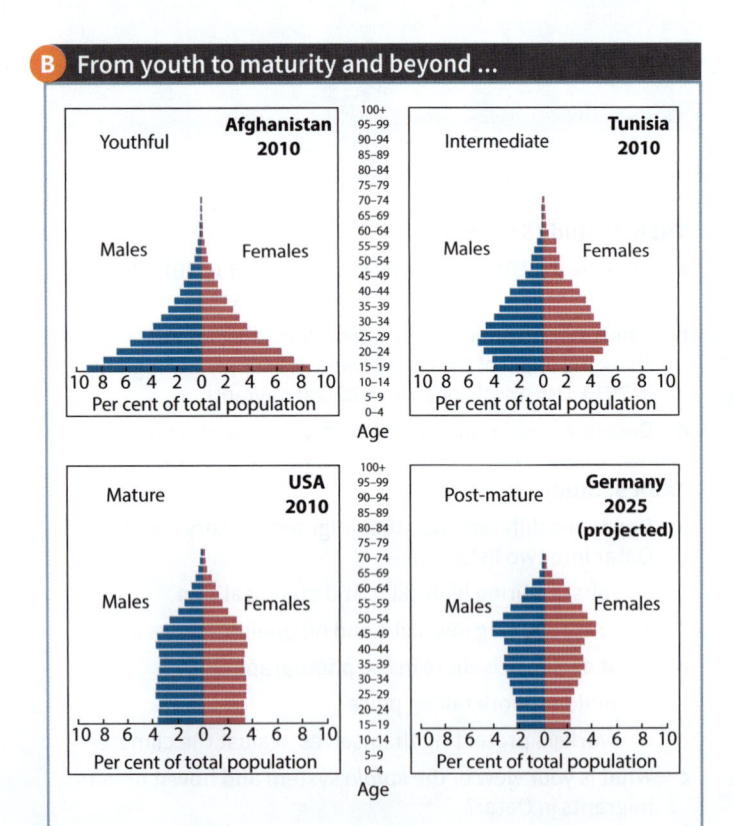

### A What a pyramid shows

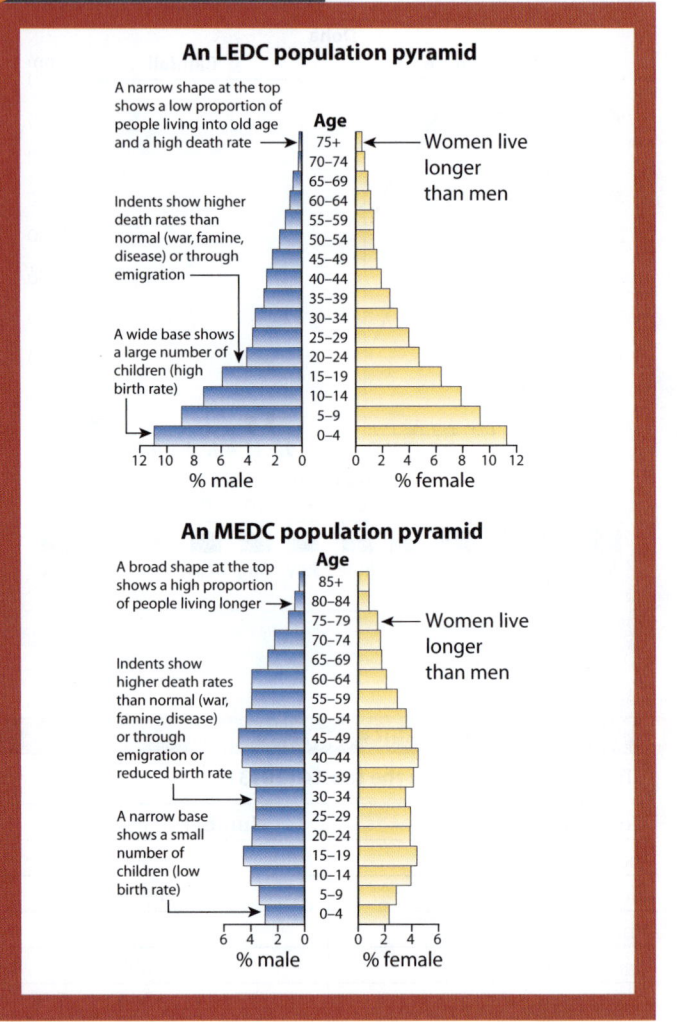

**An LEDC population pyramid**

A narrow shape at the top shows a low proportion of people living into old age and a high death rate
— Women live longer than men

Indents show higher death rates than normal (war, famine, disease) or through emigration

A wide base shows a large number of children (high birth rate)

**An MEDC population pyramid**

A broad shape at the top shows a high proportion of people living longer
— Women live longer than men

Indents show higher death rates than normal (war, famine, disease) or through emigration or reduced birth rate

A narrow base shows a small number of children (low birth rate)

### B From youth to maturity and beyond ...

**Afghanistan 2010** — Youthful
**Tunisia 2010** — Intermediate
**USA 2010** — Mature
**Germany 2025 (projected)** — Post-mature

---

**TASK 1:** Study Source **A**

a List **three** differences in the shape and structure of the two population pyramids.

b What issues would face the government of a country with a population pyramid like that of the LEDC?

c How would these issues be different for a government with a population pyramid like that of the MEDC?

**TASK 2:** Study Source **B**

a Describe the population structure of Afghanistan in 2010. Refer to age groups, workforce and dependants in your answer.

b In 2010, Tunisia's structure was different to that of Afghanistan. Suggest reasons for any differences.

c The government of the USA had different population issues to deal with in 2010 than either Afghanistan or Tunisia. Describe these differences and suggest reasons for them.

d Based on sample censuses, Germany has projected its 2025 population as shown. What should the government be doing now based on the shape of this pyramid?

# Population pyramids

Demography is the study of people or populations. Population pyramids are very useful for **demographers**. Where census information is available, a pyramid can be created which shows the population's age and gender distribution. They are one of the best tools on which to base future planning decisions by the government and local authorities. Perhaps too many babies are being born and the birth rate needs reducing; or it could be the opposite. Maybe there are going to be too many dependants and not enough workers for the jobs that will be available – so one answer might be to attract immigration. If there are going to be many old people in ten years' time, their care needs planning for.

## C Comparing population structures between countries

|  | Afghanistan | USA |
|---|---|---|
| Population (million) | 31.1 | 317.6 |
| Birth rate (per 1000 pop.) | 39.3 | 12.6 |
| Death rate (per 1000 pop.) | 14.6 | 8.1 |
| Life expectancy: Male | 59 | 75 |
| Female | 61 | 81 |
| Fertility rate (per woman) | 5.1 | 1.88 |
| Infant mortality rate (per 1000 live births) | 121 | 6.2 |
| Age structure | | |
| 65+ | 2.4% | 12.8% |
| 15–64 | 55.3% | 67% |
| 0–14 | 42.3% | 20.2% |

## D Young and old – different concerns

### AMERICA'S AGEING POPULATION
The number of old people is rapidly becoming a global issue and the pace of ageing will affect the USA in the next 30 years. By 2050, one-fifth of the USA population will be over 65. This is because the 'baby boomers' – those born after the end of the Second World War between 1946 and 1964 – are working their way up the population pyramid and are now over 65. This will put a strain on funding their health and well-being. Taxes may need raising from a smaller workforce to provide medical centres, disability equipment, care homes and drugs.

### RELIGIOUS LEADERS HELP PROMOTE BIRTH CONTROL IN AFGHANISTAN
Recent years have seen a significant increase in birth control involving some religious leaders speaking to their communities about contraceptives and the benefits of family planning. Birth spacing is also being promoted to try and reduce one of the highest birth rates in the developing world.

### US BIRTH RATE AT RECORD LOW AS COUPLES DECIDE TO STAY CHILD-FREE
The US birth rate is at a record low. In 2013 the birth rate was just 13.7 per 1000 people; a century ago it was 30.1. Much of this is due to the increase in educated women who want careers to last longer before committing to children. A materialistic lifestyle also encourages couples to enjoy their wealth without children or to have them later. With fewer young people coming through, there are concerns about the size of the working population in 20 years. Who will do the work?

### AFGHANISTAN GIVES YOUTH THE CHANCE OF A BRIGHTER FUTURE
Afghanistan has one of the world's fastest growing populations but 68% of its citizens are under 25 and 40% between 15 and 24. The government has developed a National Youth Policy to involve them in education, employment, health and well-being and to develop a workforce that will also help steer the country to peace and prosperity. Developing their skills and the economy could also help increase the life expectancy of its older citizens in a country where few people live beyond 60.

---

**TASK 3:** Study Sources **B** and **C**

a Draw comparative graphs to represent the data in Source C.

b How does the data in Source C for Afghanistan help explain the shape of its pyramid in Source B?

c How does the data in Source C for the USA help explain the shape of its pyramid in Source B?

d Suggest whether Afghanistan or the USA is the more developed. Justify your choice using the data in Source C.

**TASK 4:** Study Source **D**

a The USA and Afghanistan both have issues with birth rates. In what way are they different?

b In what ways are the issues related to an ageing population different in these two countries?

c How might the working populations be affected by the future population structures of these two countries?

**TASK 5**

a Carry out research into the population structure of your country. Try and find a population pyramid for the most recent census if your country had one.

b How does the population structure compare to the shapes in Source B?

c Discuss with a partner the issues that face your country. Refer to:
- those aged 65+
- those aged 15–64
- those aged 0–14

d Does the government of your country have any plans that will affect the population structure in the next few years? If so, write a brief summary of what they are.

**Cambridge IGCSE Geography** | **Population structure**

## Case Study

### A country with high dependency – Italy

#### Italy has a high dependent population

Italy has more than 60 million residents, with a population density of 201/km² (520/square mile) – one of the highest in Europe. One common fact in most Italian regions is the high degree of dependency of the young and old on the working population, much of which is boosted by net migration into the country. Recent census data shows that Japan and most of Europe have the highest **dependency ratios** in the world and that Italy has one of the highest in Europe. In less economically developed countries, such as Afghanistan, the dependency is mostly from the 0–14 age group as few people live to 65 or over. As a country develops, this dependency becomes more balanced between young and old, as in the case of Italy.

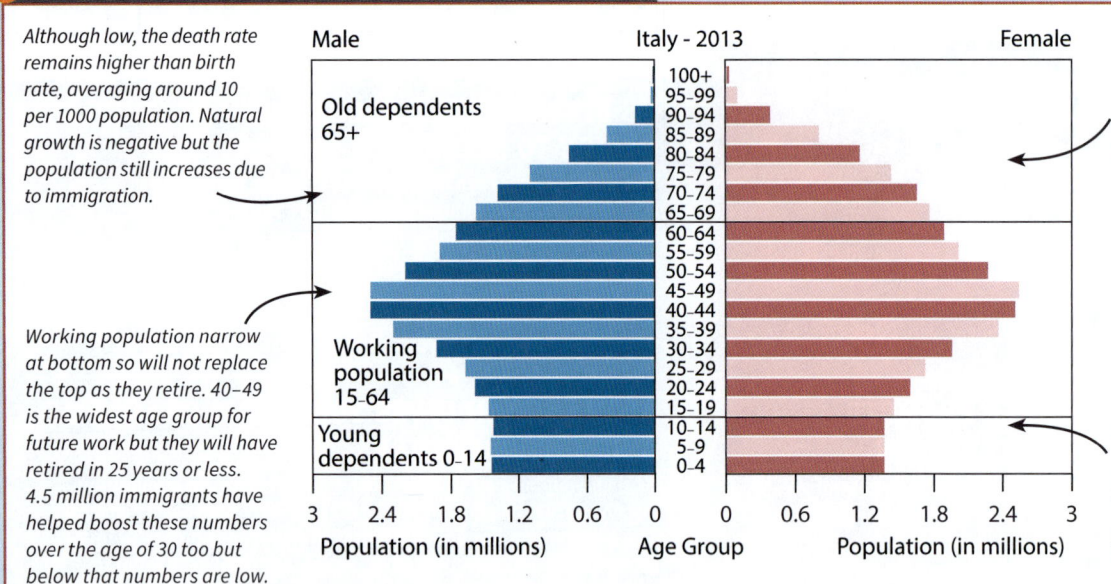

### A  Italy's population structure

*Although low, the death rate remains higher than birth rate, averaging around 10 per 1000 population. Natural growth is negative but the population still increases due to immigration.*

*Working population narrow at bottom so will not replace the top as they retire. 40–49 is the widest age group for future work but they will have retired in 25 years or less. 4.5 million immigrants have helped boost these numbers over the age of 30 too but below that numbers are low.*

Population pyramid: Italy – 2013, showing Male and Female, Old dependents 65+, Working population 15–64, Young dependents 0–14. Population in millions from 3 to 0 on each side.

*Women slightly outnumber men as elderly dependants from 65+. This is common in most population pyramids.*

*Birth rate down to around 9 per 1000 population. The 0–14 age group is the narrowest on the pyramid. About 25% of women have no child and another 25% only have one child. Birth rate is higher among immigrants than Italians.*

**Birth rate – average number of births per 1000 people per year**

| Year | 2004 | 2005 | 2006 | 2007 | 2008 | 2009 | 2010 | 2011 | 2012 | 2013 |
|---|---|---|---|---|---|---|---|---|---|---|
| Number | 9.0 | 8.9 | 8.7 | 8.5 | 8.4 | 8.2 | 8.0 | 9.2 | 9.0 | 8.9 |

**Death rate – average number of deaths per 1000 people per year**

| Year | 2004 | 2005 | 2006 | 2007 | 2008 | 2009 | 2010 | 2011 | 2012 | 2013 |
|---|---|---|---|---|---|---|---|---|---|---|
| Number | 10.2 | 10.3 | 10.4 | 10.5 | 10.6 | 10.7 | 10.8 | 9.8 | 9.9 | 10.1 |

Total population (2013): 61 482 297

---

**TASK 1: Study Source A**

a  Estimate the following:
  ■ the number of young dependants aged 10–14
  ■ the number of working population aged 60–64.
b  Comment on the differences between these figures when both age groups move into the age band above them.
c  Why is the population still increasing even though death rate is higher than birth rate?
d  Italy is a developed country. Suggest why death rates are low but birth rates are lower.

**TASK 2: Study Source B**

a  What is meant by:
  ■ a young dependant?
  ■ an old dependant?
  ■ the working population?
b  What is different about the dependent age groups in these countries?
c  Which age structure is Italy the closest to? Explain your choice.

# Case Study: A country with high dependency – Italy

## B What is dependency?

Dependants are those people who are not part of the labour force of a country. In general this means young people in the age range of 0–14 and older people of 65 and over. As a rule these people are not expected to be in the working population. Those in the 15–64 age range are the people who are part of the working population even if they are unemployed on occasions. This group forms the productive part of the population.

*If you are working and aged 15–64 you are part of the working population.*

*If you are over 64 and not at work you are an old dependant.*

### Some international age structures and dependencies

| Country | Afghanistan | Tunisia | USA | Germany | Japan |
|---|---|---|---|---|---|
| 65+ | 2.4% | 7.3% | 12.8% | 20.9% | 23.1% |
| 15–64 | 55.3% | 70.5% | 67% | 66.1% | 63.7% |
| 0–14 | 42.3% | 22.2% | 20.2% | 13.1% | 13.2% |
| Total population (million) | 25.5 | 1.8 | 317.6 | 80.6 | 127.2 |

*If you are at school and under 15 you are a young dependant.*

## C Crisis in the Cabinet of Italy

" I am concerned about the working population. More workers are reaching 65 and there are too few young people coming through to replace them. We are also losing a lot of experienced workers and may have to increase immigration to fill the jobs that our workers cannot or will not do. We may have to raise taxes to pay for the health and well-being of our ageing population; that will not be popular. My advisers suggest we raise the retirement age to 77, but who wants that? "

Minister of Labour and Social Policy

" For the next few years, while we are educating our young people to a high level, there will not be enough of them to do the jobs needed. Most schools are less than full; we may have to close some or make them join with others. This will not be popular with parents nor with teachers who may lose jobs due to the low birth rate. We could look at ways to increase the birth rate but that will only affect employment in 20 years' time! "

Minister of Education, Universities and Research

" It is the ageing population that concerns me. More people are living longer and we have increased our spending on their health and well-being, but it will not be enough. We need more hospitals, medical care, doctors and nurses and care homes. Pensions and other costs will also increase. Where will the money come from? "

Minister for Health

" We can all see that, although death rates and birth rates are low, the death rate has been above the birth rate for over a decade. With more dying than being born, we have negative natural population growth. If it wasn't for immigrants, we would have a real problem filling the jobs we need doing. We must relax our immigration laws and get another 2.2 million immigrants in to replace the people retiring. Not all Italians welcome migrants and there would be issues of border controls, housing and culture clashes to deal with. But we need their help now. "

Minister of Foreign Affairs

### TASK 3: Study Source C

a Work together in groups of five. Four group members should take on one of the roles shown in the Cabinet of Italy. A fifth member must act as the President of Italy and chair the Cabinet meeting.

b Read the comments made by the person whose role you are taking. Make a list of key points made, use data from Source A too, and add some points of your own.

c Discuss, with the President chairing the discussion, the issue of 'Italy's population structure – problems and solutions'.

d The President should summarise the problems and solutions you have suggested and the decisions made about what you are going to do! Do other groups agree?

# Factors influencing population density

## Population distribution

**Population distribution** means the pattern of where people live. World population distribution is uneven. Some places, especially those with hostile environments (e.g. Antarctica) have few people living there while others, which are easily habitable, contain many people.

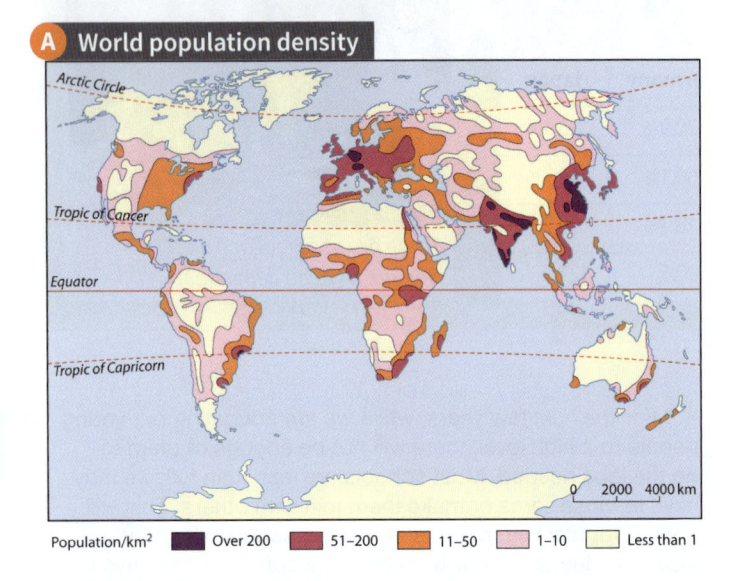

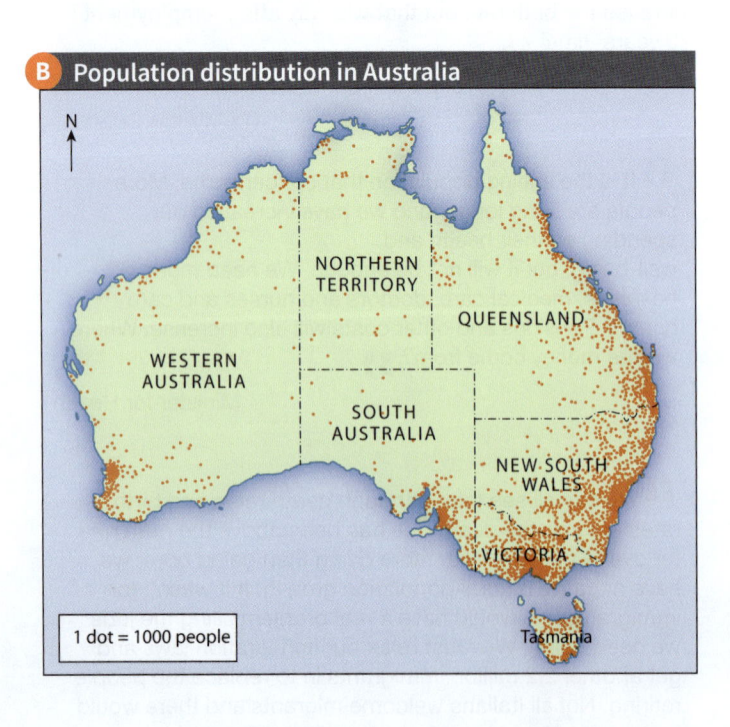

**A** World population density

Population/km²: Over 200 | 51–200 | 11–50 | 1–10 | Less than 1

**B** Population distribution in Australia

1 dot = 1000 people

## Population density

**Population density** describes the average number of people living in a given area (this is usually a square kilometre, or km²). It is calculated by dividing the total population by the area of land. If all the people living in the world were evenly spread over the surface of the land there would be about six people living in every square kilometre. However, in some areas lots of people live close together in large urban areas (towns and cities). These are densely populated or have a high population density (e.g. north-east USA). There are other areas where few or no people live, such as in mountainous regions and deserts. These are sparsely populated or have a low population density (e.g. central Australia). Over 90 per cent of the world's population lives in the northern hemisphere, where there is most land. Over half of the world's land surface has no one living on it. In contrast, Macau has more than 18 500 people living in one square kilometre.

### Where do people live?

**Source C** shows part of Shanghai, in China, where the population is 24 million. As the government has invested in the economy of urban areas such as Shanghai, the large amount of work that is available there makes it possible for many people to make a living. There is a great variety of different types of jobs, for example in offices, shops, factories, transport and hotels. Shanghai's weather is generally mild and moist, with four distinct seasons – a pleasant warm spring, a hot rainy summer, a comfortable cool autumn and a short cold winter.

**Source D** shows part of the Tröllaskagi peninsula, in northern Iceland, which lies between the fjords of Eyjafjörður and Skagafjörður. The **peninsula** is mountainous with several peaks reaching over 1000 metres above sea level, some of which are permanently covered by ice and snow. The peninsula is cut by several deep valleys that were carved by glaciers and later by the rivers that now flow down those valleys. Few people live in the area as it is hard to make a living and there is a lack of mineral resources. The slopes are difficult to build on, **access** is limited and winters are long and very cold.

Theme 1: Topic 9

**C** Shanghai, China

**D** Tröllaskagi, Iceland

**E** Factors influencing where people live

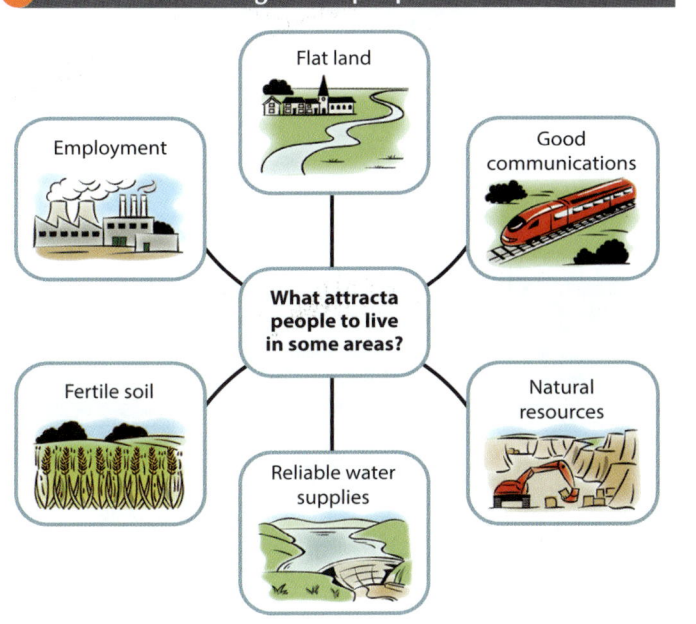

**TASK 1:** Study Source **A**

a  Explain the difference between population density and population distribution.

b  Use an atlas to name:
- **three** areas with a population density of over 200 people per square kilometre
- **three** areas with a population density of less than 1 person per square kilometre.

c  Find a map in your atlas that shows world climates. Explain how climate (temperature and rainfall) influence population density.

**TASK 2:** Study Source **B**

a  Describe the distribution of population in Australia. In your answer you should name states and use directions to help you.

b  Use information from your atlas to help you to explain why Australia's population is unevenly distributed.

**TASK 3:** Study Sources **C** and **D**

a  Describe differences between the two areas shown. Refer to:
- relief
- accessibility
- employment opportunities
- climate.

b  Explain how government policies can influence the population density and distribution in a country.

**TASK 4:** Study Source **E**

a  Find a picture of your own of an area where lots of people live. Add labels to it to explain why many people live there.

b  Find a picture of your own of an area where very few people live. Add labels to it to describe the difficulties of living there.

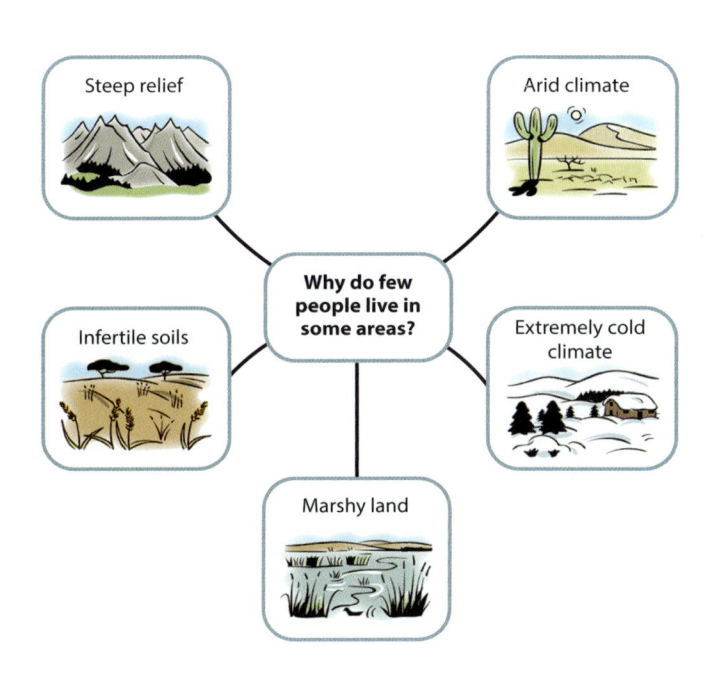

What attracts people to live in some areas?
- Employment
- Flat land
- Good communications
- Fertile soil
- Reliable water supplies
- Natural resources

Why do few people live in some areas?
- Steep relief
- Arid climate
- Infertile soils
- Extremely cold climate
- Marshy land

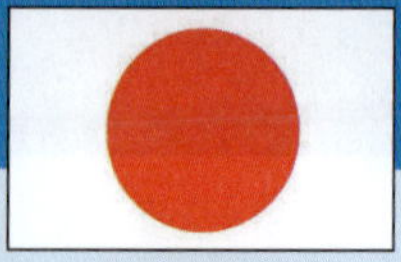

# Cambridge IGCSE Geography
## Population density and distribution

## Case Study
### High population density – Japan

### Where do people live in Japan?

Japan is one of the most densely populated countries in the world with a population density of over 350/km². However, the people are not spread out evenly across the land. Some parts of Japan are densely populated but other parts have very few people living there. Source A shows the population distribution of Japan. The distribution shows the way in which people are spread out across the country.

**A Population distribution in Japan**
- Represents 500 000 people

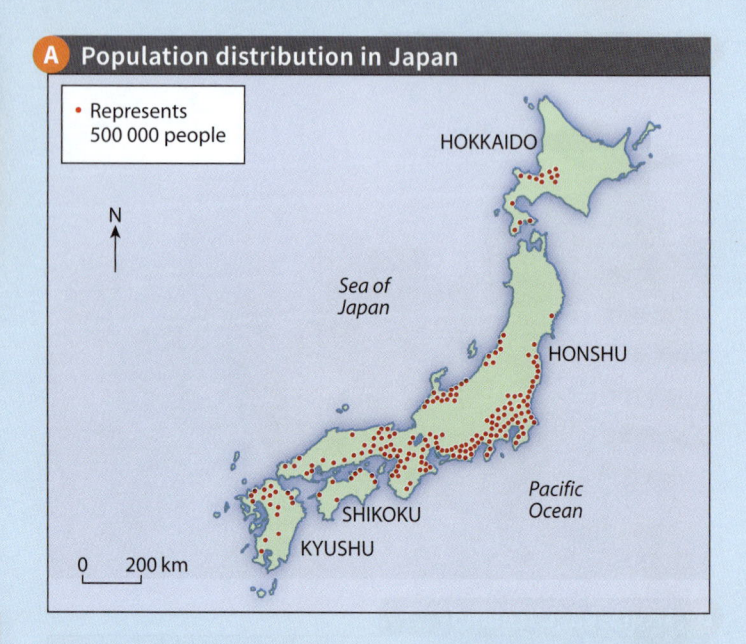

**B Population density in Japan**

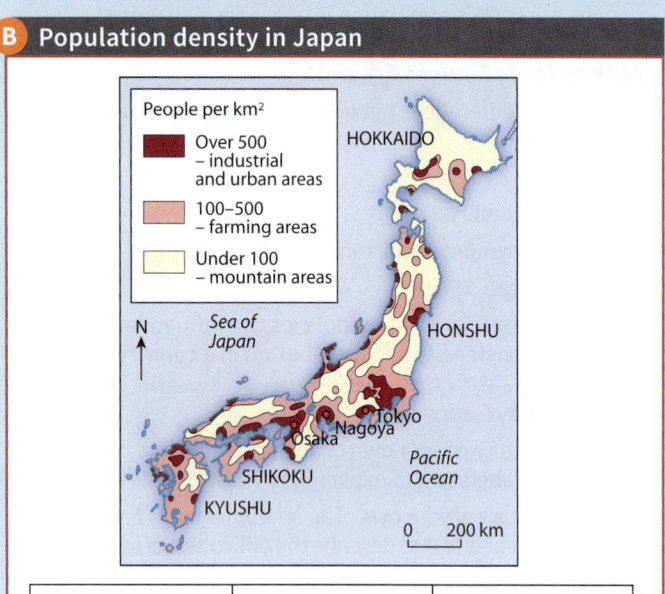

People per km²:
- Over 500 – industrial and urban areas
- 100–500 – farming areas
- Under 100 – mountain areas

|  | Population | Area (km²) |
|---|---|---|
| Hokkaido | 5 376 000 | 83 500 |
| Honshu | 98 352 000 | 230 500 |
| Kyushu | 13 169 000 | 42 150 |
| Shikoku | 4 119 000 | 18 800 |

**C Relief of Japan**
- Land over 500 m
- Land under 500 m

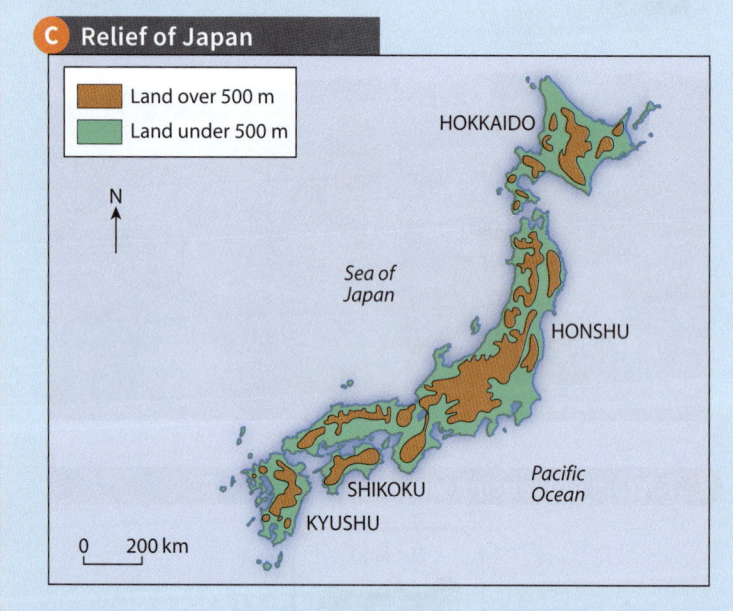

**D Land reclamation in Japan**

Kobe, with its 1.5 million inhabitants, stretches between the Rokko Mountains and the coast, a 2–4 kilometre wide and 16 kilometre-long ribbon city. The shortage of land in Kobe, and the constantly growing demand for land for its port and industries, have led, since the mid-1950s, to the increasing reclamation of land from the sea. The Japanese call this reclaimed land umetate-chi (umetate = fill in and build; chi = land, earth).

The landfill material in Kobe has consisted of rocks and soil removed from the mountains and, since 1995, also partly from earthquake rubble. The millions of cubic metres of rocks and soil from the Rokko Mountains was transported with tipper trucks to an underground conveyor belt, and then carried to its final destination in barges. After removal of the rocks and soil, the flattened mountain regions were used in many places as valuable building land for the construction of new residential districts, where over 130 000 people have found accommodation. 10 000 new houses have been built in Myodani alone.

**Adapted from** *Diercke International Atlas*

## Case Study: High population density – Japan

### E Different population densities

*Northern Japanese Alps*

*A village in Gifu prefecture, Japan*

*Tokyo cityscape*

**Low-density rural areas**
Over two-thirds of Japan is mountainous, with high land and steep slopes. These areas include the central part of Honshu Island and the southern part of Shikoku Island. Few people live here because:
- there is not enough flat land to grow food on
- soils are thin, acidic and infertile
- many areas are isolated and remote as the winding roads are poor and there are few, if any, other communications
- there is little work except forestry as there are few natural resources
- the climate is often extreme, with long, cold winters and heavy rain or snow.

**High-density rural areas**
Outside the urban areas, on the flat valley floors and gently sloping lower slopes of Honshu and Kyushu Islands, many people live in villages or small towns, between which there are many farms. Some people are farmers but others commute daily to the large cities where they work. These areas are densely populated because:
- crops can easily be grown on the fertile soils of the flat or gently sloping land
- it is easy to use farm machinery on flat land
- the warm temperate climate means a variety of crops can be grown
- good roads and railways make it possible to live in the countryside and work in the cities.

**High-density urban areas**
Towns and cities stretch along the coasts, particularly on Honshu Island. Almost a half of Japan's population live in the areas around Tokyo, Nagoya and Osaka. These areas are densely populated because:
- on the flat land it is easy to build
  – towns and cities
  – factories, offices and other commercial buildings
  – road and rail networks
  – airports
- on the coast there are many ports and harbours which have led to
  – the import of raw materials
  – the export of manufactured goods
  – the development of a fishing industry.

---

**TASK 1:** Study Source **A**
Choose the correct word to complete the following sentences about the distribution of Japan's population:
- The population is *evenly/unevenly* distributed.
- Most people live on *Hokkaido/Honshu/Kyushu/Shikoku* Island.
- Most people live along the *borders/coast/rivers/mountains*.

**TASK 2:** Study Source **B**
Work out the population density of each of the four islands which are part of Japan.
Rank the four islands from highest to lowest population density.

**TASK 3:** Study Sources **A**, **B**, **C** and **D**
a  Describe the link between population density and relief in Japan.
b  Explain how land reclamation has helped reduce the problems caused by the high population density in Kobe.

**TASK 4:** Study Source **E**
Draw a table like the one below and fill in the details.

|  | Low-density rural areas | High-density rural areas | High-density urban areas |
|---|---|---|---|
| Relief |  |  |  |
| Communications |  |  |  |
| Economy |  |  |  |

**TASK 5**
A large part of Japan's population lives in the Tokyo, Nagoya and Osaka areas.
Working in groups, carry out research on why so many people live in these areas.
You may want to use the Internet or other sources to prepare a presentation. In your presentation you should include information about:
- relief
- climate
- employment.

# Cambridge IGCSE Geography
## Population density and distribution

# Case Study
## Low population density – Namibia

### A  Regions of Namibia

| Region |  | Population density/km² |
|---|---|---|
| 1 | Caprivi | 5.5 |
| 2 | Erongo | 1.7 |
| 3 | Hardap | 0.6 |
| 4 | Karas | 0.4 |
| 5 | Kavango | 4.2 |
| 6 | Khomas | 6.8 |
| 7 | Kunene | 0.6 |
| 8 | Ohangwena | 21.3 |
| 9 | Omaheke | 0.8 |
| 10 | Omusati | 8.6 |
| 11 | Oshana | 18.7 |
| 12 | Oshikoto | 4.2 |
| 13 | Otjozondjupa | 1.3 |

### B  Climate graph of the Karas Region

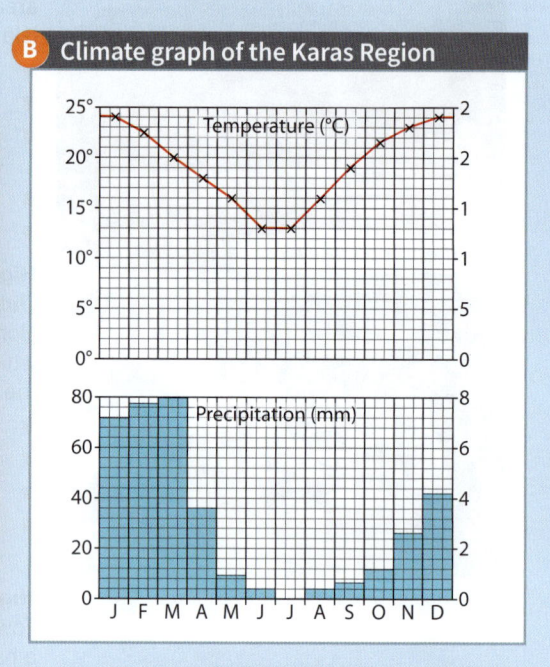

### C  The Karas Region of Namibia

#### Namibia – a country in south-west Africa

The Republic of Namibia is a country in south-west Africa on the Atlantic coast, with a low **GDP (Gross Domestic Product) per person** of US$7900. It gained independence from South Africa in 1990 and its capital city is Windhoek. With an overall population density of 2.6/km² it is one of the most sparsely populated countries in the world. The Namib Desert, an immense expanse of moving gravel plains and dunes of all shapes and sizes which includes the huge dunes at Sossusvlei, stretches along the entire coastline. Much of the country has a hot, dry climate. Rainfall is sparse and erratic and there are prolonged periods of **drought**. The economy is dependent on the extraction and processing of minerals such as diamonds and uranium for export. The Rössing Uranium Mine, for example, located in the Namib Desert near the town of Arandisis, is one of the largest opencast mines in the world. However, mining employs only about 3 per cent of the population while about half of the population depends on **subsistence agriculture**.

Case Study: Low population density – Namibia

**D** Part of the Karas Region

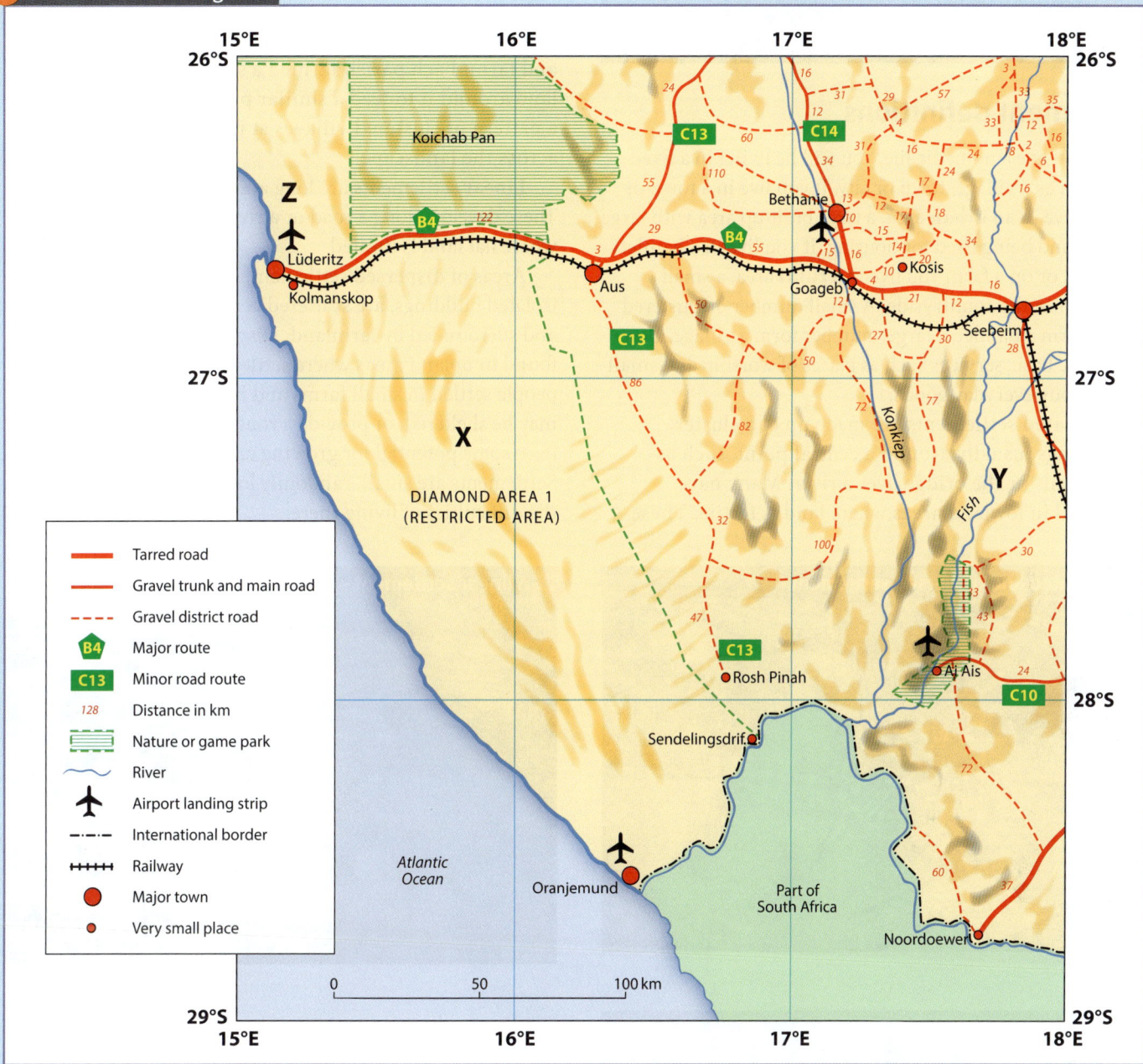

## TASK 1: Study Source A
On an outline map of Source A, produce a choropleth map to show the population density of the 13 regions of Namibia. Use three shades of the same colour for regions with:
- over 15 people/km² (*dark shade*)
- between 5 and 15 people/km² (*medium shade*)
- fewer than 5 people/km² (*light shade*).

## TASK 2: Study Source B
a What is the total annual precipitation of the Karas region?
b What is the annual temperature range of the Karas region?

## TASK 3: Study Sources C and D
The map shows part of the Karas region in southern Namibia, the most sparsely populated region in the country. The locations where the photographs were taken are shown on the map by the letters X, Y, Z.

a Use latitude and longitude to give references for the position of each photograph. (Note that 1° = 60'. The symbol ' is called a minute.)

b Write **one** sentence about each photo that clearly describes its main features.

## TASK 4
Use all the sources to explain why the Karas region of Namibia is sparsely populated. Support your answer by referring to evidence from the sources and named places on the map, Source D.

# 10 Settlement patterns

## Settlement definitions

Unless you live a nomadic life, you will be living in a fixed place such as a village, town or city. If you live in a town or city you live in an **urban** area, a large built-up area with large areas of land being used for housing. If you live in a hamlet or village, or on a farm you live in a **rural** area, a small settlement in the countryside. A small number of clustered houses form a hamlet, a larger number form a village, along with some basic services such as places of worship and small shops to buy everyday goods.

**Nucleated** settlements are made up of a cluster of buildings, usually around a central point, such as a crossroads or the bridge over a river. Many have developed in lowland areas where land is fertile. These areas attracted people many years ago to settle here and farm. Each parish farmed a similar amount of land around it to feed a similar population. This led to a pattern of clustered villages at fairly equal intervals across the landscape.

**Linear** settlements are long and thin (ribbon shaped). These develop along a road or a river valley or in an area where flat land is limited.

Areas of **dispersed** settlement, such as farms and isolated buildings, are scattered across the countryside and surrounded by farmland. Dispersed patterns are often found in upland areas where settlement is difficult. Here people settled in small farms and hamlets in areas that may be sheltered, or provide a route through the hills or have some potential for growing crops or grazing livestock. Settlements are small, randomly located and isolated due to the difficulties of living there.

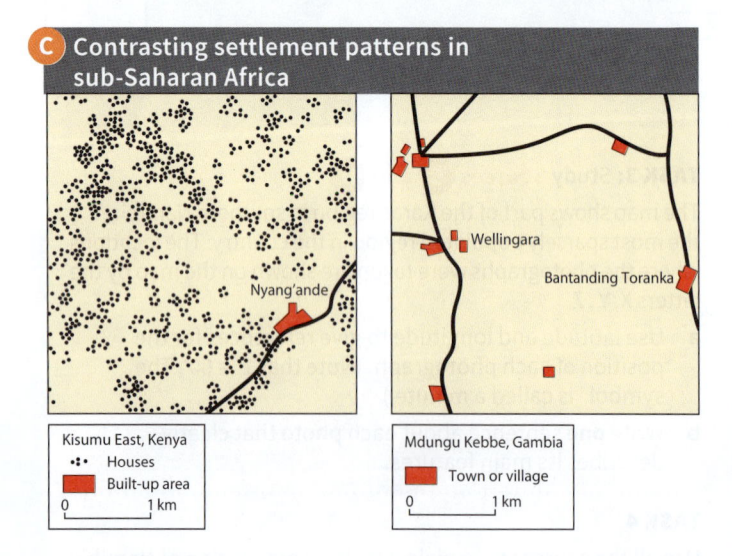

**A** Nucleated and dispersed settlement

**B** A linear settlement

**C** Contrasting settlement patterns in sub-Saharan Africa

Kisumu East, Kenya
· Houses
■ Built-up area
0    1 km

Mdungu Kebbe, Gambia
■ Town or village
0    1 km

**TASK 1:** Study **Sources A and B**
a  Write definitions of the following words:
   Urban      Rural
b  Describe the shapes of the rural settlements in Sources A and B. Use the following words in your answer:
   Nucleated     Linear     Dispersed

**TASK 2:** Study **Source C**
a  Compare the population density of the two areas.
b  How are the settlement patterns in Kisumu East and Mdungu Kebbe different?

# Theme 1: Topic 10

## D  Rural settlement in Normandy, France

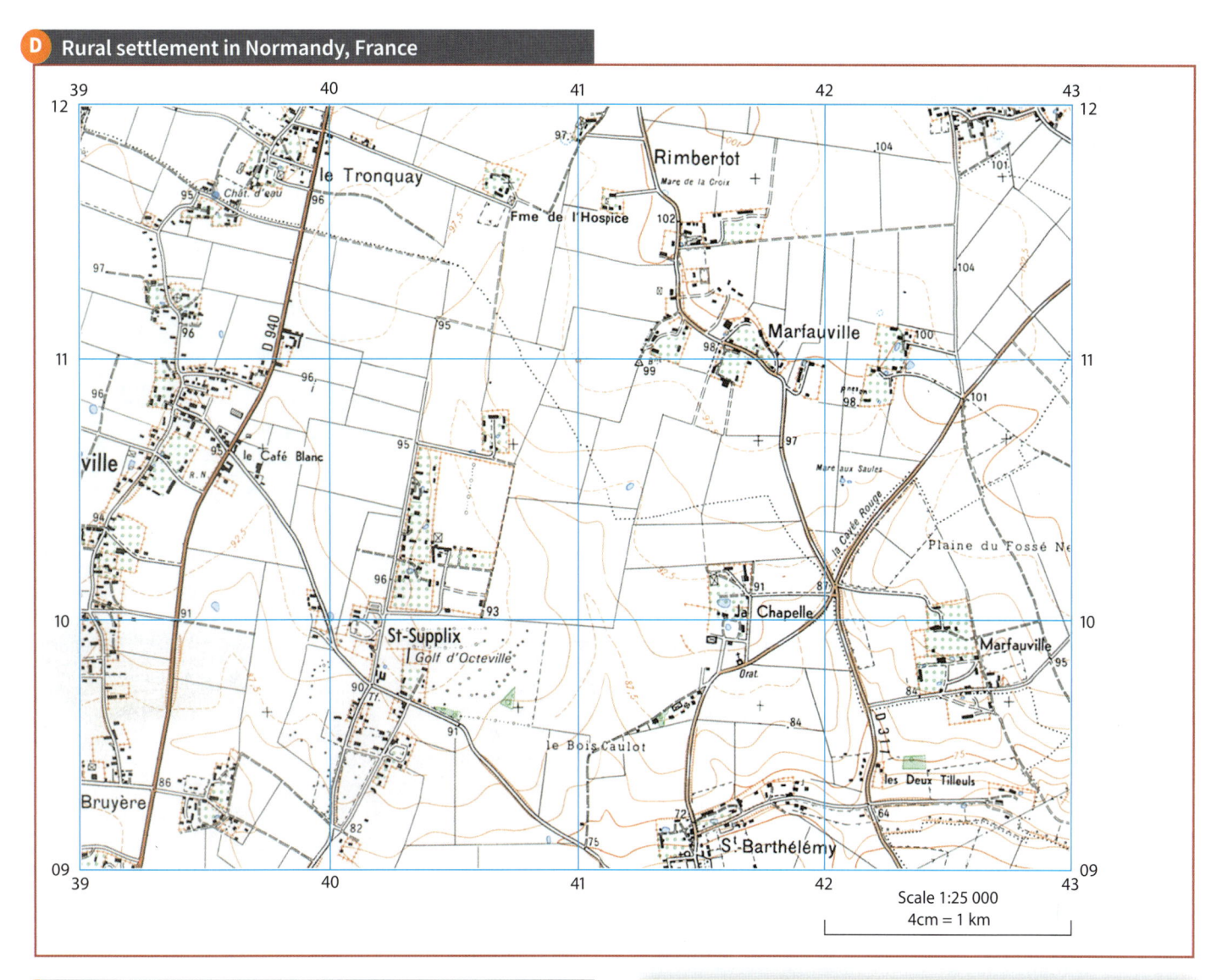

*Scale 1:25 000*
*4cm = 1 km*

## E  Rural settlement in Tanzania

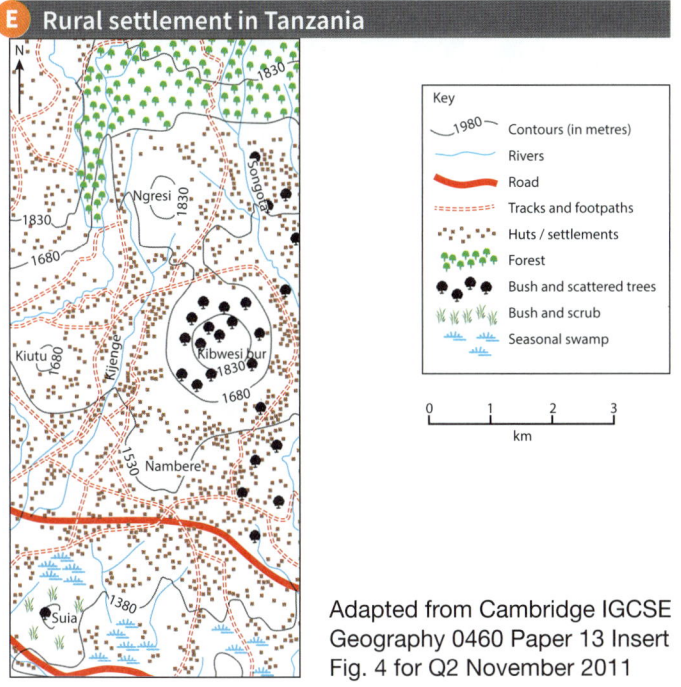

**Key**
- Contours (in metres)
- Rivers
- Road
- Tracks and footpaths
- Huts / settlements
- Forest
- Bush and scattered trees
- Bush and scrub
- Seasonal swamp

Adapted from Cambridge IGCSE Geography 0460 Paper 13 Insert Fig. 4 for Q2 November 2011

### TASK 3: Study Source D

a. What is the scale of this map? Calculate the area shown on the extract to the nearest square kilometre.

b. Describe the relief of this area of Normandy. Refer to heights given.

c. On an overlay using tracing paper, mark the settlements and name them.

d. To what extent is this pattern 'nucleated'? Give examples of settlements in your answer.

e. Identify **one** grid square that shows examples of linear settlement. Suggest why these settlements have developed in a linear pattern.

### TASK 4: Study Source E

a. Describe **three** features of the distribution of rural settlement on the map.

b. Suggest reasons for the distribution of settlement in the area.

Adapted from Cambridge IGCSE Geography 0460 Paper 13 Q2 b(i) and (ii)

# 11 Settlement sites, growth and functions

## Rural settlements

Most rural settlements initially grew up as isolated, **self-sufficient** farming communities.

Their sites (the land on which they were built) were determined by:

- **water supply:** water from springs, streams, rivers and wells was essential for human survival and farming, though areas likely to flood regularly were avoided
- **relief:** flat or gently sloping land was easier to build on and to farm
- **soils:** fertile, well-drained soils were important so large amounts of crops could be grown
- **shelter:** areas such as valleys which were sheltered from winds and rain were better sites than those that were exposed to the elements
- **defence:** threats from enemies resulted in settlements being built that were easy to defend.

In many rural areas there are still small communities that depend on farming, however they are now linked with other areas, mainly by road and sometimes by railways.

The functions (main activities or purposes) of some other rural settlements have changed as they have increased in size. As many countries have developed, farming has decreased in importance. In some areas mining villages have developed and other rural settlements are important for tourism. In areas close to large towns and cities, many people who live in rural settlements commute (travel daily) to work rather than working in the village where they live.

### A Korodegaga village near Addis Ababa, Ethiopia

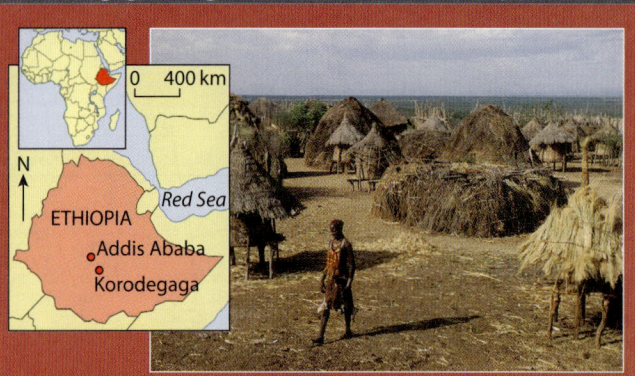

Korodegaga village consists of nine small hamlets. It has a population of about 1400 living in 300 houses. This area was first settled in the early 20th century. There were many advantages for settlement. It had access to water from two rivers, flat, fertile soil, and forests for building and firewood. Here maize, tef* and beans can be grown and cattle, sheep, goats and hens kept. There are schools, mosques and a grain mill. Although there is no market or shop here, villagers walk to Dera (25 km), Bofa (10 km) or Awash Melkase (8 km) to access these services.

*tef: an important grain crop only grown in Ethiopia from which a form of bread is made

Adapted from *Ethiopian Village Studies* – University of Bath

### B Functions of urban settlements

**Market town:** (e.g. Alençon, France and Debre Zeit, Ethiopia) where goods produced in the surrounding area are bought and sold. These:

- are found in farming areas
- have many services, e.g. shops and offices
- have good transport links – often they are route centres
- are often near bridges over rivers (mills to process farm produce were built on the river)
- have a marketplace in the town centre.

**Port:** (e.g. Olbia, Sardinia and Mar del Plata, Argentina) where goods are imported and exported by ship. These:

- are found where there are sheltered harbours, such as on an estuary, at the mouth of a river or in a bay
- have flat land for building or storage close to the water
- have deep water for large ships
- may be close to major industrial areas inland to import and export their goods.

**Industrial town:** (e.g. Pittsburgh, USA and Nowa Huta, Poland), where many people work in factories, processing raw materials or assembling products. These:

- may be found on or near coalfields
- may have old factories near to the centre of the urban area, close to railways or canals
- may have old housing areas and factories built close to each other
- may have new industrial estates on the outskirts, near main roads for transport.

**Tourist resort:** (e.g. Marbella, Spain and Pattaya, Thailand) a place which people visit to enjoy a vacation. These:

- may be on the coast with beaches or in scenic inland areas
- may be large historical cities
- may be close to industrial areas with large populations, with good rail and road links
- have hotels and entertainments of various types.

## Functions of urban settlements

The function of a settlement is its main economic activity or purpose. Most urban areas started as small settlements, growing in size and changing their function over the years. Large towns and cities developed in areas where resources were available for the growth of industry and where natural routeways and rivers met. This enabled the development of roads, railways and canals.

## Accra

Accra has been the capital city of Ghana since 1877. With a population of 2.3 million, Accra stretches along the coast and extends north into Ghana's interior. It originally developed as a fishing village; however, it soon became a major port, especially when the Europeans built three forts and trading posts there in the 17th century. Accra is now the seat of government and an important financial, commercial and administrative centre. There are main banks and department stores, and many nightclubs, restaurants and hotels. Manufacturing is important, including food processing, textiles, clothing and chemicals, and fishing is still important.

C  Accra, Ghana

**TASK 1:** Study Source A
a  Describe the function of Korodegaga village.
b  Give **three** advantages for the villagers of its site.

**TASK 2:** Study Source B
a  Define the following functions:
- Market town
- Port
- Industrial town
- Tourist resort

b  Explain why settlements develop with different functions. Use examples of different settlements in your answer.

**TASK 3:** Study Source C
a  Describe the economic activities that are shown in the different photographs of Accra.
b  Explain how and why the functions of Accra have changed over time.

## 12 Settlement hierarchies

### What is a hierarchy?

A settlement hierarchy shows how settlements in any area can be put in order based on their size or the services that they provide. Higher up the hierarchy the population size and number of services in the settlement increases, although in any area there are fewer large settlements such as cities (**high order settlements**) than towns (middle order settlements). There are even more small settlements such as villages (**low order settlements**).

Settlements in an area depend on each other as people will use a variety of services found in different settlements. The area served by a settlement is known as its **sphere of influence**. The size of this will depend on the type and number of services offered by the settlement and the transport links to it.

Rural settlements only have a few services, which are **low order** services. Low order services are those that are used often, for example a small general store which sells convenience goods. Urban settlements have a greater number and variety of services, including both low order and high order services. **High order** services are not needed so often. They may sell comparison goods, such as furniture or clothing, and people are usually prepared to travel further to buy them. The distance that people are prepared to travel to use a service is known as its **range**.

In order to make a profit, a shop or service needs a minimum number of potential customers, which is known as its **threshold population**. Services providing low order goods or services need a lower threshold population (as the service is used daily) than high order services, which need many more potential customers and thus have a higher threshold population.

**A** A settlement hierarchy

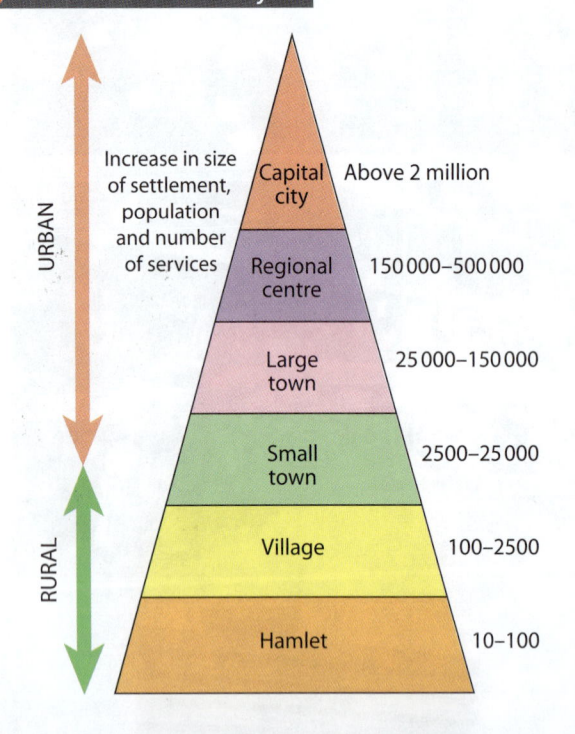

| Settlement | Population |
|---|---|
| Capital city | Above 2 million |
| Regional centre | 150 000–500 000 |
| Large town | 25 000–150 000 |
| Small town | 2500–25 000 |
| Village | 100–2500 |
| Hamlet | 10–100 |

**B** Rural settlement size and number of services in part of the Republic of Ireland

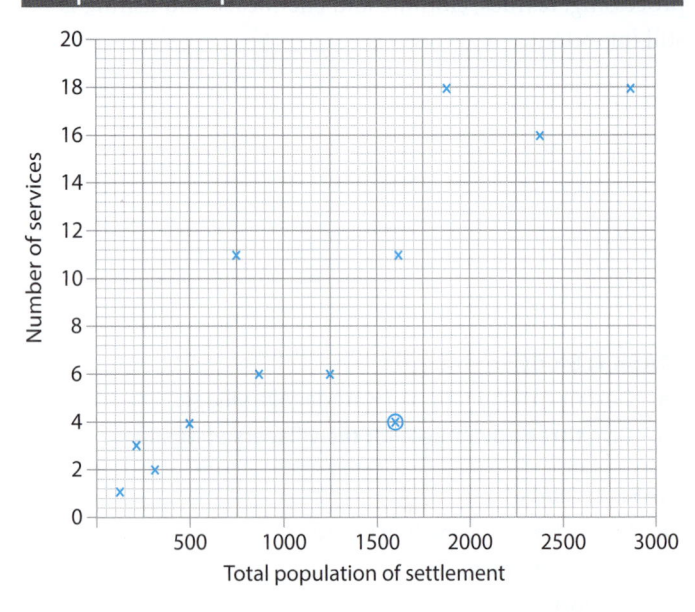

**C** Percentage of rural settlements without services in part of the Republic of Ireland

| Services | Population of settlement | | |
|---|---|---|---|
| | Less than 1000 | 1000 to 2999 | Above 3000 |
| No bus service | 69 | 41 | 23 |
| No post office | 48 | 21 | 9 |
| No village shop | 39 | 12 | 4 |
| No primary school | 21 | 5 | 2 |

Theme 1: Topic 12

## High order services in Warsaw, Poland

Warsaw is the capital city of Poland, with a population of over 1.7 million. It is the home of the Polish Parliament, the Presidential Office and the Supreme Court.

High order services in the city include:

- hospitals, e.g. Children's Memorial Health Institute and Maria Skłodowska-Curie Institute of Oncology
- theatres, e.g. the National Theatre and the Grand Theatre
- the main headquarters of TV and radio stations, e.g. Canal+ Poland and MTV Poland
- universities and schools of higher education, e.g. Warsaw School of Economics, European School of Law and Administration
- large malls containing shops, restaurants and multiscreen cinema complexes, e.g. Arkadia, Galeria Mokotów and Złote Tarasy.

The National Stadium (*Stadion Narodowy*) is located in the Praga Południe district, near Warsaw city centre. It is used mostly for international football matches but it is a multipurpose venue able to host other sporting events, concerts, cultural events, and conferences. The official stadium opening took place on 19 January 2012.

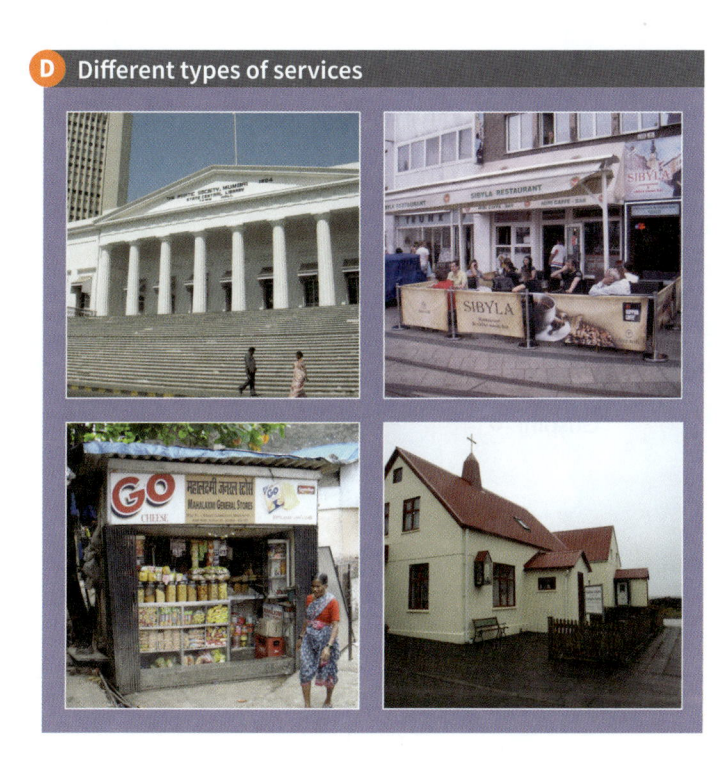

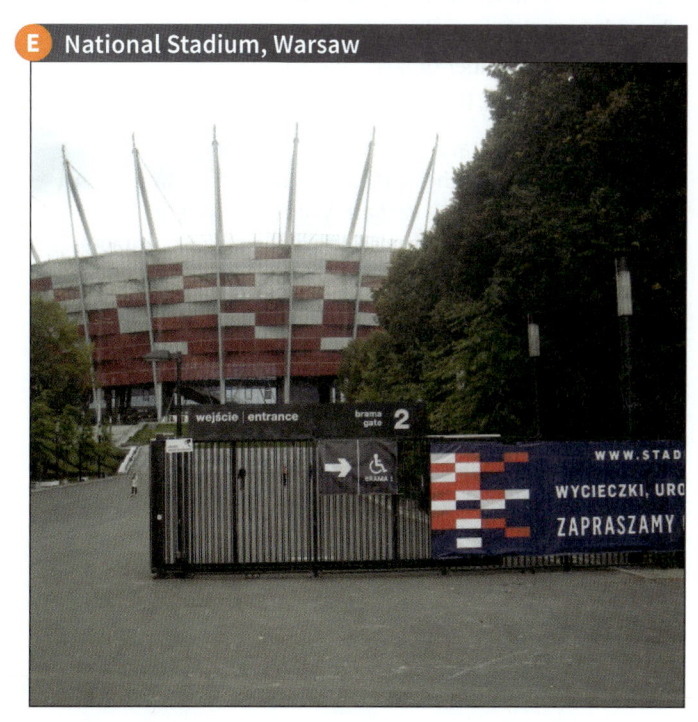

**D** Different types of services

**E** National Stadium, Warsaw

**TASK 1:** Study Source **A** and a map of the country in which you live

Draw a settlement hierarchy diagram for your country. In your diagram you should name examples of the settlements of different sizes and include their populations.

**TASK 2:** Study Sources **B** and **C**
a  What general relationship is shown between population size and the number of services available in rural settlements?
b  Suggest **two** reasons why the settlement that is circled on the scatter graph has fewer services than you would expect for its population size.
c  Using the information in Source C, draw a graph to show the percentage of rural settlements without services.
d  Write a conclusion about service provision in small rural settlements based on your graph.

**TASK 3:** Study Source **D**
Identify the services in the photographs that are:
- high order services
- services that could be found in villages, towns or cities
- services with a large sphere of influence
- services that need a high threshold population.

**TASK 4:** Study Source **E**
a  Make a list of **five** different types of high order service in Warsaw. For each one give a named example.
b  Suggest reasons why high order services are located in Warsaw.
c  Explain why venues like the National Stadium have a large sphere of influence.

**Cambridge IGCSE Geography** — Settlements and service provision

# Case Study

## Settlement and service provision in Sardinia

### Sardinia – a Mediterranean island

Sardinia is an Italian island in the Mediterranean Sea with a total population of about 1.7 million people. Until recently most of the population lived in inland areas, and the economy was based on agriculture and the mining of coal, lead and zinc. However, in the last 50 years tourist development has taken place in the coastal areas.

There are a number of large and small towns with different functions. Three examples are:

- **Cagliari**, the capital city, is the main commercial and industrial centre of the island. It has one of the largest fish markets in Italy, with a vast array of fish for sale to both the public and trade. It is also one of the biggest container terminals in the Mediterranean area.
- **Carbonia** was built to provide housing for the workforce of the nearby mines. The name Carbonia comes from the Italian word for coal, a resource that was abundant in this region. Since the mines closed in the 1970s, Carbonia has had to deal with high unemployment.
- The small town of **Bosa** is situated on the west coast of Sardinia, about 3 km inland on the bank of the Temo River. Traditionally agriculture and fishing played an important part in the economy. Its beach has been voted the most beautiful beach in Italy and the town is growing in popularity for tourism.

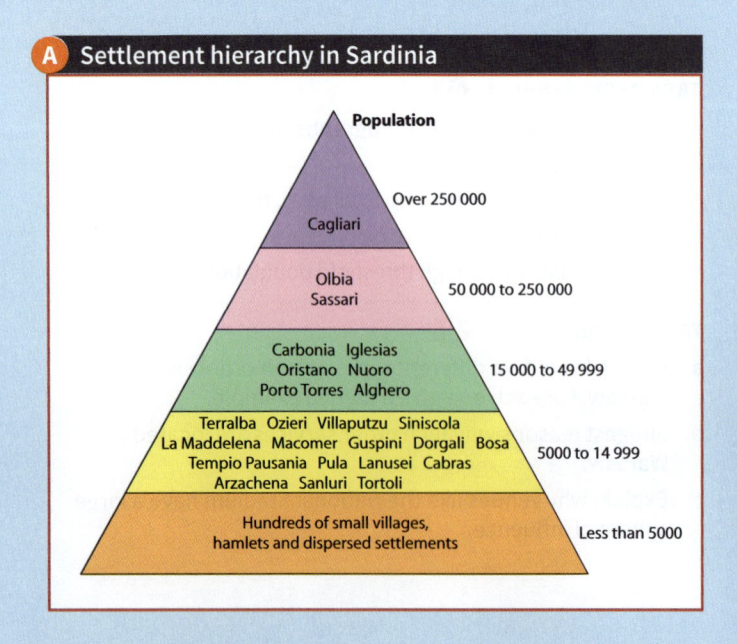

**B** Sardinia's urban population

Population
- Over 250 000
- 50 000–250 000
- 15 000–49 999
- 5000–14 999

**A** Settlement hierarchy in Sardinia

Population
- Cagliari — Over 250 000
- Olbia, Sassari — 50 000 to 250 000
- Carbonia, Iglesias, Oristano, Nuoro, Porto Torres, Alghero — 15 000 to 49 999
- Terralba, Ozieri, Villaputzu, Siniscola, La Maddalena, Macomer, Guspini, Dorgali, Bosa, Tempio Pausania, Pula, Lanusei, Cabras, Arzachena, Sanluri, Tortoli — 5000 to 14 999
- Hundreds of small villages, hamlets and dispersed settlements — Less than 5000

**C** The port of Olbia

# Case Study: Settlement and service provision in Sardinia

## An important port

Olbia is a town of over 50 000 inhabitants in north-east Sardinia. It is the main connection between Sardinia and the Italian mainland, with an airport, a passenger port, and a railway to Porto Torres and Cagliari. There is an expressway to Nuoro and Cagliari and main roads to Sassari, Tempio Pausania and Palau.

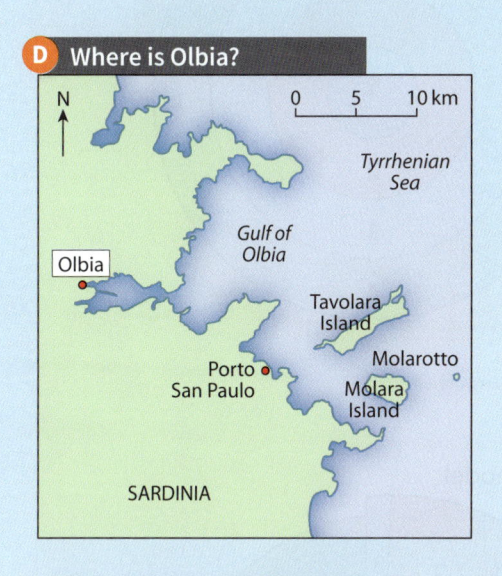

**D Where is Olbia?**

**TASK 1:** Study Sources **A** and **B**

a  Describe the hierarchy of settlements in Sardinia.

b  Suggest the likely differences between the services in Cagliari and Bosa. Give reasons for each of the differences that you suggest.

c  What are the functions of the following towns:
- Cagliari
- Carbonia
- Bosa?

**TASK 2:** Study Sources **C** and **D** and an atlas

Suggest reasons why Olbia has become an important port.

**TASK 3:** Study Source **E**

a  Make a list of the services shown in the photographs.

b  Explain why services of this type are located in Olbia. You should refer to:
- order of services
- threshold population.
- sphere of influence

c  There are many rural settlements in Sardinia. Describe the services that are likely to be found in the rural settlements. Refer to:
- shopping
- religion
- transport
- entertainment.

**E Services in Olbia**

**Cambridge IGCSE Geography** — Urban settlements

# 13 Urban land use

## Urban zones

It is possible in all urban areas to identify zones where there is a particular type of land use, e.g. the **Central Business District (CBD)**, **industrial** and **residential** zones.

Land use models are theories that attempt to describe and explain the structure of urban areas. **Source A** shows two different land use models that apply to urban areas in MEDCs and **Source B** shows a model for an LEDC.

The models are based on the idea that land values are highest in the centre of a town or city. This is because space is limited and competition is high in the central parts of the settlement. This leads to high-rise, high-density buildings being found near the CBD, with low-density, sparse developments on the edge of the town or city. The Hoyt model is based on the circles on the Burgess model, but adds sectors of similar land uses, e.g. the industrial zones that radiate out from the CBD. These could be following a main road or a railway line.

In all urban areas new developments are constantly taking place and land use changes over time, particularly at the edge of the city – the **rural-urban fringe**. Here, urban sprawl is resulting in the development of roads, housing and commercial areas in areas that were previously natural environment or farmland.

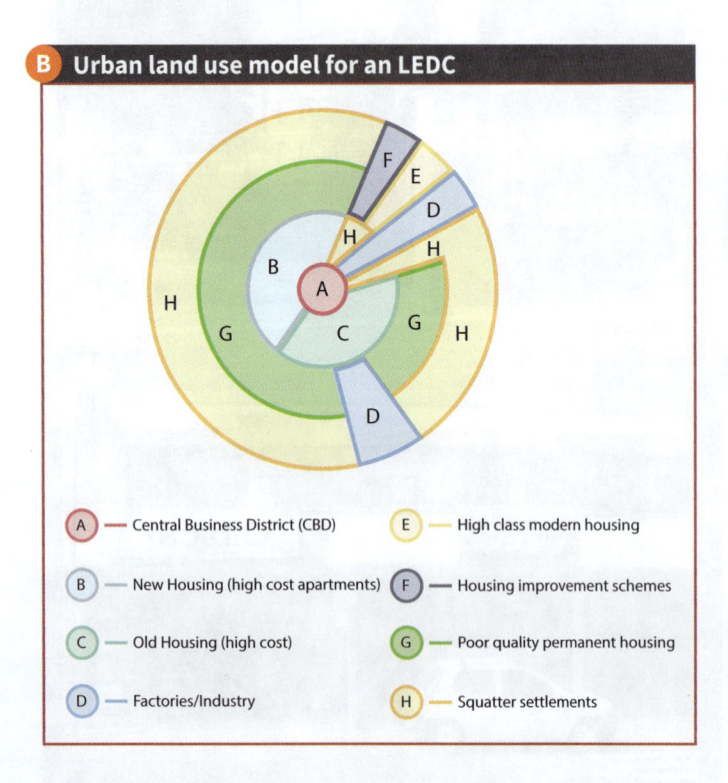

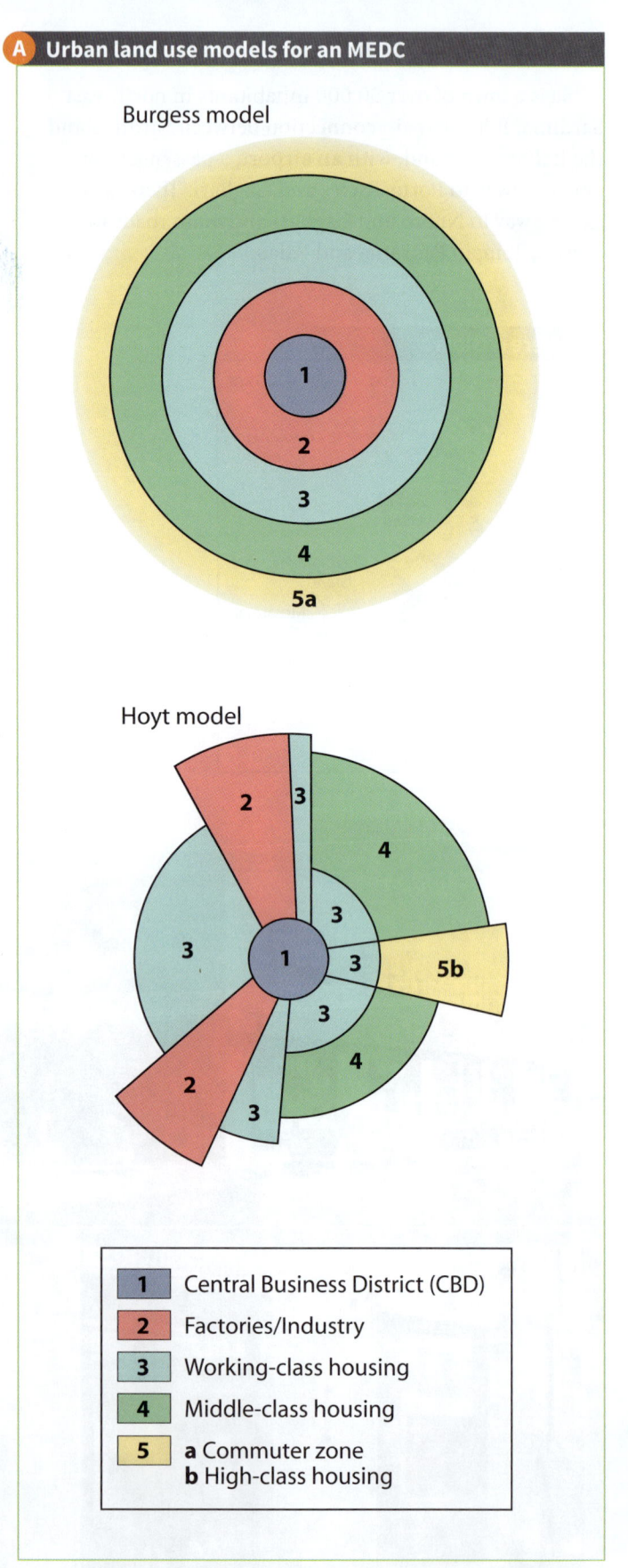

**A Urban land use models for an MEDC**

Burgess model

Hoyt model

| 1 | Central Business District (CBD) |
| 2 | Factories/Industry |
| 3 | Working-class housing |
| 4 | Middle-class housing |
| 5 | a Commuter zone  b High-class housing |

**B Urban land use model for an LEDC**

- A — Central Business District (CBD)
- B — New Housing (high cost apartments)
- C — Old Housing (high cost)
- D — Factories/Industry
- E — High class modern housing
- F — Housing improvement schemes
- G — Poor quality permanent housing
- H — Squatter settlements

Theme 1: Topic 13

## Barcelona, a city in Spain

Barcelona, located on the Mediterranean coast, has many features that are typical of a city in Western Europe. Its traditional manufacturing industries have been declining, and are being replaced by service industries and high-tech industrial parks.

In the centre of the present city, part of the medieval city still remains, with narrow streets, alleyways and small squares.

The area to the south of the medieval city is El Raval. It was the area where factories and high-rise **tenement** blocks were constructed during the **Industrial Revolution** but now much improvement is taking place. During the 19th century, the city grew with planned housing development in a grid-iron pattern. This connected Barcelona to nearby smaller towns (e.g. Gracia), which became a part of the main city.

To the north, on the slopes of the hills, a number of large villas were built in the late 19th and early 20th centuries. These formed a high-class residential zone. Between 1945 and 1975, large areas of high-rise apartments were built along the major routeways and on the edges of the city (e.g. La Mina) for migrants from other parts of Spain seeking work in the city.

In the last 20 years, two major events – the 1992 Olympic Games and the Universal Forum of Cultures 2004 – have led to massive changes. For example, in the Poblenou district, an area of old manufacturing industry, an Olympic village was constructed on an abandoned factory site. Remaining factories and workshops in the Poblenou district are being changed into a zone for new technologies.

**C** Land use in Barcelona

**D** Two residential zones

---

**TASK 1:** Study Sources **A** and **B**

a Describe the similarities and differences between the Burgess and Hoyt models of urban land use.

b Suggest reasons why in a typical MEDC city:
- high-cost, modern housing is on the outskirts
- traditional industry is close to railway lines.

c Describe **two** similarities and **two** differences between the models of urban land use in MEDCs and LEDCs. Suggest reasons why there are differences.

**TASK 2:** Study Source **C**

How well does Barcelona fit with the models of urban land use in Source A?

**TASK 3:** Study Source **D**

a Describe the residential zones shown in each of the photographs.

b In which zones do you think the photos were taken? Give reasons for your answer.

**TASK 4**

Take photographs of different zones in a town or city you know, or find photographs on the Internet of urban zones in another town or city in your country. Annotate (fully label) each one with details of the land use.

# Cambridge IGCSE Geography — Urban settlements

## 14 Urban problems and solutions

### Stress in the cities

As towns and cities increase in size they become stressful and difficult places to live in. Some parts become run-down and undesirable places to live and work, where people feel unsafe due to high levels of knife and gun crimes, drug abuse and muggings. As the land use of many cities was not planned for the current population, they are finding it more and more difficult to cope with the large numbers of people. Efforts to provide homes, services, transportation and jobs are already losing the race against rapid population growth.

**A  Urban protests**

*(Illustration: protesters holding signs — "WE NEED BETTER SCHOOLS!", "CLEAN UP THE STREETS", "BUILD MORE CHEAP HOUSES", "MORE POLICE ON THE STREETS", "BAN TRAFFIC IN THE CITY CENTRE", "WE NEED MORE JOBS!", "WE NEED CHEAPER PUBLIC TRANSPORT", "THE AIR IS UNFIT TO BREATHE")*

**B  Quality of life indicators for eight urban areas**

| Urban area | Average number of people per room | % of homes with water and electricity | Murders per 100 000 people | Levels of noise (1–10) 1 = low 10 = high | Mean traffic speed (km/hr in rush hour) | Levels of air pollution (1–10) 1 = low 10 = high |
|---|---|---|---|---|---|---|
| Cairo (Egypt) | 1.5 | 94 | 56.4 | 7 | 12.4 | 10 |
| Jakarta (Indonesia) | 3.4 | 85 | 5.3 | 6 | 16.3 | 10 |
| London (UK) | 0.6 | 100 | 2.5 | 8 | 10.4 | 3 |
| Melbourne (Australia) | 0.5 | 100 | 2.0 | 3 | 20.3 | 1 |
| Moscow (Russia) | 1.3 | 100 | 7.0 | 6 | 31.5 | 7 |
| San Francisco (USA) | 0.6 | 98 | 5.8 | 3 | 16.0 | 3 |
| Seoul (South Korea) | 2.0 | 100 | 1.2 | 7 | 13.8 | 7 |
| Shanghai (China) | 2.0 | 95 | 2.5 | 5 | 15.3 | 3 |

Major problems faced by the authorities include:

- air, noise, water and visual pollution
- inequality between the rich and poor
- poor quality housing and the growth of squatter settlements
- traffic congestion
- urban sprawl.

**C  Solving problems in LEDCs**

### Mumbai gets country's first monorail after 88-year wait for new mode of transport

*Hindustan Times* Mumbai, 1 February 2014

The 8.8 km-long Mumbai monorail between Wadala and Chembur was opened on Saturday by chief minister Prithviraj Chavan, ending the city's 88-year wait for a new mode of public transport.

Mumbai, with a population of around 17 million, has around 10 million people commuting daily by trains, buses, taxis, auto-rickshaws and private vehicles.

The stations are situated at a minimum height of around 5.5 metres — and much higher in some locations — accessed by staircases and escalators.

While this stretch is the first phase of the project, the second phase involves extending the monorail up to Jacob Circle. The 11.2 km-long Wadala to Jacob Circle line is expected to be ready by next year.

Once both the lines are complete, Chembur to Jacob Circle will be second-longest monorail corridor in the world after Osaka monorail corridor in Japan, which is 23.8 km long. The monorail will then connect the eastern suburbs to central Mumbai and is expected to carry up to 200 000 commuters daily.

Adapted from *Hindustan Times*, 1 February 2014

# Theme 1: Topic 14

## D Solving problems in MEDCs

### Urban decay

Urban decay occurs when parts of the city become run-down and undesirable to live in. Examples of urban decay are:

- slum housing, with outside toilets, overcrowding, no hot water or central heating
- buildings in disrepair with leaking roofs, draughty windows and crumbling brickwork
- empty buildings boarded up or vandalised
- areas where buildings have been knocked down and which turn into derelict land.

There have been a number of schemes to reduce the problems of urban decay. **Comprehensive redevelopment** occurs when all the buildings are knocked down and the area is completely rebuilt, for example, demolishing old housing and factories and replacing them with new flats and multi-storey high-rise buildings. This approach has been criticised as people have to move from their established communities and workplaces – they no longer know their neighbours and they are moved away from their friends and relations.

**Urban regeneration** is the renovation of existing housing and improvement of the environment and economy, including:

- rewiring the houses and fitting central heating
- fitting double glazing
- cleaning the outsides of old buildings by sand-blasting
- improving the environment by landscaping
- building or improving the social facilities such as clubs and medical centres
- encouraging new businesses and industry to set up in the areas with grants and loans.

This has proved more popular as people have been able to stay in their own area.

*Comprehensive redevelopment*

*Urban regeneration*

---

**TASK 1:** Study Source **A**

In groups of four, discuss the problems of living in cities as follows.

a   As a group, identify the **four** biggest problems of living in cities.

b   Each group member should choose **one** of the four problems that your group has identified and give a presentation using actual examples, explaining why it is a major problem.

c   Do you think all residents of the city will agree with your choice of problems? Give reasons for your answer.

**TASK 2:** Study Source **B**

a   Name **one** urban area where:
- housing is overcrowded
- the air quality is poor
- levels of traffic congestion are high.

b   Using only information from the table, identify the differences between the quality of life of people in Moscow and Shanghai.

c   Which of the cities would you prefer to live in? Explain your choice using data from the table.

**TASK 3:** Study Source **C**

a   Explain how Mumbai has attempted to solve traffic problems.

b   Suggest the advantages and disadvantages to residents of Mumbai of using a public transport system such as this.

c   Describe **three** other ways in which traffic congestion can be reduced in urban areas.

**TASK 4:** Study Source **D**

With a partner, discuss the advantages and disadvantages of comprehensive development and urban regeneration as methods of solving problems of urban decay.

# Cambridge IGCSE Geography | Urban settlements

## Case Study
### An urban area – Atlanta, USA

### A rapidly growing city

Atlanta is the capital city of Georgia state. Its population has grown from 2 million in 1970 to over 6 million in 2013 – the fastest-growing **metropolitan** city in the USA. Recent population growth has been caused by newcomers from cities around the Great Lakes and the north-east, where unemployment is high and the cost of living is expensive. This growth has resulted in many problems, including traffic congestion, air pollution, lack of affordable housing and urban sprawl. The city now has a reputation for wall-to-wall offices, shopping centres and vast suburbs.

Planners are now trying to improve the economy and environment. Plans include investment in public transport which combines light rail with new pedestrian and bike links. **Brownfield sites** are being regenerated in the city rather than further extending the city's boundaries and building on greenfield sites. For example, a former steel mill site is being turned into office space, 5000 high-rise homes, town houses and single-family homes.

### A Population growth of Atlanta

### C Atlanta BeltLine

The Atlanta BeltLine uses old, abandoned railway tracks that were built before Atlanta was a city and uses them in a redevelopment plan which forms a loop around midtown and downtown Atlanta making up 22 miles of light rail transit, trails and green space.

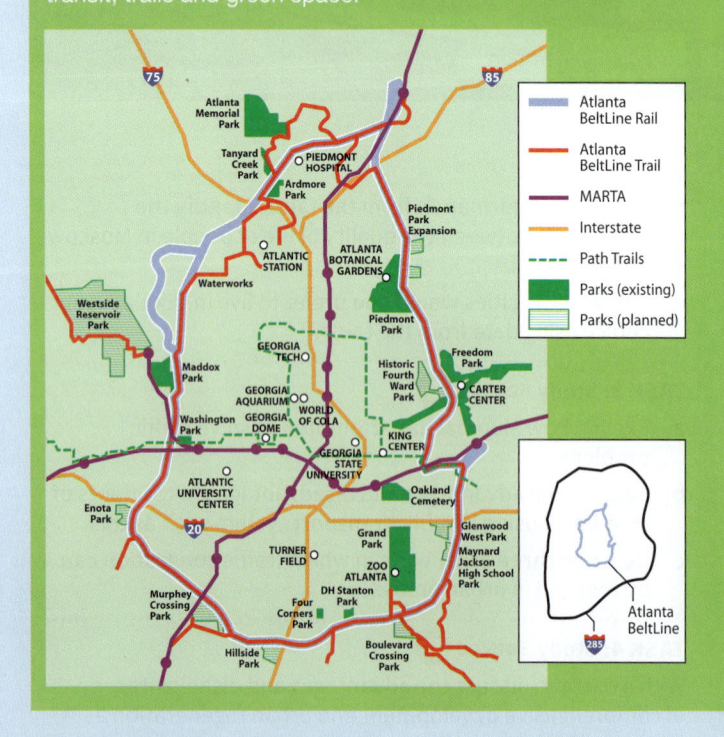

## FACTS AND FIGURES

- 527 hectares of new green space and parks
- 53 km of shared-use paths
- $20 billion of new economic development
- 30 000 new permanent jobs from new businesses in retail, entertainment, education, health care, professional services, hospitality, light industry, and the arts
- 5600 new workforce housing units
- 50 000 new housing units anticipated along the corridor
- 45 neighbourhoods gain new and greater connectivity
- 8% of the city's land mass covered in the planning area and 25% of Atlanta's residential population

The Atlanta BeltLine: A Green Future, by Ethan Davidson. US Department of Transportation: Federal Highway Administration

Case Study: An urban area – Atlanta, USA

### B Growth creates problems

**Population growth** – Atlanta is the largest metropolitan area in south-east USA. With 5.1 million people in 2006 (up from 1.4 million in 1970) urban sprawl was inevitable.

**Traffic congestion** – plus air and noise pollution is the fourth worst in the USA. There are 50 000 km of roads in Atlanta. 90% of residents drive to work experiencing 68 hours of delays per year.

**Air quality** – traffic congestion causes increases in respiratory illnesses such as emphysema, bronchitis and asthma. Air stagnates here so fumes from vehicles are rarely blown away.

**Water quality and quantity** – suburbs along the Chattahoochee river increase run-off and contaminate drinking water with pollutants. Sanitation systems cannot cope. Over 1 million Atlantans use septic tanks, which often leak. Increased water demand for industry and irrigation uses up supplies, affecting fishing habitats.

**Agricultural land** – expansion has meant that farmland has been bought and covered with shopping malls and other developments.

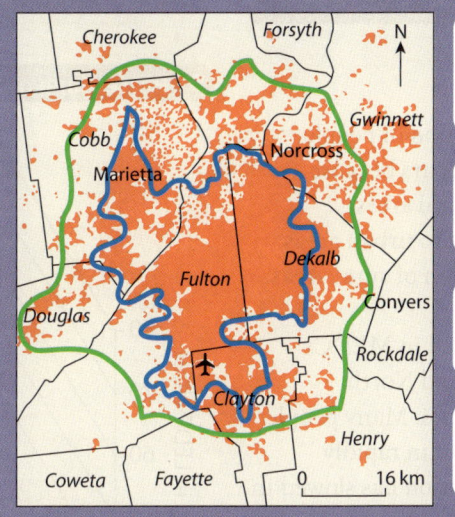

**Loss of green space/ecosystems** – between 1982 and 2002 over 38% of green space within Atlanta's city boundary was built on. The city loses an average of 125 hectares of trees per day by deforestation. Ecosystems suffer as wildlife dies or migrates away.

**Impermeable surfaces** – more concrete and asphalt replacing soil and trees means surface water cannot drain away, causing flash floods and water contamination.

**Cultural loss** – civil war battlefields surrounding Atlanta, such as the Kennesaw Mountain National Battlefield to the north, are under threat from suburban homes.

**Socio-economic division** – most sprawl is to the north where white middle-class suburbs have developed. The inner city has had less investment; this is where the poorer black population has stayed.

**Hotlanta** – the removal of trees such as maple, oak and elm and the addition of concrete encourages more heat build-up and a 'heat island' over the city. Temperatures can be up to 10°C higher than in the countryside.

- Urbanised areas
- Edge of Atlanta metropolitan area 1973
- Edge of Atlanta metropolitan area 2012

There are no large bodies of water, mountains or other obstacles to limit the city's outward growth. Atlanta's urban area has more than doubled since 1973.

### D The Atlanta skyline

**TASK 1:** Study Source A
a Describe how Atlanta has grown between 1950 and 2010.
b Explain why Atlanta has grown rapidly.

**TASK 2:** Study Source B
a Describe how Atlanta has expanded between 1973 and 2012.
b Describe **two** problems that affect people and **two** problems affecting the natural environment.

**TASK 3:** Study Source C
a List **three** ways in which the BeltLine will help to solve urban problems in Atlanta.
b In which part of the city are these ideas taking place? Why?
c What other plans do you think are needed? What should be the priorities for Atlanta?

**TASK 4:** Study Source D
a Describe the features of Atlanta that can be seen in the photograph.
b Which part of the city do you think this is? Explain your answers.

# Cambridge IGCSE Geography — Urbanisation

## 15 Rapid urban growth

### What is urbanisation?

Urbanisation is the increase in the proportion of people living in towns and cities. Urbanisation occurs because push factors cause people to move from rural areas (countryside) and pull factors attract them to urban areas (towns and cities), decreasing the population of rural areas. This is known as **rural depopulation**.

Before 1950 most **urbanisation** occurred in MEDCs. Rapid urbanisation took place in Europe and North America in the 19th and early 20th centuries. Many people moved from rural to urban areas to get jobs in rapidly expanding industries. Since 1950 urbanisation has slowed in most MEDCs, and now some of the biggest cities are losing population as people move away from the city to rural environments. This is known as **counter-urbanisation**.

Since 1950 the most rapid growth in urbanisation has occurred in LEDCs in South America, Africa and Asia. Rural to urban migration is happening on a massive scale due to population pressure and a lack of resources in rural areas. People living in rural areas believe that the standard of living in urban areas will be much better than in rural areas.

There are three main types of factors causing movement of people to major cities:

1. Physical factors such as drought or natural disasters.
2. Economic factors such as the need to make a living.
3. Social and political factors such as the desire for good education and health care and the need to be safe.

**B** Percentage of population living in LEDC cities

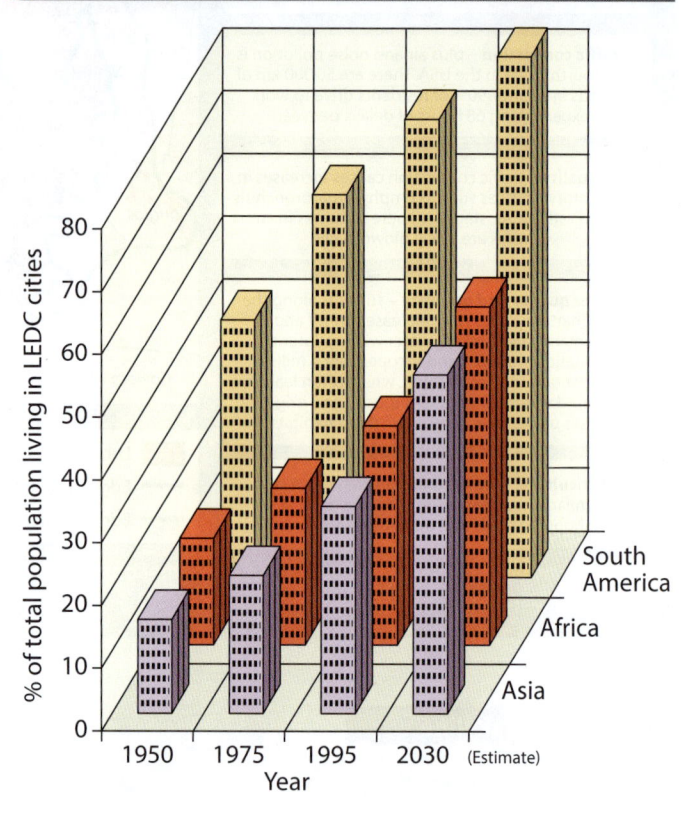

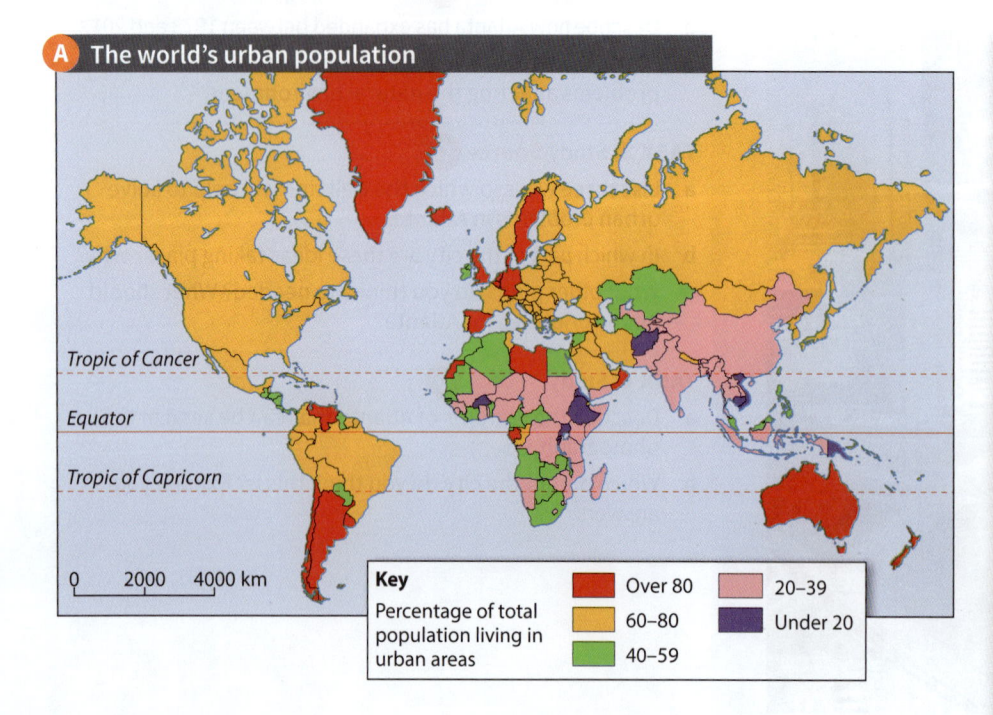

**A** The world's urban population

Key
Percentage of total population living in urban areas
- Over 80
- 60–80
- 40–59
- 20–39
- Under 20

**TASK 1:** Study **Source A** and an atlas

a Name a continent where over 60 per cent of the population live in urban areas in all the countries.

b What percentage of the population live in urban areas in:
- Brazil
- Egypt
- India?

**TASK 2:** Study **Source B**

Compare the rates of urbanisation in Africa, South America and Asia.

Theme 1: Topic 15

## C Pushes and Pulls ... and the reality

**PUSHES**: DROUGHT, NOT ENOUGH LAND, FAILED CROPS, POVERTY, FEW JOBS, NO PROSPECTS, LITTLE WORK, LOSS OF FARM WORK, NATURAL DISASTER, HIGH INFANT MORTALITY RATE, LACK OF FOOD, MALNUTRITION, POOR EDUCATION

(Dream: EDUCATION, SHOPS, HOUSING, MONEY, MEDICAL CARE)

**THE REALITY**

**PULLS**: EXPENSIVE LAND, FEW WELL-PAID JOBS, VERY LITTLE SPACE, DIRTY, NOISY AND POLLUTED, POOR-QUALITY HOUSING

## D Moving to the city

1. "You don't seem local?" — "No, I was born in the countryside."
2. "My father ran a farm but there was a drought and my brothers took the best land."
3. "So what made you come here?"
4. "I wanted a better way of life…"

## E Is moving to the city worthwhile?

**TASK 3:** Study Source **C**
a  Identify **three** reasons why people want to leave rural areas in LEDCs.
b  Identify **three** attractions of urban areas for people who live in the countryside in LEDCs.

**TASK 4:** Study Sources **D** and **E**
Many people move to urban areas in LEDCs for a better quality of life.
Do you think they achieve this? Give reasons for your answer.

53

**Cambridge IGCSE Geography** — Urbanisation

## 16 Impacts of urban growth

### Changes in the countryside and the cities

Urbanisation in many countries in Africa, Asia and South America is taking place at a rapid rate. Many inhabitants of cities expect a high quality of life but the growth of cities, largely as a result of rural to urban migration, puts a great strain on urban **infrastructure**. Road networks and public transport, power, piped water supplies and sewage systems, and health care and education services are all struggling to meet the increased demand. Traffic congestion, along with noise, air and water pollution, all add to the problems.

There are great contrasts between rich and poor. The well-built homes of the rich contrast with the **squatter settlements** of the poor and many people who have migrated from the countryside work long hours for low pay and work in the informal sector.

In areas of countryside, rural depopulation is also causing problems. As people of working age leave for the cities this may cause social problems as some families are separated. Older people may be left behind to look after the farmland and yields remain low.

### A  Change in the Indian cities

Dharavi, the largest slum in Asia, houses more than a million slum dwellers in cramped homes, close to the centre of India's financial capital, Mumbai.

The migrants who originally made Dharavi their home are the Maharashtrians from the Konkan coast, the Gujarati community, the Muslim tanners from Tamil Nadu and artisans from Uttar Pradesh.

In present-day Dharavi there are poor standards of sanitation and health care. But there is a silver lining as well, as Dharavi provides a cheap home to people who move to Mumbai to earn their living. Even in the smallest of rooms, there is usually a cooking gas stove and continuous electricity.

It has a thriving leather trade and garment industry and there are many small-scale industries that produce clothes, leather goods, pottery and plastic.

### B  A squatter settlement

### C  Working in the informal sector

**TASK 1: Study Source A**
Make a list of the advantages and problems of living in Dharavi for people who have migrated from rural areas.

**TASK 2: Study Source B**
Describe the characteristics of the squatter settlement shown in the photograph under the following headings:
- location
- homes
- quality of life.

**TASK 3: Study Source C**
a  The people in the photographs are working in the informal sector. Explain how they are making a living.
b  Explain why many people in cities in LEDCs work in the informal sector.

# Theme 1: Topic 16

# Improving living conditions in urban areas in LEDCs

As squatter settlements become more established, quality of life may improve as a result of the efforts of local communities, charities and government departments. In many countries the authorities are attempting to provide solutions by:

- offering low-interest loans so people can build their own homes
- using **site and service schemes** which give people the chance to rent or buy a piece of land that has access to essential services (e.g. water, electricity, sewage pipes) and is connected to the city by transport links
- using **self-help schemes** which give people the tools, materials and training to improve their homes for themselves
- giving people legal ownership of the land on which their squatter settlement is built
- investing and creating greater opportunities in rural areas which may prevent people from migrating to urban areas.

### D Migration to Cairo

### E Problems faced by planners in Cairo

| Planning problems | |
|---|---|
| Lack of housing | ■ Self-built brick houses are built illegally on farmlands by the river Nile. These 'informal' houses cover 80% of Cairo. |
| | ■ In the City of the Dead, 2–3 million people have set up homes among the tombs of Old Cairo. |
| | ■ Half a million people live in homemade huts on roof spaces of office blocks and flats in the city centre. |
| Traffic congestion | ■ Between 1970 and 2000 the number of cars in Cairo rose from 100 000 to over a million. |
| | ■ Travel to work times can be very slow. |
| | ■ Many drivers are aggressive and do not keep to the rules of the road, causing danger for road users and pedestrians. |
| Lack of jobs | ■ Jobs for unskilled workers are hard to find. |
| | ■ While many university graduates get jobs with the government, salaries are low. |
| | ■ Many poor people are forced to work in the informal sector, selling things on the streets to earn a meagre living. |
| Pollution | ■ The air is heavily polluted by a cocktail of vehicle exhausts and fumes from fuels used in homes and workplaces. |
| | ■ Groundwater is polluted by waste illegally dumped by factories and workshops. |
| | ■ Leaking and inadequate sewers pollute water courses. |

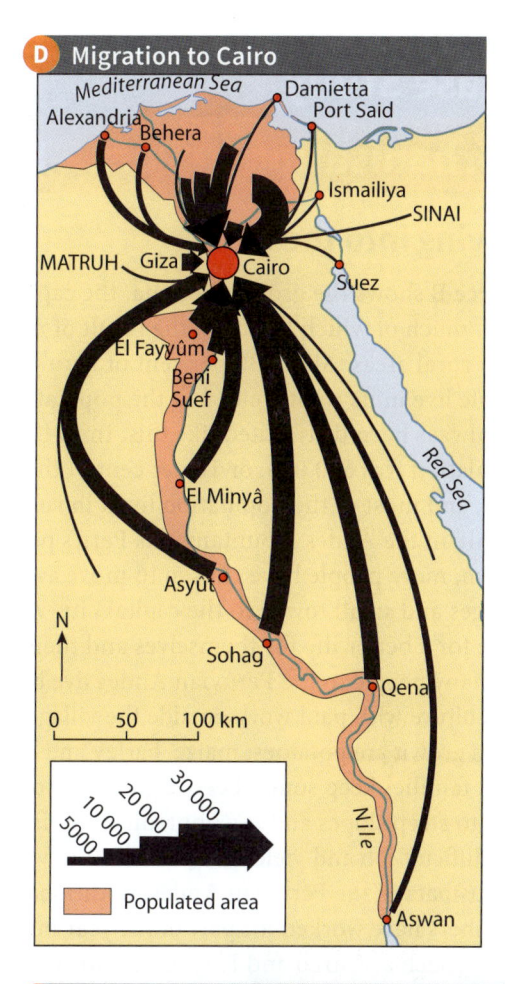

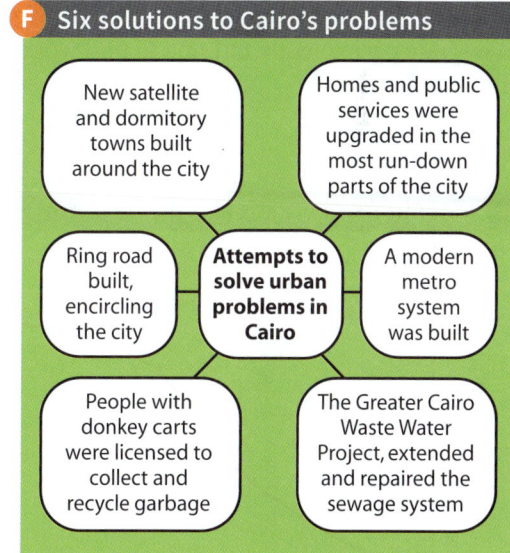

### F Six solutions to Cairo's problems

**Attempts to solve urban problems in Cairo**

- New satellite and dormitory towns built around the city
- Homes and public services were upgraded in the most run-down parts of the city
- Ring road built, encircling the city
- A modern metro system was built
- People with donkey carts were licensed to collect and recycle garbage
- The Greater Cairo Waste Water Project, extended and repaired the sewage system

---

**TASK 4:** Study Source **D**

Describe the pattern of migration to Cairo. Refer to named places or areas and use statistics in your answer.

**TASK 5:** Study Source **E**

a List the **four** main problems faced by Cairo. Use examples in your answer.

b Put the problems in a rank order 1–4 depending on which you would want to solve first. Justify your order.

**TASK 6:** Study Source **F**

a How might each solution help to solve Cairo's problems?

b Suggest **two** problems that will not be solved by these solutions.

# Cambridge IGCSE Geography — Urbanisation

## Case Study
### Urbanisation in Peru – Lima

#### Moving into the city

Source B shows the growth of Lima, the capital city of Peru, much of which has been the result of migration from rural areas. About 30 per cent of Peru's 29.5 million people live in its capital city, but the population has not always been distributed like this. In 1940, Lima's population was 600 000, or 10 per cent of the country's total, and most of the population lived in rural areas, mainly in the Andes mountains. As Peru's population has grown, more people have chosen to move away from their villages and small towns to the capital city, where they hope for a better life for themselves and their children.

Many people in the Peruvian Andes live by combining agriculture with paid work outside the village. The main crops grown are potatoes, maize, barley and beans, and most families keep some sheep, a goat and some llamas. Due to steep slopes and the unpredictable climate, farming is a difficult job and yields are often low. In villages such as Cusipata in the Peruvian Andes, traditionally family members have worked for part of the year in nearby large towns, such as Cuzco and Huancayo. However, increasing numbers of young men and women are leaving Cusipata to migrate permanently to Lima to find work in the capital city.

---

**TASK 1:** Study Source **A** and an atlas
Describe the location of Lima.

**TASK 2:** Study Source **B**
a  Describe what the graph shows about the growth of Lima between 1940 and 2020.
b  Suggest **three** pull factors which encourage people to move to Lima. You should develop your ideas by explaining why these pulls will have attracted people to move there.

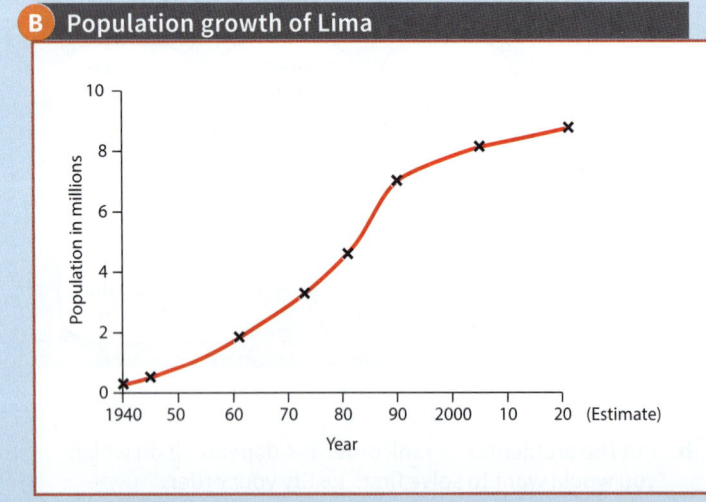

---

**A** Peru – an LEDC in South America

**B** Population growth of Lima

# Case Study: Urbanisation in Peru – Lima

## C  Population pyramids for rural Peru and Lima

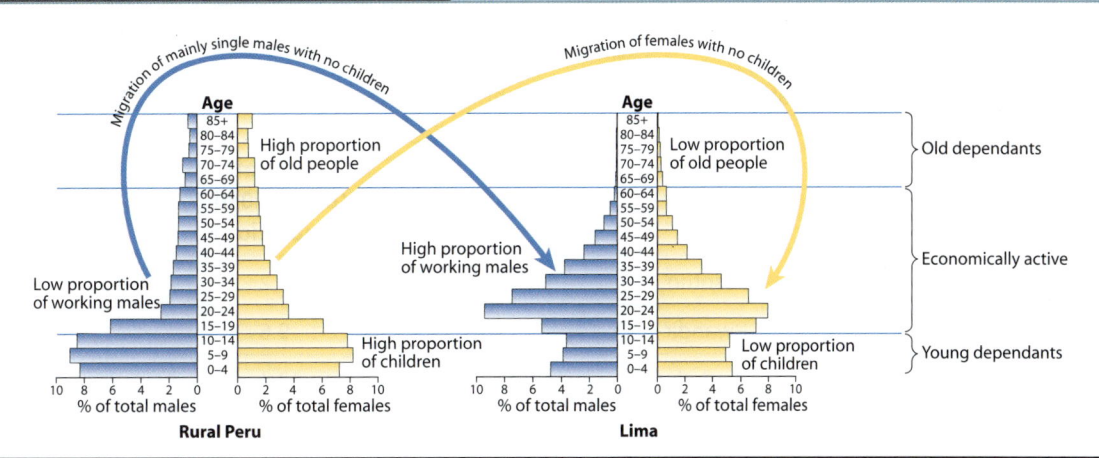

**Rural Peru:** Migration of mainly single males with no children — Low proportion of working males, High proportion of old people, High proportion of children.

**Lima:** Migration of females with no children — High proportion of working males, Low proportion of old people, Low proportion of children.

Categories: Old dependants, Economically active, Young dependants.

| Factors influencing migration to Lima from villages in Andes | What migrants experience when they get to Lima |
|---|---|
| Not enough agricultural land because it is shared between sons | Racial discrimination |
| Drought and other natural hazards | Separation from family |
| Low prices for agricultural products | Better-quality services, e.g. water, electricity |
| Cannot afford clothes and food for children | Better schools for migrants' children |
| Not much opportunity for children to go to school | Low pay and long working hours |
| No running water, electricity or sewage disposal in many villages | Forced to live in self-built houses or on the streets |

## D  Life and death in the Huancavelica region

For alpaca farmer Ignacio Huamani and his family, life in the Peruvian Andes, at almost 4700 m above sea level, has always been a struggle. His village of Pichccahuasi, in Peru's Huancavelica region, is little more than a collection of small thatched shelters and herds of alpaca surrounded by bleak, inhospitable mountains.

The few hundred people who live here are used to poverty and months of sub-zero temperatures during the long winter. But, for the fourth year running, the cold came early. First their animals and now their children are dying. There have been warnings from meteorologists in Peru that this month will see the Huancavelica region hit by the worst weather conditions in years with plunging temperatures, floods and high winds. Last month seven people died and many were injured after torrential rain caused flooding in Ayacucho, the capital of the neighbouring region.

Huamani's house is crumbling and his roof, half-collapsed from the snowstorms that battered the village last June and July, offers little protection from the wind and rain. His family, including four young children, sleep on wet ground.

Huancavelica has always been one of Peru's most deprived regions, with 80% of families below the poverty line. The area lacks basic health services and food prices are rising. Huamani says that the main problem his village faces is a lack of water, as more extreme temperatures mean there is no grass or drinking water for the alpaca that people breed for wool and meat. 'If the alpaca die, then we all die,' he says.

**Adapted from** *The Guardian*, 3 January 2010

## E  Sendero Luminoso

For the people of Ayacucho, located in a poor, remote region in the Peruvian Andes, life is very traditional. However, in the early 1980s the Maoist guerrilla organization Sendero Luminoso (Shining Path) was founded here and a brutal civil war with Peru's military government broke out. By 1992, more than 70 000 people had been killed in the conflict, mainly innocents in the villages of the region. The shadows of this terrible time are still visible and perceptible, for instance most of the elderly people are very shy or there are doors secured with eight heavy locks.

**Adapted from:** *Ayacicho, Huancavelica and Lima, Marion and Alfred blog*, 7 October 2013

**TASK 3:** Study Source **C**

How and why does migration affect the population structure of rural Peru and Lima?

**TASK 4:** Study Sources **D** and **E**

a  Use the evidence in the extracts to explain why rural depopulation has taken place in regions in the Andes.

b  Imagine you have migrated from a village in the Andes to Lima. Write a letter to your parents who still live there telling them how life is different in Lima.

# Exam-Style Question on Population Growth and Structure

a   Study Fig. 1, which shows information about the birth and death rates of three LEDCs in Africa in 2013.

| Country | Birth rate (per 1000 of population) | Death rate (per 1000 of population) |
|---|---|---|
| Lesotho | 26.3 | 15.2 |
| Rwanda | 36.1 | 9.6 |
| Zimbabwe | 32.2 | 12.4 |

Fig. 1

   i    What is meant by 'Lesotho had a death rate of 15.2 per 1000'? (1)
   ii   Which of the three countries had the highest rate of natural population growth?
        Show how you worked out your answer by including your calculations. (2)
   iii  Give **three** reasons why there are still high birth rates in many LEDCs. (3)
   iv   Explain why death rates have fallen in most countries in the world during the last century. (4)

b   Study Fig. 2, which shows population pyramids for two countries, A and B.

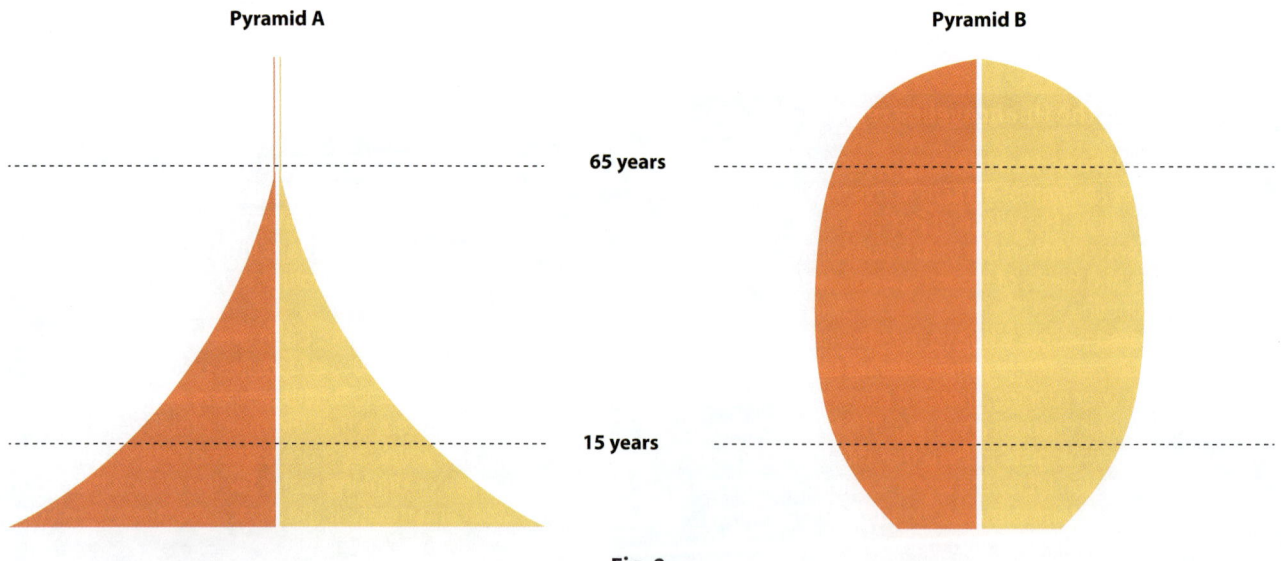

Pyramid A     Pyramid B

65 years

15 years

Fig. 2

   i    Which population pyramid shows the population structure of an LEDC? Give **three** pieces of evidence to support your answer. (3)
   ii   Describe the different problems faced by LEDCs and MEDCs in supporting their dependent populations. (5)

c   For a named example of a country which you have studied, describe the impacts of policies used by the government to influence population growth. (7)

(Total 25 marks)

# Exam-Style Question on Population Distribution

a   Study Fig. 3, which shows world population distribution.

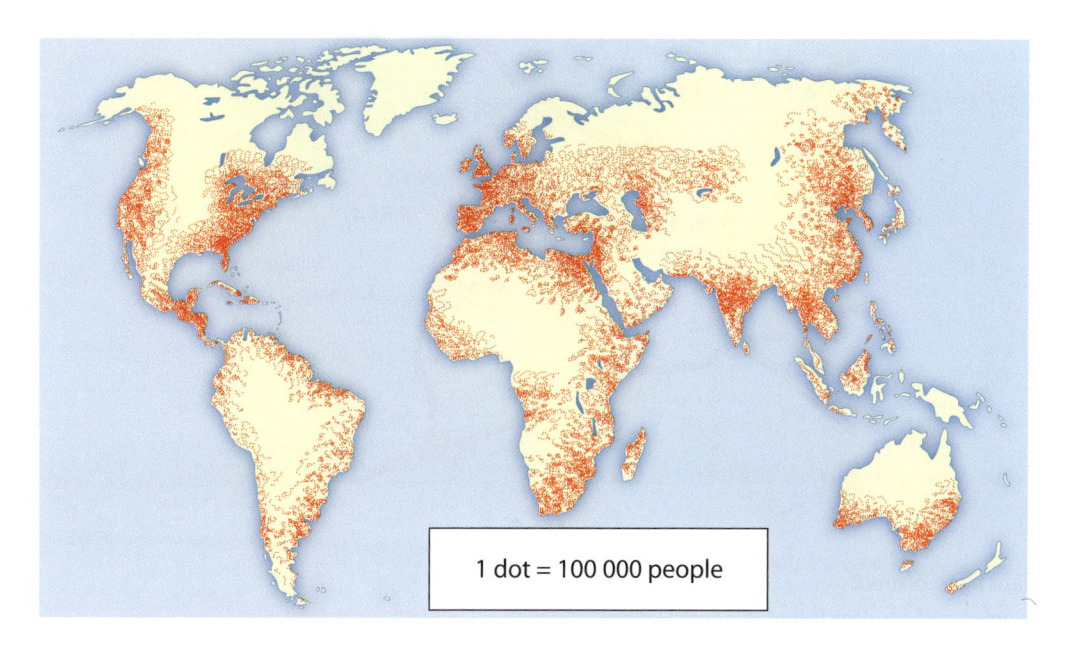

**Fig. 3**

1 dot = 100 000 people

   i    Define the term *population distribution*. (1)
   ii   Identify **two** features of world population distribution shown on Fig. 3. (2)
   iii  Suggest **three** reasons why the population of the world is not evenly distributed. (3)
   iv   Some parts of the world are over-populated. Explain why this causes problems. (4)

b   Study Photograph A, which shows a sparsely populated area from which migration is taking place.

**Photograph A**

   i    Suggest reasons why the area shown in Photograph A is sparsely populated. (3)
   ii   Describe the positive and negative impacts of migration on the areas that people move from. (5)

c   For a named area or country, explain why it has a high population density. (7)

**(Total 25 marks)**

# Exam-Style Question on Rural and Urban Settlements and Services

3  a  Study Fig. 4, a map which shows an area in an MEDC.

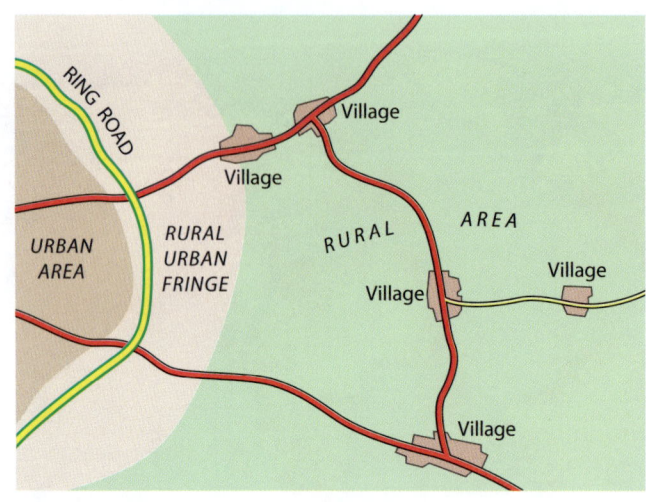

**Fig. 4**

   i   What is meant by *rural area*? (1)
   ii  Give **two** examples of services found in a small village. (2)
   iii Describe **three** likely differences between services in small villages and the urban area. (3)
   iv  Explain why new shopping areas are located in the rural-urban fringe. (4)

b  Study Photograph B, which shows part of the Central Business District (CBD) in New York, USA.

**Photograph B**

   i   Using **only** evidence from Photograph B, describe **three** features that are typical of a CBD. (3)
   ii  Describe the types of changes that are taking place in the CBDs of many urban areas. (5)

c  For a named urban area, describe the conflicts that have resulted because of a change in land use. (7)

(Total 25 marks)

# Exam-Style Question on Urbanisation

**4 a** Study Fig. 5, which shows cities that are expected to have a population greater than 5 million by 2025.

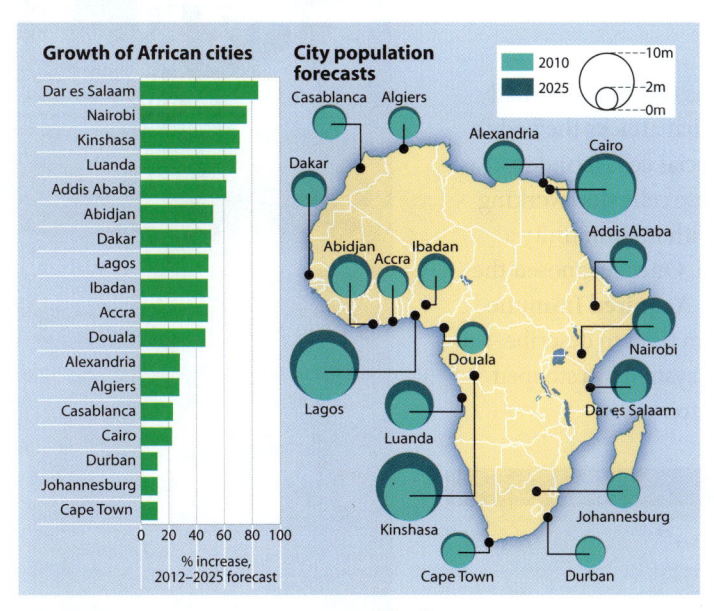

**Fig. 5**

- i Name a city with an expected population of 10 million or more by 2025. (1)
- ii Arrange the following cities in rank order according to their percentage increase in population size.
          Dakar    Kinshasa    Nairobi (2)
- iii Suggest **three** likely impacts of movement to these cities on the rural areas from which people have moved. (3)
- iv Explain why cities, such as those shown on Fig. 5, continue to attract migrants from surrounding rural areas. (4)

**b** Study Fig. 6, which shows information about the world's population who lived in urban slums between 1990 and 2010.

**Global Urban Population Living in Slums 1990–2010**

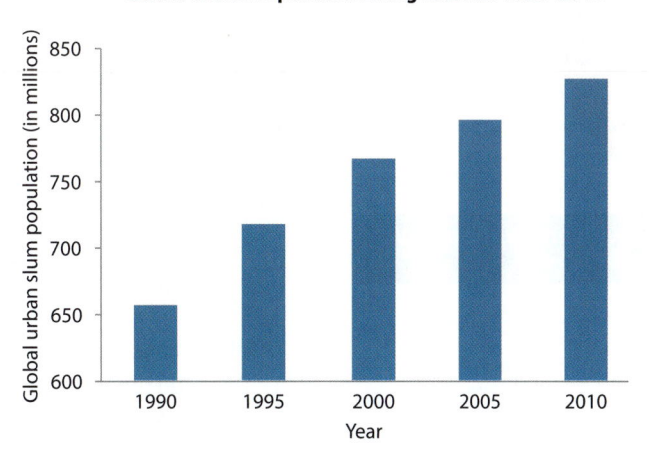

*Source*: UN HABITAT State of the World's Cities 2010/2011

**Fig. 6**

- i Describe the changes in the numbers of people living in urban slums (squatter settlements) between 1990 and 2010. Refer to statistics and years in your answer. (3)
- ii Describe the characteristics of urban slums (squatter settlements) in LEDCs. (5)

**c** Describe what has been done in a named city to improve the quality of life of families living in the slums (squatter settlements). (7)

**(Total 25 marks)**

# Cambridge IGCSE Geography — Global Theme

## 1  Global Theme: HIV/AIDS

### A  What is HIV/AIDS?

The **Human Immunodeficiency Virus (HIV)** is a sexually transmitted infection (STI) – a virus that attacks the body's immune system. The virus attacks special cells found in blood which help immunity. Once these cells stop working the immune system stops working. With no immunity a person can develop a serious infection. Once diagnosed the virus will stay with the person for life. **Acquired Immune Deficiency Syndrome (AIDS)** is a term used to describe later stages of HIV when the immune system has stopped working. At the moment there is no cure.

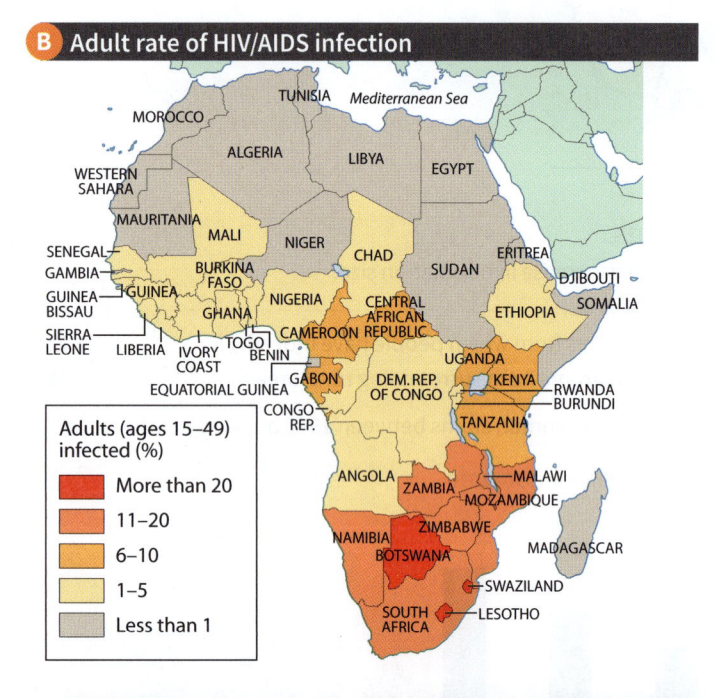

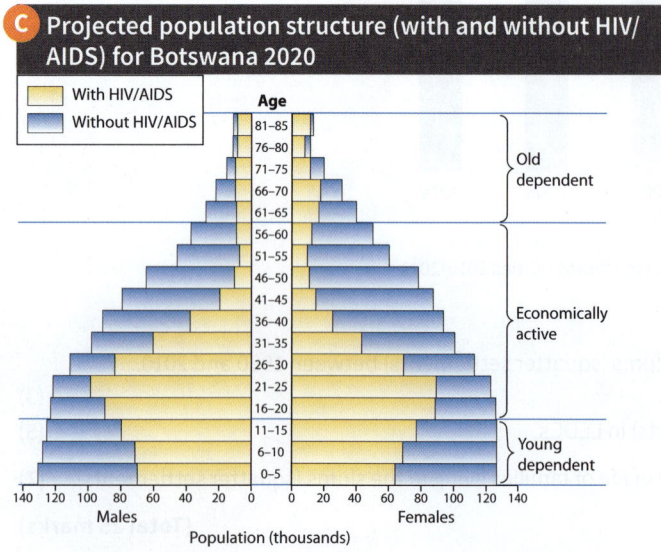

### B  Adult rate of HIV/AIDS infection

Adults (ages 15–49) infected (%):
- More than 20
- 11–20
- 6–10
- 1–5
- Less than 1

### C  Projected population structure (with and without HIV/AIDS) for Botswana 2020

- With HIV/AIDS
- Without HIV/AIDS

Age groups: 0–5, 6–10, 11–15, 16–20, 21–25, 26–30, 31–35, 36–40, 41–45, 46–50, 51–55, 56–60, 61–65, 66–70, 71–75, 76–80, 81–85

Categories: Young dependent, Economically active, Old dependent

Population (thousands): Males / Females

### D  Tackling HIV/AIDS

**HIV/AIDS – Progress in Africa threatened**

Together with conflict, HIV/AIDS poses the greatest threat to development in Africa. It has the potential to change population structures, damage economies and undermine political stability. Any progress made in recent years could be reversed.

> HIV can be transmitted in several ways: through unprotected sex, from mother to baby during pregnancy or in breast milk, or from blood-to-blood contact through sharing needles.

---

**TASK 1: Study Source A**

a  Write down what the initials HIV, STI and AIDS mean.

b  How is the body's immune system affected by HIV/AIDS?

**TASK 2: Study Source B**

a  Name two countries where over 20% of the adult population are infected by HIV/AIDS and two countries where 5% or less are infected.

b  Compare the pattern for southern Africa with that in the rest of Africa.

**TASK 3: Study Source C**

a  Describe the likely impacts of HIV/AIDS on the size and structure of Botswana's population in 2020. Refer to:
- young dependants
- the economically active
- old dependants.

b  Suggest how HIV/AIDS could prevent Botswana from developing its economy before and after 2020.

**TASK 4**

Design a poster similar to the one in Source D to advertise to people in Botswana ways to reduce the spread of HIV/AIDS.

# Theme 2:
## The Natural Environment

# 17 Types and features of earthquakes and volcanoes

## Earthquakes – power below the surface

Earthquakes are triggered from below the Earth's surface where rocks under great stress and pressure reach breaking point and make sudden jerking movements. Where this takes place is known as the **focus** or **origin**. The point on the surface immediately above the focus is the **epicentre**. Shock waves sent out from the focus cause the surface of the Earth to shake and break. These waves spread in concentric circles around the epicentre and can affect places thousands of kilometres away. How much damage is done depends on the pressure at the focus and how deep it is as well as whether there are people and places within range of the earthquake.

To decide how strong an earthquake is, scientists use the Richter scale. This measures the amount of energy produced by an earthquake. There were 58 earthquakes with a magnitude of over 6.5 on the Richter scale in 2013 alone and 176 over 2.5 magnitude on 25 December 2013 – just one day!

### A Earthquakes in the news

**185 killed in New Zealand's second largest city – chaos in Christchurch**

A magnitude 6.3 earthquake struck the Canterbury region in New Zealand's South Island on Tuesday. The epicentre was 3.2 km (2 miles) west of Lyttelton port and its focus was only 5 km (3.1 miles) down. The shallow earthquake lasted ten seconds but caused damage because of previous shocks in the region which weakened roads, bridges and buildings despite earthquake building regulations being among the strictest in the world. Over half of the deaths were in the Canterbury Television building, which collapsed and caught fire.

22 February 2011

**Major earthquake strikes Iran leaving 306 dead and over 3000 injured**

Two strong earthquakes have struck north-west Iran. The quakes struck near Tabriz and Agar but most casualties were in outlying villages. Six villages were destroyed and another 60 villages sustained 50% damage. Both quakes were measured at 6.4 magnitude. Iran is prone to seismic activity. In 2003 an earthquake in the city of Bam killed 25 000.

11 August 2012

### B The focus and the epicentre

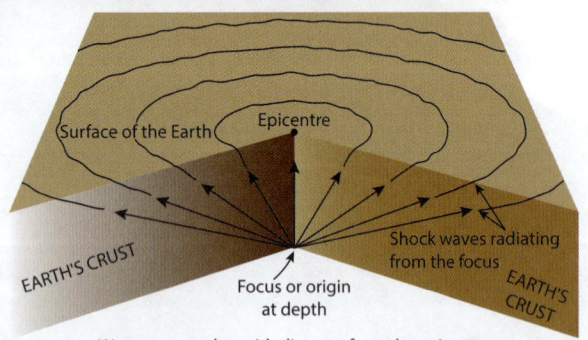

Surface of the Earth — Epicentre
EARTH'S CRUST
Focus or origin at depth
Shock waves radiating from the focus
EARTH'S CRUST
Waves get weaker with distance from the epicentre

### C The Richter scale

Scientists studying earthquakes (seismologists) use the Richter scale to measure the strength or magnitude of an earthquake. It was devised by Charles Richter in 1935. The scale goes from 0–12 but the effect is not even. Each number of magnitude is ten times the energy of the previous one so an earthquake of magnitude 7.0 is 100 times more powerful than an earthquake of 5.0.

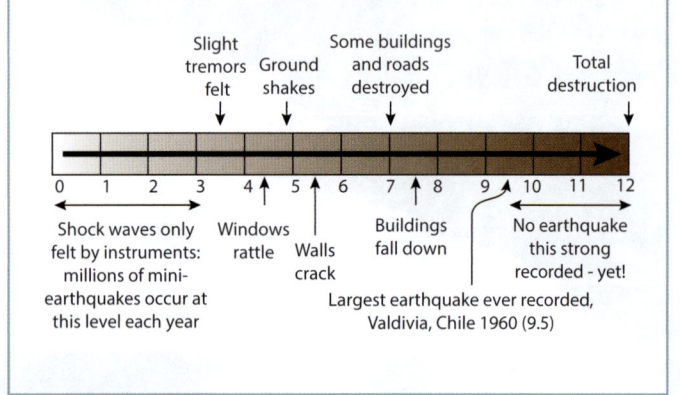

Slight tremors felt — Ground shakes — Some buildings and roads destroyed — Total destruction

0  1  2  3  4  5  6  7  8  9  10  11  12

Shock waves only felt by instruments: millions of mini-earthquakes occur at this level each year
Windows rattle
Walls crack
Buildings fall down
No earthquake this strong recorded - yet!
Largest earthquake ever recorded, Valdivia, Chile 1960 (9.5)

---

**TASK 1:** Study Source **A**

Suggest why some places have less damage from earthquakes than other places.

**TASK 2:** Study Source **B**
a Make a copy of this diagram.
b Explain the difference between the focus and the epicentre of an earthquake.
c Why can earthquakes affect places far away from the focus?

**TASK 3:** Study Source **C**
a At what strength on the Richter scale can you feel slight tremors?
b When was the Richter scale created?
c When and where was the largest earthquake recorded? What was its magnitude?
d Suggest how seismologists may have estimated the magnitude of earthquakes that took place before the scale existed.

## Volcanoes – power at the surface

A volcano is formed when a hole, crack or vent in the Earth's crust allows molten rock (magma), solid rocks, steam and other gases to escape onto the Earth's surface and into the air. There are two main types of volcano.

**Strato-volcanoes** (also known as composite cone volcanoes) are the most deadly of all volcano types. They often erupt with great violence, causing much death and destruction. They usually occur in mountain regions where great pressure can build up beneath the ground.

**Shield** volcanoes are much flatter than strato-volcanoes and are less violent, dramatic and damaging. This is because they are created where there is no great build-up of pressure so they erupt more often and are less explosive.

Volcanoes can also be classified by the frequency of their eruption. They may be:

- **active** – regular eruptions, e.g. Mount Etna, Italy, Mauna Loa, Hawaii
- **dormant** – has not erupted for many years but activity can be detected inside, e.g. Mount Fuji, Japan (its last major eruption was in 1708)
- **extinct** – will not erupt again as no activity can be detected, e.g. La Gomera in the Canary Islands.

### D  Strato-volcanoes (composite cone)

Liquid molten rock (**magma**) builds up below the Earth's crust in magma chambers. Pressure from the rocks causes an explosive eruption through a vent. Magma flows out and onto the Earth's surface and is now called **lava**. Ash clouds settle in layers on the lava as it cools. These volcanoes have steep sides as the acid lava is more viscous and cools quickly. Rocks are also thrown out of the volcano; these are known as volcanic bombs. Sometimes magma can leak through the sides, forming secondary cones. Mount Etna in Italy is an example of a strato-volcano.

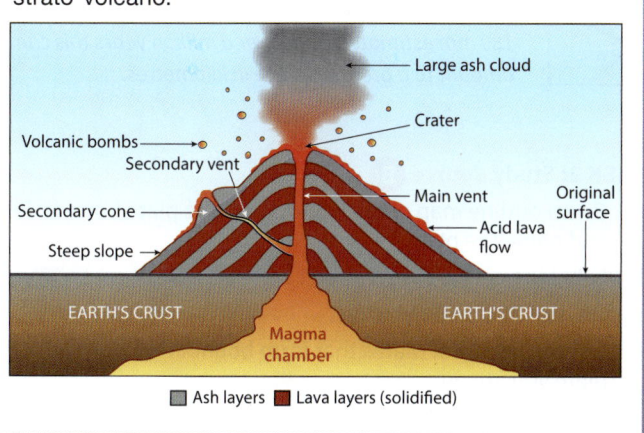

### TASK 4: Study Sources D and E

a  Draw and complete a table like the one below using the information on this page.

| Type of volcano | Type of lava | Slopes | Area covered | Potential damage | Named example |
|---|---|---|---|---|---|
| Strato-volcano | | | | | |
| Shield | | | | | |

b  Write down the meaning of the following terms:

Magma    Magma chamber    Lava    Vent    Crater

### TASK 5: Study Source F

a  Use an atlas to help you draw an outline map of southern Italy including Sicily. Write on it the names of the places mentioned in Source F, including Mount Etna.

b  Annotate the map with information about:
- the eruption and its effects
- the earthquake and its effects.

c  Collect reports on earthquakes and volcanoes during your course. You could contribute to a class wall display.

### E  Shield volcanoes

Unlike strato-volcanoes, shield volcanoes are formed where there is less pressure below the surface but there is a weakness in the Earth's crust that magma can leak through. As there is no great build-up of pressure, these eruptions are less explosive as the lava contains less acid – it is more 'basic'. This means it is less viscous and runny and flows for some distance from the vent. Once cooled, the slopes are gentle. When seen from the air they look like shields. Many of these are created beneath the ocean and their peaks form islands such as Hawaii in the Pacific Ocean. Mauna Loa in Hawaii is an example of a shield volcano.

### F  Double trouble!

## Lava flows merge in Sicilian spectacular

Mount Etna has started sending out lava flows in a week when minor earthquakes have rattled houses in Naples and much of southern Italy. The city of Catania diverted two flights after fissures in the south-east crater threw out lava and ash. The two lava flows merged into a single 'river' of molten rock that flowed down the western slope into the Bove Valley. On the same evening a 4.9 magnitude earthquake shook buildings in the Campania region around Naples, causing many people to spend the evening in their cars. The earthquake was accompanied by more than a hundred minor tremors. The epicentre was located 56 km (35 miles) north-east of Naples near the town of Piedimonte Matese, where the top floor of the hospital was evacuated and an aqueduct damaged. The earthquake's focus was at a depth of 9.6 km (6 miles).

Adapted from *The Times*, 31 December 2013

# 18 Plate tectonics

## Under and at the Earth's surface

For millions of years, since the Earth first formed as a molten sphere, powerful forces have been at work beneath and at the Earth's surface. Today scientists know a great deal about the Earth's structure. This is because they study earthquakes and volcanoes at (and close to) the surface of the Earth. These give clues to what is happening beneath the Earth's crust. With the development of aerial photography, satellites and mapping the ocean floor in the past 100 years, surface patterns have revealed a great deal about where and why earthquakes and volcanoes take place.

Earthquakes and volcanoes do not just occur anywhere. Some places regularly experience earthquakes and volcanoes; others have no record of them occurring at all. If you live in Australia, western Africa, the UK or in the east of North America you will have a different experience of earth movements compared with people who live in Peru, Alaska, Japan or Indonesia, for example. The former lie on stable sections of the Earth's crust called **tectonic plates**; the latter are often affected by earthquakes or volcanoes along **plate boundaries**.

### A Like biting an apple

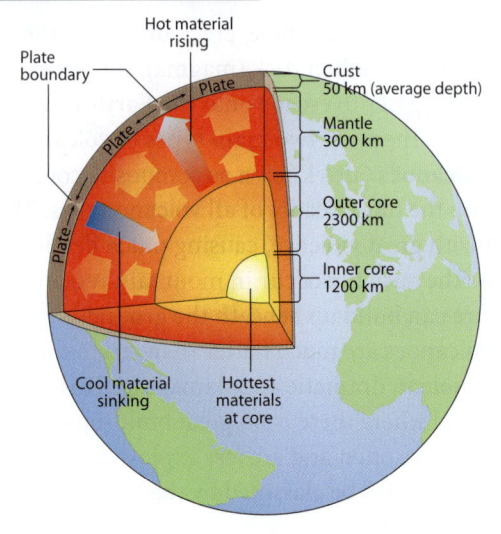

The surface of the Earth is known as the crust. This is a collection of solid tectonic plates that join together like a jigsaw puzzle. Around the core at the centre of the Earth is a layer of molten magma. This is called the mantle. Through this layer flow **convection currents**. The plates float on the mantle. The convection currents move these plates away from, or towards, or alongside each other. These movements along plate boundaries give rise to earthquakes, volcanoes and fold mountains.

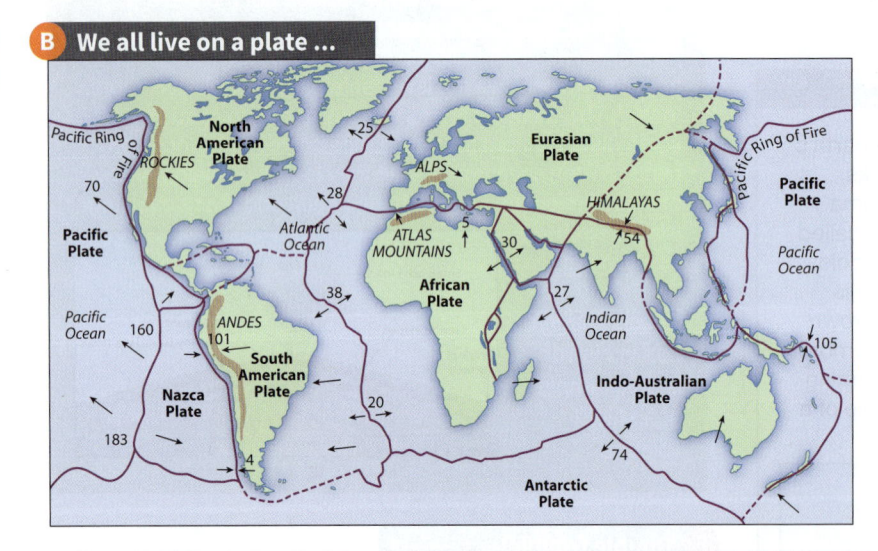

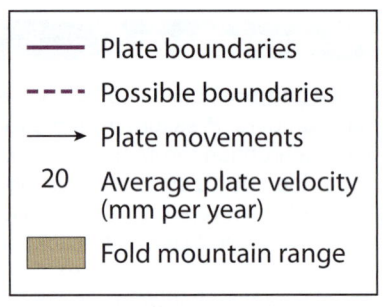

### B We all live on a plate ...

Plates are moving very slowly. The average movement is about 40 mm per year with a range of 10 mm to 180 mm estimated – but over a million years this can amount to a great distance in kilometres.

---

**TASK 1: Study Source A**

a  Make your own labelled drawing of the Earth's structure.
b  Why is the structure said to be 'like an apple'?
c  What is:
   - a tectonic plate
   - magma
   - the mantle?
d  Explain the part played by convection currents in moving the plates around the mantle.

**TASK 2: Study Source B**

a  On an outline map of the world, draw the plate boundaries and name the plates.
b  Label the country where you live.
c  On which plate do you live?
d  List the names of plates that form boundaries with the plate you are on.
e  How close do you live to your nearest plate boundary?
f  Describe the direction this plate is moving in.
g  Based on the average rate of movement of 40 mm per year, how far would a plate have moved in 10 million years? Answer in kilometres.

# Theme 2: Topic 18

## C Converging and diverging plates

**A convergent plate boundary (destructive)**

- Conical **strato-volcano**, steep-sided with lava, ash and rocks thrown out
- Horizontal layers of sedimentary rock are squeezed up into **fold mountains**
- Shape of junction is a trench. Friction here causes **earthquakes**

**A divergent plate boundary (constructive)**

- Plates pulling apart can cause **earthquakes** at ridges
- Edges of plates pushed up by convection currents to form ridges
- Shield volcano

Labels: Crust, Mantle, Continent, Plate, Subducting plate, Convection currents, Mantle, Ocean, Hot spot, Continent, Plate

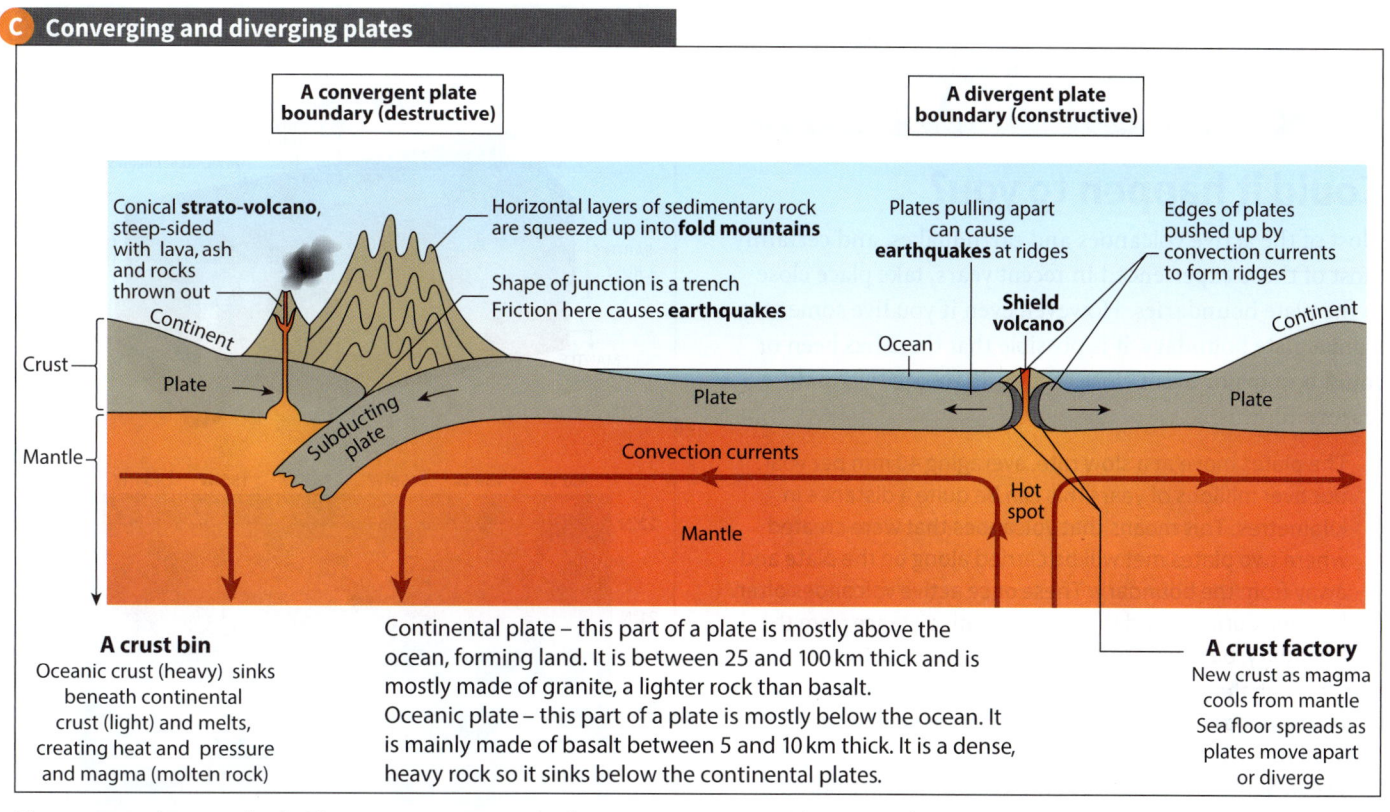

**A crust bin**
Oceanic crust (heavy) sinks beneath continental crust (light) and melts, creating heat and pressure and magma (molten rock)

Continental plate – this part of a plate is mostly above the ocean, forming land. It is between 25 and 100 km thick and is mostly made of granite, a lighter rock than basalt.
Oceanic plate – this part of a plate is mostly below the ocean. It is mainly made of basalt between 5 and 10 km thick. It is a dense, heavy rock so it sinks below the continental plates.

**A crust factory**
New crust as magma cools from mantle. Sea floor spreads as plates move apart or diverge

Plates are moving very slowly. The average movement is about 40 mm per year with a range of 10 mm to 180 mm estimated – but over a million years this can amount to a great distance in kilometres.

## D Types of plate boundary

| Type of boundary | Convergent boundary | Divergent boundary | Conservative boundary |
|---|---|---|---|
| Movement | Subduction | Spreading | The plates slide sideways by each other |
| Effect | Destructive – old crust destroyed. A crust 'bin' | Constructive – new crust created. A crust 'factory' | Crust neither created nor destroyed |
| Relief | Trench | Ridge | No major effect |
| Activity | Earthquakes and strato-volcanoes | Earthquakes and shield volcanoes | Earthquakes |

**TASK 3:** Study Source C
a Make your own copy of the diagram including labels.
b Write down the meaning and location of each of the following by referring to plates and their boundaries:
- convergent boundary
- divergent boundary
- subducting plate
- trench
- ridge

**TASK 4:** Study Source D
a Suggest why convergent boundaries are referred to as crust 'bins'.
b Suggest why divergent boundaries are referred to as crust 'factories'.
c In what way is a conservative boundary different to convergent and divergent boundaries?
d The San Andreas Fault is a conservative plate boundary in California, USA. Use two textbooks; one for you and one for partner. Your book represents the Pacific plate moving north-west at 40 mm per year; your partner's book represents the North American plate moving north-west at 15 mm per year. (Refer to Source B.) Work out where the direction north-west is. Now, between you, act out the movement of the San Andreas Fault over ten years on your desk.

# Cambridge IGCSE Geography — Earthquakes and volcanoes

## 19 Causes and effects of earthquakes and volcanoes

### Could it happen to you?

Most of the active volcanoes and earthquakes, and certainly most of those experienced in recent years, take place close to the plate boundaries. However, even if you live some way from a plate boundary, it is possible that there has been or could be a major event close to you. There are two main reasons for this:

- The plates move at a slow rate, averaging 40 mm per year, but over millions of years this can be quite a distance in kilometres. This means that volcanoes that were created where two plates met will be carried along on the plate and away from the boundary. These once active volcanoes often become dormant and then extinct with distance from the boundary, but they are evidence of volcanic activity.

- Although the plates are quite solid and stable away from plate boundaries, they can have different geological structures that cause vertical weaknesses, or faults, to occur. Some places beneath the Earth's crust are hotter than others and are called **hot spots**. These can burn a hole through the crust forming a weakness, or exploit an existing weakness, allowing molten magma to rise up to the surface to form shield volcanoes.

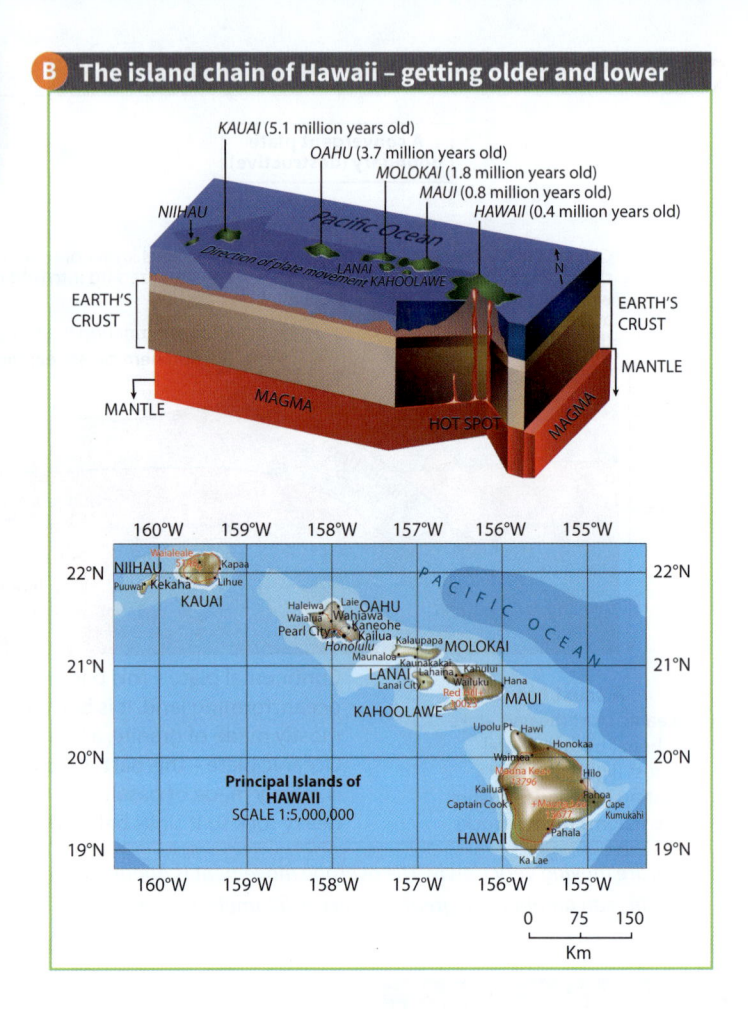

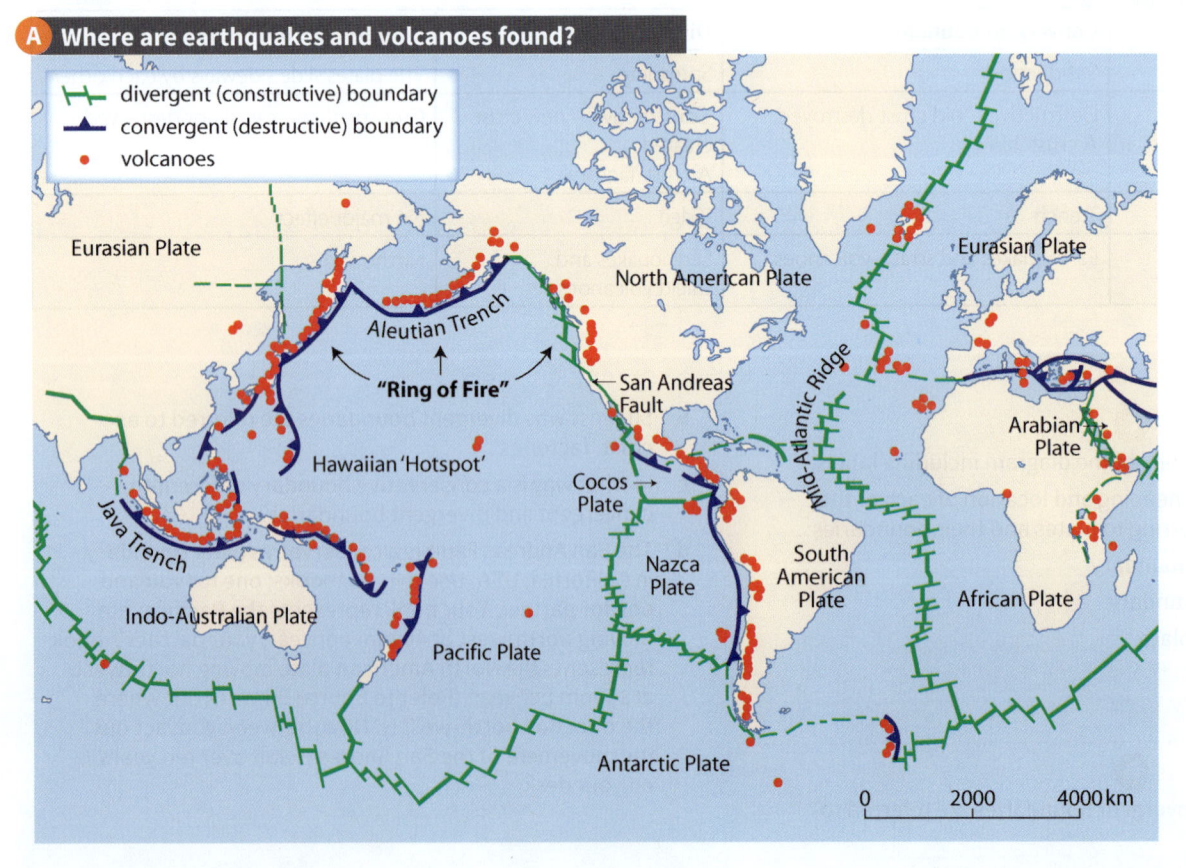

**B** The island chain of Hawaii – getting older and lower

- KAUAI (5.1 million years old)
- OAHU (3.7 million years old)
- MOLOKAI (1.8 million years old)
- MAUI (0.8 million years old)
- HAWAII (0.4 million years old)

Principal Islands of HAWAII — SCALE 1:5,000,000

**A** Where are earthquakes and volcanoes found?

- divergent (constructive) boundary
- convergent (destructive) boundary
- volcanoes

Eurasian Plate, North American Plate, Aleutian Trench, "Ring of Fire", San Andreas Fault, Hawaiian 'Hotspot', Cocos Plate, Nazca Plate, South American Plate, African Plate, Arabian Plate, Mid-Atlantic Ridge, Java Trench, Indo-Australian Plate, Pacific Plate, Antarctic Plate

Theme 2: Topic 19

## C Hawaii – a hot spot for volcanoes ...

Although located more than 1250 km from the nearest plate boundary, the island of Hawaii contains two of the world's most active volcanoes: Kilauea (1248m) and Mauna Loa (4169m). Hawaii has been constructed in the last 600 000 years and is the youngest of the Hawaiian chain of islands. This rose from the waves as the Pacific plate travelled over a hot spot in the mantle at about 100 mm per year. The moving plate carries older islands and volcanoes to the north-west, where rain and the sea erode them. Kauai's cone is now almost at sea level and beyond that there are submarine volcanic cones. Back over the hot spot, however, Hawaii is still being added to by lava flows, fluid basalt and explosive magma. This will continue until the island is transported away from the 'hot spot'.

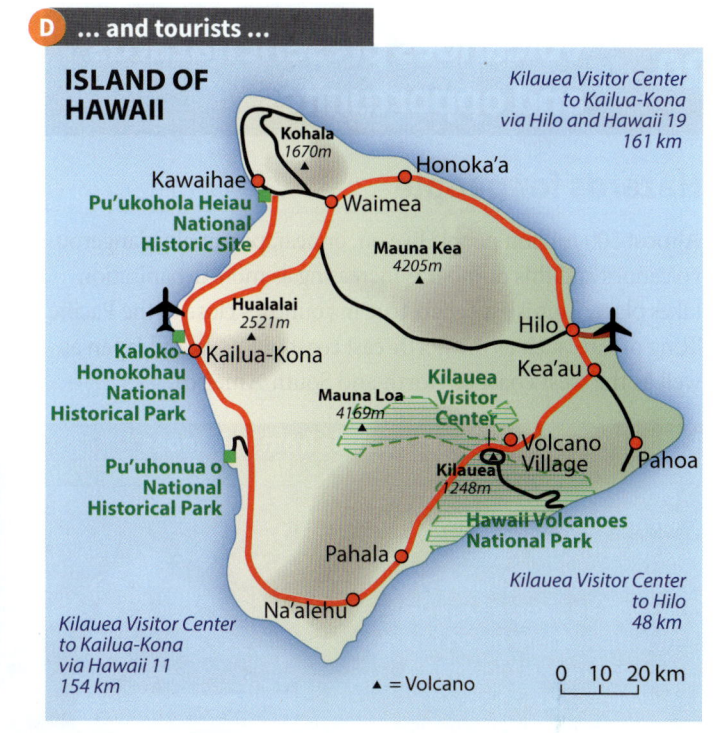

## D ... and tourists ...

**ISLAND OF HAWAII**

Kilauea Visitor Center to Kailua-Kona via Hilo and Hawaii 19 — 161 km

Kilauea Visitor Center to Hilo — 48 km

Kilauea Visitor Center to Kailua-Kona via Hawaii 11 — 154 km

Volcanoes shown: Kohala 1670m, Mauna Kea 4205m, Hualalai 2521m, Mauna Loa 4169m, Kilauea 1248m

▲ = Volcano

## E Some other impacts on people and the environment

|  | Positive | Negative |
| --- | --- | --- |
| **Earthquakes** | Underground minerals may be brought nearer to the surface. | Kills people and wildlife<br>Destroys buildings<br>Destroys roads, railways and infrastructure<br>Can create tsunamis |
| **Volcanoes** | Attractive for tourists<br>Brings in income for locals and country<br>Minerals<br>Light ash falls can add nutrients to soil<br>Can be used for geothermal power | Kills people and wildlife<br>Can destroy farms and woodland<br>Heavy ash can cover area in thick layers and cause roof collapse<br>Ash can cause problems for aircraft<br>Can destroy buildings and transport infrastructure<br>Gases can cause pollution |

**TASK 1:** Study Source **A**
a Describe where most active volcanoes are found. Refer to plates and plate boundaries.
b Why is the *Ring of Fire* so named?
c What is unusual about the location of the Hawaii volcanoes?

**TASK 2:** Study Source **B**
a Use an atlas and Source B to help you describe the location of Hawaii.
b Estimate the distance from Hawaii to the island of Kauai.
c What happens to the age of islands as you move from Hawaii to Kauai? Refer to figures in your answer.
d Explain why the islands to the north-west of Hawaii are older and lower.

**TASK 3:** Study Source **C**
a Name the **two** active volcanoes on Hawaii island and state their heights above sea level.
b Explain how these volcanoes have been formed.
c What evidence is there that the landscape of Hawaii is still being influenced by volcanic activity?

**TASK 4:** Study Source **D**
a List evidence that the Hawaiian authorities want to attract tourists to the island.
b How would you get to Hawaii from your country? Refer to mode of transport, distance, direction and time to get there.
c Describe a route around Hawaii that can be taken to see the main volcanoes on the island.

**TASK 5:** Study Source **E**
a Copy the table and add in any impacts that are missing.
b Add an extra column titled **Examples**. As you study volcanoes and earthquakes, add in the names of examples from this book and from events as they occur during your course.

69

# Cambridge IGCSE Geography — Earthquakes and volcanoes

## 20 Volcanoes present hazards and opportunites

### Hazards for people

Almost 500 million people live on, or near, potentially dangerous volcanoes and this number is increasing as more urbanisation takes place. This is especially true in countries close to the Pacific 'Ring of Fire' such as the north-east coast of Russia and Japan as well as the west coast of North and South America.

South America leads the world in the number of volcanoes that threaten lowland populations. The danger does not just come from an explosion of rocks and ash or the lava flow. Of the 204 volcanoes in the Andes mountain range, over half are covered with heavy amounts of **glacial** ice. Any lava that flows from these volcanoes melts the ice and creates floods, **mudflows** and **lahars**. These can travel many kilometres from the volcano and engulf settlements. This is just one hazard of living near volcanoes, but there are many others.

### A The environment faces hazards from volcanoes

Mount St Helens is an active strato-volcano in Washington state, USA. In 1980, scientists noticed several bulges and other activity so people were warned that there might be an eruption. An earthquake triggered a massive eruption on 18 May. It was so powerful that the volcano's height was reduced by 390 metres and a crater 3 km wide and 640 metres deep was created on the northern slope. When a volcano blows its top off like this, the crater left is called a caldera. Despite the warnings 57 people died.

*Before the eruption*

*After the eruption*

#### OTHER IMPACTS OF THE MOUNT ST HELENS ERUPTION

- Ash rose to 24 km and landed in 11 states.
- The melted ice caused a mudflow that travelled over 80 km to the south-west.
- 200 houses, 27 bridges, 24 km of railways and 298 km of roads were destroyed.
- Nearly 400 km$^2$ of forests and crops such as wheat, apples and alfalfa were destroyed.
- 1500 elks and 5000 deer perished.
- Airports and Interstate 90 highway were closed.

### B Travellers suffer

Between 14 and 20 April 2010, the Eyjafjallajökull volcano, in Iceland, erupted sending a huge amount of ash into the atmosphere. This was ejected so high by the explosion that the upper air winds, known as jet streams, carried the ash across west and north Europe. The disruption to air travel affected over 100 000 travellers.

On 4 June 2011, the Puyehue-Cordón Caulle volcano in Chile, South America, erupted. It sent out an ash cloud that reached the North Island, New Zealand over several days. Air New Zealand and Jetstar flights were cancelled or delayed for over a week.

### TASK 1
a Why are more people becoming vulnerable to the hazards caused by volcanoes?
b Why are volcanoes that are covered with ice more hazardous than similar volcanoes that have no ice cover?

### TASK 2: Study Source A
a When and where did Mount St Helens erupt?
b Describe the change in the appearance of Mount St Helens after the eruption.
c Complete a table like the **one** below by adding in facts from the information provided:

| Effect on people | Effect on infrastructure | Effect on the environment |
|---|---|---|
|  |  |  |
|  |  |  |

### TASK 3: Study Source B
a How can ash clouds affect areas a long way from the volcanic eruption?
b Suggest why airlines cancelled flights in Iceland and Chile after the eruption of these volcanoes.

# Theme 2: Topic 20

## Opportunities for people

Volcanoes create many hazards for people and the environment. But they provide opportunities and benefits too. Volcanic soils are fertile and are responsible for prosperous vineyards, farms and grain fields from Italy to Indonesia.

Volcanic heat can provide the energy for hot springs and thermal areas. Some countries, such as Iceland, Mexico and New Zealand, have used geothermal energy to produce renewable electricity.

Volcanic activity has produced much of the world's mineral wealth. As magma cools and crystallises, the process releases minerals. These are then carried in hot water which deposits them in cracks, forming veins of gold, silver, copper, zinc and lead. Diamonds are also formed by the pressures of rocks on carbon at great depths. The uplift of many rocks by plate movements has made these veins accessible to mining as they are now close to the surface though they were formed at depth.

Volcanoes are also awesome features and, with the increase in global travel in the last 50 years, many countries have taken the opportunity to market their volcanoes in what is known as *volcano tourism*. Hawaii, the Azores islands, Iceland and New Zealand have done this for years.

### C  An opportunity to farm

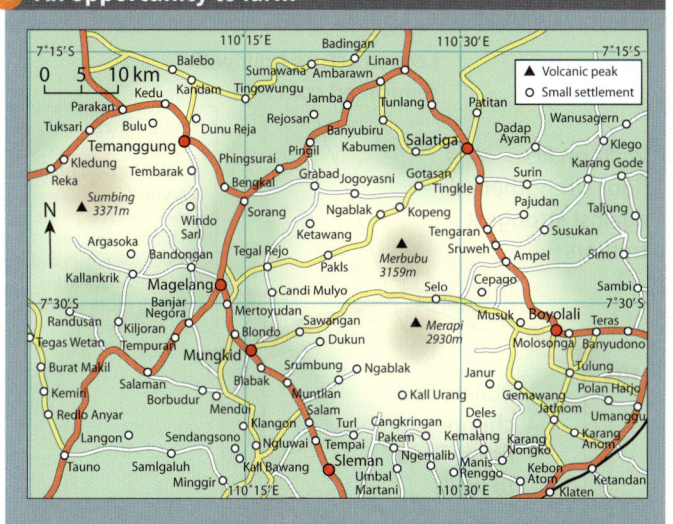

*Many small villages on the volcano slopes are not shown on this map.

### Mount Merapi erupts again – why locals don't leave

For many, the foot of one of the most active volcanoes in the world is not a desirable place to live. Yet residents here have chosen to face the risk rather than move away. Thousands of Indonesians live in small villages farming on the volcano slopes because of the fertile volcanic soils and abundant rainfall. The long-term benefits of nutrients that the ash brings outweighs the short-term destruction. Despite numerous eruptions killing people and livestock, and covering crops with ash and lava flows, the villagers keep coming back. Food is needed as Indonesia is one of the most densely populated places on Earth.

'Economic Life Slowly Returns to Indonesia's Mount Merapi', *Voice of America*, 9 January 2012

### D  Two more opportunities …

#### Heat and energy

The Taupo region of North Island is hot! Here, two of the Earth's giant plates meet, causing friction which melts rocks into molten magma that rises to the surface. The heat creates hot water springs and steaming geysers. For hundreds of years, Maori villages were sited near hot pools for cooking and washing. Heat is still used for this, but now geothermal power stations generate 13% of New Zealand's electricity using steam to drive the turbines.

#### Mining Sulphur

Sulphur is a valuable deposit which is used to make medicines, paper and gunpowder. The opportunity to work plus the foreign earnings from exporting sulphur are important to developing countries. In East Java, Indonesia, the Ijan volcanic crater is filled with one of the largest sulphur lakes in the world.

### TASK 4: Study Source C

a   Name the **three** volcanic peaks shown on the map and state their height.

b   Describe the location of Mount Merapi in relation to Mount Sumbing. Refer to distance and direction.

c   Explain why people live near Mount Merapi.

d   The government declares an exclusion zone up to 15 km around Mount Merapi when there is a major eruption. List the settlements that would be affected.

### TASK 5: Study Source D

a   State the two opportunities mentioned.

b   Choose **one** of these opportunities and:
   - describe its location.
   - describe why volcanic activity offers this opportunity.
   - explain how it affects people.

c   Suggest other opportunities that volcanoes offer to people.

# Cambridge IGCSE Geography — Earthquakes and volcanoes

## 21 Reducing the impacts

### A Earthquakes cause damage and destruction

At 12.51 pm on Sunday, 22 February 2011 a magnitude 6.3 earthquake struck Christchurch, New Zealand's second largest city. Over 185 people were killed. The total cost of rebuilding was estimated at NZ$40 billion (US$33 billion). One reason why there was so much damage was that in MEDCs, the buildings and infrastructure have been built using expensive materials and were insured. They are often multi-storey too. In LEDCs such as Haiti, where an earthquake struck in 2010, over 220 000 were killed but rebuilding costs were estimated at US$14 billion. New Zealand's GDP is US$140 billion; Haiti's GDP is US$7.8 billion.

## Reducing the impacts of earthquakes

Despite a great deal of research, it is not possible to predict when earthquakes will occur. The best advanced warning possible is about nine seconds, which is not enough time to do anything! Although earthquakes cause death and destruction through landslides, tsunamis, fires, and rock movements, the greatest loss of lives and property is due to man-made structures falling during the violent shaking of the ground. The most effective way of preventing destruction is to construct buildings that are capable of withstanding strong ground movements. Preparing for earthquakes is the only way to limit the damage caused.

### B Preparing for an earthquake

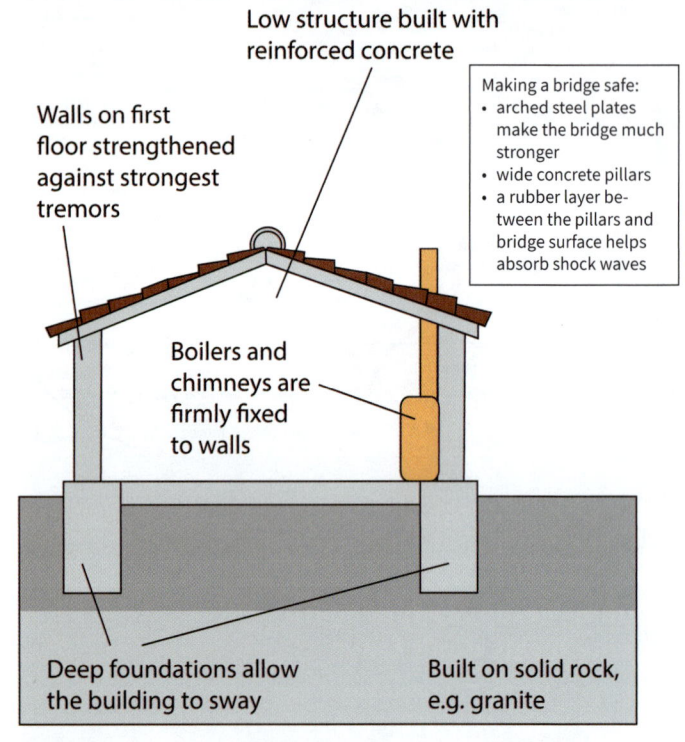

- Low structure built with reinforced concrete
- Walls on first floor strengthened against strongest tremors
- Boilers and chimneys are firmly fixed to walls
- Deep foundations allow the building to sway
- Built on solid rock, e.g. granite

Making a bridge safe:
- arched steel plates make the bridge much stronger
- wide concrete pillars
- a rubber layer between the pillars and bridge surface helps absorb shock waves

Since 2011, Christchurch has started to repair the damage. The diagrams show some solutions to make buildings and bridges more resistant to damage in future earthquakes. They should be built with deep foundations with rubber shock absorbers, and concrete reinforced with steel. They are designed to twist and sway and have sprinkler systems and gas cut-off valves.

**TASK 1:** Study Source A
a When did the earthquake strike Christchurch?
b Describe the different types of damage done in Christchurch.
c Contrast the number of deaths and cost of rebuilding in Christchurch with Haiti. Suggest reasons for these differences.

**TASK 2**
You have entered a competition. You have to give advice to the Chief Planner about how to rebuild Christchurch after an earthquake. Her job is to design buildings and bridges that will limit future earthquake damage. Prepare your entry using information from Sources A and B.

# Theme 2: Topic 21

## Reducing the impacts of volcanoes

Nothing can be done to prevent a volcanic eruption. But, unlike earthquakes, it is possible to predict to some degree when volcanoes will occur as well as prepare for their eruptions. Most volcanoes give out warning signs before a major eruption. These include steam and gas rising out of a crater, small lava flows, bulges on the volcano's slopes and minor earthquakes as the magma moves. Changes in the chemical composition of air and water around the volcano are also indicators.

The problem for authorities is that many people live close to volcanoes and do not want to evacuate until the last possible moment before an eruption. **Vulcanologists** cannot be completely accurate in predicting the exact time the volcano will erupt, but predictions of eruptions are becoming more accurate due to technological advances. Being able to predict eruptions makes it easier to prepare for them.

### C Predicting volcanic eruptions

- Checking the ground from above ... satellites can detect changes in the ground surface.

- Checking the air from above ... aeroplanes use remote sensors to test for volcanic ash.

- Checking below sea level ... plate boundaries can be explored deep beneath oceans by mini submarines.

- Checking on the volcano ... scientists can monitor ash, sulphur and other gases in the air as well as rock and water temperature and ground movement by climbing the volcano.

### D Advice – what could YOU do ...?

**IN A VIOLENT EARTHQUAKE**

- Stay indoors
- Keep calm
- Keep away from windows and heavy furniture
- Take cover in a doorway or under a strong table or other support

**When the shaking stops**

- Turn heaters off, put fires out
- Don't let your water supplies go to waste
- If the building is seriously damaged, turn off water, electricity, gas and heating oil at the mains
- Treat minor injuries
- Get in touch with neighbours – they may need help
- When help is needed, go to your closest civil defence post
- Keep alert – remember after-shocks may happen

**IN AN ERUPTION**

- Stay indoors
- Close doors and windows
- Save some water

**If you have to leave your home**

- Wear substantial clothing over your head and body
- Breathe through a handkerchief or wet cloth
- Carry a torch

---

**TASK 3: Study Source C**
a How useful are satellites and aircraft in monitoring volcanic activity?
b Suggest what evidence of volcanic activity can be found beneath the ocean.
c Why do scientists still need to climb volcanoes and use instruments?

**TASK 4: Study Source D**
a Describe and explain any differences in the advice given.
b Is your school or home near a volcano or in an earthquake zone? If so, are you prepared for such an event? Discuss what you should do.
c Have you ever experienced an earthquake or volcano? What did you do?
d In Japan, schoolchildren practise their earthquake drill on 1 September every year. Describe any drills you practise in your school.

Cambridge IGCSE Geography | Earthquakes and volcanoes

# Case Study
## An earthquake – Haiti

### Not a happy new year

Frequently damaged by hurricanes, high winds and floods, a major earthquake was about the only disaster that had not seriously affected Haiti for over 200 years, but at 5 p.m. on 12 January 2010, this changed. A powerful earthquake occurred with its epicentre just 16 kilometres south-west from the capital city of Port-au-Prince. The focus was only 10 kilometres below the surface, so the shallow shock waves caused the ground to shake violently. If the focus had been deeper, the shaking would have been less severe because the ground above would have absorbed much of the pressure.

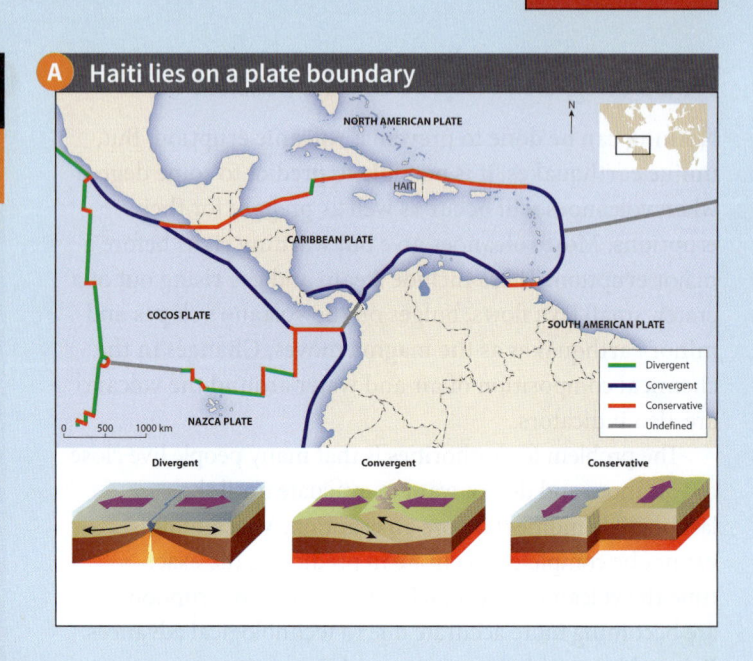

**A** Haiti lies on a plate boundary

**B** What happened on 12 January 2010?

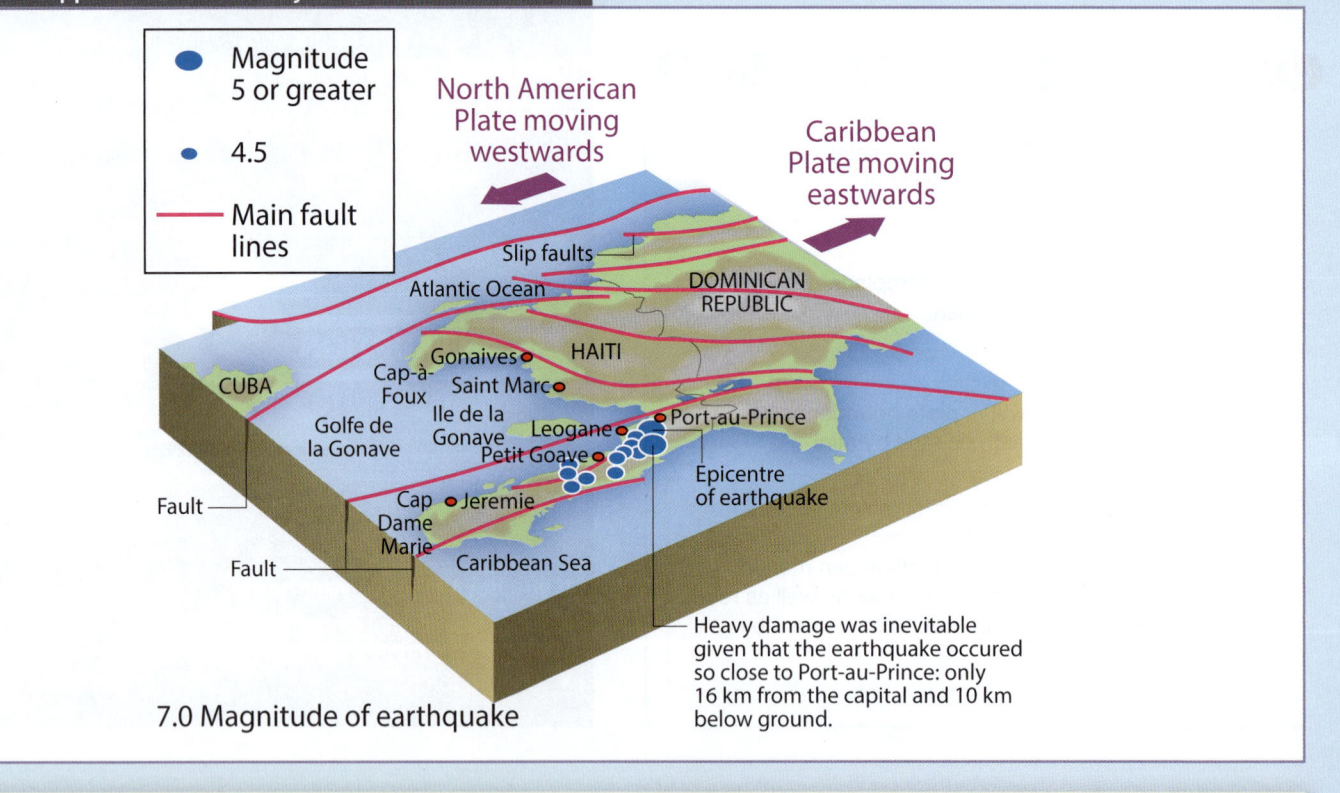

Heavy damage was inevitable given that the earthquake occured so close to Port-au-Prince: only 16 km from the capital and 10 km below ground.

7.0 Magnitude of earthquake

### TASK 1: Study Source A

a   Use an atlas and Source A to help you describe the location of Haiti. Refer to latitude, longitude and distance and direction from other countries.

b   Describe Haiti's location in relation to **two** plates.

c   Haiti lies on a conservative plate boundary. Explain what this means. Refer to the direction of movement of named plates in your answer.

d   At what time and day *in your country* did the Haiti earthquake take place? Refer to pages 284–285 to help.

### TASK 2: Study Source B

a   At what magnitude on the Richter scale was the Haiti earthquake? How severe is this?

b   Describe the location of the epicentre and the focus of this earthquake.

c   Explain the cause of the earthquake. Refer to the Caribbean plate and the North American plate.

Case Study: An earthquake – Haiti

## C The damage was devastating

### FACTFILE: DAMAGE REPORT FOR HAITI 2010

- Over 220 000 killed
- Over 250 000 houses destroyed
- Over 3 million people displaced
- Roads collapsed
- Airport control tower and runway damaged
- Hospitals collapsed or damaged
- Public telephones not working
- Over 1300 schools destroyed
- All orphanages destroyed
- Landslide damaged dam and flooding caused
- Dirty water causing cholera

**PORT-AU-PRINCE**

- CITÉ SOLEIL – Slum district less damaged
- International Airport Runway intact
- SAINT MARTIN
- Port – Damaged and closed
- Ministry of Commerce – Damaged
- National Cathedral – Badly damaged
- Parliament – Destroyed
- NAZON
- Prison – Destroyed
- National Palace – Destroyed
- BOURDON
- UN HQ Christopher Hotel – Collapsed, burying hundreds
- PACOT
- Hotel Montana – Badly damaged
- PÉTIONVILLE
- Hospital – Badly damaged

0   1km

## D On the street where I lived

Ruelle Pescaye used to be a pleasant street – quiet with comfortable homes with private gardens and views of green mountains. It was very different to the filthy slums that make up most of Port-au-Prince. Now, though, almost all homes have collapsed or are beyond repair. Debris and crushed cars lie on the road. Some residents have moved away. Others live on the road, desperate for water, food and money. Idammante Bigord, 25, a student, now lives with her two brothers on a sofa and a mattress taken from the shattered concrete and twisted steel that was their home. Her mother and younger sister were crushed in the house. 'It's very, very sad' she said quietly but the tears no longer flow. Her friend Michelle, 24, and her aunt were also buried in another house. There were 12 deaths in the street in total.

Adapted from *The Times*, 29 January 2010

## E Progress report 2014

"It is taking longer than we thought to rebuild Haiti but we are getting there with the help of aid from many countries. Since President Martelly came to office in 2011, more aid has been directed to moving the homeless out of tent camps into new housing back in their original neighbourhoods. New industrial parks and transport projects are starting up too, which will help reduce the 70% unemployment. Agricultural reform is replacing the machete with machinery to increase crop yields. Replacing charcoal as a fuel and reforestation will slow down soil erosion and provide more fertile land to grow our own crops instead of importing half of our food. Tourism is also a possibility though that is not a reliable source of income for us in the long term."

Government spokesman

**TASK 4:** Read Source **D**
a  List the damage that was done to Ruelle Pescaye.
b  How was Idammante Bigord affected by the earthquake?
c  How many people died in Ruelle Pescaye?

**TASK 5:** Study Source **E**
a  Suggest why it has been so difficult for Haiti to recover from the 2010 earthquake.
b  Describe **three** policies that the government of Haiti is carrying out to improve the country.
c  Explain how these policies should help Haiti develop its economy in future.
d  Caribbean islands have a long history of using tourism to develop their economies. Why would it not be wise to rely entirely on tourism for future wealth?

**TASK 3:** Study Source **C**
a  List **three** different types of buildings that were damaged.
b  List **three** different types of infrastructure that were damaged.
c  Describe **three** ways in which people were affected by the earthquake and the damage it caused.

# Cambridge IGCSE Geography
## Earthquakes and volcanoes

# Case Study
## A volcano – Mount Sinabung, Indonesia

### A hazardous place to live

Indonesia's 15 000 islands stretch eastwards across the Pacific Ocean, linking southern Asia to the northern seas off Australia. Java and Sumatra are the main two islands and most volcanoes in the region are found on the western coast of Sumatra. Here, spreading along the Pacific Ocean's Ring of Fire, Indonesia has more volcanoes than any other nation, which makes it a hazardous place to live. More than 3.5 million people live within 10 km of one of the region's 130 volcanoes and, being many islands, it is difficult to get away if a volcano erupts.

Although Mount Merapi in the east of Java erupted in late 2010, killing 350 people, Mount Sinabung to the north of Sumatra was dormant for over 400 years until it also erupted in late August 2010. On this occasion there were warnings for people to move away from danger. This was also the case when it erupted in September 2013. The eruptions continued for several months, but in February 2014 vast quantities of rock, toxic gas, and ash exploded out of the crater and onto nearby villages and farms. This time at least 16 people were killed; the first time the volcano has been known to claim lives.

**A Where is Mount Sinabung?**

**B Indonesia's plate boundary**

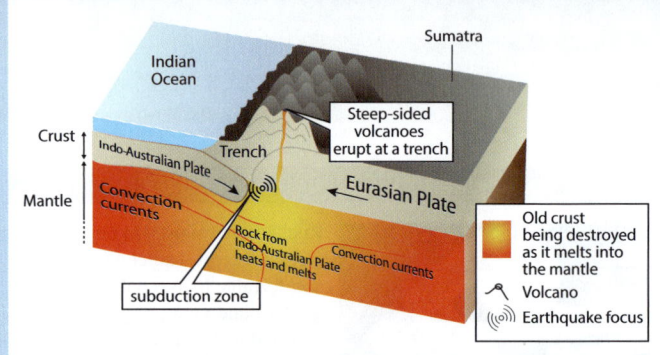

The Indo-Australian plate from the west is sliding beneath the Eurasian plate in the east.

A farmer in Ujung village, Sumatra; Mount Sinaburg simmers in the background. The villagers sell their flowers for Rp10 000 (82 US cents) per bunch of 50. The flowers are used for rituals and ceremonies by local people or sold to tourists and for export.

### TASK 1: Study Source A

a  Describe the location of Mount Sinabung in relation to:
  - Mount Merapi
  - Krakatoa.
  
  Refer to distance and direction.

b  Describe the location of Mount Sinabung in relation to lines of longitude, latitude and its location in Sumatra. Refer to sea areas and other places.

### TASK 2: Study Source B

a  Describe and explain the movement of the Indo-Australian plate.

b  Explain what is meant by a:
  - trench
  - subduction zone

c  Explain why Mount Sinaburg erupted.

# Case Study: A volcano – Mount Sinabung, Indonesia

## C The following day

### CLOUD OF DEATH AS MOUNT SINABUNG ERUPTS

An Indonesian volcano that has been rumbling for months finally erupted yesterday, killing 16 people just a day after evacuated villagers were allowed to return home. The molten lava, ash and rocks hurled out of Mount Sinabung in western Sumatra killed, among others, a television journalist and four secondary school students and their teacher who were visiting to see the eruptions. On Friday, nearly 14 000 evacuees living outside the 5 km danger zone were allowed to return home after volcanic activity decreased. Yesterday, a series of huge blasts and eruptions bellowed out of the 2600 metre volcano, covering villages, farms and trees in thick, grey volcanic ash. Within the danger zone homes, schools, and clinics have been abandoned. Only dogs, chickens and ducks left behind by farmers survive in this quiet, empty landscape. Shelters are being prepared for over 70 500 evacuees.

Adapted from the *Sunday Telegraph*, 2 February 2014

## D Why live around Mount Sinabung?

" I was born here, as were my parents and grandparents. They all farmed these slopes and I am carrying on the tradition. It is the only place I know and I can make a good living keeping a few chickens and growing some crops. This is a difficult place to get away from. The roads are poor and the bus service unreliable. I can't afford a car and, by staying here, I don't need one. "

" Why move away? There have been a few minor eruptions in recent years but, until now, nobody has been killed, so there was a good chance it would not erupt in my lifetime. If the officials had not said we could go back to our homes before the eruption, nobody would have been killed. Now it has erupted we should be safe for another 400 years. "

" More tourists are coming to Indonesia. Even more might come now it has erupted. I can earn money as a guide and my wife sells souvenirs from her roadside stall. It is a lot easier than farming though we do grow our own food. "

" I do not believe the officials or scientists. I believe in the local 'spiritualists' who give advice on our safety. However, ever since Maridjan, the 'spiritual guardian' of Mount Merapi, died in the 2010 eruption there, I am having second thoughts. I won't go but I will listen to government advice. "

" We have high temperatures and plenty of rain for most of the year, so all we need is fertile soil which the volcano's ash provides. I can grow chilli, rice, coffee and cocoa here to feed my family or to sell for a profit. "

---

**TASK 3:** Study Source **C**
a When did Mount Sinabung erupt?
b What materials were ejected into the atmosphere by the volcano?
c What damage did it do to:
- people
- the environment?
d What evidence suggests that the slopes of the volcano are densely populated?
e What decision may have caused the effects to be worse than expected?

**TASK 4:** Study Sources **A** and **D**
Explain why some people live close to Mount Sinabung.

# Cambridge IGCSE Geography — Rivers

## 22 Rivers and drainage basins

### Rivers and the water cycle

All rivers receive their water from **precipitation** – that is rain, hail, snow and sleet. But the relationship between precipitation and the amount of water in a river, known as **discharge**, is not straightforward. Only a small amount of the water that falls reaches the river, which is just part of the water, or hydrological, cycle.

Once clouds have released the precipitation, many different routes and destinations are possible for water. It may:

- evaporate back into the atmosphere
- be transpired by plants
- be kept by plants or in the soil
- stay for a time in lakes, glaciers or reservoirs
- infiltrate into the ground to become groundwater
- run off the surface immediately into rivers.

Through rivers, the water reaches the sea to be evaporated again and the water cycle continues.

### A  River terminology

| Characteristic | Definition | RIVER A | RIVER B |
| --- | --- | --- | --- |
| Width | How wide the water in the river is. The distance from bank-to-bank of the surface water of the river. | Narrow/wide | Narrow/wide |
| Depth | How deep the water in the river is. This varies across the river, so an average is usually taken from several measurements of the width. | Shallow/deep | Shallow/deep |
| Velocity | The speed at which the river is flowing. This varies with depth and width. | Slow/fast | Slow/fast |
| Wetted perimeter | Length of the wet part of the channel cross-section containing flowing water. | Low/high | Low/high |
| Cross-section area | Area of flowing water when measured from bank to bank. | Small/large | Small/large |
| Discharge | The amount of water flowing in a channel. This is calculated by multiplying cross-sectional area by velocity. | Low/high | Low/high |

*River A*

*River B*

### B  The water (hydrological) cycle

**C Condensation:** as water vapour is blown towards mountains by the prevailing winds it is forced to rise, cools and condenses back into water droplets. These form clouds and relief (orographic) rainfall or snow.

**B Evapotranspiration:** vegetation not only intercepts rainfall but also takes it up through roots from the soil. This water is eventually returned to the atmosphere by transpiration from leaves. Surface water is also evaporated from leaves.

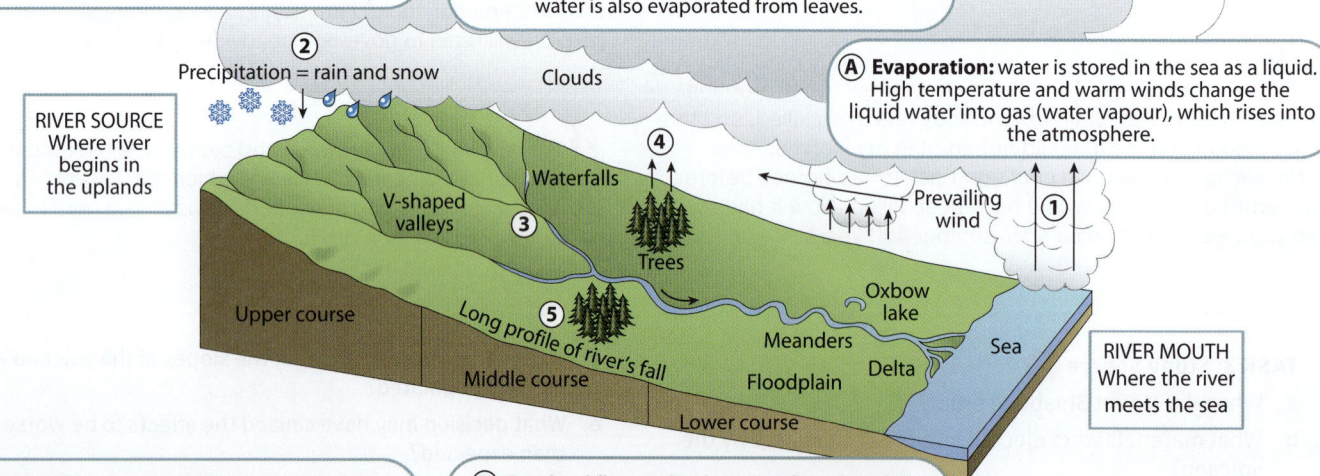

**A Evaporation:** water is stored in the sea as a liquid. High temperature and warm winds change the liquid water into gas (water vapour), which rises into the atmosphere.

② Precipitation = rain and snow

RIVER SOURCE: Where river begins in the uplands

V-shaped valleys ③
④ Waterfalls
Trees
⑤ Long profile of river's fall
Upper course
Middle course
Lower course
Oxbow lake
Meanders
Floodplain
Delta
Sea
Prevailing wind ①

RIVER MOUTH: Where the river meets the sea

**D Interception:** some rainfall is intercepted by plants and trees before reaching the ground. Some falls on land and infiltrates the ground or flows on the surface as small fast-flowing streams.

**E Overland flow:** upland streams flow downhill and join at confluences to form slower-moving, wider, deeper rivers which eventually discharge the water into lakes or the sea.

Theme 2: Topic 22

## Drainage basin characteristics

The **drainage basin** includes all the area drained by a river and its tributaries. The drainage basin is also known as the river's catchment area. The border or edge of the drainage basin is called the **watershed**. This boundary is usually on the tops of hills and mountains, or high ground, which surround the drainage basin. It is sometimes called a divide because it separates one drainage basin from others.

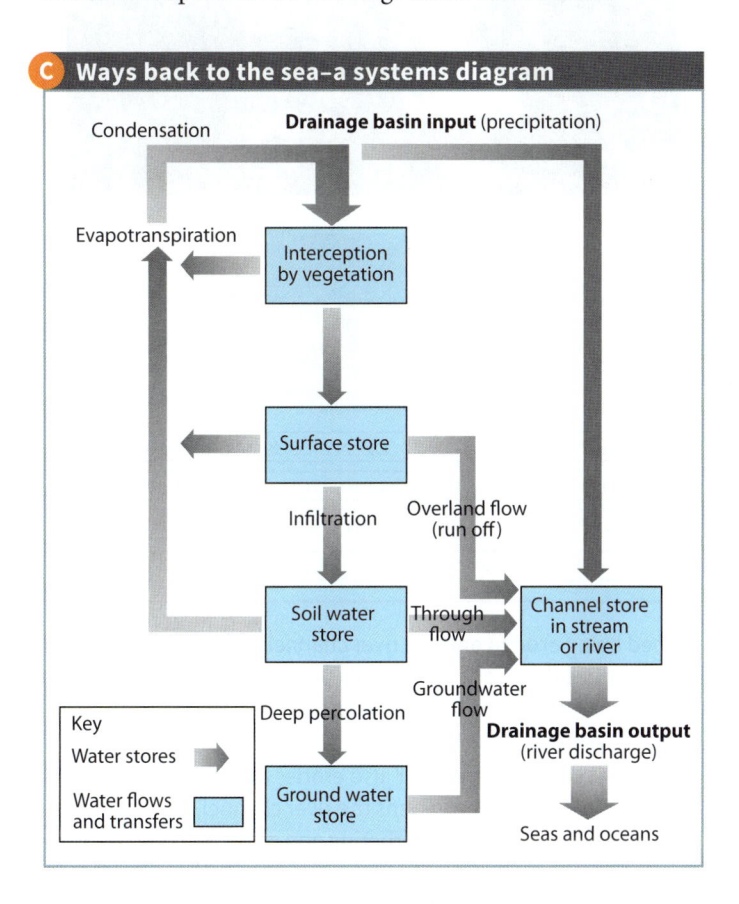

### C Ways back to the sea–a systems diagram

*[Systems diagram showing: Drainage basin input (precipitation) → Interception by vegetation → Surface store → Soil water store → Ground water store, with flows including Condensation, Evapotranspiration, Infiltration, Overland flow (run off), Through flow, Deep percolation, Groundwater flow, and Channel store in stream or river leading to Drainage basin output (river discharge) → Seas and oceans. Key: Water stores, Water flows and transfers.]*

### D People change the water cycle

---

**TASK 1: Study Source A**
a  Copy the table in Source A.
b  Look at the two photographs, which were taken at different places along the same river. Circle the correct answer in the final two columns of your table.
c  Where along the river would you expect these photographs to have been taken? Explain your decisions.

**TASK 2: Study Source B**
a  On an outline copy of the diagram, match captions A–E with locations 1–5.
b  Explain how the water cycle works.
c  How does the long profile of a river change as it moves from uplands to lowlands?

**TASK 3: Study Source C**
a  What do you understand by the terms *input* and *output*? Give an example of each from the diagram.
b  Suggest **two** places on the diagram where each of the following take place:
- water is stored
- water flows or is transferred
- water changes its state from liquid to gas.

**TASK 4: Study Source D**
a  List **five** different ways in which people are using land and water.
b  Explain how **three** of these uses change the stores, flows and transfers in the water cycle. Use Sources B and C to help.
c  Suggest how the systems diagram would change for an urban area. Explain why.

# 23 The work of rivers

## Erosion

Streams and rivers erode in various ways. There are four main processes of erosion.

- **Hydraulic action** – the force and impact of flowing water alone can remove material from the bed and banks of a river.
- **Corrasion (abrasion)** – the effect of the load grinding away at the bed and banks of a river like sandpaper. This is the most effective process of river erosion.
- **Attrition** – as material wears away the bed and banks, it also becomes smaller and more rounded and less effective in carrying out erosion.
- **Solution (corrosion)** – some rocks dissolve in the presence of water. Limestone is one example.

These processes can take place at the same time, so it is difficult to know which processes are operating at any one place in the river.

## Transport

Once eroded, materials are transported by the river. There are four types of load.

- **Solution load** – minerals are dissolved and carried in solution. This requires the *least* energy.
- **Suspension load** – very light materials are carried near the surface giving the river its colour, e.g. the Blue Nile.
- **Saltation load** – small pebbles and stones are bounced along the riverbed.
- **Traction load** – heavy boulders and rocks are rolled along the riverbed. This requires the *most* energy.

## Deposition

A river deposits material when its energy decreases. It is no longer competent to transport its load. This usually occurs because the gradient of the river channel becomes more gentle. The first material to be deposited is the heaviest and lighter ones follow. The finest material may continue to be carried which is why, as rivers approach the sea, they deposit fine material when they flood. This fine material is usually very fertile and is called alluvium. Over many years, several floods can build up the valley floor, creating a flood plain.

## Erosion of river valleys

While the water in the river is eroding the banks and bed of the river, the shape of its valley is also changing. There are two main types of erosion involved in changing the valley shape:

- **Vertical erosion** – the stream flows downhill as it tries to reach sea level from its source. This results in the

bed being eroded and the river channel getting lower. Erosion smoothes the river's long profile by removing uneven gradients in the riverbed which create waterfalls and rapids. Eventually vertical erosion creates a smooth, concave, long profile.

- **Lateral erosion** – the river also erodes away at its banks and the sideways erosion widens the river channel. However, above the river level there is weathering and erosion taking place from other processes unrelated to the river water. These processes wear away the valley sides.

Together vertical and lateral erosion create the distinctive V-shaped valley that is found in rivers in their upper course. As the river gets closer to the sea, there is more lateral erosion than vertical erosion and the V flattens out into a much wider shape.

### A Eroding the river channel away

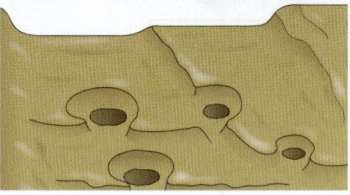

Labels:
- Width of river bed
- Direction of fast-flowing water
- Water swirls around in a depression where bed is uneven
- Pebbles carried by the water grind a hollow in the river bed
- River bed is uneven
- Deep hollows become potholes

**TASK 1:** Study Source A
a Write down the definitions of the four processes of river erosion.
b Which process is likely to be taking place in the photograph?
c Add the six labels to a copy of the potholes diagram.

**TASK 2**
Write down the definitions of the four types of load transported by the river.

Theme 2: Topic 23

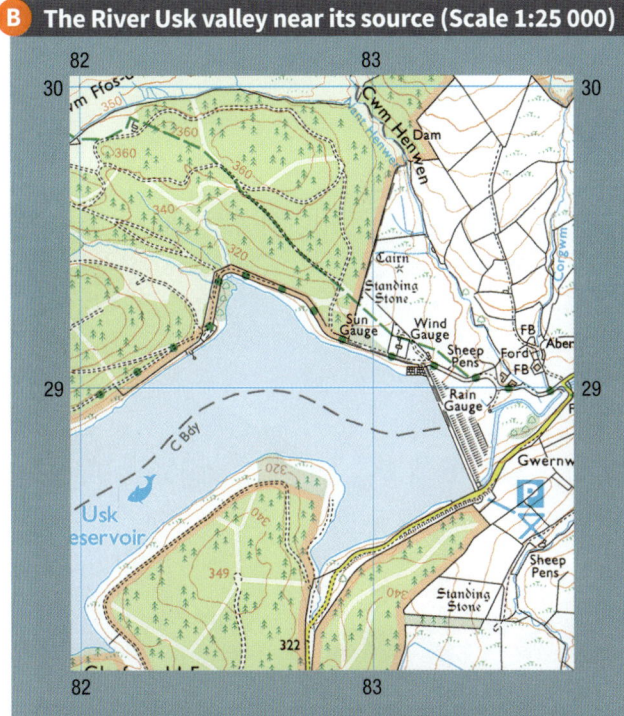

**B** The River Usk valley near its source (Scale 1:25 000)

In the upland valley, the stream flows quickly over steep ground. The main process is vertical erosion. It has a low **capacity** but a high **competence**. It flows around obstacles, creating interlocking spurs. The valley slopes are worn back by weathering processes such as freeze-thaw, soil creep and slumping. The stream erodes vertically, forming a V-shaped valley. Waterfalls are common.

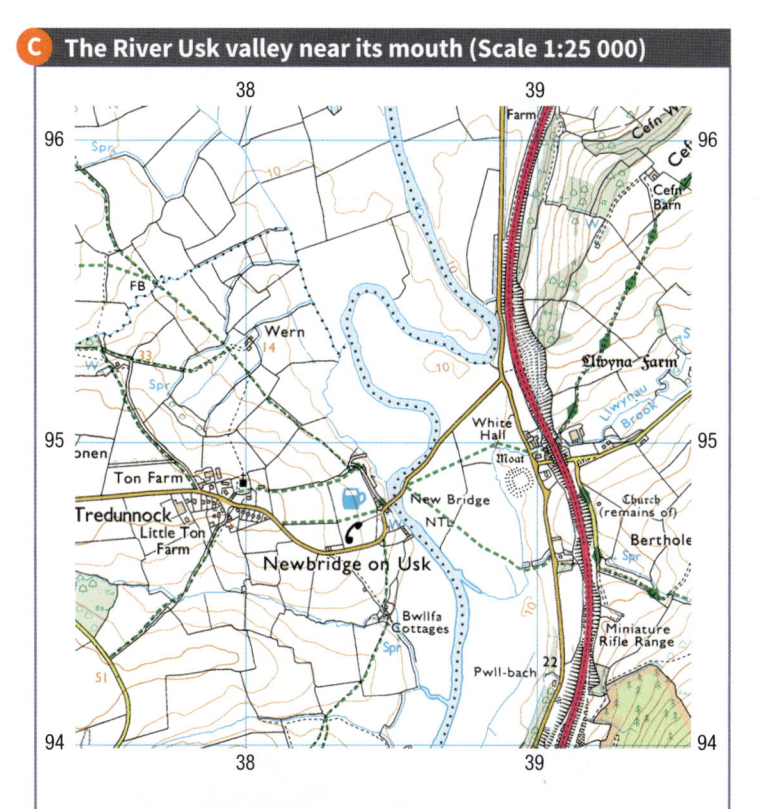

**C** The River Usk valley near its mouth (Scale 1:25 000)

In the lowland valley, the river flows more slowly over flatter ground. It has a large capacity but a low competence. It often meanders on a wide flood plain. The valley is wide due to lateral erosion of the valley sides. Deposition is the major process at times of flooding. The flat valley created can easily be seen on OS maps, e.g. in square 3895.

**TASK 3: Study Source B**
a Label the following on a sketch of the photo in Source B
- interlocking spurs
- steep slopes
- the stream.

b Annotate the sketch to explain where and how erosion is taking place.

**TASK 4: Study Sources B and C**
a Describe the view of the valley looking north from grid reference 388942.
b Compare this view with that of the Corgwm valley looking north from grid reference 835292.
c Explain why the valley shapes are different.

**Cambridge IGCSE Geography** — Rivers

# 24 River landforms – 1

## River valleys and gorges

The shape of a river valley is influenced by many factors:

- the rate of vertical erosion, or downcutting, by the river
- the rate of lateral erosion by weathering and erosion
- the geology of the valley
- the climate of the valley
- time.

The Grand Canyon is a deep river valley eroded by the Colorado river in the USA over millions of years. The Colorado river starts in the Rocky Mountains where there are large amounts of rainfall and melting snow. It is the largest natural feature in the world. It is claimed to be the most spectacular landform created by running water.

**A**

'The scale of the Grand Canyon is almost beyond comprehension. It is ten miles across, a mile deep, 180 miles long. You could set the Empire State Building down in it and still be thousands of feet above it. Indeed you could set the whole of Manhattan down inside it and you would still be so high above it that buses would be like ants and people would be invisible, and not a sound would reach you. The thing that gets you – that gets everyone – is the silence. The Grand Canyon just swallows sound. The sense of space and emptiness is overwhelming. Nothing happens out there. Down below on the Canyon floor, far, far away is the thing that carved it: the Colorado river. It is 300 feet wide (92 metres) but from the canyon lip it looks thin and insignificant. It looks like an old shoelace. Everything is dwarfed by this mighty hole.'

*The Lost Continent*, Bill Bryson
(NB 1 mile is approx. 1.6km)

**B Making the Grand Canyon**

- Resistant rock strata stick out into the valley.
- With little rainfall there are few tributaries so the Colorado plateau surface remains flat and smooth.
- The resistant rock and lack of rainfall prevent the sides of the valley being eroded. Lateral erosion is very slow.
- The North and South Rim have sharp edges due to the lack of rainfall to smooth them.
- The plateau is slowly being uplifted by forces beneath the surface. This causes the powerful Colorado river to erode downwards to reach the sea. Vertical erosion is rapid.
- Weathering on valley slopes produces scree in the valley. This is carried away by the river.
- Less resistant rock strata are worn away to give smoother slopes.

**TASK 1:** Study Sources **A** and **B**

Imagine you have just hiked from the rim of the Canyon down to the valley floor. Update your blog to describe your journey and the scale and size of the Grand Canyon.

**TASK 2:** Study Source **B**

a Label an outline copy of the photograph with the captions provided.

b Write an introduction to an illustrated tourist information leaflet entitled *How the Grand Canyon was formed*. Refer to the influence of:

- the climate
- the rock layers and plateau
- the river.

# Theme 2: Topic 24

## Waterfalls

Waterfalls are common features in the upper reaches of a river valley. Here the water is fast-flowing and vertical erosion is the main process. They can, however, occur at any point where an outcrop of hard, resistant rock obstructs the flow of the river. In these cases, the stream works at removing the waterfall by downcutting so it can achieve a smooth long profile. As a waterfall cuts down through the rock, it appears to move back upstream or 'retreat'. This has produced a **gorge** nearly 10 km long to the north of the current site.

### C Creating waterfalls

**Waterfall over horizontal hard rocks**

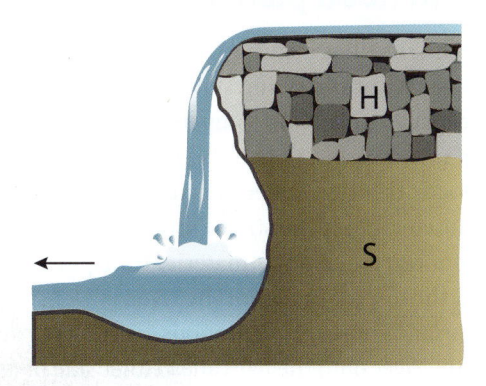

When a layer of hard rock lies across the course of a river, the water will wear away the softer rocks downstream at a faster rate. The harder rock will then overhang the softer rock, forming a waterfall. As the softer rock below is worn away, the overhang will break off and fall into the plunge pool. In this way the waterfall 'retreats' upstream, forming a gorge.

**Waterfall over vertical hard rocks**

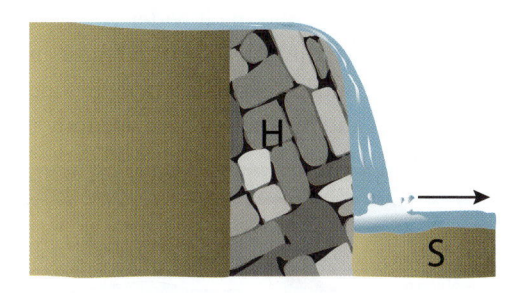

H = Harder rock    S = Softer rock

A waterfall can develop where the more resistant rock protrudes into the riverbed at a vertical angle. Here there is hardly any backward 'retreat' and no overhanging rock to fall into the plunge pool. Here the force of falling water may erode the downstream rock more deeply, but the waterfall will not alter its position.

### D The making of Niagara Falls

- The glaciers melted over 12 000 years ago.
- Meltwater poured over the Niagara Escarpment.
- The rocks of the Falls are in horizontal layers.
- The top layer of hard dolomite sandstone overlies softer rocks.
- Splashback also erodes the soft rock, undermining the hard rock above.
- Today the Falls has moved back or 'retreated' over 10 km to the south of the escarpment.
- Without this support below, the top layer continually collapses under its own weight to fall into the plunge pool below.
- This movement back has eroded the narrow Niagara Gorge or canyon.

*Niagara Falls consists of two waterfalls on the Niagara river, which mark the border between New York State, USA (The American Falls) and Ontario, Canada (the Canadian or Horseshoe Falls).*

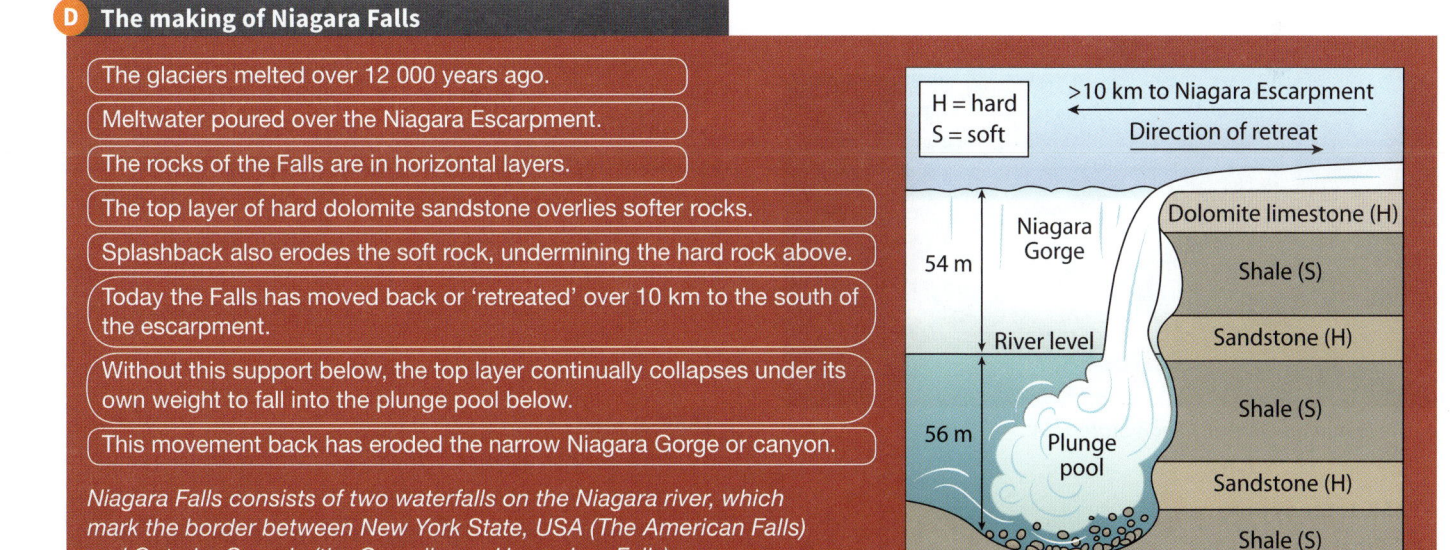

H = hard   S = soft
>10 km to Niagara Escarpment
Direction of retreat
Niagara Gorge — 54 m
River level
Plunge pool — 56 m
Dolomite limestone (H)
Shale (S)
Sandstone (H)
Shale (S)
Sandstone (H)
Shale (S)

---

**TASK 3:** Study Source C

a  Copy both diagrams and use the information to add labels that show how each type of waterfall is formed.

b  Which type of waterfall 'retreats'? Explain how this happens.

**TASK 4:** Study Source D

Use the captions in Source D to annotate a copy of the sketch to show how Niagara Falls was formed.

# 25 River landforms – 2

## Meanders and oxbow lakes

As rivers flow towards lower land, the gradient of the land they are flowing on gets less steep. This causes the water to move much more slowly. There is less vertical erosion now and the river begins to flow in bends rather than a straight line. These bends are called meanders. As these bends develop, lateral erosion is the dominant force which wears away the sides of the valley, making it wider.

As the river meanders, the fastest flow and most energy is directed towards the outside of bends where the sides are undercut by corrosion and hydraulic action, forming river cliffs. The eroded bank collapses and retreats as the meander moves further downstream. The water on the inside of the bends is slowed by friction in shallower water and deposits material there to form gently sloping slip-off slopes.

Further erosion on the outside of the bends of a meander leads to its neck getting narrower, until the river bursts through in a straight line and cuts off the meander, leaving an oxbow lake of stagnant water.

## Levées and flood plains

By the time the river has begun to create large meanders in its lower reaches, it is moving slowly. By now the river has a large capacity and a low competence. It can carry a great deal of material, but only if it is light and small as a suspended load. This fine material is usually smaller than 2 mm in diameter and is the size of sand, silt and clay which has been produced from larger material transported and eroded from the upper reaches of the river.

Over thousands of years, continuous overflowing and flooding by the river onto the flat valley either side of its main channel, and deposition onto it, has created a **flood plain**.

## Deltas

Most of the load carried by a river eventually ends up in the sea or a lake. The longer the river, the more load is carried as its capacity increases downstream. Once the river's speed is reduced when meeting the sea, it deposits its load of fine material at the mouth. The largest rivers of the world such as the Mississippi, the Nile, and the Ganges that drain the largest basins create huge areas of deposition where fresh and saltwater meet. This usually occurs where the rate of deposition by the river and tides is far more than the sea currents can remove. Over time the deposited material builds up and outwards into the sea to form **deltas** which can block the main channel. To get to the sea, the river has to divide into **distributaries**, which meander through the deposition.

### A  From meanders to an oxbow lake

### B  Future oxbow lakes?

*The Sangamon river in Illinois State, USA.*

### TASK 1: Study Source A

a  What is a *meander*?

b  Explain why lateral erosion is more effective than vertical erosion in the lower reaches of a river.

c  Explain why:
- river cliffs are found on the outside of meanders
- slip-off slopes are found on the inside of meanders.

d  Draw an annotated diagram (or a series of diagrams) to show how and why a meander can become an oxbow lake.

### TASK 2: Study Source B

a  Draw a sketch diagram of the river and its flood plain. Label:
- the river and its meanders
- where you would find river cliffs and slip-off slopes
- where erosion and deposition are taking place.

b  Where would you expect oxbow lakes to form in future? Label this on the sketch, explaining your choices.

### TASK 3

You are helping to produce a Geography DVD about river features. Imagine you are flying over the scene in Source B. Write a 50-word piece of commentary.

# Theme 2: Topic 25

Over 120 million people live in Bangladesh; one of the most densely-populated countries in the world. Yet most of the country is part of a huge, low-lying delta. This has been formed by deposition from some of the longest rivers in the world – the Ganges and its tributary, the Brahmaputra, and the Meghna river.

## C Creating flood plains and levées

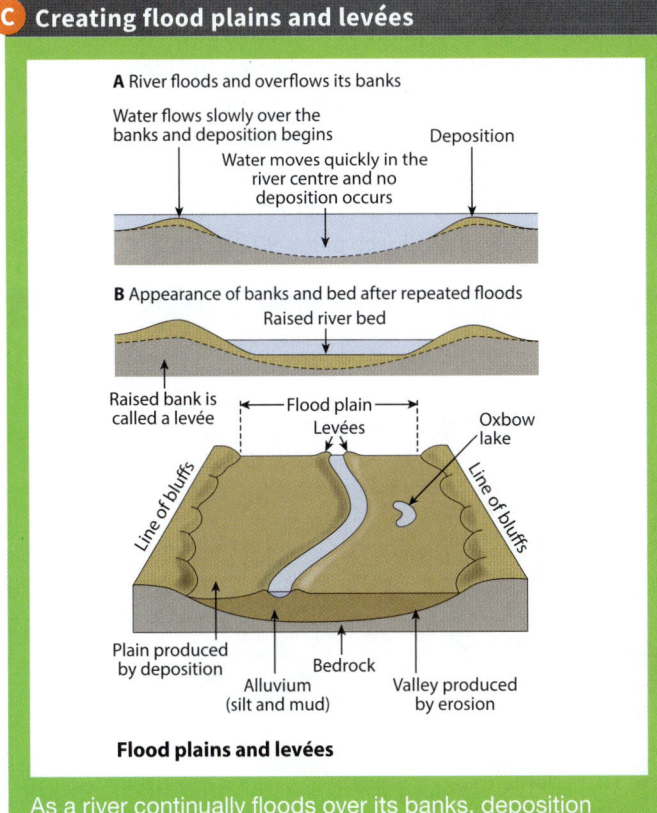

**A** River floods and overflows its banks
- Water flows slowly over the banks and deposition begins
- Water moves quickly in the river centre and no deposition occurs
- Deposition

**B** Appearance of banks and bed after repeated floods
- Raised river bed
- Raised bank is called a levée
- Flood plain
- Levées
- Oxbow lake
- Line of bluffs
- Plain produced by deposition
- Bedrock
- Alluvium (silt and mud)
- Valley produced by erosion

**Flood plains and levées**

As a river continually floods over its banks, deposition occurs on the flood plain and on the banks. As the floodwater will spend more time close to the river than further away, over time the banks build up more than the flood plain to form levées, made of slightly larger materials, sand and gravels than the rest of the flood plain. The formation of levées and deposition on the river bed means the river channel is raised and the river can flow at a higher level than before, above the level of the flood plain. These rivers cause some of the most disastrous floods when they burst through their banks and cover the lower flood plain with vast amounts of flowing water. Rivers such as the Hwang-ho, the Yangtze and the Mississippi all flow above their flood plain.

## D Making the Ganges delta

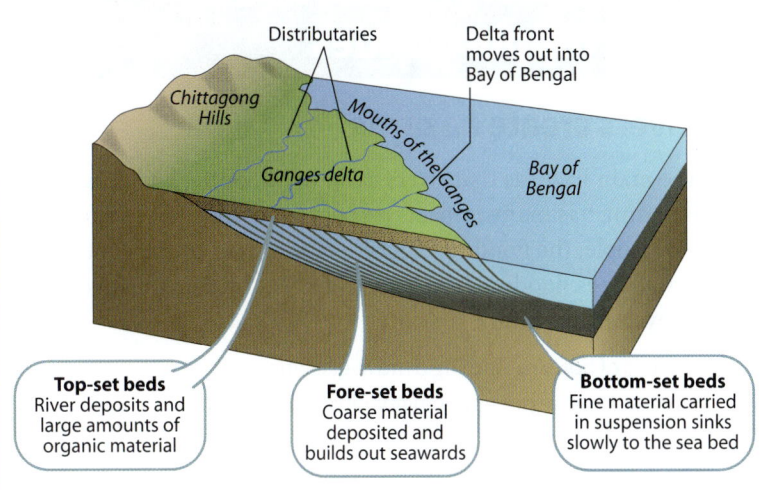

- Distributaries
- Delta front moves out into Bay of Bengal
- Chittagong Hills
- Mouths of the Ganges
- Ganges delta
- Bay of Bengal

**Top-set beds** River deposits and large amounts of organic material

**Fore-set beds** Coarse material deposited and builds out seawards

**Bottom-set beds** Fine material carried in suspension sinks slowly to the sea bed

Most of the load carried by a river is eventually deposited in a lake or the sea. If the river's journey is not too long or there is a small load then the freshwater merges into the saltwater quite easily in an estuary. Large rivers, however, often form deltas.

| Stage 1 | Stage 2 | Stage 3 |
| --- | --- | --- |
| The lower course of the slow-moving Ganges river carries a large quantity of fine silt as suspension load. The river's energy is used in transporting it. As it enters the Bay of Bengal its speed reduces and deposition takes place. The heaviest material is dropped first and builds up to form islands. | Over time more sediment is deposited as the waves are too weak to remove it quickly. The river channel becomes blocked by the silt. More flooding also takes place. The river finds its way to the sea by winding itself around the islands. These channels are distributaries. Swamps and brackish water (water that has more salinity than fresh water, but not as much as seawater) are found here. | The sediment continues to be added to the delta. Islands of dry land emerge and vegetation grows. The delta is continually moved by currents and floods. |

## TASK 4: Study Source C

a Copy the two diagrams that show cross-sections of a river as it floods and after repeated floods.
b Describe how and why the river banks and bed get raised.
c What impact does this have on the level that the river flows at in relation to the flood plain?
d Why do floods caused by rivers bursting through their levées cause so much damage?

## TASK 5: Study Source D

a Use an atlas to describe the location of Bangladesh.
b Describe the route of the Ganges through Bangladesh to the Bay of Bengal.
c Why do you think Bangladesh is called *the drain of the Himalayas*?
d Make your own copy of Source D.
e Explain, in your own words, how the delta has been formed.

# Cambridge IGCSE Geography — Rivers

## 26 Rivers – hazards and opportunities

### Rivers create hazards

The main hazards that rivers cause are flooding and erosion. Flooding has many impacts on people and the environment. For people, the flooding can be temporary or permanent. In many cases flooding is so disastrous that lives are changed forever. It can mean:

- loss of housing, forcing a move elsewhere
- lower house prices and higher insurance costs
- loss and diversion of transport routes
- loss of social, environmental and economic amenities
- stress, injuries and death.

At times of rapid flow, rivers can cause erosion that affects people and the environment too. As a river builds up its banks and bed, it can end up flowing above the level of its surrounding flood plain. If its discharge increases, especially at times of flood, it can breach the levées and flood over a far greater area than if the levée had not been built up. While artificial levées created by people may prevent flooding, there is always the risk of a breakthrough causing disaster. This was an important factor in the European floods of 2013 (see pages 90–91).

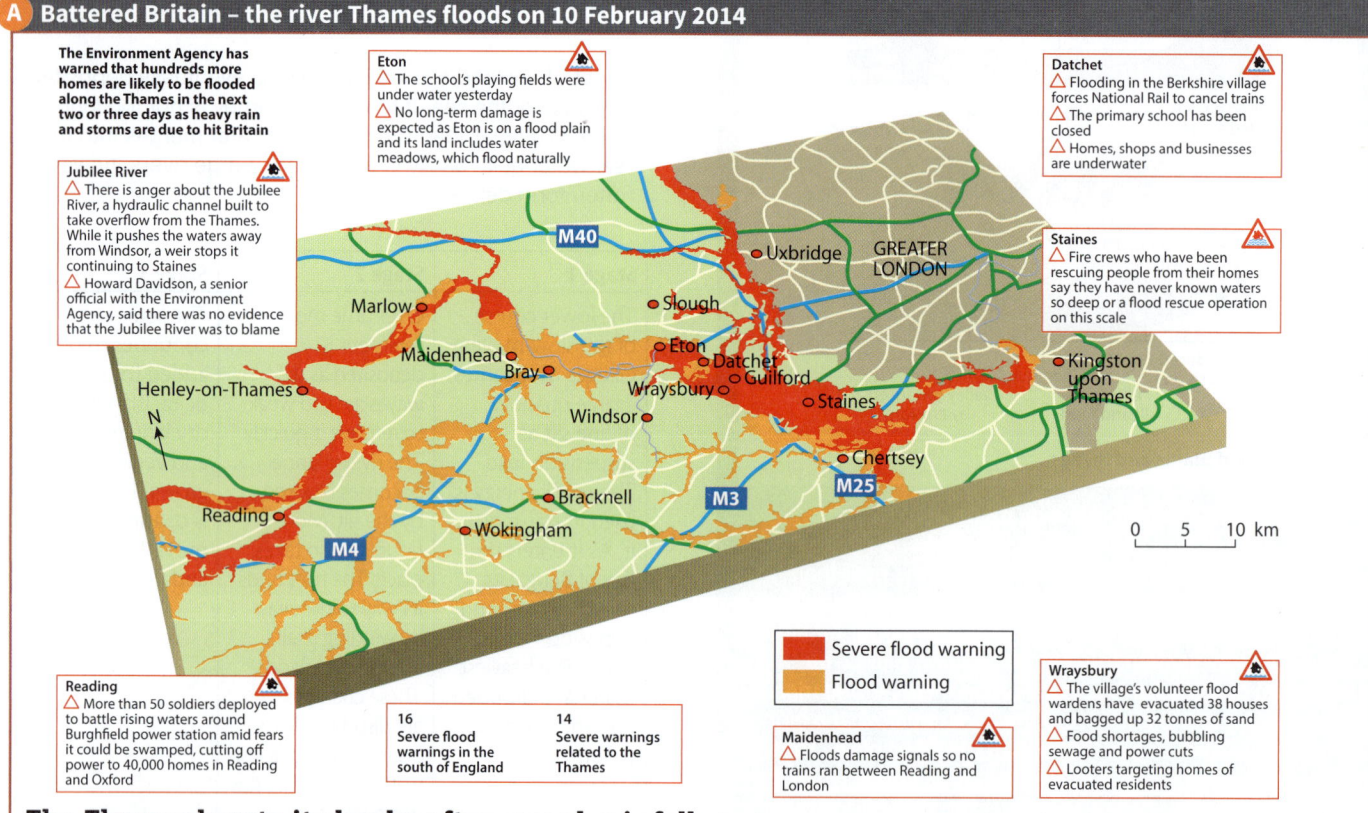

### A Battered Britain – the river Thames floods on 10 February 2014

**The Environment Agency** has warned that hundreds more homes are likely to be flooded along the Thames in the next two or three days as heavy rain and storms are due to hit Britain

**Eton**
- The school's playing fields were under water yesterday
- No long-term damage is expected as Eton is on a flood plain and its land includes water meadows, which flood naturally

**Datchet**
- Flooding in the Berkshire village forces National Rail to cancel trains
- The primary school has been closed
- Homes, shops and businesses are underwater

**Jubilee River**
- There is anger about the Jubilee River, a hydraulic channel built to take overflow from the Thames. While it pushes the waters away from Windsor, a weir stops it continuing to Staines
- Howard Davidson, a senior official with the Environment Agency, said there was no evidence that the Jubilee River was to blame

**Staines**
- Fire crews who have been rescuing people from their homes say they have never known waters so deep or a flood rescue operation on this scale

**Reading**
- More than 50 soldiers deployed to battle rising waters around Burghfield power station amid fears it could be swamped, cutting off power to 40,000 homes in Reading and Oxford

**16** Severe flood warnings in the south of England

**14** Severe warnings related to the Thames

**Maidenhead**
- Floods damage signals so no trains ran between Reading and London

**Wraysbury**
- The village's volunteer flood wardens have evacuated 38 houses and bagged up 32 tonnes of sand
- Food shortages, bubbling sewage and power cuts
- Looters targeting homes of evacuated residents

Legend: Severe flood warning (red); Flood warning (orange)

### The Thames bursts its banks after record rainfall

The record-breaking Atlantic storms have at last caused the river Thames to burst its banks. Yesterday, the soil stores were so full of water that infiltration was impossible along the river, west of London. There was only one place for the water to go. Overland flow took the water into the Thames and lower down the flood plain it reached bankfull discharge and flooded an area from Reading to Kingston-upon-Thames. This winter has seen record rainfall in the UK with 223 mm in January; the highest since 244 mm fell in January 1948. This has already caused severe flooding in the south-west of England, notably in the low-lying Somerset Levels, where much of the marshland lies below the levels that rivers now flow at.

### TASK 1: Study Source A

a Describe the different ways that the flooding of the Thames:
- affected people near the river
- affected the environment near the river.

b What caused the River Thames to flood?

# Theme 2: Topic 26

## B Opportunities along the river Nile

The sugarcane factory at Armant, near Luxor was built in 1869. Sugarcane is transported along the valley by narrow-gauge railway from the fields. The factory uses river water in its industrial processes and for transporting sugar. Main railways and roads also use the valley to travel north–south.

The Nile delta begins just after Cairo and continues for 150 km north until it reaches the Mediterranean Sea. This flat area is a rich agricultural region. It provides wheat, rice and alfalfa – in total 60% of Egypt's food supply. Over two-thirds of the 80 million population live here. However, since the Aswan High Dam was completed in 1970, less soil and nutrients reach here and farmers have to add topsoil and fertilizers. The opportunity is slowly being lost.

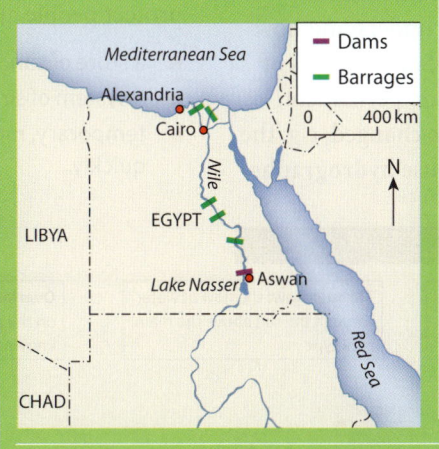

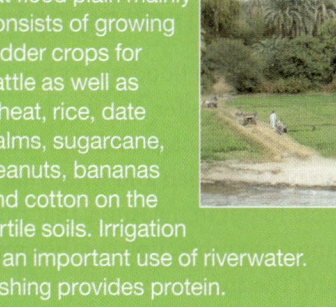

Farming along the flat flood plain mainly consists of growing fodder crops for cattle as well as wheat, rice, date palms, sugarcane, peanuts, bananas and cotton on the fertile soils. Irrigation is an important use of riverwater. Fishing provides protein.

The opportunity to trade goods along the river has been important for over 2000 years. This still happens, but today over 270 ships cruise between Luxor and Aswan where the High Dam prevents travel south. Cruising gives an opportunity for tourists to enjoy the view as well as stop at historical sites. Local people gain employment on the cruise ships or by providing many services to the tourists on shore.

Water supply to settlements for domestic use such as washing, cleaning and drinking is why houses are built by the river. 96% of Egypt is unpopulated desert; almost all the population live on the delta or in a narrow strip within a few kilometres of the river. The low water level here is controlled by dams upstream.

The High Aswan Dam was built between 1958 and 1970 (an earlier one was built too low) and holds back the world's third largest man-made lake – Lake Nasser. The opportunity for flood control has reduced the level of the river Nile in its valley and also the opportunity for depositing nutrients on the flood plain. The Hydro-electric power (HEP) dam produces half of Egypt's electricity.

## Rivers offer opportunities

Rivers have always been of importance to people because of the opportunities they provide. This was especially true when choosing a site for settlement. Rivers provide direct opportunities such as:

- water for domestic use
- water for industrial use
- water for irrigation
- water for transport
- water for generating electricity
- water for leisure and tourism.

The river also creates a valley which provides indirect opportunities such as:

- a flat flood plain for building
- fertile soils from flooding for farming
- a flat, straight transport route for roads and railways.

People who do not live close to a river are also influenced by them. They may get their water from pipelines and electricity from power stations using river water. Very dry areas may have a river flowing through them that has its source hundreds of kilometres away. Egypt is a good example of a hot, dry country that gets almost all its water from the river Nile – it is known as 'the Gift of the Nile'. To survive here the Egyptians have had to make the most of all the opportunities offered by the river and its valley.

### TASK 2: Study Source B

a What opportunities are offered by the Nile delta? Why are these being reduced?

b Describe the four uses of the river Nile shown in the photographs. List some others that might be found along a river.

c Without the opportunities offered by the river Nile, Egypt would just be one hot, dry desert. Explain, using examples, why Egypt is said to be 'the Gift of the Nile'.

# Cambridge IGCSE Geography — Rivers

## 27 Managing river flooding

### Flooding and hydrographs

Many people live on flood plains because of the opportunities they offer, but flooding is a hazard. People risk tremendous damage and loss of life. It is important to be able to predict when and where floods might take place and be able to put in measures that can prevent them from happening or to protect places they might affect. Protecting people and the environment from flooding has become a priority for many governments and local authorities.

To manage flooding, it is important to understand how and why it takes place in drainage basins. Some aspects of drainage basins cannot be changed; they are permanent, such as the rock type. Some aspects can be changed, e.g. the amount of forest in an area. Hydrologists use **hydrographs** to help them advise the authorities on flood management. A hydrograph shows how a river responds to a period of rainfall over a short period of time.

### Flood prevention

One way to manage flooding is to stop it happening in the first place. In order to do this, the hard and soft engineering techniques, shown in **Source D** can be used.

### Flood protection

A second way to manage flooding is to have procedures to protect people and property in place, such as:

- a store of sand and sandbags for emergency use
- a system of sirens and warnings and evacuation procedures
- temporary, moveable metal barriers that can be put up quickly.

### A  A 36-hour flood hydrograph

**Groundwater flow:** the flow of water below the soil on or within the main rock type.

**Throughflow:** the flow of water through the soil above the main rock type.

**Overland flow:** the flow of water on the ground surface. Also known as run-off.

**Discharge:** the amount of water in the river passing a fixed point in a second. It is measured in cumecs ($m^3$ per sec).

**Bankfull discharge:** this is the maximum amount of water in the river just before it is about to flood over its banks.

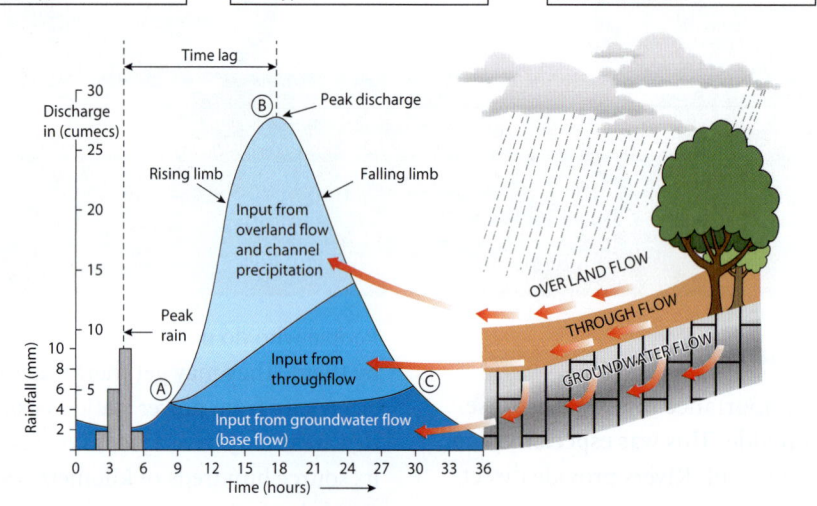

**Base flow:** the low level of water that is always in the river throughout the year. It comes from the slow movement of groundwater.

**The rising limb:** this shows how quickly the river rises during or after a storm.

**The falling limb:** this shows how quickly the river drops back to its base flow after the peak discharge (maximum flow in river).

**The time lag:** the time between the peak rainfall (the highest rainfall) and the peak discharge.

**The peak discharge:** the maximum amount of water in the river due to the rainfall.

### B  What influences the shape of the flood hydrograph

- Impermeable rock at surface
- Gentle slopes
- No rainfall in last few days
- Impermeable rock below surface
- Few buildings or roads
- Houses and roads being built
- Rough, shallow river channel
- No vegetation
- Thick soil
- Rural area mostly countryside
- Dense stream network to collect water
- Thickly forested
- Built-up urban areas in basin
- Heavy rainfall in last few days
- Few streams to collect water
- Steep slopes
- Smooth, deep river channel
- More houses and roads planned
- No plans for more building
- Thin or no soil

Theme 2: Topic 27

## C Hard and soft engineering techniques

Hard engineering involves building costly, permanent structures that will affect river flow and stop floodwater causing damage and destruction. Some may even prevent the flooding completely. These include:

- **Dams** which can control flooding by holding back water – but the reservoir can destroy settlements and ecosystems.
- **Barriers and flood walls** which can hold back water and control flooding – but are expensive and can look unsightly.
- **Embankments or levées** where the riverbanks are built up so that more water stays in the channel – but they spoil the landscape and, when the river bursts its banks, cause large-scale floods.
- **Dredging and straightening channels** which allows water to flow more quickly from one area – but can cause floods in areas further downstream.
- Canals and waterways that take water away from the river – but take up farmland.

Soft engineering involves cheaper alternatives that work with the river and do not involve permanent structures or a great deal of construction. These include:

- **Afforestation** – water is intercepted upstream by planting trees and flows more slowly into the rivers.
- **Balancing lakes and washlands** – water is allowed to overflow into land that is not valued before it can flood more valuable areas.
- **Land-use zones** – only certain buildings are allowed relative to the risk, e.g. no building near the river, high-risk buildings such as hospitals well away from it.

*Dams such as the Hoover Dam in the USA were built to control river flow and flooding. The reservoir will, however, silt up over time.*

*Purpose-built balancing lakes such as Willen Lake in Milton Keynes, UK collect surface run-off to prevent flooding.*

### TASK 1: Study Source A
a   How long did the rainfall last?
b   When was the peak rainfall and how much rain fell then?
c   How long after the rainfall stopped did the river start to rise?
d   What was the time lag between the peak rainfall and peak discharge?
e   From where did the river get its water after the rain stopped?
f   Describe how and why the river flow changed from points A-B-C. Refer to boxed labels, discharge amounts and time in hours.

### TASK 2: Study Source B
a   Draw up and complete a two-column table like this.

| What makes a river rise quickly? | What makes a river rise slowly? |
|---|---|
| Steep slopes | Gentle slopes |

b   Complete the table using words from Source B. One row has been done for you.

### TASK 3: Study Source C
a   How is *flood prevention* different from *flood protection*?
b   What is meant by *hard engineering*? Give benefits and problems of any one example.
c   In what ways is *soft engineering* a more environmentally-friendly way of controlling flooding?
d   Choose **two** *soft engineering* techniques. Suggest any additional benefits they provide that have nothing to do with flood control.

### TASK 4
a   Describe the location of your nearest river.
b   Carry out research to find out:
   - when and why it last flooded
   - what damage the flooding caused
   - what methods of flood prevention and protection were in place before the flood
   - what measures are taking place to deal with the next flood.

# Cambridge IGCSE Geography — Rivers

## Case Study
## The Elbe river

### Hazards and opportunities

The Elbe river (Labe in Czech Republic) is one of the major waterways of Europe. It rises in the Czech Republic, flowing through Germany and entering the North Sea 110 km north-west of Hamburg. Very small parts of Austria and Poland are also within its watershed. The drainage basin of the Elbe and its tributaries is over 50 000 square kilometres, the fourth largest in Europe. Over 24 million people live within the drainage basin, with major cities including Prague (1 257 000), Dresden (517 050), Magdeburg (230 450) and Hamburg (1 769 100).

Like all rivers, the Elbe offers opportunities for people, such as river transport, water supply, HEP (hydro-electric power), fertile soils and river cruises. There are also hazards, notably flooding. The management of this flooding has faced many challenges in recent years, but in 2013 some parts of central Europe experienced two months' worth of rainfall in two days. When this water had worked its way into the Elbe river and the nearby Danube river, people living close by experienced floods and subsequent damage as rivers reached their highest levels since 1954.

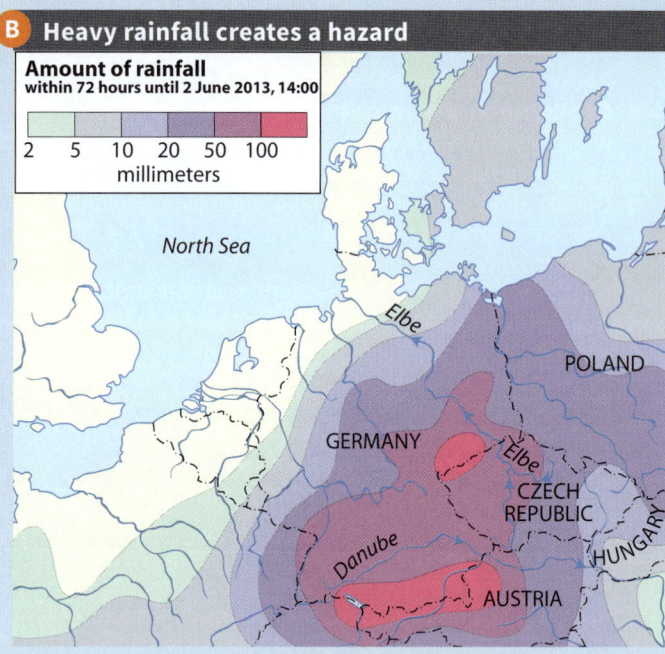

**A** The Elbe river drainage basin

Note that 'Labe' is the Czech name for 'Elbe'.

**B** Heavy rainfall creates a hazard

Amount of rainfall within 72 hours until 2 June 2013, 14:00
2  5  10  20  50  100 millimeters

### TASK 1: Study Source A
a  How long is the Elbe river drainage basin?
b  How does the basin size and river length compare between Germany and the Czech Republic?
c  Name the tributaries that join the main Elbe (Labe) river in the Czech Republic.
d  How many people live within the drainage basin?

### TASK 2: Study Source B
a  What range of rainfall fell in this region in the three days (72 hours) before 14.00 on 2 June 2013?
b  Describe the location of the area that received over 50 mm of rain in those three days.
c  Suggest why much of the flooding took place in Germany *after* 2 June 2013.

### TASK 3: Study Source C
a  What was unusual about the rainfall in late May/early June of 2013?
b  How serious a flood event was this?
c  Copy and complete the table below to summarise the effects of the flood at different places and some responses to it.

| Place | Impact of rainfall on the river | Response by people/authorities | Impact on the town/people |
|---|---|---|---|
| Prague | Rose 5 metres above normal in some places | Heavy machinery used to stop debris building up to block flow at Charles Bridge | Over 50 000 people evacuated |

# Case Study: The Elbe river

## C Flooding along the Elbe river

### 25 DEAD AND THOUSANDS LEFT HOMELESS BY ELBE RIVER FLOODS

Extreme flooding began several days after heavy rain between 30 May and 2 June, when up to 250 mm of rainfall fell in some areas; over two months' worth in normal conditions. Flood levels exceeded the 'once in a century' floods of 2002.

At Prague in the south, the Vltava river, a tributary of the Elbe river in the Czech Republic, caused havoc by rising 5 metres above normal in some places. Half the metro stations were closed and heavy machinery was brought in to stop debris building up at the historic Charles Bridge. The main railway line to Berlin was underwater so trains were diverted. Chemical factories were closed to prevent the release of toxic chemicals into the floodwaters. Over 1000 Czech troops were brought in to build flood defences while firefighters prepared to evacuate 50 000 people. Even the tigers at Prague zoo were tranquillised and moved away from their enclosure. Due to so much rainfall, the government had to open dams to let water flow away quickly, which caused flooding further down the Elbe river to the north.

In Dresden the river peaked at 7 metres above normal, flooding the city but sparing its historical centre. Bridges were closed to traffic and thousands of residents worked through the night to put up sandbags and flood barriers. Troops also pumped water back into the river.

Further north at Magdeburg the floodwaters rose to 7.5 metres, almost four times the normal height (2 m). The dykes were not built to withstand such a flood level. A state of emergency was declared and 23 000 residents were asked to leave their homes when a dam burst. 19 000 soldiers were used to help with defences and evacuating people. Helicopters were used to airlift stranded residents.

Hamburg suffered little loss due to warnings and an established flood protection scheme. Of the 25 deaths recorded, 11 were in the Czech Republic, 8 in Germany and 6 in Austria.

## D Managing the flood hazard

*Dykes, walls, sandbags and mobile metal barriers are the most common ways of protecting settlements from flooding. However, river authorities along the Elbe river are considering a 'Room for the River' project whereby space for flooding is planned in areas where minimum damage would occur. To keep raising levées and dykes is impractical and unsightly.*

**Hamburg:** Although 110 km inland, the port is vulnerable to sea and tidal flooding as well as flooding from the Elbe river. The part where 140 000 people live on the flood plain is protected by dykes and walls with a total length of 100 km. Because it is in the far north, any potential flooding from the Elbe is known about before it happens, so sirens and warnings on local radio and TV stations can be issued.

**Magdeburg:** Although the city has many dykes, they were not expected to cope with the flood levels of 2013. They are being raised to 6.5 metres and reinforced to cope in future. Dykes are also being moved back to give the river more space to flood. Unfortunately as Prague and Dresden improve their defences, more water will arrive downstream in Magdeburg!

**Dresden:** Since the floods of 2002 and 2006, the city now has higher levées, stronger walls and metal flood barriers and stocks of sandbags so they can respond quickly in times of flood. Part of an old industrial estate is being sacrificed to allow the river to flood there in future.

**Prague:** Protective metal barriers have now been strengthened and more mobile metal barriers are available. These can be erected quickly to protect the main urban area for over 7 km. Residents are used to using sandbags.

### TASK 4: Study Source D

a State what measures are referred to in Source D to minimise the impact of floods. Refer to:
- physical barriers to prevent flooding
- ways to alert people to a flood risk.

b What is meant by a 'Room for the River' project? Why are the authorities considering this along the Elbe river?

### TASK 5

Carry out research on the Internet into the Danube river, which was also affected by the same flood hazard in central Europe in 2013. Compare the impact and management of the Elbe river flood with the Danube river flood.

# 28 The work of the sea

## Changing coastlines

If you sit on a beach, you can watch the waves crashing against the shore. After each wave, the water runs quickly back into the sea, carrying and moving fine grains of sand and pebbles. If you stand in the sea, you can sometimes feel the pebbles move under your feet. In storms, large waves can move huge boulders. The waves, with their load of sand, pebbles and rocks, pound the cliffs and dislodge big pieces of rock, which fall into the sea.

Coasts are always changing. **Erosion** occurs when the sea is wearing away the land. The material that has been eroded is transported by the waves to areas where **deposition** occurs when the sea piles up sand and pebbles to form new land. Erosion is carried out by:

- **hydraulic action**: waves break against the cliffs by their sheer weight and power. They also trap air in cracks in the rock. This air is compressed by the waves, eventually causing the rocks to break apart.
- **corrasion (abrasion)**: particles carried by the waves crash against the cliffs, eroding the cliffs.
- **attrition**: particles carried by the waves crash against each other and are broken up into smaller and rounder particles.
- **solution (corrosion)**: the acids in seawater slowly dissolve the chalk and limestone cliffs. The material produced is carried away by the process of solution.

There are two types of wave: destructive and constructive. **Destructive waves** carry out erosion and scour the beach to create a steep, narrow beach, especially in the lower part. **Constructive waves** create a wide, gently sloping beach as they carry out deposition. On some coastlines, winds pick up dry sand and blow it to other areas where it is deposited to form sand dunes.

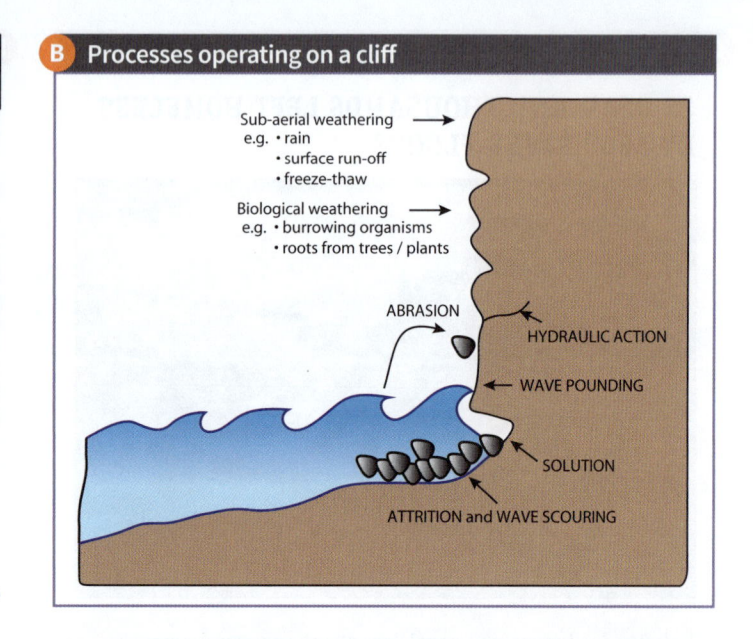

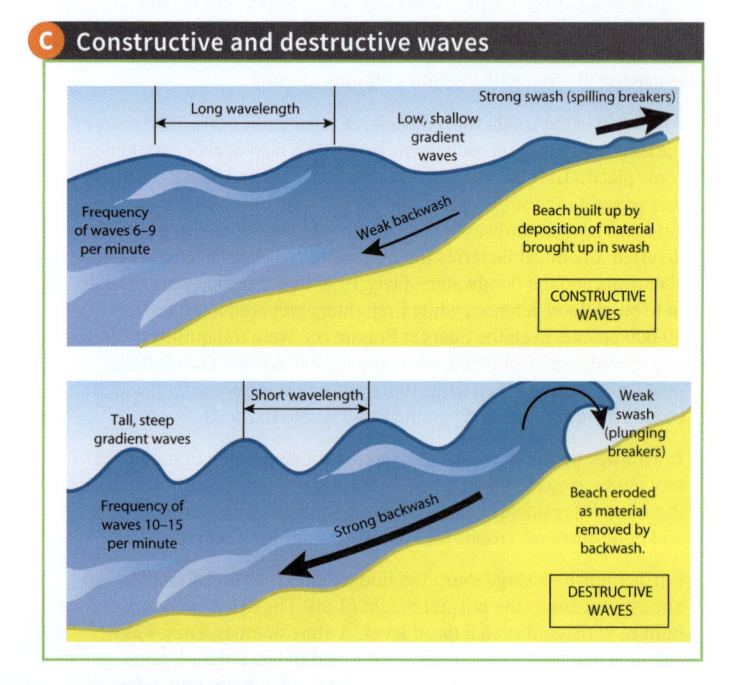

**B** Processes operating on a cliff

**C** Constructive and destructive waves

**A** Coastal erosion and deposition

# Theme 2: Topic 28

## Coastal erosion can occur rapidly

The amount and speed of coastal erosion depends on several factors:

- The type of rocks that form the cliffs – limestone, chalk and granite are resistant rocks (often forming cliffs and headlands) which erode slowly, but less resistant rocks such as clay are quickly worn away.
- The strength of the waves, which depends on the wind speed, how long it has been blowing and how large an area of sea it has blown across (the fetch).
- The shape of the coastline – on concordant coastlines, the rock strata are parallel to the sea and rates of erosion are similar along the coastline; on discordant coastlines, where bands of hard and soft rock outcrop at right angles to the sea, differential erosion may occur to form bays and headlands.
- How sheltered or exposed to waves the coast is – areas that are more exposed to wind and waves will suffer more erosion than those areas that are naturally sheltered (e.g. bays) or protected by coastal defences.

**D** The power of the sea

**TASK 1:** Study Source **A**
a. Write a paragraph describing the main features that can be seen in the photograph.
b. Explain how the waves are carrying out erosion and deposition in the area shown by the photograph.

**TASK 2:** Study Source **B**
Make a copy of the cross-section of the cliff. Annotate (fully label) your diagram to explain how weathering and erosion can change the shape of a cliff.

**TASK 3:** Study Source **C**
Describe the differences between constructive and destructive waves and the beaches they produce.

**TASK 4:** Study Sources **D** and **E**
a. Explain why some cliffs can be eroded rapidly by the sea.
b. Describe the hazards of living on or close to the coast.

**E** Coastal erosion is destructive

### An Bien, Vietnam, November 2012

During the last decade, in this south-western Vietnamese province many families have been forced from their coastal homes, as raging storms and a rising sea level lead to continued loss of land – and homes.

'Each year, sea waves have eroded about three to four metres of land,' says a 47-year-old fisherman from the Tay Yen commune. 'Our family had to move five times, and now our house is four metres from the sea.'

Many areas in Kien Giang, located about 250 kilometres from Ho Chi Min City, are actually experiencing erosion of 25 metres a year, and experts estimate that as much as one-third of Kien Giang's coast has been lost to the sea. Officials from Binh Dinh province in south-central Vietnam are equally worried about continuing erosion there. 'Every year, at least two to three rows of houses were washed away (about 80 to 90 houses),' says Do Van Sang, director of the province's Centre for Land Development.

Adapted from *'Coastal erosion reaches alarming levels in Vietnam'*, Thuy Binh, Inter Press Service News Agency, 25 November 2012

### Norfolk, UK, December 2013

Families were left devastated as their beach-side homes were destroyed after Britain's coastline was battered by the worst storm for 60 years. Beach-side houses and a lifeboat hut in Hemsby, Norfolk, were swept into the sea along with a popular café at Caister-on-Sea. Steven Connelly, 54, and his wife Jackie, 64, had been out for the evening when they returned to the scene of devastation.

Their property was one of three in Hemsby that collapsed into the sea as ferocious waves swept away huge chunks of the coastline.

Seven years ago, when they bought their home, it was about 2.4 metres (8 feet) from the edge of the cliff, but the land has slowly eroded away.

Adapted from *the Daily Mail*, 6 December 2013

### New England, USA, January 2014

Southern New England's coastline — the region's economic engine — is under siege from rising seas and storms.

Coastal communities are increasingly experiencing the impacts of an encroaching ocean. Storm waves are eroding beaches and flooding developed areas.

State and local officials are now asking how they can protect people, property and infrastructure such as drinking water supplies, utilities and roads from the advancing sea. During the past few decades, sections of the Rhode Island, Massachusetts and Connecticut shoreline have experienced an average rate of retreat of between 0.3 and 1.5 metres. A single storm, for example, can wash away some 10 metres of beach in an instant.

Adapted from *'Erosion happens: can we deal with it?'*, Frank Carini, Eco RI News

# Cambridge IGCSE Geography — Coasts

## 29 Coastal landforms created by erosion

### A Bays and headlands

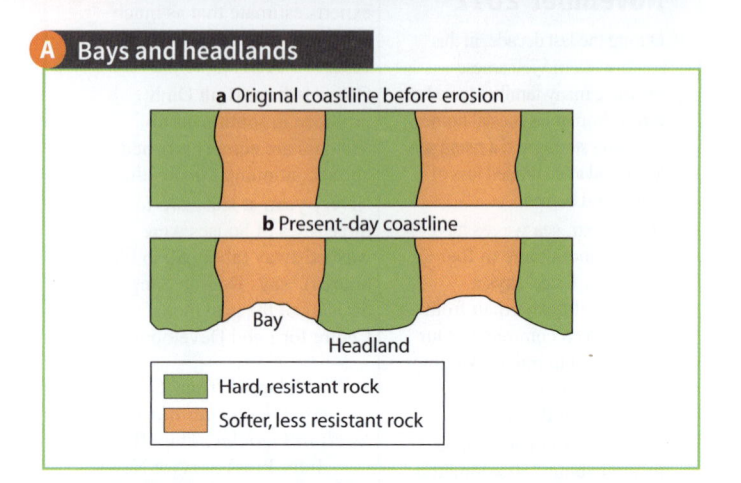

a Original coastline before erosion

b Present-day coastline

Bay
Headland

- Hard, resistant rock
- Softer, less resistant rock

### Erosional features

Look again at **Source A** on Page 92. The area where soft rock reached the coast has been eroded to form a **bay**. More resistant rocks on either side form **headlands**. On the headlands waves erode the rock face, forming cliffs. Along lines of weakness between the high and low water marks, a notch may be created along with an overhang above the notch. Eventually the overhang collapses as the notch is cut deeper into the rock. As the cliff is eroded backwards, it leaves behind a wave-cut platform at the low water mark. A line of weakness, such as a fault or joint, is increased in size until it becomes a cave and the waves continue to erode the back of the cave until a natural arch is formed. When the arch roof falls into the sea, it leaves behind a stack and after more erosion this is reduced in size to form a stump.

### B Features of headlands

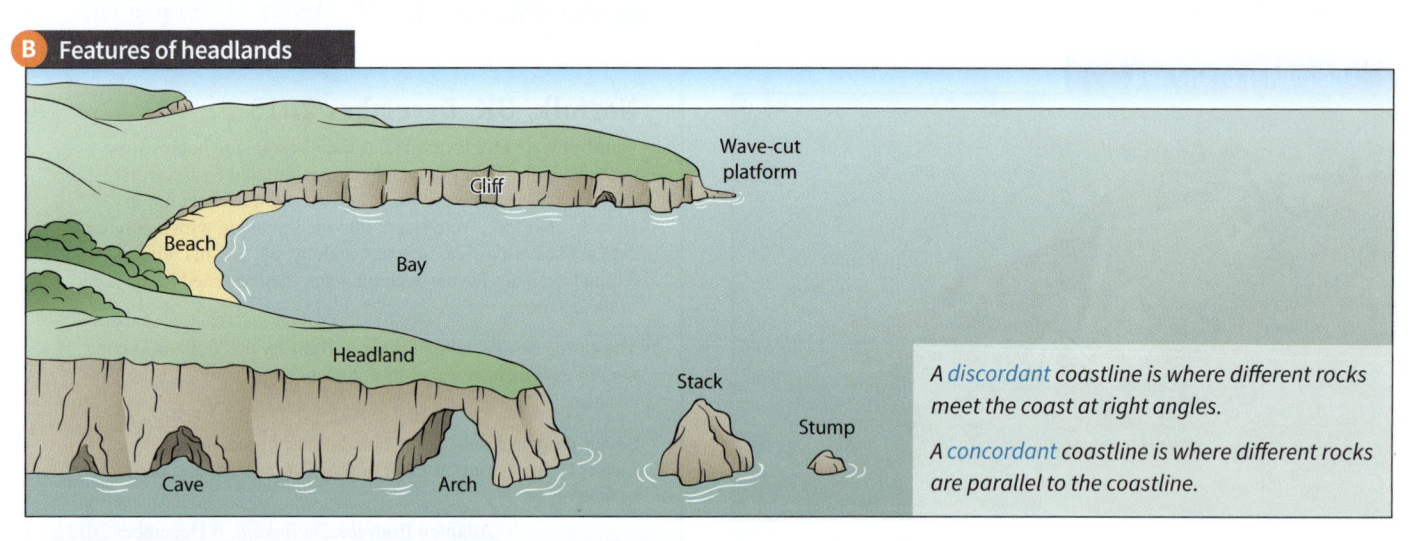

Labels: Wave-cut platform, Cliff, Beach, Bay, Headland, Stack, Stump, Cave, Arch

A **discordant** coastline is where different rocks meet the coast at right angles.

A **concordant** coastline is where different rocks are parallel to the coastline.

### C Landforms formed by erosion

## The Twelve Apostles

The Twelve Apostles are famous coastal landforms in the Port Campbell National Park, Victoria, Australia, which have been carved by the sea from the limestone cliffs. Originally the rock layers formed as horizontal beds of sediment on the sea floor over 10 million years ago to become **sedimentary rock**. Along this stretch of coast, the cliff base is constantly being eroded by the waves. Steep cliffs which reach 70 metres high, wave-cut platforms, notches, natural arches and stacks are formed.

The Twelve Apostles is a collection of stacks, the tallest reaching 45 metres high, although now there are only seven left. The rate of erosion at the base of the limestone pillars is approximately 2 cm per year and a number have fallen over as waves continue to erode their bases. The Twelve Apostles were formed as a result of different rates of erosion along the coast due to the alternate bands of hard and soft rocks. Headlands formed where the rocks were most resistant. At the bases of the cliffs on these headlands, waves eroded along lines of weakness (e.g. joints, faults and bedding planes). Back-to-back caves first formed on each side of the headlands. Continuous erosion caused these caves to extend backward until the caves met and natural arches were formed, linking the tip of the headland with the mainland. When the arches collapsed, the pillars were left standing and became stacks.

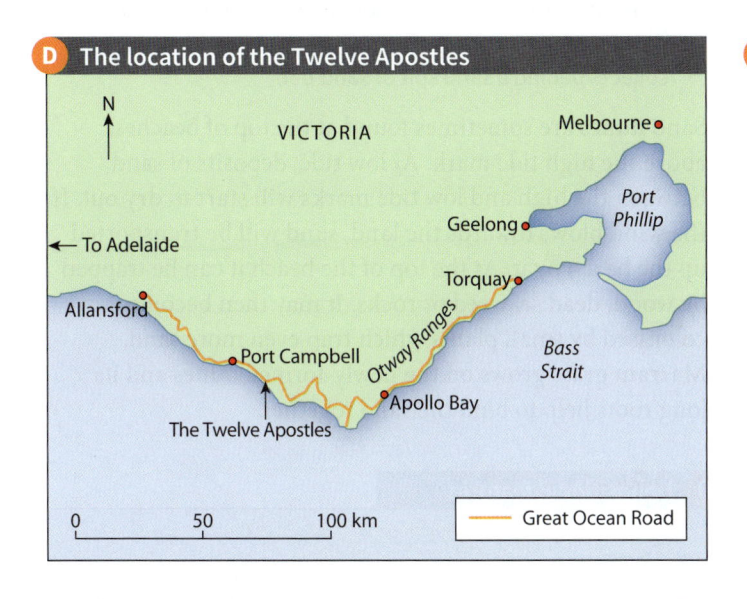

**D** The location of the Twelve Apostles

**E** The Twelve Apostles

---

**TASK 1:** Study Sources **A** and **B**
a Explain the formation of bays and headlands.
b Make a copy of Source B. Label your diagram fully to identify the features that are shown.
c When explaining how a stack is formed, why do you also need to explain how caves and arches are formed?

**TASK 2:** Study Source **C**
a Name and describe the coastal landforms shown in each photograph.
b Choose a landform from each photo and explain how it has been formed by coastal erosion.

**TASK 3:** Study Source **D**
Describe the location of The Twelve Apostles.

**TASK 4:** Study Source **E** and the text.
Design a tourist information leaflet about The Twelve Apostles. Your leaflet should include a description and a clear explanation of their formation. Use a sequence of labelled diagrams to help your explanation.

**TASK 5**
There are many other famous arches and stacks. Here are some examples.

| Stacks: | Natural arches: |
|---|---|
| Goat Rock, USA | Percé Rock, Canada |
| Old Harry Rocks, England | Holei Arch, Hawaii |
| The Needles, England | Durdle Door, England |
| Old Man of Hoy, Scotland | Porte d'Amante, France |
| Hopewell Rocks, Canada | Great Pollet Arch, Ireland |
| Po Pin Chau, Hong Kong | |
| Needle of Arsène Lupin, France | |
| Lange Anna, Germany | |

Carry out research in groups and prepare a presentation, perhaps using PowerPoint. In your presentation you need to choose **one** stack and **one** natural arch from the list, or an example from your own country.
a Describe the precise location of your chosen stack and natural arch and show them on a map.
b Find photographs to show your chosen stack and arch and describe their main features (e.g. shape, size, rock type).
c Explain clearly how each of the features was formed.

# 30 Coastal landforms created by deposition

## Coastal deposition

Coastal depositional features are formed as a result of **longshore drift**. This is the process by which beach material is transported along the coast by waves. In most areas waves do not hit the beach at right angles to the coast, and are far more likely to hit the beach at the same angle from which the prevailing wind approaches. As waves approach a beach they pick up sand, shingle and pebbles. The size of the particles moved by the wave depends on what materials are available on the sea bed, and the power of the wave. The sediment will be carried up the beach (**swash**) at the same angle; it then moves back down (**backwash**) at right angles. Gravity pulls it straight down the beach, so the backwash follows a different path to the swash and each wave can move the sediment a little further across the beach in a zigzag pattern.

If there is a change of direction in the coastline (e.g. at a river estuary), the sediment may be deposited to form the depositional features shown in **Source B**:

- **Sand spit:** a long, narrow stretch of sand and/or shingle, with one end attached to the mainland.
- **Sand bar:** develops when a spit stretches across a bay linking two headlands. Behind the sandbar an area of water may be cut off from the sea to create a **lagoon**.
- **Tombolo:** forms when a beach or sand spit joins up with an offshore island.
- **Barrier islands:** sandy islands that run parallel to the coastline forming a tidal lagoon between them and the shore.
- **Saltmarsh:** a sheltered area, flooded at high tide, where silt collects behind a sand spit or sand bar.

Sand dunes are sometimes found at the top of beaches, above the high tide mark. At low tide, deposits of sand between the high and low tide marks will start to dry out. If the wind blows towards the land, sand will be transported up the beach by it. At the top of the beach it can be trapped by wood, dead seaweed or rocks. It may then become colonised by small plants which trap even more sand. Marram grass grows on the newly-formed dunes and its long roots help to bind the sand together.

**A** Longshore drift

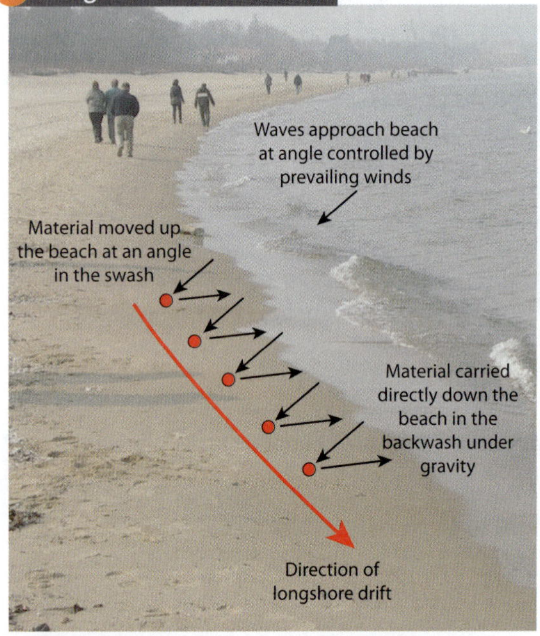

- Waves approach beach at angle controlled by prevailing winds
- Material moved up the beach at an angle in the swash
- Material carried directly down the beach in the backwash under gravity
- Direction of longshore drift

**B** Depositional features

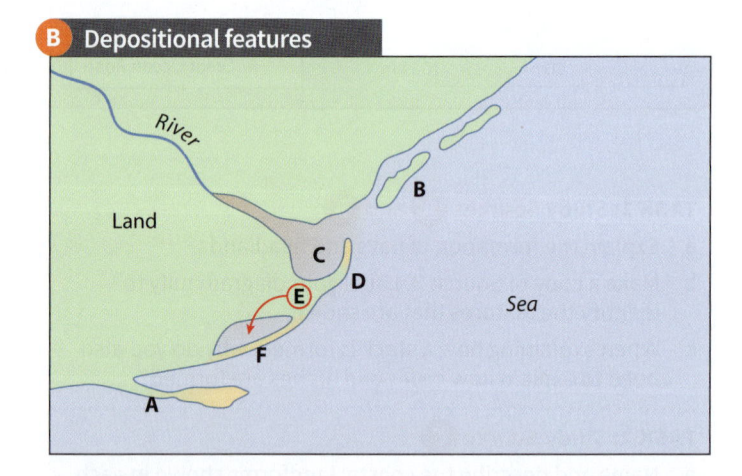

**C** Landforms formed by deposition

# Hel spit, Poland

The Hel peninsula is a sand spit situated at the western end of Gdansk Bay in northern Poland. It is long, narrow, low and relatively flat, with sand dunes in many parts. It was formed by coastal deposition, as a result of longshore drift from west to east. The predominant winds are from the west/north-west, this transports sediments from the west of the spit, where it is subject to erosion, to its eastern end where sediment builds. The beach material is sorted by the waves, resulting in large sediments (pebbles) at the top of the beach and smaller ones (sand and shingle) close to the sea.

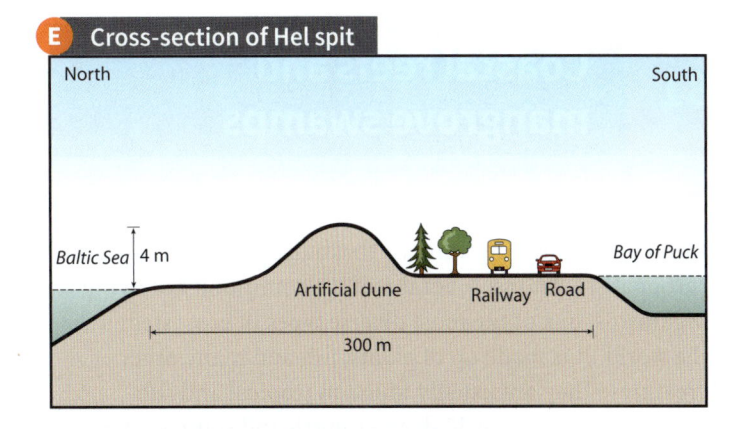

**E Cross-section of Hel spit**

**D Satellite image of Hel spit**

### TASK 1: Study Source A
Draw a diagram showing how longshore drift moves materials along a beach. Label:
- prevailing winds
- swash
- backwash
- direction of movement of beach material.

### TASK 2: Study Source B
Name the features A–F, which are formed by coastal deposition.

### TASK 3: Study Source C
a  Name and describe the coastal landforms shown in each photograph.
b  For each landform shown, explain how it has been formed by coastal deposition.

### TASK 4: Study Source D
a  Measure the length of the Hel peninsula in kilometres from Władysławowo to Hel.
b  Measure the width of the Hel peninsula between Chałupy and Władysławowo.
c  Explain in detail how the Hel sand spit was formed. Refer to:
- prevailing winds
- swash and backwash
- direction of longshore drift.

### TASK 5: Study Source E
a  Describe the features of Hel spit using the evidence.
b  The highest waves that have been observed in the area were 8 metres high when a strong wind was blowing from a northerly direction for more than two days. Explain why it is necessary to protect the sand spit from coastal erosion.

# 31 Coastal reefs and mangrove swamps

## Coral reefs

Coral polyps are tiny animals that build protective calcium carbonate skeletons. A coral reef is a community of living organisms, one of the most diverse types of ecosystem in the world. It is made up of plants, fish and many other creatures. They are usually found in tropical and sub-tropical seas between 30 degrees north and south of the equator. Fifty per cent are found in the Indian Ocean and Red Sea, 35 per cent in the Pacific Ocean and 15 per cent in the Caribbean.

Reefs are established when a large, continuous mass of coral builds upwards and outwards from a rock base. Coral has a solid skeleton of limestone, and needs three main factors for growth:

- warm water – between 23 and 25 °C is best
- clear, shallow saltwater, no deeper than 50 metres
- plenty of sunlight to aid photosynthesis.

Coral cannot grow in freshwater, and cannot tolerate silt or water high in nutrients that allow plants to use the oxygen that the coral needs.

There are three types of reef:

**Fringing reef** – Coral platforms grow out to sea attached to the mainland. A shallow lagoon lies above them.

**Barrier reef** – Coral grows in a shallower area away from the mainland. The water between is too deep for coral to grow and forms a lagoon. These reefs form off-shore barriers along coastlines.

**Atoll** – These develop around islands. Fringing reefs grow in a circle attached to the land. Sea-level rise or subsidence of the land causes the coral to grow at the height of the rising sea level to reach the light. This eventually forms a ring of coral reefs with a lagoon replacing the island in the centre.

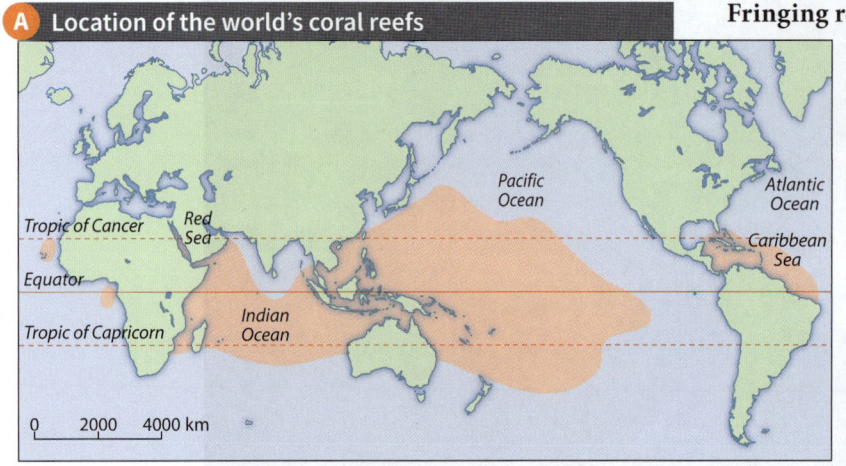

**A** Location of the world's coral reefs

**B** Three different types of coral reef

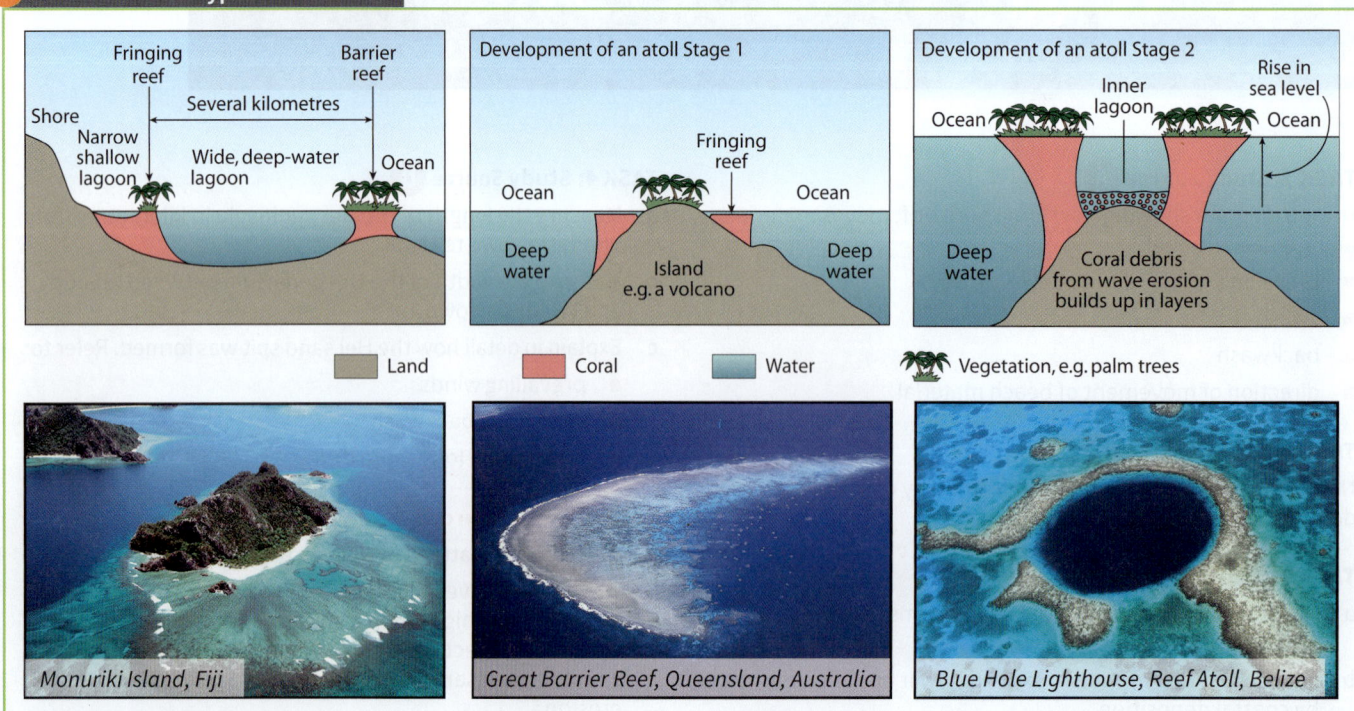

Monuriki Island, Fiji

Great Barrier Reef, Queensland, Australia

Blue Hole Lighthouse, Reef Atoll, Belize

# Theme 2: Topic 31

## Mangrove swamps

Mangrove swamps are areas of vegetation found along sheltered tropical coastlines and estuaries between 32°N and 38°S where there is a large area between high and low water mark. They are made up of different species of evergreen mangrove trees and other plants. Mangroves are halophytes (plants that need to live in salty water). They only grow in areas where the temperature remains above 20°C and the seasonal temperature range should not exceed 5°C. The areas where they grow should be calm, with no strong waves or tidal currents.

**C  A mangrove swamp**

Mangrove trees are able to withstand being covered twice a day by saltwater. They have specially adapted aerial and salt filtering roots and salt excreting leaves that enable them to occupy the wetlands where other plants cannot survive. They prop the tree up with their prop roots and take in oxygen at low tide with their aerial roots.

Mangroves are home to a diverse number of species including fish, birds, frogs, snakes, insects and crocodiles. Mammals also live in these areas, ranging from small animals such as swamp rats and monkeys to large carnivores such as tigers. Mangroves protect coastlines from erosion by acting as a natural barrier and flood defence. They also filter pollutants from rivers and prevent sediment from reaching nearby coral reefs.

Mangroves and coral reefs benefit each other – the coral reef protects the coast where the mangroves grow from being eroded by the sea, and the mangroves trap sediment washed from the land and stop it from reaching the reef.

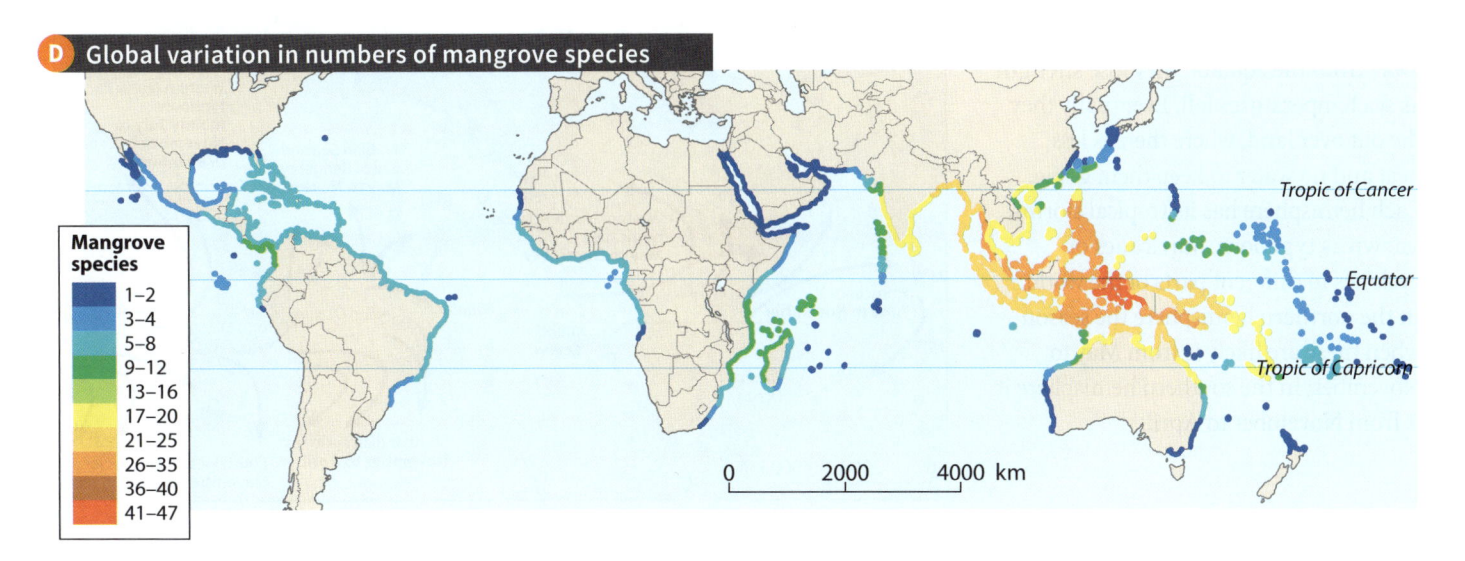

**TASK 1:** Study Source **A** and an atlas
a  On an outline map of the world, shade and name the major coral reef regions using the list below:
Philippines, Gulf of Guinea, Mauritius, Indonesia, Maldives, Taiwan and south China, Caribbean, Red Sea and Gulf of Oman
b  Name **two** oceans where coral can be found.
c  Describe the conditions required for coral to develop.

**TASK 2:** Study Source **B**
a  Name the **three** different types of coral reef.
b  Name a place where an example of each can be found.
c  Describe how a fringing reef differs from a barrier reef.
d  Explain how an island with fringing reefs can become an atoll.

**TASK 3:** Study Source **C**
Describe the characteristics of the mangroves that are growing in the area shown in the photograph.

**TASK 4:** Study Source **D** and an atlas
a  Describe the global distribution of mangroves.
b  Compare the number of species of mangroves in the Caribbean and Indonesia. Suggest reasons for the differences.
c  Describe the conditions required for mangroves to develop.

**TASK 5**
Many areas of coral reef and mangrove swamps have been destroyed in recent years. Carry out some research into an area where either coral reefs or mangrove swamps have been destroyed. Find out why the destruction has taken place and why many people are concerned about it.

**D  Global variation in numbers of mangrove species**

Mangrove species:
1–2
3–4
5–8
9–12
13–16
17–20
21–25
26–35
36–40
41–47

# 32 Hazards and opportunities

## Coasts: valuable but vulnerable

Coasts offer many opportunities for the people who live there and those who visit occasionally. In many areas the land is flat or gently sloping, making it ideal for farming and the building of settlements and communications, such as roads and railway lines. In areas where there is deep water and shelter from storms, ports develop to handle imports and exports. Manufacturing industries may grow up to process imports, and fishing may take place in nearby or more distant coastal waters. In areas with attractive scenery or climate, the tourist industry is likely to develop.

But living on the coast may sometimes be hazardous, as storms may cause death or injury, damage to property, disrupt communications and threaten livelihoods. Lowland areas close to the sea may be at risk from **tsunamis** and people need to protect their homes from coastal erosion and flooding. Homes, businesses, farmland and communications may be at risk in areas where coastal erosion is rapid. This occurs in areas where rocks are not resistant, waves are large and winds are strong.

## A hazardous place to live?

Between the Tropic of Cancer and the Tropic of Capricorn, warm air from the north meets warm air from the south. Over large oceans, where the sea temperature reaches 27 °C and the water is at least 60 metres deep, the winds begin to circulate in an anticlockwise fashion in the northern hemisphere due to the Earth's rotation. These forces create the eye of the storm, an area of intense low pressure, as the spiralling air rises to create low pressure along and close to the equator. Tropical storms develop from tropical depressions as the wind speeds increase. The easterly winds at high level (jet streams) move the tropical storms from east to west to begin with; other high-level winds then carry them in other directions. As they move north or south away from the equator, they lose strength as sea temperatures fall. Eventually they die out over land, where there is less heat and no water to keep them going. Each hemisphere has its tropical storms, known as typhoons, hurricanes or cyclones in different parts of the world. In the northern hemisphere the season when these are likely is from May to November; in the southern hemisphere it is from November to April.

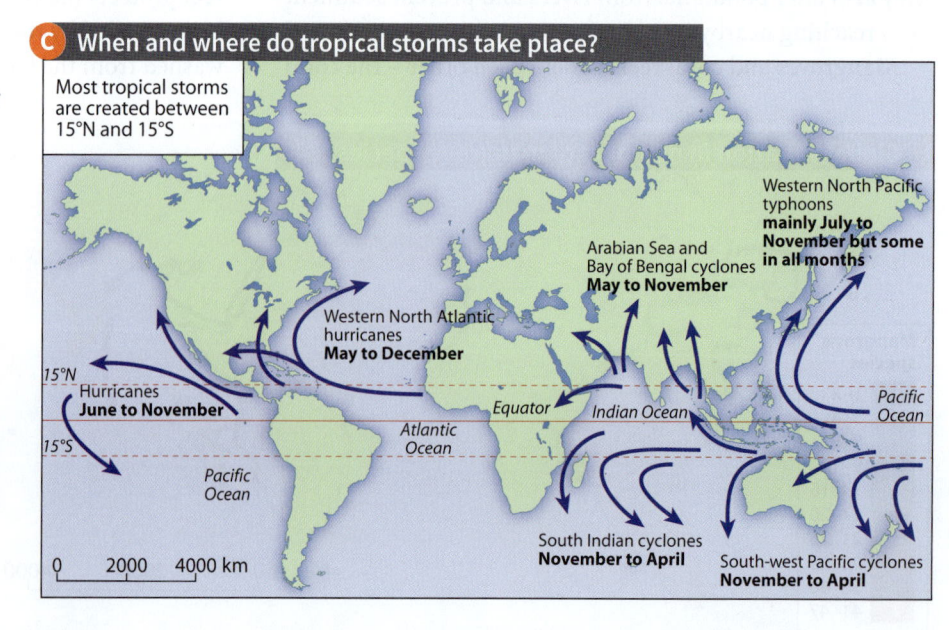

**A** Opportunities along the North Carolina coast, USA

**B** Hazards along the North Carolina coast

**C** When and where do tropical storms take place?

Most tropical storms are created between 15°N and 15°S

Western North Atlantic hurricanes **May to December**

Hurricanes **June to November**

Arabian Sea and Bay of Bengal cyclones **May to November**

Western North Pacific typhoons **mainly July to November but some in all months**

South Indian cyclones **November to April**

South-west Pacific cyclones **November to April**

# Theme 2: Topic 32

### D  Path of Typhoon Haiyan – 8 November 2013

Legend:
- Wind: 80 – 120km/h, Rainfall: 100 – 200mm
- Wind: 120 – 200km/h, Rainfall: 200 – 300mm
- Gusts up to 260km/h
- 120km/h winds

Locations shown: Laos, Thailand, Cambodia, Vietnam, Ho Chi Minh, Manila, Cebu, Philippines, Malaysia, Philippine Sea, Palau. Scale: 0 150 300 450 600 km

### E  Typhoon

## Typhoon Haiyan death toll tops 6000 in the Philippines

Nearly five weeks after Typhoon Haiyan tore through the Philippines, the government now says more than 6000 people have been reported dead. Nearly 1800 more are still missing.

More than 27 000 people have been reported injured, the country's National Disaster Risk Reduction and Management Council reported on Friday. The storm forced 3.9 million people from their homes, the agency said.

The typhoon – considered by some to be among the strongest such storms to make landfall – struck the Philippines on 8 November. Its powerful winds and enormous storm surge smashed buildings, destroyed roads and caused widespread loss of power and fresh water supplies.

The damage was particularly severe in the Leyte province city of Tacloban, which suffered a direct hit from the storm and enormous devastation.

*Adapted from CNN, 13 December 2013*

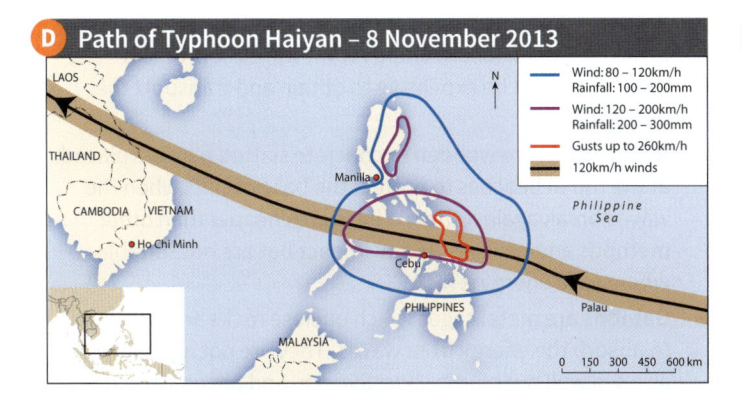

### F  The worst typhoon ever

b  Explain how the source suggests that it is possible to prepare for these hazards.

c  Suggest other examples of hazards that people may face along the North Carolina coast.

### TASK 3: Study Source C

a  Compare the distribution of cyclones with that of hurricanes.

b  What conditions are required for a cyclone or hurricane to develop?

c  Explain how the position of the sun during the year affects when tropical storms develop. Refer to the equator and the tropics.

### TASK 4: Study Source D and an atlas

Make a list of the places in the Philippines that were affected by Typhoon Haiyan.

### TASK 5: Study Sources E and F

Discuss how the Philippines could recover from the damage caused by a powerful typhoon. Decide on an action plan stating what you would do in the first two weeks and then over five years. Explain your choice of activities.

### TASK 6

The Philippines is an LEDC. Suggest why LEDCs find it difficult to prepare for, and recover from, disasters such as this, compared with MEDCs such as the USA.

### TASK 1: Study Source A

For each of the photographs, identify **two** opportunities for people in the area shown.

### TASK 2: Study Source B

a  Name the **two** types of hazard which this source suggests may occur in North Carolina.

# 33 Managing coastal erosion

## Why defend the coast?

There are numerous reasons for protecting the coast. Lots of people live and work along many coastlines and they are valuable areas economically. In some coastal areas there are fragile ecosystems which take a long time to recover if they are destroyed. Management of the coast attempts to control natural processes such as erosion, longshore drift and flooding.

Managing the coast using **hard engineering** is usually expensive. It may have a negative impact on the landscape or natural environment and be unsustainable. **Soft engineering** is usually less expensive, more long term and sustainable, with less impact on the natural environment as it works alongside natural processes.

## Hard engineering techniques

1 **Sea walls** are usually built along the base of cliffs to prevent both erosion and flooding. They are often curved, which means waves are reflected. This can cause the erosion of the beach at the base of the sea wall. They are expensive to build, are visually intrusive and the cost of maintenance is high.
2 **Groynes** are barriers, usually made from wood, built at right angles to the beach to trap sediment and stop it being moved by longshore drift. Beaches are a natural defence against erosion and attractive to tourists, but groynes are not attractive and are expensive to build and maintain.
3 **Rock armour** consists of large boulders placed along the base of a cliff to absorb energy from waves. It protects the cliff but can be expensive to obtain and transport the boulders.
4 **Revetments** are wooden or concrete slatted barriers placed at the top of beaches to protect the base of cliffs when the waves break against them. These are cheaper than other methods and have less visual impact but are not suitable when wave energy is high.
5 **Gabions** are metal cages which enclose rocks and boulders to absorb the energy from waves. They are not as expensive as a sea wall but have a short lifespan and are unattractive.
6 **Offshore breakwaters** are large concrete blocks and boulders located offshore to reduce the power of the waves or change their direction to reduce longshore drift. Beaches and cliffs retain their natural appearance but the breakwaters can be unattractive and expensive.

## Soft engineering techniques

1 **Beach nourishment** involves replacing beach material that has been removed by erosion and longshore drift, and creating higher and wider beaches by transporting sand and shingle, sometimes from off-shore. It is cheap and preserves the natural appearance of the beach. However, dredging of sand and shingle increases erosion in other areas and may affect the natural environment.
2 **Managed retreat** is when areas of coast are allowed to erode and flood, usually in areas where the land is of low value. Eroded material encourages the development of beaches and saltmarshes and the natural environment is not destroyed. However, people such as farmers lose their land.

**A** Coastal protection methods

# Theme 2: Topic 33

## Managing erosion in Hawaii

Hawaii is a state of the USA made up of many islands located in the Pacific Ocean. The coastline of many of Hawaii's islands is threatened by coastal erosion, tsunamis, hurricanes, sea level rise and flooding. The Hawaii Coastal Zone Management Program aims to reduce hazard to life and property.

Under this programme, a series of special reports have been prepared, including the Oahu Shoreline Study and Kauai Shoreline Erosion Management Study. Aerial photograph analysis of coastal erosion has been done on the islands of Kauai, Molokai, Lanai and Maui. These reports discuss coastal management alternatives, identify where most erosion is taking place and predict future erosion in these areas.

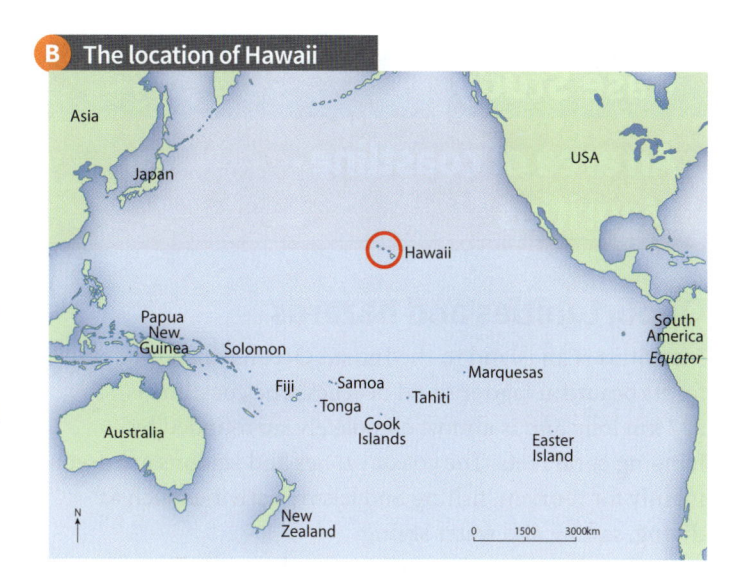

**B  The location of Hawaii**

**C  Coastal erosion in Hawaii**

### Fast-moving erosion threatens Hawaii coast

Alice Lunt didn't worry too much when she saw waves splashing close to her home on Oahu's North Shore on Christmas Eve. She had seen the ocean edge close before. But before dawn, a neighbour woke her with a call.

'Everything was washing away,' she remembered the neighbour saying.

The water claimed Lunt's deck that day, and washed away a concrete slab the next night – part of a fast-moving collapse of the shore that also ripped out a neighbour's backyard and forced another to cut away rooms to save the rest of the house.

Some property owners want to be able to install a sea wall to protect their property. Doing so, scientists say, could lead the sand on the nearby coastline – including Sunset Beach, home to some of the world's top surfing contests – to disappear.

'Do you build a sea wall and condemn the beach to extinction in front of the sea wall but at the same time buy a lot of time for homeowners on the nearby land?' asked Chip Fletcher, a University of Hawaii coastal geologist.

'Or do you not build a sea wall, condemning the homes and the developed land to extinction, but allow the beach to survive?'

He said studies show sea walls built on eroding shorelines like Sunset Beach will only lead to more erosion down the coast.

Adapted from *CBS News*, 8 January 2014

---

**TASK 1: Study Source A**
Identify which method of coastal protection is shown in each of the photographs i to iv. For each method, describe its advantages and disadvantages.

**TASK 2: Study Source B and an atlas**
a  Describe the location of Hawaii.
b  Explain why living on the coast of Hawaii is hazardous.

**TASK 3: Study Source C**
Explain why coastal management in Hawaii causes so much conflict.

# Cambridge IGCSE Geography — Coasts

## Case Study

### An area of coastline – Mauritius

### Opportunities and hazards

Mauritius is an island in the Indian Ocean which is famous for its beautiful **lagoons** and beaches. The coastline is 322 km long and is almost completely surrounded by fringing coral reefs. The coastal zones and lagoons are used mainly for tourism, fishing and leisure activities such as diving, sailing and water skiing.

Before the 1960s, there was little urban growth in the coastal areas. In 1968 there were only 15 000 tourists. The situation began to change in the 1970s when Mauritius grew economically as a result of:

- a large increase in sugar export earnings
- a growth in tourism from 27 650 arrivals in 1970 to over 950 000 in 2013
- establishment of industries and financial services.

This economic growth has led to changes in land use along the coastline, particularly the growth of settlement and tourist facilities, industry and ports.

**A** Topographical map of Grand River Bay, Mauritius

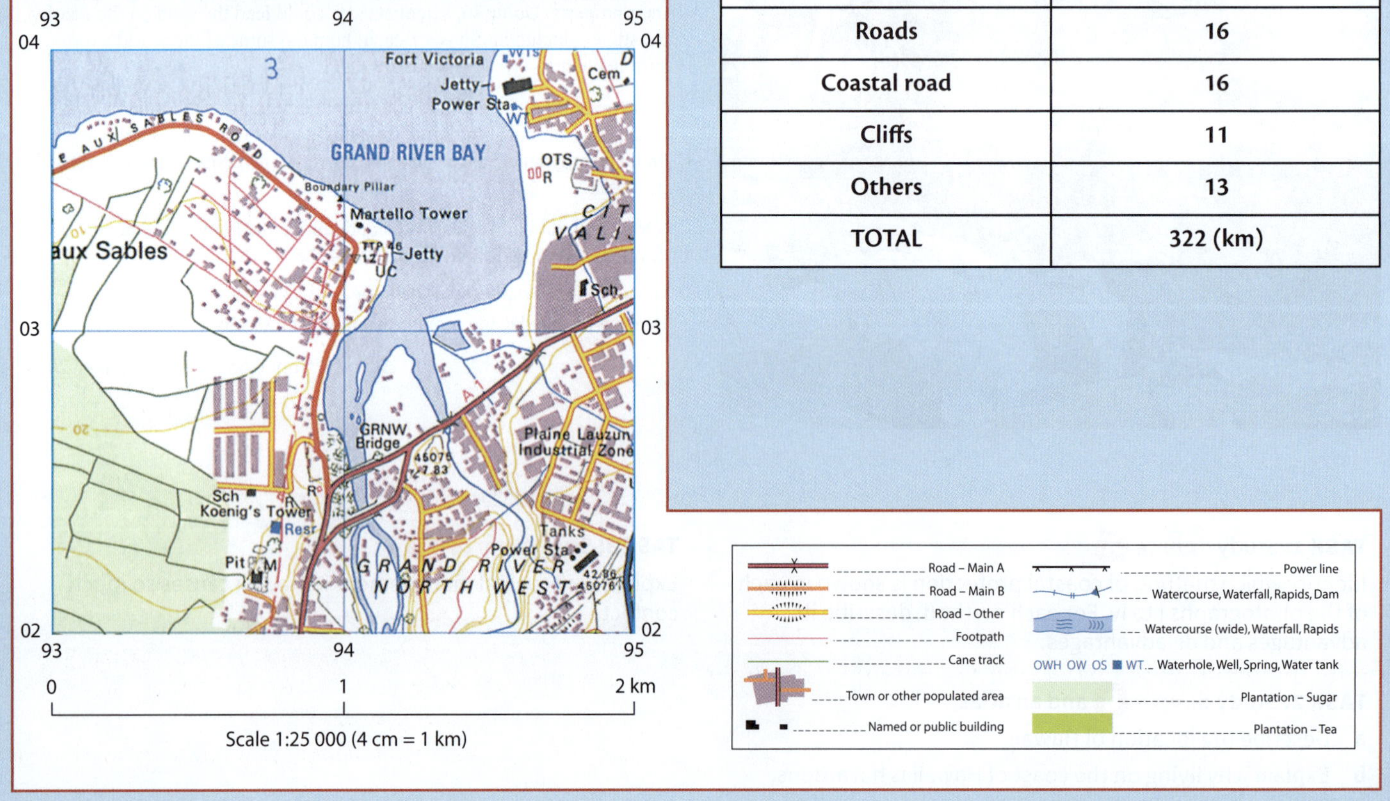

Scale 1:25 000 (4 cm = 1 km)

### Hazards along the coast

Twenty-one beaches in Mauritius experience coastal erosion and 22 sites have experienced recent flooding. Erosion rates at five key beaches around the island of Mauritius have increased in the last 10–15 years. A survey showed that there has been erosion of 0.4 m at Flic en Flac, 1 m at Morne Brabant, 1.5 m at the north-east coast of Ile aux Cerfs and 1.5 m at St Géran. In some places, sea walls have collapsed and roads have been eroded, especially after storms. The risk to life and livelihoods for people who live in coastal settlements is increasing. To manage coastal erosion, a wide range of strategies have been considered, including hard and soft engineering.

**B** Coastal land use in Mauritius (2000)

| | |
|---|---|
| Vegetation | 76 |
| Bungalows | 52 |
| Hotels | 42 |
| Grazing lands | 29 |
| Public beaches | 27 |
| Building sites | 25 |
| Cultivation | 21 |
| Roads | 16 |
| Coastal road | 16 |
| Cliffs | 11 |
| Others | 13 |
| TOTAL | 322 (km) |

# Case Study: An area of coastline – Mauritius

## C Opportunities on the coast of Mauritius

## D Cyclone warning

### Mauritius: tropical storm Bejisa is forecast to strike Mauritius as a tropical cyclone at about 06.00 on 3 January 2014

Data supplied by the US Navy and Air Force Joint Typhoon Warning Center suggests that the point of landfall will be near 20.6°S 56.5°E. Bejisa is expected to bring winds of around 166 km/h with gusts that may be considerably higher.

According to the Saffir-Simpson scale, the damage from a storm of Bejisa's strength (category 2) includes damage to roofing material, doors and windows, damage to shrubbery and trees with some trees blown down and considerable damage to mobile homes, poorly constructed signs, and piers. Small craft in unprotected anchorages may break their moorings and coastal and low-lying areas are likely to flood two to four hours before the arrival of the storm centre as sea level will rise by between 1.8 and 2.4 metres.

*Adapted from AllAfrica, 30 December 2013*

**TASK 1:** Study Source A

Look at the map and make a list to show all the different ways in which the land is used within half a kilometre of the coast.

**TASK 2:** Study Source B

a Draw a pie chart which shows how the coastline of 322 km was used in Mauritius in 2000.

b Suggest how these figures are likely to have changed in the last 15 years.

**TASK 3:** Study Source C

Use each photograph to draw a table listing how the coastline of Mauritius offers opportunities to people. Divide your table into two columns – residents and visitors.

**TASK 4:** Study Source D

a Make a list of the likely impacts of a tropical storm on the coast of Mauritius.

b To what extent is it possible to manage the impacts of tropical storms to reduce loss of life and damage to property?

# Cambridge IGCSE Geography — Weather

## 34 Collecting weather data – 1

### Studying the weather

What is the weather like today? Has it changed since you came to school this morning? What is the weather forecast for tomorrow? Weather affects so many of our daily activities. We rely on weather forecasts to plan what we are going to do and when. But how is the weather measured and how can we predict what is going to happen from these measurements?

### A Weather and climate are different

**Weather:** Short-term day-to-day changes in the atmosphere for a place. Rainfall, temperature, wind direction and strength, air pressure, sunshine, humidity and cloud cover are all studied as 'weather'.

**Climate:** The average weather conditions over a period of time – at least 30 years. Temperature and rainfall are shown on climate graphs. Climate regions cover large areas.

*Moscow, in Russia, will experience a cold and cloudy night with heavy snow, and temperatures in the morning of around minus 16 °C.*

*In Morocco, records show that desert winds from the Sahara can cause temperatures easily exceeding 40 °C on average during the summer months.*

### B The Stevenson Screen

- The screen has a roof which prevents rain and direct heat affecting the instruments. The air space between roof layers is a bad conductor of heat.
- The screen should be sited in an open area away from trees or buildings so that air can circulate freely and so that the screen is not shaded.
- The four sides are made of wooden slats to allow air to flow freely in and out of the screen.
- It should be sited on level ground.
- The screen should be sited away from any artificial source of heat such as central heating from school buildings.
- The screen is painted white to reflect sunlight.
- The screen's dimensions vary but the most common size is 65 cm high, 60 cm wide and 40 cm deep. 
- It should be sited on grass or bare earth, not concrete or tarmac which can absorb heat from the sun and re-radiate it upwards, affecting the temperature readings inside the screen.
- When sited, the door of the screen should face away from the sun so that the readings are not affected by direct sunlight, e.g. in the northern hemisphere the door should face north.
- The screen has a hinged door for access.
- It should be surrounded by a secure fence or other security measures to avoid damage by people and animals.
- The screen stands on legs which are a fixed distance of at least 125 cm from the ground to avoid any heating influence from the ground.

The Stevenson Screen was invented by Sir Thomas Stevenson (1818–1887), a British engineer and meteorologist. It is a wooden box designed to protect weather measuring instruments from rainfall and direct heat. A screen contains thermometers which are hung from a frame in the centre of the screen. These are:

- A max/min thermometer
- A wet/dry bulb thermometer (a hygrometer).

*These measure maximum and minimum daily temperatures and relative humidity. All temperature measurements are taken inside the screen to give consistent readings in the shade. Sometimes air pressure is also measured by putting a barometer inside the screen.*

# Theme 2: Topic 34

## C Measuring temperature

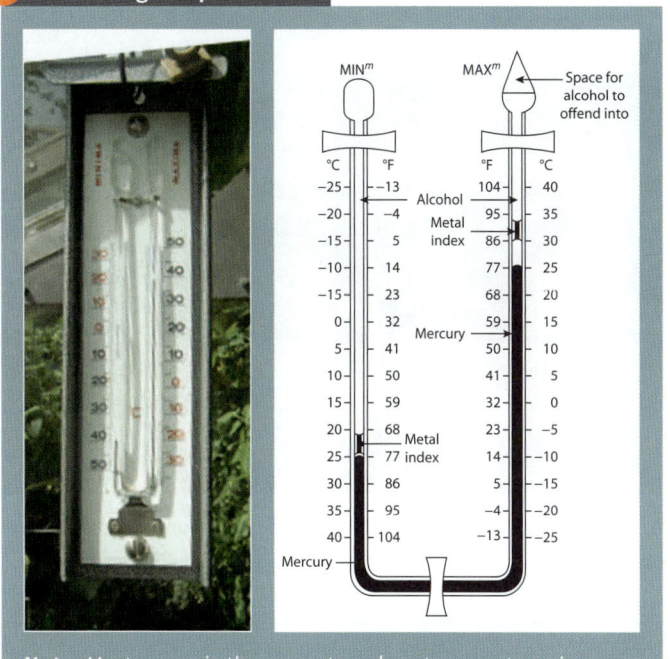

**Note:** *Most max-min thermometers show temperatures in degrees Fahrenheit (°F) and degrees Centigrade as above. All temperature references in this book are in Centigrade (°C).*

## D Measuring relative humidity

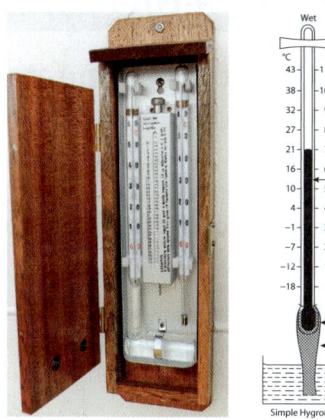

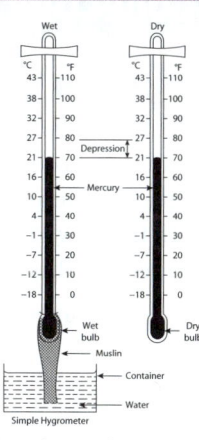

Air is never completely dry. Humidity refers to the amount of water vapour in the air. Relative humidity (RH) is a more useful measure which indicates the amount of water vapour in the air relative to the amount of water the air could hold at that temperature. So if the RH is 80% at a temperature of 30 °C, the air is holding $\frac{8}{10}$ of the water vapour it could hold. (RH tables to calculate this are used on page 111.) When air can hold no more water vapour it is saturated. Any excess vapour then condenses to form clouds, rain, mist or fog. Humidity can make a warm day feel cold and a cold day feel warm! Most people feel comfortable with 50% RH.

### TASK 1: Study Source A
a How is **weather** different from **climate**?
b Study the statement with each photograph. Decide which one is about the weather and which is about climate.
c Describe the weather outside your classroom now. How close is it to your local forecast?

### TASK 2: Study Source B
a Draw an outline sketch of the Stevenson Screen shown.
b Choose the labels that relate to its **structure**. Add them around your sketch in one colour.
c Choose the labels that relate to its **location**. Add them around your sketch in a different colour.
d Explain why locating a Stevenson Screen in the right place is important.
e Barometers are sometimes put in a Stevenson Screen. Carry out research to find out how you would use a barometer to measure air pressure (p. 248 will help).

### TASK 3: Study Source C
Copy and complete this passage by adding in the correct word from the box below.

| metal | right | falls | mercury | magnet |
| reversed | alcohol | left | bottom | pushed |

'A thermometer that measures both maximum and minimum temperatures is known as a Six's thermometer. When the temperature rises, the_____ in the minimum thermometer on the _____ expands. This pushes the_____ index down this tube and forces the mercury up the _____ tube. This pushes the other metal index up the tube on the right. The maximum temperature is read from the _____ of the metal index in the right-hand tube. When the temperature _____, the alcohol in the left tube contracts. This causes the _____ to flow in the opposite direction, pushing the metal index up the left-hand tube. Because the temperature scale is _____, the minimum temperature is read from the bottom of the metal index in the left-hand tube. Both metal indexes stay where they have been _____and are reset using a_____.'

### TASK 4: Study Source D
Copy the following passage and choose the correct word from those given in bold letters to complete it.

'The hygrometer contains **one/two/three** ordinary thermometers. The bulb of one contains **paper/tissue/muslin**, which is dipped into a container of **alcohol/mercury/water** to keep it damp. This is the **wet/maximum/dry/minimum** bulb thermometer. The other thermometer on the **left/right** is the **wet/dry** bulb thermometer. The wet muslin cools the wet bulb and this causes the mercury to **expand/stay where it is/contract**. The dry bulb thermometer on the right records the **maximum/actual/minimum** air temperature. The two thermometers show different readings. If the air was saturated, both thermometers would read the same. The difference between the two readings is an indication of the relative humidity (RH) of the air. If there is a **small/large** difference, the RH is high and the air feels damp. If there is a large difference, the RH is **low/high** and the air is dry. The difference in temperature is known as the depression of the wet bulb.'

# Cambridge IGCSE Geography — Weather

## 35 Collecting weather data – 2

### Measuring other weather elements

As we have seen, temperature, relative humidity and air pressure can all be measured by putting instruments in a Stevenson Screen. There are other weather elements that are measured with their own individual instruments without being put in a screen. These include:

- rainfall and precipitation
- amount of sunshine
- wind speed
- wind direction
- cloud type and cover.

### B Spot the instruments

*A traditional weather station at Arundel School, Harare, Zimbabwe.*

### A More weather instruments

**1: Rain gauge**

**B:** Precipitation (rain, hail, sleet and snow) falls inside the metal cylinder, down through a metal funnel into a collecting bottle. At regular intervals the contents are tipped into a standard measuring cylinder and recorded. Snow or hail must be melted first.

*Site factors:* In open space, away from overhanging buildings or trees that could drip into it. The gauge is put into the ground for stability or on a firm base. The top is 30 cm from the ground to avoid rain splash.

The direction wind is blowing from (points of the compass)

**2: Cup anemometer**

**A:** This shows wind direction. If the wind is from the west it is called a 'westerly wind' and the arrow points towards the west.

**C:** The sunshine recorder records the amount of sunshine during a 24-hour period. The sun's rays pass through a glass sphere and burn a piece of heat-sensitive black card. This has hours and minutes of the day on it so as the sun appears to move round, it burns a line which indicates when and for how long there was sunshine

**D:** The wind forces the cups to rotate. They are connected to a meter. The meter converts the rotations into wind speed.

*Site factors:* Off the ground and facing south in the northern hemisphere so that it is exposed to the sun. It must be out of the shade of buildings or vegetation.

**3: Wind vane**

Wind speed in kilometres per hour (km/h)

**4: Sunshine recorder**

Daily rainfall in millimetres (mm)

*Site factors:* On top of buildings so that it can record the true wind speed unaffected by obstacles such as other buildings and trees that can slow the wind down.

Amount of sunshine (hours and minutes)

*Site factors:* On top of buildings so that the arrow can move freely in any direction the wind is blowing without any interference.

---

**TASK 1: Study Source A**

Create a four-column table. In the first two columns match the instruments (numbered 1–4) with their descriptions (labels A–D). Then, in the last two columns, add the site factors and units each weather element is measured in.

**TASK 2: Study Source B**

a Name all the weather instruments you can identify.
b Do you think this weather station meets the requirements for its ideal location? Explain your view. (Refer to page 106 for help)

Theme 2: Topic 35

## Recording the weather

The final weather element to measure and note is cloud amount and the type of cloud present. This is done by observation rather than using special instruments.

Once they are taken, all measurements have to be recorded. A common code of symbols is required so that weather can be compared between different regions. In the UK, the Meteorological Office uses the system shown in **Source C**.

### C Measuring cloud cover and identifying types

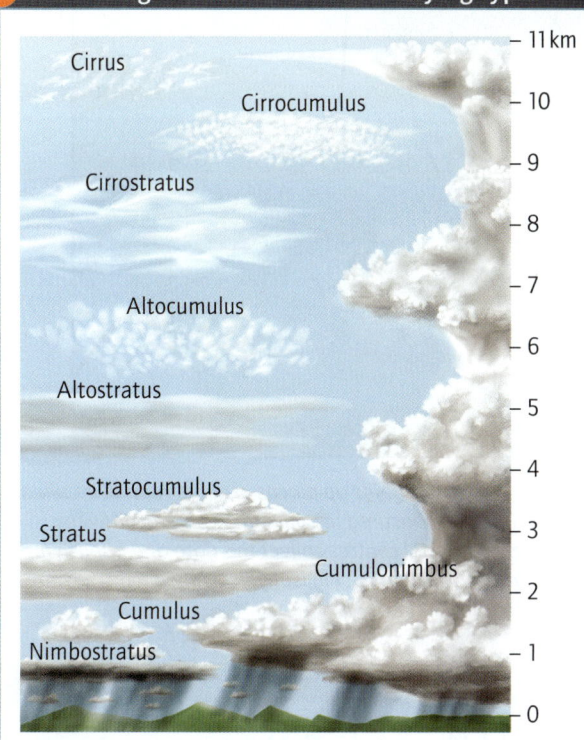

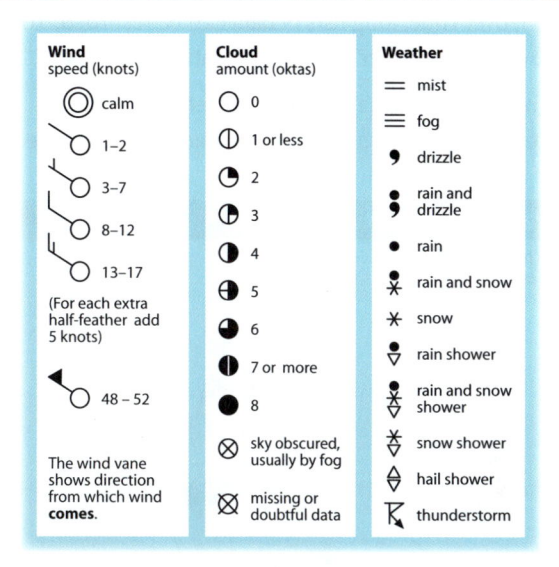

Cloud types by altitude (km):
- Cirrus — 11 km
- Cirrocumulus — 10
- Cirrostratus — 9
- 8
- Altocumulus — 7
- 6
- Altostratus — 5
- 4
- Stratocumulus
- Stratus — 3
- Cumulonimbus — 2
- Cumulus
- Nimbostratus — 1
- 0

**Wind speed (knots)**
- calm
- 1–2
- 3–7
- 8–12
- 13–17
- (For each extra half-feather add 5 knots)
- 48–52

The wind vane shows direction from which wind **comes**.

**Cloud amount (oktas)**
- 0
- 1 or less
- 2
- 3
- 4
- 5
- 6
- 7 or more
- 8
- sky obscured, usually by fog
- missing or doubtful data

**Weather**
- mist
- fog
- drizzle
- rain and drizzle
- rain
- rain and snow
- snow
- rain shower
- rain and snow shower
- snow shower
- hail shower
- thunderstorm

**Note:** The knot is an international measurement used in meteorology for measuring wind speed. (8 km/hour = 5 knots)

**Cloud cover** is estimated by looking up at the sky and judging how many eighths (or oktas) are covered.

### D A weather station circle

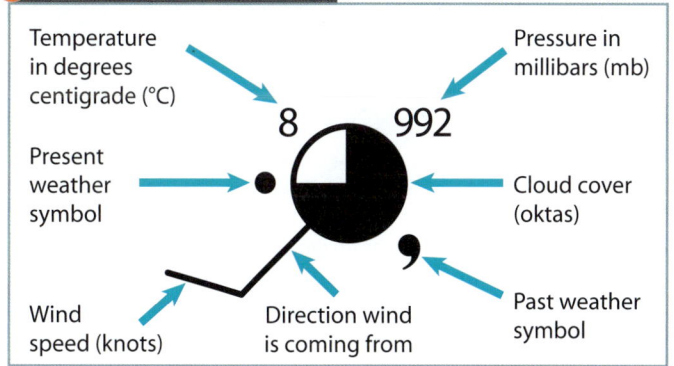

- Temperature in degrees centigrade (°C): 8
- Pressure in millibars (mb): 992
- Present weather symbol
- Cloud cover (oktas)
- Wind speed (knots)
- Direction wind is coming from
- Past weather symbol

### E Measuring weather in a digital age

*This displays the relative humidity as well as the actual temperature.*

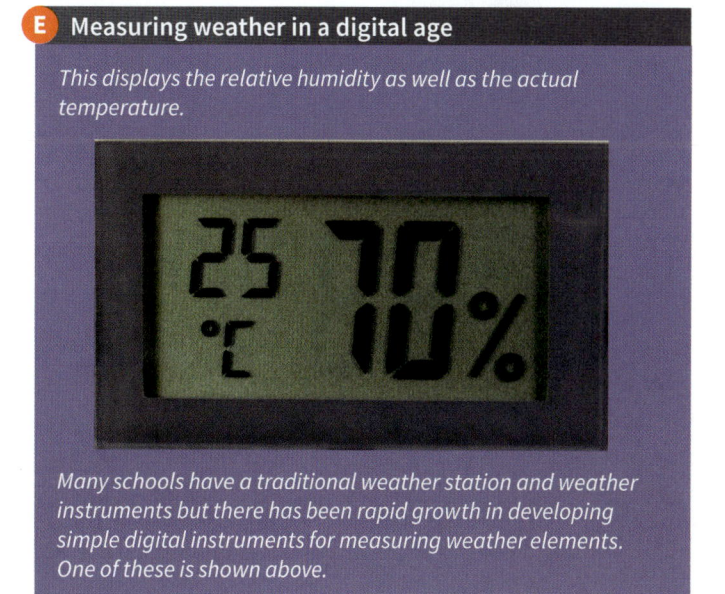

Display shows: 25 °C  70%

Many schools have a traditional weather station and weather instruments but there has been rapid growth in developing simple digital instruments for measuring weather elements. One of these is shown above.

**TASK 3:** Study Source **C**
a  How many different types of cloud are shown?
b  At what height will you find **stratus** and **cirrus** clouds?
c  How is cloud cover estimated? In what units?
d  Is there any cloud cover outside your school? If so, identify the type and estimate its cover.

**TASK 4:** Study Sources **C** and **D**
Describe the weather shown on the station circle in Source D.

**TASK 5:** Study Source **E**
Suggest advantages and disadvantages of using digital instruments instead of traditional instruments to measure weather elements.

# Cambridge IGCSE Geography — Weather

## 36 Using weather data

### Refining and presenting data

Collecting weather data is just the start of investigating weather and climate. When collected on a daily basis recording sheets are used and, over time, long lists of data can be recorded. To make sense of these weather records, the data needs to be:

- refined by carrying out calculations of useful statistics
- presented so that patterns can be seen and analyses made.

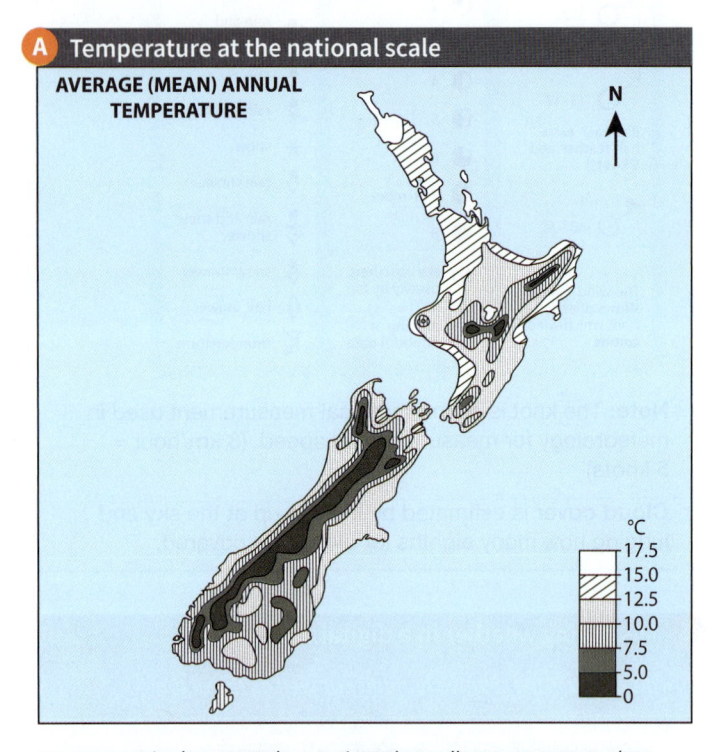

### A Temperature at the national scale

Many countries have weather stations that collect temperature data and send it to the national meteorological centre. It can then produce a map of average temperatures. This map shows the average annual temperature in New Zealand. A line on a map that joins up places of equal temperature is called an **isotherm**.

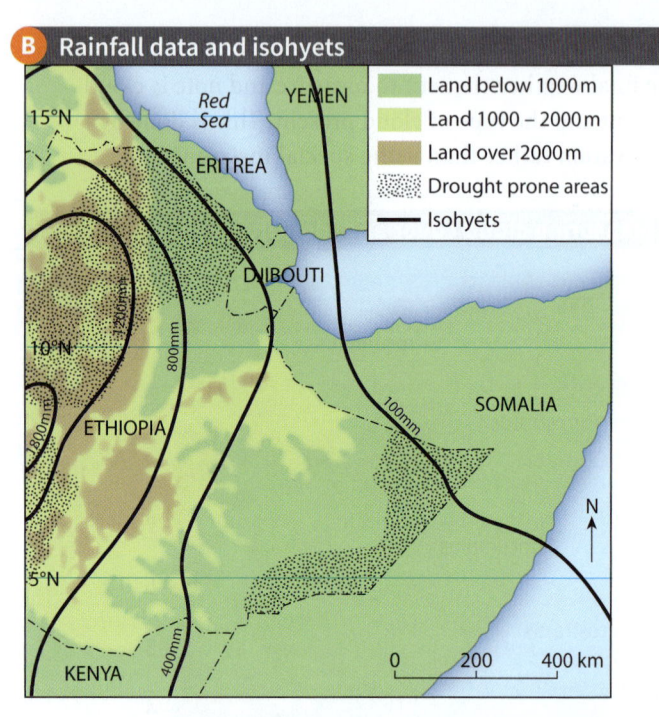

### B Rainfall data and isohyets

A line drawn on a map that joins up places of equal rainfall is called an **isohyet**. Rainfall is measured in millimetres and recorded by weather stations. National centres collect this data and publish maps showing the pattern of rainfall using isohyets as shown by the map of eastern Ethiopia above.

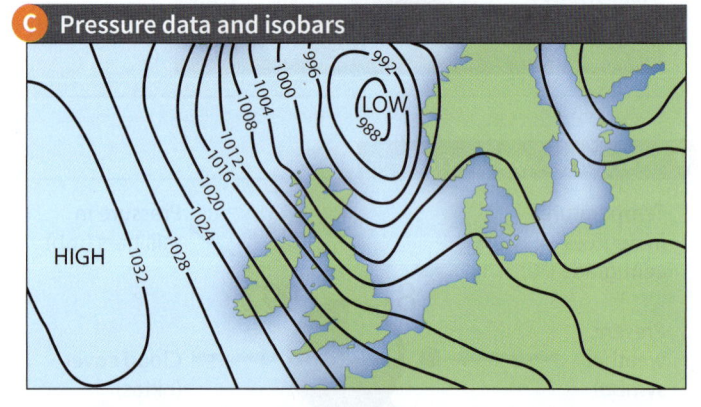

### C Pressure data and isobars

A line drawn on a map that joins up places of equal pressure is called an **isobar**. They are usually drawn at 4 mb intervals. Isobars over 1000 mb indicate high pressure; isobars below 1000 mb indicate low pressure. The above weather map shows isobars over northern Europe for December.

---

**TASK 1: Study Source A**

a  What is an isotherm?
b  The map shows the average (mean) annual temperature range in New Zealand. Is this a good technique to show this information? Give reasons for your answer.
c  Describe the average (mean) annual temperature pattern in New Zealand.

**TASK 2: Study Source B**

a  What is an isohyet?
b  State the highest and lowest isohyets on the map.
c  Describe the pattern of rainfall over Ethiopia.
d  To what extent does this pattern explain the drought-prone areas shown?

**TASK 3: Study Source C**

a  What is an isobar?
b  Use an atlas to describe the location of the LOW and HIGH pressure centres.
c  What is the isobar interval?
d  State the range of isobars from *Low* to *High*.

# Theme 2: Topic 36

## D Calculating relative humidity

"I recorded the dry bulb temperature of 12 °C this morning."

"And the wet bulb reading was 9 °C."

"So the difference is 3 °C. Did you know this is known as the depression of the wet bulb?"

"Of course. We need to check the RH table to see what that gives us."

"I'll look along the top line of the table for 3 °C. You look down the side for the dry bulb temperature of 12 °C."

"Got it – where they meet gives a RH of 67%."

"I thought the air felt a bit damp today!"

| Dry-bulb temperature (°C) | Difference between wet-bulb and dry-bulb temperatures |||||||||||||||| 
|---|---|---|---|---|---|---|---|---|---|---|---|---|---|---|---|
| | 0 | 1 | 2 | 3 | 4 | 5 | 6 | 7 | 8 | 9 | 10 | 11 | 12 | 13 | 14 | 15 |
| 0 | 100 | 81 | 63 | 45 | 28 | 11 | | | | | | | | | | |
| 2 | 100 | 83 | 67 | 51 | 36 | 20 | 6 | | | | | | | | | |
| 4 | 100 | 85 | 70 | 56 | 42 | 27 | 14 | | | | | | | | | |
| 6 | 100 | 86 | 72 | 59 | 46 | 35 | 22 | 10 | | | | | | | | |
| 8 | 100 | 87 | 74 | 62 | 51 | 39 | 28 | 17 | 6 | | | | | | | |
| 10 | 100 | 88 | 76 | 65 | 54 | 43 | 33 | 24 | 13 | 4 | | | | | | |
| 12 | 100 | 88 | 78 | 67 | 57 | 48 | 38 | 28 | 19 | 10 | 2 | | | | | |
| 14 | 100 | 89 | 79 | 69 | 60 | 50 | 41 | 33 | 25 | 16 | 8 | 1 | | | | |
| 16 | 100 | 90 | 80 | 71 | 62 | 54 | 45 | 37 | 29 | 21 | 14 | 7 | 1 | | | |
| 18 | 100 | 91 | 81 | 72 | 64 | 56 | 48 | 40 | 33 | 26 | 19 | 12 | 6 | | | |
| 20 | 100 | 91 | 82 | 74 | 66 | 58 | 51 | 44 | 36 | 30 | 23 | 17 | 11 | 5 | | |
| 22 | 100 | 92 | 83 | 75 | 68 | 60 | 53 | 46 | 40 | 33 | 27 | 21 | 15 | 10 | 4 | |
| 24 | 100 | 92 | 84 | 76 | 69 | 62 | 55 | 49 | 42 | 36 | 30 | 25 | 20 | 14 | 9 | 4 |
| 26 | 100 | 92 | 85 | 77 | 70 | 64 | 57 | 51 | 45 | 39 | 34 | 28 | 23 | 18 | 13 | 9 |
| 28 | 100 | 93 | 86 | 78 | 71 | 65 | 59 | 53 | 47 | 42 | 36 | 31 | 26 | 21 | 17 | 12 |
| 30 | 100 | 93 | 86 | 79 | 72 | 66 | 61 | 55 | 49 | 44 | 39 | 34 | 29 | 25 | 20 | 16 |

Relative humidity is calculated using a relative humidity table like that above. A wet-dry bulb thermometer (hygrometer) kept in a Stevenson Screen will provide a wet-bulb and dry-bulb temperature at the time of measurement.

## E Wind direction and wind speed

**January 2014**

| Wind direction | Number of days |
|---|---|
| N | 2 |
| NNE | 0 |
| NE | 0 |
| ENE | 2 |
| E | 1 |
| ESE | 2 |
| SE | 2 |
| SSE | 3 |
| S | 4 |
| SSW | 5 |
| SW | 4 |
| WSW | 3 |
| W | 1 |
| WNW | 1 |
| NW | 1 |
| NNW | 0 |
| Total: | 31 days |

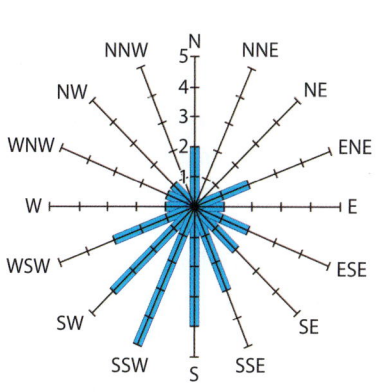

*Each mark on the direction line = 1 day.

A wind rose is one way to present information about wind direction. It is usually drawn after taking daily readings for a month so that a pattern of direction can be seen. It is useful for seeing from which direction most winds blow, i.e. the prevailing wind. Wind roses use the 8- or 16-point compass. Wind directions in between the compass points are recorded as being nearest to each stated direction, e.g. a wind blowing from 173° would be recorded as a wind from the south.

### TASK 4: Study Source D

a Use the relative humidity (RH) tables to work out the RH in the following cases:
- a dry-bulb temperature of 24 °C and a wet-bulb temperature of 16 °C
- a dry-bulb temperature of 8° C and a wet-bulb temperature of 7 °C.

b Which of these would be the most 'comfortable' to experience? Explain why.

c Make up a few situations involving dry- and wet-bulb temperatures and get a partner to calculate RH.

### TASK 5: Study Source E

The wind rose is for the month of January 2014 from a school on the west coast of France. The students wanted to test the hypothesis that **'The prevailing wind direction is mostly from the south-east.'**

Do you agree with the hypothesis? Make a decision and support your view with evidence from the wind rose.

# Cambridge IGCSE Geography — Weather

## 37 Using weather and climate data

### What happens to weather data?

Most countries have weather stations scattered over the country to record the key weather elements at the same time each day. These are then sent to a national meteorological centre where **meteorologists** analyse the information and produce weather maps to show a pattern of weather over a large area. From these, and previous weather patterns, they produce a forecast. This can be for the next 24 hours, a week, three months or a long-range forecast for the year. Weather forecasts are usually given several times a day on the TV, radio or websites and there is usually one in local newspapers.

### A Weather data from a Botswana school

**Maru a Pula School — Weather Records Enrichment**
09.00

| Date Feb | Day | MAX. (°C) | MIN. (°C) | WIND DIR. | WIND SPEED (KM/HR) | CLOUD | Rain (mm) |
|---|---|---|---|---|---|---|---|
| 07 | Thu | 34°C | 19°C | NE | 18 | Yes | 0.2 |
| 08 | Fri | 34°C | 20°C | NNE | 18 | Yes | 3 |
| 09 | Sat | 33°C | 19°C | N | 0 | Yes | 2 |
| 10 | Sun | 29°C | 17°C | NE | 8 | A Few | 0 |
| 11 | Mon | 30°C | 17°C | ENE | 8 | A Few | 0 |
| 12 | Tue | 30°C | 17°C | NE | 6 | NONE | 0 |
| 13 | Wed | 32°C | 17°C | NW | 5 | A Few | 0 |
| 14 | Thu | 32°C | 16°C | NNE | 8 | A Few | 0 |

The Maru a Pula School in Gaborone, Botswana takes regular weather readings from its weather station. The above recording sheet covered a week in February 2013 from Thursday 7–14 February.

### B Gaborone's climate

Gaborone, (25°S 26°E) Botswana, Africa    Altitude: 1010 metres

|  | J | F | M | A | M | J | J | A | S | O | N | D |
|---|---|---|---|---|---|---|---|---|---|---|---|---|
| Temperature (°C) | 26 | 25 | 24 | 21 | 17 | 13 | 13 | 17 | 20 | 23 | 24 | 25 |
| Rainfall (mm) | 97 | 63 | 70 | 30 | <1 | <1 | <1 | 2 | 13 | 21 | 73 | 63 |

Average annual rainfall = 432 millimetres

Temperatures are average (mean) for each month

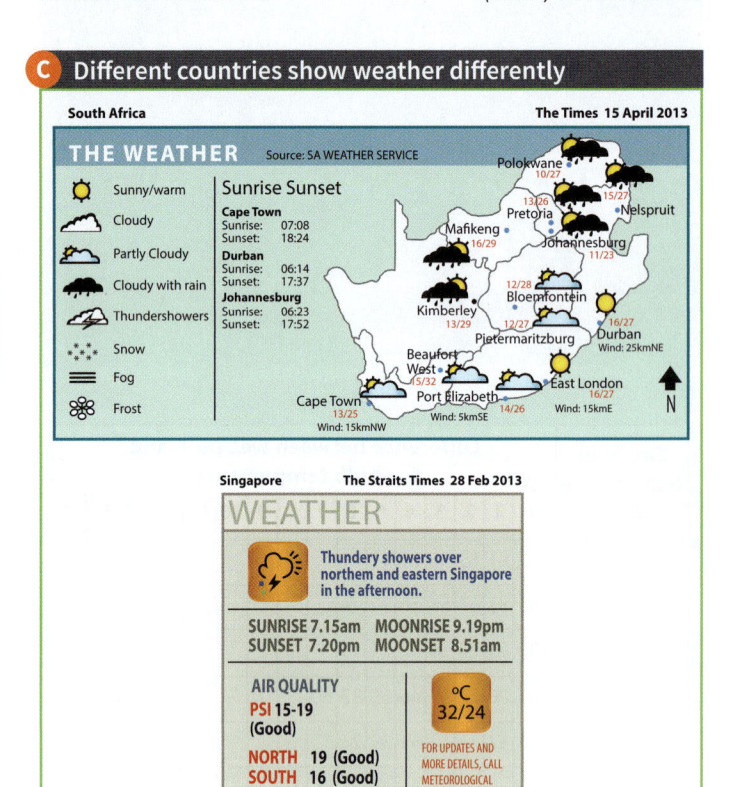

### C Different countries show weather differently

*South Africa — The Times 15 April 2013*
THE WEATHER — Source: SA WEATHER SERVICE
- Sunny/warm
- Cloudy
- Partly Cloudy
- Cloudy with rain
- Thundershowers
- Snow
- Fog
- Frost

Sunrise Sunset
- Cape Town — Sunrise: 07:08  Sunset: 18:24
- Durban — Sunrise: 06:14  Sunset: 17:37
- Johannesburg — Sunrise: 06:23  Sunset: 17:52

Polokwane 10/27; Pretoria 13/26; Nelspruit 15/27; Mafikeng 16/29; Johannesburg 11/23; Kimberley 13/29; Bloemfontein 12/27; Pietermaritzburg; Durban 16/27 Wind: 25kmNE; Beaufort West 15/32; East London 16/27 Wind: 15kmE; Cape Town 13/25 Wind: 15kmNW; Port Elizabeth 14/26 Wind: 5kmSE

*Singapore — The Straits Times 28 Feb 2013*
WEATHER
Thundery showers over northern and eastern Singapore in the afternoon.
SUNRISE 7.15am   MOONRISE 9.19pm
SUNSET 7.20pm    MOONSET 8.51am

AIR QUALITY
PSI 15-19 (Good)
NORTH 19 (Good)
SOUTH 16 (Good)
EAST 17 (Good)
WEST 18 (Good)
CENTRAL 15 (Good)

°C 32/24

FOR UPDATES AND MORE DETAILS, CALL METEOROLOGICAL SERVICE SINGAPORE 6542-7788 OR GO ONLINE TO www.nea.gov.sg

---

**TASK 1: Study Source A**

a   For the week shown, state or calculate all of the following:
- The maximum temperature
- The minimum temperature
- The average minimum temperature
- The average maximum temperature
- The average temperature range

b   State the most common direction the wind was blowing from.

c   What was the range of wind speed?

d   How could the cloud cover be estimated more accurately?

e   What evidence suggests this was quite a dry week?

**TASK 2: Study Sources A and B**

Look at the information on Gaborone's climate in Source B. How close would you say the readings in Source A were to the climate expected in February?

**TASK 3: Study Source C**

a   Discuss as a group what weather information you would want to see in a weather forecast.

b   List the type of weather information that is:
- common to both forecasts.
- different between the forecasts.

c   Weather information is presented in different ways. Which of these two styles do you prefer? Why?

d   Find a weather forecast for your local area.

Compare its presentation and the type of information provided with the two forecasts shown here.

# Theme 2: Topic 37

## Climate graphs and world climates

Many people mix up weather and climate. Climate is an average of weather conditions and describes what we expect to happen over a large area based on weather records over at least 30 years. Weather stations send information to meteorologists for daily forecasts while **climatologists** keep these records to produce climate data. As these records accumulate, climate data and graphs can be produced. From these emerge patterns which are used to produce a world map showing different climate types.

To decide how the climate we live in compares with others, we must have an idea of what an average climate is like. We need a place where it is neither too hot nor too cold, not too wet nor too dry, as a reference point. The United Kingdom (UK) has a climate with no extremes. It is between the cold Arctic region (north of 66½°N) and the hot Tropic of Cancer (23½°N). Cambridge (52°N) is a good reference point for a climate between the two.

### E Reading a climate graph

Cambridge, UK (52°N 0°E) Altitude: 6 metres

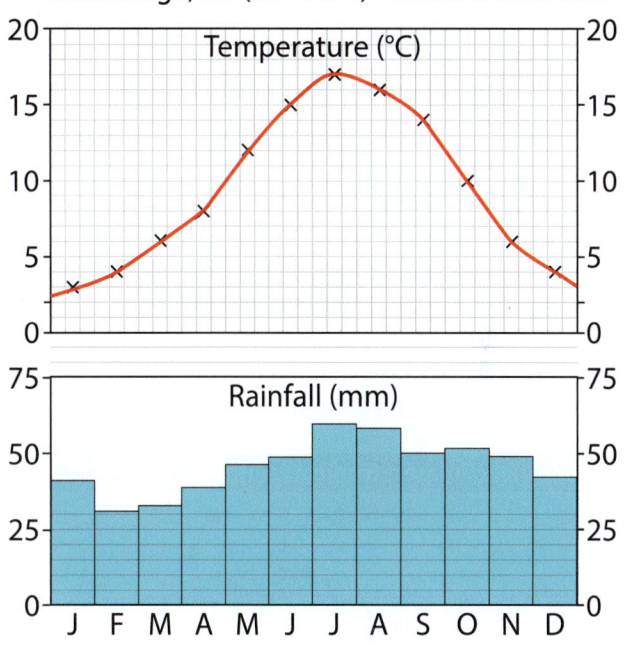

|  | J | F | M | A | M | J | J | A | S | O | N | D |
|---|---|---|---|---|---|---|---|---|---|---|---|---|
| Temperature (°C) | 3 | 4 | 6 | 8 | 12 | 15 | 17 | 16 | 14 | 10 | 6 | 4 |
| Rainfall (mm) | 41 | 31 | 35 | 38 | 46 | 48 | 60 | 57 | 50 | 53 | 49 | 44 |

*Average annual rainfall = 552 millimetres*
*Temperatures are average (mean) for each month*

### D World climates

- Tropical wet rainforest
- Semi-arid
- Mediterranean
- Temperate maritime
- Continental cool summer
- Tundra
- Mountain
- Tropical wet and dry savanna
- Arid or desert
- Humid sub-tropical
- Continental warm summer
- Sub-arctic
- Ice cap

---

### TASK 4: Study Source D

a Which type of climate is experienced in the place where you live?
b What type of climate does Cambridge in the UK experience?

### TASK 5: Study Sources B, D and E

a Using Source E, describe the climate of Cambridge. Refer to:
- average monthly temperatures
- annual temperature range
- average annual rainfall
- rainfall distribution.

b Referring to Source B, using exactly the same scales as for Cambridge, draw a climate graph for Gaborone.

c From Source D, identify Gaborone's climate type.
d Compare the climate of Gaborone with that of Cambridge. Refer to the same elements as in Task 1.
e How can you tell from the graph that:
- Gaborone is in the southern hemisphere?
- Cambridge is in the northern hemisphere?

### TASK 6

a Find climate data for where you live. Draw a climate graph using the same scales as used in Task 5b.
b Compare your climate with that of Cambridge and Gaborone.

# Cambridge IGCSE Geography
## Climate and natural vegetation

## 38 The equatorial climate

### Equatorial climates – hot and wet

The equatorial climate is also known as the tropical rainy climate, tropical wet climate or equatorial lowlands climate. This climate type is hot and very wet and supports tropical rainforest. It is found between the Tropic of Cancer (23½°N) and the Tropic of Capricorn (23½°S), usually within 10° of the equator, and normally extends up to 1000 metres above sea level where the air becomes too cool to support lowland rainforest. It is characterised by:

- low pressure all year along the equator – an area known as the Doldrums
- the midday sun almost always at a vertical angle, giving maximum **insolation**
- average temperature around 26 °C – lower than some other climate types due to heavy cloud and rainfall
- a small annual and daily (diurnal) temperature range
- heavy convectional rainfall and thunderstorms in the afternoon after the sun has warmed the ground, causing air to rise
- average annual rainfall of over 1500 millimetres distributed fairly evenly throughout the year
- high relative humidity, usually above 75%.

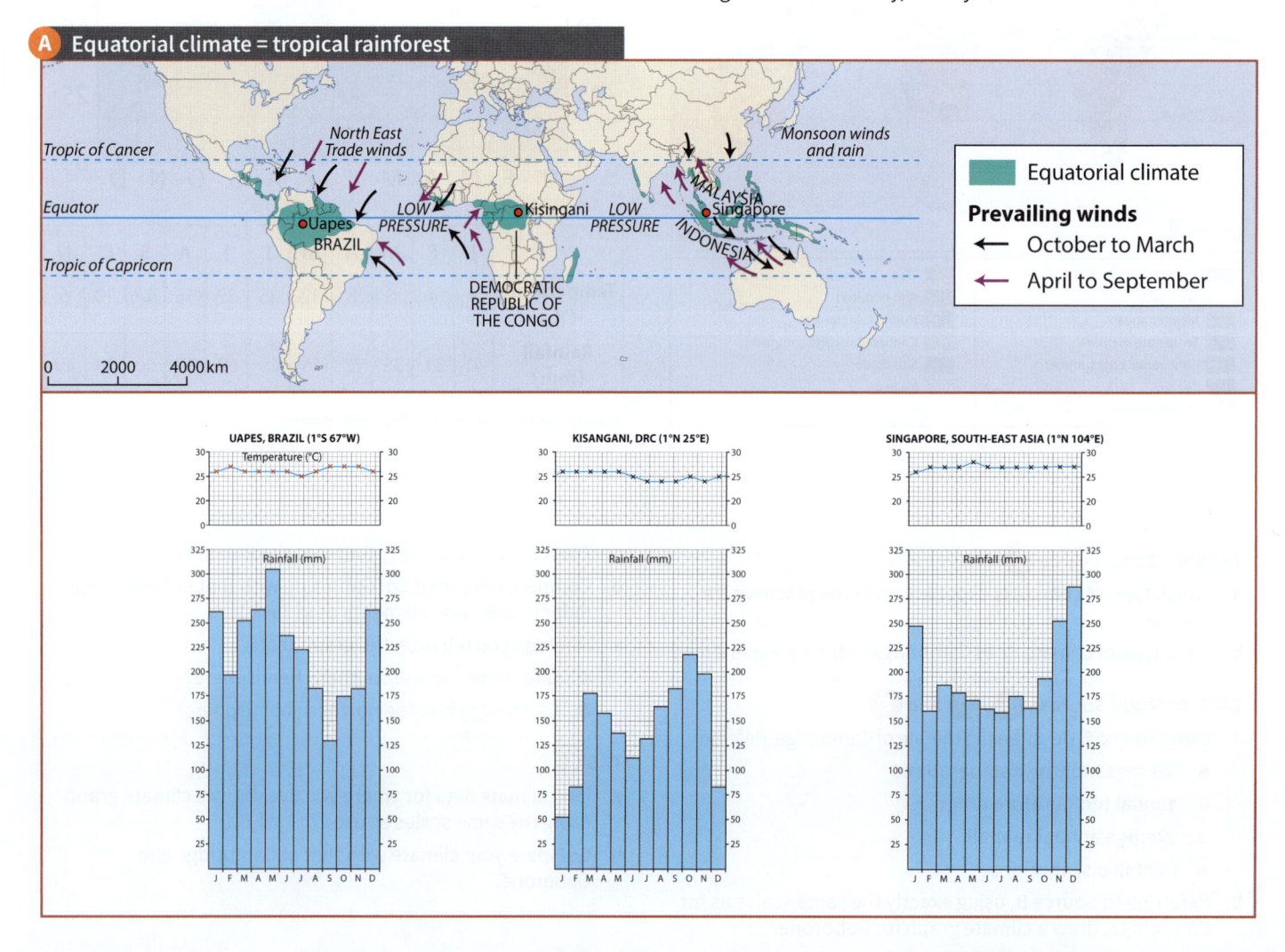

### TASK 1: Study Source A

a  Write down **four** characteristics of the equatorial climate that support tropical rainforest.
b  On an outline map of the world, shade and label areas that experience an equatorial climate and have tropical rainforests.
c  Name and label Uapes, Kisingani and Singapore on the map.
d  Describe the global distribution of rainforests.
e  Write down **three** similarities between the climate of the three places.
f  Write down **three** differences between the climates of the three places.
g  Suggest why the temperature and rainfall are lower at Kisangani than that at Uapes and Singapore.
h  Compare the climate for Cambridge on page 113 with any one of those in Source A.

**A** Equatorial climate = tropical rainforest

# Theme 2: Topic 38

## B  What causes the equatorial climate?

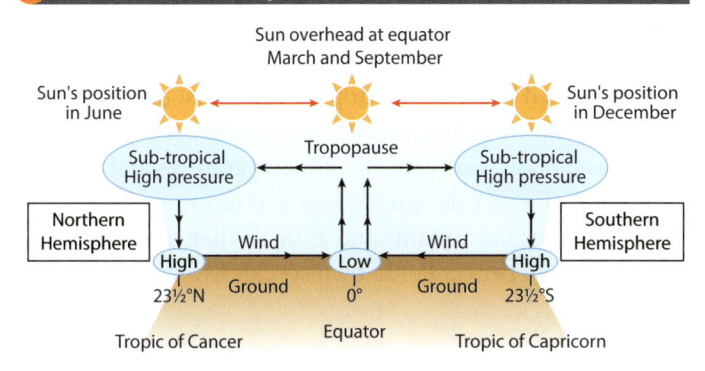

This diagram shows the position of the sun, pressure systems and wind movement in March and September when the sun is directly overhead the equator. The low and high pressure belts move north and south with the sun during the year, giving summer and winter seasons to both hemispheres as follows:

**21 March:** sun overhead equator (Equinox)
**21 June:** sun overhead Tropic of Cancer (Solstice) – northern summer/southern winter
**21 September:** sun overhead equator (Equinox)
**21 December:** sun overhead Tropic of Capricorn (Solstice) – northern winter/southern summer.

## D  2014 World Cup worries about the weather

### ITALY AND MANAUS TOO HOT FOR ENGLAND IN WORLD CUP OPENER
**England 1 Italy 2**

'It's going to be hot in all respects,' a spokesman for the World Cup organisers had warned. 'From the weather to the warmth of the fans. They're going to experience an Amazonian summer.' He was proved right. As the evening kick-off time approached, temperatures soared to 34°C. Manaus was the city that the England manager had wanted to avoid when the draw was made. There were other weather-related problems. In constructing the new stadium all the welding was delayed by tropical storms and the new grass, which was grown locally, was either saturated with heavy rain or dried out in the tropical heat. Players of both teams had trained with equipment that simulated the equatorial climate, so it was only in the second half that players began to show fatigue – but not before Mario Balotelli had headed the winning goal to leave England with an uphill struggle to qualify for the next stage.

From *Our man in Manaus* – 15 June 2014

**Average climate statistics for June**

|  | Manaus, Brazil | London, England | Rome, Italy |
|---|---|---|---|
| Daily temperature – high (°C) | 31 | 21 | 27 |
| Average daily temperature (°C) | 26 | 16 | 21 |
| Daily temperature – low (°C) | 23 | 13 | 15 |
| Average monthly rainfall (mm) | 256 | 50 | 34 |
| Relative humidity (%) | 87 | 76 | 58 |

## C  Convectional rainfall

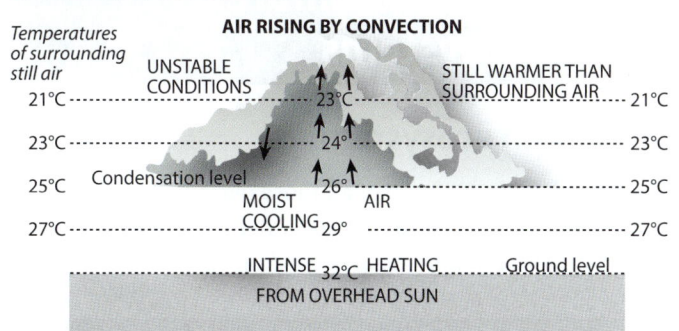

The mean annual rainfall of the equatorial climate is high – usually over 1500 mm. This is caused by air masses from the sub-tropics converging here as winds blow from high pressure to low pressure at the equator. Warm, unstable air rises to give **convectional rainfall**. Where highlands occur along the equator, such as in eastern Brazil, there can also be **orographic (relief) rainfall**.

### TASK 2: Study Sources B and C

a  Describe the location of the sub-tropical high pressure areas in March and September.

b  Explain how and why air from the sub-tropical high pressure systems converges at the equator.

c  Explain why heavy cloud and thunderstorms:
  - take place along the equator
  - take place mostly in the afternoon.

d  Explain why areas to the north and south of the two tropics have summer and winter seasons, whereas the equatorial climate has no real seasons during the year.

### TASK 3: Study Source D

a  What is meant by **convectional rainfall**?

b  Explain how and why convectional rainfall takes place along the equator.

c  Suggest how the presence of mountains along the equator can increase the amount of rainfall in these regions.

### TASK 4: Study Source D

a  How different was the climate likely to be in June in Manaus for both the England and Italian teams? Use data in your answer.

b  Suggest how this might have affected their performance over 90 minutes during the game.

c  How did the climate in Manaus affect other preparations for the match?

d  Suggest why using average climate figures from London and Rome may not be the best way of judging how players would adapt to the climate in Manaus.

e  USA and Colombia also played in Manaus. Which of these teams should have been more comfortable in this climate? Explain your answer.

# 39 Tropical rainforest ecosystems

## What is an ecosystem?

The **biosphere** is made up of all those plant and animal components in the world that are either living or have lived (organic). These components depend on each other. They also depend upon non-living parts (inorganic) such as sunshine, rocks and air. The interaction of all these parts takes place in an ecosystem. Large ecosystems at the global scale are called **biomes**. The tropical rainforest biome has the ideal conditions for developing a complex ecosystem, with the equatorial climate of high temperatures and heavy rainfall every day giving heat and moisture. This biome contains more plants and animals than any other ecosystem – 90 per cent of known species live there.

### A  Tropical rainforest structure

These broad-leaved evergreen forests show dense growth and extremely diverse **fauna** and **flora**, forming unique ecosystems. There can be 40–100 species of tree per hectare. Large amounts of shade prevent much growth at low levels, so most plant and animal species are in the canopy where there is light.

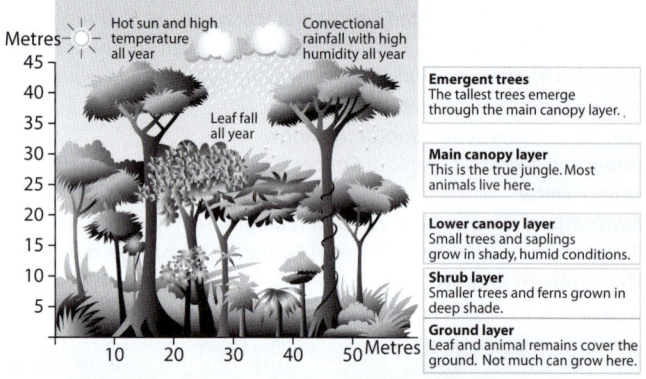

Hot sun and high temperature all year
Convectional rainfall with high humidity all year
Leaf fall all year

**Emergent trees** The tallest trees emerge through the main canopy layer.
**Main canopy layer** This is the true jungle. Most animals live here.
**Lower canopy layer** Small trees and saplings grow in shady, humid conditions.
**Shrub layer** Smaller trees and ferns grown in deep shade.
**Ground layer** Leaf and animal remains cover the ground. Not much can grow here.

All the plants compete for light to **photosynthesise** – this causes vegetation to grow in layers. Those that reach the sky – the emergents – form islands of green above the main forest. Rainforests are called the 'lungs of the Earth' due to the oxygen they produce.

### B  Plants adapt to survive in tropical rainforests

**CHARACTERISTIC ELEMENTS OF LOW-LATITUDE FORESTS**

1. Buttress roots
2. Epiphytic plants with high light requirement invade a 'host' tree
3. Lianas and climbers
4. Drip-tip leaves

*Buttress roots* – tall, heavy trees develop these as a support. Trees are mostly shallow rooted.

*Epiphytes* – plants that live on trees above ground level to get light have their roots in debris or decaying plants, e.g. orchids, bromeliads.

*Lianas, climbers and vines* intertwine around trees to get to the light at the top.

*Drip-tip leaves* – plants develop pointed tips and glossy leaves to remove water quickly.

Trees give the impression they are 'evergreen' as they lose and renew their leaves throughout the year rather than in any one season. Leaf-growth, flowering, fruit-fall and leaf-fall occur all the time so that the rainforest looks the same all year.

**TASK 1:** Study Source A

a. Make your own labelled copy of the vertical structure of the rainforest.

b. Are there any forests near where you live? If so, how does their structure compare with that of the rainforest?

c. Why does so little rainfall and light reach the ground in the rainforest? How does this affect the growth of vegetation in the lower levels shown in the photo?

d. Explain how competition for light leads to layers of vegetation in the rainforest.

**TASK 2:** Study Source B

It shows four ways in which plants have adapted to survive in the rainforest. Describe **two** of these ways.

**TASK 3:** Study Source C

Describe what happens to nutrients once organic matter lands on the forest floor.

## C Nutrient recycling

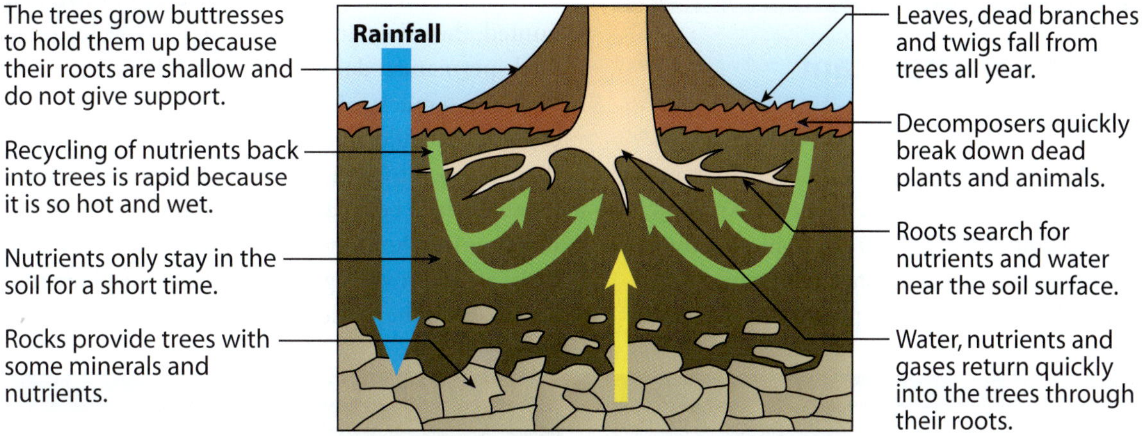

- The trees grow buttresses to hold them up because their roots are shallow and do not give support.
- Recycling of nutrients back into trees is rapid because it is so hot and wet.
- Nutrients only stay in the soil for a short time.
- Rocks provide trees with some minerals and nutrients.

*Rainfall*

- Leaves, dead branches and twigs fall from trees all year.
- Decomposers quickly break down dead plants and animals.
- Roots search for nutrients and water near the soil surface.
- Water, nutrients and gases return quickly into the trees through their roots.

## D A rainforest food web from the Virunga rainforest region of the D.R. Congo, Africa

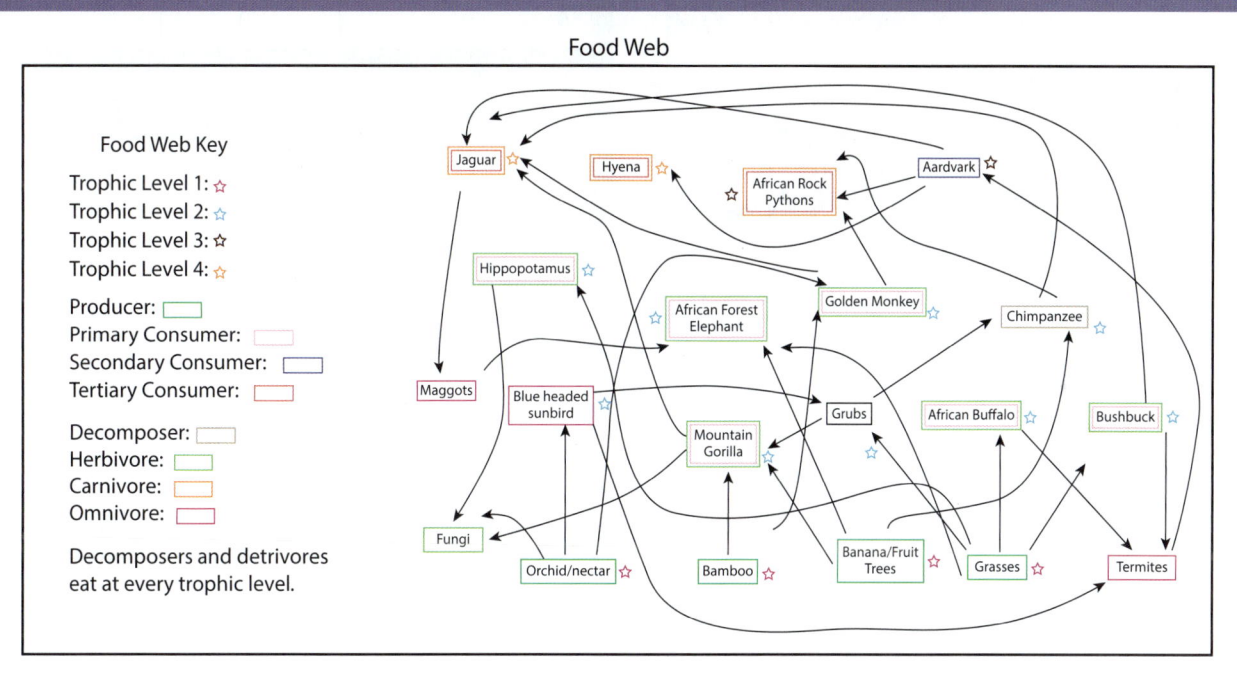

**Food Web**

**Food Web Key**

Trophic Level 1: ☆
Trophic Level 2: ☆
Trophic Level 3: ☆
Trophic Level 4: ☆

Producer: ☐
Primary Consumer: ☐
Secondary Consumer: ☐
Tertiary Consumer: ☐

Decomposer: ☐
Herbivore: ☐
Carnivore: ☐
Omnivore: ☐

Decomposers and detrivores eat at every trophic level.

Organisms in the food web: Jaguar, Hyena, African Rock Pythons, Aardvark, Hippopotamus, African Forest Elephant, Golden Monkey, Chimpanzee, Maggots, Blue headed sunbird, Grubs, African Buffalo, Bushbuck, Mountain Gorilla, Fungi, Orchid/nectar, Bamboo, Banana/Fruit Trees, Grasses, Termites.

### Some definitions

**Producers** – plants are producers because they capture the sun's energy by photosynthesis. All consumers depend on producers.

**Consumers** – primary consumers feed on the producers, then secondary and tertiary consumers feed on producers and/or other consumers.

**Trophic levels** – these are levels of energy. Plants form the first trophic level, then primary, secondary and tertiary consumers form the second, third and fourth trophic levels.

**TASK 4: Study Source D**

a What is meant by a **producer** and a **consumer**?

b At what trophic level is:
- a chimpanzee
- a banana
- a jaguar?

c Draw **one** example of a food chain for:
- the African rock python
- the jaguar.

d The mountain gorilla is close to becoming extinct. Discuss and write down any likely consequences on the food web if this takes place.

# Cambridge IGCSE Geography — Climate and natural vegetation

## 40 Rainforest deforestation

### Deforestation – an important rainforest issue

Deforestation of the tropical rainforest has been an issue for many years. Most concerns have been about the Amazon rainforest, which accounts for over 50 per cent of all the deforestation taking place. Most deforestation began with small-scale subsistence farmers' practice of shifting cultivation. Clearings were made, crops grown and animals hunted, then the tribes moved on to allow for regrowth. Little permanent damage was done. However, in the last 50 years so much rainforest has been removed that there are concerns it could all disappear in the 21st century. While there is much to gain from exploiting rainforest resources, there needs to be an awareness of the part they play in maintaining the planet by supplying oxygen, absorbing carbon and providing water to the atmosphere for rainfall elsewhere in the world.

### A  Where is deforestation taking place?

Share of rainforest and its share of deforestation
- Dense forest
- recent deforestation

| South America | Africa | Asia |
|---|---|---|
| 48% / 56% | 15% / 10% | 37% / 34% |

### B  Why are forests being cleared?

**Percentage of global deforestation**

| South America | Africa | Asia |
|---|---|---|
| 56 | 10 | 34 |

**Why deforestation is taking place (Figures in %)**

|  | South America | Africa | Asia |
|---|---|---|---|
| Small-scale agriculture | 40 | 50 | 40 |
| Commercial crops | 20 | 20 | 24 |
| Cattle ranching | 20 | 5 | 1 |
| Logging | 12 | 15 | 25 |
| Fuelwood | 8 | 10 | 10 |
| All figures in % | 100 | 100 | 100 |

---

**TASK 1: Study Source A**

a  On an outline map of the world, create your own map of deforestation.

b  Compare the share of rainforest that each of the three main regions has.

c  Which region is causing:
- most concern about deforestation
- least concern about deforestation?

Give reasons for your answer.

**TASK 2: Study Source B**

a  Using a radius scale of 1 mm = 1%, draw three circles using the figures shown for the percentage of global deforestation.

b  Within the three circles, draw pie charts using the figures showing why deforestation is taking place.

c  List the **five** main reasons for deforestation.

d  Which land use accounts for most deforestation in all three continents?

**TASK 3: Study Source C**

a  Describe the scene in the photograph.

b  What is:
- slash-and-burn farming?
- shifting cultivation?

c  Put the eight captions into the correct time order. Use them to produce your own storyboard.

d  Suggest some consequences of deforestation for the rainforest and the wildlife that live there.

# Theme 2: Topic 40

## C Deforestation affects soils and vegetation

- The ash supplies nutrients.
- Heavy rainfall eventually washes nutrients and soil into rivers.
- People set fire to the trees – a practice called slash-and-burn farming.
- Rainforest is destroyed.
- Crops grow well for a number of years.
- Crops no longer grow on the infertile soil.
- Animals lose habitats and food.
- People go elsewhere to remove more rainforest. This is called shifting cultivation.

### RAINFOREST STILL FAIRLY INTACT!

The 135 million hectares of rainforest of Central West Africa in D.R. Congo still remains largely intact. This is due to the government's heavy taxes on forestry investment, wars, plus the Livingstone Falls on the Congo river which limits access. More than half the population, 35 million people, live or depend on the forest resources. Logging production is low as yet, but the forests have been opened up to farmers and commercial hunters who supply bushmeat to cities. Species such as bonobo, elephants and the white rhino are becoming endangered. Yet if controls are put in place, and the Amazon continues to be destroyed, D.R. Congo may soon have the world's greatest rainforest.

**Adapted from** *Rainforests* – The Burning Issue

**Tribal issue:** The 'Pygmy' tribes are all under threat across central Africa; tribes such as the Twa, Aka, Baka and Mbuti. All have different languages and hunting traditions but all face the same threats: racism, logging and conservation, leading to loss of tribal lands, serious health issues and violent abuse.

**Adapted from** *Survival* – The Pygmies

## D What are the main threats?

### BRAZIL ALLOWS MORE CATTLE RANCHING WHILE PROTECTING TRIBES

Vincente Riva has been farming in the rainforest area for 30 years. He owns 10 000 hectares of rainforest and has been given a licence to clear 1000 more hectares and expand his herd of 850 cattle. In the 1970s, the government sold large amounts of rainforest cheaply to people to reduce the population of its cities. In return, the farmers had to provide infrastructure such as roads to open up the rainforest. Now the local economies of small towns depend on cattle ranching for jobs . 'If the government gave us US$750 per hectare we can preserve the forest while still earning from the cleared land,' he said.

**Adapted from** *Rainforests* – The Burning Issue

**Tribal issue:** The Brazilian government has promised to drive out illegal loggers from the Amazon reserve of the Awa tribe, listed as one of the world's most threatened people. The loggers have already cut down 30% of the rainforest in the tribal territory. About 100 members of the tribe have had no contact with the outside world. They are vulnerable to disease and are afraid to hunt in case they meet armed loggers.

**Adapted from** *The Times*, 8 January 2014

### A WORLD WILLING TO FRY FOR PRIZE OF 'GREEN GOLD'

From the air, the palm oil plantations are quietly impressive. Up close it is ecological chaos. Burning, cutting and noise from chainsaws taking down rainforest and palms. Indonesia and Malaysia form 90% of the market, but China and other growing economies also have an appetite for fried food. Over 3.8 million people depend on palm oil for employment in this region. Palm oil has two main uses: for cooking and in vehicles as a renewable fuel. In the many islands of Indonesia, though, there remain tribes that are under threat from the outside world.

**Tribal issue:** The Kajang tribe live on the island of Sulawesi in Indonesia, and have asked for a legal court ruling to own their land before too much logging occurs. Other tribes have lost their tribal lands to clove, cocoa and coffee plantations

**Adapted from** *The Times*, 11 December 2009

---

**TASK 4: Study Source D**

a List the different land uses that cleared rainforest land is being used for.

b To what extent are local people dependent on using rainforest land for their livelihoods? Refer to examples.

c In what ways are remote tribes threatened by rainforest being cleared?

d Why might the rainforest in D.R. Congo become the world's greatest rainforest in future?

e Source D refers to several different tribes in different rainforests. In groups of three, allocate each person a different tribe. Carry out research on the Internet into:
- the way of life of the tribe
- how it has been affected by deforestation
- what the future holds for the tribe.

119

# Cambridge IGCSE Geography
## Climate and natural vegetation

# Case Study
## The tropical rainforest – Ecuador

### 'Republic of the Equator'

Ecuador is the second smallest country in the continent of South America. In the east is the tropical rainforest of the upper Amazon basin, known as the Oriente. This region contains one of the richest and most diverse rainforest ecosystems in the world. Puyo (population 25 000) is the capital of Pastaza, a province in the Oriente region. It experiences a very hot and wet equatorial climate and its tropical rainforest vegetation lies on the western edge of the Amazon basin. Despite the remoteness of this rainforest, it is under threat from logging, tourism and oil companies. Conserving the rainforest and the way of life of the tribes that live there has been one of the country's priorities, but there are also huge oil reserves – the income from drilling for oil would allow a great deal of development in this LEDC.

### A  Ecuador and its rainforest

The Oriente is home to over 25 000 species of plants, 1600 bird species, 300 mammals and 460 species of amphibians – mostly frogs! Lianas (thick, dangling vines) hang from high in the canopy. Spread across the forest are the buttress roots of tropical hardwoods. Equally impressive are the forest's giant leaves which are thick and waxy and have pointed 'drip tips', which help water run off during downpours. Home to poisonous snakes, toxic plants and flesh-eating fish plus caiman and jaguars, the rainforest may not seem like the most inviting habitat. But for the tribes who have always lived there, the rainforest has everything needed for survival.

*The Lonely Planet Guide to Ecuador & the Galapagos Islands*

### B  The climate of Puyo

**Puyo (2°S 78°W), Ecuador, South America**
**Altitude: 950 metres**

|  | J | F | M | A | M | J | J | A | S | O | N | D |
|---|---|---|---|---|---|---|---|---|---|---|---|---|
| Temperature (°C) | 25 | 25 | 25 | 25 | 24 | 24 | 24 | 24 | 25 | 25 | 25 | 25 |
| Rainfall (mm) | 214 | 222 | 305 | 366 | 353 | 338 | 301 | 225 | 259 | 302 | 289 | 237 |
| % Humidity | 85 | 86 | 86 | 87 | 86 | 83 | 80 | 79 | 79 | 79 | 81 | 85 |

Average annual rainfall = 3411 millimetres
Temperatures are average (mean) for each month
Average daily temperature: Max: 30 °C Min 19 °C
Average relative humidity: 80%

### C  Does Puyo tick the boxes?

| Beginnings . . . | . . . endings |
|---|---|
| Temperatures over 20 °C for most months of the year . . . | . . . so photosynthesis can take place all year. |
| High rainfall in each month of the year . . . | . . . result in the rapid recycling of nutrients. |
| Long hours of daylight and sunshine . . . | . . . so there is water available for growth all year. |
| High temperatures and high rainfall . . . | . . . so plant growth is not limited by low temperatures. |

### TASK 1: Study Source A
a  Use Source A to describe the location of:
   - Ecuador
   - the capital Quito
   - the region of Oriente
   - the town of Puyo.
b  What evidence shows the Oriente region has a large diversity of plants and animals?
c  Which plant adaptations are mentioned in the extract?
d  Why is the rainforest and the way of life of the tribes who live in the Oriente region under threat?
e  Describe the location of the Yasuni National Park.

### TASK 2: Study Sources B and C
a  Draw a climate graph using the same scales as on the previous work on climate data and graphs (see page 113).
b  Match the **Beginnings . . .** and **. . . endings** in Source C.
c  Explain why the climate of Puyo is better for rapid plant growth than the climate at Cambridge (see page 113).

# Case Study: The tropical rainforest – Ecuador

## D The rainforest food web in Ecuador

The food web shows a fraction of the main links between plants and animals in Ecuador. Missing from here is the Andean Condor – a huge bird of prey with a wingspan of 3.2 metres. It is a member of the vulture family and feeds mostly on carrion (dead carcasses) such as deer and cattle. It is the national emblem of many South American countries. It is somewhere on page 120; can you find it?

## E Conserving the rainforest – the Yasuni National Park

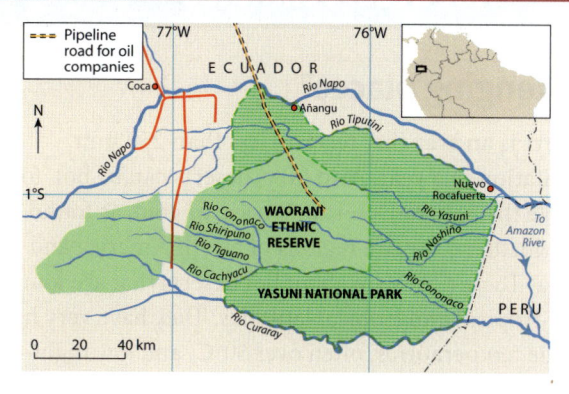

The Yasuni National Park is an international biosphere reserve, established in 1979. It covers an area of 1 million hectares in the north-east of Ecuador. It is home to the most diverse ecosystem of plants, animal and insect species in the world. The soils beneath the rainforest in the park are tropical red soils (see page 117). The park has been created to the east of the Waorani tribe's reserve where, due to the area's inaccessibility, hunter-gatherers have survived for centuries by living off the rainforest. Now the park and the reserve are both threatened by road-building, tourism and oil drilling.

## F Newspaper extract

### WORLD FAILS TO SAVE AMAZON FROM OIL DRILLERS

Ecuador's parliament has voted to drill for oil in an Amazon nature reserve after failing to attract enough funds from other countries to leave the area untouched. President Correa said that he would not approve the exploitation of oil reserves under the Yasuni National Park unless rich countries contributed US$ 3.6 billion to his poor country. The park is home to some of the most diverse fauna and flora in the world, as well as indigenous tribes. Only US$13 million was raised so the state oil company, Petroamazonas, will now take charge of oil extraction. This has not gone down well with local people. 'We want them to respect our territory,' said Alicia Cauilla, who represents the Waorani people. 'Let us live how we want.' The President claims that the drilling will only affect a small part of the park and it would raise US$22 billion to be used among the poor for welfare and education programmes. The problem is this, he said: 'Do we protect 100% of the Yasuni and stay poor, or do we save 99% of it and have US$18 billion to defeat poverty?'

Adapted from *The Times*, 5 October 2013

## TASK 3: Study Source D

a From Source D identify:
- a producer
- a primary consumer
- a secondary consumer
- a tertiary consumer.

b Draw **one** food chain that involves a producer and all three different types of consumer.

c At what trophic level are parrots?

d Imagine parrots became extinct. Write down **three** consequences at the trophic level(s):
- below that of the parrot
- above that of the parrot.

## TASK 4: Study Source E

a Why is it such an important area for conservation?

b Why has the area managed to survive in its natural state for so long?

c The Waorani tribe are hunter-gatherers. What do you understand by that term?

d State **three** different activities that threaten the future of the rainforest and the Waorani tribe's way of life.

## TASK 5: Study Source F

a What did President Correa propose as a way of saving the Yasuni National Park but also gaining some income for his country?

b The policy failed, so oil drilling will take place here. Comment on the question posed by President Correa at the end of the article.

# Cambridge IGCSE Geography | Climate and natural vegetation

## 41 Hot desert climates

### Challenging places?

A **desert** is an area that receives less than 250 mm precipitation in a year. Arid (dry) deserts can be hot, for example the Sahara Desert in Africa; or cold, as found in the northern **tundra** regions of North America and Eurasia. These pages are about hot deserts that are found in sub-tropical and tropical latitudes. They have very high daytime temperatures, often over 50°C, and low night-time temperatures, well below 0°C with clear skies and sometimes a ground frost. They are mostly found on the western edge of continents because the **prevailing winds** in tropical regions are off-shore, blowing from the east across land, so they cannot pick up moisture from the sea. Hot deserts are extreme environments which present challenges for people who live there or visit there.

### A  A desert scene

**Monument Valley, the Mojave Desert, USA**

The Mojave Desert is a dry, barren desert. The Monument Valley area was originally a basin of sandstone and limestone layers. It has slowly been uplifted to become a flat plateau up to 3 km above sea level. Heat, wind and water have eroded the land for over 50 million years, cutting it up and peeling away the rock layers. Hard horizontal rocks have been left as isolated caps above softer sandstone. These are called 'mesas'. Due to low rainfall, the features are not rounded.

### B  The world's hot deserts

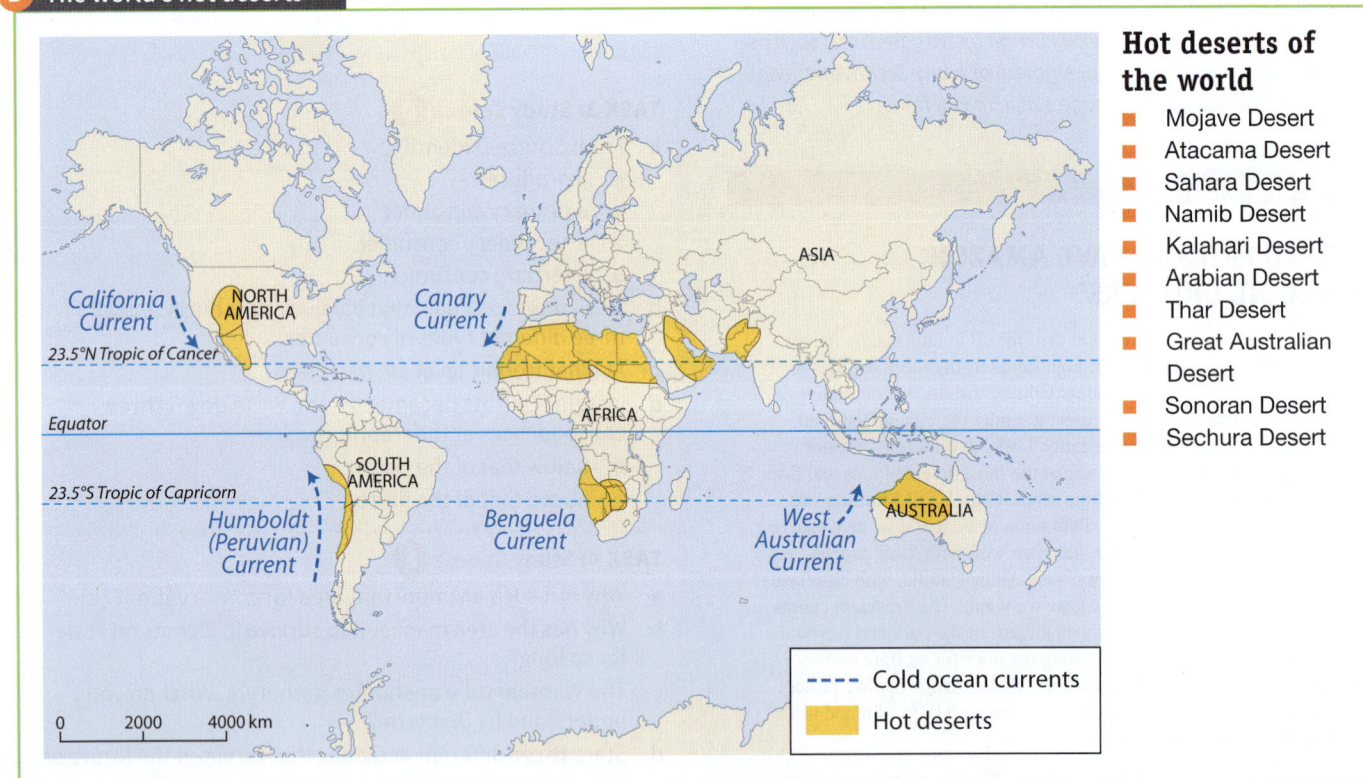

**Hot deserts of the world**
- Mojave Desert
- Atacama Desert
- Sahara Desert
- Namib Desert
- Kalahari Desert
- Arabian Desert
- Thar Desert
- Great Australian Desert
- Sonoran Desert
- Sechura Desert

---

**TASK 1:** Study Source **A**

a  Describe the scene. Give at least **three** reasons that suggest this is an area of low rainfall.

b  Explain how mesas have been formed here.

**TASK 2:** Study Source **B**

a  On an outline map of the world, add the borders of the ten hot deserts and the cold ocean currents shown.

b  On your map, name all ten hot deserts from the box provided. Use an atlas to help.

c  Describe the distribution of hot deserts.

Theme 2: Topic 41

## C A hot desert climate

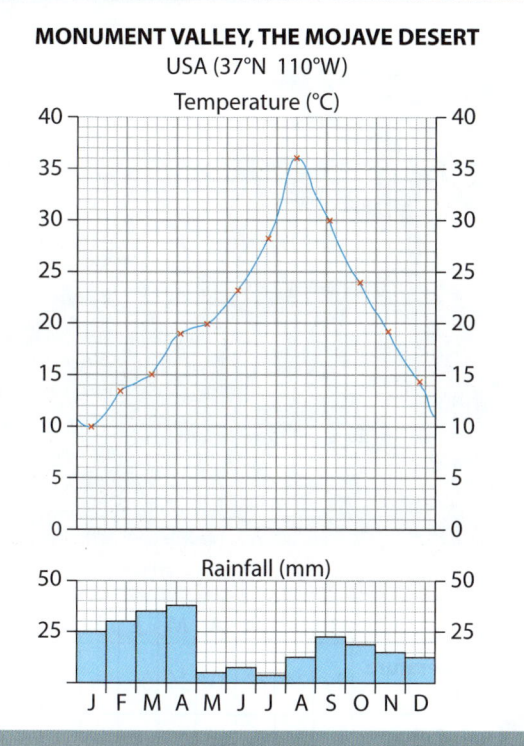

**MONUMENT VALLEY, THE MOJAVE DESERT**
USA (37°N 110°W)

Monument Valley (37°N 110°W), the Mojave Desert, USA

|  | J | F | M | A | M | J | J | A | S | O | N | D |
|---|---|---|---|---|---|---|---|---|---|---|---|---|
| Temperature (°C) | 10 | 13 | 15 | 19 | 20 | 23 | 28 | 36 | 30 | 24 | 19 | 14 |
| Rainfall (mm) | 25 | 30 | 34 | 37 | 4 | 6 | 3 | 12 | 22 | 18 | 15 | 13 |

Average annual rainfall = 219 mm
Temperatures are average (mean) for each month

**TASK 3: Study Source C**
a What is the mean temperature of the hottest month?
b What is the mean temperature of the coldest month?
c Work out the annual mean temperature range.
d How much below 250 mm is the average annual rainfall? Describe its distribution.
e Monument Valley is a famous desert that has been featured in many films. Suggest the best time of year for tourists to visit or film-makers to make films. Justify your choice.

**TASK 4: Study Source D**
a Explain how sub-tropical high pressure zones are created.
b Why is it difficult for rain to form in these areas?
c Name **two** hot deserts in each of:
   - areas of sub-tropical high pressure
   - the western side of continents close to cold ocean currents.
d Use Source B to help you name **three** cold currents that flow to the west of **three** named hot deserts.
e Suggest why these ocean currents are cold.
f How can cold ocean currents help create fog but also cause a lack of rainfall in some hot deserts?

## D Creating hot deserts

The **tropopause** is the boundary between the atmosphere and space. Rising air cannot penetrate it so it is diverted towards the tropics.

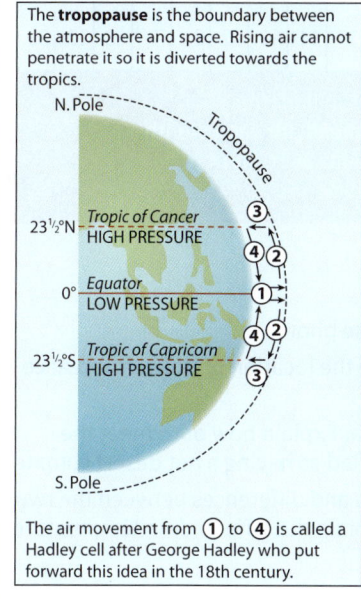

N. Pole
Tropopause
23½°N — Tropic of Cancer — HIGH PRESSURE
0° — Equator — LOW PRESSURE
23½°S — Tropic of Capricorn — HIGH PRESSURE
S. Pole

The air movement from ① to ④ is called a Hadley cell after George Hadley who put forward this idea in the 18th century.

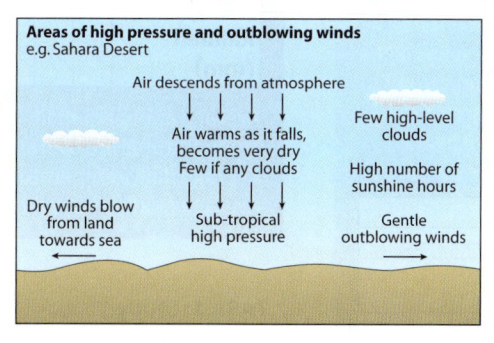

**Areas of high pressure and outblowing winds** e.g. Sahara Desert

Air descends from atmosphere
Air warms as it falls, becomes very dry — Few if any clouds
Few high-level clouds
High number of sunshine hours
Dry winds blow from land towards sea
Sub-tropical high pressure
Gentle outblowing winds

**Areas with cold ocean currents offshore** e.g. Namib and Atacama Deserts

Wind usually offshore but any cold moist air moving inland from the sea is warmed rapidly by the land
Fog forms around coast as cold air reaches very warm land
Air soon warms: able to hold more moisture Little condensation
Cold moist air flowing over cold current
Cold current in ocean
Very warm land

**Key to diagram** (left)
① Due to the heat of the sun, which is overhead at the equator, the land surfaces are warmed up and air rises. This gives low pressure at the surface along the equator. This rising air cools and condenses to give thunder clouds and heavy rainfall in equatorial regions.
② Once this rising air reaches the tropopause it then travels to the north and south towards each tropic.
③ As it moves away from the equator at high altitude it cools. Between 20° and 35° north and south of the equator the air begins to sink or subside towards the surface.
④ This gives permanent sub-tropical high-pressure systems (anticyclones) in these areas. Rainfall cannot occur where air sinks. These areas of aridity are the hot deserts of the world.

123

# Cambridge IGCSE Geography — Climate and natural vegetation

## 42  Hot desert ecosystems

### Living conditions in hot deserts

Hot desert biomes are found in North America, South and Central America, Africa, the Middle East, South Asia and Australasia. They are found around and within tropical regions, mostly around the Tropic of Cancer and Tropic of Capricorn. These biomes are characterised by:

- hot seasons for most of the year
- average annual rainfall below 250 millimetres
- extreme daily variation in temperature from up to 50 °C during the day to below 0 °C at night
- clear skies all day and night
- coarse sandy soils with good drainage, little sub-surface water but low in nutrients and organic matter.

To survive in these conditions requires special adaptations for plants and animals. Yet the hot desert ecosystem is much richer than at first sight.

### B  Adapting to desert life

*The Saguaro cactus is the state flower of Arizona, USA. The blossoms open during desert nights and close in the day. It has a tall, thick stem with smooth waxy skin and 20 mm spines. The stem can expand to store water.*

*Camels are called 'ships of the desert' because they can cross the desert better than any other animal. They have bushy eyebrows and two pairs of eyelashes to keep sand out of their eyes. They only have two toes and thick padded feet so they can walk easily across sand. The hump stores fat reserves that can be used as food as the animals travel. If the hump shrinks the camel's reserves are low.*

| Beginnings … | … endings |
|---|---|
| Plants are low-growing … | … to avoid water loss by strong winds. |
| Some animals can store food and water for days … | … to prevent water loss by evapotranspiration. |
| Animals are often small … | … to reach underground water supplies. |
| Plants store water in thick stems … | … to use in dry periods. |
| Small animals can hide in burrows or under stones … | … to reach the maximum area for water and to find any surface moisture. |
| Some rodents are nocturnal … | … so there is less water loss from a small surface area. |
| Plants have roots that travel horizontally … | … so they can avoid intense daytime heat. |
| Insects and reptiles have waterproof skins … | … so they can hunt in cooler nights. |
| Plants have long roots … | … so they can retain water in their bodies. |
| Plants have small, thick leaves or needles … | … so they can travel far without the need for daily supplies. |

### A  Living conditions are harsh

Makkah (21°N 40°E), Saudi Arabia; Altitude: 277 metre

| | J | F | M | A | M | J | J | A | S | O | N | D |
|---|---|---|---|---|---|---|---|---|---|---|---|---|
| Temperature (°C) | 24 | 24 | 27 | 31 | 34 | 36 | 36 | 36 | 35 | 32 | 28 | 25 |
| Rainfall (mm) | 21 | 1 | 6 | 12 | 1 | 0 | 1 | 6 | 5 | 14 | 22 | 21 |

Average annual rainfall = 110 millimetres
Temperatures are average (mean) for each month
Average daily temperature: Max 43 °C Min 18 °C
Average relative humidity: 46%

Alice Springs (24°S 134°E ), Australia; Altitude: 545 metres

| | J | F | M | A | M | J | J | A | S | O | N | D |
|---|---|---|---|---|---|---|---|---|---|---|---|---|
| Temperature (°C) | 28 | 28 | 25 | 20 | 15 | 13 | 12 | 15 | 18 | 23 | 26 | 28 |
| Rainfall (mm) | 38 | 37 | 30 | 13 | 14 | 12 | 12 | 8 | 7 | 18 | 22 | 32 |

Average annual rainfall = 243 millimetres
Temperatures are average (mean) for each month
Average daily temperature: Max 36 °C Min 4 °C
Average relative humidity: 19%

**TASK 1:** Study Source A

a  Describe the scene in the photo.
b  Use an atlas to describe the location of Makkah and Alice Springs.
c  Look at the climate data. Explain how both meet the criteria for being classified as having a hot desert climate.
d  Describe the similarities and differences between the two sets of climate data. Explain the difference in temperature distribution.
e  Suggest any difficulties facing plants, animals and people who need to survive in these environments. Refer to the photo and climate data.

Theme 2: Topic 42

### C  A hot desert food web

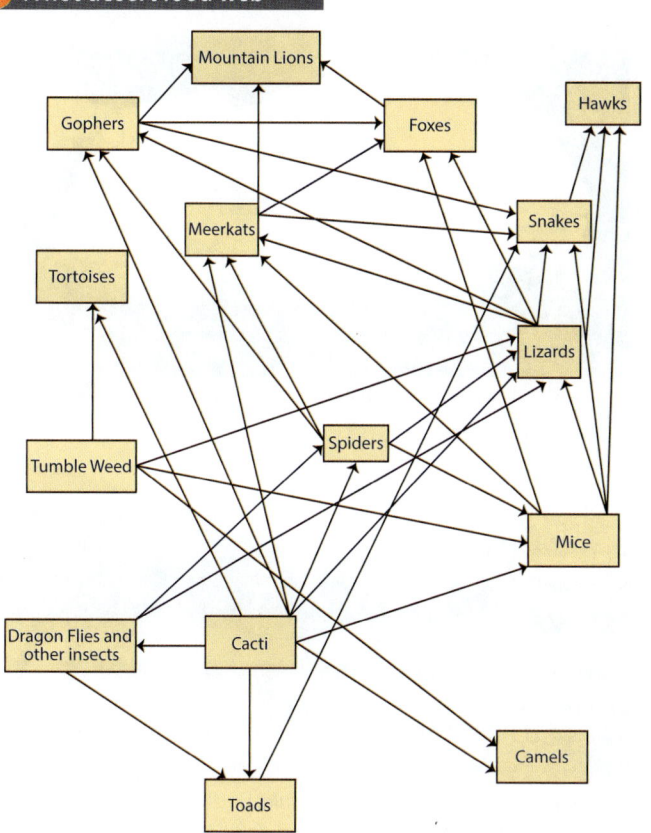

*Food web showing: Mountain Lions, Gophers, Foxes, Hawks, Meerkats, Snakes, Tortoises, Lizards, Tumble Weed, Spiders, Mice, Dragon Flies and other insects, Cacti, Camels, Toads.*

**TASK 2:** Study **Source B**

a  Match the **Beginnings ...** and **... endings** in two different tables: one for plants and one for animals.

b  Draw an annotated sketch showing your design for a plant or animal that would survive the conditions found in a hot desert.

**TASK 3:** Study **Source C**

a  Name **one** example of each of the following:
  - a producer
  - a primary consumer
  - a secondary consumer
  - a tertiary consumer.

b  Draw **one** food chain that involves four trophic levels from producer to tertiary consumer.

c  Imagine all the snakes are taken out of this food web. Describe any benefits or problems that this change to food chains might cause for some plants and animals.

**TASK 4:** Study **Source D**

a  Describe changes that will affect plants and animals in hot desert ecosystems. Explain your choices.

b  Suggest advantages and disadvantages of any of these changes for hot desert ecosystems and for people who live and work in them.

### D  Desert ecosystems face changes

Less rainfall and more drought will increase desertification and extend desert areas. People may have to migrate into more crowded areas.

Increased development of settlements and roads as countries develop their economies will change the nomadic way of life.

Many scientists think that hot deserts are ideal places to develop solar energy, as they receive intense sunlight and have plenty of space to build solar farms.

Increased winds will blow more sand grains onto agricultural land. Food supplies will suffer.

Tourists are looking for exciting desert activities such as camel trekking, off-road dune buggying, and star-gazing. Local people earn good money as guides, camel owners or buggy drivers.

Diverting rivers for irrigation or HEP reservoirs will reduce water flow through desert areas. People may migrate into towns for water supplies.

Modern mines excavate below the water table and pump out water, making it lower. Abandoned mines leave copper, lead and nitrate to pollute drinking water and affect irrigation as well as plants and animals. Each mine causes dust, noise and damage. Roads and oil and gas pipelines also affect the desert ecosystem.

People have lived and worked in hot deserts for thousands of years. Nomads have moved their herds of sheep, goats and camels to find water or settle in semi-permanent oases, where the water table reaches the surface. Camel trains have trekked across the Sahara Desert carrying gold, ivory and other goods to the south and, in previous centuries, returned with slaves. Where a river is close by, some irrigation has allowed people to carry out subsistence farming and settle in villages and market towns.

Cambridge IGCSE Geography  Climate and natural vegetation

# Case Study

## A hot desert – the Sahara and Mali

### The Sahara and the Sahel

The Sahara, sprawling across north Africa, is the world's largest and hottest desert – it covers roughly the same area as the USA. About one-quarter is covered by sand desert – known as ergs. The rest consists of gravel-strewn plains called reg and areas of barren rocks called hamada. Fossil evidence shows the desert used to be wetter 1000 years ago, but human activity and climate change – through natural and human causes – have turned the Sahara into a true desert. Today the Sahara is growing even larger, spreading to the south due to more overgrazing and deforestation. This moving edge of the desert is called the Sahel – an Arabic word that means 'fringe'. This is where desertification is increasing.

**TASK 1: Study Source A and an atlas**

a Describe the distribution of rainfall from north to south. Use figures in your answer.

b List all the countries in which the Sahel can be found.

c How will desertification affect these countries if the 300 mm isohyet moves further south?

**TASK 2: Study Source B**

a What are the causes of desertification?

b How is this different from land degradation?

c Explain how:
- the lack of rain since 1969 has led to the Sahel extending south
- population pressure has led to the Sahel extending south.

**TASK 3: Study Source C and an atlas**

a Describe the location of Mali. Refer to lines of latitude, neighbouring countries, the Sahara Desert and the Sahel in your answer.

b Describe and suggest reasons why the population of Mali is not evenly distributed.

**TASK 4: Study Source D**

a Draw a climate graph for Timbuktu. Use the same scales on the axes as used for Monument Valley on page 123.

b Compare and contrast the two hot desert climates.

c How have the fennec fox and the acacia tree adapted to survive in northern Mali?

**A  The desert moves south**

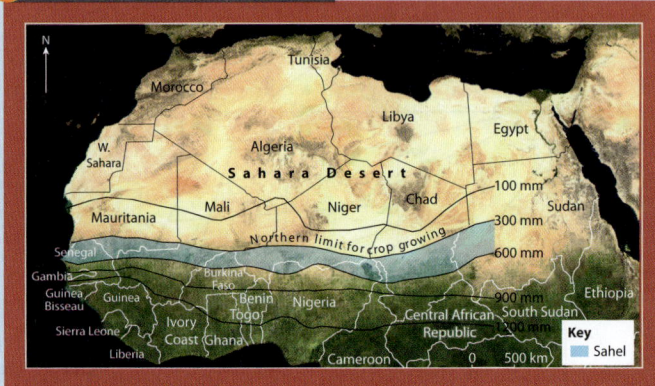

*A camel train travelling from Timbuktu to Taoudenni to exchange goods for salt*

**B  The changing Sahel**

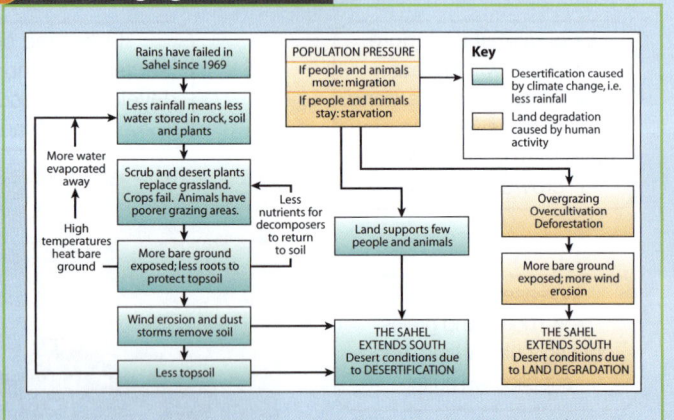

The Sahel is a semi-arid belt of poor, dry soil 300–500 km wide from north to south. It stretches from west to east across north Africa between the Sahara Desert and the savanna grasslands. In the Sahel, average rainfall ranges from 300 to 600 mm per year. When – and if – it rains, up to 90 per cent of the moisture evaporates. Drought is natural to the Sahel but desertification and land degradation by people have moved the limit for growing crops and grazing animals further south each year. Countries like Mali now have even less inhabitable land to survive on.

# Case Study: A hot desert – the Sahara and Mali

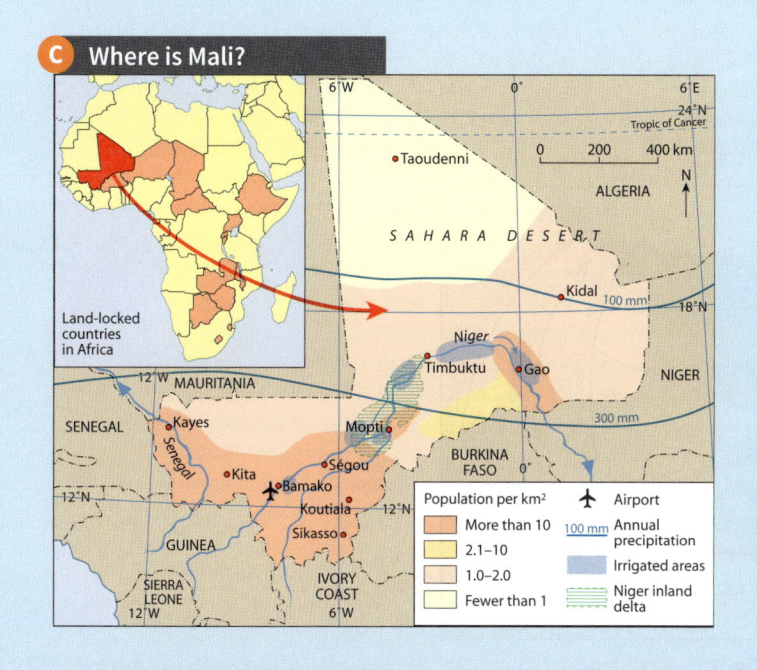

## C  Where is Mali?

## Mali – a land-locked country

Once home to one of Africa's greatest empires, Mali is a vast, land-locked country nestled between the Sahara Desert and six neighbouring countries in West Africa. It is the largest country in West Africa but one of the poorest countries in the world. Bordering the Sahel region of West Africa in the north, 65 per cent of Mali's land is desert or semi-desert. In these areas Malians suffer from periods of drought and widespread food shortages. Population density is only 5 per km². It is an extreme environment for plants, wildlife and people to survive in.

The Niger river is the most important feature in Mali. It provides a reliable water supply and is a vital transport route for goods and people. The Niger's high-water flood season is from August to December.

## D  Surviving the desert climate

The fennec fox is a mammal and is the world's smallest fox. It has enormous ears to help radiate heat to help it stay cool. It lives deep in the ground in long, cool burrows and emerges around dusk to hunt when the day is less hot. Most of northern Mali has less than 100 mm of rainfall a year – sometimes none. In most places the main source of moisture for animals is dew. The desert is fiercely hot by day but can freeze at night. Most animals are small so they can lose heat more easily, as their surface area is large compared with their size.

The acacia tree has developed a long, shallow root system which enables it to find moisture. It has thorny leaves to prevent water loss, and its crown is wide so the foliage can absorb the maximum amount of sunlight. Smaller shrubs and cacti have little foliage above ground but rely on long or deep roots and fleshy stems for water storage.

| Timbuktu, Mali (17°N 3°W) | J | F | M | A | M | J | J | A | S | O | N | D |
|---|---|---|---|---|---|---|---|---|---|---|---|---|
| Temperature (°C) | 23 | 24 | 26 | 31 | 35 | 34 | 34 | 33 | 33 | 32 | 27 | 23 |
| Rainfall (mm) | 0 | 0 | 10 | 0 | 14 | 30 | 77 | 50 | 20 | 17 | 0 | 0 |

*Average annual rainfall = 218 mm     Temperatures are average (mean) for each month*

Signs like this, found all over West Africa, indicate the remoteness of Timbuktu from other places. It was founded as a trading post in the 11th century midway between the north and south of West Africa.

**TASK 5: Study Source D**

Imagine you are to lead a camel train from Timbuktu to Taoudenni. The round trip will take four weeks.

a  At what time of year would you **not** go? Why?

b  Discuss and list the equipment and supplies you would need.

c  How would you ensure the health and safety of the people and the camels?

# Cambridge IGCSE Geography — Exam-Style Questions

## Exam-Style Question on Rivers

a  Study Fig. 1, which shows a river and the land around it.

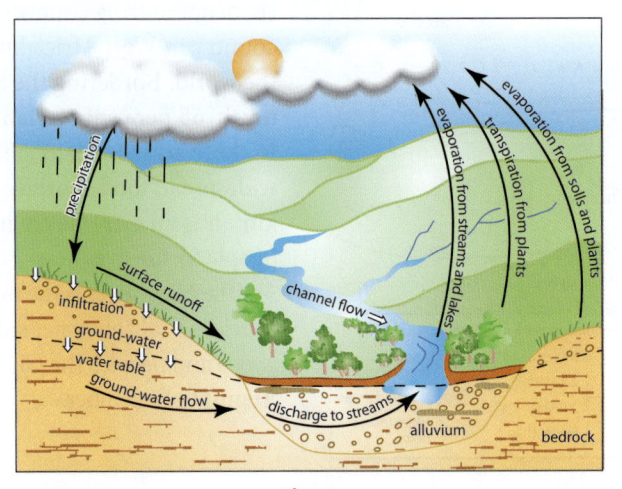

**Fig. 1**

   i   Which one of the following describes what Fig. 1 shows?
       - Causes of flooding
       - Formation of river landforms
       - Methods of river erosion
       - Processes operating in a drainage basin [1]
   ii  What is meant by:
       - evaporation
       - groundwater flow? [2]
   iii Give **three** ways in which the river shown is likely to change as it flows downstream from its source. [3]
   iv  Use ideas from Fig. 1 to explain why some rivers are more likely to flood than others. [4]

b  Study Photograph A, which shows a waterfall.

**Photograph A**

   i   Describe the features of the waterfall shown in Photograph A. [3]
   ii  Draw a fully labelled diagram (or sequence of diagrams) to explain how river processes form a waterfall. [5]

c  For a named example of a river you have studied, describe how it is managed to reduce flooding hazards. [7]

[Total 25 marks]

# Exam-Style Questions

## Exam-Style Question on Earthquakes and Volcanoes

a   Study Fig. 2, which shows tectonic plates and earthquakes around the Pacific Ocean.

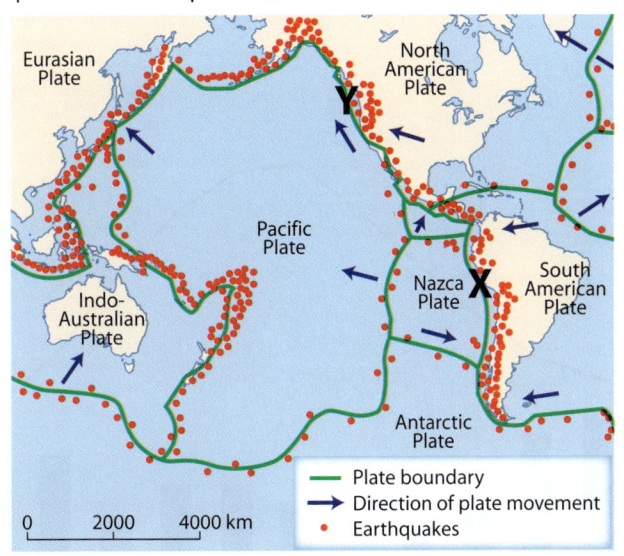

**Fig. 2**

| i | Define the term *tectonic plate*. | [1] |
|---|---|---|
| ii | Name the type of plate boundaries at each of X and Y on Fig. 2. | [2] |
| iii | Explain why earthquakes occur at plate boundaries. | [3] |
| iv | Describe what can be done to reduce the impacts of earthquakes in large urban areas | [4] |

b   Study Fig. 3, information about a volcanic eruption.

### Volcanic eruption creates new land off coast of Japan

A volcanic eruption has created a new island in the sea off the coast of Nishinoshima, a small, uninhabited island which lies close to the destructive plate boundary between the Pacific plate and Eurasian plates. Television footage on Thursday showed heavy smoke, ash and rocks exploding from the crater, as steam billowed into the sky. The last recorded volcanic eruption in this area was in the mid-1970s. Much of the volcanic activity occurs under the sea, which is thousands of metres deep at the site of the Izu-Ogasawara-Marianas Trench.

**Adapted from** *Associated Press, The Guardian*, 21 November 2013

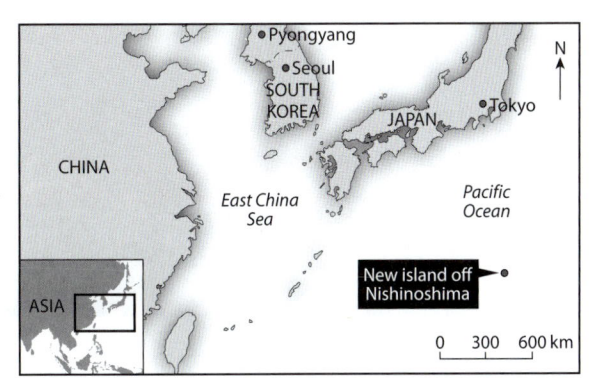

**Fig. 3**

| i | Describe the location of the new island referred to in Fig. 3. | [3] |
|---|---|---|
| ii | Suggest reasons why the volcanic eruption described in Fig. 3 occurred. | [5] |

c   For a named area or country, explain why people live close to volcanoes.  [7]

**[Total 25 marks]**

# Cambridge IGCSE Geography — Exam-Style Questions

## Exam-Style Question on Climate and Vegetation

**a** Study Fig. 4, a climate graph for part of the Coachella Valley, an area of hot desert in Southern California, USA.

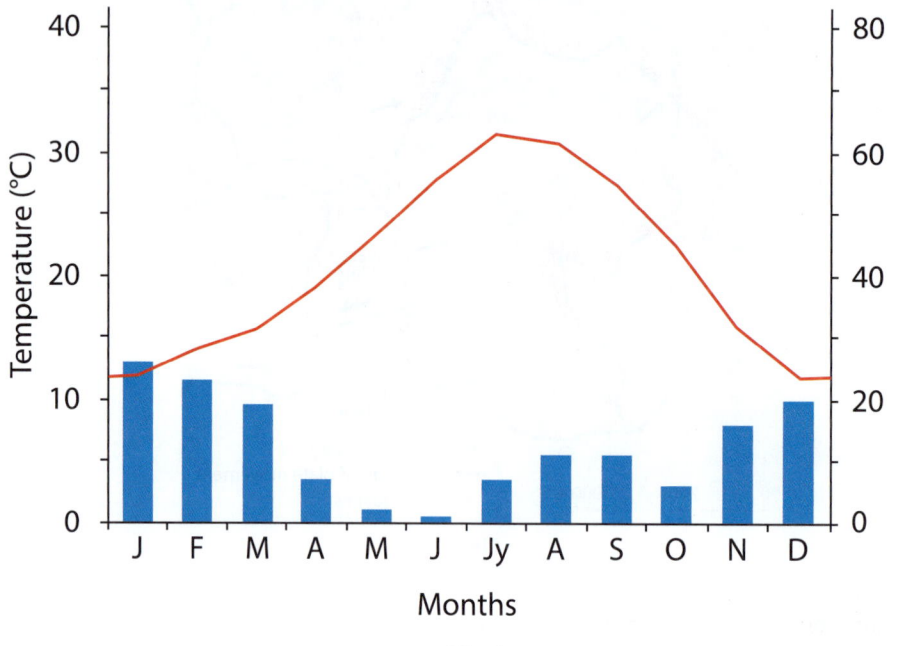

**Fig. 4**

    **i** Use Fig. 4 to estimate the total precipitation for the year. [1]
    **ii** Describe the difference between the climate of January and June in the Coachella Valley [2]
    **iii** How and why do temperatures change between day and night in a desert? [3]
    **iv** Explain why tropical deserts are dry. [4]

**b** Study Photograph B, which shows an area in a hot desert.

**Photograph B**

    **i** Describe **three** features of the area of hot desert shown in Photograph B. [3]
    **ii** Explain how natural vegetation is able to survive in a desert. [5]

**c** The equatorial climate is another climatic zone.

For a named example you have studied, describe the ecosystem of an area with an equatorial climate. [7]

[Total 25 marks]

# Exam-Style Question on Coasts

a   Study Photograph C, which shows an area of coastline.

**Photograph C**

   i    Name a feature formed by coastal erosion that can be seen in Photograph C. [1]
   ii   Give **two** pieces of evidence from the photograph that attempts have been made to manage coastal erosion. [2]
   iii  Suggest why management of coastal erosion is necessary in the area shown in the photograph. [3]
   iv   Name and describe **four** different processes by which coastal erosion takes place. [4]

b   Study Fig. 5, a map showing longshore drift.

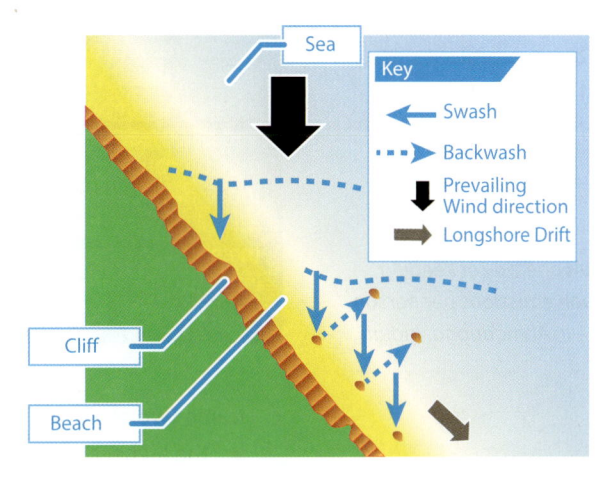

**Fig. 5**

   i    Define the following terms:
        - Prevailing wind direction
        - Swash
        - Backwash. [3]
   ii   Explain how the processes shown in Fig. 5 may result in the formation of a sand spit. [5]

c   Describe the opportunities offered by a named area of coastline you have studied. [7]

[Total 25 marks]

# Cambridge IGCSE Geography — Global Theme

## 2. Global Theme: Reducing carbon emissions

### Enhanced global warming

There have been cold and warm periods throughout the Earth's history; global cooling and warming are natural phenomena. Nobody is really sure, however, how much human activity is responsible for additional 'enhanced' global warming. This is the extra global warming and increased temperatures that people may have been responsible for in the past 250 years due to industrialisation and using carbon-based energy and fuel sources. These increased greenhouse gas emissions, especially carbon dioxide. As a greenhouse gas $CO_2$ traps heat leaving the Earth's surface, causing temperatures to rise.

**B  The top six polluters**

| Country | % of world's total carbon emissions | Emissions per person (tonnes) | Amount from burning fossil fuels (million tonnes) | Amount from transport (million tonnes) |
|---|---|---|---|---|
| China | 22.9 | 4.9 | 6550 | 334 |
| USA | 15.5 | 18.4 | 5596 | 1456 |
| India | 5.1 | 1.25 | 1428 | 121 |
| Russia | 4.9 | 11.2 | 1394 | 112 |
| Japan | 3.5 | 9 | 1151 | 203 |
| Germany | 2.2 | 9.8 | 804 | 140 |
| WORLD | 100 | | | |

Sources: *The Atlas of Climate Change (2011)* plus various sources

*Here's one way of keeping carbon emissions per person low – in Ahmadabad, India!*

**A  The Kyoto Protocol**

### Agreed targets at Kyoto

In December 1997 the Third United Nations Conference on Climate Change took place in Kyoto, Japan. The conference adopted the Kyoto Protocol which agreed on the following:

- MEDCs to reduce greenhouse gas emissions by 5% below 1990 levels by 2012.
- LEDCs to continue to reduce carbon levels to 1990 levels by 2005.

*Air pollution from a factory in Moscow, Russia. The country was the third highest polluter in 1990 but carbon emissions are less now.*

**C  Do as we say, not as we did!**

Few countries met their targets for 2005 or 2012 when the Kyoto Protocol expired. One barrier to progress is that many of today's MEDCs became wealthy by developing industry and transport using fossil fuels, especially coal and oil. These are responsible for the air pollution that may be causing global warming. Now LEDCs, especially those developing rapidly such as the BRICS countries (Brazil, Russia, India, China and South Africa), are following the same route and do not want to be held back by international agreements that restrict developing their economies by not using fossil fuels.

---

**TASK 1: Study Source A**

a  Why is it important to reduce carbon emissions?
b  How were targets set at Kyoto different for MEDCs and LEDCs? Suggest why.

**TASK 2: Study Source B**

a  Draw a horizontal bar graph to show the countries in rank order of percentage of the world's total carbon emissions produced.
b  On the graph rank the countries from 1 (most carbon emitted per person) to 6 (least carbon emitted per person). Comment on your findings.

c  Name **two** countries for each of the following:
- the highest emissions per person.
- the highest amount of carbon emitted from fossil fuels.
- the highest amount of carbon emitted from transport.

**TASK 3: Study Source C**

a  Suggest why it is difficult for countries to reduce their carbon dioxide emissions.
b  Why are countries such as China and India reluctant to reduce their emissions? Can you justify their view?

# Theme 3:
# Economic Development

# 43 Indicators of development

## How is development measured?

Development measures how economically, socially, culturally or technologically advanced a country is. It can be measured so that countries can be compared with each other, or the same country's progress can be compared over a period of time. The aspects of development that can be measured are **economic development** and **social development**.

Economic development measures a country's wealth. Social development measures the access the people in a country have to wealth, education, food, health and political freedom.

There are a number of ways in which development can be measured. These are known as development indicators.

**Economic indicators include:**

- **Gross Domestic Product (GDP):** the total value of goods and services produced by a country in a year.
- **Gross National Income (GNI):** the total income of a country, including earnings from abroad. This is also known as **Gross National Product (GNP)**.
- **GNI per capita (per person):** the country's GNI divided by its population.

**Social indicators include:**

- life expectancy: the average age to which a person lives.
- infant mortality rate: the number of babies, per 1000 live births, who die under the age of one.
- the percentage of people living below US$1 per day.
- the percentage of the population with access to clean water and sanitation.
- the average number of people per doctor.
- the percentage of children and young people who attend primary school, secondary school and higher education.
- literacy rate: the percentage of adults who can read and write.
- the percentage of the population who have possessions such as mobile phones, television and the Internet.

**A** Aspects of development

**B** Relationship between GNI per capita and life expectancy

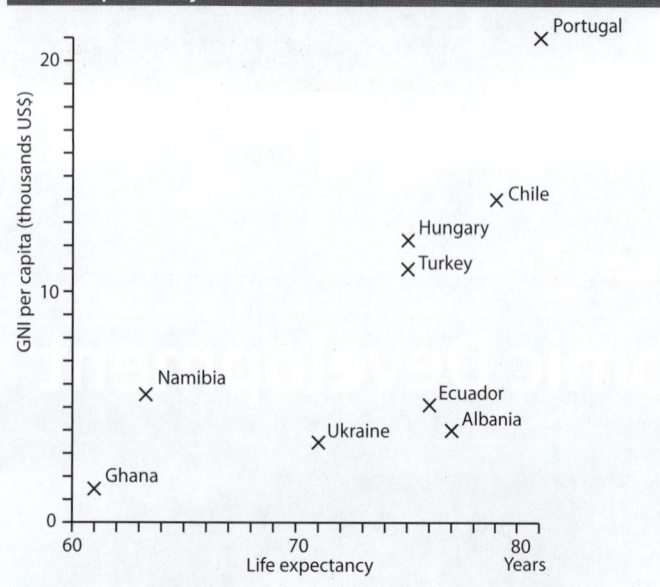

**TASK 1: Study Source A**

For each photograph describe the aspect of development that is shown and explain how it can be measured.

**TASK 2: Study Source B**

a What relationship is shown by the graph between GNI per capita and life expectancy?

b Explain why there is a relationship between GNI per capita and life expectancy.

**TASK 3**

Carry out a short investigation into the link between GNI per capita and literacy by using statistics from http://data.worldbank.org/

You will need to follow these steps:

a Choose a representative sample of countries.
b Obtain the statistics from the website.
c Present the information using a scatter graph.
d Analyse the graph and state your conclusions.

Theme 3: Topic 43

## Human Development Index

The Human Development Index (HDI) was created by the United Nations Development Programme in 1990. It uses a number of development indicators to give each country in the world a score on an index from 0 to 1. Countries with a score close to 1 are the most developed while those with the lowest score are the least developed.

The index is created by combining indicators of life expectancy, education and income. It classifies the countries of the world into four broad bands – very high, high, medium and low human development.

### C Components of the HDI

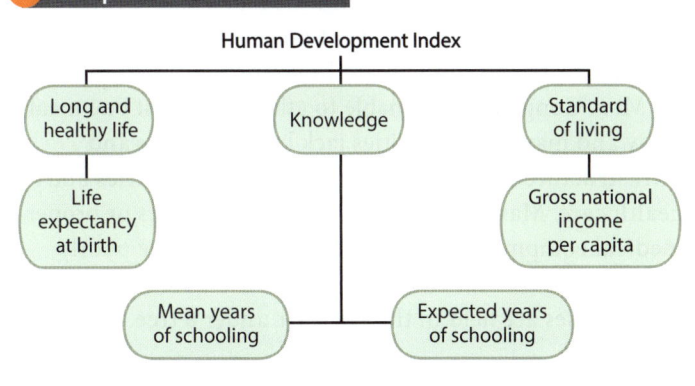

Human Development Index
- Long and healthy life
  - Life expectancy at birth
- Knowledge
  - Mean years of schooling
  - Expected years of schooling
- Standard of living
  - Gross national income per capita

### D HDI Rankings of 20 selected countries (2013)

**Very High Development**

| Rank | Country | HDI Index |
|------|---------|-----------|
| 1 | Norway | 0.955 |
| 3 | USA | 0.937 |
| 10 | Japan | 0.912 |
| 26 | UK | 0.875 |
| 36 | Qatar | 0.834 |

**High Development**

| Rank | Country | HDI Index |
|------|---------|-----------|
| 55 | Russia | 0.788 |
| 57 | Saudi Arabia | 0.782 |
| 64= | Malaysia | 0.769 |
| 64= | Libya | 0.769 |
| 85 | Brazil | 0.73 |

**Medium Development**

| Rank | Country | HDI Index |
|------|---------|-----------|
| 101 | China | 0.699 |
| 103 | Thailand | 0.69 |
| 112 | Egypt | 0.622 |
| 121 | South Africa | 0.629 |
| 136 | India | 0.554 |

**Low Development**

| Rank | Country | HDI Index |
|------|---------|-----------|
| 161 | Uganda | 0.456 |
| 165 | Gambia | 0.439 |
| 173 | Ethiopia | 0.396 |
| 175 | Afghanistan | 0.374 |
| 186 | D.R. Congo | 0.304 |

### E Global variation in HDI

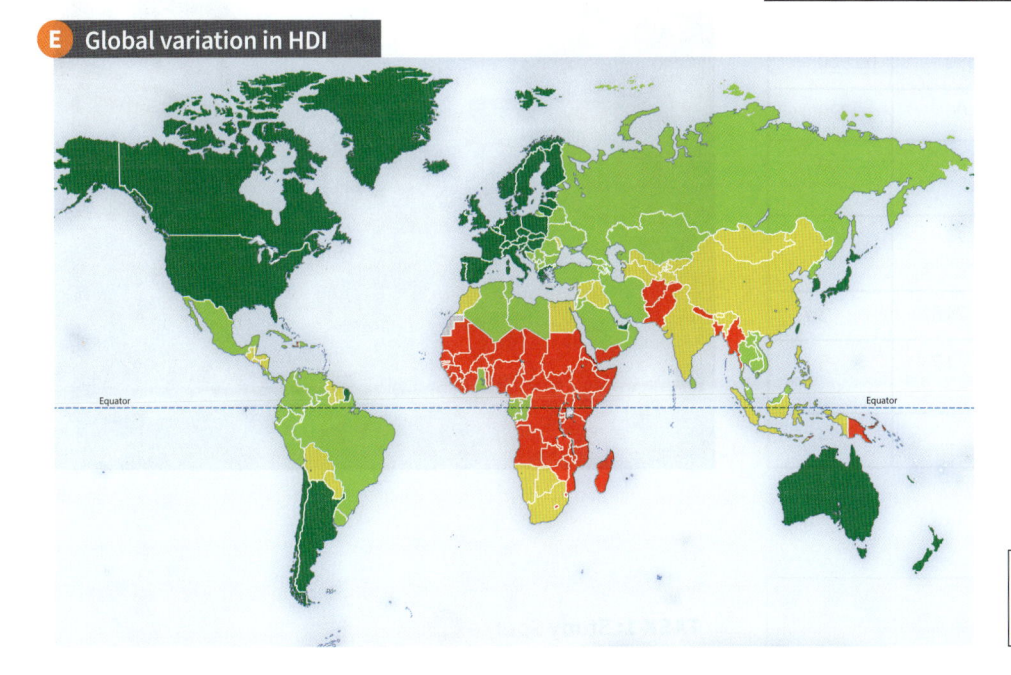

HDI
- 0.8 and over (very high development)
- 0.7 - 0.79 (high development)
- 0.5 - 0.69 (medium development)
- below 0.5 (low development)

---

**TASK 4: Study Source C**

a Explain how HDI is different from the indicators of development described on page 134.

b What are the advantages and disadvantages of using HDI as an indicator of development?

**TASK 5: Study Sources D and E and an atlas**

a Describe the distribution of those countries with:
- very high development
- high development
- medium development
- low development.

In your answer you should refer to examples.

b Are there any countries in Source D that surprise you? Explain why.

c Use the Internet to find out the latest HDI figures for your own country. How is your country classified according to the HDI figure?

**Cambridge IGCSE Geography** — **Development**

## 44 Identifying inequalities

### Inequalities between countries

The Democratic Republic of the Congo, a country in central Africa with a population of over 75 million, is the least developed country in the world, according to its Human Development Index (HDI) of 0.304. In contrast Norway, a country in northern Europe with a population of just over 5 million, is the most developed, with a Human Development Index of 0.955.

Norway, like many other countries in Europe, has an advanced economy with a long history of economic and commercial development. Large amounts of income are earned from obtaining and processing its raw materials, especially oil, and there is a great variety of manufacturing industries and commercial organisations.

The Democratic Republic of the Congo is a former Belgian colony which has a great variety of natural resources; however, much of its population live in extreme poverty and unemployment is high as the country's infrastructure was only developed for the purpose of extracting raw materials. Since its **independence** in 1960 it has suffered several civil wars and a long, brutal dictatorship. Since 1994, over 5.4 million Congolese have died due to armed conflicts in the country.

Most Congolese are unable to afford even just one meal a day and many communities lack basic facilities and infrastructures such as community centres, libraries and health care. Many hospitals lack beds, medicines or proper medical equipment. The schools that do exist are poorly resourced, most students have no books and in many rural areas classes are held in the open air under a tree.

**A  Factfile – D.R. Congo and Norway**

| Indicator | D.R. Congo | Norway |
|---|---|---|
| Human Development Index | 0.304 | 0.955 |
| Life expectancy (years) | 49 | 80.44 |
| Adult literacy (percentage) | 67 | 100 |
| GNI per capita (US$) | 390 | 66 960 |
| People per doctor | 9100 | 320 |
| Access to an improved drinking water source (percentage) | 45 | 100 |
| Access to improved sanitation (percentage) | 24 | 100 |
| Infant mortality rate (per 1000) | 74.87 | 3.47 |
| Population with access to Internet (percentage) | 1.7 | 95 |
| Car ownership (per 1000 people) | 5 | 584 |

**B  Alesund, Norway**

**C  Kinshasa, D.R. Congo**

### TASK 1: Study Source A

a  Use the indicators of development to describe the differences in the level of development between D.R. Congo and Norway.

b  Suggest reasons why Norway is more developed than D.R. Congo.

### TASK 2: Study Sources B and C

a  Use only evidence in the photographs to compare Alesund, Norway and Kinshasa, D.R. Congo.

b  Find additional pictures of Alesund and Kinshasa and use them to extend your answer to a.

# Inequalities within countries

In all countries some areas develop faster because of human and physical advantages and become the **core area**, while other areas become the less important **periphery**. Usually urban areas develop as the core, especially the capital city, and rural areas develop as the periphery. Core areas are likely to experience greater growth, investment and inward migration, while the periphery may well be exploited and suffer from lack of investment.

Core areas usually have areas of flat land that make construction easy. Good transport links, e.g. international airports, roads and railways are located there and they are the areas where there are the best education and health care facilities (e.g. universities and major hospitals).

## Core and periphery in Indonesia

Indonesia is a country consisting of over 17 000 islands, about 9000 of which are inhabited. On some islands many people are crowded into a relatively small area, including the capital city of Jakarta on the island of Java which forms part of the core area of Indonesia. Many of the other inhabited islands are under-populated and underdeveloped and they form the periphery of Indonesia. During the late 20th century the Indonesian government gave people incentives to move from the over-populated islands of Java and Bali to the islands of West Papua, Kalimantan, Sumatra and Sulawesi. The purpose of this **transmigration** was to:

- reduce the poverty and over-population on Java
- provide opportunities for hard-working poor people
- provide a workforce to make better use of the natural resources of the underdeveloped outer islands.

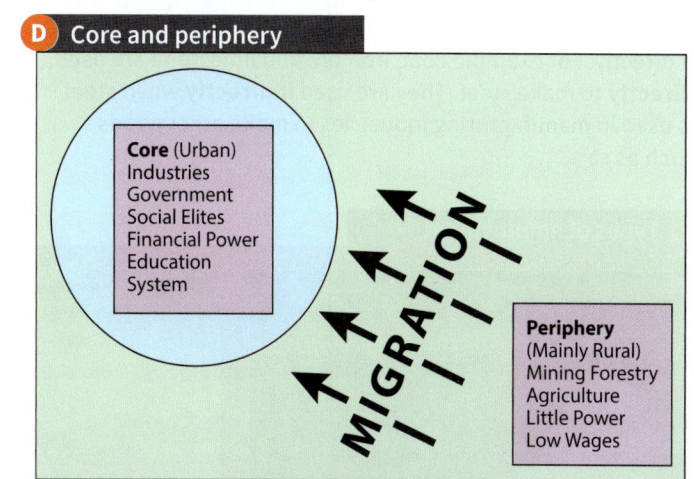

**D Core and periphery**

Core (Urban)
Industries
Government
Social Elites
Financial Power
Education System

MIGRATION

Periphery (Mainly Rural)
Mining Forestry
Agriculture
Little Power
Low Wages

**E Inequalities in Indonesia**

| Island | % of Indonesia's land | % of Indonesia's population | Human development index |
|---|---|---|---|
| Java | 6.9 | 60.2 | 0.716 |
| Bali | 0.3 | 1.6 | 0.719 |
| Sumatra | 24.7 | 20.3 | 0.720 |
| Kalimantan | 28.1 | 4.8 | 0.738 |
| Sulawesi | 9.9 | 7.2 | 0.751 |
| West Papua | 22.0 | 0.8 | 0.679 |

**TASK 3: Study Source D**

Describe how and explain why there are inequalities within countries.

**TASK 4: Study Source E**

a Draw a graph or graphs using the statistics about the percentage of population, the area and the HDI of the six Indonesian islands.

b What does the graph(s) show about inequality within Indonesia?

# 45 Classifying production

## Sectors of production

Employment is classified into four sectors:

**Primary:** the part of a country's economy that grows or extracts raw materials. It includes fishing, agriculture, forestry and mining.

**Secondary:** the part of a country's economy that is concerned with the manufacturing and processing of goods. It uses the products of primary industry either directly or indirectly. For example coal, iron ore and limestone are used **directly** to make steel. They are used **indirectly** when steel is used in manufacturing industries to make other goods such as cars.

**Tertiary:** the part of a country's economy that provides services. People may pay directly for a private service, e.g. paying for a taxi. The government, using money taken indirectly through taxes, may provide public services such as schools and hospitals.

**Quaternary:** the part of a country's economy that provides information services, such as computing, information and communication technologies (ICT), consultancy (offering advice to businesses), research and development, and financial services.

The quaternary sector is sometimes included with the tertiary sector, as they are both service sectors.

### A Types of employment

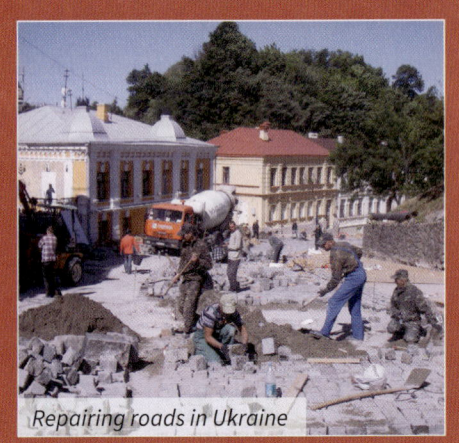

Scientist in Jordan

Rice farmer in Indonesia

Cutting stone slabs in Lesotho

Drying tuna in the Maldives

Waitress in China

Repairing roads in Ukraine

**TASK 1: Study Source A**
a Describe the work being done by each of the people in the photos.
b Decide which of the photos show primary, secondary, tertiary and quaternary employment. Explain your choices.

**TASK 2**
Collect adverts for and photographs of different types of jobs from the media. Decide whether the jobs are for the primary, secondary, tertiary or quaternary sectors of the economy. These could be mounted on a wall display or presented as a PowerPoint presentation.

# Hi-tech – a growing sector

Hi-tech industries involve making and using silicon chips, computers, semi-conductor devices and computer-controlled machinery. They use micro-electronics to make computers, pharmaceuticals, communications equipment and equipment for the aerospace industries. Hi-tech industries have been growing rapidly.

**Source C** shows 'Silicon Valley' near San Francisco in California, USA. This is one of the earliest concentrations of hi-tech industry and this is still one of the most important locations in the sector.

Silicon Valley lies along the south side of San Francisco Bay, from Palo Alto in the west to San Jose in the east. Companies involved in the research, development and manufacturing of micro-electronics have been present in the region since the second half of the 20th century. Many software companies, internet-related businesses and companies in the fields of biotechnology and aerospace are also located here. In this area average incomes are among the highest in the USA.

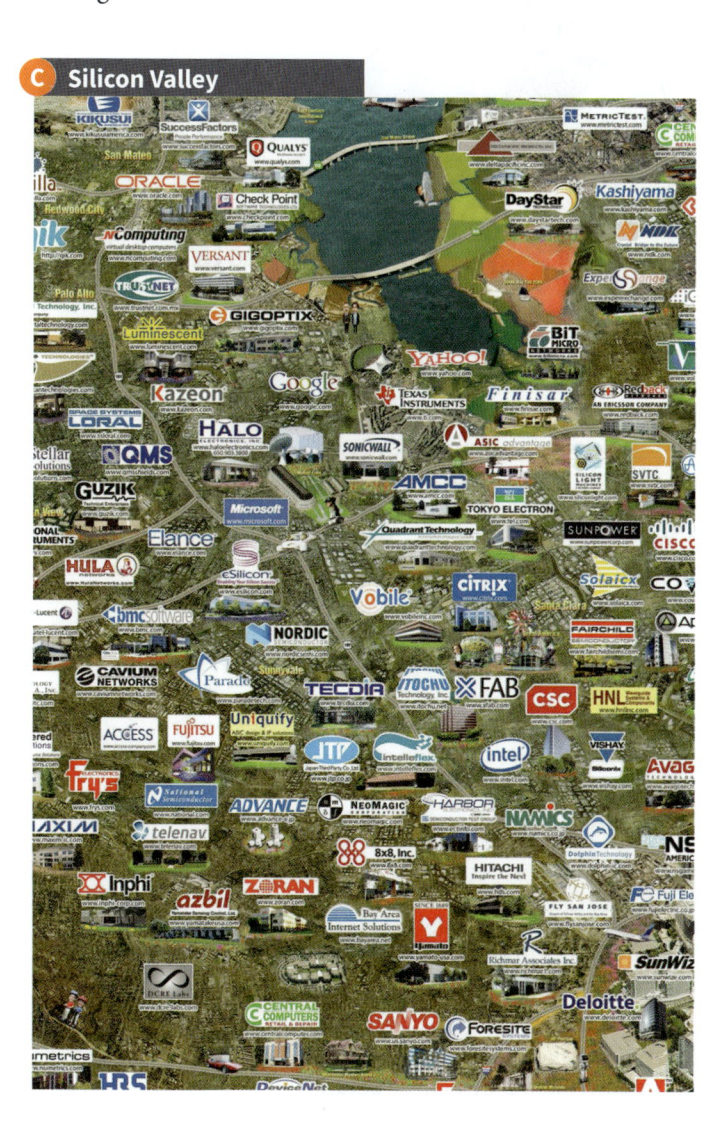

**B  Products of hi-tech industry**

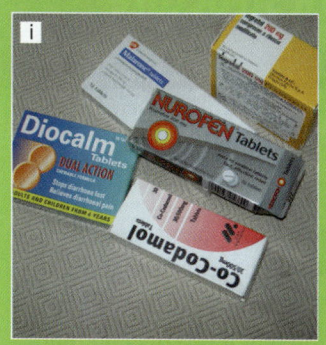

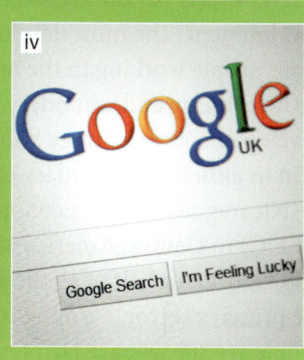

i

ii

iii

iv

**C  Silicon Valley**

### TASK 3: Study Source B

a  Identify the products of hi-tech industry that are shown in each of the photographs i to iv.

b  Explain why industries producing products such as those shown in the photographs are growing rapidly.

c  Explain why the firms producing the products shown in the photographs employ people in each of the secondary, tertiary and quaternary sectors.

### TASK 4: Study Source C

Choose a major company that is located in Silicon Valley.

a  Use the Internet to carry out research about the company and write a short paragraph describing the business in which it is involved.

b  Describe the exact location of the company.

c  Explain why the company located in Silicon Valley.

d  List **three** different types of job that the company will offer in Silicon Valley.

# 46 Employment structure varies

## Employment structure and development

The employment structure of a country shows the percentage of workers in the primary, secondary and tertiary/quaternary sectors. The workforce is divided in different ways in countries at different levels of economic development. The most developed countries usually have more people working in the tertiary/quaternary sector than in the primary and secondary sectors. However in the least developed countries more people work in the primary sector than in either the secondary or tertiary sectors.

Nicaragua is a Less Economically Developed Country (LEDC) in Central America with a GNI per capita of US$3960. Over half of all the working population work in the primary sector. Farming is important because many people are subsistence farmers, eating the food they produce; also crops such as fruit are a major export. Much of the work on farms is done by hand rather than by machinery.

Malaysia is a **Newly Industrialised Country (NIC)** in Asia with a GNI per capita of US$10 440. Almost half of its population works in secondary industry, not all of which is mechanised as the cost of workers is relatively low. Many people are employed in tertiary industries, partly because it has a growing tourist industry, but mainly because of improvements in services such as health care and education.

New Zealand is a More Economically Developed Country (MEDC) with a GNI per capita of US$35 520. It has a low proportion of people working in primary industry. This is partly because of mechanisation which has replaced the jobs of people in the primary and the secondary sectors. Also, New Zealand now imports many of its raw materials and manufactured goods as this is cheaper than producing them domestically. The tertiary sector is the main employment sector as many people work in hospitals, schools, offices and financial services. As people become wealthier and have more free time there is a greater demand for leisure services.

**A** Employment structure of selected countries

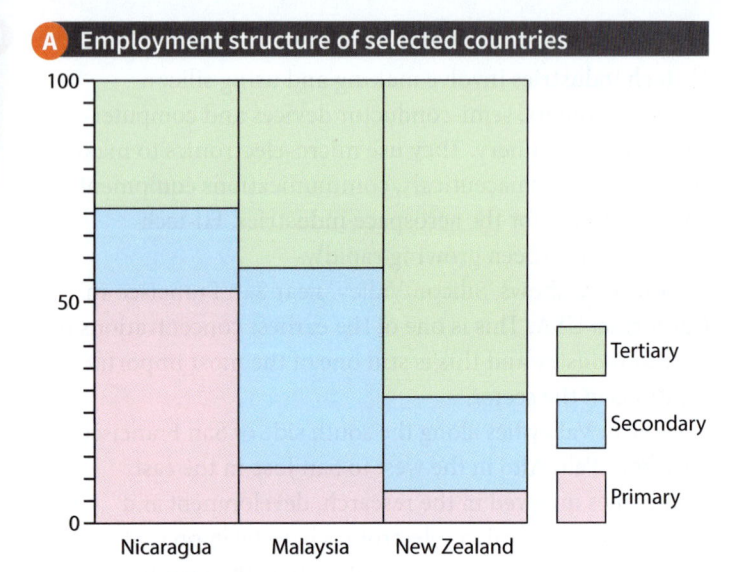

**B** Exports of Malaysia
1970
other, manufacturing, rubber, tin, oil/gas

2010
other, palm oil, textiles, chemicals, gas/oil, electronics

---

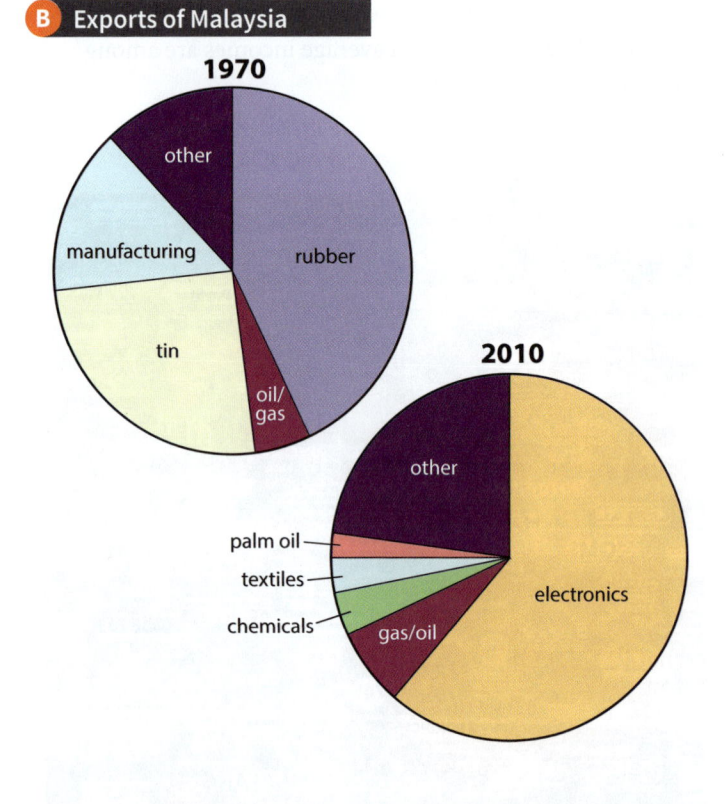

**TASK 1:** Study Source **A**
a Compare the employment structures of Nicaragua, Malaysia and New Zealand.
b Give reasons why the employment structure of Nicaragua differs from that of New Zealand.

**TASK 2:** Study Source **B**
a Describe how the exports of Malaysia have changed between 1970 and 2010.
b What do you think Malaysia's employment structure was like in 1970?
c How do the changes in Malaysia's exports help to explain its current employment structure?

Theme 3: Topic 46

## Changes in employment structure

Employment structures change over time as a country develops. In many countries in Western Europe in 1800 many people worked in the primary sector. During the Industrial Revolution many people were needed in the growing secondary sector and migrated to urban areas to work in coal mines or do jobs such as shipbuilding, working in steelworks and manufacturing textiles. This led to the growth of major industrial regions.

Since 1900 mechanisation has meant that machines could do most of the work that people previously did, so fewer people were needed to work on the land, in mines and in factories. Also raw materials, such as coal, began to run out or became too expensive to mine. Manufactured products, raw materials and food from other countries became more affordable so were imported, which led to a further reduction in primary and secondary sector employment.

Jobs increased in schools, hospitals, the leisure industry and shops so that by the year 2000 much of the workforce in most countries in Western Europe was employed in tertiary industries. Many workers prefer well paid, less dirty jobs to physical work on the land and in factories. In some of these countries quaternary industries have recently been established and this sector is growing as many firms want to carry out research and development for their products and take advantage of ICT opportunities, consultancy and financial services. Improvements in technology have encouraged industries such as micro-electronics and biotechnology to grow.

**E** Employment structure of Tunisia

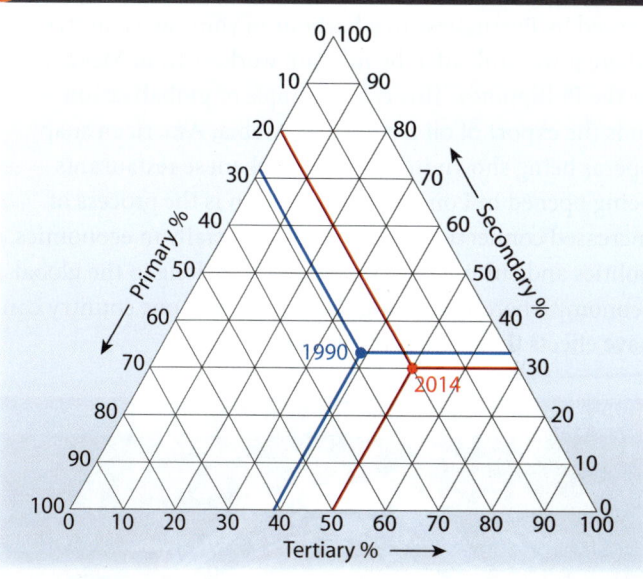

**C** Changing employment structure as a country develops

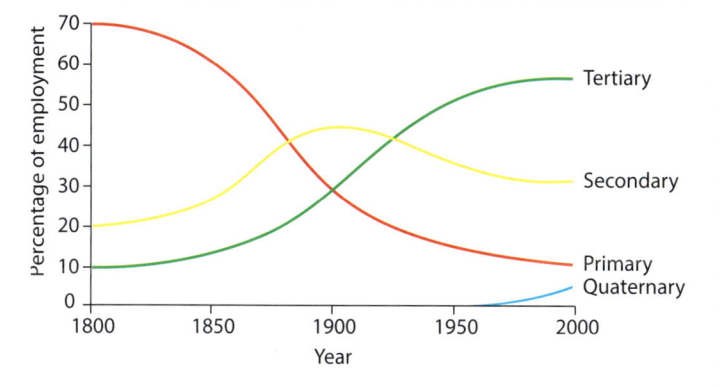

**D** Employment structure changes over time

|  | Primary | | Secondary | | Tertiary | |
|---|---|---|---|---|---|---|
|  | 1990 | 2014 | 1990 | 2014 | 1990 | 2014 |
| Tunisia | 28 | 20 | 33 | 30 | 39 | 50 |
| China | 72 | 43 | 15 | 25 | 12 | 32 |
| India | 54 | 28 | 16 | 29 | 30 | 43 |
| South Africa | 13 | 9 | 26 | 24 | 61 | 68 |

**TASK 3:** Study Source **C**
a Describe the changes in employment structure in Western Europe between 1800 and 2000.
b Explain:
- the reduction in primary sector employment
- the increase in secondary sector employment
- the increase in tertiary sector employment.
c Choose one other country from Source D or find data for the country in which you live. Compare the changes in employment structure with Tunisia.

**TASK 4:** Study Source **D**
a Place the countries in rank order for 2014, using employment structure as an indicator of economic development.
b Decide which country has made most progress with economic development since 1990. Give reasons for your choice.

**TASK 5:** Study Sources **D** and **E**
a Describe how Tunisia's employment structure has changed since 1990.
b Plot the information about the other countries in Source D on a copy of the triangular graph.

141

# Cambridge IGCSE Geography — Development

## 47 Globalisation

### What is globalisation?

If you look at the labels on your clothing you are likely to see that each garment was made in a country other than the one in which you are living. Before you bought it, your T-shirt it could have been made in Bangladesh with Indian cotton, shipped abroad on a French cargo ship crewed by Portuguese to a harbour in your own country, where it was unloaded by migrant workers from Mexico or the Philippines. This is an example of **globalisation** – so is the export of oil from Saudi Arabia, American soap operas being shown in Israel, and Lebanese restaurants being opened in London. Globalisation is the process of increased connection of countries, especially in economics, politics and culture. All countries now belong to the global economy where something that happens in one country can have effects throughout the world.

**A  Companies across the globe**

**B  Footballers playing in Europe (2012/13)**

| Competition | Country | Number of players | Players from home country | Players from other countries |
|---|---|---|---|---|
| Premier League | England | 470 | 163 | 307 |
| Serie A | Italy | 519 | 238 | 281 |
| Bundesliga | Germany | 429 | 201 | 228 |
| Ligue 1 | France | 494 | 271 | 223 |
| La Liga | Spain | 490 | 293 | 197 |
| Eredivisie | Netherlands | 399 | 248 | 151 |

### What has caused globalisation to occur?

Globalisation has been taking place for hundreds of years, but its speed has increased over the last half century due to:

- **increased trade** – trade is important to the economies of most countries around the world as companies rely on it to make large profits. International organisations promote **free trade** between countries and many countries have created free trade agreements with other countries.
- **labour availability and skills** – LEDCs have lower labour costs than MEDCs and many also have people with many skills. Industries that use lots of workers can take advantage of cheaper costs of labour and land, along with fewer government restrictions.
- **improvements in transport** – larger ships mean that the cost of transporting goods between countries has decreased and that goods and people can travel more quickly. People can travel internationally for work or leisure. Also money for investment can be moved electronically between countries.
- **quick communications** – the Internet and mobile technology has allowed greater communication between people in different countries. Miles of fibre-optic cable now connect the continents, allowing people around the world to communicate instantly through the World Wide Web. People can read information about foreign countries as easily as they read about their local news and become aware of incidents thousands of miles away in seconds.

**TASK 1: Study Source A**
a  Explain what is meant by globalisation. Use examples from the source.
b  Explain why globalisation has occurred. In your answer refer to:
  - technology
  - transnational corporations
  - economic factors.

**TASK 2: Study Source B**
a  Draw a suitable graph to show the information in Source B.
b  Explain how the information in Source B is an example of globalisation.
c  In a group prepare a presentation to explain how globalisation has changed **either** a sporting competition such as the English Premier League **or** another leisure activity.

# Theme 3: Topic 47

## Transnational corporations (TNCs)

The global spread of McDonald's has become a symbol of globalisation. Some things on the menu, such as the Big Mac, are the same all over the world.

The Hong Kong Shanghai Banking Corporation (HSBC) was set up in 1865 for people trading between China and the UK. Today, HSBC is the world's largest bank, with offices in 88 different countries.

The world's biggest companies are no longer national firms but transnational corporations which operate in many countries. Not only are markets for goods and services global, but also many businesses have set up offices, factories or shops in other countries. When companies based in MEDCs move factories and jobs to LEDCs, this is called outsourcing. They can pay lower wages, because the standard of living in LEDCs is much lower. Laws protecting workers' safety and the natural environment are less strict in LEDCs, which also lowers costs for the corporation.

Globalisation has **benefits**:

- Money is invested in LEDCs, providing new jobs and skills. They are able to develop their technology and people are able to improve their standard of living.
- TNCs bring wealth and foreign currency to LEDCs. The extra money created by this investment can be spent on education, health and infrastructure.
- Global competition helps to keep prices low.
- Many problems facing the world today cross national borders (e.g. international crime, deforestation and global warming) and aid agencies can respond quickly to natural disasters.
- There is a greater access to foreign culture such as films, music, food and clothing.

. . . but also **problems**:

- The richest countries dominate world trade at the expense of LEDCs which provide the rest of the world with cheap labour and raw materials.
- There are no guarantees that investment will benefit the local community as profits are sent back to MEDCs where TNCs are based and TNCs may put local companies out of business.
- Outsourcing takes away manufacturing jobs from MEDCs as industry locates in LEDCs.
- If it becomes cheaper to operate in another country, the TNC might close down the factory and make local people redundant.
- As different cultures from around the world interact, they begin to lose their individuality.
- Due to the lack of strictly enforced laws, the safety of workers and the natural environment are put at risk.

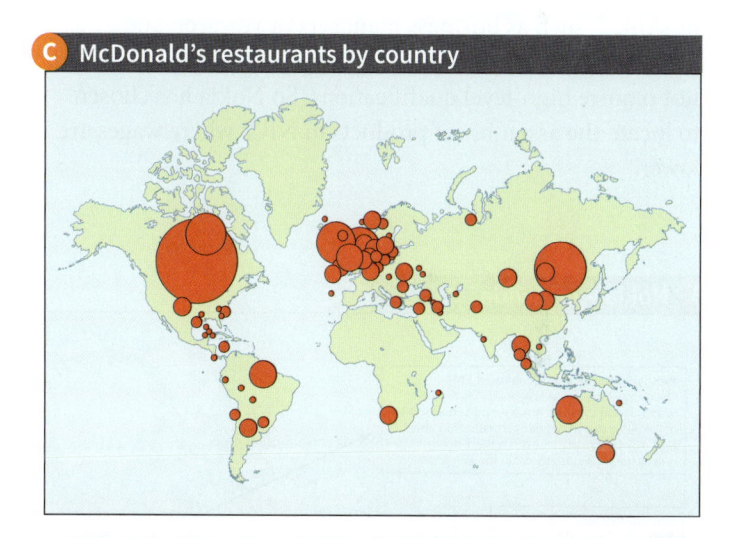

**C** McDonald's restaurants by country

**D** Globalisation is here to stay

> It has been said that arguing against globalisation is like arguing against the laws of gravity.
> Kofi Annan (Former UN Secretary-General)

---

**TASK 3:** Study **Source C** and an atlas
a  Describe the global distribution of McDonald's restaurants.
b  Suggest reasons why McDonald's restaurants are located in many different countries.
c  Choose a country other than the United States where there are McDonald's restaurants. Describe the advantages and problems of this to people who live in the country you have chosen.

**TASK 4:** Study **Source D**
Do you agree with the message in the source? Give reasons for your answer.

# Cambridge IGCSE Geography — Development

## Case Study
### A transnational corporation – Nokia, Finland

### Location of Nokia factories and offices

Nokia, a company that produces mobile phones, has branches in many countries because it wants to reduce costs by opening factories and offices in regions of the world that have low labour costs, cheap land and building costs, and low business rates. Another reason is to be close to its customers, who are spread right across the world. Mobile phone ownership has grown rapidly in Newly Industrialising Countries (NICs) and as people in LEDCs have become wealthier, Nokia has expanded its business opening new sales offices in Asia, Africa and South America.

Nokia employs many workers. Some are highly qualified or skilled, such as business managers or research and development staff. Others, such as assembly workers, do not require high-level qualifications. So Nokia has chosen to locate the assembly of products in NICs where wages are lower.

However, the more highly trained research and development staff work in Europe where Nokia develops new products which use the latest technology and need highly trained staff to develop and produce them.

### A  The development of the Nokia corporation

|  |  |
|---|---|
| 1865 | Mining engineer Fredrik Idestam set up his first wood pulp mill at the Tammerkoski Rapids in south-western Finland. A few years later he opened a second mill on the banks of the Nokianvirta river after which the company was named 'Nokia Ab'. |
| 1898 | The Finnish Rubber Works was set up, which later became Nokia's rubber business, making everything from rubber boots to tyres. |
| 1912 | The Finnish Cable Works was established, the start of Nokia's cable and electronics business. |
| 1962 | The Finnish Cable Works started branching out into electronics. It made an electronic device for use in nuclear power plants. |
| 1963 | It started developing radio telephones for the army and emergency services. |
| 1982 | Nokia introduced the first car phone and digital telephone. |
| 1987 | Nokia introduced the first handheld mobile phone. |
| 1998 | Nokia was the world leader in mobile phones. |
| 2005 | Nokia sold its billionth phone – in Nigeria. |
| 2014 | Microsoft acquired Nokia's devices and services business. |

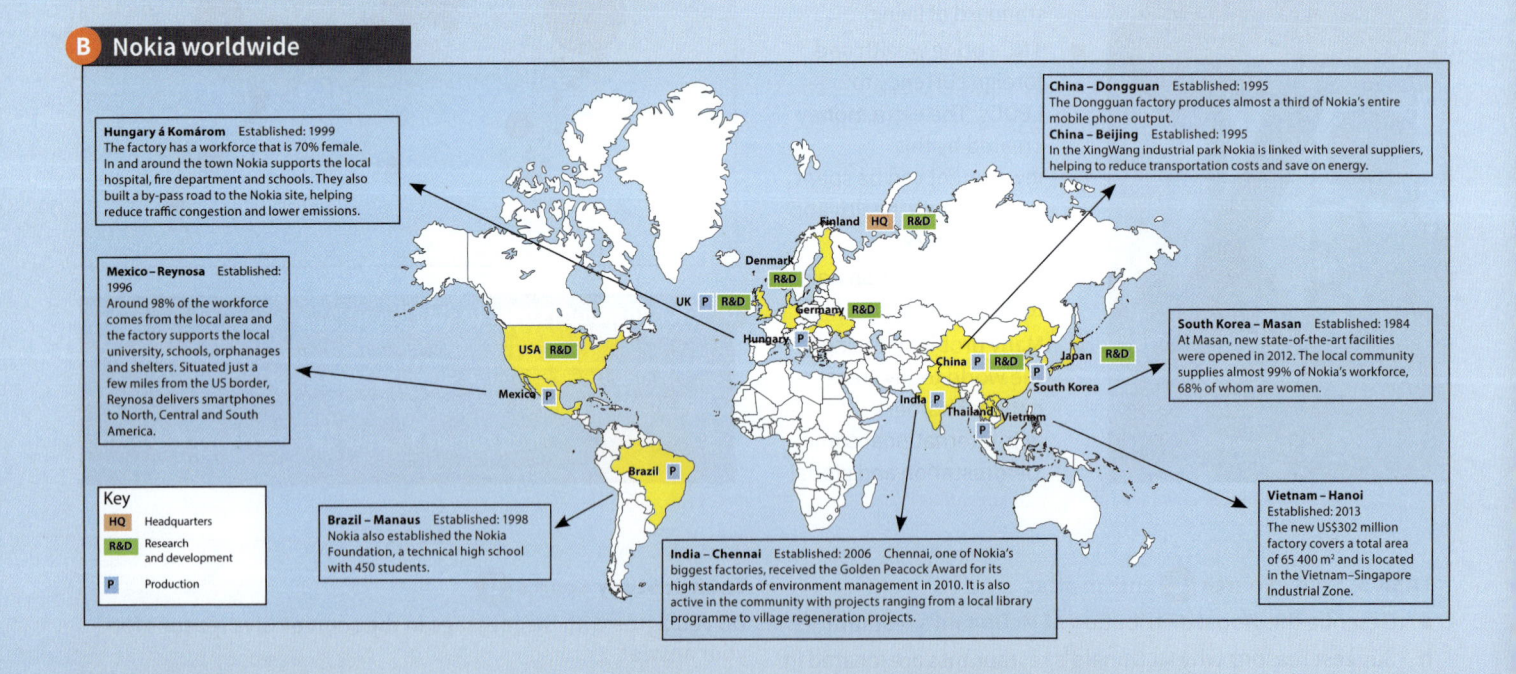

### B  Nokia worldwide

**Hungary á Komárom** Established: 1999
The factory has a workforce that is 70% female. In and around the town Nokia supports the local hospital, fire department and schools. They also built a by-pass road to the Nokia site, helping reduce traffic congestion and lower emissions.

**Mexico – Reynosa** Established: 1996
Around 98% of the workforce comes from the local area and the factory supports the local university, schools, orphanages and shelters. Situated just a few miles from the US border, Reynosa delivers smartphones to North, Central and South America.

**China – Dongguan** Established: 1995
The Dongguan factory produces almost a third of Nokia's entire mobile phone output.

**China – Beijing** Established: 1995
In the XingWang industrial park Nokia is linked with several suppliers, helping to reduce transportation costs and save on energy.

**South Korea – Masan** Established: 1984
At Masan, new state-of-the-art facilities were opened in 2012. The local community supplies almost 99% of Nokia's workforce, 68% of whom are women.

**Brazil – Manaus** Established: 1998
Nokia also established the Nokia Foundation, a technical high school with 450 students.

**India – Chennai** Established: 2006
Chennai, one of Nokia's biggest factories, received the Golden Peacock Award for its high standards of environment management in 2010. It is also active in the community with projects ranging from a local library programme to village regeneration projects.

**Vietnam – Hanoi** Established: 2013
The new US$302 million factory covers a total area of 65 400 m² and is located in the Vietnam–Singapore Industrial Zone.

**Key**
- HQ  Headquarters
- R&D  Research and development
- P  Production

---

**TASK 1:** Study Source A
Write a paragraph which describes how Nokia developed from a small company to a transnational corporation.

**TASK 2:** Study Source B
Using the evidence in the resource, explain why Nokia is a good example of a transnational corporation.

# Case Study: A transnational corporation – Nokia, Finland

## C Nokia moves to Asia

### Nokia factories shift to Asia: Did it have any choice?

Nokia is hoping it can become competitive by moving most of its manufacturing to Asia, a move which will see 4000 jobs moved from Finland, Hungary and Mexico to China and South Korea.

The company said that it made sense to move its manufacturing closer to the component suppliers, which are largely located in China.

Of course, the job losses and cuts in Finland will not be popular in Nokia's home country but the company had few options. Within a generation, China has become not only one of the cheapest electronic manufacturing markets in the world, but also the one that has the greatest amount of expertise.

**Adapted from** gigaom.com, 8 February 2012

## D Nokia opens new factory in Vietnam

### Nokia's new Vietnam phone factory gets excellent reception

HANOI – Nokia yesterday opened its first cell phone manufacturing base in Vietnam.

Stephen Elop, of Nokia worldwide, said the inauguration ceremony marked 17 years since its first activities in the Vietnamese market. He also said the company was committed to working closely with the local government.

Speaking at the ceremony, Vietnam's Deputy Minister of Planning and Investment Dang Huy Dong said that Nokia's investment in Vietnam had contributed to developing the hi-tech industry in Vietnam and that the country was committed to becoming an important manufacturing hub in the region.

**Adapted from** vietnamnews.vn, 29 October 2013

## E Nokia closes last factory in Finland

### Nokia Shuts Down Last Factory in Finland

Nokia has confirmed that it is shutting down its last factory in Salo, Finland resulting in a loss of 780 jobs. The final phone to carry the 'Made in Finland' label was made on Wednesday.

The closing of the plant in Salo will also be accompanied by the closure of research and development centres in Germany and Canada. This should help them to save around US$2 billion by the end of the year.

**Adapted from** fonearena.com, 29 July 2012

## F Nokia closes factory in Romania

### Nokia to axe 3500 jobs and close factory

Nokia will close a manufacturing plant in Romania. Nokia, the world's largest maker of mobile phones said the closure of the factory in Cluj would result in 2200 job losses, with a further 1300 losses at its Location and Commerce division. Manufacturing operations at Nokia's Cluj factory will be moved to Asia. Nokia has factories in China, South Korea and India and is building a further facility in Vietnam.

The Cluj factory, which took seven months to build at a cost of US $88m, was only opened in 2008 as a replacement for a plant in Bochum, Germany.

**Adapted from** ft.com, September 2011

---

**TASK 3:** Study Sources **C** to **F**

Using all the resources on this page, along with the information on page 144, describe the impacts of Nokia on different places in the world. You should include both positive and negative impacts and develop the points you make.

# 48 Agricultural systems

## Many different systems
Agriculture (or farming) is the production of food and other resources through the growing of plants and the raising of domesticated animals. There are many different types of agricultural system in the world.

## Arable, mixed or pastoral farming?
Arable farmers grow crops while pastoral farmers keep animals. A mixed farm does both.

## Extensive or intensive farming?
**Extensive farming** involves a low input of capital, material and labour with large amounts of land. It produces a low yield of product from a large area of land.

**Intensive farming** involves high inputs of capital, fertilisers and labour, and labour-saving technologies such as pesticides or machinery. The object is to get as high a yield of product as possible from a small area of land.

## Subsistence or commercial farming?
**Subsistence farmers** produce enough crops and keep just enough animals to feed their families. Any surplus will be stored or sold in a local market but the primary object is to produce enough food to survive. Most subsistence farming takes place in LEDCs.

With some types of subsistence farming, traditional farmers move around forests practising shifting cultivation. In desert areas, where water is scarce, many farmers live a nomadic life herding their animals between areas where they hope to find water or better grazing land.

**Commercial farmers** produce crops and/or animals to sell in order to make a profit. Whilst most commercial farming takes place in MEDCs, it also takes place in some LEDCs where cash crops are grown mainly for export.

**A** Arable or pastoral?

**B** Extensive or intensive?

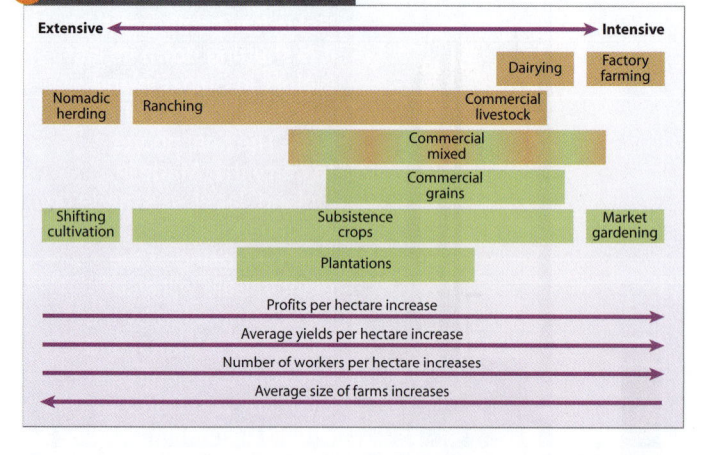

---

**TASK 1:** Study Source **A**
a  Suggest **three** differences between the two types of farming shown.
b  What are the benefits and difficulties of each type of farming?

**TASK 2:** Study Source **B**
a  Find out the meaning of the following farming types:
   - market gardening
   - plantation
   - dairying
   - factory farming.
b  Give **two** examples of *extensive farming* and **two** examples of *intensive farming*.
c  Using the information in the diagram compare *shifting cultivation* with *commercial livestock farming*.

## C Farming as a system: inputs, processes and outputs

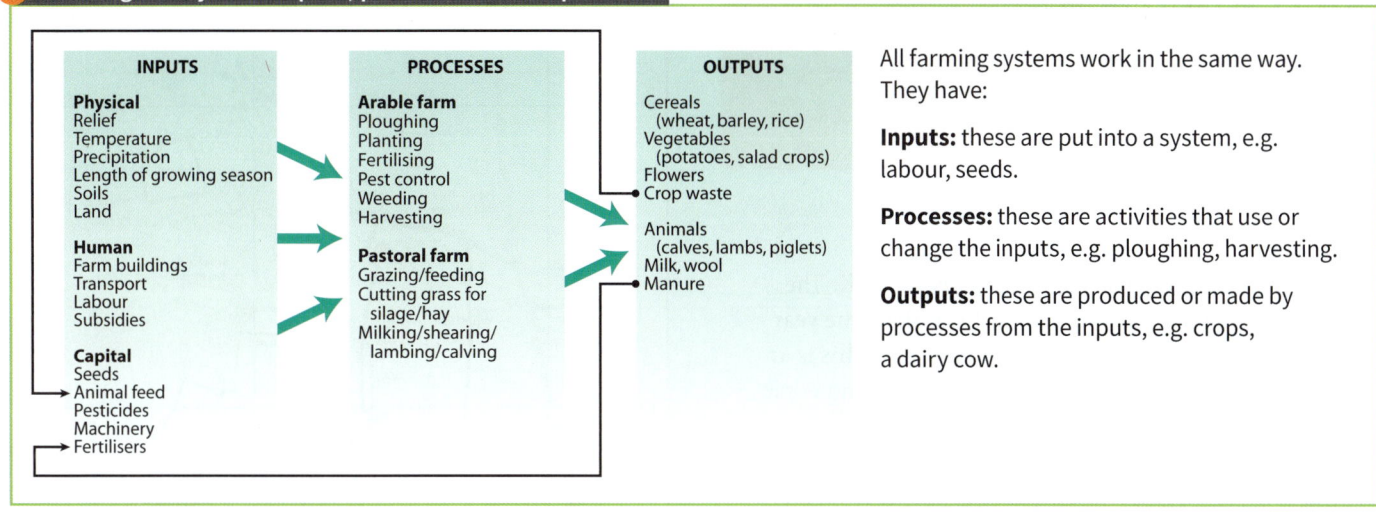

**INPUTS**

Physical
- Relief
- Temperature
- Precipitation
- Length of growing season
- Soils
- Land

Human
- Farm buildings
- Transport
- Labour
- Subsidies

Capital
- Seeds
- Animal feed
- Pesticides
- Machinery
- Fertilisers

**PROCESSES**

Arable farm
- Ploughing
- Planting
- Fertilising
- Pest control
- Weeding
- Harvesting

Pastoral farm
- Grazing/feeding
- Cutting grass for silage/hay
- Milking/shearing/lambing/calving

**OUTPUTS**

- Cereals (wheat, barley, rice)
- Vegetables (potatoes, salad crops)
- Flowers
- Crop waste
- Animals (calves, lambs, piglets)
- Milk, wool
- Manure

All farming systems work in the same way. They have:

**Inputs:** these are put into a system, e.g. labour, seeds.

**Processes:** these are activities that use or change the inputs, e.g. ploughing, harvesting.

**Outputs:** these are produced or made by processes from the inputs, e.g. crops, a dairy cow.

## D A subsistence farming system

Shifting cultivation is practised by **indigenous** tribes in rainforests. The Erigbaagtsa tribe live in the tropical rainforest of the Amazon Basin in Brazil. There is a clear **division of labour** here. The men obtain food by hunting animals in the forest while women grow crops such as maize, rice and cassava in small clearings. The nutrients in the soil are obtained by burning trees. After a few years, heavy rainfall has removed these from the soil so the tribe moves to another area. They will move between clearings several times before returning to allow the trees to grow back again, making this a **sustainable** agricultural system.

## E How shifting cultivation works

- Forest clearance: small trees cut by hand, bushes and branches burned. Some trees may be left standing to provide food and protect soil.
- Fire destroys natural seeds. Ash dug into soil to provide fertiliser.
- Crops planted (e.g. yams, manioc).
- Lack of vegetation cover subjects soil to leaching and erosion.
- Crop yields decrease after 2–3 years.
- Farmers move on to clear a new plot elsewhere.
- Plants can be restored after 20 years but fewer species then grow.

## TASK 3: Study Source C

a Give **one** example of a physical input into a farm and **one** example of a human input.

b Give **one** example of a process that takes place:
- on an arable farm.
- on a pastoral farm.

c Give **one** example of an output from:
- an arable farm
- a pastoral farm.

d Explain, using examples, how some outputs feed back into the system as inputs.

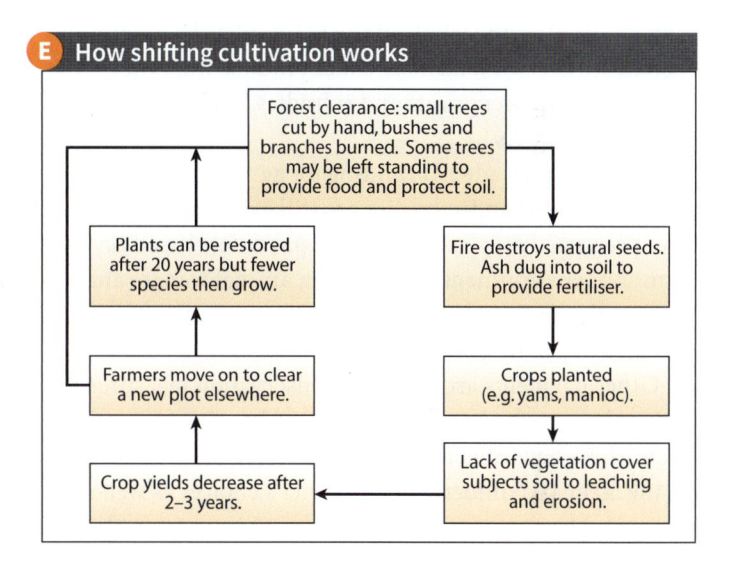

## TASK 4: Study Source D

a Describe the scene in the photo.
b Where do the Erigbaagtsa tribe live?
c How is the work divided between men and women?
d How do they obtain nutrients to grow crops?
e Why is *shifting cultivation* a sustainable agricultural system?

## TASK 5: Study Source E

a Draw a systems diagram based on Source C above to show the inputs, processes and outputs of the Erigbaagtsa tribe's shifting cultivation system.

b Why does the tribe have to move to another area after a few years?

c The Amazon Basin is being deforested at an alarming rate – see page 118. Suggest how this might affect the farming system practised by the Erigbaagtsa tribe. Refer to inputs, processes and outputs.

# Cambridge IGCSE Geography | Food production

## Case Study
## An arable farm in Lincolnshire, UK

### Glebe Farm

Glebe Farm is an arable farm in Lincolnshire, UK. The farm was bought by a new owner in 1973; the same year that the UK joined the **European Union (EU)**. This is an organisation of 28 countries and over 500 million people that trade with each other as a common market.

The money that member countries contributed to a central fund to belong to the EU was available to farmers as **grants** and **subsidies**. These were used to produce the food required by the whole of the EU. Under the **Common Agricultural Policy**, farmers could produce what they wanted but only get grants and subsidies if they met EU production targets.

In the past decade EU funding for agriculture has changed. Grants and subsidies are still available but they have been partly replaced by **direct payments** based on farm size, environmental protection, animal welfare and keeping the land in good condition. Farmers can grow what they like depending on market conditions.

Other payments are given for conservation measures such as keeping hedges for wildlife and keeping footpaths open. These have affected the inputs, processes and outputs on the farm and influenced the farmer's choices as well as changed the appearance of the rural environment in the UK.

### A Inputs

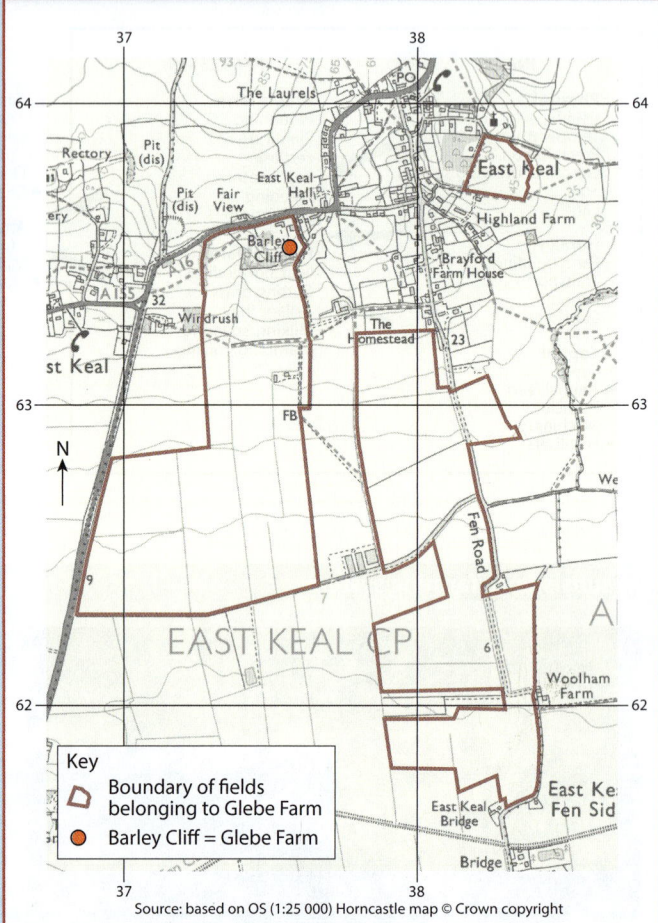

Source: based on OS (1:25 000) Horncastle map © Crown copyright

*Barley Cliff is the name of the farmhouse. The farm and its fields make up Glebe Farm.*

> " Glebe Farm is about 127 hectares in area and is almost ideal for arable farming. We get rainfall every month of the year and most of the year temperatures are above the growing season temperature of 6 °C. Warm temperatures in the summer make the sandy soil too dry for grass to grow well enough to feed cattle or sheep successfully. I wouldn't want to milk the cows twice a day anyway; pastoral farming is not for me! The farm faces south so the higher northern fields drain down the hill to a wet area as we are not very high above sea level. I have to put in drains to take the surplus water away. I plan my work so the crops needing less attention are further away from the farm buildings. The sandy soil drains well and warms up quickly but lacks nutrients so I feed it with fertilisers. I also use sprays to protect sprouts and cereals from insects and disease. To carry out this work I have two tractors, a plough, seed drill and I hire a combine harvester in late summer for the cereals.
> I do most of the work myself and hire workers at busy times "
> 
> Farmer

---

**TASK 1:** Study Source A

a  Draw a labelled map to show:
  - Barley Cliff farmhouse
  - the village of east Keal
  - roads and drains
  - the fields owned by the farmer

b  Refer to Source c on page 147. Add labels around the map you have drawn to show:
  - the *physical inputs* that influence farming here
  - the *human inputs* that influence farming here
  - the *capital inputs* that influence farming herer

c  How does the farmer overcome problems on his farm?

d  Explain why the farmer chose to run an arable rather than a pastoral farm here.

# Case Study: An arable farm in Lincolnshire, UK

## B Processes

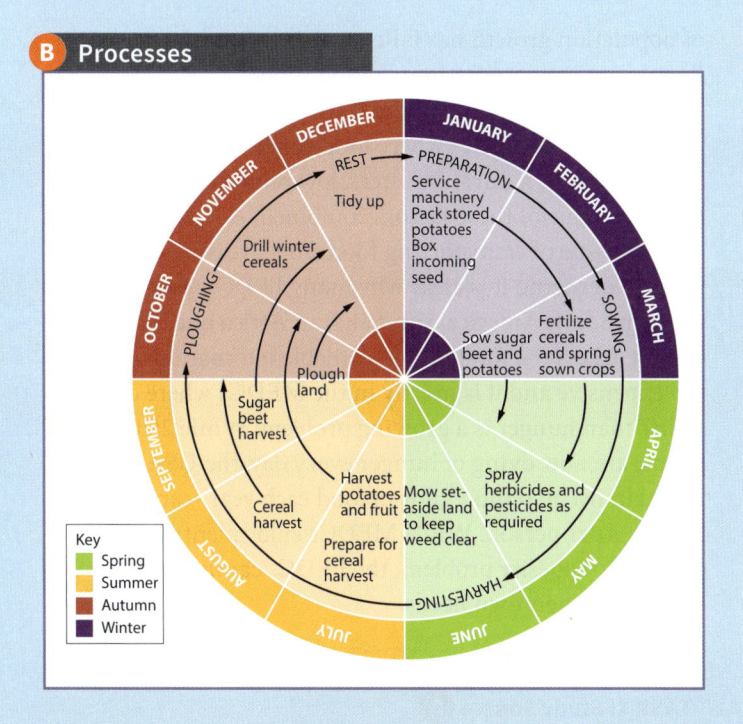

*Farming calendar showing activities through the year:*

**Winter (December–February):** REST – Tidy up; PREPARATION – Service machinery, Pack stored potatoes, Box incoming seed.

**Spring (March–May):** SOWING – Sow sugar beet and potatoes, Fertilize cereals and spring sown crops; Spray herbicides and pesticides as required; Mow set-aside land to keep weed clear; Prepare for cereal harvest.

**Summer (June–August):** HARVESTING – Cereal harvest; Harvest potatoes and fruit.

**Autumn (September–November):** Sugar beet harvest; Plough land; PLOUGHING; Drill winter cereals.

Key: Spring, Summer, Autumn, Winter

## C Outputs

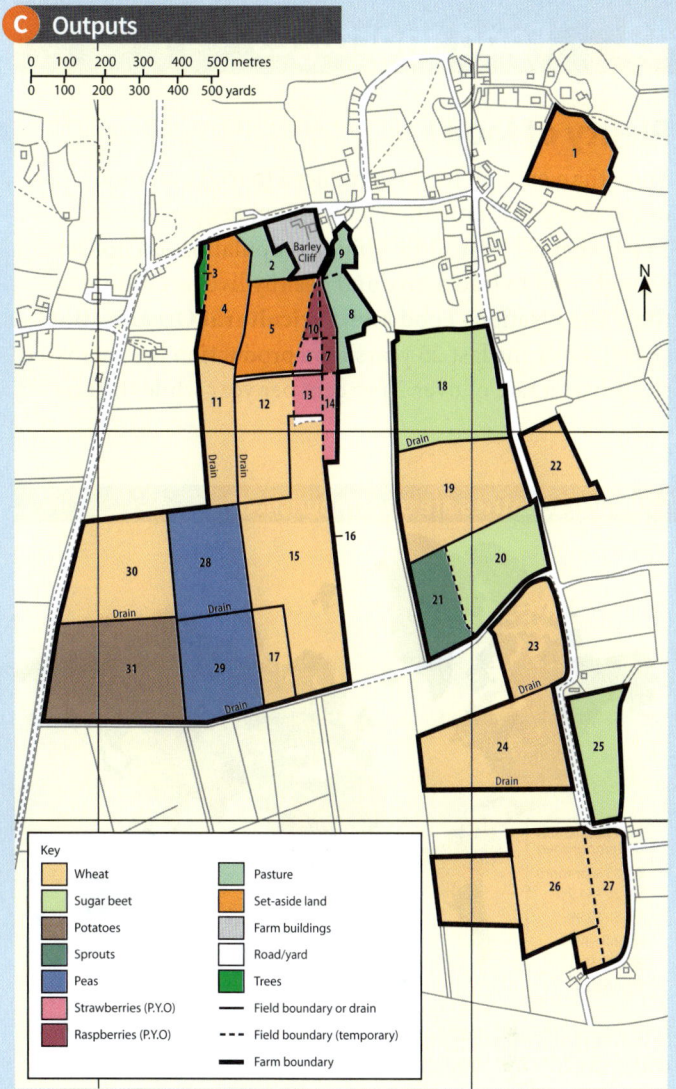

*Map of Glebe Farm showing fields numbered 1–31.*

Key:
- Wheat
- Sugar beet
- Potatoes
- Sprouts
- Peas
- Strawberries (P.Y.O)
- Raspberries (P.Y.O)
- Pasture
- Set-aside land
- Farm buildings
- Road/yard
- Trees
- Field boundary or drain
- Field boundary (temporary)
- Farm boundary

## TASK 2: Study Source B

a Find out what a *cereal* crop is.

b From the farming calendar, list the main activities carried out in each season.

c When do you think the farmer's year is:
- at its busiest
- least busy?

Explain your choices.

d Suggest advantages and disadvantages of working as a self-employed farmer compared with being employed as an office worker. Which would you prefer?

## TASK 3: Study Source C

a Which cereal crop is grown at Glebe Farm? To what extent does it dominate the land use here?

b List the vegetables and fruit that are grown here.

c Suggest why access to fields may cause difficulties in running Glebe Farm efficiently.

## TASK 4: Study Sources C and D

a What is meant by diversification?

b How has the farmer diversified his farm business in the last 30 years?

c Suggest advantages and disadvantages of diversification for the farmer.

d How have EU policies affected the land use and appearance of the rural environment at Glebe Farm?

## TASK 5

Refer back to the systems diagram on page 147. Draw a detailed diagram that shows the **inputs–processes–outputs** for Glebe Farm in Lincolnshire, UK.

## D Diversification

> Since I bought the farm much of what I do has been influenced by the EU. I used to grow a lot more wheat but, because of overproduction in the EU, we were asked to set aside 15% of our usual wheat area. For this we could claim an EU Area Payment and then another payment for growing a crop the EU did want on the same land such as oil-seed rape and linseed. I have also diversified into growing fruit – mainly strawberries and raspberries – close to the main road as a pick-your-own (PYO) enterprise. I now use land for a Caravan Club site for five caravans. Without the EU grants, subsidies and payments for these activities, farmers would be bankrupt; people just wouldn't pay the full price to cover costs. I still claim grants for planting hedges and trees, creating ponds and for not farming a 10-metre strip around the edge of many fields which encourages wildlife. After all it's in the farmers' interests to look after the environment.

Farmer

# Cambridge IGCSE Geography | Food production

## 49  Food shortages

### Plenty of food?

More than enough food is produced to feed everyone in the world yet more than 850 million people, about 13 per cent of the world's 7 billion population, do not get enough food to lead active and healthy lives according to the United Nations **Food and Agricultural Organisation (FAO)**. Over the last 25 years food production has increased steadily at a rate of over 2 per cent per year while the rate of population growth has fallen to 1.1 per cent per year. Population is not outstripping food supply.

Why is there hunger in the world? Most undernourished people live in countries where food is in short supply because of war, natural disasters, low productivity, rising prices or some of these factors combined. Add to this the difficult issue of transporting food from areas of surplus to areas of need and it is clear why many LEDCs, especially those in South America, sub-Saharan Africa and Asia, cannot access the food that is available internationally. It is too expensive and it is mostly in the MEDCs where obesity rather than hunger is a growing problem. While 25 000 people are now dying of hunger every day, the USA throws away almost 50 billion kilos of food each year – around 150 kilos per person. While MEDCs enjoy plenty of food, creating an obesity problem, the LEDCs cannot produce enough for their own needs.

### A  Which countries are undernourished?

% of population undernourished
- 35% or more
- 20–34.9%
- 5–19.9%
- 2.5–4.9%
- < 2.5%
- no data

Undernourishment means not eating enough food to have a healthy and active life. The Food and Agricultural Organisation (FAO) regards 2300 calories as the minimum quantity required per day. The average amount of food produced per person in the world is 2720 calories.

**TASK 1:** Study **Source A**

a  List **four** areas of the world where less than 2.5% of the population are undernourished.

b  Describe the distribution of countries where 35% or more of the population is undernourished.

**TASK 2:** Study **Source B**

a  On an outline map of Africa, and with the help of an atlas, create your own choropleth map using the data in the table 'The 25 hungriest countries'. Use a different key and group interval to that used in Source A.

b  List the countries in the list that are **not** in Africa.

c  Suggest why using a world outline map for this exercise would not have been a good idea.

### B  The 25 hungriest countries

% of population undernourished

| | | | | | | | | | |
|---|---|---|---|---|---|---|---|---|---|
| 1 | Somalia | 77% | 10 | Ethiopia | 37% | 19 | Chad | 30% |
| 2 | D.R. Congo | 69% | 11 | Mozambique | 37% | 20 | Rwanda | 30% |
| 3 | Burundi | 67% | 12 | Swaziland | 36% | 21 | Uganda | 3% |
| 4 | Eritrea | 64% | 13 | Sudan | 34% | 22 | Liberia | 29% |
| 5 | Haiti | 50% | 14 | Tanzania | 33% | 23 | Namibia | 29% |
| 6 | Comoros Islands | 46% | 15 | Guatemala | 31% | 24 | Sierra Leone | 29% |
| 7 | Zambia | 43% | 16 | North Korea | 31% | 25 | Yemen | 29% |
| 8 | Angola | 41% | 17 | Tajikistan | 31% | | | |
| 9 | Timor-Leste | 38% | 18 | Zimbabwe | 31% | | **World average** | **12%** |

Data from World Bank (2013)

Theme 3: Topic 49

### C Food shortages – different causes

### Over 1.6 million need food aid in Zimbabwe

It was once the 'bread basket' of Africa, people in Zimbabwe need food aid. Many farmers have had their land taken over by the government and many fields are going to waste. Drought, rising prices and a lack of investment in fertilisers and machinery are also being blamed.

### Food shortage major issue after typhoon hits Philippines

Food shortages are the greatest threat that survivors of typhoon Haiyan face. All the coconut plantations have been destroyed. Food aid will run out in three months but the next coconut harvest cannot be for another year.

### Locust plague aggravates food shortage in Yemen

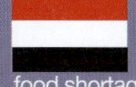

A plague of locusts has devastated crops in Yemen. The country already faces a food shortage due to poor investment in farming and droughts. 75% of the people depend on farming for their food but it is either too dry or, when the rains come, the locusts can breed and eat any crops that are grown.

### Access for food and water a problem in Afghanistan

Ongoing drought and the continuing problem of difficult access into the mountains means that almost 9 million people face food shortages. The wheat crop failed due to a lack of rain. Transporting food and water for irrigation into the mountains is an almost impossible task.

### El Salvador hit by floods

Floods in El Salvador have left over 50 000 people homeless and without food. About 10 000 people are in need of food aid after heavy rains washed away crops.

### Food shortages trigger protests in Venezuela

Six weeks of violence against the government has plunged the country into crisis. Rationing and a fingerprinted ID card have been introduced to stop people stockpiling food. In state-run shops people queue for hours for basic food such as flour, cooking oil and chicken.

### Civil war puts Syria children at risk

Lack of access to food, rising food prices and a collapse in food production have put children in Syria at risk of malnutrition. More than 4 million people – half of whom are children – are unable to produce or buy enough food as the war continues. Many have fled to neighbouring countries such as Iran where food supply cannot provide for the extra refugees.

151

### TASK 3: Study Source C

a Copy and complete the following table by naming a country with a food shortage for the reason given. Add any effects of the food shortage in column three.

b Which of the reasons listed for food shortages do you think people can influence either for better or worse? Explain your choices.

| Natural causes | Named country(ies) | Effects |
|---|---|---|
| Drought/soil erosion | | |
| Floods | | |
| Tropical storms | | |
| Pests | | |

| Economic/political causes | | |
|---|---|---|
| Low investment | | |
| Access/transport issues | | |
| Wars and civil unrest | | |
| Rising prices | | |

### TASK 4

a A Chinese man, Lao Tzu, once wrote 'Give a man a fish and you feed him for a day. Teach him how to fish and you feed him for a lifetime'. What did he mean by this?

b How does this relate to providing food aid to LEDCs with food shortages?

c Decide, as a group, the best way to solve food shortages. Use some of the ideas discussed or use your own.

**Cambridge IGCSE Geography** — **Food production**

# Case Study

## Food shortages in Darfur, Sudan

### Drought + conflict = food shortage

Before separating into two countries in 2011, Sudan was the largest country in Africa. Bordering the Red Sea, it is a region of contrasts – both physical and human. Its landscape changes from desert in the north to forests in the south and grassy plains and swamps in the centre. The river Nile provides water in the east but many areas receive no rainfall. One reason for separation into two countries was the contrast in people: the Arabs in the north and Africans in the south. Tension between these two groups has led to two civil wars since independence in 1956; the second civil war began in 2003 and ended in 2011 with independence for South Sudan. The north of Sudan has kept the country's original name.

During the second civil war there were periodic droughts and, by 2009, many parts of Sudan required large amounts of food aid. Most of these people were concentrated in Darfur, a region in the west of Sudan and north of the newly created South Sudan. In the last ten years Darfur has seen one of the world's largest concentrations of human suffering and food shortages. Local conflicts and drought continue to cause major problems in this region.

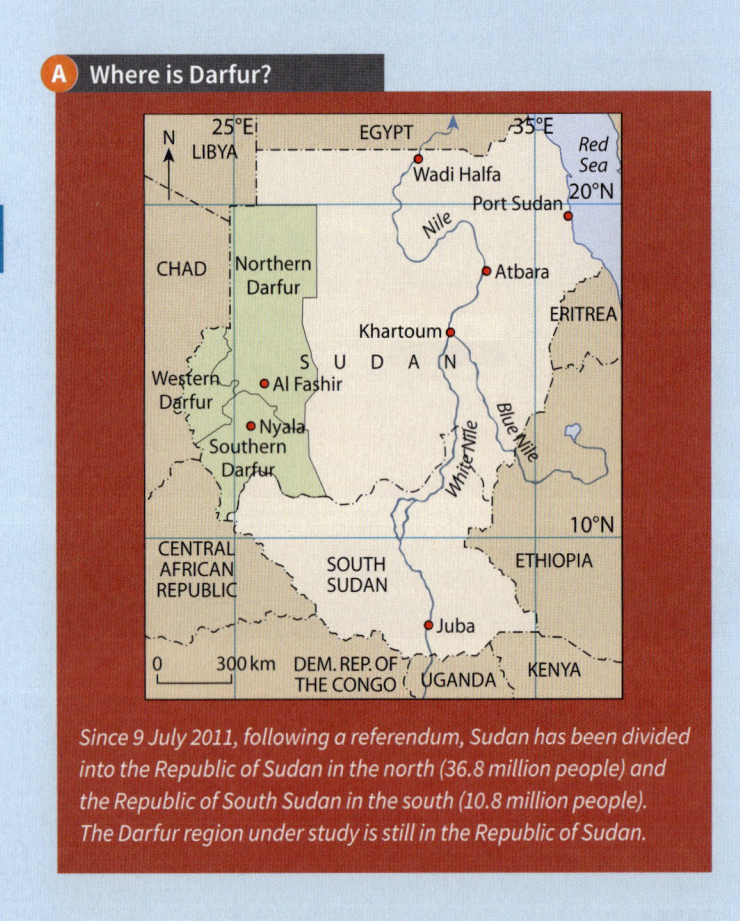

### A  Where is Darfur?

Since 9 July 2011, following a referendum, Sudan has been divided into the Republic of Sudan in the north (36.8 million people) and the Republic of South Sudan in the south (10.8 million people). The Darfur region under study is still in the Republic of Sudan.

### B  Darfur – a difficult area to live and work in

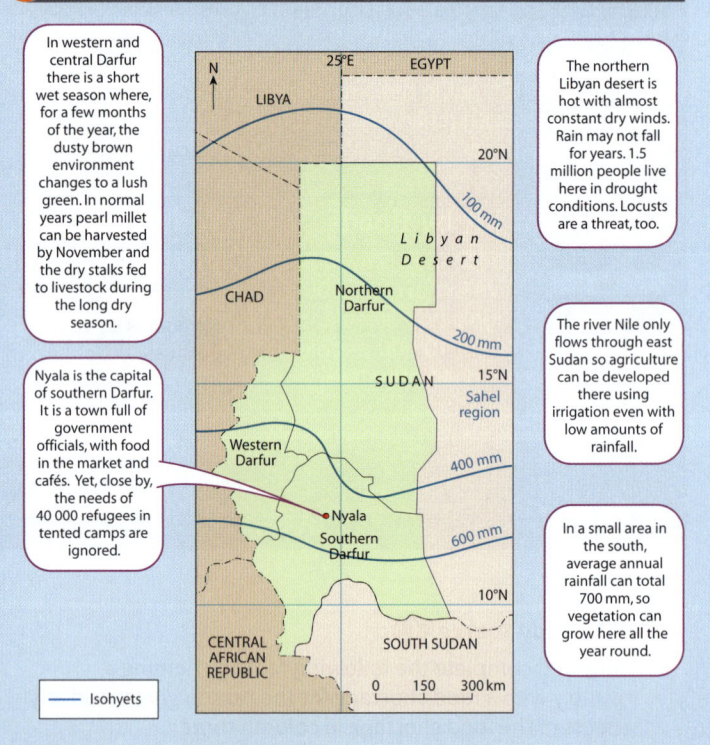

In western and central Darfur there is a short wet season where, for a few months of the year, the dusty brown environment changes to a lush green. In normal years pearl millet can be harvested by November and the dry stalks fed to livestock during the long dry season.

Nyala is the capital of southern Darfur. It is a town full of government officials, with food in the market and cafés. Yet, close by, the needs of 40 000 refugees in tented camps are ignored.

The northern Libyan desert is hot with almost constant dry winds. Rain may not fall for years. 1.5 million people live here in drought conditions. Locusts are a threat, too.

The river Nile only flows through east Sudan so agriculture can be developed there using irrigation even with low amounts of rainfall.

In a small area in the south, average annual rainfall can total 700 mm, so vegetation can grow here all the year round.

---

**TASK 1: Study Source A**

a  Describe the location of Darfur. Refer to a continent, lines of latitude and longitude, the Red Sea and neighbouring countries.

b  Suggest **three** reasons why it has been easier to develop the country east of, and around, the capital Khartoum.

**TASK 2: Study Source B**

a  Write a heading 'Why I would not want to live in northern or western Darfur'. List **five** reasons.

b  Compare your lists with those of your classmates. How many different reasons have you all suggested?

# Case Study: Food shortages in Darfur, Sudan

## C Diary of a disaster

**1956** Independence granted to Sudan from Egypt and the UK. Leaders begin to develop areas that could sustain rain-fed agriculture along the Nile river valley.

**2003** Rebels in Darfur, a western region of Sudan that is predominantly African, rise up against the government, claiming that they have been neglected while the rest of Sudan and the capital Khartoum – mostly Arab – have been favoured. Since 2003, many villages have been burned to the ground and around 200 000 people have died. More than 2 million people (1 in 3 from Darfur) have been forced to flee their homes because of the violence. They are known as **internally-displaced people** (IDPs) who live in vast, crowded refugee camps – tented villages on the edge of towns – in Darfur and Chad. The camps hold about 130 000 people with 200 000 refugees in Chad. Most have been there since 2003. There are no toilets, medical facilities, food or water supplies. Many have died of disease, water shortage, heat and malnutrition in overcrowded conditions. Up to 4.5 million depend on international aid.

**2007** In an attempt to protect people the United Nations and **African Union** have provided a joint UN–AU peace-keeping force of 26 000 soldiers but only one-third had arrived by October 2008.

**January 2011** A referendum is held in the south of Sudan where people voted overwhelmingly to separate from the north.

**9 July 2011** Republic of South Sudan becomes an independent country. The north of Sudan becomes the Republic of Sudan.

## D Newspaper extract

### Displacement And Food Shortages Continue In Darfur

Four areas in Southern Darfur – Gereida, Sheria, Adila and Nitega – are suffering from food shortages and insecurity. The people have fled from their farms as they don't feel safe and also the lack of rain is causing a drought. Here, close to Nyala, the capital of Southern Darfur, thousands of men, women and children have been abandoned by those that should help them. There is no food, toilets, drainage or medical facilities. These illegal camps hold over 80 000 people between them; some are close to the road from the airport where relief aid arrives. But the government does not distribute the food or allow relief agencies to operate there. It wants the displaced people to go back to their villages but the refugees are too frightened of the military to return. Fighting between rebels and government forces continues; more than 215 000 people have fled their homes since January 2014.

Child malnutrition is commonly seen in the region's health centres. Ms Khadjia Abdullah is one of many thousands of mothers in camps for displaced people in Darfur. She says that during the rainy season, from June to October, she returns to her home area of Korma, Northern Darfur, to cultivate her land so she can put food on her family's table. When she travels to Korma she takes her young son, Mustapha with her. 'I don't have anyone to care for my child while I am away,' she says. 'I try to bring as much food and water as I can with me to care for him.'

At the clinic Mustapha, who is 21 months old, weighed 7.8 kg and was being treated for severe malnutrition and skin eczema.

*Adapted from* Voices of Darfur, *April 2014*

## TASK 3: Study Source C

a When did Sudan gain independence from Egypt and the UK?
b What caused rebels in Darfur to rise up against the government in 2003?
c What is an IDP? How many people have become IDPs since 2003?
d List other ways in which people have suffered due to the war.
e What significant events took place in 2011? How did this affect the Darfur region under study?

## TASK 4: Study Source D

a What are the main causes of the food shortages in Darfur?
b What basic services are missing in the refugee camps? How will this affect the IDPs who are living there?
c Why won't the government distribute overseas aid?
d Why won't the displaced people return to their villages?
e Why does malnutrition rise between June and October?
f What impact is the food shortage having on children like Mustapha?

# 50 Industrial systems

## Secondary industry

Secondary industry involves making things. It is the production of goods by industrial processes. It takes raw materials from the primary industries of farming, fishing, forestry, mining and quarrying and processes them into manufactured goods and products. In doing so it adds value to the raw materials. Secondary industry, or manufacturing, can be studied as a system with inputs, processes and outputs. A large-scale industry employs many people, takes up a lot of space, has a large capital investment and produces a high volume of products aiming for high profits. A small-scale industry employs few people, uses up a small amount of land, has low investment and produces a low volume of products aiming for a modest profit.

Although making products and profit are two positive outputs of manufacturing industry, industrial waste is an inevitable negative output too. Most secondary waste from factories causes different types of pollution in the form of:

- air pollution – e.g. chemicals given out in smoke
- water pollution – e.g. chemicals discharged into local rivers
- ground pollution – e.g. contamination of soil by acid rain
- visual pollution – e.g. derelict factories and wasteland.

### A Different types of secondary industry

**Manufacturing** refers to the conversion of raw materials from the primary sector into finished products on a large scale. Steelmaking produces many manufactured products, some of which are then used in processing industries, assembly lines and hi-tech industries.

**Processing** involves taking materials and creating a finished product from combining and changing them in some way. It is common in the food industry, where recipes produce a final unique product from many sources, e.g. canned food.

**Assembly** industries involve putting together parts made elsewhere. Parts are added to other semi-finished parts in a sequence that usually involves conveyer belts, assembly lines and workers using specialised skills at each stage. Every extra stage added leads to the final assembled product.

**Hi-tech** products are manufactured using 'cutting edge' technology and involve advanced computer techniques. Biotechnology, telecommunications, aerospace, pharmaceuticals, IT developments are all in this category. However, the pace of change can mean that a hi-tech industry may not be so hi-tech in a short space of time.

---

**TASK 1:** Study Source **A**

a What is meant by secondary industry?
b Explain why developing secondary industry is important if a country wants to become an MEDC.
c Explain why:
- making steel is a manufacturing industry
- manufacturing canned food is a processing industry
- car-making is an assembly industry
- developing new iPads, smartphones and tablets is a hi-tech industry.

d Suggest which activities in the photographs would produce the *most* and the *least* industrial waste. Justify your choices.

# Theme 3: Topic 50

## B Inputs–processes–outputs in a large-scale industry

**SECONDARY INDUSTRY AS A SYSTEM**

**INPUTS**
- Capital
- Enterprise
- Land
- Raw material
- Power
- Labour

**PROCESSES**
e.g.
- smelting
- weaving
- spinning
- dyeing
- printing
- knitting
- stitching
- tanning
- moulding

**OUTPUTS**
1. Processed goods such as (i) cement, cotton yarn, ghee, lime, sugar and wheat flour which may be raw materials for other industries or sold directly to the public (ii) soft drinks, packets of tea and tinned fruit which are sold directly to the public.
2. Manufactured goods which may be raw materials for other industries such as (i) bottles, cotton cloth, nuts and bolts, steel sheets and wire which may be raw materials for other industries or sold directly to the public (ii) axles, electric motors, fan guards and wheel hubs which are almost entirely the raw materials for other industrial units.
3. Manufactured goods such as drugs, fans, garments, motor cycles and tractors which are final products sold directly to the public.
4. The products of the construction industry such as factories, office blocks, blocks of flats, hospitals, schools.

Waste — IF RECYCLED
Profit — PROFIT RE-INVESTED

## TASK 2: Study Source B

a List **one** example of each input, e.g. capital = a bank loan.
b Suggest **one** type of manufacturing industry for each of the listed processes, e.g. smelting = iron and steel industry.
c Give **one** example of:
  ■ an output that is a final product sold directly to the general public
  ■ an output that becomes a raw material for another industry.
d Suggest what may happen to the outputs 'Waste' and 'Profit'.

## TASK 3: Study Source C

a Read Mohammed's story and then copy and complete this table based on what he says about his work.

| Inputs | Processes | Outputs |
|--------|-----------|---------|
|        |           |         |
|        |           |         |

b Why is Mohammed's pottery a small-scale manufacturing industry?
c What happens to any 'Waste' and to 'Profit'?
d Suggest some social, economic and environmental consequences of making pottery in this area.

155

## C Inputs–processes–outputs in a small-scale industry – Tamagroute, Morocco

### Mohammed's story

'I have been here for over ten years as a potter. I pay rent on the land but for that I can use the shed and kilns. I use red clay from the bank of a nearby river but buy some in if I get short. We use donkeys to bring clay and water here in plastic bottles and use dung and local wood for fuel. To get the clay ready, three large holes are dug in the ground and filled with water. The raw clay is mixed in to create a wet, slushy material. We then shovel out the wet clay into a large puddle on the ground and walk on it to flatten it and squeeze out surplus water. The clay is cut into large chunks and stored in a cool place in plastic bags. I have a wheel where I throw the clay into pots, plates and bowls; I use my feet to drive the wheel. Most of my day is spent throwing pots using water and fingers to create the shape I want. Once there are enough pots made, they are left to dry in the sun, then they are stacked in the kilns which are sealed. Dung or firewood is lit to fire the pottery. We are hoping to get gas bottles here soon. The fired pottery is left for a day to cool. The unglazed pots are then removed for decorating. There are three of us working here – one to prepare the clay, one to throw it and another to glaze and sell the pottery. Tourists buy a great deal but some villagers come here too. Any profit goes back into the pottery after paying rent. There is no waste unless a pot breaks before it is fired; the clay can then be reused. One day we hope to buy the pottery from the landlord.'

*Throwing - pedal power is used to turn the wheel*

# Cambridge IGCSE Geography — Industry

## 51 Industrial location

### Deciding on where to locate

There are many different types of secondary industry. One thing that they all have in common is a site – or several sites – where they produce their goods. This site may have been chosen many years ago but, whenever it was chosen, a number of location factors would have been considered. These include:

- Land – amount required and cost.
- Weather and climate – working conditions and impact on processes.
- Raw materials – amount and location of inputs needed.
- Power – fuel and electricity requirements.
- Labour – amount required and cost.
- Transport – communication by road, railway, rivers, sea or air.
- Market – location of customers.
- Government aid or grants – may reduce costs.
- Internet and telecommunications access – for buying and selling materials and goods.

In addition to these factors the person owning the factory may have a personal preference related to where they live and their personal situation.

There are three main types of industrial location:

- **Located close to raw materials** – these industries use heavy, bulky raw materials which are expensive to transport and produce waste. They locate close to the raw materials. The final product weighs less so transport costs to the market are low. Iron and steelworks are examples of locations near to raw materials.
- **Located close to the market** – the raw materials for these industries are often small and light so the transport costs for them are low but the final product is heavier, usually due to the addition of water, and in some cases perishable. It needs to be consumed quickly so these industries locate close to the market, e.g. bakeries, drink bottling factories.
- **Footloose** – these industries can locate almost anywhere; raw materials and market locations are not as important as the availability of suitable labour and good transport and communications. Examples include computer software development.

### A  Locating industry … the past

A great deal of heavy industry, such as iron and steelmaking, began over 200 years ago in Western Europe. The main influences on location were more to do with the location of raw materials (iron ore, limestone, water), power (from burning coal) and the market at that time. Transport costs were a major influence in deciding on the location for manufacturing a product. These included:

- moving raw materials to the factory
- moving finished product to market.

*Margam steelworks at Port Talbot, Wales, UK in 1929.*

---

**TASK 1:** Study Source A
a  How and why is a location close to raw materials different to a location close to the market?
b  What is meant by a 'footloose' location?
c  State the **three** main influences on the location of the early iron and steelworks.
d  What **two** different types of transport costs would influence industrial location?
e  In what ways would these different transport costs influence the location of:
- an iron and steelworks
- a bakery
- a computer software company?

**TASK 2:** Study Sources A and B
a  Describe the features of the steel works and its location.
b  Search the Internet to see what has happened to the Port Talbot steelworks in recent years.

# Theme 3: Topic 51

## B  Decisions, decisions …

| | Location factor | Questions to ask |
|---|---|---|
| **PHYSICAL** | Site requirement | Is there cheap land available? |
| | Natural routes | Is there a natural land or sea route, which provides speedy and cheap transportation? |
| | Availability of raw materials | Are sufficient raw materials available near by? |
| | | Will the supply of raw materials be reliable? |
| **HUMAN** | Access to market | What is the distance from the site to the market? |
| | | What is the cheapest form of transport available? |
| | Skilled labour | Are there enough skilled workers available? |
| | Power supply | What sources of power are available and at what cost? |
| | Industrial linkage | Are there any industries in the area that we can benefit from? |
| | Capital | Is capital available for developmental purposes? |
| | Government policies | Are there government incentives to develop a new industry? |

**TASK 3:** Study Source **B**

a  Make a copy of the table. Leave space in column **two** to add **one** other question you could ask about each factor.

b  Choose **two** physical factors and **two** human factors from the table. Suggest how each could influence the location of a factory.

**TASK 4:** Study Source **C**

Many new industries such as electronic and cell phone manufacturing have developed in recent years. Although transport costs and markets are considered in deciding on a location, there are other influences now.

a  Name **two** industrial areas shown on the map.

b  Name **three** examples of secondary industry shown on the map.

c  Use map evidence to suggest why industries have been developed in this area.

d  How might each of the following benefit from the building of new hi-tech industries in the area? Explain your views:

- a school leaver with no qualifications
- a young university graduate
- the owner of a food store at the local KIADB shopping complex.

## C  Locating industry…the present

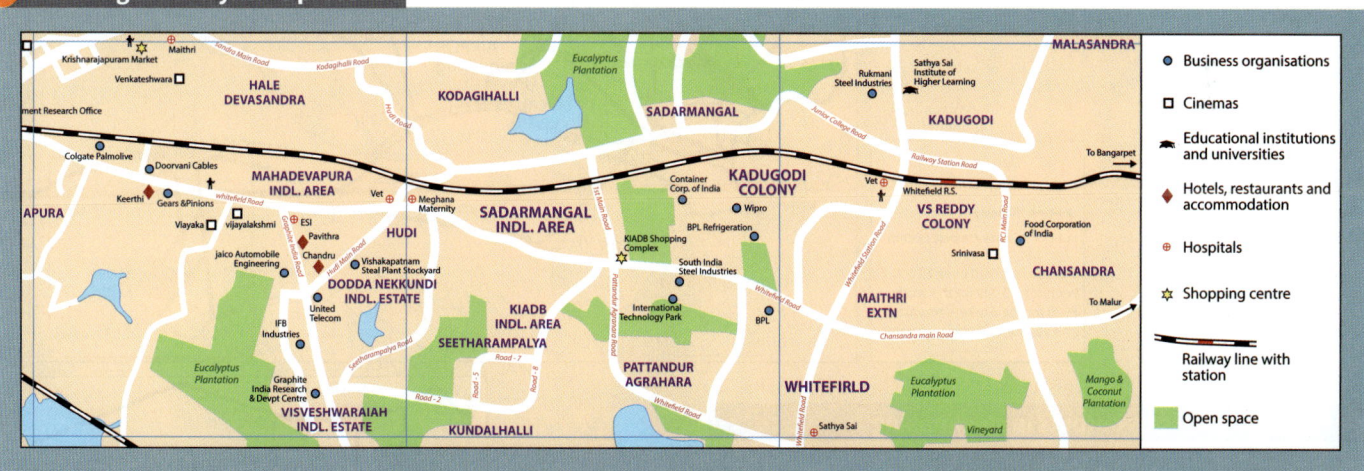

Bangalore is India's fifth largest industrial city. In 1991 a Software Technology Park of India (STPI) was created by the government and since then many transnational IT companies have arrived. It is now known as the 'IT capital of India'. The reasons for the growth of this industry here are:

- an agreeable climate, with temperatures between 10 °C and 33 °C and some monsoon rains
- an international airport with 70 flights a day
- a central position with road and rail routes in all directions
- highly trained, qualified workers
- excellent social, educational and health facilities
- a diverse cosmopolitan culture
- the best telecommunication infrastructure in the country
- government incentives and support
- the creation of science and technology parks.

# Cambridge IGCSE Geography — Industry

## Case Study
## The Pakistan Steel complex at Pipri, near Karachi

### Forty years of Pakistan Steel

After independence from India in 1947, Pakistan realised that it needed an iron and steelmaking industry to build houses, factories and infrastructure such as railway lines. Without its own industry, the country would be paying huge import bills for many years as well as being reliant on other countries. Its own economy would not develop. After much debate lasting many years, the first steel factories for Pakistan Steel were built in 1973. The project was so large it took another 12 years before the steel complex was completed and formally opened in 1985.

Today Pakistan Steel produces 1.1 million tonnes of steel and is the country's largest industrial activity. This provides for a quarter of Pakistan's steel demand with the rest being imported.

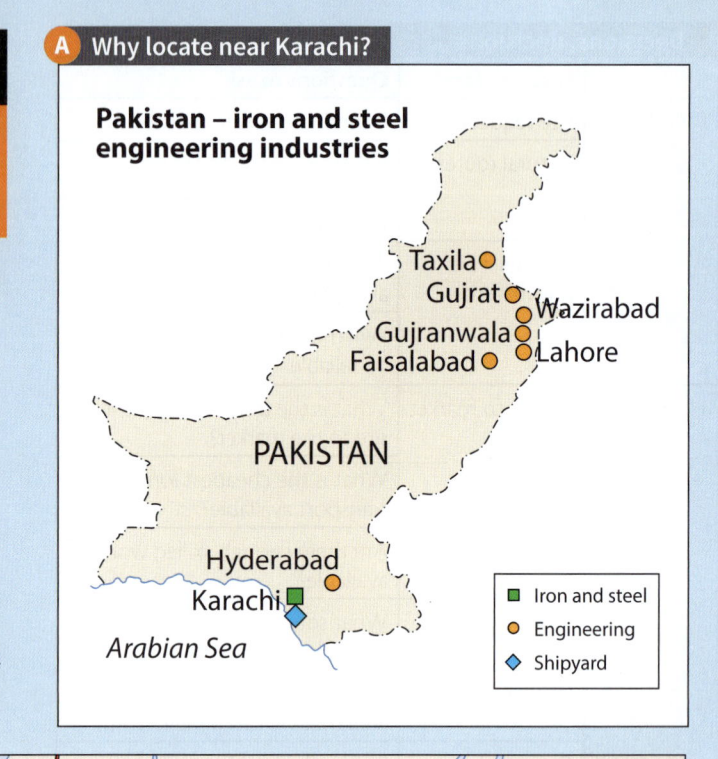

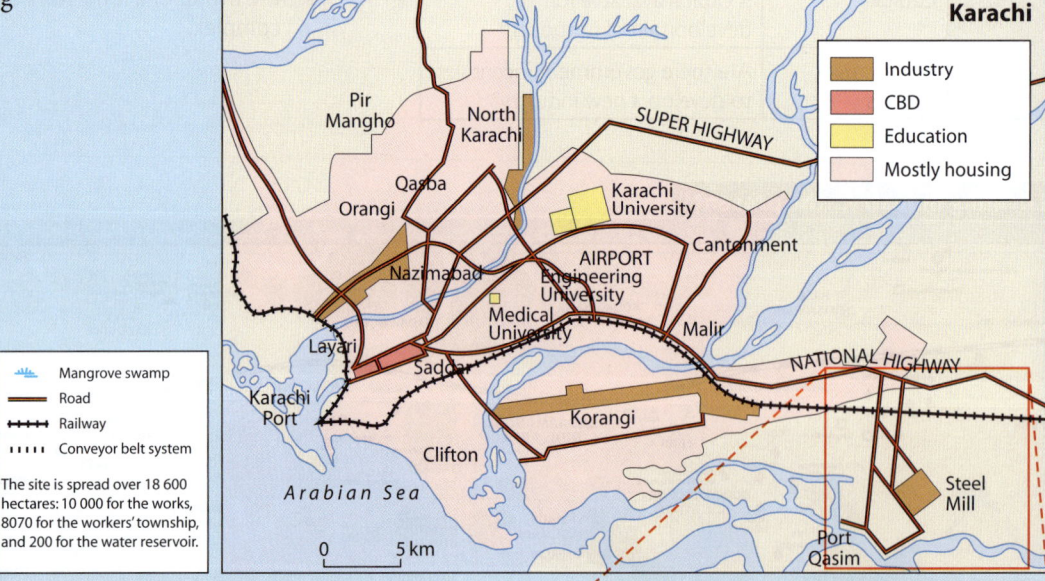

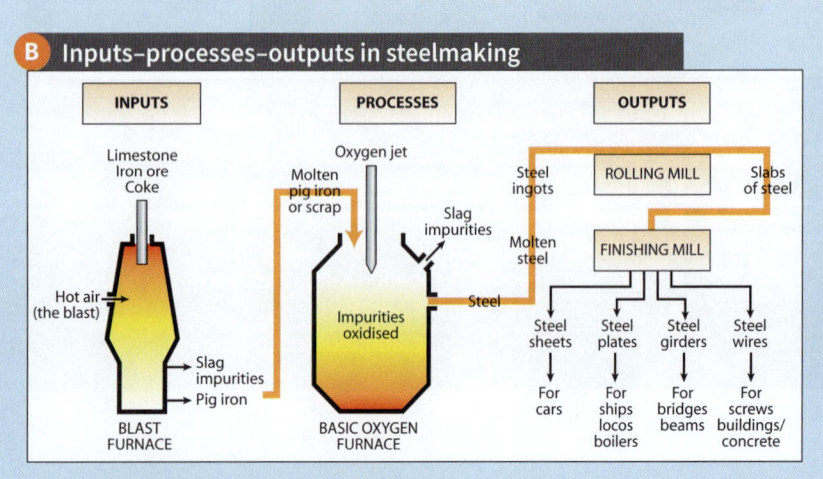

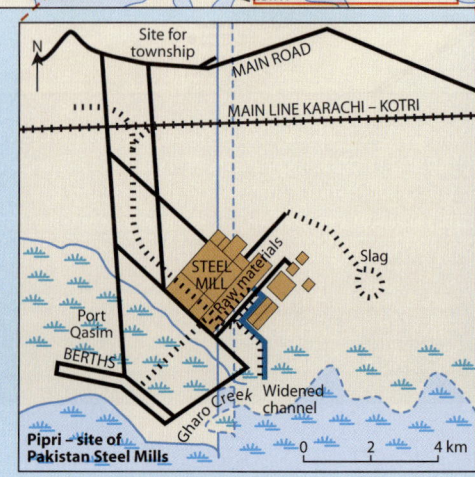

### A  Why locate near Karachi?

**Pakistan – iron and steel engineering industries**

Locations shown: Taxila, Gujrat, Wazirabad, Gujranwala, Lahore, Faisalabad, Hyderabad, Karachi.

Legend:
- ■ Iron and steel
- ● Engineering
- ◆ Shipyard

### Karachi map

Legend:
- Industry
- CBD
- Education
- Mostly housing

Places: Pir Mangho, North Karachi, Qasba, Orangi, Nazimabad, Karachi University, Cantonment, Airport, Engineering University, Medical University, Layari, Saddar, Malir, Karachi Port, Clifton, Korangi, Port Qasim, Steel Mill. Super Highway, National Highway.

Map legend:
- Mangrove swamp
- Road
- Railway
- Conveyor belt system

The site is spread over 18 600 hectares: 10 000 for the works, 8070 for the workers' township, and 200 for the water reservoir.

### B  Inputs–processes–outputs in steelmaking

**INPUTS**: Limestone, Iron ore, Coke; Hot air (the blast) → BLAST FURNACE → Slag impurities, Pig iron

**PROCESSES**: Molten pig iron or scrap, Oxygen jet → BASIC OXYGEN FURNACE → Slag impurities, Impurities oxidised → Molten steel

**OUTPUTS**: Steel ingots → ROLLING MILL → Slabs of steel → FINISHING MILL → Steel sheets (for cars), Steel plates (for ships, locos, boilers), Steel girders (for bridges, beams), Steel wires (for screws, buildings/concrete)

### Pipri – site of Pakistan Steel Mills

Features: Site for township, Main Road, Main Line Karachi–Kotri, Steel Mill, Raw materials, Slag, Port Qasim, Berths, Gharo Creek, Widened channel.

# Case Study: The Pakistan Steel complex at Pipri, near Karachi

## C  Why locate at Pipri?

| Factors influencing location | Reason |
|---|---|
| **PHYSICAL** | |
| Site | |
| Natural routes | |
| Raw materials | |
| **HUMAN** | |
| Capital | |
| Energy | |
| Labour | |
| Markets | |
| Transport | |

Port Qasim has a natural harbour that can deal with imports of materials and exports of steel to the countries neighbouring the Arabian Sea and east and west of the Indian Ocean. The 2.5 km long seawater channel is kept navigable for ships.

Iron ore, manganese and most of the coking coal can be imported through Port Qasim. Limestone, needed as a flux, can be brought by road from the nearby Makli Hills near Thatta. Large quantities of water required for making steel can be brought from Lake Haleji, 50 km to the east (saltwater is not suitable).

Port Qasim and Karachi had the highest electricity-generating capacity in the country. Pipri thermal power station produced 21% and Koranga thermal power station produced 15% of the total. Karachi also has a nuclear power station.

Plenty of skilled and unskilled cheap labour was available locally from Karachi.

Flat, cheap unused land was available at Pipri near Gharo Creek.

The former USSR (now Russia) provided economic assistance in the form of technical expertise, finance and capital.

Pipri was connected to the main Karachi–Kotri railway. Metalled roads also connected this area to the main road system

Many steel-using industries were located in Karachi such as tool-making. It supplies rolled sheets, galvanised sheets, pig iron and coal tar to the rest of the country. Over half the steel is used in the Punjab at Taxila where many factories were established with Chinese finance in 1979.

---

**TASK 1:** Study Source **A**

a  Why did Pakistan need an iron and steel plant of its own after 1947?
b  State **one** advantage of Karachi's location for building a steelworks.
c  Describe the situation of the steel mill in relation to Karachi. Refer to distances and directions.
d  Describe the site of the steel mill. What advantage does this site have for moving raw materials and products around?

**TASK 2:** Study Source **B**

a  List the main raw material inputs from the diagram. List **three** other inputs apart from raw materials that would be needed.
b  Describe the processes that turn these raw materials into steel.
c  Draw a detailed inputs–processes–outputs diagram using Source B and other information on these pages. Source B on page 155 will also help.
d  Making steel is a large-scale industry. How might the social, economic and environmental consequences of manufacturing steel in Pakistan be similar and different to the small-scale pottery manufacturing studied on page 155?

**TASK 3:** Study Source **C**

On a copy of the table, write in the 'Reason' column the matching label from those around the photograph.

**TASK 4**

Is there a factory near you or that you could study? If so:
a  Find out what it manufactures.
b  Draw a detailed inputs–processes–outputs diagram.
c  Suggest why the factory was located there.
d  What are the factory's social, economic and environmental influences on the local community? Decide if they are positive or negative.

# Cambridge IGCSE Geography — Tourism

## 52 The growth of tourism

### Tourism – a rapidly growing industry

Tourism is the fastest growing industry in the world. It is the world's largest employer, providing over 250 million jobs, and generating income of over US$900 billion per year. It is the main source of income for 80 per cent of the world's countries. There are several reasons that explain the growth in tourism:

- People in many countries earn more money and therefore have more **disposable income**.
- More people have paid time off work for holidays and many people have more than one holiday per year.
- The speed of travelling is much quicker than it used to be so it is easier to travel long distances. Motorways and railways can be used to travel quickly on land and aircraft can be used to get to different countries.
- More people own cars which gives them greater freedom to choose when and where to travel to.
- Life expectancy has increased in most countries and many people who are retired from work remain active and have the time and wealth to travel.
- Television programmes and advertising make people more aware of how and where they can choose to spend their free time.
- The Internet makes it easier for people to search for and book holidays from home.
- There is now more choice of holiday destinations and many different types of holiday available.

### The main attractions for tourism

The physical and human landscape found in an area may attract tourists to it.

**Physical attractions** are ones that are natural such as beaches, lakes, rivers, mountains, ecosystems or an attractive climate. While many tourists want hot, dry weather for sunbathing and beach holidays, others may want to get away from the heat or travel to destinations where there is snow for winter sports activities.

**Human attractions** have been made by people, such as historical buildings, monuments, theatres and theme parks.

### A  International tourism

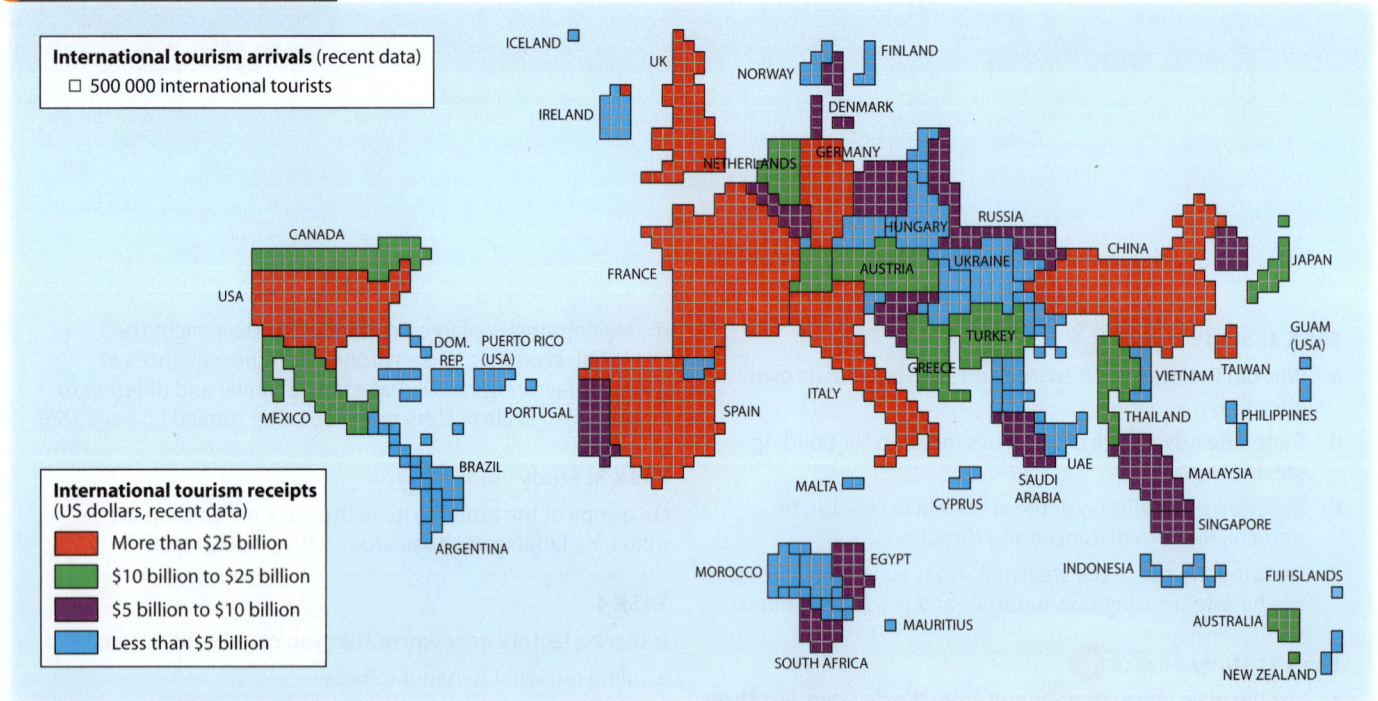

**International tourism arrivals** (recent data)
- □ 500 000 international tourists

**International tourism receipts** (US dollars, recent data)
- More than $25 billion
- $10 billion to $25 billion
- $5 billion to $10 billion
- Less than $5 billion

---

**TASK 1:** Study Source A

a  How many international tourists visited Portugal?
b  How much income was earned from international tourism by Egypt?
c  Put the following countries in rank order from the highest to the lowest number of international tourist arrivals.
- China
- France
- Italy
- Spain
- USA

# Theme 3: Topic 52

## B International tourism is growing

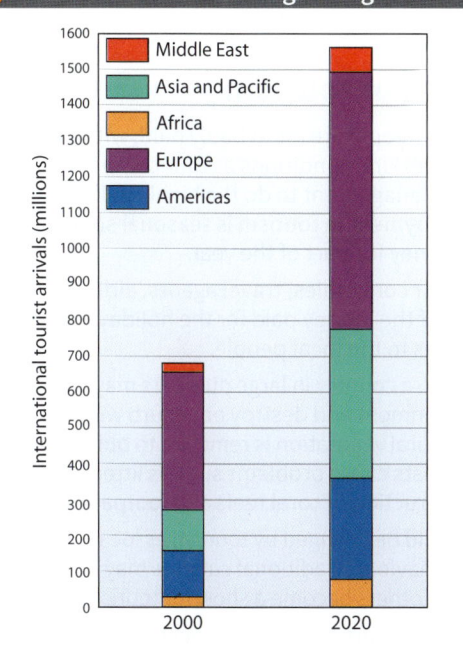

Bar chart showing international tourist arrivals (millions) in 2000 and 2020, by region: Middle East, Asia and Pacific, Africa, Europe, Americas.

## D Bergamo in March

## C The climate of Bergamo (northern Italy)

Climate graph for Bergamo (52°N 0°E) showing maximum and minimum temperature (°C) and rainfall (mm) by month.

## E Different tourist destinations

- New York, USA
- Hlane, Swaziland
- Pas de la Casa, Andorra
- Loch Ness, Scotland
- Rome, Italy
- Flic en Flac, Mauritius

---

### TASK 2: Study Source B

a By how much was the total number of international tourists expected to increase between 2000 and 2020?

b Identify the part of the world that:
- had over 50% of the world's international tourist arrivals in 2000
- is likely to increase its number of international tourist arrivals from 115 million in 2000 to over 400 million in 2020.

### TASK 3: Study Sources C and D

Suggest reasons why Bergamo is a popular destination for tourism all year round.

### TASK 4: Study Source E

a In pairs, look at each photograph and make a list of the different types of tourist destination they show.

b For each photograph make a list of the attractions of that area. For each attraction identify whether it is a natural (physical) or human (built) attraction.

c In groups, choose any tourist destination and carry out research to find out its main attractions. Produce either a poster or a PowerPoint presentation on the attractions of your chosen destination.

# 53 The benefits and disadvantages of tourism

## The impacts of tourism

In both MEDCs and LEDCs tourism has benefits and disadvantages. It brings overseas investment and economic growth into an area, creating work for local residents – for example, 30 per cent of all people in the Bahamas are directly employed in tourism, and if you add the people who are indirectly employed in tourism the percentage rises to about 64 per cent.

## Benefits of tourism

- Employment is provided for many local people, including formal work (e.g. construction of hotels, working in restaurants) and informal work (e.g. selling fruit on the beach), improving their living standards.
- Local people can learn new skills and languages.
- Tourism benefits the economy as people spend money in bars, restaurants, and other local businesses, so tourism can have a positive **multiplier effect**.
- The infrastructure of the area is developed as new roads, airports, electricity, water supplies and sanitation are provided for tourists. These also benefit the local residents.
- Income from tourism may be used to help protect the natural environment (e.g. national parks and wildlife conservation areas) and historical buildings.
- Tourism may help to preserve local cultures and festivals as they become a tourist attraction.
- Foreign currency earned and taxes raised from tourism can be invested in education and health care.

## Disadvantages of tourism

- Jobs for the local people are often badly paid, with long hours and poor working conditions as tour companies bring in foreign management to do the highly paid jobs. Sometimes employment in tourism is seasonal so people can only earn money for part of the year.
- Transnational tour companies, travel agents, airlines and hotels get most of the money paid for the holiday, so only a small amount gets to the local people.
- Tourists coming to a country in large numbers may damage the natural environment and destroy or disturb wildlife and habitats. Natural vegetation is removed to build tourist facilities and tourists cause problems such as litter, water and air pollution, destruction of coral reefs and footpath erosion.
- Local cultures could be changed by tourism as locals imitate tourist behaviour. Traditional cultures may became 'westernised' and others become a show for tourists to watch.
- Supplying water for tourists can leave local people, plants and animals short of water.
- Land and property prices rise which makes houses too expensive for locals.
- Areas of settlement, local fishing grounds and good quality farmland may be lost when hotels and other tourist facilities are built.
- Tourism can easily be affected by local and world events (e.g. economic recession, terrorism, natural disasters) and the number of tourists can drop very quickly.
- Tourism may increase the crime rate or cause conflict as illegal economic activities may develop, such as drugs, sex tourism, alcohol abuse and trading in endangered species.

### A Working in the tourist industry

### B Costs of tourism in Thailand

I was born in 1972 and when I was eight or nine it was still mainly rainforest here on the island. By the late 1980s, though, it was mostly developed. We have now lost so much of the biodiversity and primary forest and the soil is eroding in many places. The construction of hotels upstream is creating a lot of sediment in the water and this causes damage to the coral reefs when it washes out to sea. It also affects the mangroves on the east coast. A lot of our waste water – about 40 per cent – is still being pumped out to sea on the west coast where all the resort areas are. Land is now so expensive here due to tourism that it has meant many local people have been forced to sell off their homes and farmland. The corals are also damaged by tourism. Snorkellers actually cause more damage than divers because they touch the coral more often …

Leo Hickman, *The Final Call – In Search of the True Cost of our Holidays*, 2007

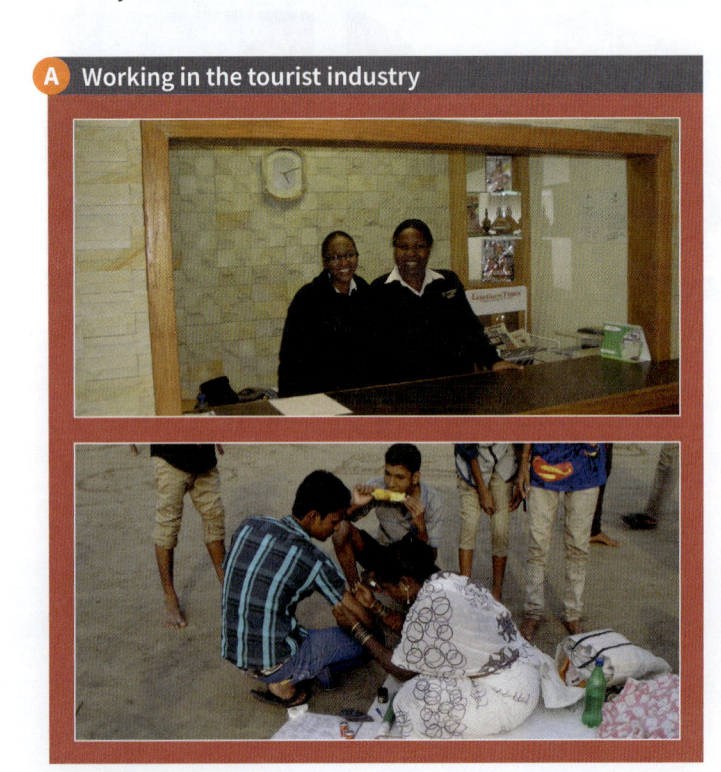

Theme 3: Topic 53

## The Seychelles

The Seychelles is made up of 115 islands in the Indian Ocean, 1500 km east of mainland Africa, north-east of the island of Madagascar.

The traditional economy is based on the growing of coconut palms and tea on plantations and the cultivation of spices such as cinnamon and vanilla on small farms. There are also craft industries, and some fishing, especially for tuna, takes place around the coast.

Since independence in 1976 the government has encouraged foreign investment in order to build hotels and other tourist amenities. Now the tourist industry provides the islands with 70 per cent of their income and it employs about 30 per cent of the labour force.

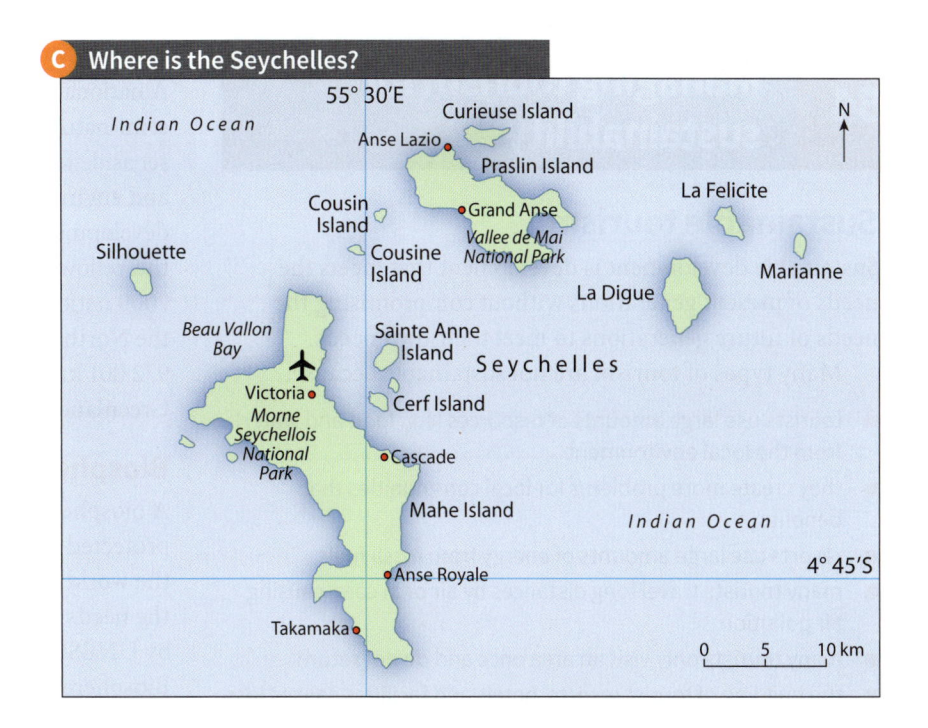

### C Where is the Seychelles?

### TASK 1: Study Source A
a  Describe the jobs in the tourist industry that are shown in the photographs. Explain whether you think each one is formal or informal and low or high paid.
b  What other jobs does tourism bring to an area?
c  Explain how getting a job in tourism can benefit people in an area visited by tourists.
d  In what other ways does tourism benefit the local people?

### TASK 2: Study Source B
a  Explain how tourism may threaten the natural environment in Thailand. You should refer to threats to natural vegetation (flora), wildlife (fauna), coral and mangroves.
b  How does the extract suggest that local people have been affected by tourism? Is this a benefit or a problem? Explain your answer.

### TASK 3: Study Source C
a  Name the three largest islands in the Seychelles.
b  Name **two** national parks.
c  Anse Royale is a resort in the Seychelles.
 - State its latitude and longitude.
 - Give its distance and direction from the airport at Victoria.

### TASK 4: Study Source D
a  In what ways does the tourist industry contribute to water shortages in LEDCs such as the Seychelles?
b  The Minister of Tourism of the Seychelles wants to limit tourist numbers to 200 000 per year. In groups, discuss the benefits and problems of this policy.

### D Water shortages may affect tourism in Seychelles

The reality of water shortages in Seychelles became all too apparent this week. In a chic restaurant in town some tourists were heard complaining about the filthy toilet without a drop of water next to the restaurant. The poor owner was trying to explain to the tourists that around this time of the year there is a drought in Seychelles and everywhere they go they will encounter the same problem.

The government took out a loan of US$25 million not so long ago to invest in a desalination plant but there are still water restrictions and water shortages. We lose 75% of our water because of old and leaking water pipes. One wonders if the money could have been better spent building reservoirs everywhere around our islands similar to the one being built at upper Anse La Mouche, especially since there is an abundance of water during the rainy season which ends up in the sea. Better still, why was the money not used to purchase and install new water pipes? One also questions the wisdom of taking such a large foreign exchange loan to invest in a desalination plant.

**Adapted from** *Seychelles Weekly*, August 2006

# 54 Managing tourism for sustainability

## Sustainable tourism

Sustainable development is development that meets the needs of present generations without compromising the needs of future generations to meet their own needs.

Many types of tourism are not sustainable because:

- tourists use large amounts of resources (e.g. food and water) from the local environment
- they create more problems for local communities than benefits
- resorts use large amounts of energy from fossil fuels
- many tourists travel long distances by air or in cars, causing air pollution
- many tourists only visit an area once and do not return
- the building of tourist resorts, hotels and facilities causes loss of natural vegetation and habitats.

**Sustainable tourism** can be defined as:

'Tourism that takes full account of its current and future economic, social and environmental impacts, addressing the needs of visitors, the industry, the environment and host communities.' (United Nations World Tourism Organization (UNWTO))

Examples of sustainable tourism include:

## Ecotourism

Ecotourism is defined as 'Responsible travel to natural areas that conserves the environment and improves the well-being of local people.' (The International Ecotourism Society, 1990)

Ecotourism sets out guidelines for how tourists should behave when visiting fragile environments:

- Protect the environment – keep to footpaths, don't leave litter or start fires.
- Don't interfere with wildlife – don't scare or feed the animals.
- Protect resources – don't take too many showers or use air conditioning.
- Support local communities – stay in locally owned accommodation and buy produce from local people.
- Eat local food and drink – avoid products that have been imported.
- Respect local customs and traditions – do not offend local people by wearing inappropriate clothes in religious places, or by not covering up appropriately on the beach. Try to learn the local language and show an interest in the culture.

## National parks

A national park can be defined as a reserve of natural or semi-natural land, declared or owned by a government, set aside for human recreation and enjoyment, animal and environmental protection and restricted from most development. The first national park, established in 1872, was the Yellowstone National Park in the USA. There are about 7000 national parks in the world and the largest is the Northeast Greenland National Park which protects 972 001 km$^2$ of the interior and north-eastern coast of Greenland, which is almost three times larger than Germany!

## Biosphere reserves

A biosphere reserve is an area of land or water that is protected by law to conserve ecosystems to help to protect the world's plant and animal species while dealing with the needs of the population. These areas were created by UNESCO under a programme called 'Man and the Biosphere' in 1968.

**A** The Arusha Declaration – October 2012

Sustainable tourism is one of the most effective ways to preserve Africa's national parks and protected areas while creating jobs and income for local communities. This was one of the main conclusions of the First Pan-African Conference on Sustainable Tourism in African National Parks, organised by UNWTO and the Government of Tanzania (Arusha, Tanzania, 15–18 October 2012) and attended by tourism ministers, tourism private sector representatives and conservation officials.

'Nature is one of Africa's greatest assets,' said UNWTO Secretary-General, Taleb Rifai, opening the conference. 'Many of the 50 million international tourists visiting Africa each year are driven by the continent's unparalleled wildlife and natural scenery. These tourists spend money in the local economy, sustain jobs and provide an incentive for conservation, making tourism a powerful engine for sustainable development.'

Signatories to the Arusha Declaration underlined the importance of good management of tourism, calling for 'the need to directly involve local communities in the management of parks and protected areas to ensure they gain concrete benefits in terms of employment and income generation'.

Adapted from traveldailynews.com

# Theme 3: Topic 54

There are three main parts to a biosphere reserve. The first part is called the core zone, which is protected to make sure that different types of plants and animals are safe from human impact. The second part is called a buffer zone, and surrounds the core zones, providing a space for environmental research, recreation and tourism. The last part is called a transition zone, and this area is for local communities to manage the resources of the area through farming, fisheries, and other activities.

## B Ecotourism in the Galapagos Islands

Many of the plants and animals found in the Galapagos Islands are not found anywhere else in the world. This is because the islands are cut off from the rest of the world by the Pacific Ocean.

Tourists who visit have to pay an entry fee of US$100 and keep to strict rules:

- They should not touch, feed or disturb wildlife.
- They can only visit on small ships of 10 to 16 tourists, most of which are owned by local people.
- They can only visit a limited number of places on the islands so other parts are protected.
- They should keep to paths and not leave litter.
- They are given information on how to conserve the islands before they visit.

## C Biosphere reserves in Cuba

Cuba, an LEDC in the Caribbean, has six UNESCO biosphere reserves that protect the country's natural attractions. Highlights include the La Boca crocodile-breeding farm at the **Ciénaga de Zapata** Biosphere Reserve, where rare Cuban crocodiles are carefully nurtured. This reserve contains the largest wetlands in the Caribbean, and one of its most diverse ecosystems. The world's smallest bird, the bee hummingbird, lives there. Tourism is very important and brings more than 800 000 people to the area each year, for the benefit of the local communities.

At the eastern end of the island, untouched rainforests flourish in the **Cuchillas del Toa** reserve near Baracoa.

The **Buenavista** Biosphere Reserve protects ecosystems including mangroves, coral reefs and sand dunes. There are caves with historical paintings. Around 7000 tourists visit the area annually and some of the main activities are fishing, beach tourism and diving.

The **Baconao** Reserve has 1800 plant species that are of interest for their medicinal properties. There are a reported 939 indigenous species of wildlife living here, too, including butterflies, mammals, reptiles and the endangered hot-cave bat. The Sierra Maestra mountain range is protected within the Baconao biosphere, as are the first coffee plantations in Cuba.

**Sierra del Rosario**, created in 1985, was Cuba's first biosphere reserve. Here there are rainforests containing one of the world's smallest frogs and the colourful reptile, the chipojo.

The **Península de Guanahacabibes** Reserve includes the Guanahacabibes National Park. Its vegetation includes mangroves, marsh grasslands, coastal scrublands and forests and there are many species of birds and lizards.

---

**TASK 1: Study Source A**

a What is sustainable tourism?

b Explain how the Arusha Declaration might help to ensure that tourism in Africa is sustainable.

**TASK 2: Study Source B**

a What is ecotourism?

b Explain why the Galapagos Islands attract tourists. Use the Internet to find out and include more details in your answer.

c Suggest **two** reasons why tourists have to pay an entry fee of US$100 before they can visit the Galapagos Islands.

d Explain why each of the rules are important to ensure that tourism in the Galapagos Islands is sustainable.

**TASK 3: Study Source C**

a What is a 'biosphere reserve'?

b Describe the attractions of the biosphere reserves in Cuba for tourists.

c Explain why it is important that biosphere reserves are protected.

d Explain how the creation of a biosphere reserve is likely to affect the people who live there.

**Cambridge IGCSE Geography** — Tourism

## Case Study
### An area where tourism is important – Dubai, UAE

#### From a desert to a top tourist destination

Dubai is one of the seven **emirates** that make up the United Arab Emirates (UAE) on the Arabian Peninsula. It is located on the southern shore of the Persian Gulf. Dubai city is a busy urban area but, outside the city itself, it is a sparsely populated desert area.

Dubai has a sub-tropical, arid climate. Rainfall is infrequent and irregular, falling only on about five days per year. The mean daily temperature maximum is 30 °C in January, rising to over 40 °C in July.

Dubai's growing tourist industry accounts for over 30 per cent of its GDP. In 1998 there were only 2 million tourists, but by 2014 this increased to over 5 million. Growth continues to increase at 10% per year. Hotels and apartments record over 9 million guests per year, generating revenues of more than US$4 billion. In a short period of time tourism has transformed an area of desert into one of the world's top tourist destinations of the 21st century.

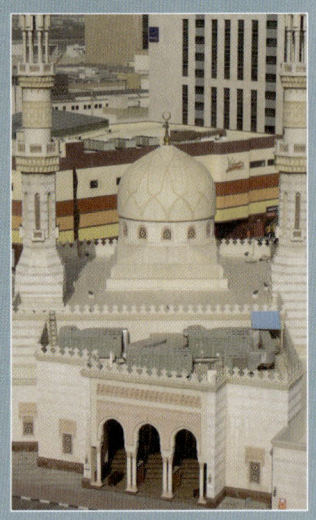

**A** Where is Dubai?

**B** Dubai – attractions for tourists

# Case Study: An area where tourism is important – Dubai, UAE

## What is the likely future for Dubai?

Dubai used to rely on its oil reserves to survive but now tourism is the most rapidly increasing sector of the economy and it has one of the fastest rates of tourism growth in the world. However, this means there may be an impact on the natural environment.

In a recent survey the United Arab Emirates was the least environmentally friendly country due to its extensive use of air conditioning and desalinated water. Cheaply available oil is used to desalinate the water which is used to water the tropical landscapes planted in hotel grounds. It is used to fuel cars in a city designed for cars rather than pedestrians. People are becoming aware that such a lifestyle may not be sustainable and that Dubai's low-lying reclaimed coasts are at risk from flooding as sea levels rise.

Building tourist hotels and facilities in the desert has great environmental costs and building The World islands on land reclaimed from the sea resulted in 33 million cubic metres of sand being dredged up from the sea bed to make the islands. Areas of coral have also been damaged by sediment deposits.

This rapid growth needs effective management. The government is creating new laws and the ruling family is managing new projects to meet the challenge of building a sustainable tourist destination in the desert.

### C Al Maha Desert Resort and Spa

**Al Maha Desert Resort and Spa, Dubai, United Arab Emirates**

The Al Maha Desert Resort and Spa is at the centre of the 225 km² Dubai Desert Conservation Reserve in the Arabian Desert, built in old-style Arabian architecture. Conservation of the desert's ecosystem was a part of the development project. A wildlife reserve was developed which has 33 indigenous mammal and reptile species, 100 bird species, and nearly 300 Arabian oryx.

The 37 suites each measure 75 m² and contain a king-size bed, minibar, bathroom with a king-size bath, walk-in-shower and vanity areas. The main restaurant is cool and airy, and serves international cuisines. It has a shaded terrace with views of the reserve and mountains. The resort also offers a personal dining facility in a secluded spot in the sand dunes within the reserve.

The Al Maha's spa and fitness facility overlooks the mountains, and includes treatment rooms, a sauna, a steam room and a jacuzzi. There is a swimming pool and gymnasium and the services of a personal trainer. Al Maha has a library featuring original artworks and paintings, and is furnished with rustic furniture and woven traditional rugs.

Guests can rest in Majlis, a traditional Arabic seating area. There is a souvenir shop selling a range of antiques and artefacts.

The resort protects one of the largest underground water reservoirs of the United Arab Emirates. Before it was turned into a resort the land was used for farming and the water was used for irrigation. Since the opening of the hotel there has been no reduction in the quality and level of the water. All glass, plastic, cans and paper used in the hotel are recycled and all kitchen oils and organic wastes are carefully disposed of.

**Adapted from** www.hotelmanagement-network.com

---

**TASK 1:** Study Source A and an atlas
a  Describe the location and growth of Dubai as a tourist destination.
b  Explain why Dubai is perfectly positioned to attract tourists from all parts of the world.

**TASK 2:** Study Source B and the Internet
The growth of Dubai into one of the top tourist destinations in the world has been rapid and spectacular.

In groups, prepare a presentation about the physical and human attractions for tourists in Dubai.

**TASK 3:** Study Source C
a  To what extent is the Al Maha resort environmentally friendly? You should explain how care has been taken to protect the environment but also comment on any problems that the resort could cause.
b  Explain why it is important for tourism to be carefully managed in Dubai.

# 55  Energy use varies

## Using non-renewable fossil fuels

People's use of energy sources has changed over time. Up to the 18th century wood-burning provided most of the world's energy supplies. With the Industrial Revolution affecting Western Europe and the USA in the 19th century, coal became the most used energy source. The 20th century saw the rise of transport and industry, which required large amounts of fuel, usually oil for direct use, e.g. petrol for cars or for indirect use, e.g. in power stations, for producing electricity.

In the 21st century oil is the most sought-after energy source. Only a few countries have major oil reserves so they dictate who gets it at what price. They can also decide not to sell it to some countries for political reasons and develop a power base and alliance with other countries. Many countries are looking at alternative ways of meeting their energy demand. Some are trying to develop their own renewable resources; others are looking at a process called 'fracking' which involves extracting gas and oil from shale deposits underground by blasting water and chemicals into the rock. If countries become less dependent on importing their energy resources, they can move towards self-sufficiency and control of their energy policies instead of being controlled by the countries that have energy sources they need.

### A  Non-renewable energy

*Oil provides 31% of the world's energy supplies.*

*Natural gas provides 25% of the world's energy supplies.*

*Coal provides 24% of the world's energy supplies.*

The most important non-renewable fossil fuels used as energy sources are coal, oil and natural gas. These are derived from the remains of plants and animals that have been buried and fossilised over thousands of years. They are non-renewable because there is a limited amount; they will run out one day so they are not sustainable.

### B  World fossil fuel producers, 2013

| Top 6 oil producers | Million tonnes (mt) | Top 6 coal producers | Million tonnes (mt) | Top 6 natural gas producers | Billion cubic metres (bcm) |
|---|---|---|---|---|---|
| Saudi Arabia | 544 | China | 3549 | USA | 681 |
| Russia | 520 | USA | 935 | Russia | 656 |
| USA | 387 | India | 595 | Qatar | 160 |
| China | 206 | Indonesia | 443 | Iran | 158 |
| Iran | 186 | Australia | 421 | Canada | 157 |
| Canada | 182 | Russia | 354 | Norway | 115 |
| Others | 2117 | Others | 1534 | Others | 1508 |
| WORLD TOTAL | 4142 | | 7831 | | 3435 |

**TASK 1:** Study Source A

a  What is meant by *non-renewable* and *renewable* sources of energy?

b  Name the **three** non-renewable sources of energy shown.

c  What percentage of the world's energy use is produced from these **three** sources of energy?

d  Suggest why it is important for countries to try and become self-sufficient in energy supplies.

**TASK 2:** Study Source B

a  Represent this data on an outline world map. Add a title and a key.

b  Describe the global distribution of fossil fuel production.

c  List countries that are in the top six for:
- all **three** types of energy production
- any **two** types of energy production.

Theme 3: Topic 55

## Renewable energy sources

Renewable sources of energy are obtained from natural resources, e.g. sun, wind, waves, and can be used continuously and will not run out unless people interfere with nature – they are sustainable. About 13 per cent of the world's energy use is now based on renewable energy sources. These include geothermal supplies, wind, hydro-electric power (HEP), wave and tidal power, solar power and biofuels. As an energy source biofuels can either be used:

- directly to produce heat, e.g. by burning fuelwood
- indirectly after converting it to various forms of biofuels, e.g. ethanol.

Using biofuels in the form of fuelwood is renewable if reforestation restores the trees; if this does not happen they become non-renewable sources.

### C Renewable energy

*Hydro-electric power (HEP) supplies 3% of the world's energy supplies.*

*Wind power provides 2% of the world's energy supplies.*

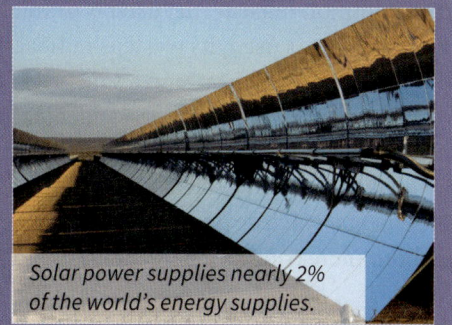

*Solar power supplies nearly 2% of the world's energy supplies.*

### D Energy sources in an MEDC and LEDC (2013)

**France – An MEDC**

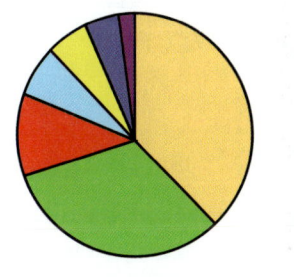

Legend: Nuclear, Oil, Natural Gas, HEP, Biofuels, Coal, Others

France is the most important producer and consumer of electricity from nuclear power stations in the European Union (EU). Much oil and gas is imported and so is coal as the country has none of these resources left. Renewable uses have risen to 13%. More nuclear power stations are due to be built by 2020.

**Democratic Republic of the Congo – An LEDC**

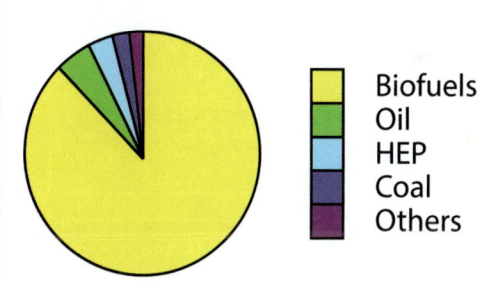

Legend: Biofuels, Oil, HEP, Coal, Others

Over 90% of the energy used is based on burning biofuels in the form of fuelwood for heating and cooking as only 6% of the population are connected to an electricity source. Any electricity used comes from HEP and some imported coal and oil. D.R. Congo has the greatest potential for HEP in Africa with a huge HEP project planned along the Congo river – the Inga project.

**TASK 3:** Study Source C
a  Name the **three** renewable sources of energy shown.
b  Use Source C to describe the importance of renewable energy supplies:
  - compared to non-renewable supplies
  - compared to each other.
c  Suggest why many countries are developing their own renewable energy sources.

**TASK 4:** Study Source D
a  Describe, using data, **three** differences between energy consumption in France and D.R. Congo.
b  Suggest reasons for these differences.
c  Predict how the percentage figures for consumption in both countries might change over the next few years. Justify your answer.

# 56 Nuclear power or renewables

## Nuclear power

All **thermal power** stations produce heat that changes water into steam. This drives the turbines that produce electricity. In nuclear power stations the heat is generated by splitting atoms – a process known as fission. The neutrons released bounce against each other, generating heat. The most common nuclear fuel used is uranium. While only a small amount is used, its waste is radioactive for thousands of years. Storing the waste in a safe place is a great concern for many people. Disasters or accidents that result in the release of this waste are also of great concern. This is why nuclear power stations are built a long way from settlements. Nuclear power and renewable energy sources are both increasing as a percentage of global energy use.

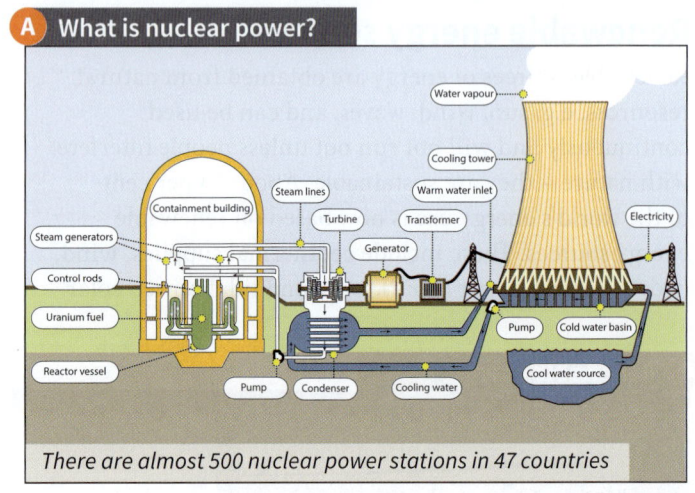

### A What is nuclear power?

*Diagram labels: Water vapour, Cooling tower, Steam lines, Warm water inlet, Containment building, Turbine, Transformer, Electricity, Steam generators, Generator, Control rods, Uranium fuel, Pump, Cold water basin, Reactor vessel, Pump, Condenser, Cooling water, Cool water source*

There are almost 500 nuclear power stations in 47 countries

* Please note: the cool water source e.g. a river will be sited next to the cooling tower, not beneath it.

Nuclear power is the more controversial energy source with its supporters and opponents producing strong views on its benefits and its disadvantages.

### B Nuclear power – benefits and disadvantages

- Nuclear power is cheap and reliable once the stations are built.
- For most countries uranium would have to be imported.
- Nuclear power stations are clean and safe.
- The disposal of nuclear waste poses unacceptable health hazards such as the risk of cancers.
- Safe disposal stores for radioactive waste could be found.
- Nuclear power stations can provide all of a country's energy needs without using coal, oil and gas.
- Nuclear accidents can never be completely ruled out.
- Building a nuclear power station provides about 1200 construction jobs for local people.
- Nuclear power stations are expensive to build.
- Radioactive gases and waste can pollute the environment for hundreds of years.
- Operating a nuclear power station provides jobs for over 500 staff for about 35 years, often in isolated areas where jobs can be hard to find.
- Nuclear power stations can be built in remote areas to reduce dangers to health.

### TASK 1: Study Source A

a Describe the path of cold water from its starting point in the 'cool water source' to it being turned into steam to generate electricity and then its return to the cool water source.

b Suggest the *inputs* needed to build and operate a nuclear power station.

c Suggest the *processes* that take place in a nuclear power station.

d Electricity and waste are the two main *outputs*. Describe what happens to these after processing has taken place.

### TASK 2: Study Source B

As a group, discuss your views on the benefits and disadvantages of developing nuclear power stations.

### TASK 3

Accidents involving nuclear power stations are rare but they do happen. For **one** of the following accidents, find out when it happened, what took place and the causes and consequences.

- Three Mile Island, USA.
- Chernobyl, Ukraine.
- Fukushima, Japan.

# Renewable energy sources

At present nuclear power accounts for 8 per cent of energy of all the electricity produced in the world; slightly less than the 13 per cent that all the renewable sources of energy produce. One general disadvantage of renewables is that the set-up and distribution costs are more than fossil fuels and nuclear power to produce the same amount of energy. The use of renewable sources is growing as it can provide several benefits.

- Renewable sources are constantly available and will never be used up.
- Renewable sources cause less environmental impact and issues than fossil fuels or nuclear power so are often termed 'green' energy.
- Many countries, such as the USA, which rely heavily on other countries for energy sources, can become self-reliant without using fossil fuels.
- Governments can avoid the controversy and disadvantages of using nuclear power.

## C Comparing renewable energy sources

| Energy source | Benefit | Disadvantage | *Average Cost |
|---|---|---|---|
| Geothermal | Replenished by nature.<br>Good for heating and cooling. Individual houses can benefit.<br>Partially built underground so little surface impact.<br>Reliable and consistent supply once available.<br>Very low carbon emissions from equipment. | Location-specific; needs to have correct geology and access to the hot water underground.<br>Might cause small earthquakes.<br>High set-up costs.<br>Only sustainable if underground reservoirs managed carefully so that use of water equals replacement by rainwater. | US$200 |
| Wind | Wind is free.<br>Once built no air pollution.<br>Although tall, only takes up small amount of land. Surface below can continue to be farmed.<br>Useful in remote areas away from national electricity grid.<br>Various sizes and costs for use in MEDCs and LEDCs. | Needs reliable wind but this can range from zero to storms.<br>Storage of electricity problem. Visual issues of wind farms.<br>Can be as noisy as a car travelling at 112 km/h (70 mph).<br>Manufacture produces some air pollution.<br>Largest turbine can only produce electricity for 475 homes. Many needed for a town. | Onshore: US$185<br>Offshore: US$260 |
| Hydro-electric power (HEP) | No pollution issues.<br>Reliable once built as simple structures; few breakdowns reported.<br>Have a long life.<br>Provides drinking water plus other opportunities, e.g. boating, fishing, a road across the dam, tourism.<br>Can respond to supply and demand quickly.<br>Can control flooding downstream. | Site requirements mean often have to locate in remote mountain areas.<br>High cost of building dam and electricity infrastructure.<br>Requires large area for reservoir and may involve relocating people.<br>Dam prevents seasonal flooding of ecosystems which affects wildlife.<br>Relies on rain/snowmelt; droughts mean no electricity can be produced so a back-up power source needed. | US$340 |
| Wave and tidal power | Renewable while there are tides which rely on the sun and the moon.<br>Very efficient in converting energy into electricity.<br>Predictable, unlike other renewables that rely on the weather.<br>No greenhouse gas pollution. | Very high set-up costs.<br>It takes 7 years to build and 2 years before it generates electricity.<br>Storm waves can damage machinery.<br>Limited to sites with high tidal ranges to turn the turbines.<br>Works for 10 hours a day during tidal surges – need back-up power source.<br>Disrupts fish migration and can damage marine creatures. | US$285 |
| Solar power | The sun's energy is free.<br>Renewable while there is a sun.<br>No noise and no air pollution.<br>Little maintenance needed once set up.<br>Easy to install in individual homes or as solar farms.<br>Can be used in remote areas away from a national electricity grid. | Limited availability of sun in many areas.<br>Very high set-up costs.<br>Cannot be generating during cloudy days or at night.<br>Limited storage capacity.<br>Can take up large amount of land.<br>Visual issues of solar farms. | US$155 |

*All costs are in US Dollars (US$) equivalent per megawatt of electricity generated.
Other electricity generating costs (average US$/megawatt): coal US$155, gas US$130, nuclear US$160, biofuels US$210.

### TASK 4: Study Source C
a Put the average cost of generating electricity from the different energy sources in rank order from highest to lowest. Include those listed below the table.

b Choose **one** of the five renewable sources listed. Make a list of benefits and disadvantages. Carry out some extra research to add other points to your list.

### TASK 5
a 'The benefits of using nuclear power to generate future supplies of electricity far outweigh the benefits of using renewable energy.'

Make **two** lists of points:
- one that supports the statement
- one that argues against the statement.

b Write down your view of this statement and explain why you hold that view.

# Cambridge IGCSE Geography — Energy

## Case Study
### Energy supply in Iceland

**Renewable energy – a model for the world?**

Renewable energy, while supported at many international conferences, still plays only a small part in the global energy mix. However, Iceland has reached the stage where 66 per cent of its energy use comes from geothermal sources and 15 per cent from **HEP (hydro-electric power)** – 81 per cent of its energy needs comes from its own sustainable energy resources. The remaining 19 per cent consists of imported fossil fuels, coal and oil, for motor vehicles and ships. It is the only western country that produces all its electricity from emission-free and sustainable natural resources in the form of geothermal power and HEP.

### A  Iceland sits on a hotspot

Iceland, a country of just 300 000 people, is located on the Mid-Atlantic Ridge. This is a constructive plate boundary between the North American and Eurasian plates. These are moving apart at a rate of 2 cm a year, creating volcanic activity and rising heat in the gap. Precipitation here is also high with over 800 mm per year. Consequently Iceland has a wealth of geothermal sources and water for HEP. Three-quarters of its population live in the south-west (with 60 % in the capital Reykjavik) where most geothermal sources are found.

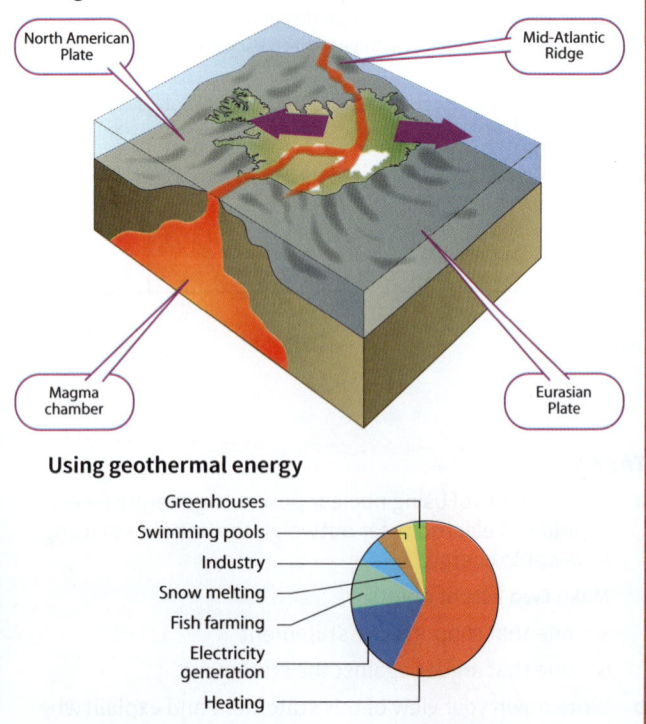

*Diagram labels: North American Plate, Mid-Atlantic Ridge, Magma chamber, Eurasian Plate*

**Using geothermal energy**
Pie chart categories: Greenhouses, Swimming pools, Industry, Snow melting, Fish farming, Electricity generation, Heating

### B  Volcanic zones and geothermal areas

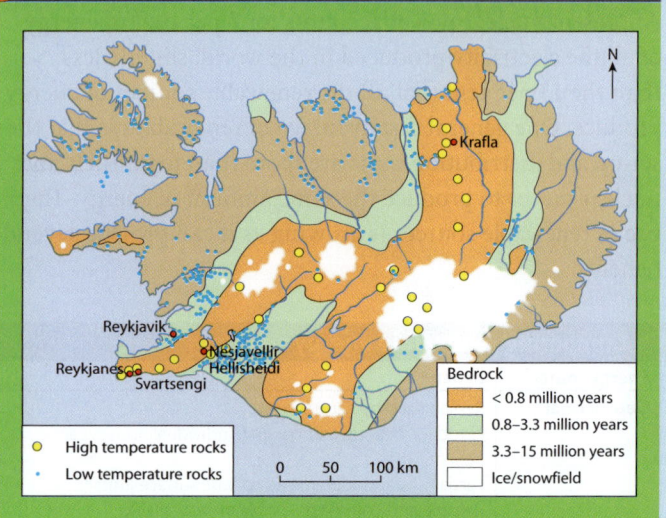

*Map of Iceland showing: Krafla, Reykjavik, Reykjanes, Nesjavellir, Hellisheidi, Svartsengi*

- High temperature rocks
- Low temperature rocks

Bedrock:
- < 0.8 million years
- 0.8–3.3 million years
- 3.3–15 million years
- Ice/snowfield

0   50   100 km

**Low temperature activity** – located away from the main volcanic zone close to the surface at about 1 km depth. Rock temperature varies from 50° to 150°C. Water from precipitation is heated by the rock to create hot, boiling springs at the surface.

**High temperature activity** – located within the active volcanic zones at a depth below 1 km where temperatures are at least 200°C. Here groundwater exists in deep reservoirs so hot water is not seen at the surface but steam is.

### TASK 1: Study Source A

a  With the help of an atlas and the diagram, describe the location of Iceland. Refer to latitude, longitude, the Mid-Atlantic Ridge and diverging plates.

b  Explain why Iceland can create energy from geothermal and water sources but is not able to create energy using fossil fuels of its own or solar power.

c  Draw a pie chart to show the percentages of energy use produced from geothermal power, HEP and fossil fuels in Iceland.

d  List in order (by percentage) the different uses of geothermal energy.

e  What is the major use of geothermal energy? Suggest why it is used to melt snow.

### TASK 2: Study Source B

a  Describe the location of Reykjavik.

b  Where are most of the high-temperature rocks?

c  How does this compare with the distribution of low-temperature rocks?

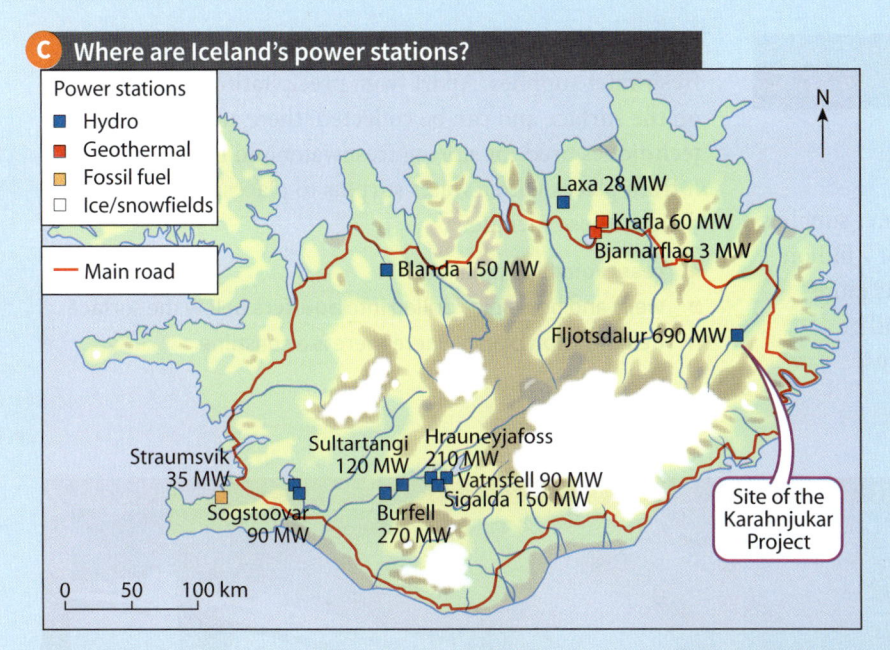

# Case Study: Energy supply in Iceland

## C Where are Iceland's power stations?

**Power stations**
- ■ Hydro
- ■ Geothermal
- ■ Fossil fuel
- □ Ice/snowfields
- — Main road

Laxa 28 MW
Krafla 60 MW
Bjarnarflag 3 MW
Blanda 150 MW
Fljotsdalur 690 MW
Straumsvik 35 MW
Sultartangi 120 MW
Hrauneyjafoss 210 MW
Vatnsfell 90 MW
Sigalda 150 MW
Sogstoovar 90 MW
Burfell 270 MW
Site of the Karahnjukar Project

HEP is the source of 75% of Iceland's electricity, with geothermal sources producing the other 25%. Landsvirkjun is the company responsible for producing electricity in Iceland. It was founded in 1965 and is now run as a state-owned national energy provider. Ten HEP stations have been constructed since 1965. Today the company not only produces electricity for Iceland but has a surplus that is exported to earn foreign currency. The reservoirs and HEP stations are built on glacial rivers which are largely fed by snowmelt. Some of the snowmelt is activated by using heat from geothermal energy.

### TASK 3: Study Source C

a How many of each type of power station does Landsvirkjun run in Iceland?
b Compare the distribution of the different types of power stations shown.
c Explain why many HEP stations are close to ice and snowfields.
d State the range of capacities (in megawatts) of the HEP stations shown.
e How do the HEP capacities compare to the geothermal and fossil fuel capacities?

### TASK 4: Study Source D

a Draw an outline, labelled sketch of the photograph.
b Give **two** advantages and **two** disadvantages of the Karahnjukar project for Iceland.
c What does Alcoa produce?
d Suggest why Iceland was an attractive location for Alcoa to move to from the USA.

## D The Karahnjukar project

Hálslón reservoir created behind the two dams
Vatnajokull glacier
Second dam
River Jokulsa a Bru
Main dam
River Jokulsa a Dal

The largest HEP station was completed in 2009 in the north-east of Iceland at Fijotsdalur away from the populated south-west. The Karahnjukar project is the largest construction project ever built in the country. It involved damming two glacial rivers that flowed from the Vatnajökull glacier and creating the Hálslón reservoir covering 57 km² behind the dams. The project created controversy because it is in one of Europe's largest wilderness areas with 2000 reindeer grazing here. The diversion of water plus submergence of land also removed habitats for birds such as the pink-footed goose and harbour seals which breed on the river deltas. The government built it for Alcoa (Aluminium Company of America) which wanted to move here because of pollution problems created by its US plant. Using coal, oil and gas to smelt 1 kg of aluminium creates between 9 and 14 kg of carbon dioxide but HEP only produces 2 kg. Iceland offered cheap electricity and a clean environment. The project has provided over 750 jobs plus foreign currency for Iceland which has little industry. However, it has been criticised for its impact on the environment and for employing foreign migrant workers.

# Cambridge IGCSE Geography — Water

## 57  Using water

### No water … no life

There will be an increasing demand for more water supplies in the future as the world's current population of 7 billion is increasing by 78 million people per year and as more countries move towards MEDC status. Water will be needed for agriculture, domestic and industrial use.

There are several different methods of providing freshwater supplies. Apart from precipitation that flows on the surface and can be collected, there are various techniques used for storing freshwater and for transferring it from places with a water surplus to places with a water deficit. These include:

- **reservoirs** and pipelines
- wells and boreholes drilled into **aquifers** below the surface
- **desalination** plants where there is a coastline.

### A  Different uses of water

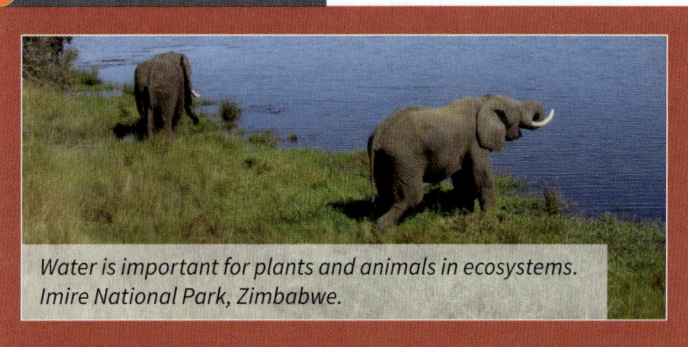

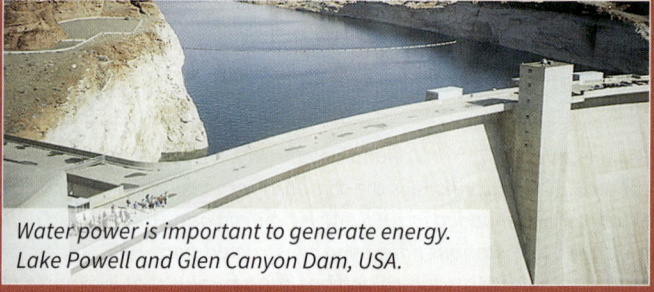

*Water is important for plants and animals in ecosystems. Imire National Park, Zimbabwe.*

*Water power is important to generate energy. Lake Powell and Glen Canyon Dam, USA.*

*Water is important for drinking and staying clean and healthy. Ntalikwa village, Tanzania.*

*Water is important for waste disposal. Near Tozear, Tunisia.*

### B  Water use and levels of development

**Percentage of water use by sector in countries at different levels of development**

|  | USA | Brazil | UK | Mali | India | Australia |
|---|---|---|---|---|---|---|
| Agriculture | 41 | 62 | 3 | 90 | 86 | 75 |
| Domestic | 13 | 20 | 22 | 9 | 9 | 15 |
| Industry | 46 | 18 | 75 | 1 | 5 | 10 |

Source: *The Atlas of Water*, earthscan 2009

**TASK 1:** Study Source **A**
a  For each photo list the uses of water shown.
b  Add other uses of water to your list.
c  Mark these uses with an:
- (S) if essential for survival
- (Q) if desirable for a high quality of life.

**TASK 2:** Study Source **B**
a  Draw pie charts on an outline world map to show this information.
b  Choose **one** country that you regard as more economically developed and **one** country that you regard as less economically developed. Compare the water use in your chosen countries.
c  Suggest reasons for the differences in water use between these two countries.

**TASK 3:** Study Source **C**
a  What is meant by an *aquifer*?
b  How is water obtained from an aquifer?
c  Annotate a copy of the cross-section to suggest why water is trapped in the chalk.
d  What is meant by the *water table*?
e  Suggest why its level varies during the year.

# Theme 3: Topic 57

## C Wells, boreholes and aquifers

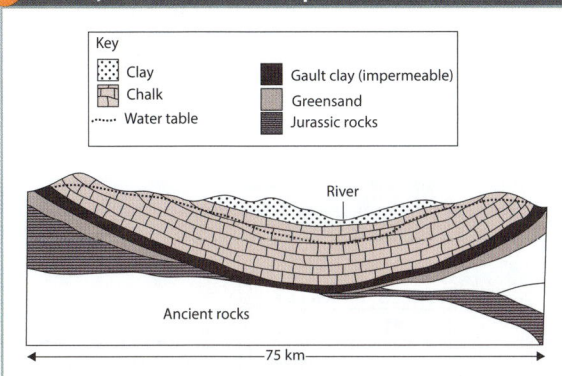

**Key**
- Clay
- Chalk
- Water table
- Gault clay (impermeable)
- Greensand
- Jurassic rocks

River
Ancient rocks
75 km

If rock at the surface is **impermeable** the water can't infiltrate into the ground. It will run off quickly over the ground into a stream, river or reservoir. But if the rock at the surface is **permeable**, the water will infiltrate. It will then collect above any impermeable rocks below the surface. This underground reservoir of water is an aquifer. Its highest level is known as the water table. This varies depending on how much water is extracted compared to how much rain is keeping it topped up. Aquifers are mainly found in **porous** rocks such as chalk and sandstone. From these, water supplies can be extracted by drilling wells or pumping it from the aquifer.

## D Reservoirs and dams

**Wimbleball reservoir is located in the Exmoor National Park in the UK. It is one of three major water-supply reservoirs serving the south-west of England.**

**The environment:** the structures are designed to blend in with the landscape. Over 12 000 trees screen the lake and car parks.

**Leisure and recreation:** the site includes play areas, tea and gift shops and picnic areas on paths. There is a sailing club, trout fishery and nature reserve.

Unlike many reservoirs, Wimbleball was only built for water supply; it is not an HEP project where the main function is to produce electricity. The dam was built across the river Haddeo which is a tributary of the larger river Exe. The reservoir can store over 21 000 megalitres of water and covers an area of 150 hectares. It supplies water to the south-west of England by releasing it into the river Haddeo which then flows into the river Exe to urban areas such as Tiverton and Exeter. This extra water can then be taken out (abstracted) and transferred by pipelines to where it is needed. There are 15 000 km of pipelines in the area serving over 1.5 million people.

**TASK 4:** Study **Source D**
a  Suggest **two** reasons why this reservoir and dam were located here.
b  Describe the way that water is transferred from this reservoir to places like Tiverton and Exeter.
c  Suggest advantages and disadvantages that building this reservoir has created for local people and the environment.

**TASK 5**
a  What is meant by 'desalination'?
b  Carry out research to find out which countries are using desalination to obtain freshwater supplies.

# 58 Managing water

## Water supply varies

The world is not 'running out of water'. The water cycle is a closed system so the amount of water circulating in it – whether as gas, water or solid – is fixed. But it is not always available when and where people need it. The distribution of global rainfall varies. Countries that receive heavy rainfall may have a water surplus but suffer heavy floods. Countries that have low amounts of rainfall may have a water deficit and suffer from droughts. They may have to rely on a river flowing through their dry country; for example, the river Nile, which flows through Egypt and Sudan.

A large proportion of the world's population – about 1 billion people – are without safe drinking water and 2.5 billion are without access to sanitation. It is very difficult for people to influence their natural water supplies. However, as you have seen, there is large-scale technology that can be used to transfer water from areas of surplus to areas of deficit by building reservoirs and dams and using pipelines and tunnels. These techniques depend on having money, expertise and the will to do it. Small-scale techniques can also be effective in small communities. Conserving and recycling water also helps to make the best of the amount received.

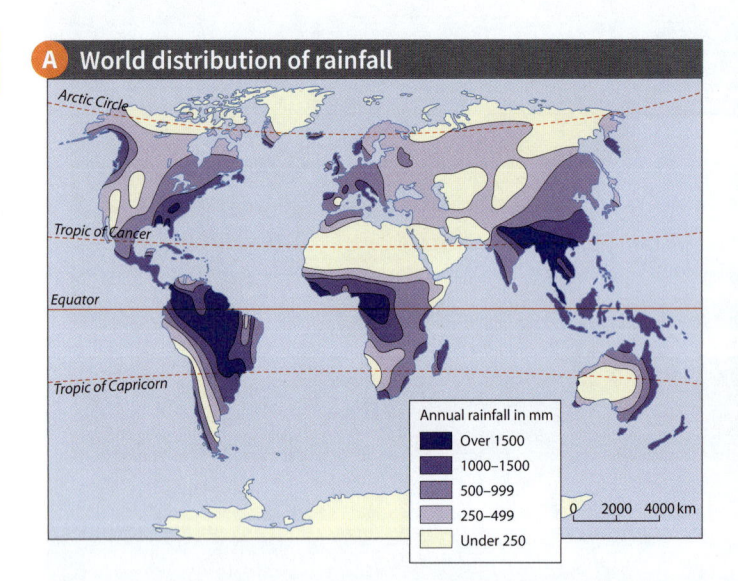

**A** World distribution of rainfall

Annual rainfall in mm
- Over 1500
- 1000–1500
- 500–999
- 250–499
- Under 250

**B** Managing water supply – further solutions

### Stop water leakages

NEW SOURCES OF WATER
1. NEW DAMS
2. RIVER SHARING
3. RAIN-WATER HARVESTING
4. DESALINISATION
5. ICE-BERGS

JUST PLUG THE LEAKS!!

*The World Bank estimates that in LEDCs 60% of treated water that enters the distribution system is lost by leakage.*

### Agree on river sharing

More than 260 river basins are shared between countries; 13 river basins are shared by 5 or more countries. Very few river basins are controlled entirely by one country. So countries upstream along a river can control the water flow into another country by building dams, altering river flows, extracting water for agriculture, industry and domestic use and reducing its quality by pollution. This makes countries downstream vulnerable and conflict or 'water wars' possible. There is no international law on water-sharing so international co-operation is the only way to ensure the water is shared.

---

**TASK 1:** Study Source **A**

a  Describe the distribution of areas with over 1500 mm of rainfall per year. Refer to continents in your answer.

b  Use an atlas to help you suggest **two** countries or regions that may:
- experience a water surplus
- experience a water deficit.

**TASK 2:** Study Source **B**

a  What is the message of the cartoon?

b  Use an atlas to find:
- a river basin that is entirely in the control of one country
- a river basin that is shared by **two** countries or more.

For the second river basin, list some problems that a country upstream can cause for a country downstream of it.

c  For the country you live in, find out whether the water you receive by river flow is shared with other countries or is entirely within your country's control. Have there been any recent issues involving water sharing between your country and neighbouring countries?

# Theme 3: Topic 58

## C  Access to clean water

Rapid urban growth, increasing industrialisation, mining and modern farming methods – especially in LEDCs – are causing increased water pollution. This has several impacts:

1. Death or illness of people from polluted water in surface streams and rivers. In LEDCs 90% of human sewage is discharged untreated into rivers as is 70% of industrial waste. This causes diseases such as cholera, typhoid and dysentery, reducing the health of people who could work. An estimated 10% of global disease could be prevented by improving water supplies, sanitation and hygiene behaviour.
2. If polluted water is used for irrigating farmland then the crops and livestock may be contaminated too, as will food from these sources.
3. Polluted groundwater from solid waste tips, industrial and farmyard drains, leaking sewers, pesticides and insecticides reduces the quality of water from aquifers.

*A polluted river in Rui'an city, China. One-fifth of the water in China's rivers is toxic to touch and two-fifths is seriously polluted due to China's economic boom which is fuelled by factories that dump industrial waste into rivers.*

## D  Local water management

Creating a water-management scheme is not always about large-scale technologies involving reservoirs, dams, tunnels and pipelines. The village of Thunthi Kankasiya, in Gujarat, India is an example of how local people can develop their own water management scheme at the local level. During the 1990s the villagers created an all-year-round water supply by damming a river and digging 23 wells. This enabled them to irrigate 153 hectares of land; almost twice the 85 hectares under cultivation before the villagers acted. They are now able to grow three crops a year and have quadrupled the production per hectare. This has raised average annual incomes to almost 100 000 rupees (US$1570) and reduced the need for people to migrate away from the rural area for months to earn money in nearby towns and cities.

---

**TASK 3:** Study Source C
a  Why is water pollution increasing in countries like China and LEDCs?
b  Explain how increased water pollution can:
- affect the health of people
- affect the size of working population
- affect the economic development of a country.

**TASK 4:** Study Source D
a  Use an atlas to describe the location of Gujarat state in India.
b  How did the villagers create their own all-year round water supply?
c  Describe the benefits the villagers gained by doing this.

# Cambridge IGCSE Geography — Water

## Case Study

### Water supply in Lesotho

#### Supplying water to ourselves... then others

The Lesotho Highlands Water Project (LHWP) is the largest civil engineering project in Africa. It is the world's second largest water-transfer project after the Three Gorges Dam in China and is Africa's largest water transfer scheme. There are two major objectives of the project:

- To provide Lesotho with its own reliable water supply by transferring water into rivers that flow through areas that need water, especially for irrigation.
- To transfer, for a fee, any surplus water to South Africa which has a water deficit in areas around Johannesburg. This income could then be used to improve the quality of life and standard of living of people in Lesotho.

The project was developed in partnership between the governments of Lesotho and South Africa with advantages for both countries. Construction began in 1988 and, when completed (estimate 2027), the project will divert about 40 per cent of the Sequa/Orange river water through five large-scale dams in Lesotho. After taking the water that Lesotho needs for its own agriculture, domestic and industrial use, the rest can be sent to South Africa along the River Vaal which rises in Lesotho and flows down to Johannesburg.

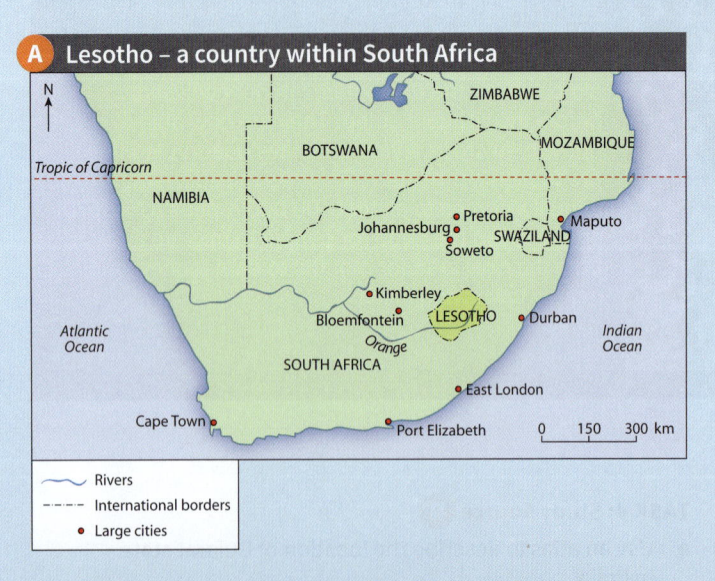

**B   Rainfall provides a water surplus**

Average rainfall 1020 mm

**A   Lesotho – a country within South Africa**

A mountainous and land-locked country, the kingdom of Lesotho is completely surrounded by South Africa. Most of the highlands are to the east where villages can only be reached on horseback, on foot or by a light plane. These highlands receive heavy rainfall, so the valleys are ideal for building dams and reservoirs.

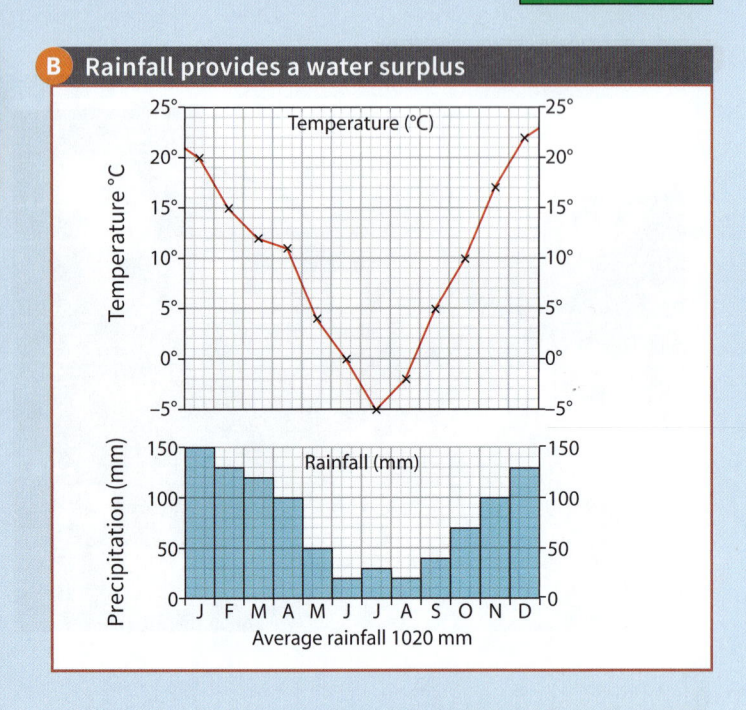

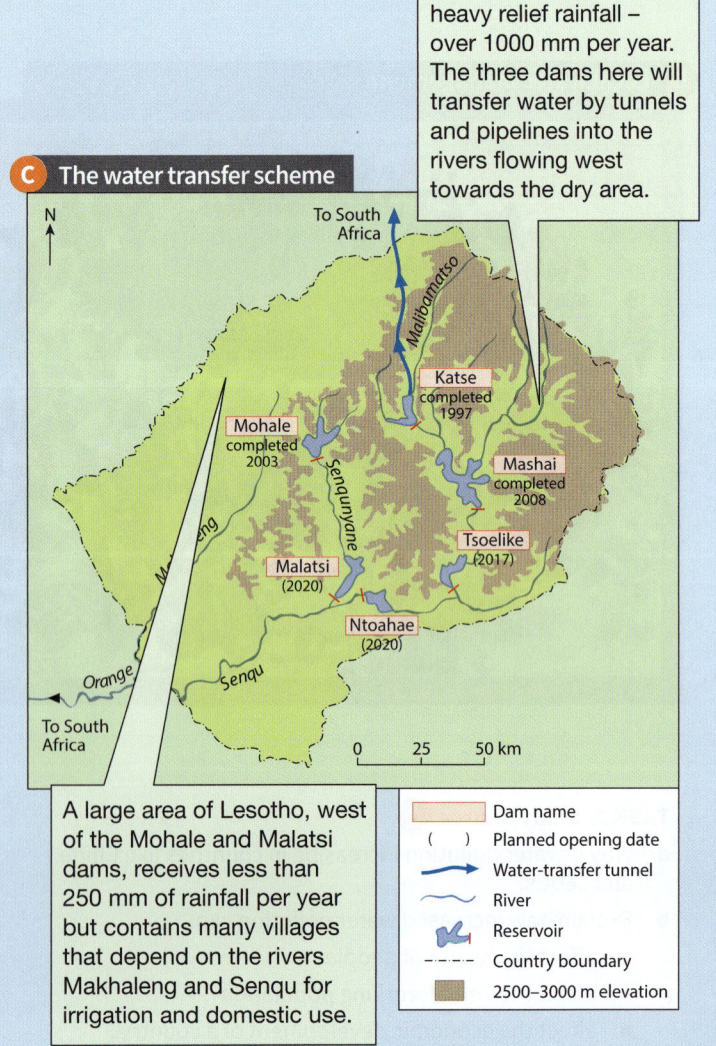

**C   The water transfer scheme**

The highland area of the east of Lesotho receives heavy relief rainfall – over 1000 mm per year. The three dams here will transfer water by tunnels and pipelines into the rivers flowing west towards the dry area.

Dams: Katse (completed 1997), Mohale (completed 2003), Mashai (completed 2008), Tsoelike (2017), Malatsi (2020), Ntoahae (2020)

A large area of Lesotho, west of the Mohale and Malatsi dams, receives less than 250 mm of rainfall per year but contains many villages that depend on the rivers Makhaleng and Senqu for irrigation and domestic use.

Key: Dam name; ( ) Planned opening date; Water-transfer tunnel; River; Reservoir; Country boundary; 2500–3000 m elevation

# Case Study: Water supply in Lesotho

## D The Katse dam

*Completed in 1997, the Katse dam is the first of the six major dams forming the LHWP. It is 185 metres high and was built from basalt rock. It has a surface area of about 36 square kilometres. It is the most efficient storage dam in Africa due to its great depth and small surface area which reduces evaporation. The dam was built on the Malibamatso river. It is kept full from summer rain and winter snow. The tunnel that flows north into South Africa is 82 kilometres long and has a diameter of 4.8 metres.*

## E Different views

"We rely heavily on the river Senqu for our livelihood. We use the water for drinking, washing and cooking as well as to irrigate our crops. But this is a dry area and the river is not always full enough to provide irrigation all year. Once the water scheme is completed we will have water all year round which will be controlled by the Malatse dam. We should then be able to grow a surplus for sale and develop the local economy. Fewer people will need to be farmers; they can do another job."

*Farmer living in the west of Lesotho near the Senqu river*

"Over 30 000 of us were moved when the Katse dam was built. Our farms are now under water. Some villagers were relocated to steeper slopes where nothing can grow. People in the west will benefit but we have seen no benefits from building the dam despite many promises from the government. We are hoping that tourism will eventually provide new jobs, though our culture and way of life may be changed by that."

*Villager who used to farm in the valley now covered by the Katse dam*

"We are a poor country. We only grow a little corn and wheat and import 90% of our products. We have nothing to export. Farming is subsistence and heavy rainfall in the mountains causes soil erosion. But we do have water and good sites for reservoirs in the east so we can provide water to our people living in the dry west. What is left over can be sold to South Africa. We can also use our dams to generate hydro-electric power (HEP) and large reservoirs will attract tourists. We will use the money to develop industry and other services so there will be better jobs than subsistence farming. We are being paid $50 million a year for 50 years. A poor country can do a lot with that money."

*Minister of Natural Resources, Lesotho*

"Lesotho will now be dependent on South Africa for future income. We will have to do what they want us to. If South Africa wants more water than we can supply, we could have a water war here. We are a small, land-locked country with no real defence against a country like South Africa."

*Opposition politician in Lesotho parliament*

## TASK 1: Study Source A
a Describe the location of Lesotho. Use distances and directions in your answer.
b Give **one** advantage and **one** disadvantage of the relief of Lesotho for development. Explain your choices.

## TASK 2: Study Source B
a Describe the distribution of temperature and rainfall throughout the year. Refer to data from the graphs.
b Give **two** advantages and **two** disadvantages of this climate for providing a reliable and regular water supply all year round.
c Suggest why the LHWP can provide water all year for the people of Lesotho.

## TASK 3: Study Source C
a Name the six dams making up the LHWP and add the years in which they were, or will be, completed.
b Describe and explain why the west of Lesotho has a water deficit but the east has a water surplus.
c Explain how the LHWP will improve the water supply in the west of Lesotho.

## TASK 4: Study Source D
a On a sketch of Source D, label the following:
- the Katse dam
- steep valley sides
- the reservoir
- the river outflow
- an area of overland flow
- an area of evaporation.

b Suggest **two** reasons why this site was chosen for the reservoir. Explain your reasons.
c Suggest benefits that the Katse dam and its reservoir could bring to Lesotho that are not to do with water supply.

## TASK 5: Study Source E
a Read the different views. Make a table with two columns: one for reasons in favour of the LHWP and one for reasons against it.
b Briefly summarise your views on whether the LHWP scheme should continue to be built. Justify your answer.

179

# Cambridge IGCSE Geography — Environmental risks of economic development

## 59 Economic activities pose threats

### A growing problem for over 250 years

The period 1750–1900 was when the Industrial Revolution took place in the UK and Western Europe. Until then agriculture dominated economic activity and had only changed the appearance of the landscape by creating hedgerows which separated fields for arable and pastoral farming. Once the Industrial Revolution had started, however, the natural environment was threatened by:

- coal mining and the consequences of burning coal in factories which increased carbon dioxide and other greenhouse gases in the air
- towns and cities expanding to cope with people moving from rural areas to work in factories
- the development of transport – roads, railways and canals – which crossed the landscape as they linked the growing industrial urban areas.

In the 20th century and more recent times increased energy use, vehicle ownership, air travel and tourism have also caused environmental impacts.

Many countries have copied the industrial route to economic development and, in their rush to move from LEDC to MEDC status, the impact on the natural environment – especially any long-term impact – has only been a minor consideration. Today there is great concern about the impact of economic activities that were established hundreds of years ago, as well as current economic activities, on the natural environment.

### A Economic activity creates different types of pollution

**Air pollution**
*Avoiding breathing in polluted air in Tokyo, Japan.*

**Water pollution**
*A polluted lake in Wuhan, Hubei province, China.*

**Noise pollution**
*Noise from traffic in Tahrir Square, Cairo, Egypt.*

**Visual pollution... or thing of beauty?**
*Light pollution in Las Vegas, Nevada, USA.*

---

**TASK 1**

a Explain why economic activities had no real effect on the natural environment until around 250 years ago.

b Suggest ways in which primary, secondary and tertiary economic activities can change the natural environment.

**TASK 2:** Study Source A

a List the four different types of pollution and suggest which type of economic activity has caused them.

b Write down **one** example of each type of pollution from an area you know.

## Theme 3: Topic 59

### B  Secondary economic activity: mining, industry and air pollution in Albania

#### Albania at risk of disaster from pollution

According to experts Albania is facing disaster due to growing pollution caused by poisonous gases.

Tirana, Albania's capital city is one of the most polluted cities in the world. Experts said that deaths due to illnesses caused by pollution have increased by 20% in Tirana in the past two years.

90% of the vehicles are too ol, 70% use diesel and 30% petrol, but mostly petrol with lead and a huge quantity of sulpur, banned in the European Union countries.

Until recently the worst air pollution was in Elbasan, the centre of heavy industry, where pollution from dust and sulpur gas was 15 times above acceptable levels.

Here there has been an increase in the number of babies born with deformities. There have also been reported cases of deformed animals being born: four-legged roosters and two-headed calves and rabbits.

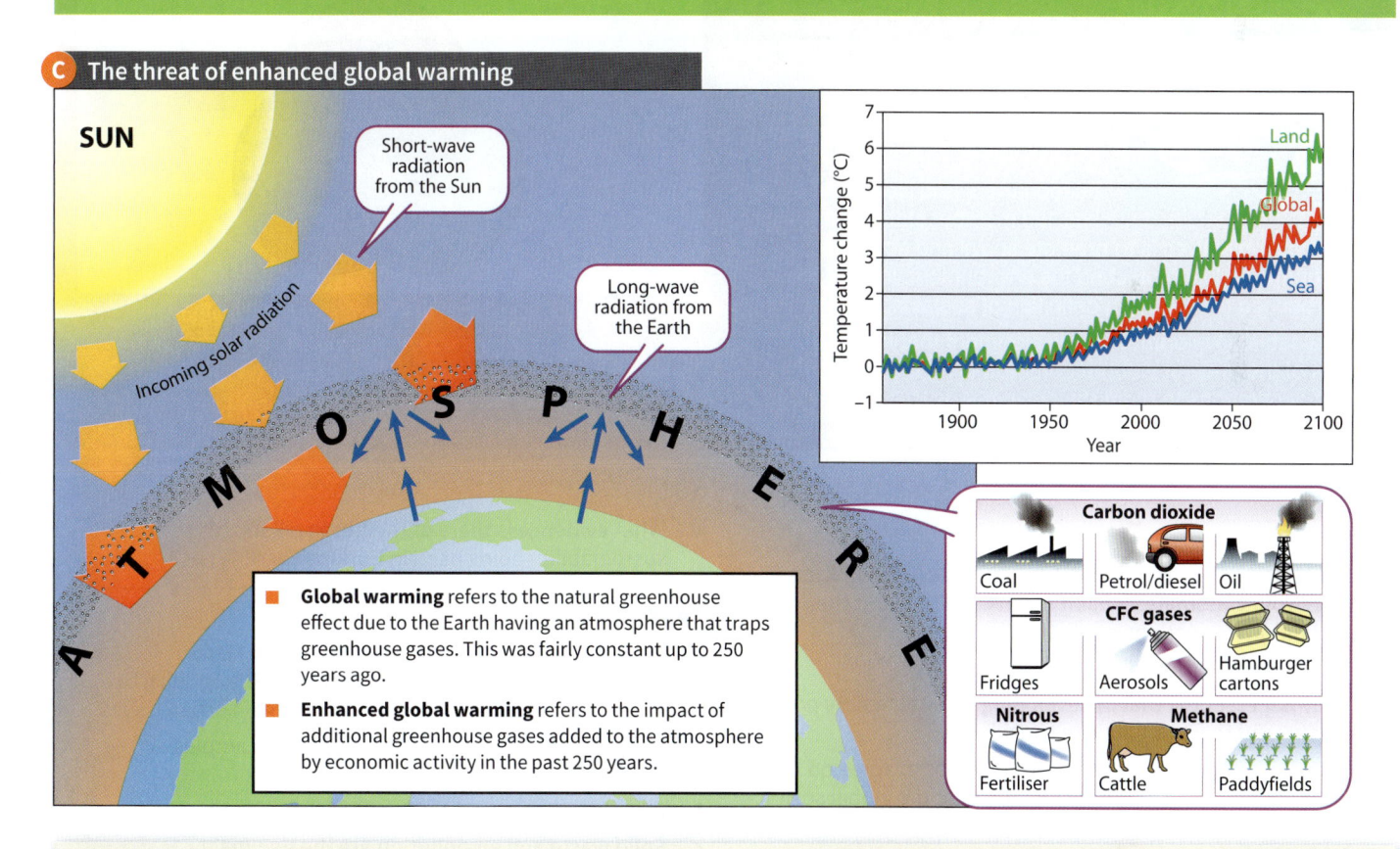

Map legend:
- Hazardous industrial site
- Mining site
- Waste disposal site
- Mining industry hotspots
- Serious water pollution

### C  The threat of enhanced global warming

- **Global warming** refers to the natural greenhouse effect due to the Earth having an atmosphere that traps greenhouse gases. This was fairly constant up to 250 years ago.
- **Enhanced global warming** refers to the impact of additional greenhouse gases added to the atmosphere by economic activity in the past 250 years.

Carbon dioxide: Coal, Petrol/diesel, Oil
CFC gases: Fridges, Aerosols, Hamburger cartons
Nitrous: Fertiliser
Methane: Cattle, Paddyfields

---

**TASK 3: Study Source B**

Albania is one of the most polluted countries in Europe. Write a paragraph, including named examples, to describe the location of areas where mining and industry are causing pollution in Albania.

**TASK 4: Study Source C**

a  Explain how natural and enhanced global warming takes place.

b  Describe how global temperatures are expected to change between 1900 and 2100. Refer to data and years in your answer.

c  Which human activities are believed to have caused these temperature changes?

# 60 Managing for sustainable development

## Sustainability and management

**Sustainability** involves fulfilling the resource requirements of the present generation without reducing the ability of future generations to have the same access to the benefits of these resources. To be sustainable the Earth's resources must be used at a rate that allows for replenishment.

In rural areas sustainability involves ensuring that activities such as agriculture, forestry, mining and tourism allow the resources to be used to benefit the present generation in a way that ensures they will still be available for future generations.

In urban areas sustainability involves ensuring that activities such as the growth of housing, industrial development, the development of transport and infrastructure and any subsequent pollution are managed to ensure the town or city can continue to function in a way that allows future generations to enjoy living and working there.

Managing for sustainability involves putting into action policies that conserve resources for the future. Many international conferences take place to try to agree on environmental policies but this is difficult as each country has its own agenda and priorities for economic development. Politicians are often more interested in the short-term future of their own country than the long-term future of the planet.

### A  What is sustainability?

The United Nations (UN) is an international organisation established on 24 October 1945 to promote international co-operation. It was created after the Second World War to prevent another conflict and its main headquarters is in New York. It has 193 member states. One of its main objectives is to promote social and economic development while protecting the environment. In 1987 the UN produced the following definition of sustainability:

'Sustainable development is development that meets the needs of the present without compromising the ability of future generations to meet their own needs.'

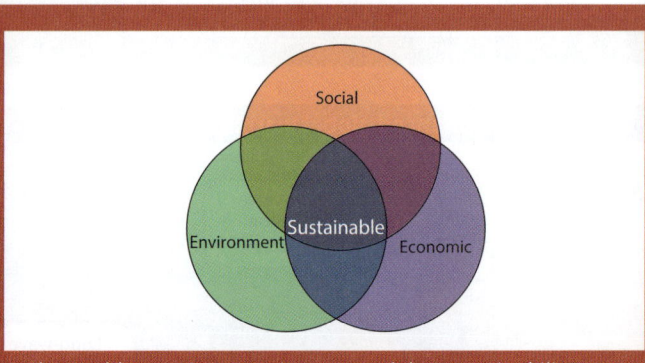

*At the World Summit in 2005 it was noted that sustainability requires social, environmental and economic demands to work together to create true sustainability – these are known as the 'three pillars' of sustainability.*

### TASK 1: Study Source A

a  Write down the UN's definition of sustainability. Discuss with your classmates what it means and then put the definition into your own words.

b  What are the 'three pillars' of sustainability?

c  Why is it essential that in developing a sustainability policy all three of these 'pillars' are considered?

d  Why is it difficult to get separate countries to agree on international policies on sustainability at the global scale?

### TASK 2: Study Source B

a  Why are the government of Burkina Faso and Mr Lagware worried about soil fertility?

b  How are the government and villagers managing the challenge of developing a sustainable approach by villagers?

c  Choose **three** ways being used in Burkina Faso to provide a sustainable future in the country for the next generation.

d  What evidence is there of the 'three pillars' of sustainability being used in Burkina Faso?

### TASK 3: Study Source C

Source C is an extract from an interview with Marco Kusumawijaya, founder and director of the Ruang Jakarta Center for Urban Studies – an NGO focusing on urban issues.

a  What is an NGO? Find out and give **two** examples of other NGOs.

b  What is an ecological city?

c  Solid waste and air pollution are the two main environmental concerns in Jakarta. Why is this?

d  What indicates that Jakarta is not following sustainable policies?

e  What solutions are suggested to make Jakarta a more ecological city?

## B Sustainability in rural areas: Burkina Faso

### BURKINA FASO PROTECTS ITS FRAGILE SOILS
by Jean-Marie Sawadogo, Ouagadougou

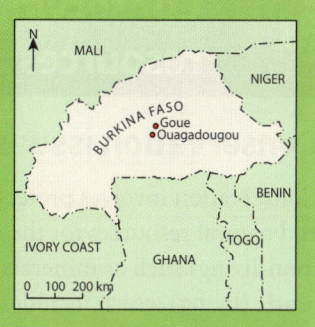

Like other farmers in the village of Goue, 30 km from Ouagadougou, Mr Pierre Lagware is worried about the fertility of his land which has been declining each year from over-exploitation and poor farming practices. Here methods to combat soil erosion and restore fertility are not well known but, with agriculture employing 86% of the population, the government is just as concerned. It is in debt to the World Bank for loans and needs to produce more to improve its trade balance.

Local communities have been made responsible for managing their farmlands, pastures and forests to ensure environmental protection and sustainability. Several strategies are taking place.

- Overcultivation and overgrazing have reduced soil nutrients, so increased phosphate and organic fertilisers are being used to overcome the deficiency.
- Many farmers were unaware that their soil fertility can be improved. Farmers now apply organic compost with mineral fertilisers to improve soil-water retention.
- Farmers are encouraged to grow fodder crops to avoid overgrazing.
- In the north, farmers have been taught to build bunds with stones, earth and vegetation to allow water run-off and prevent topsoil erosion.
- Higher-yielding seeds for rice and grain and small-scale irrigation projects are being developed.
- The villagers are now involved in replanting seedlings, regulating tree cutting and increasing the use of domestic stoves. The Long Live The Farmer Association shows farmers how to cut fuelwood selectively while conserving vegetation that provides soil nutrients.

## C Sustainability in urban areas: Jakarta – an ecological city?

### AN EDITED VERSION OF THE INTERVIEW REPORTED IN *THE JAKARTA POST* ON 22 APRIL 2014

**Question:** *What is an ecological city?*
**Answer:** One that minimises the use of non-renewable energy. By exploiting this type of energy we cause depletion of resources and pollute the environment. If it continues the environment cannot sustain our lives.

**Q:** *Solid waste has always been a problem in Jakarta. The city produces over 6000 tonnes of rubbish every day. What actions should we take to deal with this problem?*
**A:** Jakarta has not dealt with this problem. We should be recycling solid waste into compost fertiliser and get rid of non-organic waste. Fortunately 60% of the city's solid waste is still organic so it is biodegradable. As for the rest, we should get rid of plastic and replace it with biodegradable material.

**Q:** *Have we handled waste properly?*
**A:** No. We still use lorries using non-renewable fuel to transport waste to its final dumping site. We still use incinerators which produce gas emissions. We use a lot of energy to get rid of waste. So by burning waste we add to the city's air pollution.

**Q:** *Air pollution is one of Jakarta's most pressing problems. How should we deal with this?*
**A:** We need better planning. Many people work in Jakarta and commute from the suburbs using cars, trucks and motor bikes – every vehicle produces emissions. Planners need to develop workplaces near to where these people live so their vehicles are used less. Another problem is that the city's green spaces – which can limit the effects of air pollution – are now being built on with hotels, apartments and shopping malls.

**Q:** *Do your comments mean that the city authorities have a low priority for dealing with solid waste and air pollution?*
**A:** There is certainly a lack of knowledge on out how to manage the city for a sustainable future. Instead of spending money on rubbish trucks and incinerators they could educate Jakartans on how to transform organic waste into compost and provide them with the tools to do this. There are also ways to reduce the use of plastic. We must sit down together and agree on actions that will transform Jakarta into an ecological city with a sustainable future.

*On 22 April 2014 the city of Jakarta (population 10 million – the capital of Indonesia) held activities for the annual Earth Day. The theme was 'Green Cities' which are sometimes called ecological cities.*

# 61 Conserving natural resources

## Conservation issues

Conservation involves protecting the natural environment and natural resources for the future. These can be **abiotic** (non-living) such as minerals, soil and the atmosphere, or **biotic** (living) which includes the biodiversity of plants and animals and their habitats. Today there are many global **conservation** movements such as Greenpeace and the World Wildlife Fund (WWF). These organisations are particularly focused on conserving plants and animal species, especially endangered species under threat of extinction such as mountain gorillas.

These animals are all part of **ecosystems** which are environments where plants and animals grow and live together. There are several different types of ecosystem on land, in freshwater and in the oceans. Every day more habitats are lost and creatures become extinct due to human activity. As species disappear, the natural balance of nature will change unless people increase their awareness of and involvement in conservation, sustainability and the management of ecosystems and natural resources.

**A** A tundra ecosystem in the Arctic

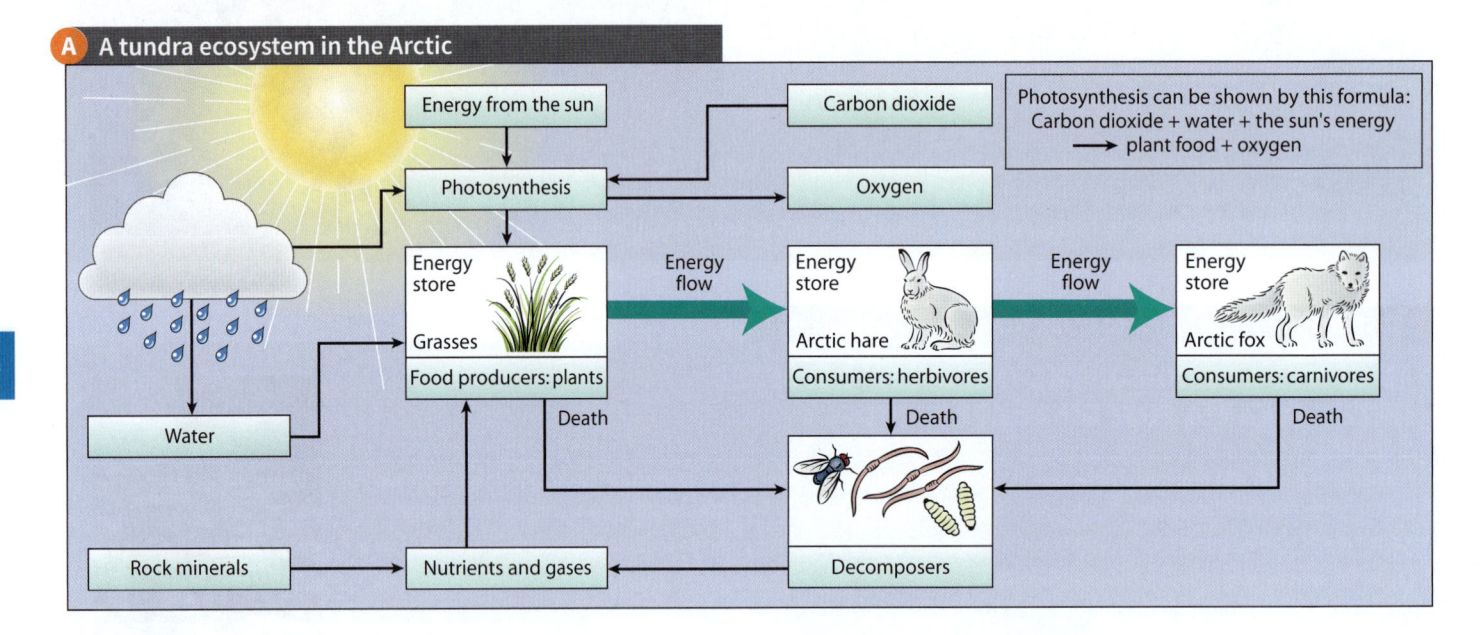

Photosynthesis can be shown by this formula:
Carbon dioxide + water + the sun's energy ⟶ plant food + oxygen

## Antarctica – the white continent

Antarctica is a frozen **continent** south of the Antarctic Circle (66½°S). It is larger than Europe. The ice cap covering the land rises to over 4 km above sea level. The continent was once covered by an ice sheet but today, due to enhanced global warming, there is less ice and more land is being exposed due to higher temperatures.

While it remains a challenging environment to live and work in, as more land is exposed, it is becoming more accessible each year. Today tourists take cruises there and many countries are staking a claim to its natural mineral resources by establishing bases. As the continent becomes colonised by human activity, the sustainability of fragile ecosystems, on land and sea, becomes an important issue for conservationists.

**B** An environment at risk

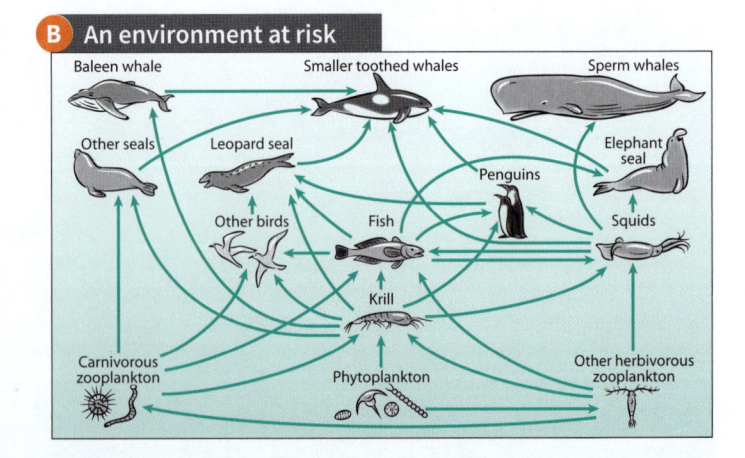

# Theme 3: Topic 61

## C Conserving natural resources: Antarctica

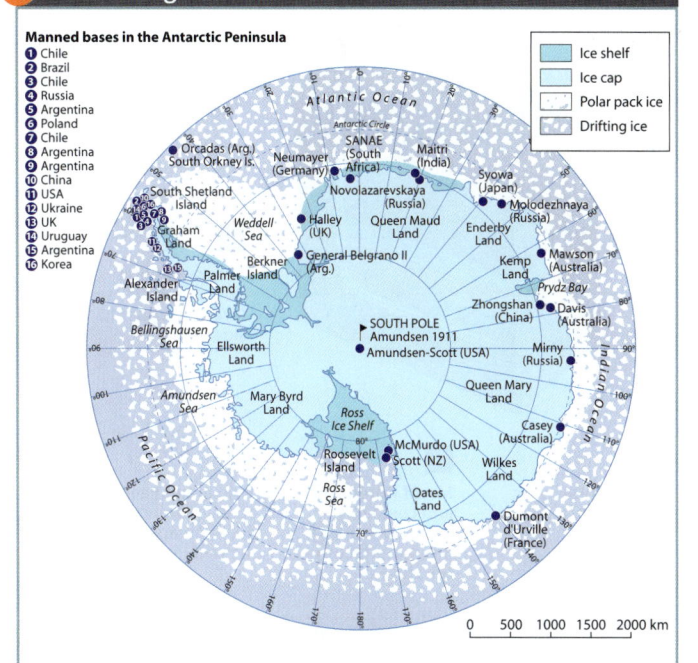

**Manned bases in the Antarctic Peninsula**
1. Chile
2. Brazil
3. Chile
4. Russia
5. Argentina
6. Poland
7. Chile
8. Argentina
9. Argentina
10. China
11. USA
12. Ukraine
13. UK
14. Uruguay
15. Argentina
16. Korea

*Note: under the Antartic Treaty of 1959 all territorial claims are held in abeyance in the interest of international co-operation for scientific purposes.*

## D Antarctica – safe for now?

### The Power Games that Threaten World's Last Pristine Wilderness
by James Bone, Eduardo Frei Montalva Base, Antarctica

Antarctica, once the torment of explorers such as Scott and Shackleton, is slowly being settled by mankind. Global warming, shrinking ice and soaring oil prices have forced countries to compete for the world's final frontier.

The Frei base sits on King George Island off the tip of the Antarctic Peninsula, a territory claimed by Britain and Argentina as well as Chile. Once a remote whaling station, the island is now known as the unofficial 'capital of the Antarctic'. The first surprise on landing in a Chilean C130 transport airplane is that my Blackberry works. I check my email and call my wife in New York to tell her I am surrounded by turquoise-tinted icebergs. As well as a mobile phone signal Frei base has a bank, post office, hospital, supermarket, bar, chapel, a school and an FM radio station called Sovereignty.

Flying over Antarctica we see colonies of sea-lions and penguins among corrugated shelters that are the international bases. However, despite all the overlapping territory claims, there is no conflict between countries yet. All the countries with bases are signed up to the 1959 Antarctic Treaty, which prevents exploitation and territorial claims. The 1991 Madrid Protocol to the Antarctic Treaty declares the icy continent 'a natural reserve devoted to peace and science' and outlaws mining or oil-drilling for 50 years. The British Antarctic Territory issues its own postage stamps, visitors' passports get stamped, and Chile and Argentina fly out pregnant mothers to have Antarctic-born children. However, polar scientists fear conflict is inevitable as global warming and deglaciation make it tempting to exploit the exposed land for oil and gas. Other minerals include gold, silver, chromium and uranium. In 2049 the unanimous ban on exploitation of Antarctica's resources will expire.

**Adapted from** *The Times*

---

**TASK 1:** Study **Source A**
a Explain what happens when photosynthesis takes place.
b What type of food producer is shown?
c Suggest what might happen in this tundra ecosystem if:
- arctic hares increased because there were fewer arctic foxes to eat them
- grasses increased because of higher temperatures
- oil pollution destroyed most of the decomposers.

**TASK 2:** Study **Source B**
a How important is krill to the baleen whale?
b Describe how **two** other Antarctic animals would be affected if krill was removed from this marine ecosystem.
c Penguins and seals spend part of their lives living on land as well as the sea. Suggest how they might be affected by:
- primary economic activity such as mining companies and their equipment
- secondary economic activity including manufacturing in countries far from Antarctica
- tertiary economic activity such as tourists visiting from cruise ships.

**TASK 3:** Study **Source C** and an atlas
a On an outline map of the world shade in all the countries that have manned bases in Antarctica. Suggest explanations for the pattern that you have produced.
b With the help of an atlas suggest why most manned bases are located in a similar area.

**TASK 4:** Study **Source D**
a Give **three** reasons why countries want to own part of Antarctica.
b What prevents countries exploiting these resources?
c Give examples of ways in which countries are trying to justify their ownership.
d List some mineral resources that lie beneath the Antarctic ice cap.
e Why might conflict occur in Antarctica before 2049?

**TASK 5**
'Antarctica is a remote, isolated continent.'
To what extent do you think this is true?
Use evidence from the sources to justify your views.

**Cambridge IGCSE Geography** — Environmental risks of economic development

# Case Study
## Fracking in California, USA

### Fracking – a 21st century energy solution?

Fracking is a process for extracting oil and natural gas from the ground by blasting water and chemicals into underground rocks. It is not a new process for extracting energy but it used to be extremely expensive. What is new is that the technology has improved and costs have come down so that it can now be used economically on land. In addition, recent global events have meant that more countries want to find and use their own energy sources and not rely on others.

Economic development usually requires energy and fuel sources. The exploitation of all energy sources has some effect on the world we live in.

- Coal produces gases that may cause global warming.
- Nuclear power produces dangerous waste that is difficult to store.
- Oil can produce spills that damage the natural environment.
- HEP and tidal power change river flow and ecosystems.
- Wind farms affect the landscape.

While these impacts are undesirable, the consequences of an energy shortage are far worse. While energy production has social, economic and environmental costs, so too do shortages. Fracking is seen as a way that countries such as the USA and UK can free themselves from being dependent on oil and gas from countries like Russia, Saudi Arabia and Iraq.

### A What is fracking?

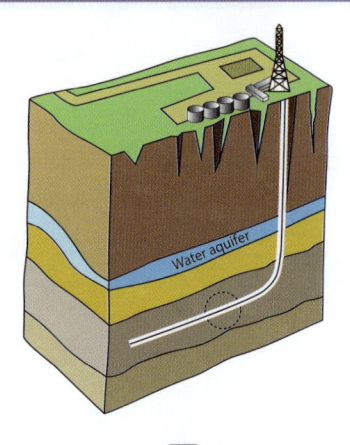

Modern techniques mean vast new resources can be tapped

**1** Companies drill down to shale layer, then go sideways

**2** Small holes blasted into the rock

**3** Mix of water, sand and chemicals pumped in at high pressure, fracturing the shale

**4** Sand grains keep fractures open, allowing trapped gas to escape into the well

### TASK 1: Study Source A
a  What is meant by *fracking*?
b  Is this a primary, secondary or tertiary economic activity?
c  Give **two** reasons why fracking is taking place.
d  Describe how fracking releases oil and gas from the ground.

### TASK 2: Study Source B
a  Describe the location of the Monterey and Santos shale areas in California.
b  Name **four** settlements that could be affected by drilling for oil and gas from the Monterey and Santos shale deposits.
c  How much fracking is already taking place in California? How will California benefit from more fracking?

### B Fracking in California

There are two major shale-bearing rock formations in California: the Monterey shale formation and the Santos formation. Together they are estimated to contain 15.4 billion barrels of oil which is almost 80 times California's annual production from other sources. At current rates of oil refining these reserves could supply California for the next 21 years. The reserves lie about 3 km beneath the ground. In 2013 fracking activity in the two basins covered over 4000 km² in 10 Californian counties using over 600 wells. Oil companies have also fracked offshore of Los Angeles.

Case Study: Fracking in California, USA

## C  The economic case for fracking

❝ We have the opportunity to become the world leader in oil and gas by 2020 thanks to fracking. Rising oil prices and global conflicts mean that the USA simply has to find its own energy resources otherwise we will continue to depend on countries who have the oil and gas but whose governments we have had problems with. These include Russia, Saudi Arabia, Iraq and others in the Middle East.

The shale deposits under California contain 65% of the USA's oil deposits; enough to meet the USA's demand for many years. USA production can increase from 8 million to around 11 million barrels per year by 2020 and gas from 604 billion cubic metres to 747 billion.

Current unemployment in California is 8%; only three other states are higher. Fracking here could create 200 000 jobs and put millions of dollars into the state economy. Last year fracking supported over 2 million jobs in the country and contributed US$284 million to the US economy. Also the USA reduced its oil imports from 60% to 28% and achieved the highest levels of oil production for 25 years. Unfounded fears from those against fracking must not get in the way of the most promising and exciting energy revolution since the famous Spindletop gusher set off the Texas oil boom a century ago. ❞

*Oil company executive*

## D  The environmental case against fracking

### AN OPEN LETTER TO THE GOVERNOR OF CALIFORNIA

Dear Governor,

We believe that fracking is simply too risky for our water, air and wildlife. Fracking involves toxic chemicals such as methanol and benzene which are used with water in the fracking process; once these make their way into aquifers and drinking water, wildlife, the environment and human beings will all be at risk of illness and death. Water quality is seriously threatened. Fracking involves a huge amount of water and, if waste water is laced with chemicals, it cannot be cleaned or reused. In a state where droughts are frequent, we cannot afford to lose any of our freshwater supply.

Fracking can also pollute our air. There will be oil and gas emissions at the wellheads which will reduce the air quality but so will the waste water when it is dumped into waste pits once it evaporates in the California heat. Fracking also releases methane, a highly potent greenhouse gas that is at least 56 times more effective in trapping heat than carbon dioxide. It should be added that most of California's oil is dirty, heavy crude with a strong carbon concentration.

Wildlife will suffer. Losing their habitats by clearing forest and vegetation to create the well head sites will cause death or migration. Endangered species such as the California condor, San Joaquin kit fox and blunt-nosed leopard lizard live in places where fracking is likely to expand.

Fracking is poorly regulated in California. It is not included in the Safe Drinking Water Act, the Clean Water Act or the National Environmental Policy Act. In addition several minor earthquakes have taken place close to fracking sites and cracks have appeared in houses which is another concern. The idea of fracking in a state that includes the San Andreas fault is beyond belief! It is time that this dangerous practice was stopped and there was more research and development of sustainable energy practices such as wind and solar energy.

From 50 organisations representing more than 2 million Californians

---

**TASK 3: Study Source C**

a  Give **three** reasons why the USA does not want to depend on other countries for its energy supplies.

b  How important will California be in providing the USA with future oil supplies?

c  In what ways will people and the local economy benefit from fracking?

**TASK 4: Study Source D**

a  Read the letter to the Governor of California. Make a list of ways in which:
- people could suffer if fracking continues
- wildlife (plants and animals) could suffer if fracking continues
- other aspects of the natural environment will suffer.

b  Do you think fracking should go ahead in California? Justify your answer.

**TASK 5**

Fracking is being considered in many countries. Carry out research into your own country to see whether fracking is taking place or might be taking place in future. If so write down the arguments:
- in favour of fracking from an economic viewpoint.
- against fracking from the point of view of the natural environment.

# Cambridge IGCSE Geography — Exam-Style Questions

## Exam-Style Question on Development

a   Study Fig. 1, which shows Gross National Income (GNI) per capita in North and South America.

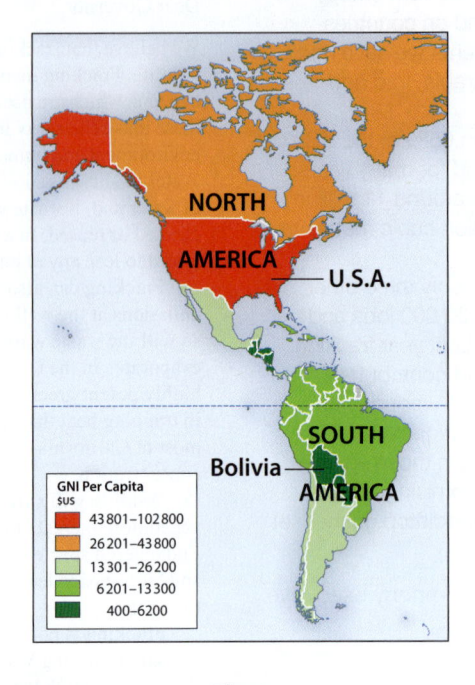

**Fig. 1**

i   What is meant by Gross National Income (GNI) per capita? [1]
ii  Using information from Fig. 1, compare the GNI per capita of the USA and Bolivia. [2]
iii Suggest reasons for the differences in the GNI per capita of the USA (an MEDC) and Bolivia (an LEDC). [3]
iv  State **two** other indicators of development and for each one explain how it can be used to assess the level of development of a country. [4]

b   Study Fig. 2, which shows changes in the employment structure in a country in Europe between 1930 and 2010.

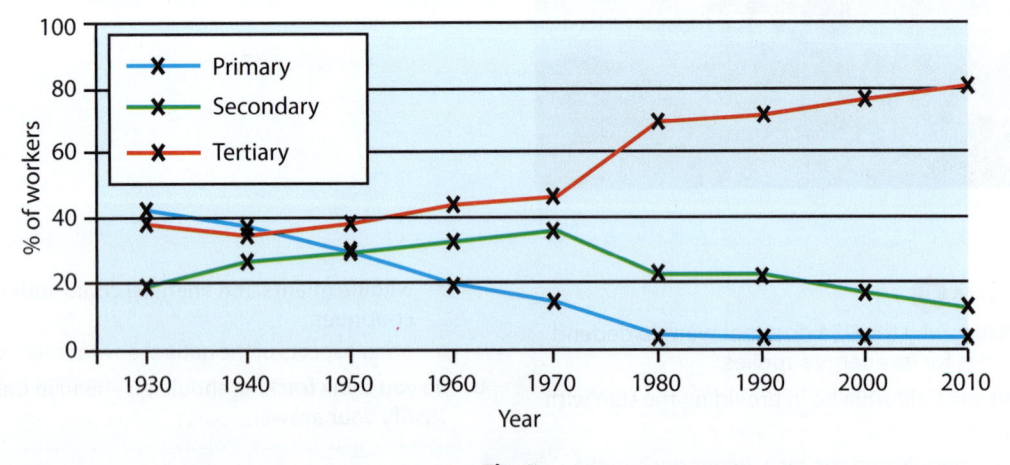

**Fig. 2**

i   Identify the main changes in the employment structure between 1930 and 2010. [3]
ii  Explain why the employment structure of a country changes as development occurs. [5]

c   Describe the impacts of a named transnational corporation on an area that you have studied. [7]

[Total: 25 marks]

# Exam-Style Questions

## Exam-Style Question on Tourism

a   Study Fig. 3, which shows information about tourist attractions in Buleleng, in northern Bali, Indonesia.

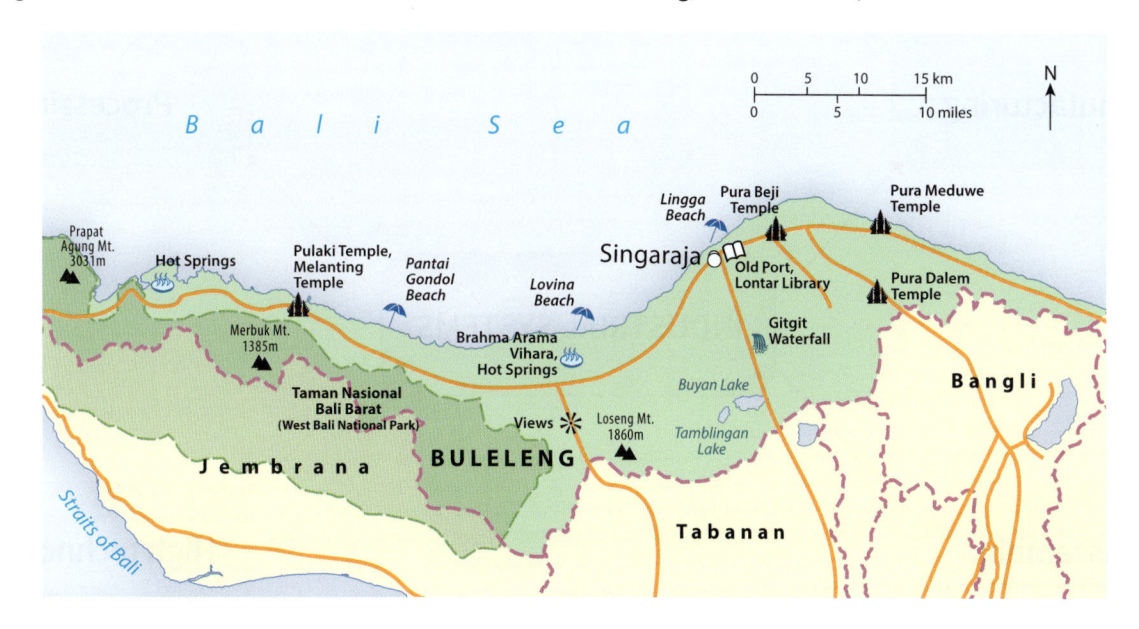

**Fig. 3**

   i   From Fig. 3, identify **one** example of an attraction of the human landscape for tourists to Buleleng. [1]
   ii  Using only evidence from Fig. 3, suggest reasons why the natural landscape of Buleleng attracts different types of tourists. [2]
   iii  Describe **three** different problems that tourism might cause for the natural environment in Buleleng. [3]
   iv  Explain how the climate of an area might be an attraction for tourists. [4]

b   Study Photograph A, which shows an artist's image of new tourist apartments being buit in Montenegro (an MEDC in Europe).

**Photograph A**

   i   Describe the main features of the tourist apartments. [3]
   ii  Explain how the building of the tourist apartments might have benefits and disadvantages for local people. [5]

c   For a named area or country explain how tourism is managed so that it is sustainable. [7]

**[Total: 25 marks]**

**Cambridge IGCSE Geography** — Exam-Style Questions

## Exam-Style Question on Industry/Food Production

a   Study Fig. 4, which shows examples of industrial systems.

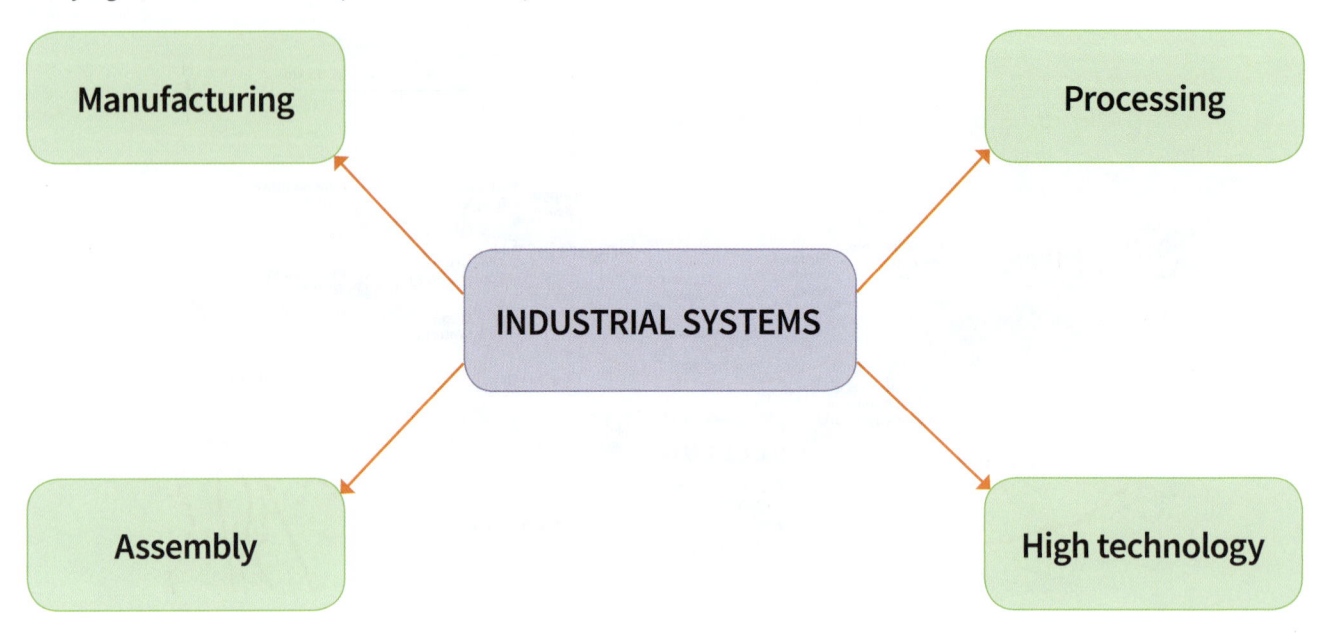

```
Manufacturing                           Processing

              INDUSTRIAL SYSTEMS

Assembly                                High technology
```

**Fig. 4**

| | | |
|---|---|---|
| i | Define the term *industrial system*. | [1] |
| ii | Explain how the inputs of an assembly industry are likely to differ from those of a processing industry. | [2] |
| iii | Give **three** examples of outputs of high technology industries. | [3] |
| iv | Explain how and why the market for a product can influence the location of industry. | [4] |

b   Study Photographs B and C, which show two different agricultural systems.

**Photograph B**           **Photograph C**

| | | |
|---|---|---|
| i | Describe **three** differences between the agricultural systems shown in Photographs B and C. | [3] |
| ii | For **either** Photograph B **or** Photograph C suggest how natural and human factors have influenced the agricultural system. | [5] |

c   For a named country or region that you have studied describe the effects of food shortages. [7]

**[Total: 25 marks]**

# Exam-Style Questions

## Exam-Style Question on Energy/Water

a   Study Fig. 5, which shows information about global electricity generation.

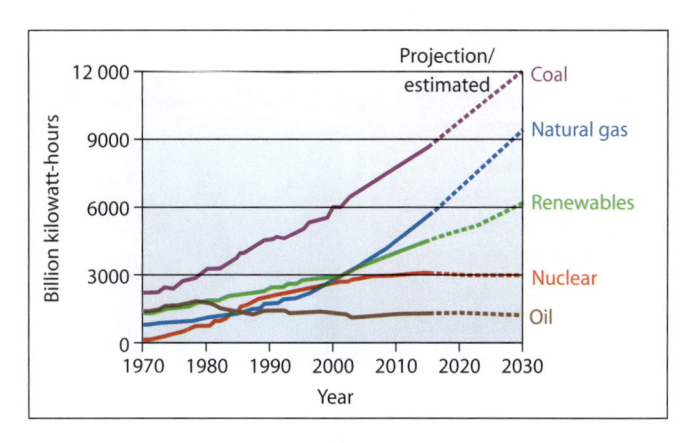

Fig. 5

i    By how much did the amount of electricity generated by coal increase between 1970 and 2010? [1]
ii   Identify **two** changes that are likely to occur in the generation of electricity by 2030. [2]
iii  Name **three** types of renewable energy. [3]
iv   Explain why some countries are trying to reduce their dependence on non-renewable forms of energy. [4]

b   Study Fig. 6, which shows nuclear power stations in the United States of America (USA).

Fig. 6

i    Describe the distribution of nuclear power stations in the United States. [3]
ii   Explain why the generation of electricity in nuclear power stations causes conflict. [5]

c   Explain how a named country or area that you have studied obtains its water supplies. [7]

[Total: 25 marks]

**Cambridge IGCSE Geography** — **Global Theme**

# 3 Global Theme: Reduce, re-use, recycle

## A Recycling across the world

*Recycling in an LEDC – the Philippines*

Brothers and sisters aged 9 or less scavenge plastic items on a beach in Manila Bay in the Philippines. They can sell the scrap for recycling, earning about 100 pesos (US$2) a day to buy food for the family. In most LEDCs recycling takes place as part of the informal economy as a desperate way to earn some money.

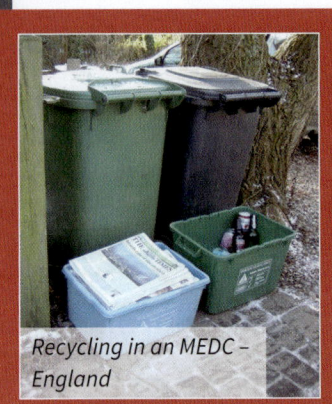

*Recycling in an MEDC – England*

Most houses are provided with green bins (garden waste) and black bins (non-recyclable waste) for collection by the council each week. Boxes for newspapers and for glass and cans are also provided. Each town has a council tip where people can take other items for recycling, e.g. computers, plastic bottles, wood and furniture. These services are funded by householders who have to pay council tax.

## A waste of resources

Many goods that we buy, from drinking bottles to newspapers, are disposable: we throw them into a bin as soon as we have finished with them. But much of this waste is not useless: glass, plastic, metal and paper are valuable materials that can be recycled. Recycling saves energy. Making new paper from old uses only 50 per cent of the energy used in making brand new paper, which conserves trees and their ecosystems. Using less plastic reduces demand for oil resources, making them last longer. Recycling also solves the problem of what to do with the waste.

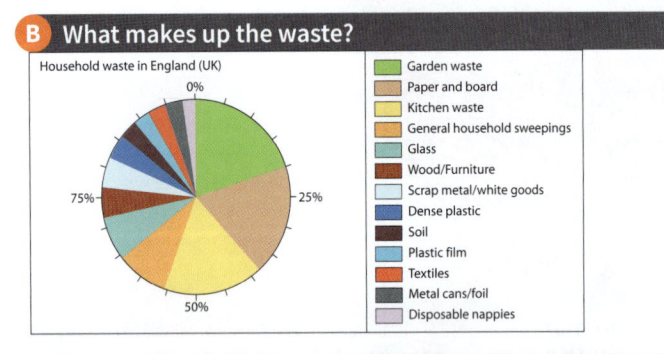

### B What makes up the waste?

Household waste in England (UK)

- Garden waste
- Paper and board
- Kitchen waste
- General household sweepings
- Glass
- Wood/Furniture
- Scrap metal/white goods
- Dense plastic
- Soil
- Plastic film
- Textiles
- Metal cans/foil
- Disposable nappies

## C Meet Sustainable Dave …

### A rubbish life for LA marathon recycler

Dave Chameides has spent almost an entire year living a life full of utter garbage. The Los Angeles cameraman has lived in his Hollywood home without throwing away a single piece of trash. Instead the 39 year old – nicknamed 'Sustainable Dave' – recycles his garbage or stores it in his basement. Instead of the usual 725 kg of trash the average American family produces each year, Dave, his wife and two daughters have amassed only 15 kg. This has been done by:

- drinking filter tap water instead of bottled water
- buying rice and pulses loose by the kilo in bulk and putting them in containers instead of cardboard packaging
- buying fresh fruit and vegetables loose from a weekly farmers' market instead of using paper bags or plastic wrapping
- using worms to mince up organic waste such as banana skins and eggshells to create a compost
- fitting his Californian home with solar panels
- using cooking oil to fuel his car
- wrapping presents in comics or other existing paper sources.

---

**TASK 1:** Study Source **A**

a Who carries out the recycling in LEDCs like the Philippines? Discuss your views on this with your classmates.

b How is recycling carried out in an MEDC like the UK?

c Why is it important to increase the amount of recycling in the world?

**TASK 2:** Study Source **B**

a Which **three** types of waste make up over 50% of the household waste in England?

b How do the different types of waste and their amounts compare to waste in your home?

**TASK 3:** Study Source **C**

a What is Dave Chameides' nickname? Why?

b What difference has recycling made to the amount of waste his family now produce compared with the average American family?

# Part B

# Geographical Skills

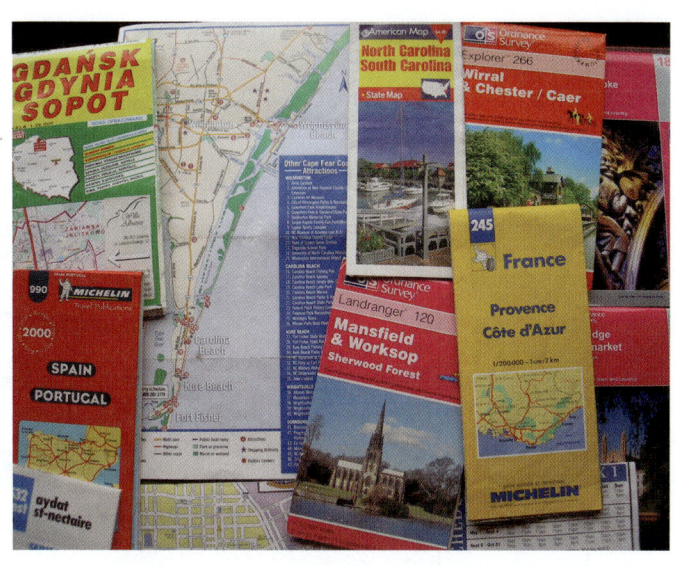

Part B of this coursebook covers the geographical skills set out in the Cambridge syllabus: application, interpretation and analysis of geographical information, e.g. topographical maps, other types of maps, diagrams, graphs, tables of data, written material, photographs and pictorial material.

Part B provides six examples of large-scale (1:25 000 or 1:50 000) topographical maps including updated exercises on maps from Peru, Zimbabwe, Jamaica and Indonesia, plus two Ordnance Survey map exercises from the UK; one at 1:25 000 and the other at 1:50 000. For each country an extract of a map is provided with guidance and tasks on the main map skills required, along with further tasks to develop other geographical skills.

A series of exam-style questions, including questions based on a 1:50 000 scale map of Ireland, is provided to enable students to practise their geographical skills. Example answers to these questions are provided on the teacher CD, which also contains sample answers to all the tasks in Part B.

The student CD contains support sheets and extension sheets for some of the topics in Part B.

**Cambridge IGCSE Geography** | **Geographical Skills**

## 1  Monsefu, Peru

### Peru – a country of varied relief

Peru, in western South America, covers almost 1.3 million km². The country borders Ecuador and Colombia to the north, Brazil to the east, Bolivia to the south-east and Chile to the south. The Andes mountains run parallel to the Pacific Ocean, dividing the country into three regions:

- The Costa (coast), in the west, is a narrow plain.
- The Sierra (highlands) is in the Andes mountains. It includes the Altiplano plateau as well as the highest peak of the country – Huascarán at 6768 m.
- The selva is a wide expanse of flat terrain covered by the Amazon rainforest in the east.

The 1:50 000 map extract below shows the area around Monsefu and Puerto Eten, in the northern part of the Costa region.

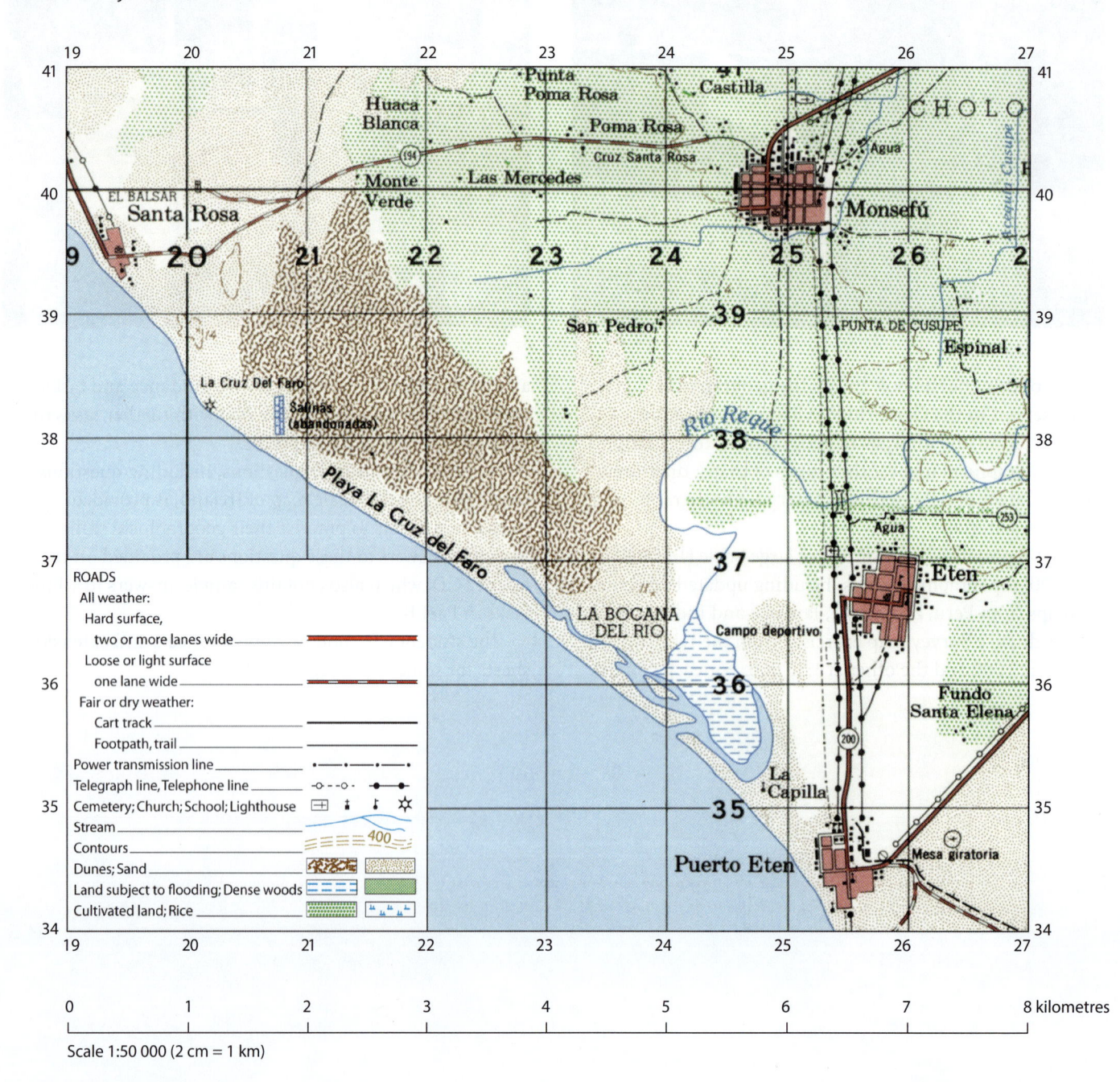

Scale 1:50 000 (2 cm = 1 km)

# Geographical Skills

## A Grid references

## SKILLS Working out distance and area

The scale of the Monsefu map is 1:50 000. This means that every centimetre on the map represents 50 000 centimetres (0.5 kilometres) in reality. Therefore the map has a scale of 2 cm = 1 km. This scale is shown by the line below the map.

To work out a **distance**, place a piece of paper with a straight edge between the two points you are measuring. Mark off these points, then transfer the piece of paper to the line below the map. Make sure that the first point marked on the paper is level with zero, then read off the distance between the two points. If you do this on the grid in **Source A** to measure line A–B you should get 2.5 km as your answer.

Each grid square on the map measures 2 cm × 2 cm and therefore it represents 1 square kilometre of land. To work out an **area**, count the total number of grid squares, or estimate areas that are smaller than a grid square, giving your answer in square kilometres. In **Source A**, the forest occupies a total of three grid squares so it is 3 km². The quarry takes up about half a grid square so this is an area of 0.5 km².

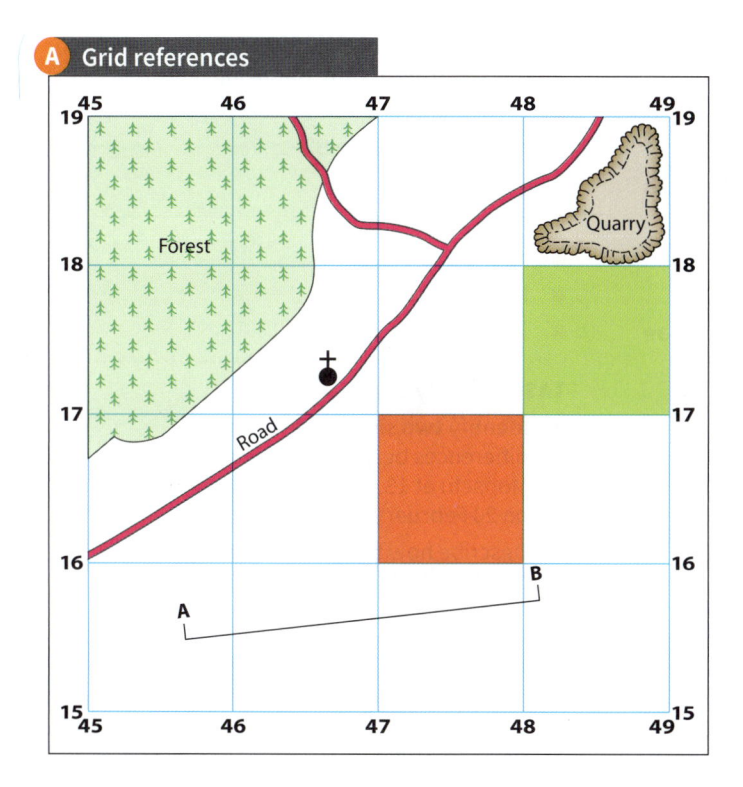

## SKILLS Giving 4-figure and 6-figure references

1:25 000 and 1:50 000 maps have a grid of numbered squares on them. To see how a 4-figure grid reference is given, look at the grid in **Source A** and follow these instructions to give the reference for the red shaded square.

- 47 is the line left of the square.
- 16 is the line below the square.

Put these two numbers together and you have a 4-figure grid reference: 4716.

The 4-figure grid reference of the green shaded square is 4817 because the line on the left is line 48 and the line at the bottom is 17.

6-figure grid references are used to identify a location within a square. To see how a 6-figure reference is given, follow this example using **Source A**.

- For the church symbol 467 is the easting. 46 is the grid line to the left and 7 is the number of tenths along towards the next grid line.
- 173 is the northing. 17 is the grid line below and 3 is the number of tenths up towards the next grid line.
- The 6-figure reference is 467173.
- The 6-figure reference of the road junction is 475182. This point is halfway (five-tenths) between eastings 47 and 48 and two-tenths of the way between northings 18 and 19.

**TASK 1:** Study the 1:50 000 map extract of Monsefu.
a  Name the small settlements in the following squares:
   2338    2635    2638
b  What is at the following 6-figure references?
   248352    195396    202383

**TASK 2:** Study the 1:50 000 map extract.
a  What is the distance:
   - along the telephone line from Puerto Eten to where it crosses the road north-east of Monsefu
   - along the road from Monsefu to Santa Rosa?
b  Estimate the area:
   - of sand dunes between Santa Rosa and La Bocana del Rio
   - of land subject to flooding at La Bocana del Rio.

**TASK 3:** Study the 1:50 000 map extract.
Find the following settlements:
- Eten (in and around grid square 2536)
- Monsefu (in and around grid square 2539)
- Puerto Eten (in grid square 2534)
- Santa Rosa (in grid square 1939)

The built-up area in each settlement is shown in pink.
Estimate the area of land covered by each settlement and then write the names of the four settlements in a list, from the largest one to the smallest.

# Cambridge IGCSE Geography — Geographical Skills

## Monsefu – some physical features

**A** Part of the 1:50 000 map

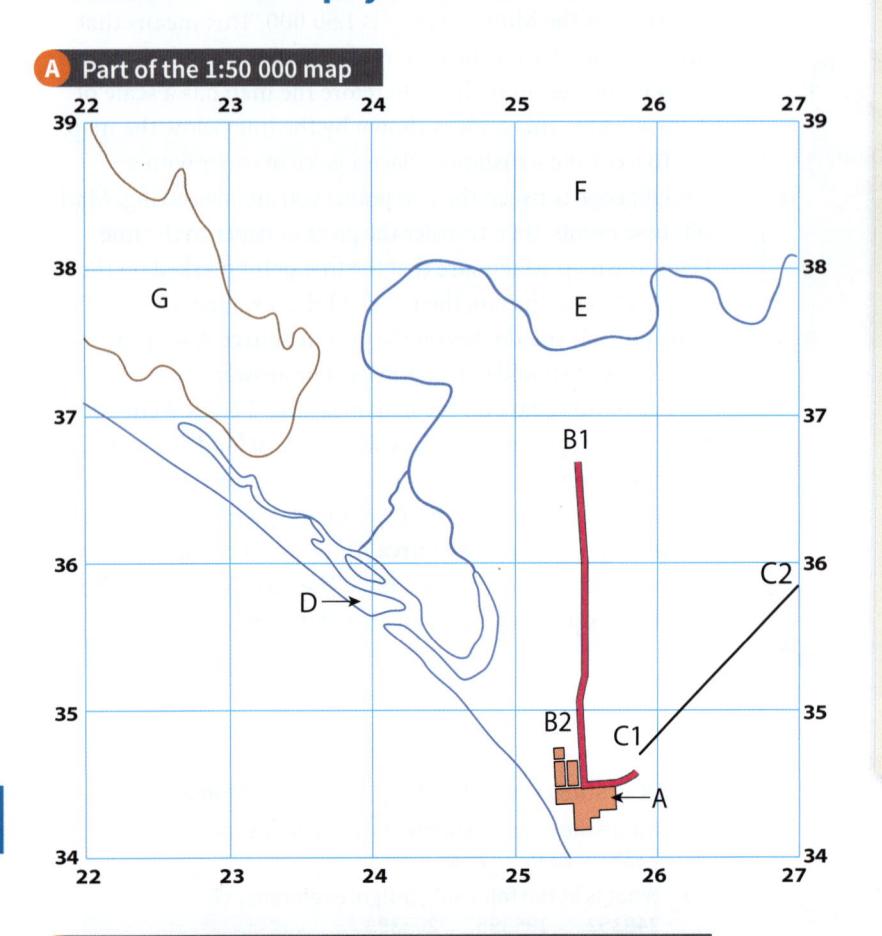

**TASK 1:** Study the 1:50 000 map extract and Source **A**. Identify the following features:
- settlement A
- road number B1 to B2
- line C1 to C2
- coastal landform D
- river E
- land use at F
- landform G.

**TASK 2:** Study Source **B**
a Identify **two** similarities and **two** differences between the weather at Monsefu at 13.00 on 18 February and 07.00 on 20 February 2014.

b Describe how the weather changed between 01.00 and 19.00 on 19 February.

**B** Weather at Monsefu, 18–21 February 2014

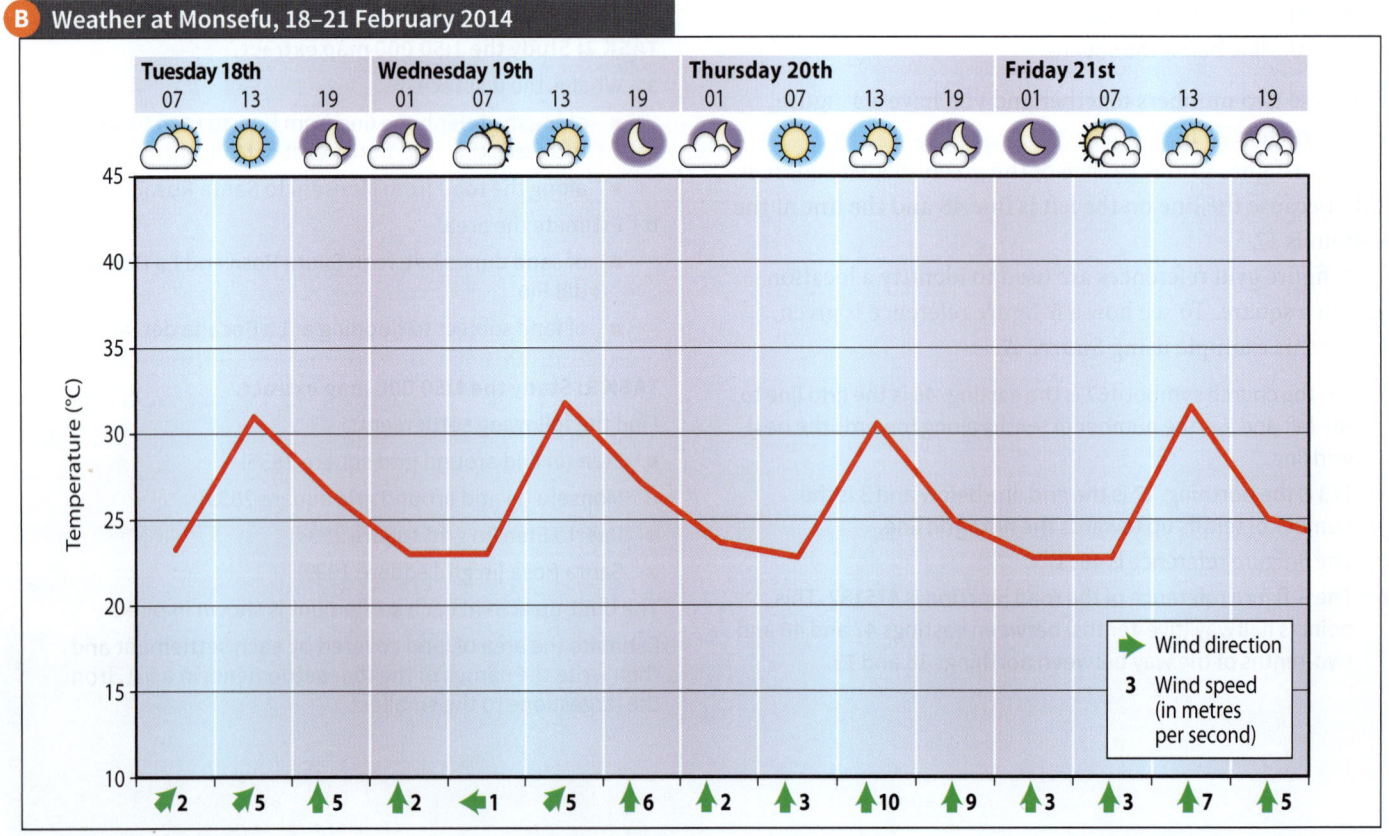

Tuesday 18th: 07, 13, 19
Wednesday 19th: 01, 07, 13, 19
Thursday 20th: 01, 07, 13, 19
Friday 21st: 01, 07, 13, 19

Wind speeds (m/s): 2, 5, 5, 2, 1, 5, 6, 2, 3, 10, 9, 3, 3, 7, 5

Wind direction (arrow)
3 Wind speed (in metres per second)

# Geographical Skills

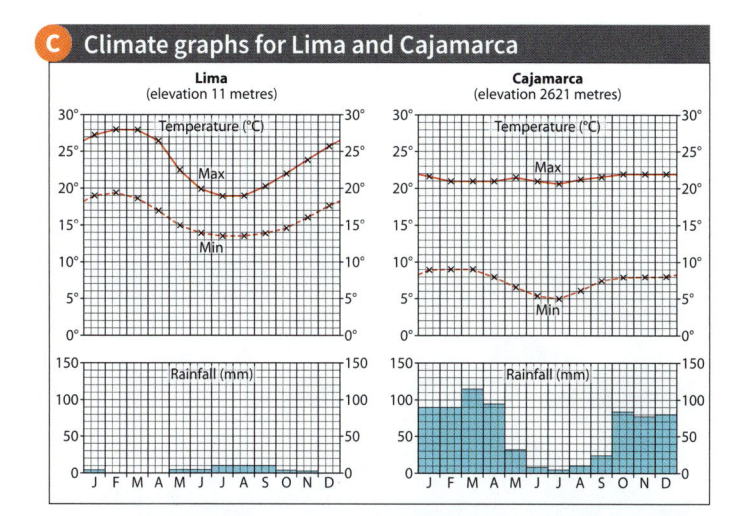

**C** Climate graphs for Lima and Cajamarca

**TASK 3:** Study Sources **C** and **D**

a  What is the average maximum temperature in Lima in April?
b  Which month in Cajamarca has the highest rainfall?
c  What is the average range of temperature in Lima in January?
d  What is the average annual rainfall in Lima?
e  Suggest why there is more rainfall in Cajamarca than in Lima.
f  Suggest why January temperatures are higher in Lima than in Cajamarca.

**TASK 4:** Study Sources **C** and **D**

a  Compare the relief of the three regions in Peru.
b  Suggest reasons why over 40% of the population of Peru live in the Costa region.
c  Give **two** advantages and **two** difficulties of living in the Sierra region.
d  Oil and natural gas have recently been discovered in the Selva region. Explain why it is difficult to exploit these resources.

**TASK 5**

In recent years the tourist industry has become important in parts of Peru. In groups, carry out research and prepare a presentation that identifies, locates and describes the attractions of Peru as a tourist destination.

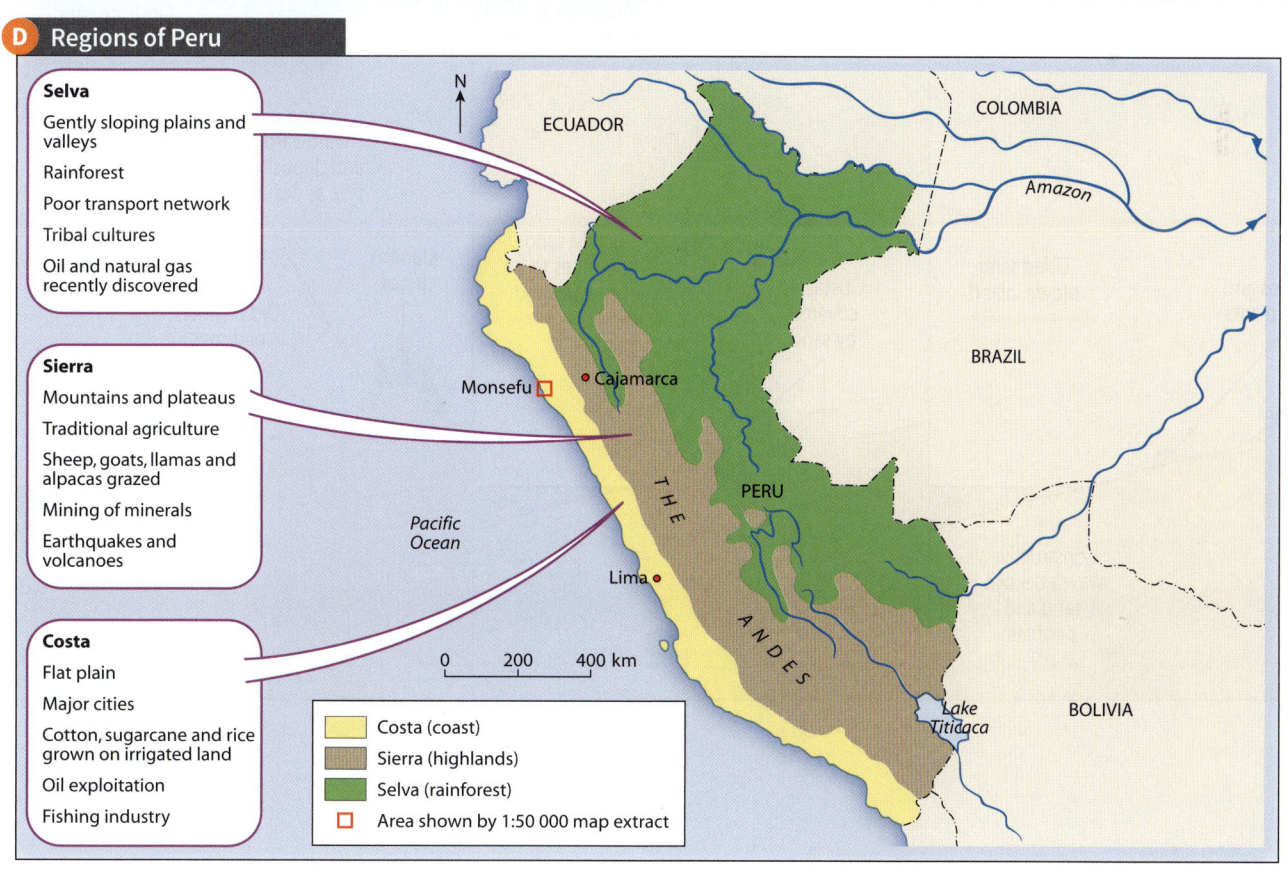

**D** Regions of Peru

**Selva**
- Gently sloping plains and valleys
- Rainforest
- Poor transport network
- Tribal cultures
- Oil and natural gas recently discovered

**Sierra**
- Mountains and plateaus
- Traditional agriculture
- Sheep, goats, llamas and alpacas grazed
- Mining of minerals
- Earthquakes and volcanoes

**Costa**
- Flat plain
- Major cities
- Cotton, sugarcane and rice grown on irrigated land
- Oil exploitation
- Fishing industry

- Costa (coast)
- Sierra (highlands)
- Selva (rainforest)
- ☐ Area shown by 1:50 000 map extract

# Cambridge IGCSE Geography — Geographical Skills

## Sand dunes on the coast of Peru

The 1:50 000 map on page 194 shows an area of sand dunes between Santa Rosa and La Bocana del Rio. Coastal sand dunes form where constructive waves encourage the deposition of sand on a beach, and where prevailing onshore winds blow this sand inland. An obstacle, such as a plant or a pebble, traps the sand and as the particles get trapped they start to accumulate to create a mound of sand. The wind then erodes particles from the **windward** side and deposits them on the **leeward** side. Gradually this action causes the dune to move inland. As it does so it accumulates more and more sand.

**A** Coastal sand dunes

**TASK 1:** Study Source **A**
Draw a sketch of the sand dunes shown in the photograph. Label **four** different features of the dunes on your sketch.

**TASK 2:** Study the 1:50 000 map on page 194 and Source **B**
Explain how the sand dunes between Santa Rosa and La Bocana del Rio were formed.

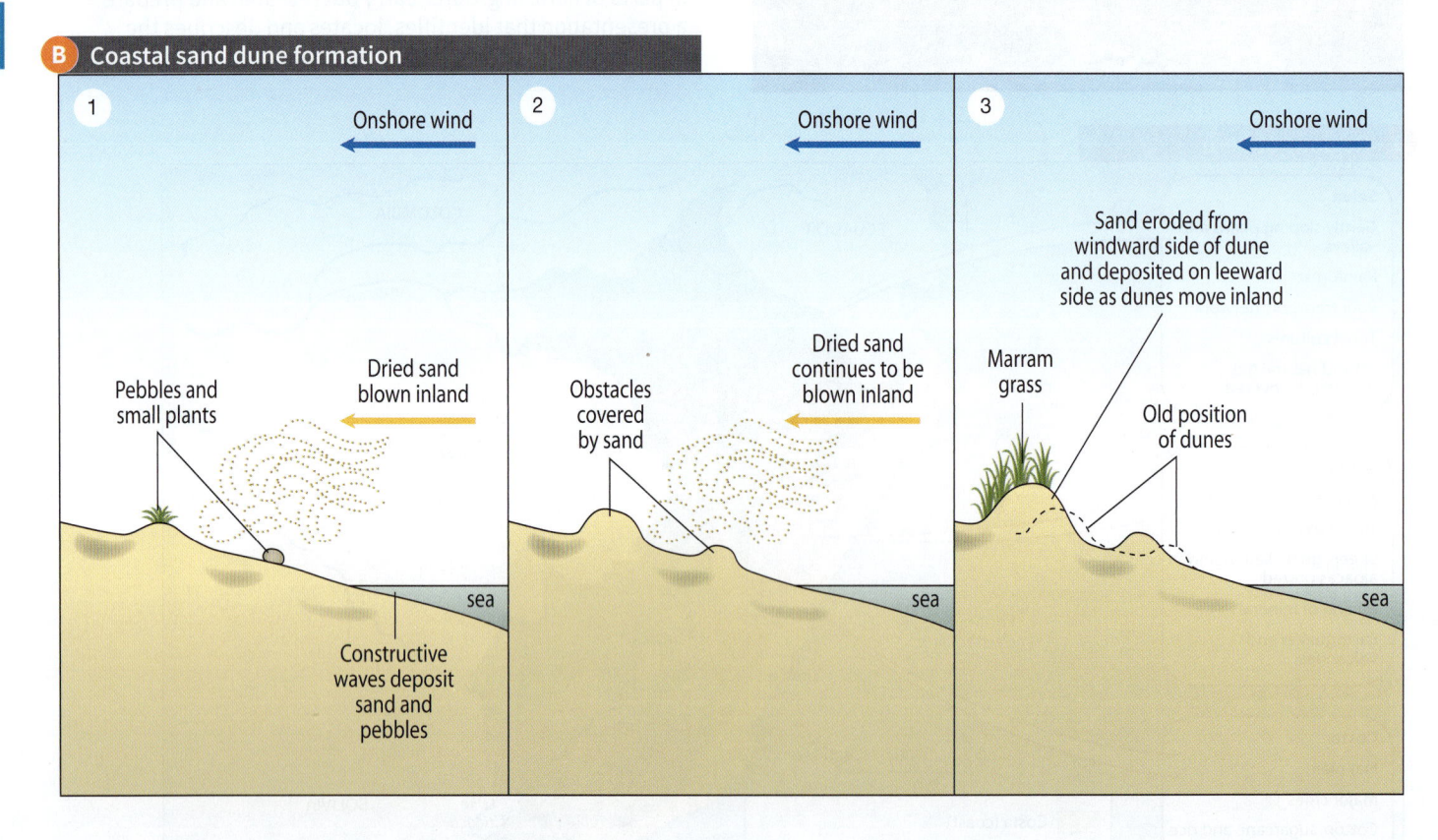

**B** Coastal sand dune formation

**1** Onshore wind — Pebbles and small plants; Dried sand blown inland; Constructive waves deposit sand and pebbles; sea

**2** Onshore wind — Obstacles covered by sand; Dried sand continues to be blown inland; sea

**3** Onshore wind — Marram grass; Sand eroded from windward side of dune and deposited on leeward side as dunes move inland; Old position of dunes; sea

# Geographical Skills

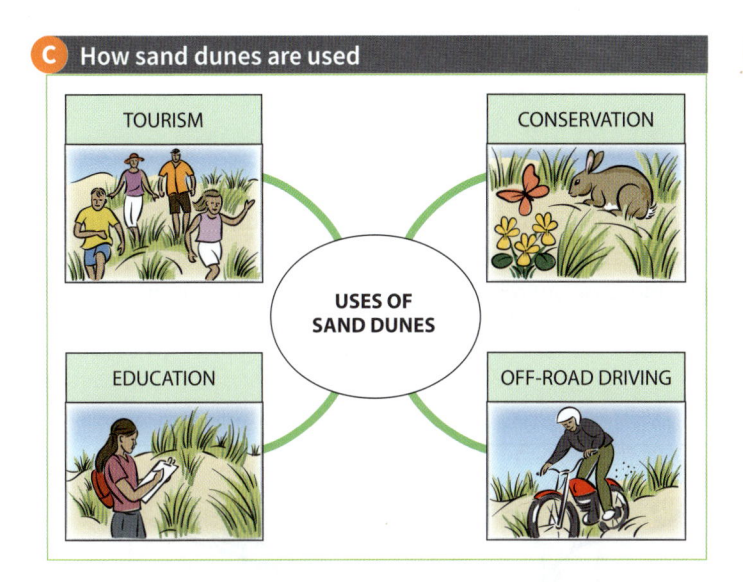

### C | How sand dunes are used

TOURISM — CONSERVATION — EDUCATION — OFF-ROAD DRIVING

**USES OF SAND DUNES**

### D | Tourists using sand dunes

### E | Schools use sand dunes

### F | A conflict matrix

|  | TOURISM | EDUCATION | CONSERVATION | OFF-ROAD DRIVING |
|---|---|---|---|---|
| TOURISM |  | ? | ? | ? |
| EDUCATION | ? |  | ✓ | ✗ |
| CONSERVATION | ? | ✓ |  | ✗ |
| OFF-ROAD DRIVING | ? | ✗ | ✗ |  |

✗ Conflict
? Possible conflict
✓ No conflict

### G | Dune management

### TASK 3

There are conflicts arising over the use of the sand dunes between Santa Rosa and La Bocana del Rio. They are being used for many different purposes and the dunes and ecosystems are being damaged.

Study **Sources C to G**

The table shows information about four possible schemes being considered to manage the dunes.

In groups, choose the scheme that you think will be most useful to manage the dunes. Explain your reasons for choosing this scheme. You should do this by describing the advantages of the scheme you have chosen and the disadvantages of the schemes you have rejected.

| Scheme 1 | Scheme 2 |
|---|---|
| Ban all human activities on the dunes, and use 24-hour security patrols and CCTV. | Fence off areas of the dunes so that different activities can take place in each. |

| Scheme 3 | Scheme 4 |
|---|---|
| Provide a free information centre and guides for students and visitors. | Allow unlimited use but charge an entrance fee to all users of the dunes. |

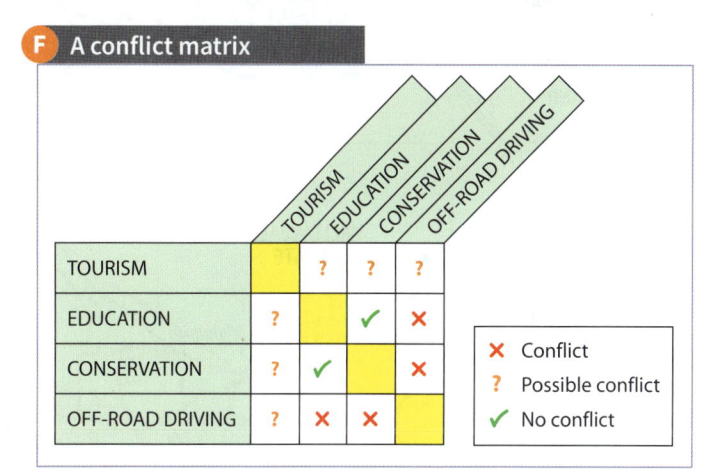

**Cambridge IGCSE Geography** | **Geographical Skills**

# 2 Harare, Zimbabwe

## Harare – Zimbabwe's largest city

The 1:50 000 map below shows part of the rural-urban fringe on the western edge of the city of Harare, the capital of Zimbabwe. According to the 2012 census Harare had a population of 2 098 199. It is Zimbabwe's largest city and its administrative, commercial and communications centre.

The city has important manufacturing industries (e.g. steel, textiles and chemicals) and it is a trade centre for crops produced on surrounding farmland (e.g. tobacco, maize, cotton, and citrus fruits).

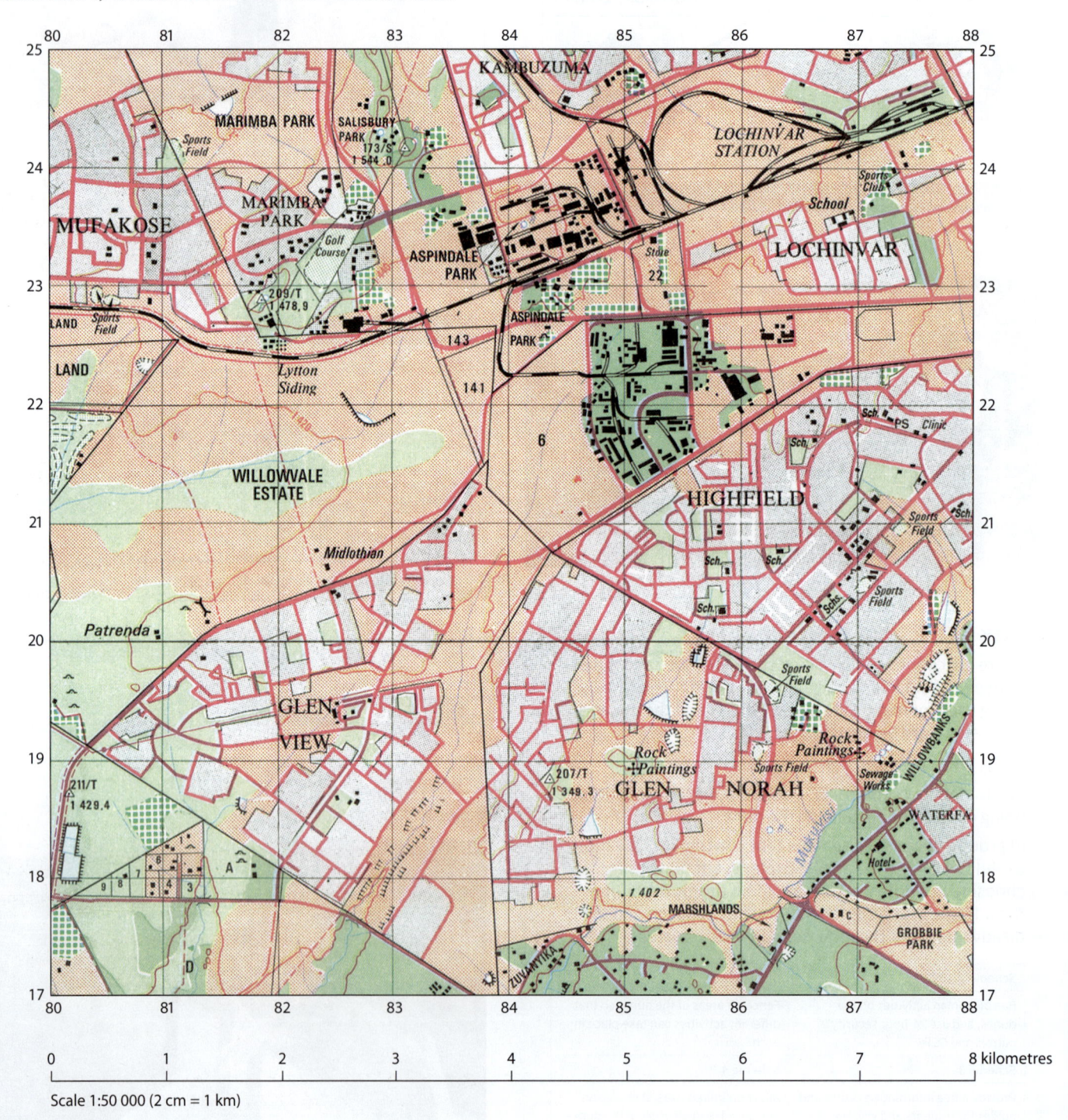

Scale 1:50 000 (2 cm = 1 km)

# Geographical Skills

## SKILLS  Giving a compass bearing

A bearing is a numerical measurement of direction between two points. Bearings use all 360° of a compass to indicate direction. The bearings on a compass are numbered clockwise with north as 0°, east 90°, south 180°, and west 270°. So a bearing of 135° would be south-east and a bearing of 315° would be north-west. A protractor can be used to measure the bearing.

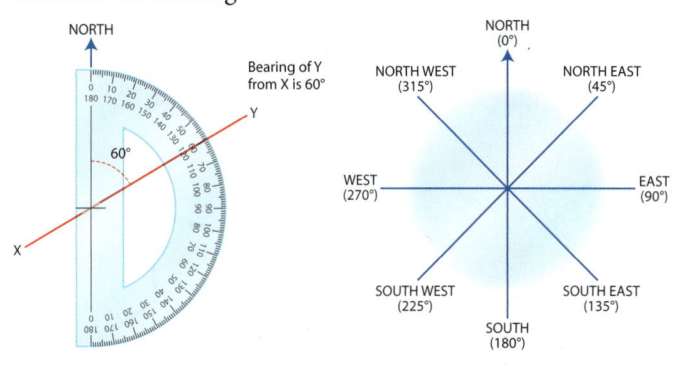

| Key for 1:50 000 map | |
|---|---|
| Road, Wide tarred | |
| Road, Narrow tarred | |
| Road, Gravel or earth, Bridge | |
| Railway, with embankment, Cutting, Tunnel | |
| Built-up area, Buildings | |
| Church | |
| Dip tank | |
| River, Watercourse | |
| Dam | |
| Contours at 20 metre vertical interval, with Cliff feature | |
| Cultivation | |
| Medium bush | |
| Sparse bush | |
| Orchard or plantation | |

**TASK 1:** Study the 1:50 000 map extract.

Find where the railway line crosses the road at 832228. Imagine that a train is travelling along this railway to the eastern edge of the map.

a   Use the scale of the map to work out the distance of this journey.

b   Work out the compass direction in which the train will be travelling.

c   What is the compass bearing from where the railway crosses the road to the eastern edge of the map?

d   Imagine you are sitting on this train, looking out of the window on your right-hand side (i.e. to the south of the railway line).

Write a paragraph to describe what you would see from the window on this part of your journey. You will need to use the map key.

**TASK 2:** Study the 1:50 000 map extract.

a   Give evidence from the map which shows that Highfield (in and around grid square 8621) is a densely populated area.

b   Suggest reasons why the land around the Mukuvisi river (in and around grid square 8618) does not have many people living on it.

**TASK 3:** Study the 1:50 000 map extract.

Much of the the land in grid square 8423 is used for manufacturing industries.

a   Use map evidence to suggest the advantages of the site for manufacturing industries.

b   Suggest benefits and problems of this manufacturing industry for local people and the natural environment.

# Cambridge IGCSE Geography — Geographical Skills

## Urban farming in Harare

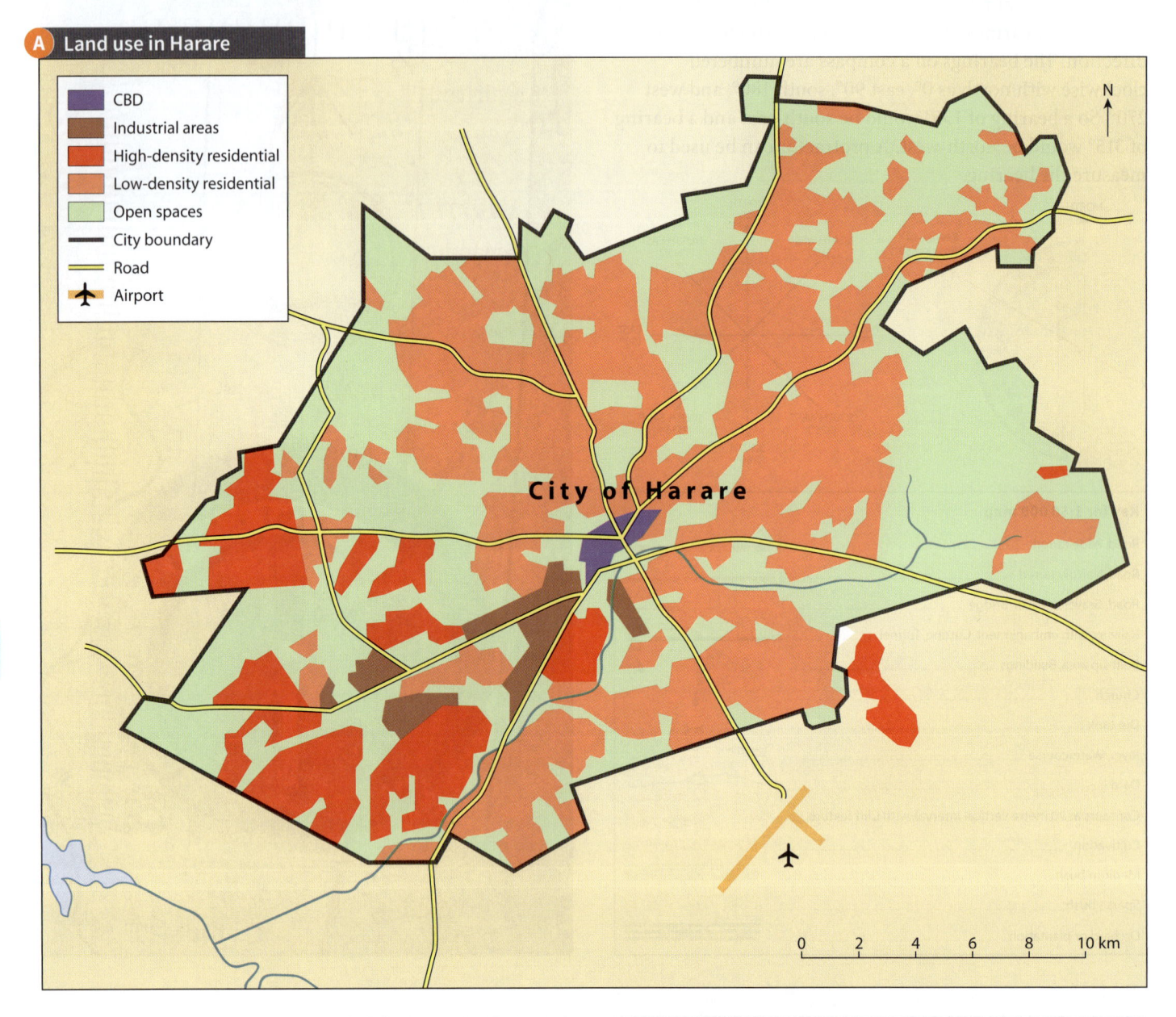

### A  Land use in Harare

**Legend:**
- CBD
- Industrial areas
- High-density residential
- Low-density residential
- Open spaces
- City boundary
- Road
- Airport

While farming is often thought of as a rural activity, many poor families who live in cities in LEDCs would not have food to eat without growing crops in their backyards, on roadside verges or allotments, and any other areas of open space. Harare has a warm, wet climate and there are some open spaces in and around the city. River floods in the long, wet season prevent building on low land, but provide water for irrigation for farmers. Tomatoes, green vegetables and maize are the main crops. Urban farmers, mainly women, grow the crops to eat, or to sell at market to earn money to buy meat and pay for their children's education. In some parts of the city more than two-thirds of households carry out some farming, either around their homes or on public land such as roadside verges.

**TASK 1: Study Source A**

a  What is the distance and direction from the airport to the CBD?

b  Estimate the percentage of land within the boundary of Harare that is open space.

c  Suggest reasons why large areas of land are likely to be used for farming within the city boundary to the south-west of the CBD of Harare.

# Geographical Skills

## B  Three urban farmers in Harare

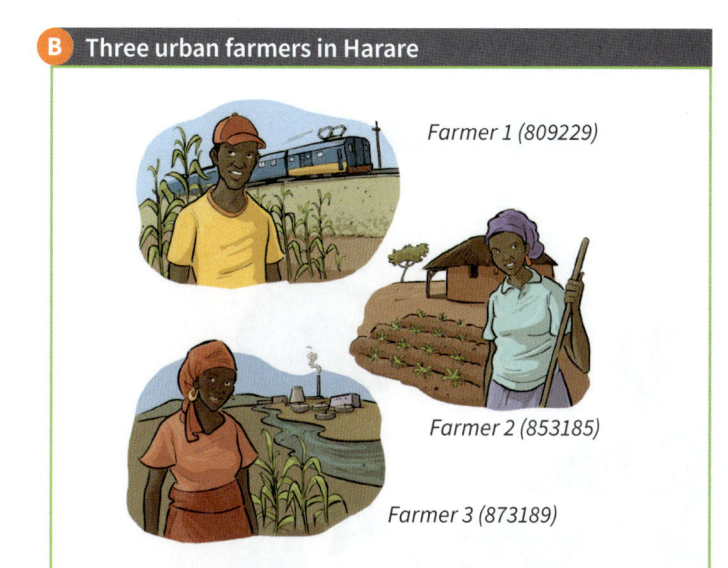

Farmer 1 (809229)

Farmer 2 (853185)

Farmer 3 (873189)

## C  Benefits and problems of urban farming in LEDCs

### Benefits
- Food is produced for poor families.
- Surplus food sold on local markets for income to reduce poverty.
- Use made of land that may otherwise be wasted.
- Plants grown help reduce atmospheric pollution.
- Producing food locally saves transport and storage costs.
- Waste water and organic solid waste can be used on the farms.

### Problems
- Chemicals used may pollute local drinking water supplies.
- Farmers will be at risk from mosquitoes when farming near rivers.
- Conflict occurs over the use of land and farmers can lose their land at any time.
- Crops grown close to roads and railways could be contaminated by fumes.
- The use of land for farming competes with other urban land uses, especially public open spaces.
- Use of water for crops reduces scarce supplies and increases cost.

## D  The growth of urban farming

### Urban agriculture threatened from all sides

Urban farming is part of the lifestyle of most urban residents in Zimbabwe, providing healthy home-grown food and extra income. Maize and sweet potatoes are the most popular crops planted and as the rainy season approaches, residents begin to cultivate areas of undeveloped land around Harare.

This year, however, far fewer people will be able to use land to grow crops due to the increase in property construction, particularly on the city outskirts.

Christine Gadzikwa, a domestic worker in Borrowdale West, told *Harare News* that she will not be able to plant this season as her usual piece of land located near Groombridge shopping centre has been developed by its owner. Gadzikwa said she will continue to look for another undeveloped piece of land to farm as her 100 square metre field allowed her to supplement both her diet and income through selling fresh and boiled mealie cobs to other residents in the area.

Building developments are not the only threat. Historically, the Harare municipality has destroyed crops planted in illegal spaces, especially on roadsides and along footpaths. 'I am not sure if I will plant this season because last year my maize was slashed by council workers,' said Roddy Magaya from Budiriro.

Environmentalists are also concerned over poor farming methods by the urban farmers which include planting in wetlands, stream bank cultivation and the use of chemicals which threaten human and environmental health.

However, it remains to be seen whether urban farming will stand the test of time as developers, council and environmentalists take a tougher stance against the practice.

Adapted from *Harare News*, 24 November 2013

---

**TASK 2:** Study the 1:50 000 map extract on page 200 and Source **B**

a  Use the 6-figure reference to name the suburb and describe the characteristics of the area where each of the urban farmers grows crops.

b  Suggest a different difficulty faced by each of farmers 1, 2 and 3 when growing their crops.

**TASK 3:** Study the 1:50 000 map extract on page 200 and Sources **C** and **D**

a  Give **two** reasons why some urban farmers in Harare are no longer able to grow crops.

b  Imagine you are an adviser to the Harare Municipality. Consider the arguments for and against allowing urban land to be used for farming and decide whether urban agriculture should be allowed to continue in suburbs such as Glen Norah and Glen View. Prepare a report to justify your decision.

**Cambridge IGCSE Geography** — Geographical Skills

# Quality of life

**A** Children collect stagnant water for use in Glen View, Harare

**B** Access to clean water in Africa

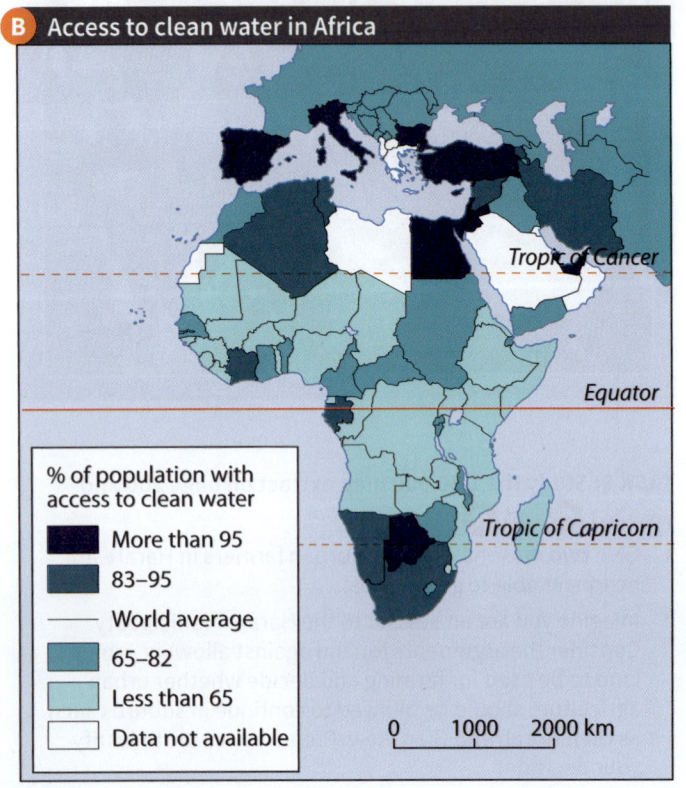

% of population with access to clean water
- More than 95
- 83–95
- World average
- 65–82
- Less than 65
- Data not available

0  1000  2000 km

**TASK 1:** Study **Source A** and the 1:50 000 map on page 200.

a  Give a 4-figure reference for the grid square in which the photograph could have been taken.

b  Suggest what the quality of life will be like for the children shown in the photograph. Give reasons for your answer.

**TASK 2:** Study **Source B** and an atlas.

a  Put the following countries in rank order according to the percentage of their population that has access to clean water. Rank from high to low.
- Algeria
- Egypt
- Mali
- Zimbabwe

b  Name **three** countries where between 83% and 95% have access to clean water.

c  Describe the distribution of those countries where less than 65% of the population have access to clean water.

d  Suggest reasons why the access of the population to clean water varies from country to country.

# Geographical Skills

**C** Quality of life indicators for selected LEDCs

| Country | GDP per person (US$) | Energy use per person (kg oil equivalent) | Number of doctors (per 1000 people) | Adult literacy (percentages) |
|---|---|---|---|---|
| Algeria | 7500 | 1108 | 1.21 | 73 |
| Bangladesh | 2100 | 205 | 0.36 | 58 |
| Egypt | 6600 | 978 | 2.83 | 74 |
| Ethiopia | 1300 | 381 | 0.03 | 39 |
| India | 4000 | 614 | 0.65 | 63 |
| Mexico | 15 600 | 1588 | 1.96 | 93 |
| South Africa | 11 500 | 2741 | 0.76 | 93 |
| Zimbabwe | 600 | 697 | 0.06 | 84 |

Source: The World Factbook (Central Intelligence Agency)

**D** GDP and energy use

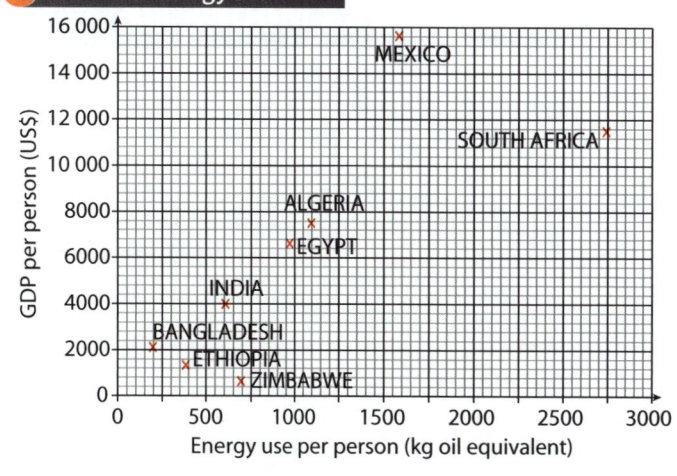

(scatter graph: GDP per person (US$) vs Energy use per person (kg oil equivalent); points plotted for Mexico, South Africa, Algeria, Egypt, India, Bangladesh, Ethiopia, Zimbabwe)

**E** Assessing quality of life 1

**F** Assessing quality of life 2

**G** A bi-polar chart for quality of life

| Clean | +3 | +2 | +1 | 0 | −1 | −2 | −3 | Dirty |
|---|---|---|---|---|---|---|---|---|
| Healthy | +3 | +2 | +1 | 0 | −1 | −2 | −3 | Unhealthy |
| Quiet | +3 | +2 | +1 | 0 | −1 | −2 | −3 | Noisy |
| Safe | +3 | +2 | +1 | 0 | −1 | −2 | −3 | Dangerous |

**TASK 3: Study Source C**

a 'People in Zimbabwe have a lower quality of life than people in Egypt.' Give **two** pieces of evidence from the table to support this statement.

b Which country in the table do you think has the highest quality of life? Give reasons for your answer.

**TASK 4: Study Sources C and D**

a To what extent is there a relationship between GDP per person and the use of energy? Use examples of countries and give figures in your answer.

b Draw a scatter graph showing the relationship between GDP per person and adult literacy.

c Explain why there is a positive relationship between GDP per person and adult literacy.

d Suggest reasons why Zimbabwe does not fit into the pattern shown by the scatter graph.

**TASK 5: Study Sources E, F and G.** Source G is a chart which can be used to assess the quality of life in an urban area.

a The photographs in Sources E and F show areas where people live in the same city. Use Source G to compare the quality of life in the two areas. To do this you will need to give each of the areas a score between +3 and −3 on each line. When you have done this you can work out an overall score for each area.

b Use a suitable method to plot your figures on a graph.

c Which area would you want to live in: the one shown in Source E or Source F? Give reasons for your answer.

# Cambridge IGCSE Geography — Geographical Skills

## 3 North Yorks Moors, UK

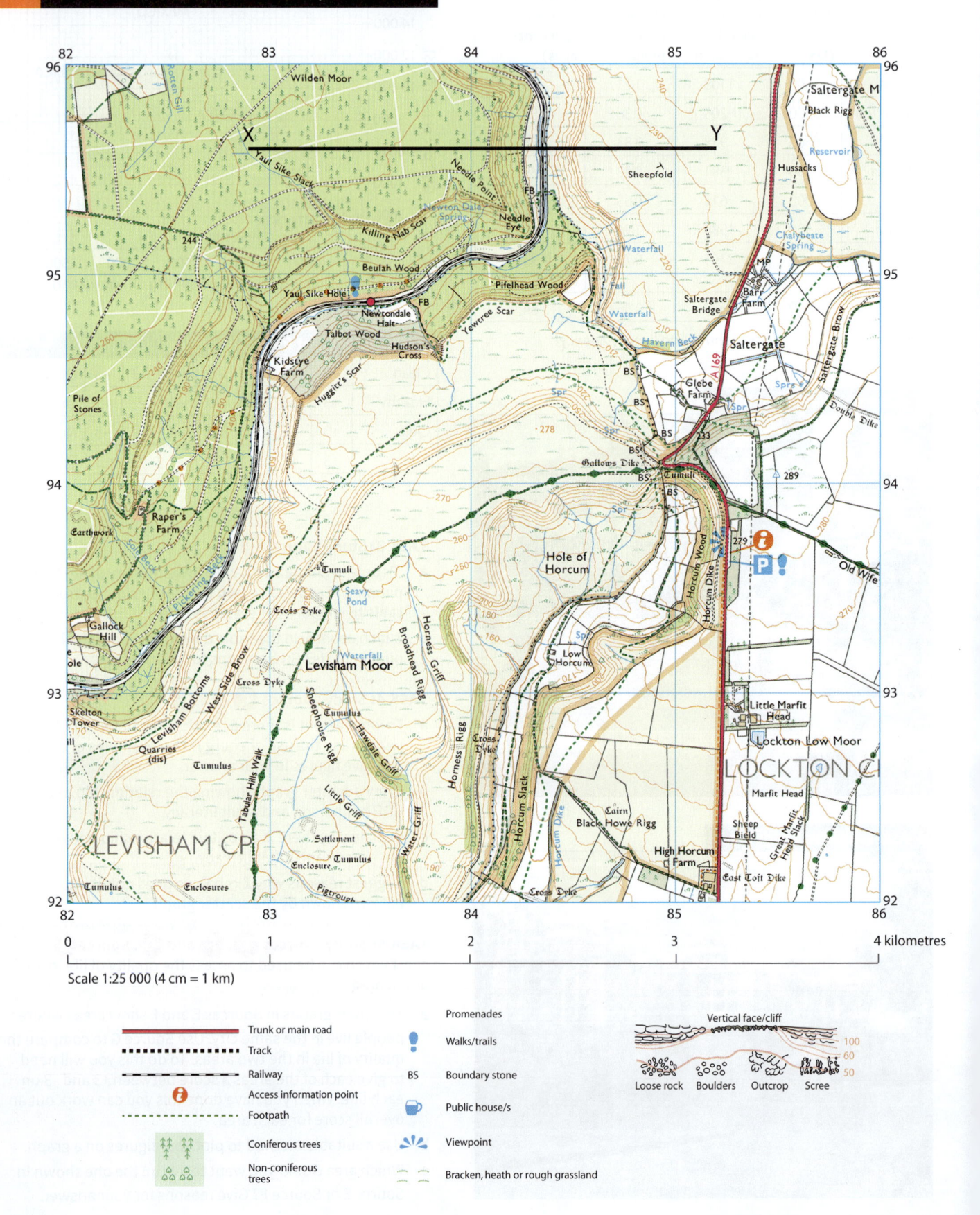

Scale 1:25 000 (4 cm = 1 km)

**Legend:**
- Trunk or main road
- Track
- Railway
- Access information point
- Footpath
- Coniferous trees
- Non-coniferous trees
- Promenades
- Walks/trails
- BS Boundary stone
- Public house/s
- Viewpoint
- Bracken, heath or rough grassland
- Vertical face/cliff
- Loose rock
- Boulders
- Outcrop
- Scree

# Geographical Skills

## The North York Moors National Park

The North York Moors is a national park in North Yorkshire, England. It covers an area of 1436 km² and is sparsely populated with an average of 16 people per km² who live in small towns, villages or on scattered farms. Much of the area consists of moorland plateaus with many deep valleys. The moors are largely used by local farmers for grazing sheep but some of the valleys are cultivated. Large areas are covered with coniferous forests. The area is popular with tourists. Many visitors enjoy outdoor pursuits, such as walking, cycling, horse-riding and gliding.

### Representing height

To represent height on a map, spot heights and contours are used.

**Spot heights** are dots placed anywhere on the map with a number next to them. This tells us the exact height of that spot in metres above sea level. Sometimes spot heights show the highest part of a hill, but they can show any height, anywhere on the map.

**Contours** are brown lines on a map that join together places of equal height. These can be used to work out what the relief of the land is like (its height and shape).

**Triangulation stations** (also known as trig points) are shown on maps by a small dot within a triangle. The height in metres is written on the map. If you went to this location you would find a concrete or brick pillar used for surveying purposes. They are usually built on the top of hills.

> **TASK 1:** Study the 1:25 000 map extract and Source A
> Give a 4-figure reference for a grid square for each of the following.
> a   An area of gentle slopes covered with coniferous forests
> b   A plateau
> c   A deep and steep-sided valley

**A** The Hole of Horcum

*Steep slopes are represented by contours that are close together.*

*A plateau is a large area of flat land on the top of a hill. This is represented by widely spaced contours at a height that is greater than the surrounding land.*

*Gently sloping land is represented by contours that are widely spaced.*

# Describing the physical landscape

**SKILLS** Describing relief and drainage

When you are describing the **relief** of an area you should begin by referring to the main relief features, e.g. glaciated upland, coastal plain or escarpment, etc. Name any such feature and describe it if possible, e.g. 'This map area forms part of a coastal plain with gentle slopes.'

Then refer to relief features within the area, e.g. valleys, spurs, ridges, plateaus, stating where they are (possibly by the use of grid references), and describe them. It is useful to describe slopes on the map, e.g. flat, gently sloping, steep, and to add some references to height. You can get this information from contour lines or spot heights, e.g. 'The river, which flows around interlocking spurs through grid square 3498, has steep valley sides which lie between 240 and 475 metres and its source is on the ridge at 337976 at 512 metres above sea level. The ridge has steep north-facing slopes, although those that face south are gentler.'

When you are describing the **drainage** of an area you should note the following:

- Name the main rivers and state the direction(s) of flow.
- Density of surface drainage. This can be judged by the number of rivers and streams shown and how close together they are, e.g. 'There are many rivers in the east of the map but very few in the west.'
- Width of rivers, e.g. 'The wide river that flows through grid square 9811 is joined by many narrow tributaries.'
- Long profile of rivers: this can be judged by how close together the contours are where a river crosses, e.g. 'The river has a steep and irregular long profile and there is a waterfall at grid reference 348512.'
- The course of the rivers, e.g. are they meandering or straight? Perfectly straight drainage is usually artificial, and used for drainage or irrigation.

When you have described the relief and drainage it should be possible to summarise your comments on a sketch map to show the main aspects of the physical landscape. Label significant features in each region, e.g. plateau, ridge, valley, and add information about the drainage by marking on the main rivers and their valleys.

**A** Contour patterns and slopes

Convex slope

Concave slope

Uniform slope

Convex and concave slope

**TASK 1:** Study the map extract of the North York Moors on page 206 and Source **A** on page 207.

a The photograph in Source A was taken from the viewpoint at 852937.
Describe the landscape shown in the photograph.

b Describe the relief and drainage in grid square 8392.

**TASK 2**

Study the map extract again. Give evidence from the map to identify **three** ways in which the area is used by people. For each piece of evidence you should give a grid reference.

# Geographical Skills

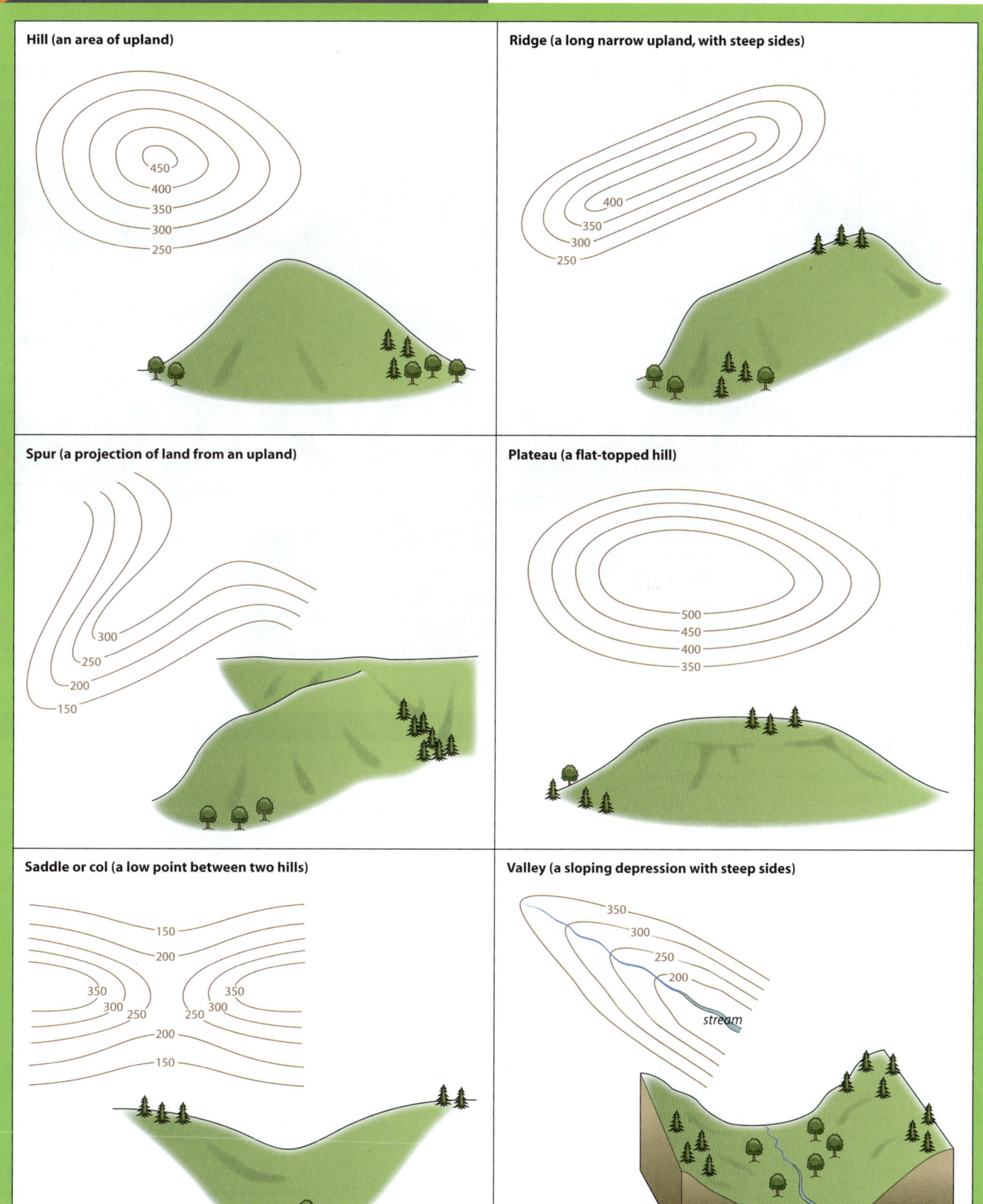

## B Contour patterns and landforms

**Hill (an area of upland)**

450
400
350
300
250

**Ridge (a long narrow upland, with steep sides)**

400
350
300
250

**Spur (a projection of land from an upland)**

300
250
200
150

**Plateau (a flat-topped hill)**

500
450
400
350

**Saddle or col (a low point between two hills)**

150
200
350 350
300 300
250 250
200
150

**Valley (a sloping depression with steep sides)**

350
300
250
200
stream

209

# Gradients and cross-sections

## A Gradients

### SKILLS How to calculate a gradient

The gradient of a slope measures the steepness of the slope. The steepness of a slope is important to walkers and cyclists. Roads are sometimes constructed along slopes with steep gradients, although railways are usually built on more gentle slopes.

On many maps roads are marked with one arrow if the gradient is between 1 in 7 and 1 in 5, and with two arrows if it is steeper than 1 in 5. A gradient of 1 in 5 can also be expressed as a 20% gradient. This means that for every 5 metres of horizontal distance there is a change in height of 1 metre. This is shown in **Source B**.

To work out the average gradient of a slope on a map:

- Measure the horizontal distance along the slope in metres. This is known as the **horizontal equivalent**.
- Find the difference in height between the two end points of the slope (this can be worked out in metres by looking at contours or spot heights). This is known as the **vertical interval**.
- Divide the vertical interval by the horizontal equivalent.

So if the difference in height between the top and bottom of a slope is 10 metres and the distance along the slope is 100 metres:

$$\text{Gradient} = \frac{\text{Vertical interval}}{\text{Horizontal equivalent}} = \frac{10}{100} \text{ or 1 in 10 or 10\%}$$

## B A 1 in 5 gradient

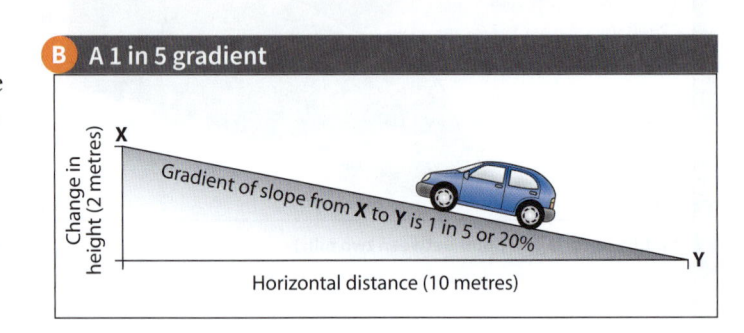

Gradient of slope from **X** to **Y** is 1 in 5 or 20%
Change in height (2 metres)
Horizontal distance (10 metres)

### TASK 1

a Why can roads be constructed on steeper gradients than railway lines?

b Which gradient is steeper?
- 1 in 3 or 1 in 10
- 10% or 20%

### TASK 2: Study the map extract of the North York Moors on page 206.

Calculate the average gradient on the A169 main road between the viewpoint at 852937 and High Horcum Farm at 852921. The height at High Horcum Farm is 215 metres above sea level.

# Geographical Skills

## SKILLS How to draw a cross-section

A cross-section is a diagram showing variations in height and slope along a line drawn on a map. To draw a cross-section:

- Place a piece of paper with a straight edge along the cross-section line on your map. Mark the beginning and ending of the line with the letters X and Y.
- Along the straight edge of your paper mark the point where each contour crosses it, labelling the height of each contour. You will need to estimate the heights at the end of the line. Also mark the points where features such as rivers, roads and railway lines cross the line of the cross-section (see **Source C** Stage 1).
- Draw a frame for your cross-section on graph paper. The base of the frame should be the same length as your cross-section line. Use a vertical scale that shows the height in metres.
- Put the straight edge of your piece of paper along the base of the frame and mark a small cross at the correct height, using the vertical scale, where each contour line is marked on the straight edge (see **Source C** Stage 2).
- Join the dots with a smooth line and shade the land. Draw arrows and label the position of rivers, roads, railway lines and any other features (see **Source C** Stage 3).

**TASK 3:** Study the map extract of the North York Moors on page 206.

a   Draw a cross-section along the line from X to Y. (From 829956 to 852956)

b   On the cross-section you have drawn, mark the positions of a coniferous forest, a railway line and a track.

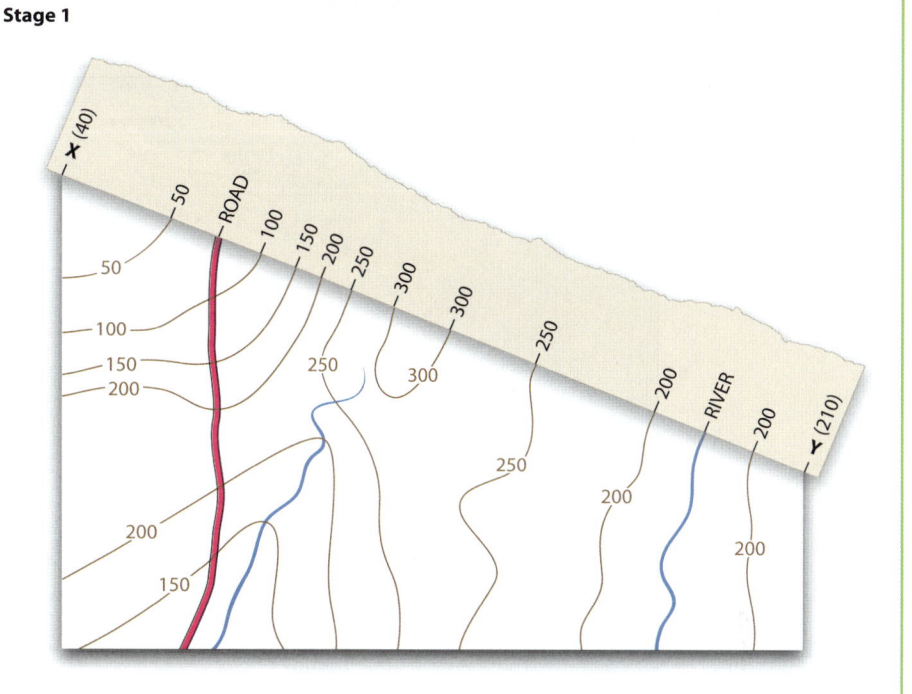

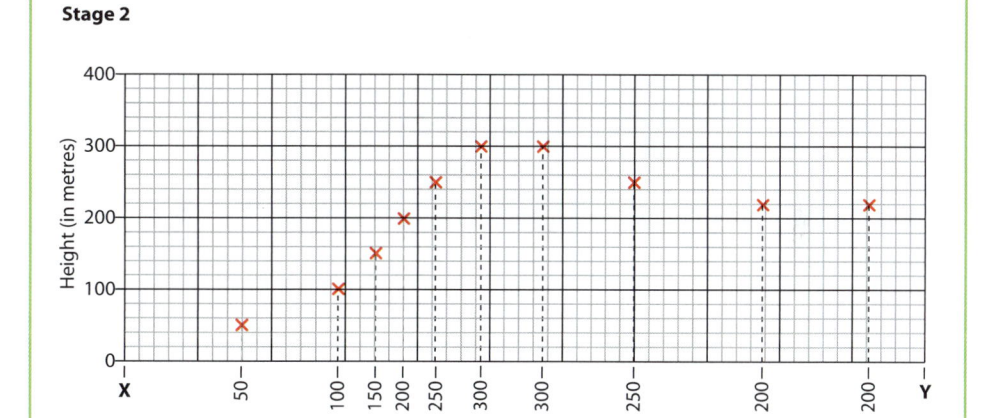

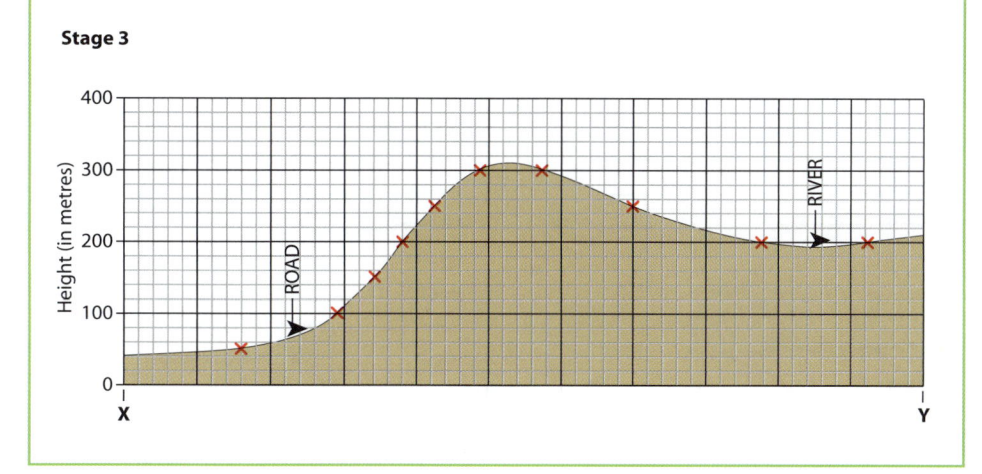

### C Drawing a cross-section

**Stage 1**

**Stage 2**

**Stage 3**

# Cambridge IGCSE Geography — Geographical Skills

## 4  Montego Bay, Jamaica

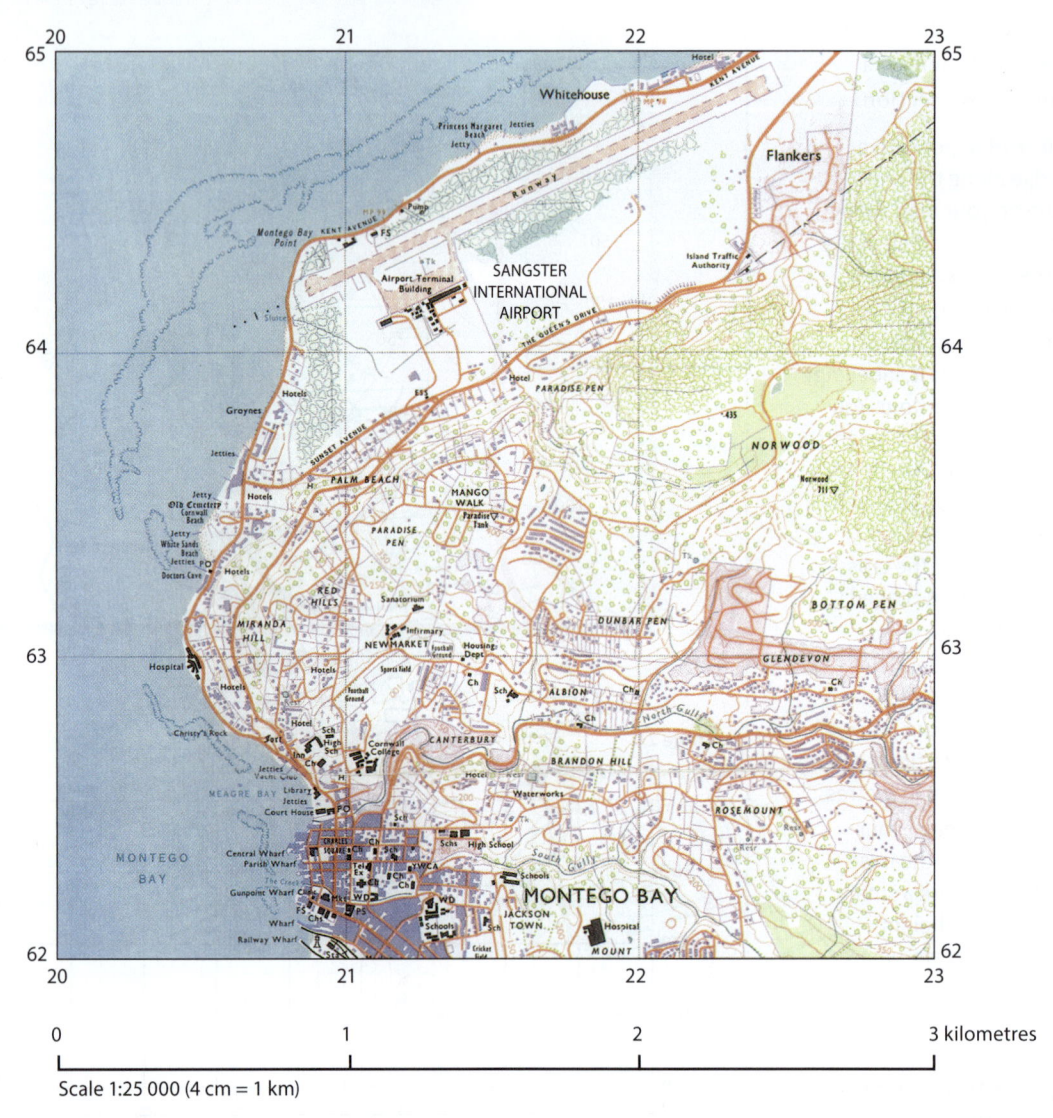

Scale 1:25 000 (4 cm = 1 km)

### Map Key

**Transport and infrastructure**
- Road - 1st Class (Mile Post)
- Other
- Track or Footpath
- Railway
- Light or Siding
- Disused
- Power Line
- Telephone Line
- Telephone Line along Road

**Relief and features**
- Contours (VI 50 feet)
- Contour showing Depression
- Antiquity — Fort
- Cemetery
- Ruin
- Mangrove

**Natural features**
- Swamp or Marsh
- Line of Small Trees, Palms
- Bamboo
- Well, Waterhole, Spring — W, WH, S
- Reservoir, Tank — Resr, T

**Buildings and services**
- Church — Ch
- Electricity Sub Station — ESS
- Fire Station — FS
- Hospital — Hosp
- Hotel — H
- Market — Mkt
- Mission — M
- Police Station — PS
- Post Agency — PA
- Post Office — PO
- Pump House — Pump
- School — Sch
- Wireless Station — WS
- Works Department — WD

**Settlement**
- Town
- Building - Public, Other
- Areas of small or semi-permanent buildings

**Boundaries and stations**
- Boundary - County
- Parish
- Trigonometrical Station - Primary
- Secondary
- Tertiary
- Spot Height (Photogrammetric)

**Vegetation**
- Dense Woodland
- Trees and Bushes
- Forest Plantation
- Plantation - Banana
- Citrus
- Coconut
- Sugar
- Unclassified Plantation or Pasture
- Mixed or Scattered Cultivation

# Geographical Skills

## Montego Bay

Montego Bay is an important tourist resort on the north-west coast of the island of Jamaica. It has a population of about 110 000 people and close by is Jamaica's largest airport, the Sangster International Airport. Flights to and from Montego Bay provide access for increasing numbers of tourists from countries such as the USA, the UK, Germany and Canada.

Sangster International Airport is located at the centre of the country's main tourism region and close to a wide range of hotels and tourist resorts. The airport is within easy driving distance of the cruise ports at Montego Bay and Ocho Rios as well as the popular tourist town of Negril.

### SKILLS  Describing site and situation

**Site** is a description of the actual land on which a feature is built. This includes the relief of the land (its height above sea level, its slope and its aspect) and the size of the area of land.

**Situation** is a description of where the feature is built in relation to other features around it. This includes natural features such as rivers or the coast, and built features such as settlements. Distance and direction from these features should be used to describe the situation accurately.

**A  Sangster International Airport**

### TASK 1

a  In the box below, there are 11 statements about Sangster International Airport. You will find **three** correct statements about the site of the airport and **three** about its situation.

- It is on low land, less than 50 feet above sea level.
- It is 2 km north of the resort of Montego Bay.
- It is in the Montego Hills.
- It is within 1 km of the coast.
- It is on a gentle, south-facing slope.
- It is built on flat land.
- It is about 1.5 km² in size.
- It is the largest airport on Jamaica.
- It is called the Sangster International Airport.
- It is between Kent Avenue, Sunset Avenue and Queens Drive.
- It is 2 km east of Flankers.

Draw a table like the one below and fill in the columns with the correct statements:

| Site of Sangster International Airport | Situation of Sangster International Airport |
|---|---|
|  |  |
|  |  |
|  |  |

b  Think about why the airport was built there. Use map evidence to explain why the site and situation of Sangster International Airport are good ones.

c  Choose **two** other features shown on the map. For each feature:
- give a grid reference
- describe its site and situation.

### TASK 2: Study the map opposite.

a  In which grid square is the airport terminal building? You will need to give a 4-figure reference.

b  Use the scale to work out the length of the runway. Give your answer in kilometres and metres.

c  Look at the symbol used to show the vegetation between the runway and the coast. Use the key to identify this vegetation.

d  Find the symbol at 211644. Use the key to identify this building. Why do all airports need this type of building?

### TASK 3: Study Source A and the map opposite

In which direction do you think the camera was pointing? Give reasons for your answer.

# Cambridge IGCSE Geography — Geographical Skills

## Using the airport in Montego Bay

**SKILLS  How to describe a trend**

Look for any overall changes shown by the graph between the first and last dates. For example, you may be able to use descriptive words such as 'increased', 'decreased' or 'stayed the same'. Possibly the first and last years will have similar figures, but in between they might have gone up or down.

Write about the rate of change – was it large or small? Did it differ during the time period shown? Perhaps there was a time when it increased or decreased very rapidly.

Always use figures from the graph to support your comments, and remember to give the units, e.g. millions.

**A** Destinations served by direct flights from Sangster International Airport

**B** Passenger arrivals

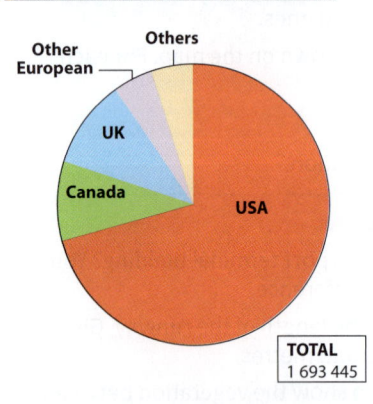

TOTAL 1 693 445

**C** Annual passenger arrivals at Sangster International Airport 1992–2013

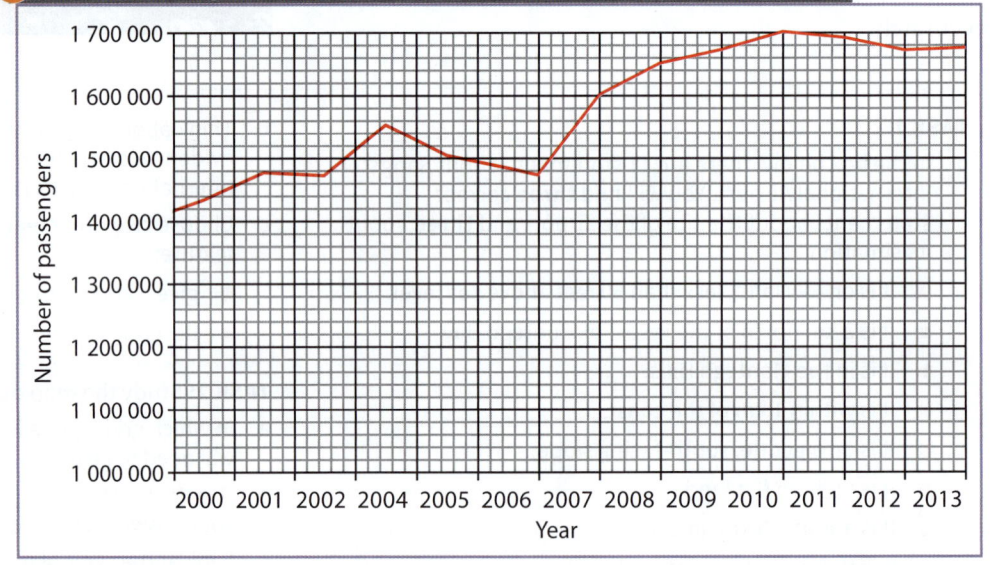

---

**TASK 1:** Study Source **A** and an atlas.
Identify the following places to which there are direct flights from Sangster International Airport.
- One city in the UK.
- Two cities in Germany.
- Two cities in Canada.
- Two cities in the west of the USA.
- Two cities in the centre of the USA.
- Three cities near or on the east coast of the USA.

**TASK 2:** Study Source **B**
a  Work out the approximate number of passengers who arrive at Sangster International Airport from the USA.
b  Suggest reasons why more passengers arrive at Sangster International Airport from the USA than from any other part of the world.

**TASK 3:** Study Source **C**
Describe the trends in passenger arrivals at Sangster International Airport. Make sure you use descriptive words and figures in your answer.

Geographical Skills

**D** **Benefits and problems of an airport for local people**

Benefits
- Jobs will be created in building and operating the airport.
- Local businesses grow (the multiplier effect).
- People will be attracted to the area and extra houses will be built.
- More services will be opened, such as shops, schools and hospitals.
- New railway lines and roads will be built.
- More flight destinations may be available from the airport.

Problems
- Farmland and historic buildings may be lost for runways and new houses.
- Natural countryside and wildlife habitats may be destroyed.
- There will be more demand for water from the terminal and from new houses.
- More flights will create more noise and atmospheric pollution.
- Homes and listed buildings may be destroyed.
- Many of the jobs created may be seasonal.

**TASK 4:** Study the map on page 212.

For each of the three individuals and one couple shown here, decide what they will feel about the continued growth in the number of flights using Sangster International Airport. Give reasons for their views.

Owner of construction firm in Montego Bay at 212621

Plantation worker living in Flankers at 225645

Owner of hotel on Kent Avenue at 223649

Retired couple living in Canterbury at 213627

215

# Cambridge IGCSE Geography — Geographical Skills

## Tourism in Jamaica

**A** Money earned from tourism as a percentage of exports

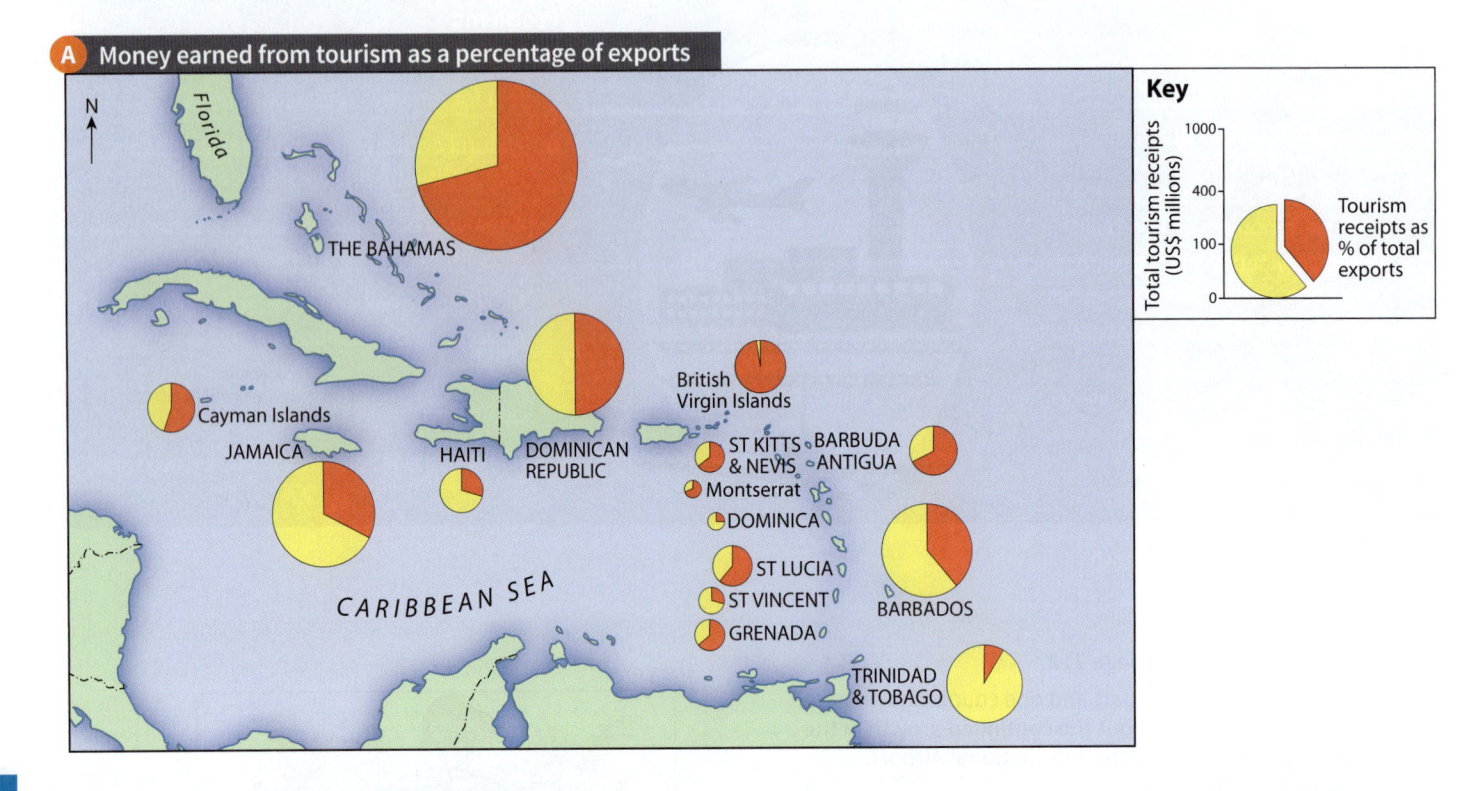

**B** Temperature and rainfall in Montego Bay

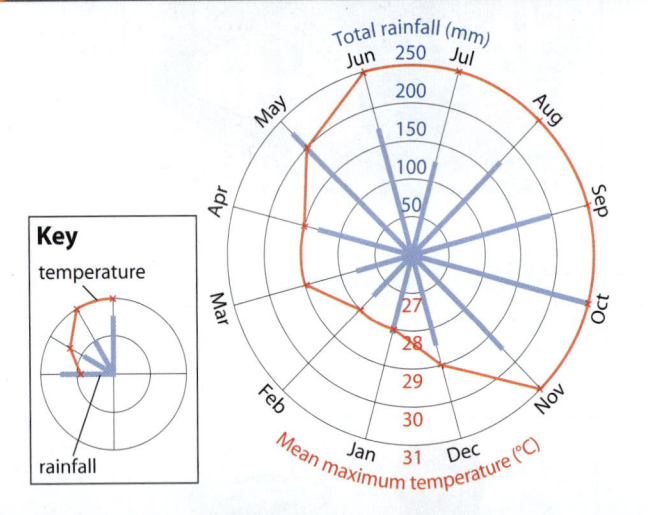

**C** Average number of tourists visiting Montego Bay, per month (2013)

| Month | Visitors | Month | Visitors |
|---|---|---|---|
| January | 139 568 | July | 162 841 |
| February | 140 286 | August | 143 021 |
| March | 177 927 | September | 90 059 |
| April | 147 249 | October | 105 357 |
| May | 133 805 | November | 131 135 |
| June | 151 711 | December | 170 486 |

**TASK 1: Study Source A.**

List the islands below in rank order from the highest to the lowest amount based on:

a  their total tourism receipts
b  the money they earn from tourism as a percentage of total exports.

- Jamaica
- Dominican Republic
- Barbados
- Bahamas
- Cayman Islands
- Trinidad and Tobago
- Grenada
- Haiti

**TASK 2**

a  Using Sources B and C, investigate whether the climate of Montego Bay influences the number of international visitors.
b  Suggest what factors, other than the local climate, may help explain the variation in visitor numbers throughout the year.

# Geographical Skills

## Montego Bay Marine Park

In 1992, Jamaica's first national park, the Montego Bay Marine Park, was established. It is 15.3 km² in area. It begins at the high-tide mark on land, and extends to the 100-metre depth at sea. It stretches from Sangster International Airport to Rum Bottle Bay, 9 km west of Montego Bay. It includes mangrove forests and islands, white sand beaches, river estuaries, sea-grass beds and corals. However, years of overfishing, of mangrove destruction, and of sewage disposal had almost destroyed the rich underwater life in the area. Now fishing, shell collecting, and all activities that can have a negative impact on the coral reefs, are forbidden. Water sports are regulated and park patrols keep a careful watch over the area.

**Source D** shows Doctor's Cave Beach. You will find this at grid reference 205632 on the map on page 212.

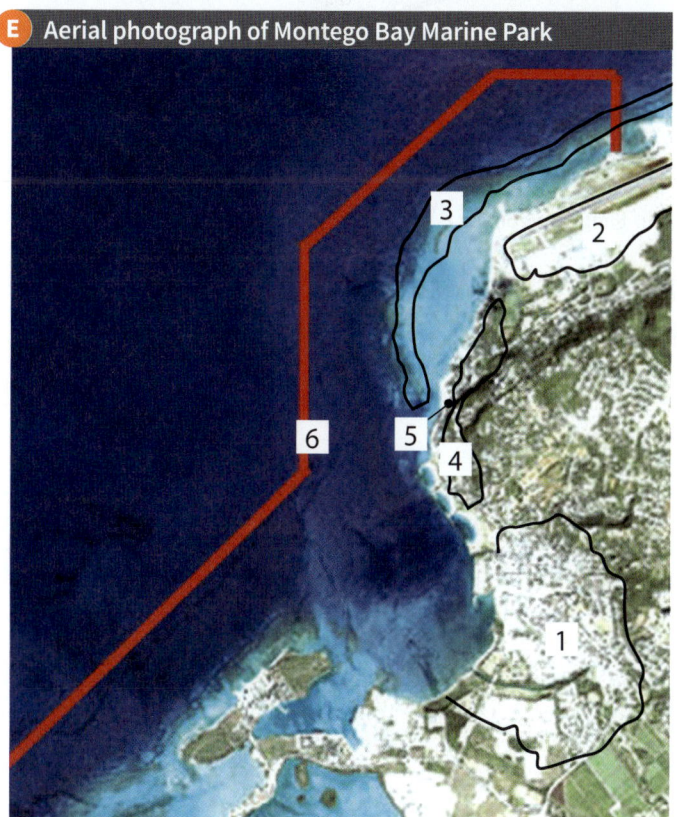

**D** Doctor's Cave Beach

**E** Aerial photograph of Montego Bay Marine Park

### TASK 3

a Using **Source D**, explain why Doctor's Cave Beach is attractive to tourists.

b The Montego Bay Marine Park was established to protect the coastal area around Montego Bay. Explain **three** different ways in which tourists in and around Doctor's Cave Beach may damage the natural environment.

### TASK 4: Study the map on page 212.

Match the features labelled 1 to 6 on Source E with the following:

- Sangster International Airport
- Marine National Park
- Main town of Montego Bay
- Coral reef
- Main area of hotels boundary
- Doctor's Cave Beach

# Cambridge IGCSE Geography — Geographical Skills

## 5  Negara, Indonesia

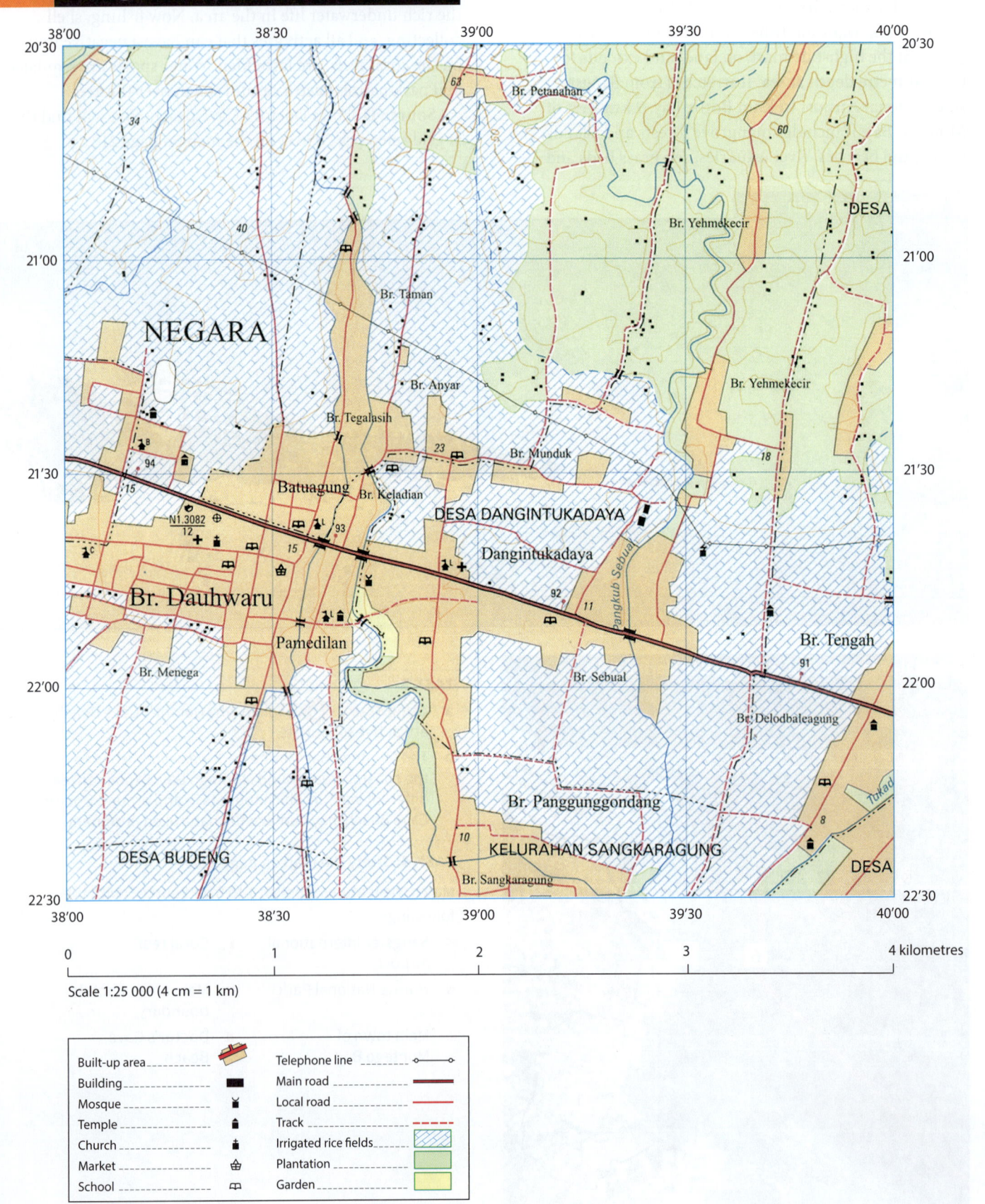

Scale 1:25 000 (4 cm = 1 km)

**Key:**
- Built-up area
- Building
- Mosque
- Temple
- Church
- Market
- School
- Telephone line
- Main road
- Local road
- Track
- Irrigated rice fields
- Plantation
- Garden

# Geographical Skills

## Indonesia – a country of islands

The country of Indonesia, in south-east Asia, covers an area of 2 million km². With over 253 million people, it has the world's fourth largest population. It consists of more than 17 500 islands, 6000 of which are inhabited. The largest islands are Java, Sumatra, Kalimantan and Sulawesi. The capital city of Jakarta lies on the island of Java. The map shows part of the town of Negara in West Bali. It is surrounded by agricultural land.

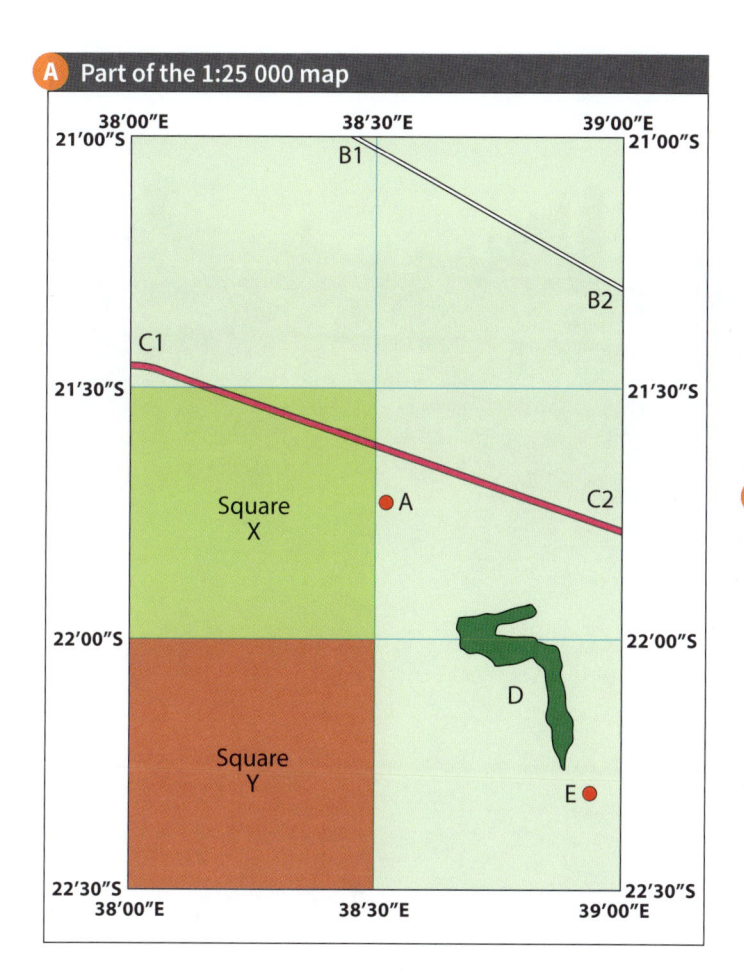

**A** Part of the 1:25 000 map

**B** Photograph taken in square Y

**C** Photograph taken in square X

**TASK 1:** Study the 1:25 000 map extract on page 218.
a  Give examples of **three** different places of worship.
b  Count the number of schools in the built-up area of Negara.

**TASK 2:** Study the 1:25 000 map extract and Source **A**
Identify the following features:
- building A
- line B1 to B2
- type of road C1 to C2
- land use D
- spot height E.

**TASK 3:** Study the 1:25 000 map extract and Sources **A**, **B** and **C**
Compare the land use in squares X and Y.

**Cambridge IGCSE Geography** — Geographical Skills

## Farming in Indonesia

Almost 70 per cent of Indonesia's 253 million people are farmers. Many of them grow rice on small plots of land using traditional methods. The traditional method for cultivating rice involves flooding the fields while, or after, setting the young seedlings. Large amounts of labour are needed, and sometimes animals such as oxen are used to pull simple wooden ploughs. While many traditional farmers produce rice for themselves and their families, they aim to produce a surplus to sell at local markets. However, as few farmers can afford fertilisers, or any form of pesticides, yields are low.

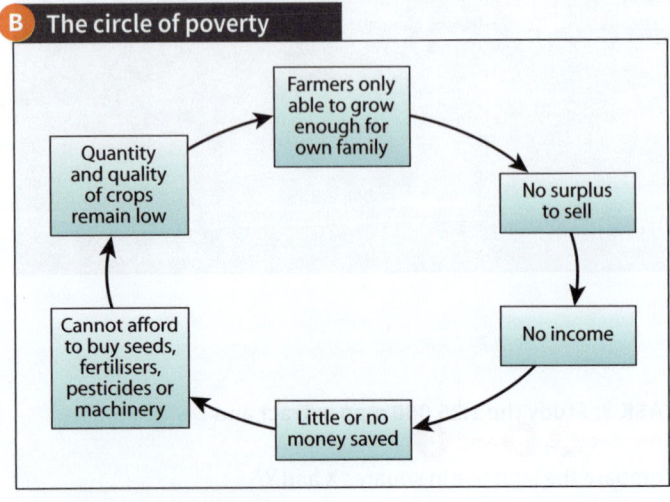

**A** Traditional rice farming

**B** The circle of poverty

- Farmers only able to grow enough for own family
- No surplus to sell
- No income
- Little or no money saved
- Cannot afford to buy seeds, fertilisers, pesticides or machinery
- Quantity and quality of crops remain low

**TASK 1:** Study Source **A** and the map extract of Negara on page 218

a Describe the relief (height and slope) of the land that is used for growing rice.

b Explain why relief of this type is needed by traditional rice farmers.

**TASK 2:** Carry out your own research using reference books or the Internet to find out the climatic conditions that are needed for rice growing.

**TASK 3:** Study Source **B**
Use your own words to explain why it is difficult for many traditional rice farmers in Indonesia to escape from poverty.

# Geographical Skills

## C  Production and trade in rice

*[Map showing world rice production and trade. Rice-producing countries shaded orange: USA, Brazil, Nigeria, Iran, Pakistan, India, Bangladesh, Myanmar, Thailand, China, Vietnam, Philippines, Indonesia, Japan. Bar charts showing % of world production for Bangladesh, China, India, Myanmar, Japan, Vietnam, Philippines, Indonesia, Thailand, Brazil. Red arrows indicate rice imports to Iran, Nigeria, Brazil, Philippines. Green arrows indicate rice exports from USA, and from the India/Thailand/Vietnam region.]*

Key
% of world production
Scale: 1 mm = 5% of world rice imports (red arrow)
Scale: 1 mm = 5% of world rice exports (green arrow)

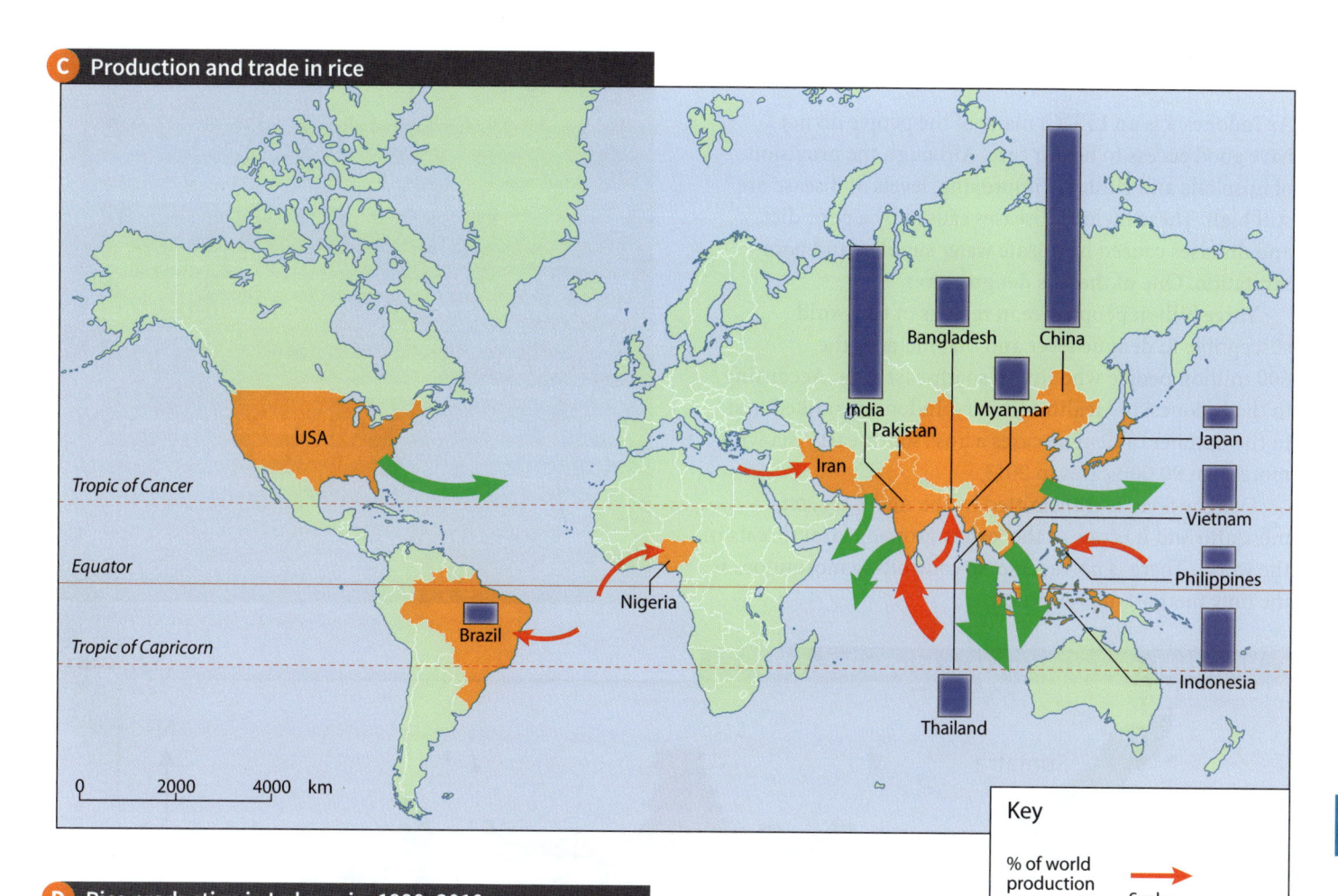

Scale: 0   2000   4000 km

## D  Rice production in Indonesia, 1990–2010

|  | 1990 | 1995 | 2000 | 2005 | 2010 |
|---|---|---|---|---|---|
| Area harvested (million hectares) | 9.9 | 10.5 | 11.4 | 11.7 | 12.1 |
| Yield (tonnes/hectare) | 3.9 | 4.3 | 4.3 | 4.2 | 5.0 |
| Total production (million tonnes) | 39.1 | 45.2 | 49.7 | 49.2 | 55.9 |
| Total fertiliser consumption (million tonnes) | 1.9 | 2.4 | 2.5 | 2.8 | 2.9 |
| Tractors used in agriculture (nearest thousand) | 12 | 28 | 60 | 70 | 72 |

### TASK 4: Study Source C

a List the top **three** rice producers in the world in rank order from highest to lowest.

b Name **two** countries that export a greater percentage of the world's rice than they produce.

c What percentage of the world's rice does Indonesia produce?

d Suggest reasons why Indonesia has to import rice even though rice farming is an important agricultural activity.

### TASK 5: Study Source D

a Use suitable graphs to plot the statistics in the table. Remember to use titles for your graphs and label their axes.

b Suggest reasons for the increase in total production of rice in Indonesia between 1990 and 2010.

# Cambridge IGCSE Geography — Geographical Skills

## Dengue Fever in Indonesia

As Indonesia is an LEDC, many of the people do not have good access to health care. Although the provision of hospitals and clinics is improving, levels of disease are still high. These include diseases caused by a poor diet, and diseases caused by unsafe water supplies and poor sanitation. One of these is **dengue fever**.

Three billion people live in regions of the world susceptible to dengue fever and that includes the 600 million people who live in south-east Asia. According to the Indonesian Health Ministry, Indonesia ranked first in the number of dengue cases across south-east Asia with more than 90 000 cases in 2013.

Dengue fever is transmitted by the *Aedes aegypti* mosquito and it is one of the fastest-growing viral threats in the world. There is no vaccine, so controlling mosquitoes is the only method of prevention.

### B  Indonesia fights dengue fever

Indonesia is trying to contain an outbreak of dengue fever which has killed 91 people in six provinces since the start of the year. Health officials say around 4500 people have been taken to hospital with the disease – twice as many as in last year's outbreak.

Dengue fever is carried by mosquitoes which bite and infect about 100 million people worldwide each year. Java island has been the worst hit, with at least 38 people reported dead in East Java province and 17 others in the capital Jakarta. Symptoms of the disease include fever, body ache and, in the most serious cases, internal bleeding.

Officials in Jakarta have said that the increased number of cases could be to do with heavy rains and pools of stagnant water in the city which serve as a breeding ground for mosquitoes.

Workers in Jakarta have been spraying neighbourhoods with insecticide to try and prevent the disease from spreading.

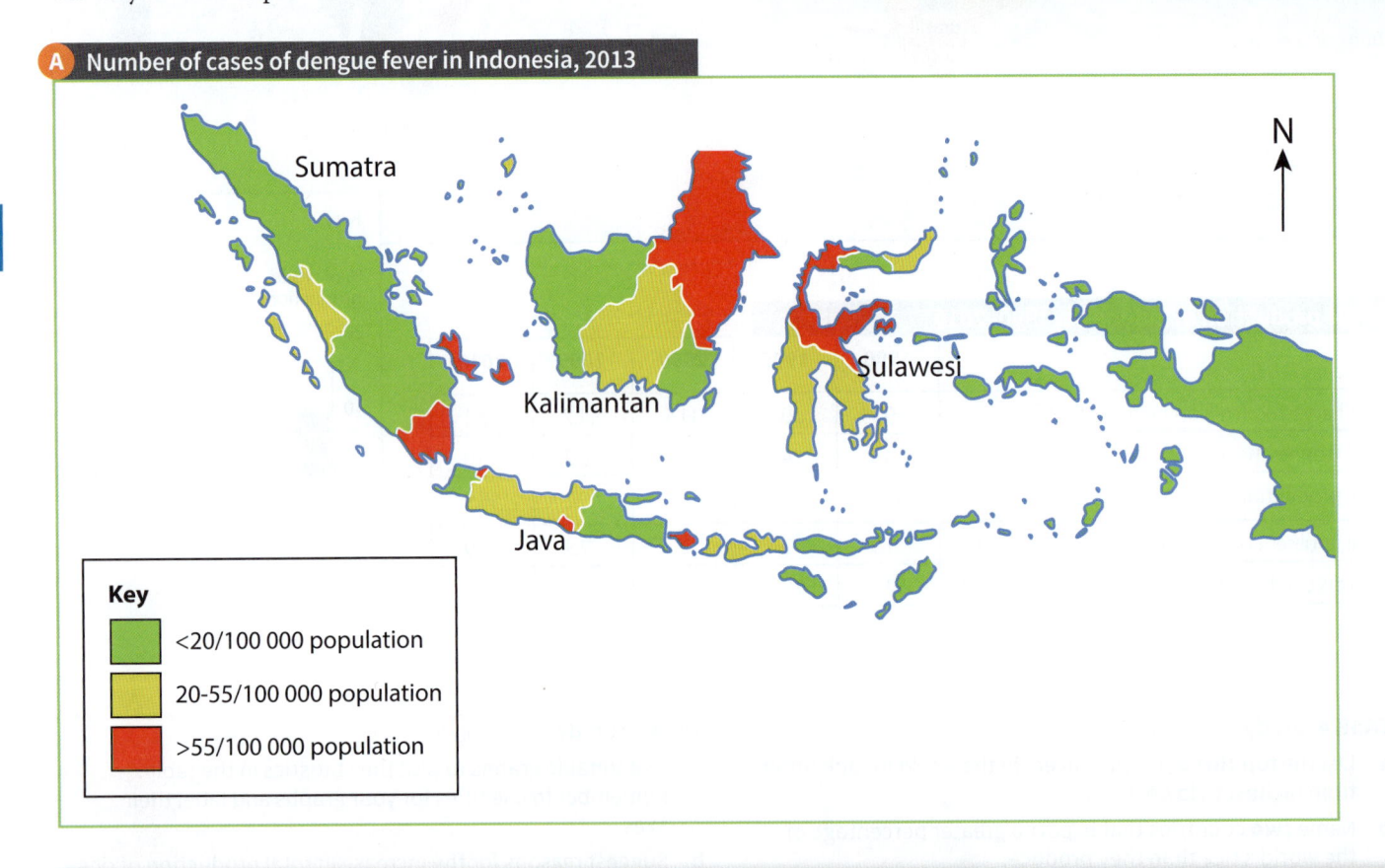

### A  Number of cases of dengue fever in Indonesia, 2013

**Key**
- <20/100 000 population
- 20-55/100 000 population
- >55/100 000 population

### TASK 1: Study Sources A and B
a  Use your own words to describe the causes and effects of dengue fever.
b  Describe how the numbers of people (per 100 000) with dengue fever in Sulawesi differ from those in Sumatra.

### TASK 2: You should work in pairs on this task.
a  Think of **four** indicators that can be used to compare levels of health care between countries.
b  Use the Internet to find out recent statistics for the **four** indicators you have chosen. You will need to find statistics for Indonesia and **three** other countries of your choice.
c  Explain what the indicators tell you about levels of health in Indonesia compared with the other **three** countries you have chosen.

# Geographical Skills

## C Dengue fever in Indonesia, 1990–2013

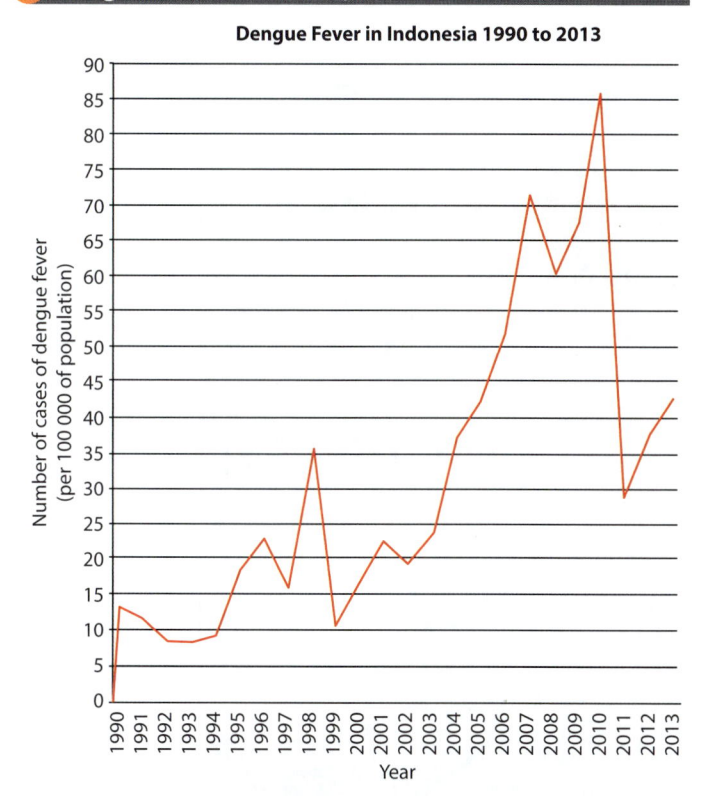

**Dengue Fever in Indonesia 1990 to 2013**

(Line graph showing Number of cases of dengue fever per 100 000 of population by Year, 1990–2013. Values start near 0 in 1990, rise to around 13 in 1991, fall to about 8 by 1993–94, rise to a peak of about 35 in 1998, drop to around 10 in 2000, then rise generally to about 71 in 2007, dip to about 60 in 2009, peak at about 85 in 2010, fall sharply to about 28 in 2011, then rise to about 42 in 2013.)

## E Controlling dengue fever

### PLANS TO STOP THE SPREAD OF DENGUE FEVER

To stop the spread of the disease the Health Agency will run a campaign on the prevention of dengue fever in February and March. The campaign will stress that the best way of preventing the disease, which is spread by the Aedes aegypti mosquito, is to make sure that pools of still water around houses are drained or covered so that mosquitoes cannot lay their eggs there. The Agency also plans to use groups of local people, working together, to spray the streets with insecticides.

## D Interviews with health professionals

"In the first three days of March there were 71 cases of dengue fever, compared with 50 cases for all of January. The hospital is like a war zone with patients sleeping in camp beds in any available space – corridors, hospital mosques and maternity wards. The health system was unprepared for the outbreak. The problem is that the number of cases is increasing – it is very high. So our staff are tired, but they are still working very hard. Some of the nurses, they should be home at 4 p.m. but they go home at 10 p.m. We are asking the government to give us more nurses and doctors. Anyway, we can still handle the situation."

Extract from an interview with the nursing director at the Persahabatan Hospital

"The hospitals are well equipped and staffed. The main problem is the increase in the number of mosquito breeding sites. A large number of construction projects came to a halt in Jakarta after the Asian financial crisis. The unfinished buildings collected pools of water where the mosquitoes bred. The people living in slums make the problems worse by dumping increased amounts of rubbish in urban slum areas."

Extract from an interview with Indonesia's Health Minister

### TASK 3: Study Source C

a Describe the changes in the number of cases of dengue fever in Indonesia between 1990 and 2013.

b Suggest reasons for the changes in the number of cases of dengue fever:
- from 2000 to 2007
- from 2010 to 2011.

### TASK 4: Study Sources D and E and the 1:25 000 map of Negara on page 218.

a The Health Agency is planning a campaign, using posters, to advise the local people how to prevent the spread of dengue fever. Produce a poster that could be displayed in the local clinic in Negara. Your poster should inform people what they can do around their homes to prevent dengue fever.

b To what extent do you think people in Negara are at risk from dengue fever? Give reasons for your opinions.

# Cambridge IGCSE Geography
## Geographical Skills

## 6 Leicester, UK

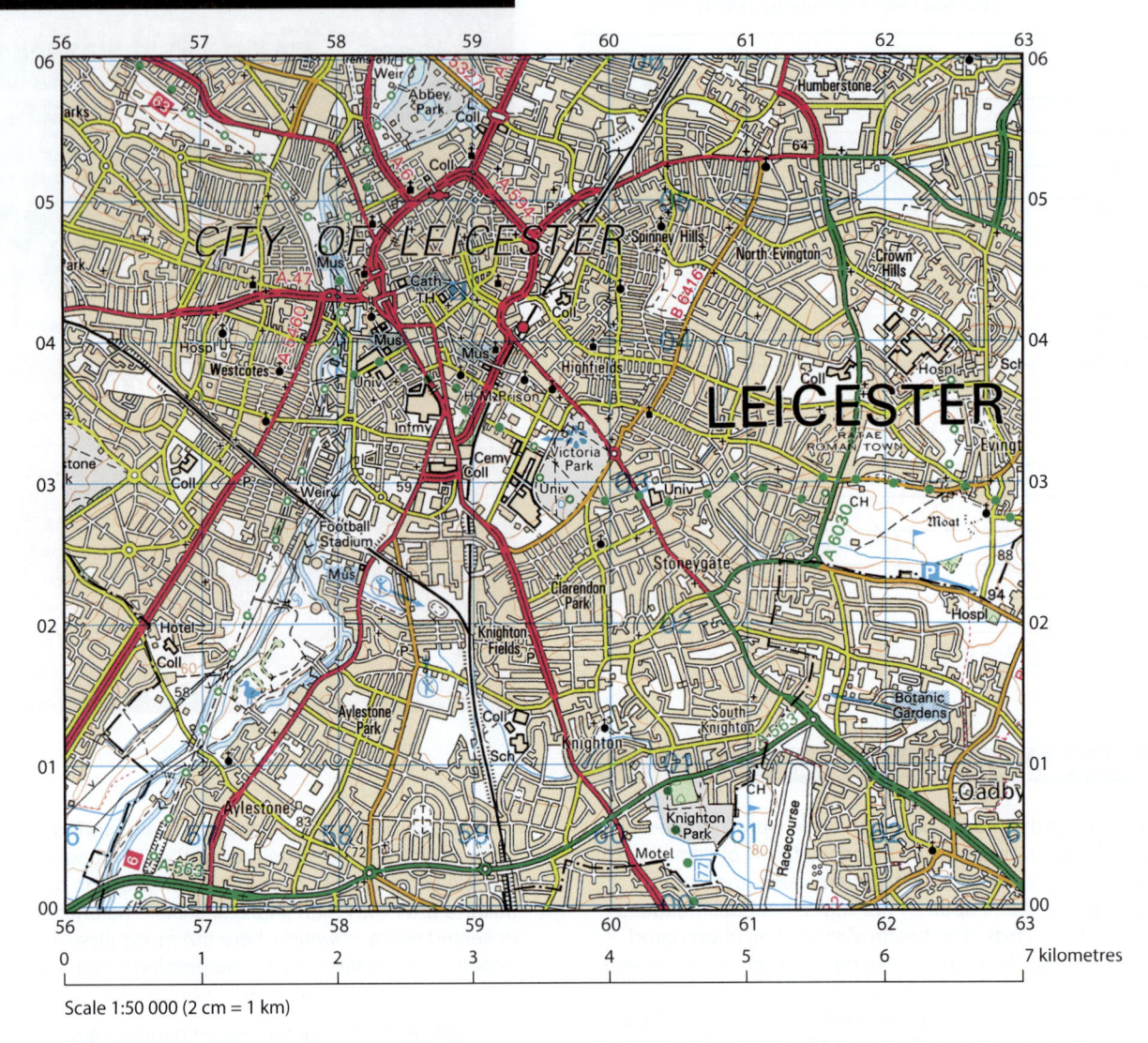

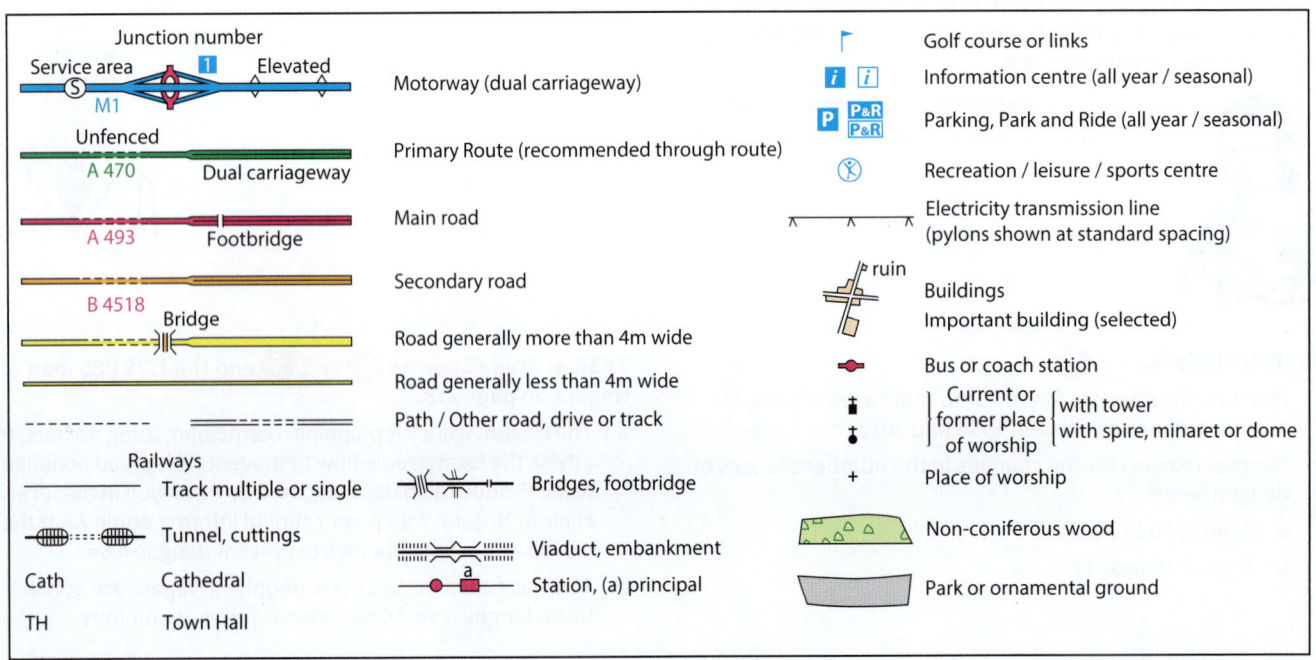

Scale 1:50 000 (2 cm = 1 km)

### Legend

- Motorway (dual carriageway) — Junction number, Service area, Elevated, M1, Unfenced
- Primary Route (recommended through route) — A 470 Dual carriageway
- Main road — A 493 Footbridge
- Secondary road — B 4518 Bridge
- Road generally more than 4m wide
- Road generally less than 4m wide
- Path / Other road, drive or track
- **Railways**: Track multiple or single; Tunnel, cuttings
- Cath — Cathedral
- TH — Town Hall
- Bridges, footbridge
- Viaduct, embankment
- Station, (a) principal
- Golf course or links
- Information centre (all year / seasonal)
- Parking, Park and Ride (all year / seasonal)
- Recreation / leisure / sports centre
- Electricity transmission line (pylons shown at standard spacing)
- ruin
- Buildings
- Important building (selected)
- Bus or coach station
- Current or former place of worship — with tower / with spire, minaret or dome
- Place of worship
- Non-coniferous wood
- Park or ornamental ground

224

# Geographical Skills

## The growth of Leicester's population

Leicester is a city in the East Midlands region of England, in the county of Leicestershire. The settlement was originally developed on the River Soar, which flows through the city. In the 2011 census, the population was 329 839, making Leicester the tenth largest city in the United Kingdom. The 1:50 000 map shows part of the built-up area of the city.

## SKILLS Map interpretation – describing urban features

Maps contain many details which allow us to build up a picture of what an urban area is like. They show information about the extent of the built-up area, with details of any large buildings such as services or industries. The communications within the urban area are shown, including the roads and railway lines. The density and pattern of the roads can be used to work out what the urban landscape is like. Four examples are shown in **Source A**.

### A Interpreting the human geography of an urban area

**1. The CBD** – Main roads may meet here or perhaps an inner ring road will surround the central part of the urban area. There will also be many minor roads, tightly packed together, where the shops and other services are located and there will be little open space (unshaded areas on the map extracts). Larger buildings such as a cathedral, town hall or railway station may be shown by symbols.

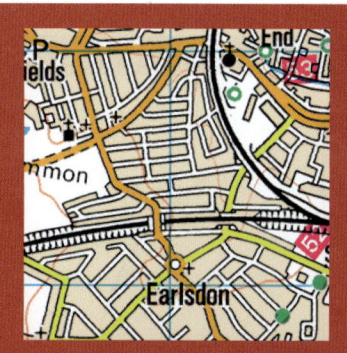

**2. The inner city** – Main roads and railways may pass through the area and many minor roads in a grid pattern indicate terraced housing. Areas of industry or other land uses may be marked and labelled and there will not be much open space.

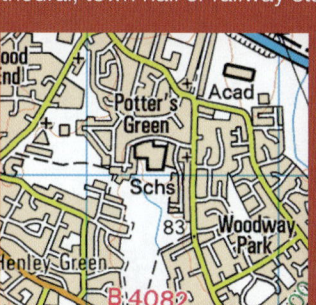

**3. The outer suburbs** – Between the main roads that radiate out from the centre there will be large, built-up areas with many minor roads arranged according to a set pattern. In most places these will not be so close together as in the inner city and there will be areas of open space as well as parks or woodlands. Large buildings such as schools will be shown.

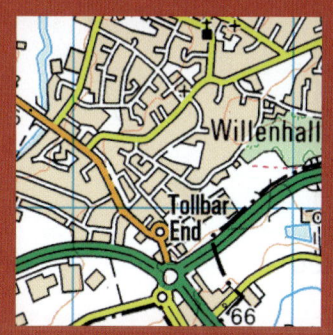

**4. The rural-urban fringe** – this is easy to recognise as the shading for the built-up areas begins to be replaced by open areas with scattered farm buildings labelled or areas shaded as woodlands. There may be a ring road or bypass around the urban area and there could be large buildings shown where there are new developments such as out-of-town shopping malls or business parks.

**TASK 1:** Study the 1:50 000 map extract on page 224 and **Source A**
a Give the 4-figure reference of the CBD of Leicester.
b Use map evidence to list **six** services that are in or close to the CBD.
c What other evidence tells you that the grid square you have chosen is the CBD?

**TASK 2:** Study the 1:50 000 map extract and **Source A**
a Compare the urban land use in grid squares 5703 and 6200. Which of these grid squares is the inner city and which is the outer suburbs?
b Give the 4-figure reference of a grid square which is in the rural-urban fringe. Justify your choice.

## International migration to Leicester

In 2011, 34% of the 329 839 people living in Leicester were not born in the UK, the highest proportion of any place in the East Midlands region.

People born in India are the largest non-UK-born group in Leicester (37 224 residents), followed by people born in Kenya (7118); Poland (6417); Pakistan (3534), and Zimbabwe (3377).

The city also had the largest growth in the migrant population between 2001 and 2011, with 46 283 international migrants moving to the city.

Migration over the last century means that ethnic minority groups in Leicester may soon make up the majority of the population.

Today more than a third of people living in Leicester are migrants or second generation migrants. Some migrants have been here for many years; others have moved more recently to find work or live close to families.

There are around 70 languages spoken in the city. In addition to English, eight languages are commonly spoken. Gujarati is the main language of 16% of the city's residents, along with Punjabi 3%, Somali 4% and Urdu 2%. Other languages spoken include Hindi, Bengali and Polish.

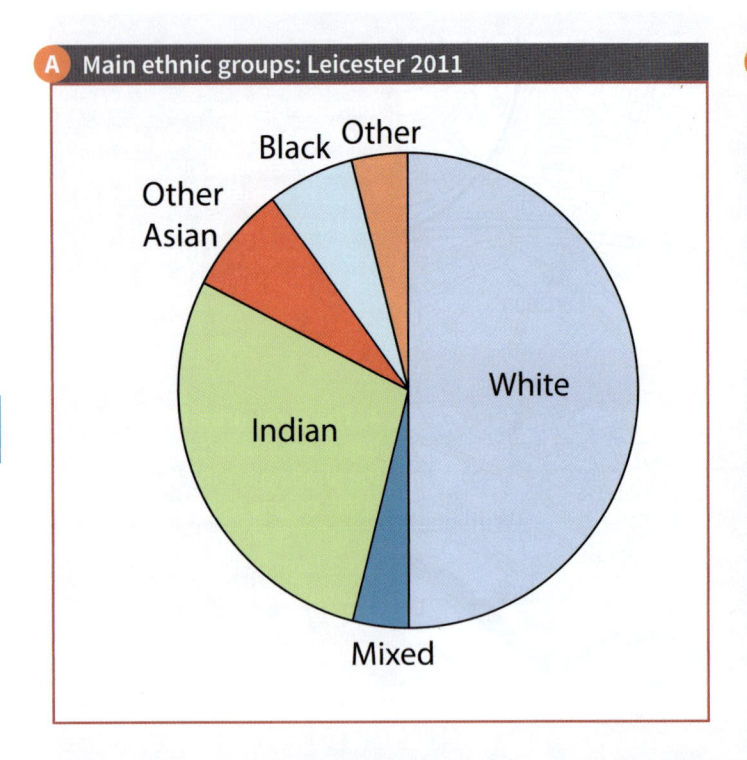

**A** Main ethnic groups: Leicester 2011

**C** Services in Highfields, Leicester

**B** Leicester – a multicultural city (2011 census data)

|  | Leicester | England |
| --- | --- | --- |
| Total population | 329 839 | 53 012 456 |
| Born overseas | 33.6% | 13.8% |
| White | 50.6% | 85.5% |
| South Asian | 31.8% | 5.5% |
| Black | 6.3% | 3.4% |
| Mixed | 3.5% | 2.2% |
| East Asian and other | 5.3% | 2.2% |
| Christian | 32.4% | 59.4% |
| Muslim | 18.6% | 5.0% |
| Hindu | 15.2% | 1.5% |
| English as a main language | 69.3% | 90.9% |

# Geographical Skills

**D** Part of the Highfields area of Leicester

**KEY**
- A road single/dual carriageway
- One-way street
- Railway
- Woodland
- Park
- Built-up area
- Retail building
- Post Office
- Public library
- Church/chapel
- Schools and mosques

0  1  2  3  4 kilometres

227

**TASK 1:** Study Source **A**

a  Work out the approximate percentage of the population of Leicester who in 2011 were:
- white
- Indian
- other Asian
- black

b  How many of Leicester's total population of 329 839 in 2011 were white? Do you think they were all British born? Give a reason for your answer.

**TASK 2:** Study Source **B**

a  Plot the figures using a suitable graph to show how Leicester's population compares with England as a whole.

b  How do these figures show Leicester's importance as a major destination for international migrants in the UK?

**TASK 3:** Study Sources **C** and **D**

a  Name two different services shown in the map in Source D that are likely to be mainly used by migrants. For each one locate it by using the number and letter of the grid square.

b  Describe the street pattern in grid square M7. What do you think the houses will be like on these streets?

c  Use evidence from the photographs and map to suggest why many international migrants choose to live in the Highfields area of Leicester.

# Cambridge IGCSE Geography | Geographical Skills

## Sprawl – different causes, same result!

A century ago, nine in every ten people lived in villages and the countryside. Now almost 50 per cent of the planet's population jostles for space in fast-growing congested cities. By 2050 the figure is expected to reach 75 per cent. All these people will hope for or expect housing, work, services and a high quality of life.

As population increases in towns and cities, **urban sprawl** takes place. This happens in both MEDCs and LEDCs but the causes are different. Urban sprawl tends to be unplanned in LEDC cities and planned in MEDC cities – but the outcome is similar. In both cases the urban area expands into the countryside, affecting people and changing the environment at the **rural-urban fringe**. Land use changes around the urban area for the benefit of some and to the disadvantage of others.

### A  The rural-urban fringe

Map 1 shows the rural-urban fringe to the south-west of Leicester in 1992.

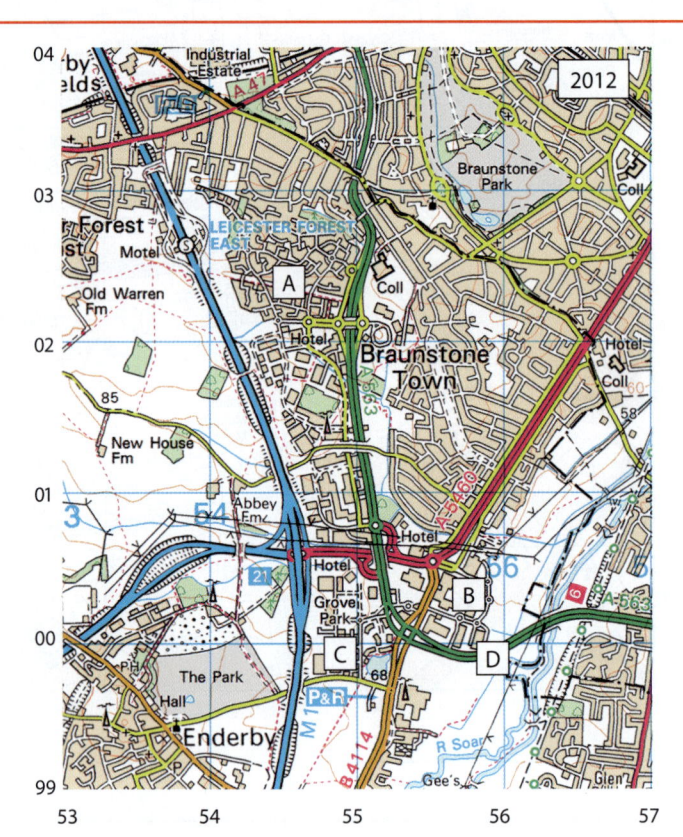

Map 2 shows how the same area has changed due to urban sprawl over the 20-year period 1992–2012.

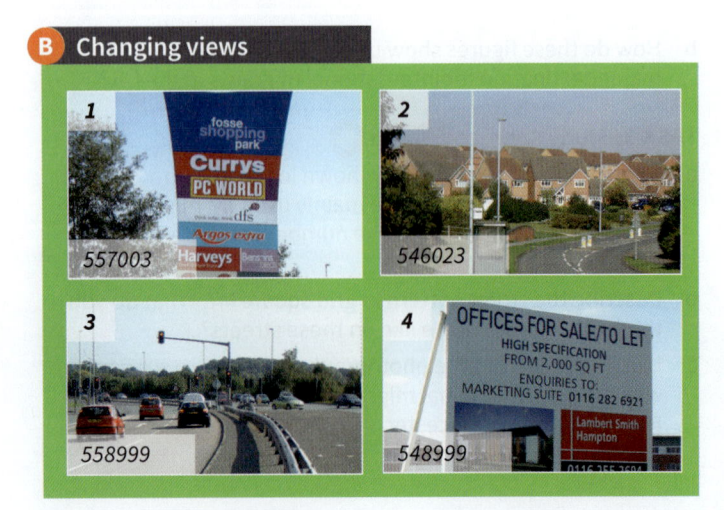

### B  Changing views

1  557003
2  546023
3  558999
4  548999

**TASK 1:** Study **Source A**

a  Estimate the land use in km² that was built on in 1992. How had this changed by 2012? (Note: The scale is 1:50 000 or 2 cm = 1 km.)

b  In which direction do you think sprawl will take place in the next 15 years? Justify your decision.

**TASK 2:** Study **Sources A** and **B**

a  Match photos 1–4 with locations A–D on Map 2.

b  List the **four** different land uses shown.

c  Suggest why these have been located in the rural-urban fringe.

# Geographical Skills

## Fosse Park

Fosse Park is an out-of-town retail area which was opened in 1989 on the south-western edge of Leicester. It is shown on Map 2 on page 228. The **retail park** is in an area of mixed industrial and commercial development, about two kilometres from Junction 21 of the M1, where it meets the M69. Junction 21 also connects the M1 with the A5460 (Narborough Road), and Leicester's main ring road, the A563.

There is a wide range of **chain stores**, usually found in the CBD of UK cities, including Boots, Gap, Marks & Spencer, Next, SportsDirect.com, Carphone Warehouse and WHSmith, along with many food outlets such as McDonald's, Costa and KFC.

There are 2500 free car parking spaces and there is a regular bus service to and from Fosse Shopping Park from the centre of Leicester, its suburbs and surrounding villages.

**C Shopping out of town at Fosse Park**

**TASK 3:** Study Map 2 on Page 228 and **Source C**

a Give reasons why the location of Fosse Park is suitable for an out-of-town retail area.

b Suggest reasons why Fosse Park attracts many customers.

c Suggest how the opening of Fosse Park affected businesses in the CBD of Leicester, 5 km to the north-east. Give reasons for your answer.

d Suggest groups of people, who live in the area shown by Map 2, who will benefit from or be disadvantaged by this urban sprawl. Explain your choices.

# Cambridge IGCSE Geography — Geographical Skills

## Exam-Style Questions: Geographical Skills

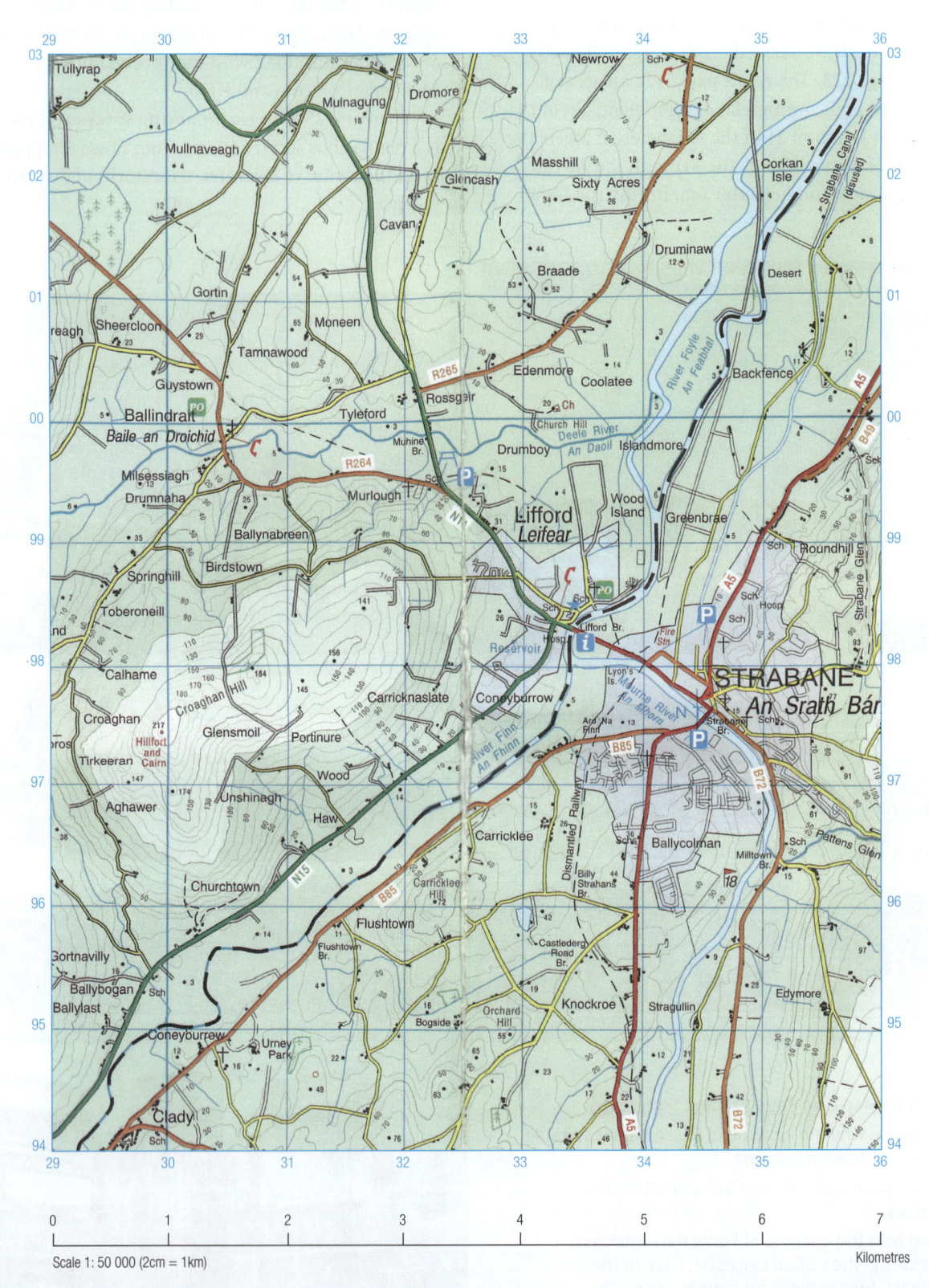

# Geographical Skills

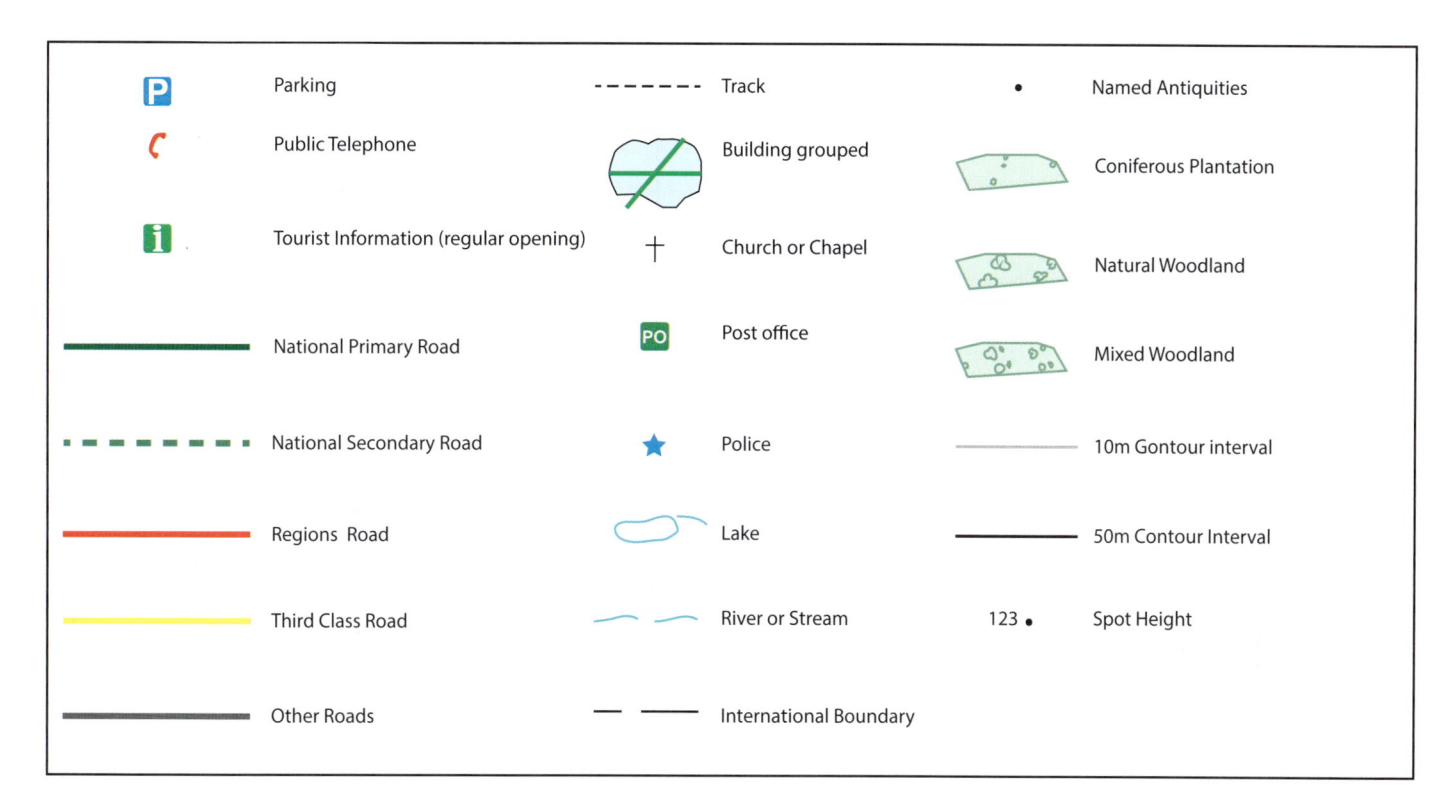

| | | | | | |
|---|---|---|---|---|---|
| **P** | Parking | ------- | Track | • | Named Antiquities |
| C | Public Telephone | | Building grouped | | Coniferous Plantation |
| **i** | Tourist Information (regular opening) | + | Church or Chapel | | Natural Woodland |
| ——— | National Primary Road | PO | Post office | | Mixed Woodland |
| - - - - | National Secondary Road | ★ | Police | ——— | 10m Gontour interval |
| ——— | Regions Road | | Lake | ——— | 50m Contour Interval |
| ——— | Third Class Road | | River or Stream | 123 • | Spot Height |
| ——— | Other Roads | — — | International Boundary | | |

The following pages (232–7) contain a selection of exam-style questions. They use the map and key on these pages and a selection of other resources. You should answer them in a copy of the question and answer booklet which can be printed from the student CD.

231

# Cambridge IGCSE Geography
## Geographical Skills

1. This question uses the map extract of Strabane, Northern Ireland and east Donegal in the Republic of Ireland on page 230 and the key on page 231. The scale is 1:50 000.

   (a) Fig. 1 shows some of the features in the north-west part of the map extract. Study Fig. 1, the map extract and the key, and answer the questions below.

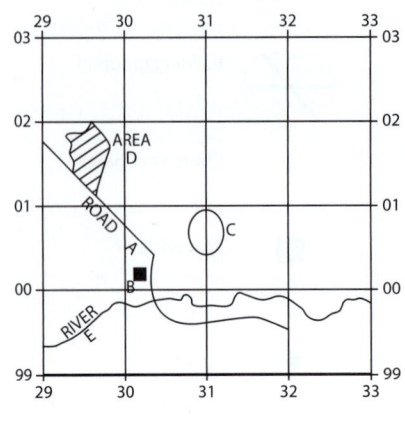

   **Fig. 1**

   Using the map extract, identify the following features shown in Fig. 1.
   (i) The number of road A. [1]
   (ii) The type of building at B. [1]
   (iii) The height along contour line C. [1]
   (iv) The land use in area D. [1]
   (v) The name of river E. [1]

   (b) Study the settlement of Strabane, in and around grid square 3497.
   (i) Identify **three** different types of service in the built-up area of Strabane. [3]
   (ii) Using map evidence only, suggest reasons for the growth of a large settlement at Strabane. [4]

   (c) Find the spot height where the hillfort and cairn are located in grid square 2997.
   (i) What is the 6-figure grid reference of this spot height? [1]
   (ii) What is the bearing, from grid north, from this spot height to the bridge over the river Foyle, between Strabane and Lifford? Choose from the following answers:
   
   15°   75°   105°   285° [1]
   
   (iii) Calculate the average gradient between this spot height and the bridge over the river Foyle, between Strabane and Lifford. [2]

   (d) Fig. 2 shows the area to the north of Strabane.

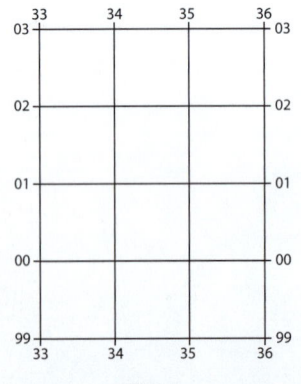

   **Fig. 2**

   Look at the river Foyle from Strabane to the northern edge of the map in the area shown on Fig. 2. Describe the features of the river Foyle and its valley. [4]

   **[Total: 20 marks]**

2   Study Fig. 3, which shows information about the number of international tourists visiting different parts of the world in 1990 and 2013.

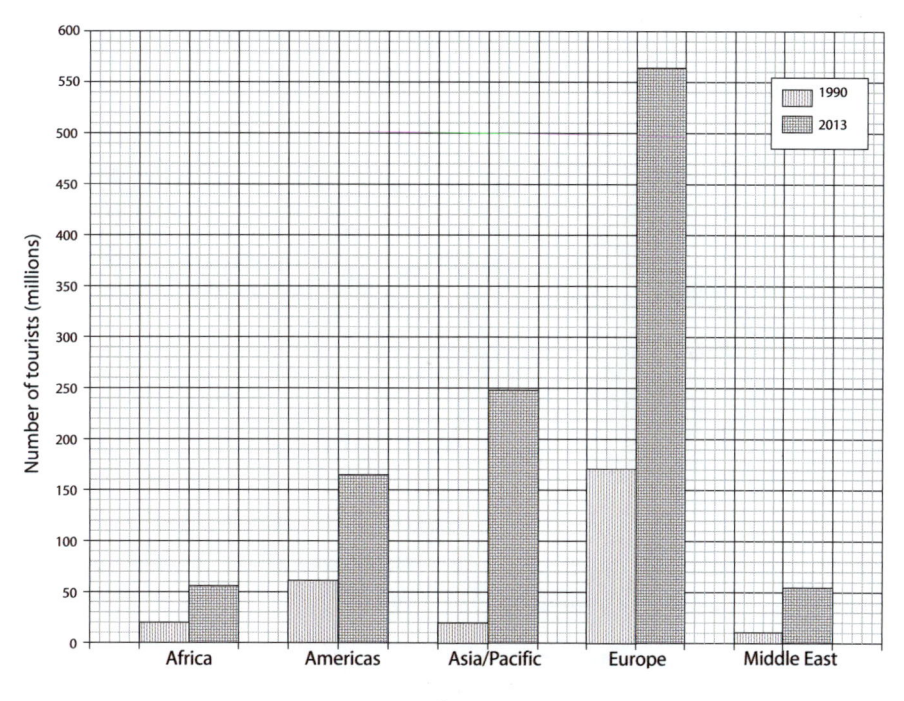

Fig. 3

(a) (i)   What is a tourist? [1]
    (ii)  State the **two** regions that attracted the most tourists in 2013. [2]
    (iii) Compare the change in importance of tourism in Asia/Pacific and the Americas between 1990 and 2013. Use statistics in your answer. [2]
(b) Photograph A shows an area where tourism is an important industry.

**Photograph A**

Identify **three** natural attractions for tourists which are shown in the photograph. [3]

[Total: 8 marks]

**Cambridge IGCSE Geography** — **Geographical Skills**

3  Study Fig. 4a, a map showing information about the sugar industry in Reunion, an island in the Indian Ocean and Fig. 4b, which shows information about Reunion's exports.

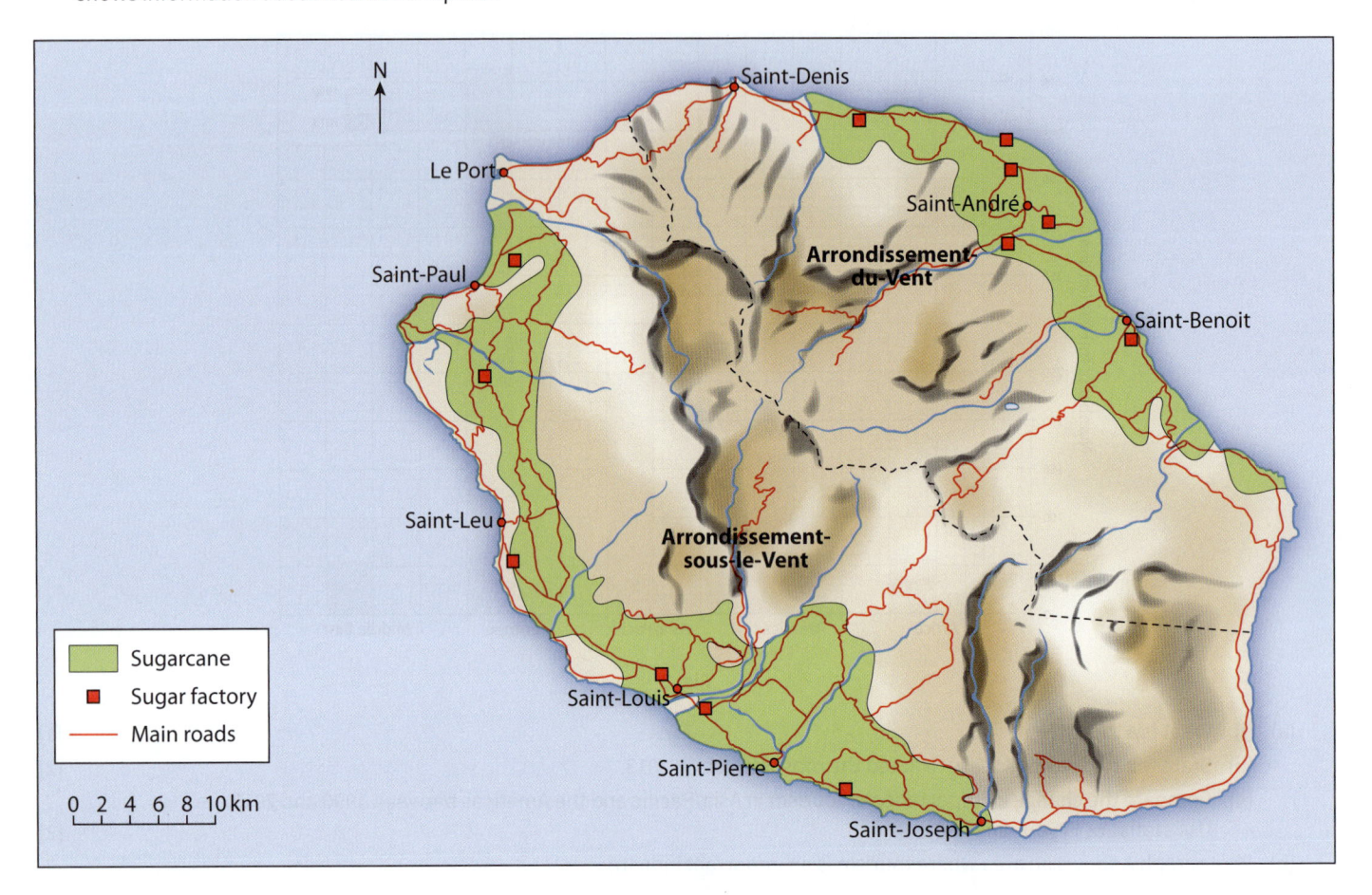

Fig. 4a

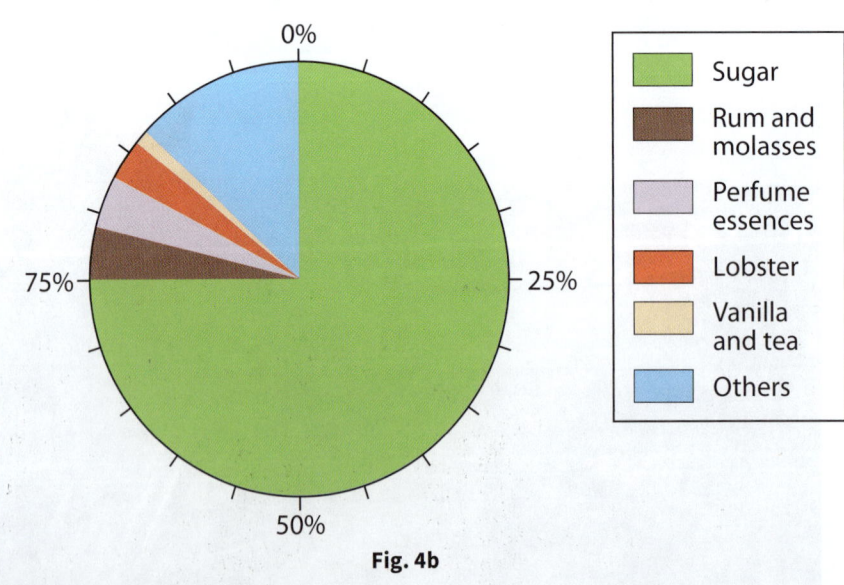

Fig. 4b

(a) (i)   What percentage of Reunion's total exports is sugar? [1]
    (ii)  Describe the distribution of the areas where the sugarcane is grown in Reunion. [3]
    (iii) Explain the location of the sugar factories. [4]

[Total: 8 marks]

4  Study Fig. 5, a map of the Great Barrier Reef Marine National Park, an area of coral reefs off the coast of Australia.
   (a) (i)  A and B on the map mark the ends of the Great Barrier Reef National Park. Estimate the straight line distance between A and B in kilometres. [1]
       (ii) Which **one** of the following locations is an area of coral reef?
           15°S   147°E
           17°S   146°E
           20°S   147°E [1]
   (b) Fig. 6 shows the areas of coral reef at risk in different parts of the world.

**Coral reefs at risk from human activities**

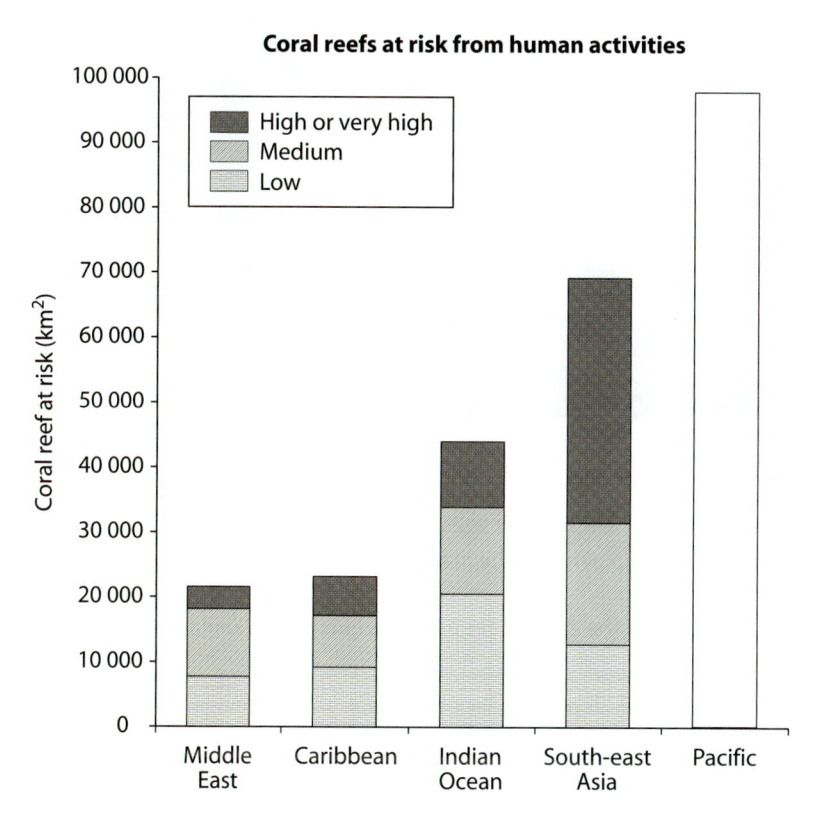

Fig. 6

   (i)   Complete the bar for the Pacific on Fig. 6 above using the following information:
         High or very high risk 10 000 km²
         Medium risk 30 000 km²
         Low risk 60 000 km² [3]
   (ii)  How many square kilometres of coral reef are at risk in the Middle East? [1]
   (iii) In which area is:
         • the largest area of coral reef at risk?
         • the largest area of coral reef at high or very high risk? [2]

         **[Total: 8 marks]**

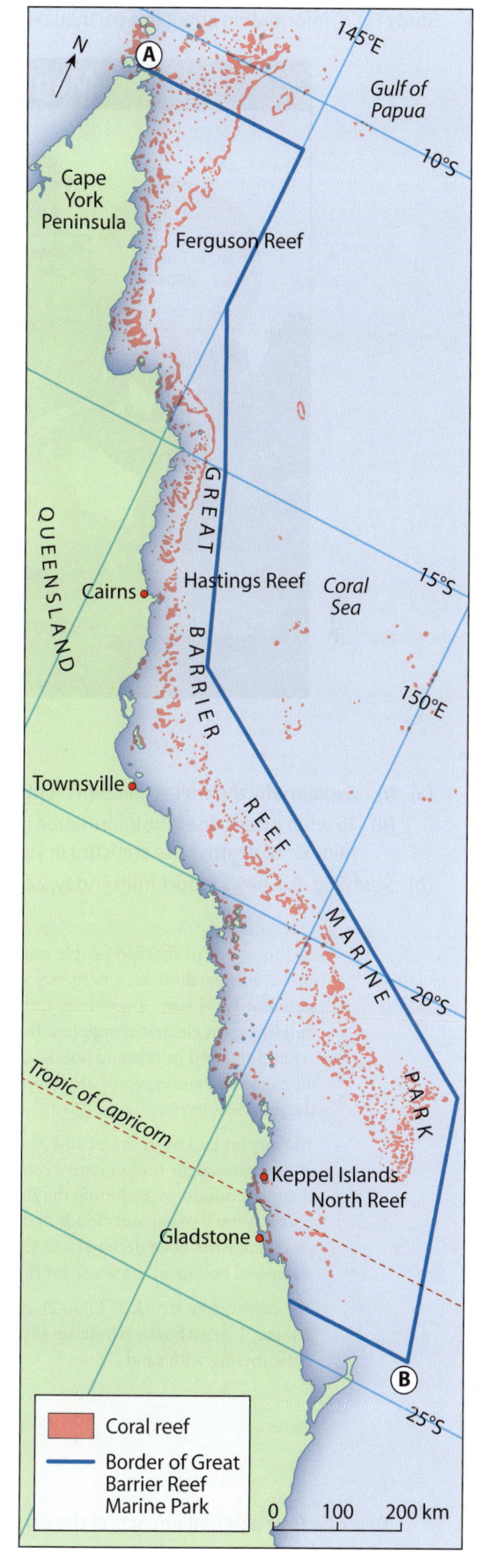

Fig. 5

5  Study Fig. 7, information about five earthquakes.

**Magnitude of five earthquakes**

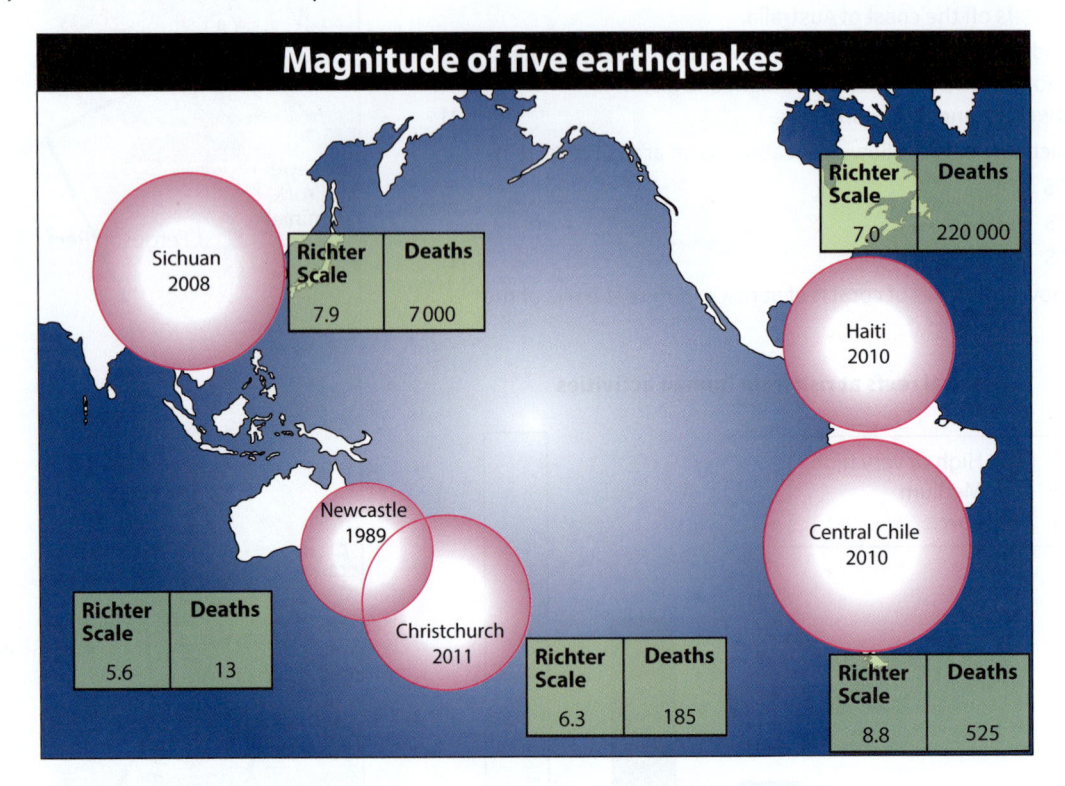

| Earthquake | Richter Scale | Deaths |
|---|---|---|
| Sichuan 2008 | 7.9 | 7 000 |
| Haiti 2010 | 7.0 | 220 000 |
| Newcastle 1989 | 5.6 | 13 |
| Christchurch 2011 | 6.3 | 185 |
| Central Chile 2010 | 8.8 | 525 |

**Fig. 7**

(a) (i)  Explain why the circles that represent the earthquakes on Fig. 7 are different sizes. [1]

   (ii) To what extent does the information in Fig. 7 show a relationship between the magnitude of an earthquake and the number of deaths? Use statistics in your answer. [3]

(b) Study Fig. 8, a news report from Friday, 22 February 2011, the day of the earthquake in Christchurch, New Zealand.

> As thousands of shocked people wandered the rubble-strewn streets of Christchurch after today's devastating and deadly earthquake, emergency workers were searching for survivors. The 6.3 magnitude earthquake struck at 12.51 p.m., a very busy time with people at work and children at school. The tremor brought down buildings, cut electricity supplies, fractured gas and water mains and badly damaged phone networks. People are still trapped in cars and buildings. Many buildings and roads in the centre of Christchurch were badly damaged and some people are trapped. Christchurch Hospital had more than 40 injured people and expected the numbers to rise.
>
> The airport had been closed and all flights across the country were initially grounded across the country as the national air traffic control centre in Christchurch was checked. Emergency crews worked amid the shattered buildings, including the cathedral, to evacuate the city centre and rescue those trapped. There was a strong smell of gas and clouds of dust and burst water mains have caused flooding in some areas. A state of emergency has been declared and Civil Defence officials said anyone remaining in the city should conserve water and boil drinking water for three minutes.
>
> The earthquake struck 20 kilometres from the city. It happened at a shallow depth of 5 to 6 kilometres below ground. Christchurch is built on silt, sand and gravel, with a water table under it. In an earthquake, the water rises, mixing with sand.
>
> Adapted from *The Age*, 22 February 2011

**Fig. 8**

Describe **four** different impacts of the earthquake on the infrastructure of Christchurch. [4]

[Total: 8 marks]

6  Study Figs. 9a and 9b, information about the population structure of Kerala in India (an LEDC).

**Kerala population structure in 1991**

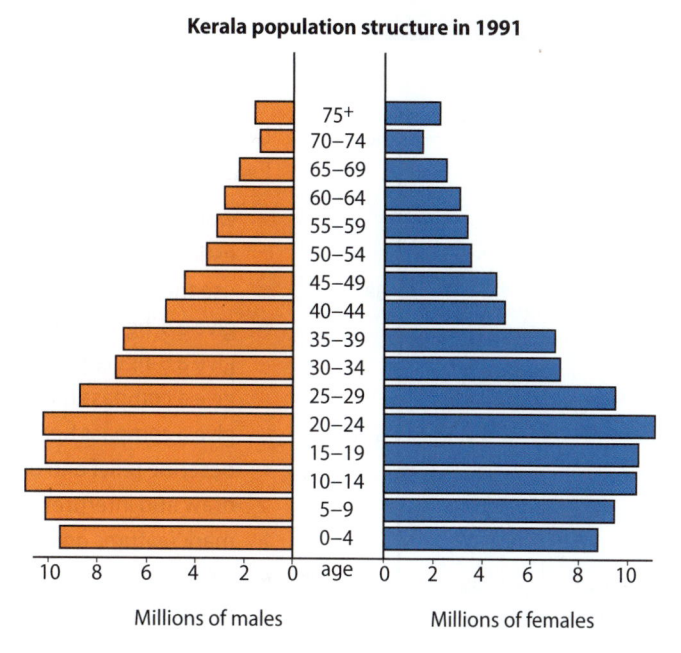

Fig. 9a

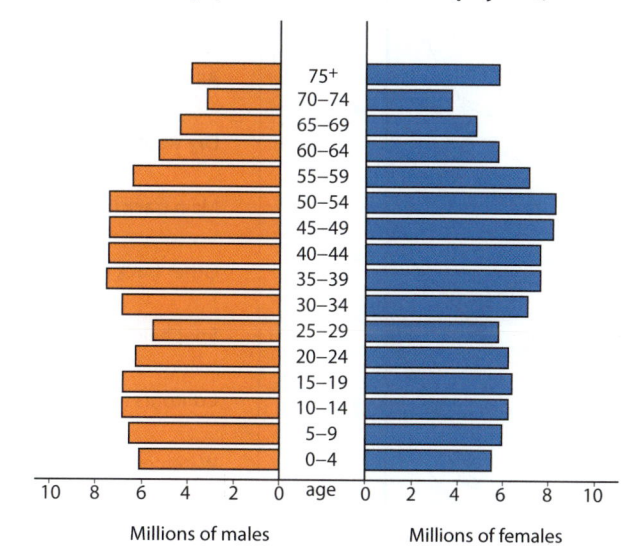

**Kerala population structure in 2021 (projected)**

Fig. 9b

(a) (i)   How many people were aged between 60 and 64 in Kerala in 1991? [1]
    (ii)  By how much is the number of people aged between 60 and 64 in Kerala expected to increase by 2021? [1]
    (iii) Describe **three** differences between the population pyramid for Kerala in 1991 and the one that is expected in 2021. [3]
(b) The evidence on the two population pyramids suggests that birth rates are likely to have fallen in Kerala between 1991 and 2021. Suggest **three** different reasons for this fall in birth rate. [3]

[Total: 8 marks]

# Cambridge IGCSE Geography
## Geographical Skills

## Map skills checklist

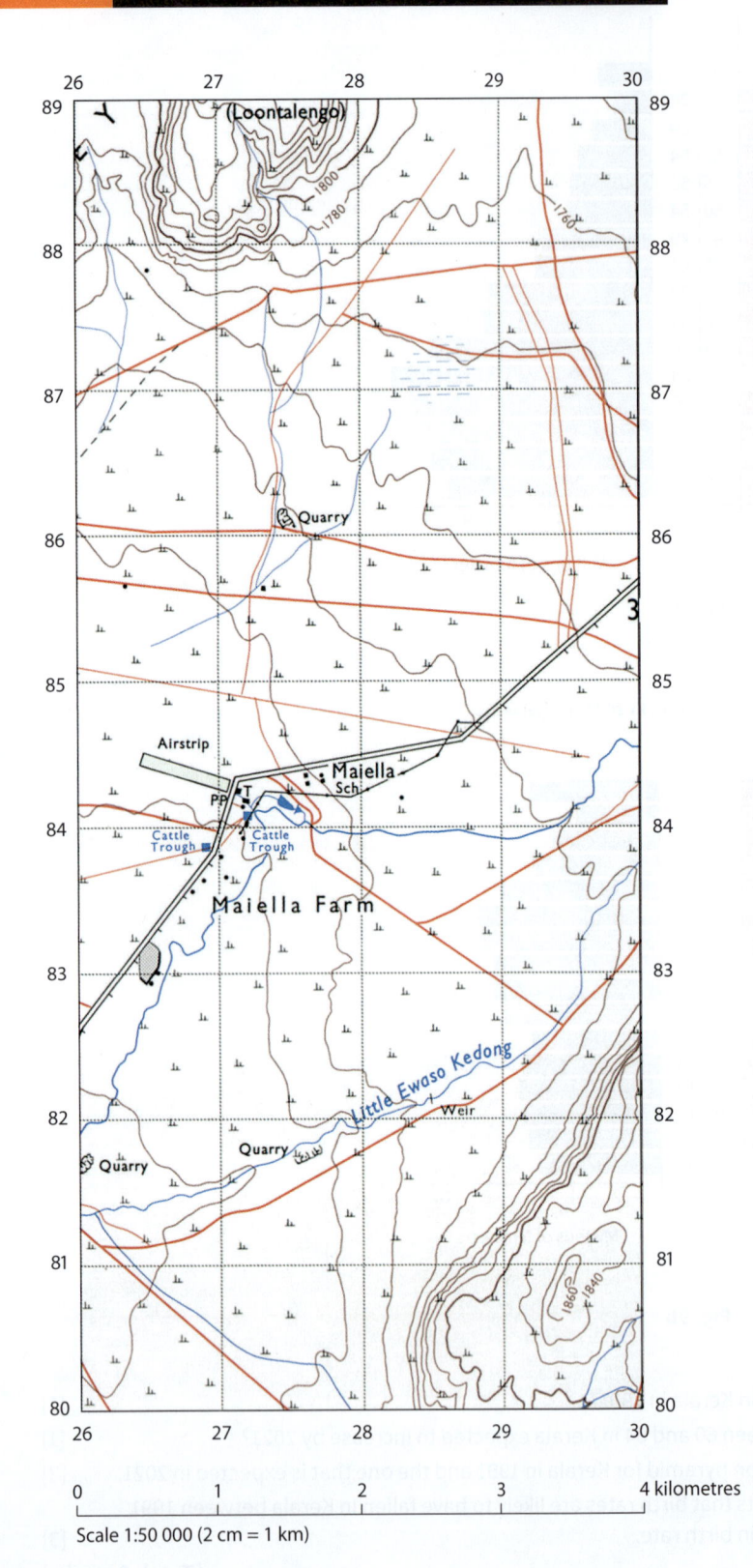

Use this extract from a 1:50 000 map of part of Ewaso Kedong, Kenya to check that you can:

- work out distances (in straight lines and along a road)
- estimate the area of a section of land
- use the key to identify buildings and land use
- give a 4-figure grid reference
- give a 6-figure grid reference
- give a compass direction
- give a compass bearing
- describe relief and drainage
- draw and interpret a cross-section
- mark features on a cross-section
- calculate a gradient
- describe patterns of settlement
- describe and suggest reasons for transport routes.

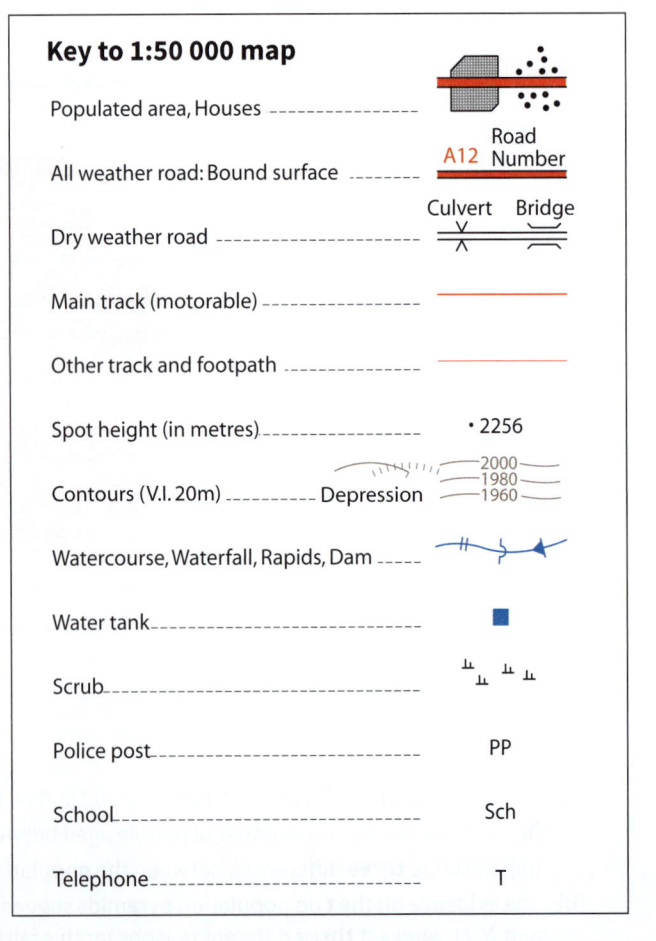

### Key to 1:50 000 map

|  |  |
|---|---|
| Populated area, Houses | |
| All weather road: Bound surface | A12 Road Number |
| | Culvert   Bridge |
| Dry weather road | |
| Main track (motorable) | |
| Other track and footpath | |
| Spot height (in metres) | • 2256 |
| Contours (V.I. 20m) ...... Depression | 2000 / 1980 / 1960 |
| Watercourse, Waterfall, Rapids, Dam | |
| Water tank | ■ |
| Scrub | |
| Police post | PP |
| School | Sch |
| Telephone | T |

Scale 1:50 000 (2 cm = 1 km)
0   1   2   3   4 kilometres

# Part C

# Geographical Enquiry

Geography is about people and places and, consequently, is a subject that is best studied (as much as possible) in the real world rather than in a classroom. When feasible, teachers should organise fieldwork so that students can carry out research into the world around them. In some places it is difficult to carry out the requirements of a full coursework assignment due to health and safety issues as well as difficulties with access but, even in these cases, schools and their grounds offer many opportunities for small-scale investigations e.g. weather measurements, pedestrian surveys, carrying out questionnaires and sampling techniques. Students who have not taken part in fieldwork during their geographical studies will have missed out on a vital experience that is crucial to being a geographer.

Part C covers coursework which involves students completing one assignment set by teachers of up to 2000 words. The coursework assignment can be based on physical geography, human geography or an interaction between both. The assignment must be related to one or more of the three syllabus Themes. In this part of the coursebook a brief summary of what is involved in setting up a coursework assignment and some examples of suitable titles are provided for reference. It is not the purpose of this coursebook to provide extensive advice and guidance on organising a coursework assignment as that is covered in the Cambridge syllabus with further guidance available from www.cie.org.uk.

Part C covers in more detail four popular topics: the CBD (Central Business District), Rivers, Tourism and Weather. Each topic uses a double-page spread to suggest how each could be investigated through fieldwork. Students should undertake some fieldwork activities as their examination may test their knowledge and understanding of fieldwork techniques, e.g. questionnaires, sampling, surveys and use of equipment. Some of this can be carried out in the classroom and school grounds if there are difficulties in getting out of the school.

There is an exam-style question covering two topics. The teacher CD contains mark schemes that can be used with the exam-style questions. It also contains sample answers to all the tasks in Part C. The student CD contains support sheets and extension sheets for some of the topics.

# Cambridge IGCSE Geography — Geographical Enquiry

## Fieldwork skills in examination

## Choosing the right option

The Cambridge IGCSE offers two main routes to assess your fieldwork skills: the Coursework Assignment or the Alternative to Coursework paper. Your teacher will advise you on which option you will be taking and will make the decision based on a number of factors, such as safety issues, the school's location and whether there is enough teaching time to complete the Coursework Assignment.

Both options require you to have fieldwork experience and some experience of coursework methodology. Fieldwork skills involving sampling, questionnaires and measuring weather are techniques that need not involve leaving the school's premises, but will give you vital practice.

Whichever option you are taking you should be familiar with the '*Route to Geographical Enquiry*' illustrated in **Source A**. This gives step-by-step help on how to set up and work through coursework in a logical, enquiry-based way.

### A  The Route to Geographical Enquiry

| | | |
|---|---|---|
| 1. | Identification of issue, question or problem | 'Given the location of your school, what local issue would be interesting and possible in a period of five to six weeks of study? Many studies look at the physical environment such as weather over a period of time or river processes. Other studies take place in settlements close to the school such as identifying the CBD or land use in buildings of different heights or traffic and pedestrian surveys. The impact of tourism is popular where there are plenty of visitors to carry out questionnaires. Wherever your school is located, there is usually an issue nearby that would make a good Coursework Assignment.' |
| 2. | Objectives of the study are defined | 'Once you have identified the issue, you need to think carefully about a few objectives and aims. In the time you have to carry out the fieldwork you cannot research into everything! Consider testing two or three hypotheses and focus your enquiry on these. Otherwise you might collect too much information to make sense of, and lose the focus of your investigation.' |
| 3. | Collection of data | 'You need to make a list of the data you want to collect and consider how to collect it. This might involve group or individual work collecting:<br>■ primary data involving questionnaires and sampling techniques, field sketches and maps, observation, measuring and recording counts<br>■ secondary data involving a census, the Internet, books and newspapers.<br>You might also consider carrying out a pilot study to check if your data collection methods will work or need improving in the real study.' |
| 4. | Selection and collation of data | 'The data you or your group collects may need to be put together so you have a full set of information to select from for presenting as tables, graphs, maps or diagrams.' |
| 5. | Presentation and recording of the results | 'Presentation plus analysis and interpretation, and the evaluation and conclusions that follow below, are the key areas in the mark scheme where the best answers score well. Here you need to show that you can present a range of relevant techniques – not just multiple pie and bar charts – as is often seen!' |
| 6. | Analysis and interpretation | 'You need to go beyond basic description of what you have found. The best answers give reasons and explain what they have found, including anomalies that were not expected. They also refer to data and evidence in maps, graphs, tables or diagrams to support their statements.' |
| 7. | Making effective conclusions, evaluation and suggestions for further work | 'This is where you need to think through your analysis and interpretation and provide a brief summary of the main findings with conclusions.<br>■ What has your investigation shown?<br>■ Do you agree with the hypothesis you stated at the start?<br>■ Could you have done the investigation better? How?<br>■ What further work, if any, should be done to be complete this investigation?' |

*From the Cambridge IGCSE syllabus, reproduced by permission of Cambridge International Examinations.*

# The Coursework Assignment

## B So what coursework could we do?

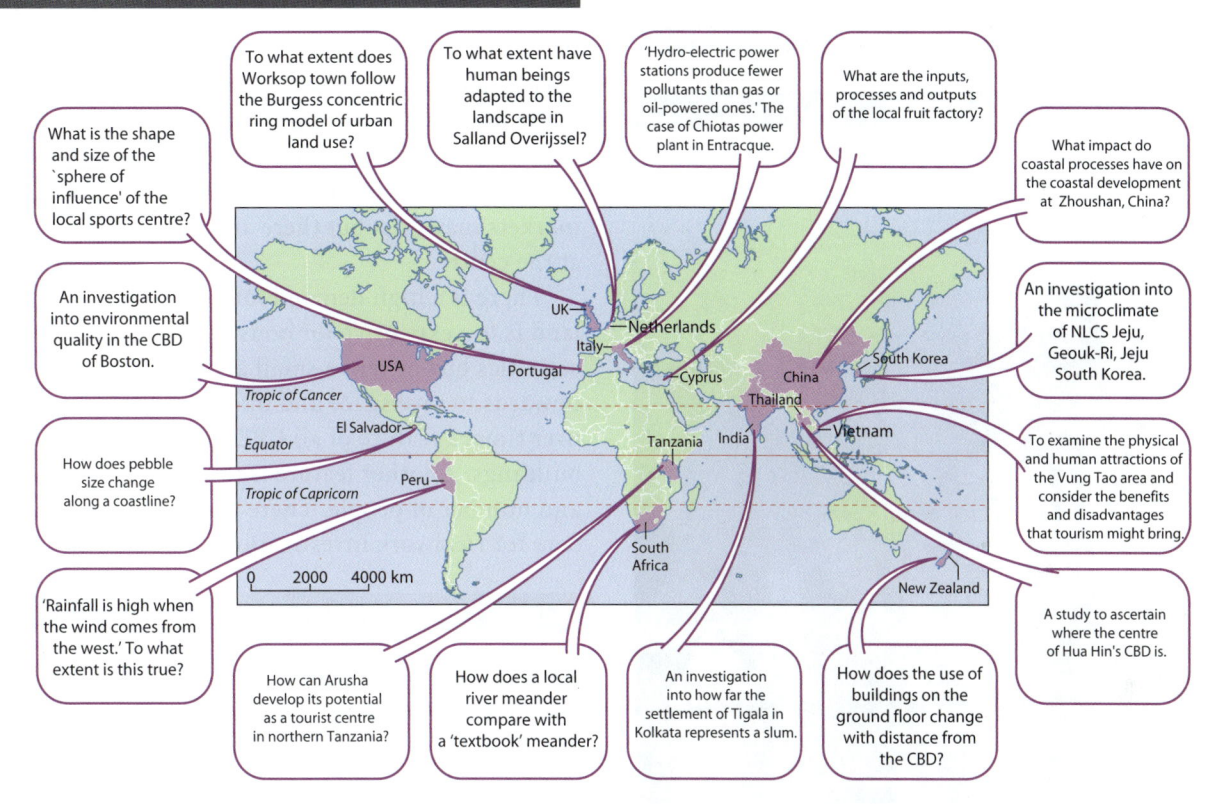

World map showing possible coursework titles in different countries:

- What is the shape and size of the 'sphere of influence' of the local sports centre? (UK)
- To what extent does Worksop town follow the Burgess concentric ring model of urban land use? (UK)
- To what extent have human beings adapted to the landscape in Salland Overijssel? (Netherlands)
- 'Hydro-electric power stations produce fewer pollutants than gas or oil-powered ones.' The case of Chiotas power plant in Entracque. (Italy)
- What are the inputs, processes and outputs of the local fruit factory? (Portugal)
- What impact do coastal processes have on the coastal development at Zhoushan, China? (China)
- An investigation into the microclimate of NLCS Jeju, Geouk-Ri, Jeju South Korea. (South Korea)
- An investigation into environmental quality in the CBD of Boston. (USA)
- How does pebble size change along a coastline? (Peru)
- 'Rainfall is high when the wind comes from the west.' To what extent is this true? (South Africa)
- How can Arusha develop its potential as a tourist centre in northern Tanzania? (Tanzania)
- How does a local river meander compare with a 'textbook' meander? (India)
- An investigation into how far the settlement of Tigala in Kolkata represents a slum. (India)
- How does the use of buildings on the ground floor change with distance from the CBD? (Thailand)
- To examine the physical and human attractions of the Vung Tao area and consider the benefits and disadvantages that tourism might bring. (Vietnam)
- A study to ascertain where the centre of Hua Hin's CBD is. (Thailand)

## How coursework is assessed

If you are carrying out the Coursework Assignment your teacher will give you specific guidance on what you need to do to meet the course requirements. You should also make sure that you check the syllabus for the year that you are entering the examination to ensure that you understand how you will be assessed. The coursework assignment will involve you carrying out fieldwork and producing a report.

Five different geographical skills are assessed, and all are of equal value. The skills are:

- knowledge with understanding
- observation and data collection
- organisation and data collection
- analysis and interpretation
- judgement and decision making, which includes evaluation and conclusions.

The same skills are tested in coursework or alternative to coursework examinations.

The world map in **Source B** illustrates many different courscwork types that schools could use. All these titles are either:

- enquiry questions
- statements to investigate
- hypotheses to test.

## Coming up next …

The following pages provide guidance and classroom practice for schools when they carry out fieldwork. The following popular investigations are covered:

- The Central Business District (CBD)
- Rivers
- Tourism
- Weather.

These are followed by two questions set out in the style of an Alternative to Coursework examination which provides further practice for students. Sample answers can be found on the Teacher CD.

### TASK 1
a   Describe the location of your school.
b   Suggest fieldwork techniques that you could practise:
- within the school grounds.
- within walking distance of the school grounds.
- some distance from the school that would involve organising transport.

### TASK 2: Study Source B

Look at the titles of coursework assignments that it would be possible to carry out in different countries. Write down **two** assignments from these titles that you could carry out in or around your school.

241

# Cambridge IGCSE Geography — Geographical Enquiry

## 1 Investigating the CBD

**A** Part of the CBD of New York, USA

### The Central Business District (CBD)

All urban areas, whether in an MEDC or an LEDC, will have a central area. The CBD has usually developed at the most accessible point for people surrounding the urban area to travel to. In some LEDC cities it is characterised by market functions; in MEDC cities markets may exist but there are mainly shops and offices at the centre.

There is a high demand for land in the CBD so the land is too expensive for housing. Instead commercial activities buy or rent a small area of land and build upwards to save space and money. Consequently, over time, a feature of all CBDs is the presence of tall buildings. Another feature is the large amount of traffic and number of people. There are many opportunities here for fieldwork investigations.

**B** In the CBD we could investigate …

> Your enquiry can start as a hypothesis or a question. A hypothesis is a statement which your fieldwork may prove to be true, partially true, or false. A question needs an answer from your fieldwork.

> Where does the CBD start and end?

> The function of buildings changes with height.

> To what extent are pavements congested during the day?

**TASK 1:** Study Source **A**
a Describe the main features of the scene.
b Where is your closest CBD? List any similarities and differences between it and the CBD of New York.
c To what extent is this photograph useful for describing New York's CBD?

**TASK 2:** Study Source **B**
a Suggest **one** other topic that could be investigated in the CBD.
b Choose **one** topic from those suggested in Source B or use your suggestion. Using the 'Route to Geographical Enquiry' on page 240, plan how you would carry out an investigation into this topic.

# Investigating the CBD

## C Investigating traffic flow in New York

New York is a busy city. Vehicles travelling into the CBD have increased by 7 per cent per year since 1995. If that trend continues until 2035, over 1 million vehicles per day will be entering the CBD. In some places the average speed will drop to less than 22 km (14 miles) per hour. At present drivers spend more than the equivalent of a working week each year stuck in New York's traffic. As traffic causes noise as well as emissions that can cause cancer and asthma, monitoring traffic flow is an important part of identifying problems and proposing solutions to the traffic issue.

©AA Media Limited 2009
Cartographic data ©Tele Atlas N.V. 2009

### Our Route to Enquiry

**Enquiry question:** How does traffic flow vary at a major junction in New York during the day?

**Equipment needed:** Clipboard, watch, recording sheet, pens/pencils, camera, 16 students making 8 pairs.

**Method:** At 09.00, 12.00 and 15.00 (equal three-hour intervals) 8 pairs of students will carry out a traffic count for 10 minutes. Two pairs of students will be responsible for each of the roads merging at the junction. Each pair will stand on opposite sides of the road and record the numbers of different vehicles using a tally system on a recording sheet.

**Safety issues:** Clothing, ID, money, check if permission needed, stay in pairs, cell phone / school or teacher contact location, choose a safe position.

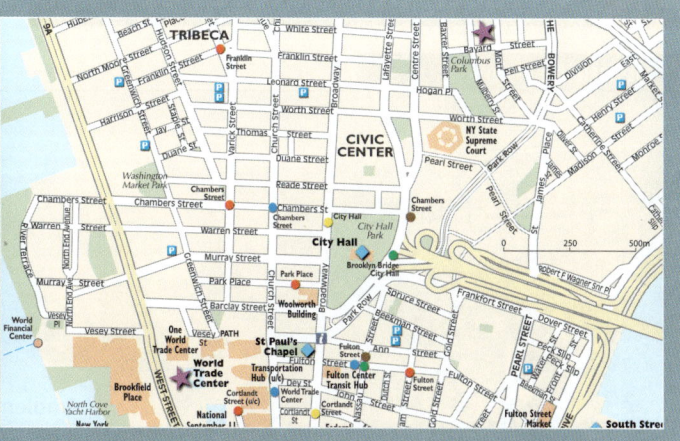

## D The traffic survey recording sheet

**TRAFFIC SURVEY SHEET**

Name .................................... Day/date ..........................

Location of junction .................. Name of street ..............

Measuring traffic flow in/out of the CBD?      IN/OUT

Time period    09.00   12.00   15.00

| Bicycle | Motorbike | Private car | Taxi |
|---------|-----------|-------------|------|
|         |           |             |      |

| Minibus/van | Bus/coach | Lorry |
|-------------|-----------|-------|
|             |           |       |

\* Use a tally system in groups of five (𝍧).

Comments on survey

---

**TASK 3:** Study Source **C**

A group of students in a New York school decided to study traffic flow at the junction of Broadway and Chambers Street.

a  Describe the location of the junction. Refer to distances and directions.

b  Do you think this is a good choice of location for this enquiry? Explain your views.

c  Read the group's plan. Comment on its strengths and any weaknesses. What would you do differently?

**TASK 4:** Study Source **D**

a  Comment on the layout and content of the traffic survey sheet. Could it be improved?

b  Consider how the group might present the results of the survey.

c  Suggest what conclusions the group might expect to draw from their fieldwork before they carry it out. Explain your views.

# Cambridge IGCSE Geography — Geographical Enquiry

## 2 Investigating rivers

**A** Measuring rivers

*Labels on photograph: Gradient of valley side; Gradient of channel; Width; Speed of flow; Depth*

### Measuring rivers

Measuring river features and processes is a popular fieldwork exercise. The students in **Source A** are measuring the width of a river in Wales, UK as part of their coursework investigation. They are working near to its source where, because the river is shallower and not too wide, measurements can be taken easily, quickly, safely and accurately. The labels show some of the measurements that can be recorded at any site. As the river gets wider and deeper, this becomes more difficult. Providing two or more sites are used, it is possible to describe and compare river features and processes along its length.

**B** Along a river we could also investigate …

### SUGGESTION BOX
**Enquiry questions and hypotheses to test**

**Channel size and shape**
Does the river channel increase in width and depth as the river moves downstream away from its source?

**Load size and shape**
The bedload of a river will be smaller and rounder as it moves away from its source.

**Speed of flow**
The river does not increase its speed as it moves downstream towards its mouth.

**Valley shape**
How does the shape of the valley change as the river moves downstream from its source?

**Gradient**
Does the river bed gradient decrease as the river moves downstream from the source to its mouth?

**Impact of human activity**
People have changed some parts of the river and its valley.

**TASK 1:** Study **Source A**
a Identify **three** different river characteristics that can be measured.
b Suggest how each could be measured accurately.
c Compare the health and safety issues that must be considered in river studies with those in the CBD (see pages 242–243).

**TASK 2:** Study **Source B**
Every investigation needs a clear purpose. This can be written as a hypothesis to test or an enquiry question to be answered.
a Write down **one** investigation that is a hypothesis to test.
b Write down **one** investigation that is an enquiry question to answer.
c Suggest **one** other investigation that could be carried out on a river.

# Investigating rivers

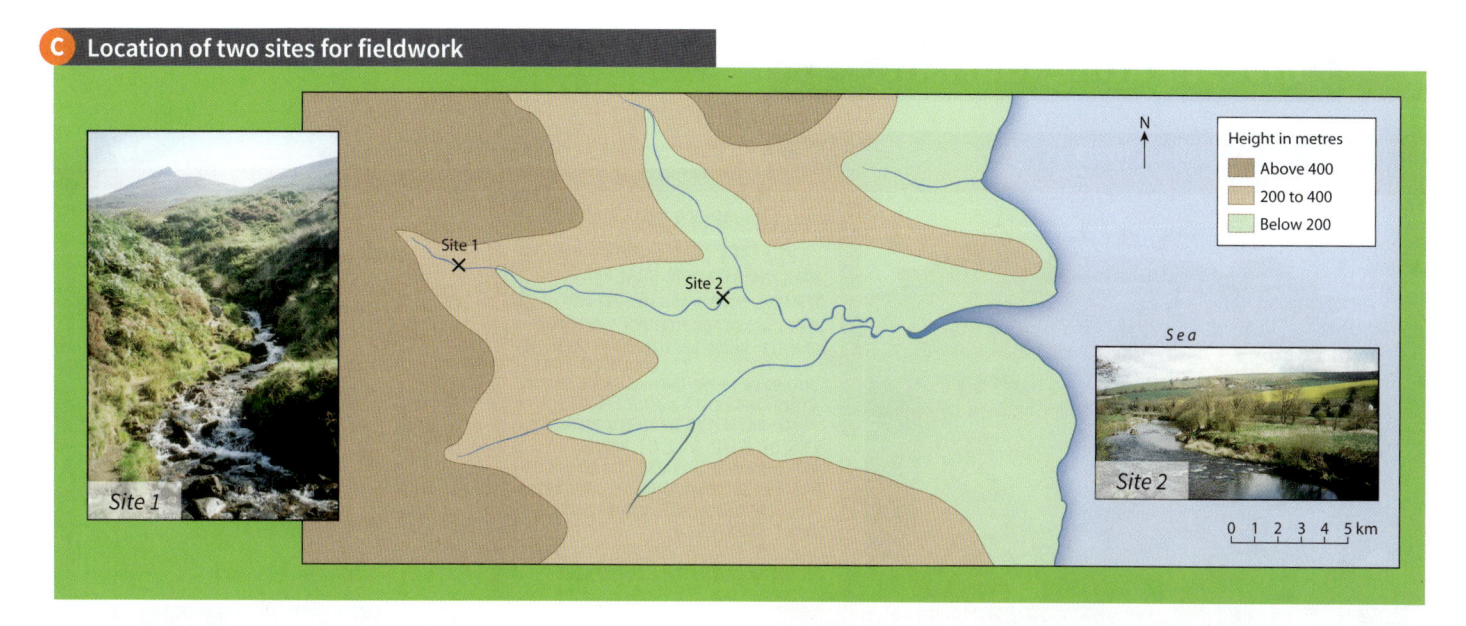

## C Location of two sites for fieldwork

Height in metres:
- Above 400
- 200 to 400
- Below 200

## Comparing two sites

A group of students carried out an investigation comparing Sites 1 and 2 along a river. **Source C** shows a photograph taken at each site and also the location of each site on a map. The students chose this hypothesis from those suggested in **Source B**.

'The bedload of a river will be smaller and rounder as it moves away from its source.'

At each site they randomly selected 25 pebbles from the bed of the river and measured the long axis. They also used Powers' scale of roundness to make a judgement about how rounded each pebble was.

## E Powers' scale of roundness

| very angular | angular | sub-angular | sub-rounded | rounded | well rounded |
|---|---|---|---|---|---|
| 1 | 2 | 3 | 4 | 5 | 6 |

## D Measuring the long axis of a pebble

## F Recording the results

Partial bedload data-collection tables for site 1 and site 2.

Site 1:
| Bedload sample | Long axis (cm) | Roundness |
|---|---|---|
| 1 | 11 | 2 |
| 2 | 9 | 4 |
| 3 | 13.5 | 3 |
| 4 | 10 | 5 |
| 5 | 10 | 3 |
| 6 | 11 | 5 |
| 7 | 12 | 2 |
| 8 | 2.3 | |

Site 2:
| Bedload sample | Long axis (cm) | Roundness |
|---|---|---|
| 1 | 6 | 5 |
| 2 | 12 | 3 |
| 3 | 10 | 5 |
| 4 | 13 | 3 |
| 5 | 5 | 5 |
| 6 | 2.5 | 2 |
| 7 | 8 | 4 |
| 8 | 16 | 2 |
| 9 | 7 | |

**TASK 3:** Sources **D** and **E** show how to measure size and roundness. Source **F** is an extract from the group's results. Some preliminary conclusions can be drawn from these extracts.

a Draw graphs to present the data for the first seven results at Sites 1 and 2.
b Describe any relationship that appears to exist between:
- size and roundness
- distance from the source and size
- distance from the source and roundness.

**TASK 4**
Decide whether you think the hypothesis is true, partially true or false. Support your decision with evidence from the data and graphs you have drawn.

**TASK 5:** Study **Source B** again.
a Choose **one** other hypothesis or question or the one you suggested in Task 2c.
b Use the 'Route to Geographical Enquiry' on page 240 to plan how you would investigate this topic.

# Cambridge IGCSE Geography — Geographical Enquiry

## 3 Investigating tourism

### A  The City Palace, Jaipur, India

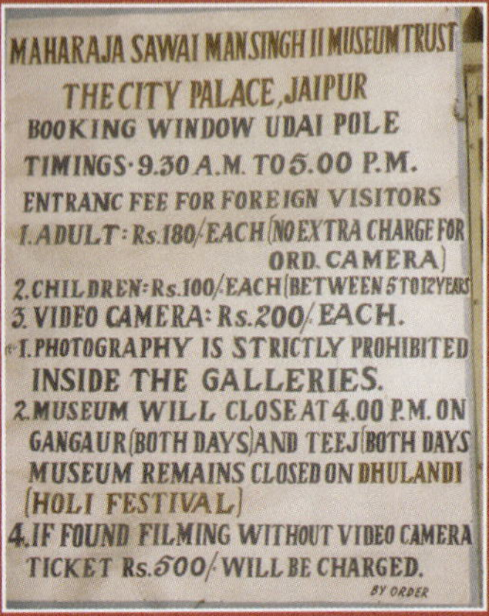

**MAHARAJA SAWAI MAN SINGH II MUSEUM TRUST**
**THE CITY PALACE, JAIPUR**
BOOKING WINDOW UDAI POLE
TIMINGS: 9.30 A.M. TO 5.00 P.M.
ENTRANCE FEE FOR FOREIGN VISITORS
1. ADULT: Rs.180/- EACH (NO EXTRA CHARGE FOR ORD. CAMERA)
2. CHILDREN: Rs.100/- EACH (BETWEEN 5 TO 12 YEARS)
3. VIDEO CAMERA: Rs.200/- EACH.
- 1. PHOTOGRAPHY IS STRICTLY PROHIBITED INSIDE THE GALLERIES.
- 2. MUSEUM WILL CLOSE AT 4.00 P.M. ON GANGAUR (BOTH DAYS) AND TEEJ (BOTH DAYS)
- 3. MUSEUM REMAINS CLOSED ON DHULANDI (HOLI FESTIVAL)
- 4. IF FOUND FILMING WITHOUT VIDEO CAMERA TICKET Rs.500/- WILL BE CHARGED.
BY ORDER

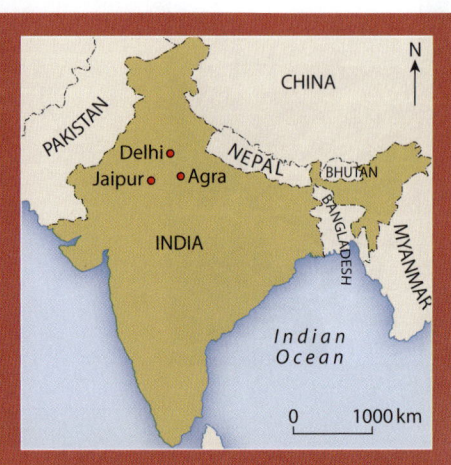

Jaipur is the capital city of Rajasthan, a state in the northern part of India. It is located in a very dry and sandy area but attracts tourists who usually visit the Delhi-Agra-Jaipur triangle of cities. Known as the 'pink' city, Jaipur has many historical buildings. One is the City Palace.

## International tourism to India

Many countries rely on income from tourism. This is especially true of LEDCs such as India. Almost 3 million visitors travel from overseas countries to India, of which more than 83 per cent travel by air, with the majority landing at Delhi. Western Europe provides over one-third of these visitors, with more travelling from the UK (16 per cent) than any other country. The most popular period is October to December whereas the least visitors arrive between April and June. Carrying out fieldwork investigations of visitor patterns is a popular coursework topic in many countries.

### B  So what shall we investigate … and how?

"Next month we are going to spend time at the City Palace in Jaipur. We will be carrying out a survey of visitors to the building. I want you to think about what hypothesis or question we could investigate using questionnaires. Also bear in mind that we cannot ask every visitor so we will have to take a sample. Think about the best way to do that too."

---

**TASK 1:** Study Source **A** and an atlas.

a  Describe the location of Jaipur in relation to:
- Delhi, Agra and other features on the map
- the country you live in.

b  In what ways does the local economy benefit from tourists? Refer to evidence from the photograph and your own ideas.

**TASK 2**

The teacher in an international school in Jaipur (Source B) decided to take a group of students to the City Palace to carry out a survey of tourists, using questionnaires. He obtained permission from the authorities to do this outside the main entrance for a period from 10 to 11 a.m. on one day in June.

a  Do you think this was a good time and month to carry out this work?

b  Suggest how the results might differ at other times of day or in other months.

**TASK 3:** Study Source **C**

a  Why is sampling necessary in many geographical investigations?

b  What is systematic sampling? How is it different from random sampling?

c  In what situations might you use stratified sampling?

d  Take a sample of six students from your class using systematic, random and stratified sampling methods. Comment on your findings.

# Investigating tourism

## Sampling and questionnaires

Sampling is a necessary part of many geographical investigations. There is never enough time, money, energy, equipment or students to ask questions of every visitor to a tourist attraction. The larger the sample the more reliable the data. Group work is one way of obtaining more results in a fixed time. But how do we sample the 'population' of tourists?

### C  Random or systematic sampling?

**Random sampling for questionnaires**
There are several ways of using this method. It is best to use random number tables. Using the extract below (see shaded numbers) you could ask questions of the 61st, 2nd, 10th and 54th person you meet. It avoids bias and any subjectivity but does take time to set up.

Extract from a random numbers table

| 23 | 17 | 59 | 66 | 38 | 61 | 02 | 10 | 86 | 10 | 51 | 55 |
|----|----|----|----|----|----|----|----|----|----|----|----|
| 03 | 04 | 10 | 33 | 53 | 70 | 11 | 54 | 48 | 63 | 94 | 60 |
| 38 | 67 | 23 | 42 | 29 | 65 | 40 | 88 | 78 | 71 | 37 | 18 |

**Systematic sampling for questionnaires**
The people asked are chosen by a system that is evenly distributed, e.g. every 3rd person. This avoids bias such as only asking people who might appear to be cooperative or of a certain age group. It is easy and simple to use.

**Stratified sampling for questionnaires**
This can be used when the proportions of people in a sample are very different, e.g. in a class of students two-thirds may be girls and one-third boys. In this case you could use either systematic or random sample methods to choose four girls and two boys. This would reflect the gender balance.

### D  Which is better: Questionnaire 1 or Questionnaire 2?

The hypothesis: 'The characteristics of visitor patterns to the City Palace in Jaipur show that they are mostly from overseas rather than from India.'

**VISITOR QUESTIONNAIRE 1**

1. Why have you come here?
2. Have you been here before?
   Yes   No   Can't remember
3. How long do you intend to stay here?
   < 4 hours   > 4 hours
4. Are you aware that by visiting this place you may cause damage?
5. Where have you come from?
6. How did you get here?   Car   Train   Bus

**VISITOR QUESTIONNAIRE 2**
Good morning. I am carrying out a geography investigation for my IGCSE examination. Could I ask you a few questions please?

Time/date            Weather            Place

1. Have you ever visited this site before?   Yes   No
2. How did you get to hear about this place?
   Advert   Television   Friend   Other
3. How far have you travelled to get here today?
   < 5 km   5–20 km   > 20 km
4. If you did not arrive by car, how did you travel to the site?
   Bus   Walk   Bike   Motorbike   Train   Other
5. Why are you attracted to this site?
   _____
6. How long do you intend staying here?
   < 2 hours   2–4 hours   > 4 hours   Longer
7. In which country or place are you a permanent resident?
   _____

Gender:   Male   Female
Age estimate:   < 20   20–35   36–50   51–65   > 65

---

**TASK 4:** Study Source D and note the hypothesis.
The teacher divided the class into six groups of four students and set each group a task of devising a questionnaire. The questionnaires were shown to each group to vote on the best one to use. Questionnaire 1 received least votes and Questionnaire 2 received most votes.

a. List **three** differences between the two questionnaires.
b. Discuss in a group why Questionnaire 2 was judged to be the best one to use.
c. Following your discussion, write down **four** reasons why Questionnaire 2 would be more effective for this investigation than Questionnaire 1.

**TASK 5**
When devising questionnaires it is useful to carry out a pilot survey.

a. Use a copy of Questionnaire 2 with friends or family to see if it could be improved. They will have to imagine they are visiting a tourist destination in your country.
b. Check the 'Route to Geographical Enquiry' on page 240. Devise a plan for the investigation into visitor patterns at a tourist destination of your choice.

# Cambridge IGCSE Geography — Geographical Enquiry

## 4  Investigating weather

### Measuring the weather

The weather refers to day-to-day changes in, for example, temperature, cloud cover, air pressure and rainfall. Providing a school has a Stevenson Screen and appropriate weather instruments, many different investigations into weather can be carried out within the school grounds.

**A  Siting a Stevenson Screen**

*A weather station in the Brecon Beacons National Park, Wales, UK*

**B  Not all weather is measured in a Stevenson Screen**

| Rainfall | Maximum temperature |
|---|---|
| Hours of sunshine | Wind speed |
| Cloud cover | Relative humidity |
| Air pressure | Wind direction |

**C  Measuring air pressure**

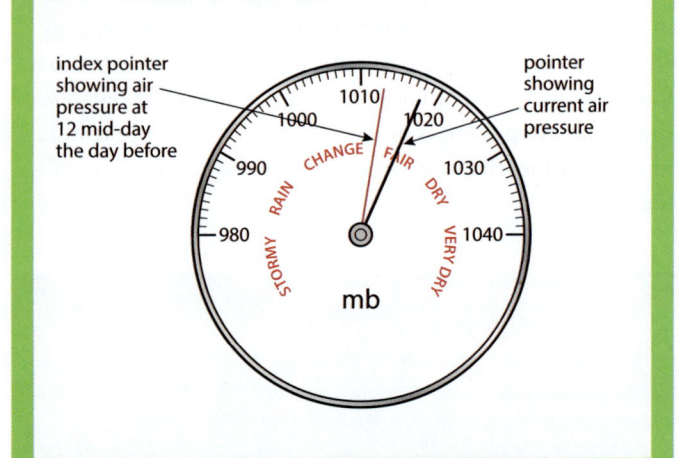

Aneroid barometers are sometimes kept in a Stevenson Screen but many are hung on walls for convenience of checking. They measure air pressure in millibars (mb). The pressure of air on the glass moves levers which move a pointer around a dial. If pressure is high on the glass, the pointer moves around to HIGH. If pressure is low on the glass, the pointer moves towards LOW.

Most barometers have two pointers. An index pointer can be moved by a central dial so the pressure from the previous day can be fixed. The other pointer moves with current air pressure so a comparison can be made.

Average sea level pressure is set at 1000 mb. Above this is high pressure; below this is low pressure. Pressure in the world can range from 950 mb to 1050 mb. Many barometers also indicate the weather expected, so
LOW = Rising air = Clouds and rain;
HIGH = Sinking air = Clear, dry weather.

---

**TASK 1:** Study **Source A**

a  Is this Stevenson Screen in a good location? Refer to page 106 to help you decide.

b  Answer the following:
- Why is it painted white?
- Why does it have slatted sides?
- Why is it mounted on legs?

**TASK 2:** Study **Source B**

List the elements of weather that are not measured using instruments in the Stevenson Screen.

**TASK 3:** A teacher decided to get her class to investigate some aspects of weather around the school. She was confident they understood how to use most weather instruments but was less sure about their ability to measure air pressure using an aneroid barometer. Using **Source C** she set them the following questions.

a  What units is air pressure measured in?

b  Explain how an aneroid barometer works.

c  Explain how and why the index pointer on the barometer is used.

d  From the diagram, work out the difference between the pressure at 12 midday the day before and the current air pressure.

e  What decides whether air pressure is termed *High* or *Low*?

f  Under what air pressure can we expect:
- clouds and rain?
- clear, dry weather?

Give reasons for your answer.

# Investigating weather

## Recording the weather

Once measurements are taken, they need to be recorded. A common code of symbols is required so that weather can be compared between different regions. In the UK the Meteorological Office uses the system that is shown on page 109.

A geography class in the UK decided to investigate the hypothesis:

**'The weather around the school showed little change on three consecutive days in March.'**

The class carried out the fieldwork using traditional weather measuring instruments. They were divided into seven groups of four students. Each group was responsible for measuring or observing one aspect of the weather at the same time on three consecutive days. After taking their readings they presented these on weather station circles.

### D Overall recording sheet – observations from 7 groups

| | Time | Temp. (°C) | Pressure (mb) | Direction wind from | Wind speed (knots or km/hour) | Cloud cover (oktas) | Cloud type | Current weather |
|---|---|---|---|---|---|---|---|---|
| **Day 1** (17 Mar) | 09.00 | 6 | 1010 | South-west | 10 kn (16 km/hr) | 4 | Stratus | Drizzle |
| **Day 2** (18 Mar) | 09.00 | 7 | 1015 | West | 14 kn (22 km/hr) | 3 | Cumulus | Mist |
| **Day 3** (19 Mar) | 09.00 | 9 | 1024 | South | 6 kn (10 km/hr) | 1 | Cirrus | Clear |

**Note:** For an explanation of 'knot' and 'okta', refer to **Source C** on page 109.

### E The weather station circle for 09.00 hours on Day 1

Temperature in degrees centigrade (°C) — 6
Pressure in millibars (mb) — 1010
Present weather symbol
Cloud cover (oktas)
Wind speed (knots or Km/h)
Direction wind is coming from
Past weather symbol

### F The Beaufort scale

| Beaufort Scale No. | Wind Description | Effect on land features | Speed (km/h) |
|---|---|---|---|
| 0 | Calm | Smoke rises vertically | less than 1 |
| 1 | Light air | Direction shown by moving smoke but not by wind vane | 1–5 |
| 2 | Light breeze | Wind felt on face; leaves rustle; wind vane moved | 6–11 |
| 3 | Gentle breeze | Leaves and twigs in constant motion; flag moved | 12–19 |
| 4 | Moderate breeze | Raises dust and paper | 20–29 |
| 5 | Fresh breeze | Small trees begin to sway | 30–36 |
| 6 | Strong breeze | Large branches in motion | 37–49 |
| 7 | Moderate gale | Whole trees in motion | 50–60 |
| 8 | Fresh gale | Twigs broken off trees | 61–73 |
| 9 | Strong gale | Slight structural damage occurs, especially to roofs | 74–86 |
| 10 | Whole gale | Trees uprooted | 87–100 |
| 11 | Storm | Widespread damage | 101–120 |
| 12 | Hurricane | Widespread devastation experienced | above 121 |

---

**TASK 4: Study Sources D and E**

a Look at the station circle describing the weather recorded by the students at 09.00 hours on Day 1. Check that this matches the weather for Day 1 shown in the table.

b In pairs, draw two weather station circles – one each. One of you should use the Day 2 data and the other the Day 3 data to add symbols to your station circle. When you have finished, check each other's station circle against the data.

c To what extent do you think that the hypothesis is **true, partially true** or **false**? Support your views with evidence from the table.

**TASK 5: Study Source F**

Some students also decided to use the Beaufort scale as well as anemometers to record the effects of the wind as well as its speed.

a Why and how is the Beaufort scale useful?

b Look at the wind speeds recorded on anemometers by the students in Source D. What effect of the wind could be seen by the students on each day of the investigation?

c At what ranges of wind speeds would:
- trees be uprooted
- wind vanes be moved by the wind
- chimney pots be removed?

Give your answers in kilometres per hour (km/h).

**TASK 6**

a If your school has a weather station:
- describe the location of the weather station and the Stevenson Screen.
- list all the instruments that are in the Stevenson Screen and in the area of the weather station.
- list any other instruments you can use to measure the weather that are not in the weather station or the Stevenson Screen.

b Here is a hypothesis you could test: **'Changes in rainfall amounts are related to changes in air pressure.'** Discuss how you could carry this out at your school.

c Discuss other hypotheses that you could test without leaving your school grounds.

# Cambridge IGCSE Geography — Geographical Enquiry

# Fieldwork checklist

## Collecting primary data

### Measuring

If you are carrying out a coursework assignment then the instruments you need to know about will be limited to the requirements of that investigation.

If you are preparing for an Alternative to Coursework examination however you will be expected to know how to use many different types of instruments. Most instruments are required in investigations into physical geography. These include:

- quadrats
- clinometers
- pebbleometers
- callipers
- rulers
- measuring tapes
- ranging poles
- floats
- stopwatches
- Stevenson Screen
- max–min thermometers
- hygrometers (wet and dry bulb thermometer)
- sunshine recorders
- anemometers
- wind vanes
- cloud type charts
- cloud cover estimates by eye
- barometer
- rain gauge
- simple digital instruments
- click counters

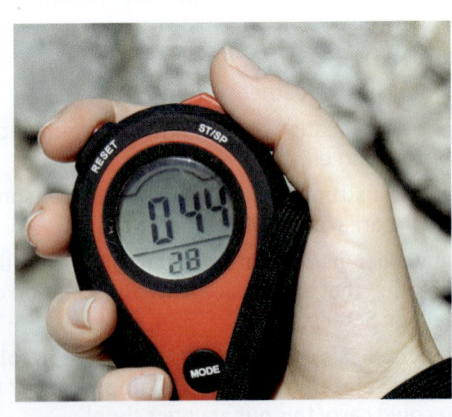

# Fieldwork checklist

## Sampling

Check that you know when and how to use the following three sampling techniques:

- systematic sampling
- random sampling
- stratified sampling

## Observation

- field sketches and maps
- photographs
- recording sheets
- cloud types and cover

## Surveys and counts

Before carrying out a survey you need to consider if a pilot survey is needed. You need to know how to carry out investigations in, for example:

- urban land use
- pedestrian count
- traffic count.

## Questionnaires

Check that you know what makes a good questionnaire and the appropriate circumstances to use it.

You need to understand how to create a questionnaire. Consider, for example:

- its layout
- the format of the questions
- the number of questions
- the wording of the questions
- age and gender issues.

You need to understand how to carry out a questionnaire and what questions to ask:

- Where will it be carried out?
- How many people should be asked?
- How long should the interview last?
- Whom shall we ask?
- In pairs or groups?
- Who will ask the questions?
- Who will fill the answers in?
- How should we conduct ourselves?
- What problems might be met?

## Collecting secondary data

This would include any data or information collected by other people or organisations found in, for example:

- books, newspapers and magazines
- census data
- libraries
- internet information
- official records and archives.

## Refining and presenting data

Check that you know how and when to use these techniques to refine and present data:

- line graphs
- bar graphs
- divided bar graphs
- histograms
- flow diagrams
- wind-rose diagrams
- isoline maps
- scatter graphs
- pie charts
- triangular graphs
- radial graphs
- dispersion graphs
- choropleth maps
- kite diagrams
- pictograms

# Cambridge IGCSE Geography — Geographical Enquiry

# Fieldwork safety

## Health, safety and welfare

Fieldwork is an activity involving risks and hazards. The health, safety and welfare of students is of major importance when carrying out fieldwork. It is important that students are also aware of the risks and how accidents can be avoided.

Some guidance applies to all types of fieldwork in different environments. This includes:

- Never work alone; always work in pairs or a group.
- Always have a means of contact such as a mobile phone/cell phone or a whistle.
- Have contact numbers/addresses for teachers and parents.
- Make sure you know the location of meeting points and at what time you should meet.
- Check the forecast for any extreme weather.
- Take a map and compass and know how to use them.
- Dress appropriately for the occasion, e.g. waterproof boots, warm clothing, a hat.
- Use sunblock or suncream where temperatures may be high.
- Put on insect repellent if necessary.
- Take basic first aid supplies such as plasters; teachers will have a more complete kit for the group.
- Tell the teacher about any medical condition you have and carry medication with you.
- Carry out the fieldwork in daylight hours.

### Urban environment

**Safety points**
- Be aware of traffic and busy roads.
- Don't wear ear muffs or headphones.
- Be careful crossing roads.
- Avoid surveys at heavily polluted or very noisy sites.
- Avoid areas that may be dangerous or unsafe.
- Beware of approaches by strangers.
- Be polite if interviewing passers-by.
- Avoid dogs or stray animals.

**Sample question**: Before the group visited the CBD, the teacher called a meeting to discuss safety procedures that should be observed in the city centre. Suggest **three** pieces of advice that the teacher gave them and explain their importance.

### Coastal environment

**Safety points**
- Check tide tables.
- Carry out your work at low tide.
- Only work in shallow water.
- Don't touch any driftwood or other beach materials.
- Avoid any sea-life that is on or near the beach.
- Don't go near the edge of cliffs.
- Don't stand beneath cliffs, or wear a helmet.
- Stay on coastal paths.
- Wear safety goggles if studying rocks.

**Sample question**: Before the students began their fieldwork their teacher reminded them of the need to be safe on the beach and near the sea. Suggest **three** safety precautions that they could take to reduce the risk of accident and explain why they are important.

### TASK 1
On this page are two examples of different environments where students could carry out fieldwork. As well as the above guidance, some specific safety points that apply to each have been listed. Choose **one** of these environments and answer its sample question.

### TASK 2
Two other environments in which fieldwork is carried out are rivers and forest environments. Choose **one** of these environments and make a list of safety points that would apply to it.

## Geographical Enquiry

# The Alternative to Coursework

These two questions are in the style of questions that students may encounter in Alternative to Coursework examinations. Full versions of the exam-style questions with lines to write the answers on can be printed off from the Student CD. Mark schemes for the questions are available on the Teacher CD.

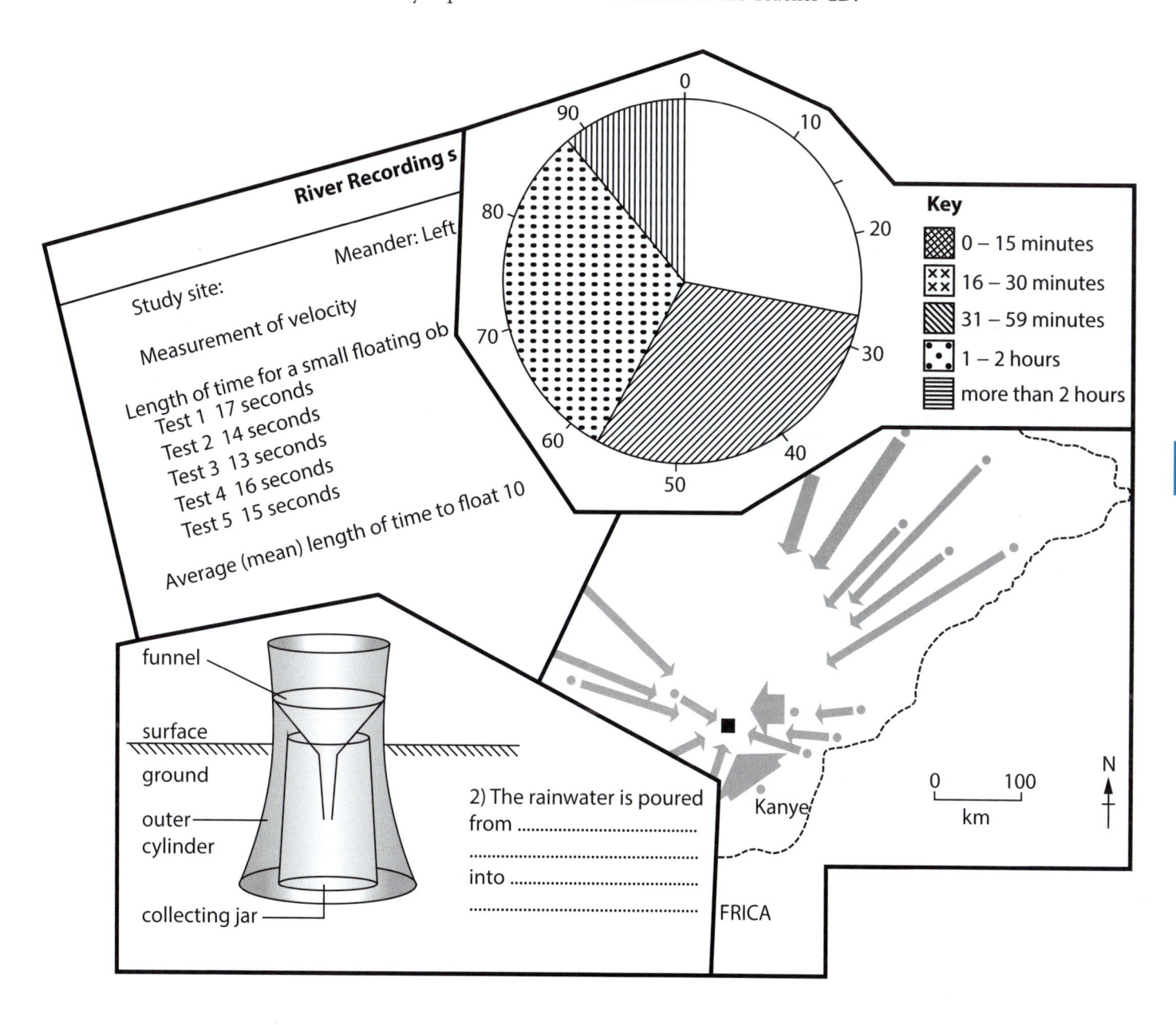

**River Recording s**

Study site: ........................................ Meander: Left

Measurement of velocity

Length of time for a small floating ob...

Test 1  17 seconds
Test 2  14 seconds
Test 3  13 seconds
Test 4  16 seconds
Test 5  15 seconds

Average (mean) length of time to float 10

**Key**
- 0 – 15 minutes
- 16 – 30 minutes
- 31 – 59 minutes
- 1 – 2 hours
- more than 2 hours

funnel
surface
ground
outer cylinder
collecting jar

2) The rainwater is poured from ..........................................
.................................................................
into ..........................................
.................................................................

Kanye

FRICA

0   100
km

N

# Cambridge IGCSE Geography — Geographical Enquiry

## Exam-Style Question 1

A class of students in the UK was carrying out fieldwork in the main shopping area of a small town near to their school. They wanted to find out whether a small town (population 92 500) showed the features of a CBD (Central Business District) and whether people who shopped there used it for different reasons. They decided to test the following hypotheses:

**Hypothesis 1:** 'The shops and services in the small town do not show the features expected in a CBD.'

**Hypothesis 2:** 'People who are shopping are attracted to the small town for different reasons.'

(a) First the students completed a land-use survey and then they produced a land-use map of the central area of the small town. Their map is shown as Fig. 1 opposite.

　(i)　Use the map and its key to identify the land uses at X and Y marked on Fig. 1. [2]

　(ii)　Describe the distribution of banks shown on Fig. 1. [2]

　(iii)　What type of shop or service is located immediately south of the building at point X? [1]

　(iv)　What type of shop or service is located 30 metres west of the building at point Y? [1]

　(v)　How many public car parking spaces are there on the map? Circle your answer below.

　　　　　170　216　298　318 [1]

(b) (i) Before the survey, the teacher had asked the students to write a list of features that they would expect to find in a CBD. The teacher was surprised by the suggestions and said that only four of these features were correct.

In the table below tick the **four** CBD features that you think the teacher agreed with.

| | |
|---|---|
| High order services | |
| Reservoir | |
| Tall buildings | |
| Convenience shops | |
| Football stadium | |
| Noise pollution | |
| Public car parks | |
| Water pollution | |

[2]

　(ii)　State **one** other feature you would expect to find in a CBD. [1]

Exam-Style Question 1

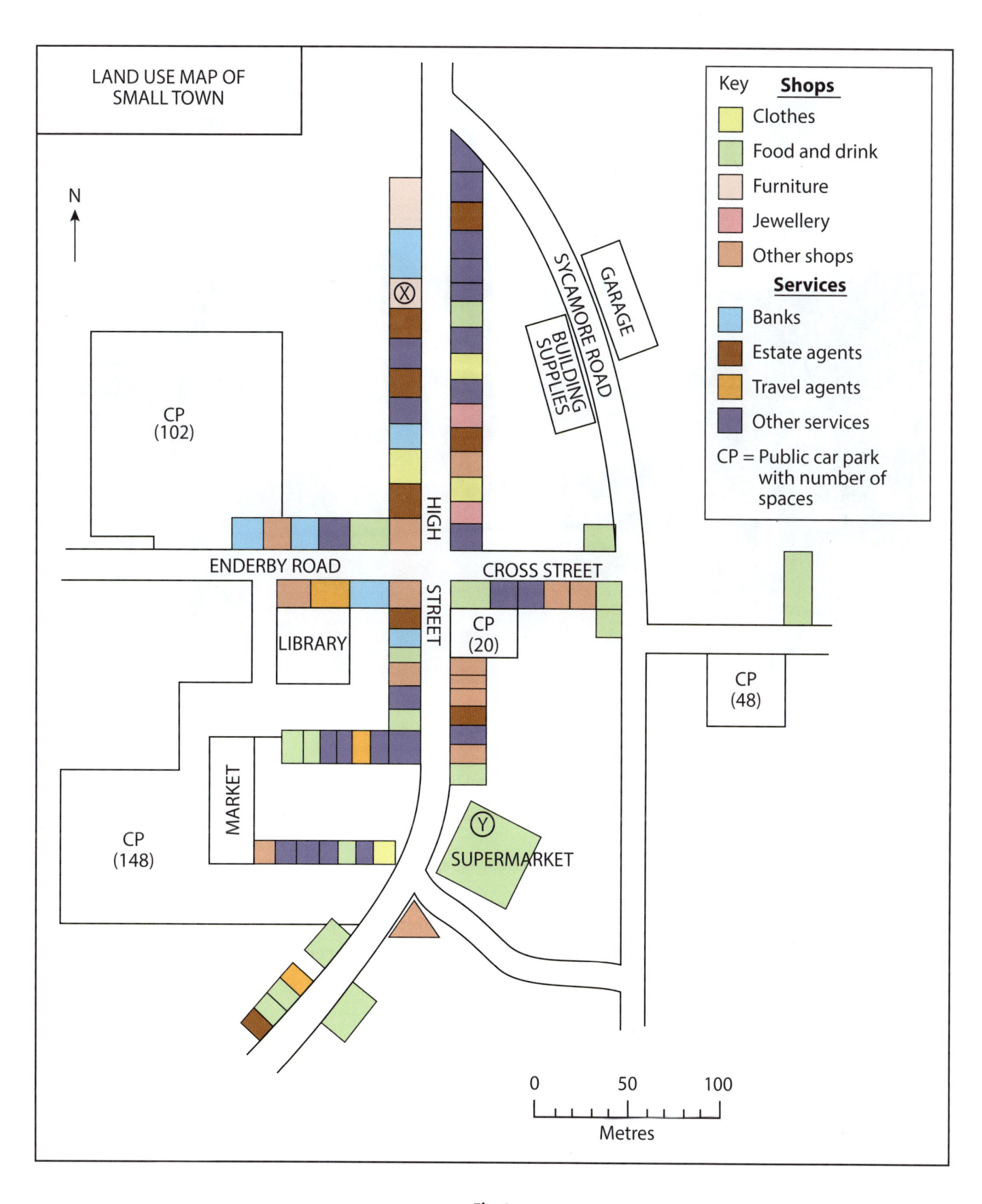

LAND USE MAP OF SMALL TOWN

**Key** **Shops**
- Clothes
- Food and drink
- Furniture
- Jewellery
- Other shops

**Services**
- Banks
- Estate agents
- Travel agents
- Other services

CP = Public car park with number of spaces

Fig. 1

(c) Look again at Fig. 1 and Photograph A below. The photograph was taken at the crossroads where Cross Street meets High Street.

**Photograph A**

(i) Suggest **one** reason why the students only mapped the ground-floor land use. [1]

(ii) The students agreed that *Hypothesis 1: 'The shops and services in the small town do not show the features expected in a CBD'* was mostly true.

What evidence supports this decision? Refer to Fig. 1 and Photograph A in your answer. [3]

(d) To investigate *Hypothesis 2: 'People who are shopping are attracted to the small town for different reasons'*, the students decided to carry out a questionnaire of people leaving the large supermarket at Y on Fig. 1.

Each group of students created a questionnaire and showed it to the teacher. The questionnaire she chose as the best one is shown in Fig. 2 opposite.

(i) Suggest **two** reasons why the teacher thought this was a good questionnaire. [2]

# Exam-Style Question 1

**SHOPPING QUESTIONNAIRE**

Name of town ..............................................

Where the questionnaire was used .............................

    Date ............................ Time ................................

I am a student studying geography at the local school. Could you please answer two questions to help me with my fieldwork project?

1. What is the main reason you are shopping in this small town today?
   - ☐ *Near home*     ☐ *Near work*
   - ☐ *Visitor to the area*     ☐ *Plenty of free parking*
   - ☐ *Wide range of shops*     ☐ *Wide range of services*

2. Apart from this supermarket, which other shops will you be buying items from today?
   - ☐ *Clothes*     ☐ *Food and drink*
   - ☐ *Furniture*     ☐ *Jewellery*
   - ☐ *Other*     ☐ *None*

3. What are the main services you will be using today?
   - ☐ *Bank*     ☐ *Estate agent*
   - ☐ *Travel agent*     ☐ *Library*
   - ☐ *Other*

   **Gender:**  Male      Female

   **Age:**  ☐ 16 and under  ☐ 17–30  ☐ 31–45
           ☐ 46–60  ☐ Over 60

   Thank you very much for your help and time

**Fig. 2**

(ii) A small group of students decided that they would take it in turns to carry out the questionnaire in pairs. They agreed to question people leaving the supermarket during a Friday morning. Each pair of students carried out the questionnaire for 30 minutes then the next pair took over. They could not ask every person leaving the supermarket so took a systematic sample.

    How would the students take a systematic sample of the shoppers? [1]

(iii) The teacher told the students that not every shopper asked would want to take part in the questionnaire. Give **one** reason why this might be true. [1]

iv  Fig. 3 below shows the results of Question 1 in the questionnaire.

**Answers to Question 1: What is the main reason you are shopping in this small town today?**

|  | Percentage | Key |
|---|---|---|
| Near home | 15 |  |
| Near work | 7 |  |
| Visitor to the area | 2 |  |
| Plenty of free parking | 26 |  |
| Wide range of shops | 20 |  |
| Wide range of services | 30 |  |
| Total | 100 |  |

Fig. 3

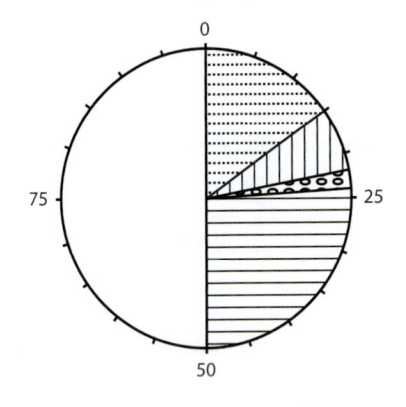

Fig. 4

Use the results from the table in Fig. 3 to complete the pie chart for the small town in Fig. 4 above. [2]

(v) Fig. 5 below shows the combined results of Question 2 and Question 3 in the questionnaire.

**Answers to Question 2: Apart from this supermarket, which other shops will you be buying items from today?**
**Answers to Question 3: What are the main services you will be using today?**

| Shops | Percentage | Services | Percentage |
|---|---|---|---|
| Food and drink | 10 | Bank | 30 |
| Furniture | 4 | Estate agent | 12 |
| Clothes | 12 | Travel agent | 21 |
| Jewellery | 5 | Library | 10 |
| Other shops | 35 | Other services | 35 |
| None | 40 |  |  |

Fig. 5

**SHOPS**

[Bar chart showing percentages for:
- Food and drink: ~10
- Furniture: ~1
- Clothes: ~13
- Jewellery: ~5
- Other shops: ~35
- None: ~40]

Percentage

**SERVICES**

[Bar chart showing percentages for:
- Bank: ~30
- Estate agent: ~13
- Travel agent: ~1
- Library: ~10
- Other services: ~35
- Use the results from]

Percentage

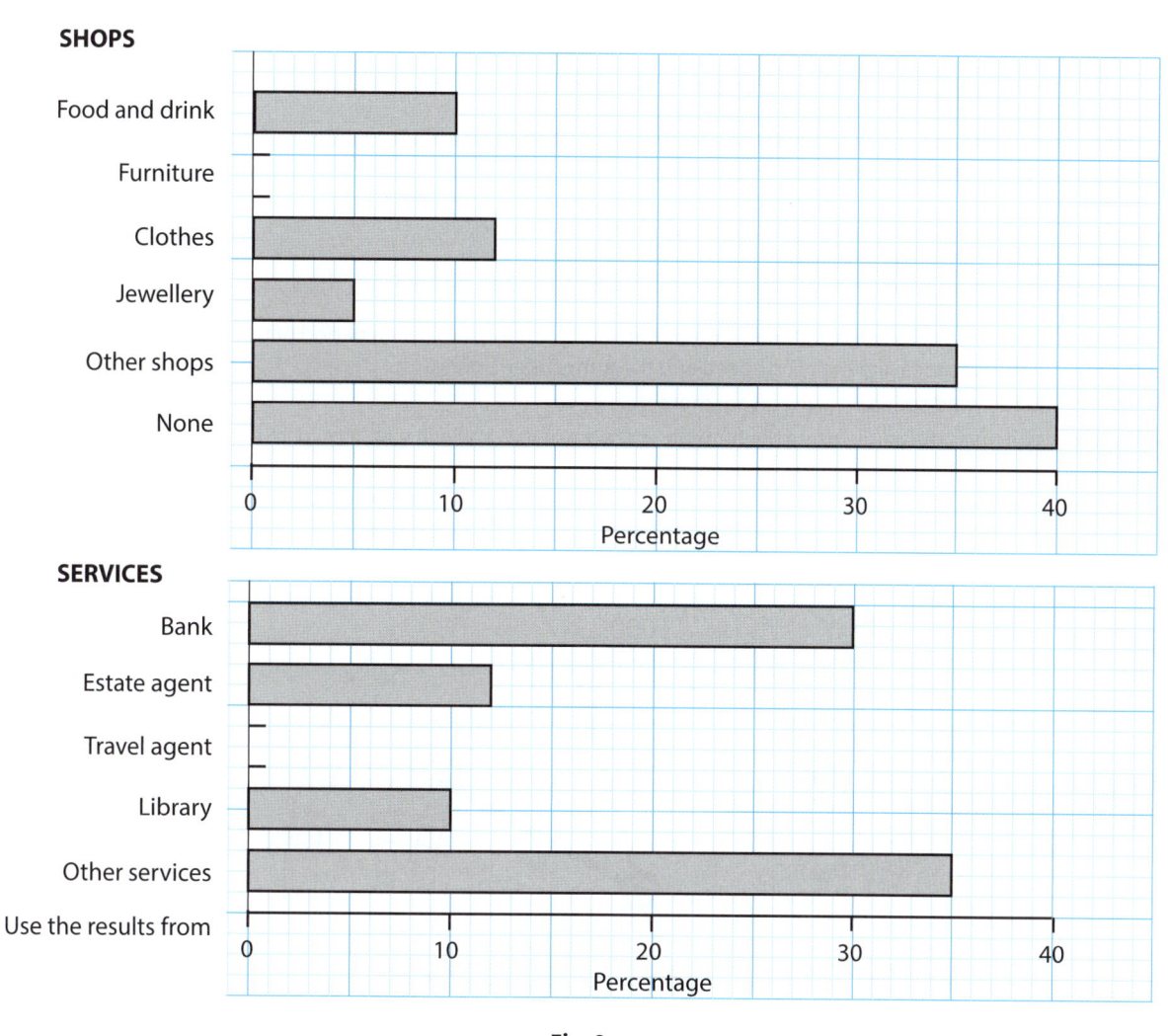

**Fig. 6**

Use the results from Fig. 5 to complete the bar graphs on Fig. 6 above. [2]

(vi) Do the results of the questionnaire support *Hypothesis 2: 'People who are shopping are attracted to the small town for different reasons'*? Use evidence from Figs 4, 5 and 6 to support your conclusion. [4]

(e) To extend their fieldwork, the students decided to investigate the sphere of influence of the shops and services in the town. The sphere of influence is the area where people who use the shops and services live. Describe how they could carry out the fieldwork and show their results. [4]

**[Total: 30 marks]**

**Cambridge IGCSE Geography** — Geographical Enquiry

# Exam-Style Question 2

As part of their coursework, a class of students at a school wanted to measure and analyse various aspects of the weather in the school grounds. They decided to test two hypotheses:

**Hypothesis 1:** 'As atmospheric pressure increases so does wind speed.'

**Hypothesis 2:** 'The school receives most of its rainfall when the wind blows from the south and south-west.'

(a) The students decided to take their weather measurements during school days over a period of two weeks. For Hypothesis 1, pairs of students took it in turns to measure the wind speed and the atmospheric pressure.
Students recorded the wind speed by using an anemometer.
Atmospheric pressure was measured using the barometer shown in Fig. 1, which was kept in a Stevenson Screen.

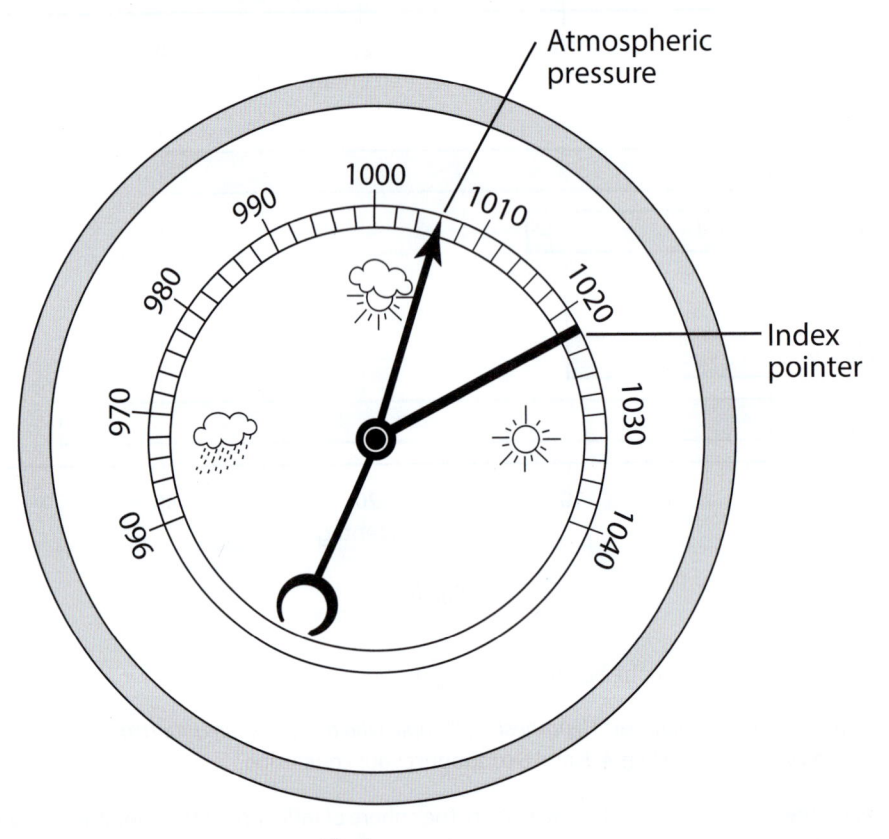

**Fig. 1**

(i) Describe how the barometer shown in Fig. 1 measures atmospheric pressure. [3]
(ii) What is the atmospheric pressure shown in Fig. 1? [1]
(b) (i) Complete the sentences below to explain the structure of a Stevenson Screen. [3]

| |
|---|
| It is painted white so that ................................................................................................ |
| The box has gaps in its side so that ..................................................................................... |
| The instruments are kept in a box at least 1.25 metres from the ground so that ........................ ................................................................................................................................. |

**Fig. 2**

# Exam-Style Question 2

(ii) A pair of students took it in turns to record the wind speed indicated by an anemometer while another pair took it in turns to record the atmospheric pressure at the same times. They agreed to take the readings at 09.00, 12.00 and 15.00 on school days only. Their results for the two-week period in June are shown in Fig. 3 below.

**Wind speed readings (km) recorded by students at 09.00, 12.00 and 15.00**

| Day/Date | 09.00 | 12.00 | 15.00 |
|---|---|---|---|
| Monday 9 | 35 | 24 | 30 |
| Tuesday 10 | 32 | 22 | 25 |
| Wednesday 11 | 28 | 24 | 22 |
| Thursday 12 | 30 | 22 | 20 |
| Friday 13 | 28 | 16 | 28 |
| Saturday 14 | | | |
| Sunday 15 | | | |
| Monday 16 | 34 | 8 | 20 |
| Tuesday 17 | 24 | 30 | 12 |
| Wednesday 18 | 20 | 11 | 6 |
| Thursday 19 | 18 | 9 | 12 |
| Friday 20 | 12 | 6 | 10 |
| **Average wind speed** | 26.1 | 17.2 | 18.5 |

**Atmospheric pressure readings (mb) recorded by students at 09.00, 12.00 and 15.00**

| Day/Date | 09.00 | 12.00 | 15.00 |
|---|---|---|---|
| Monday 9 | 996 | 1008 | 998 |
| Tuesday 10 | 998 | 1008 | 1000 |
| Wednesday 11 | 1000 | 1012 | 1004 |
| Thursday 12 | 1002 | 1010 | 1005 |
| Friday 13 | 1002 | 1014 | 1006 |
| Saturday 14 | | | |
| Sunday 15 | | | |
| Monday 16 | 998 | 1022 | 1010 |
| Tuesday 17 | 1004 | 1024 | 1022 |
| Wednesday 18 | 1008 | 1020 | 1022 |
| Thursday 19 | 1010 | 1016 | 1024 |
| Friday 20 | 1014 | 1018 | 1002 |
| **Average pressure** | 1003.2 | 1015.2 | |

Work out the average atmospheric pressure for 15.00 hours and insert it into the table above. [2]

**Fig. 3**

(iii) What does 'mb' stand for? [1]
(iv) The students chose to measure the weather every three hours. Circle below what this type of sampling technique is called.
  Random       Stratified       Systematic [1]
(v) Suggest **two** reasons why the students chose to take the measurements every three hours at 09.00, 12.00 and 15.00. [2]
(vi) The students produced a scatter graph from these recordings. This is shown as Fig. 4.

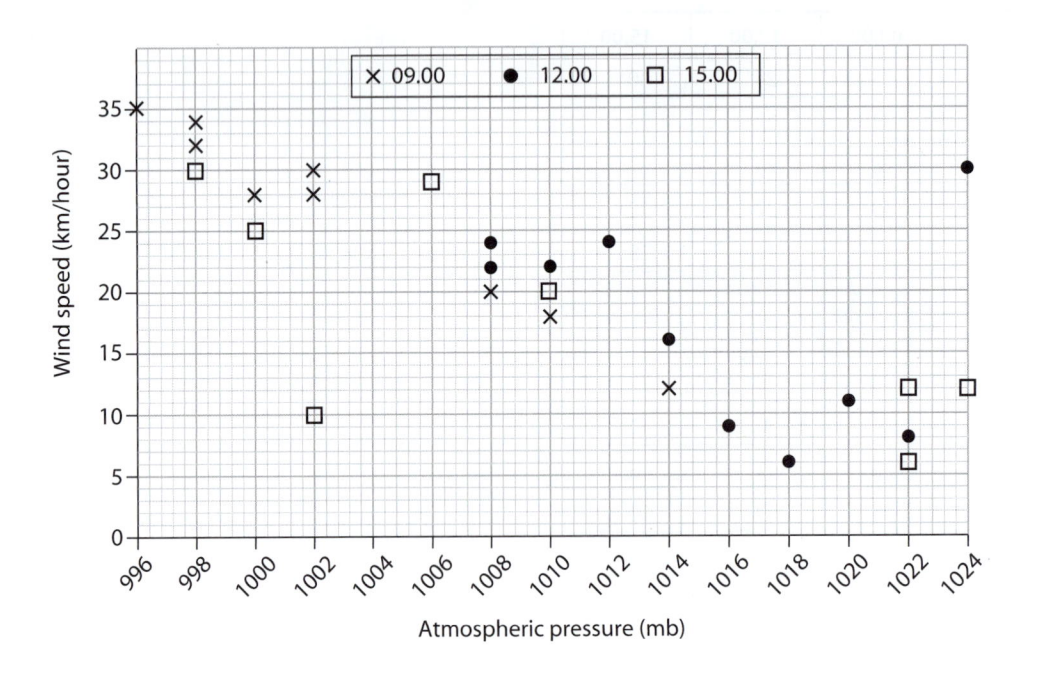

**Fig. 4**

Complete the graph for 15.00 hours by plotting the data from Fig. 3 for Wednesday, 11 June and Thursday, 12 June and then adding a best-fit line to this graph. [3]

(vii) What was the students' conclusion about *Hypothesis 1: 'As atmospheric pressure increases so does wind speed'*?
Use evidence from Figs 3 and 4 to support your decision. [4]

(c) While some students had been recording atmospheric pressure and wind speed, another group of students took it in turns to monitor wind direction and rainfall. To do this they used a wind vane and a rain gauge. Both instruments are shown below in Fig. 5.

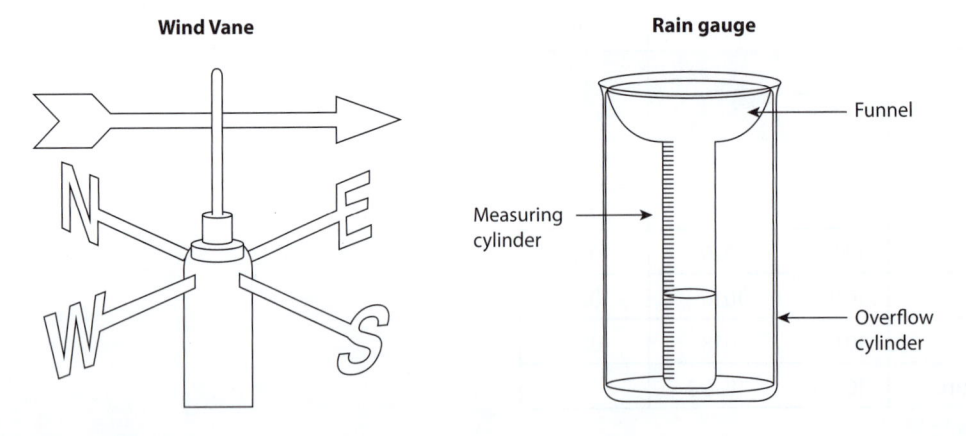

**Wind Vane**    **Rain gauge**

**Fig. 5**

(i) Choose **one** of these instruments and describe where it should be located and why it should be located there.
Circle instrument chosen:     Wind vane        Rain gauge
Location – where and why? [3]

**Exam-Style Question 2**

(ii) These students recorded their data at 09.00 for the same two-week period as shown in Fig. 6 below.

| Day/Date | Wind direction | Rainfall (mm) |
|---|---|---|
| Monday 9 | South-west | 8 |
| Tuesday 10 | South | 6 |
| Wednesday 11 | West | 3 |
| Thursday 12 | South | 9 |
| Friday 13 | North-west | 2 |
| Saturday 14 | | |
| Sunday 15 | | |
| Monday 16 | South | 5 |
| Tuesday 17 | South-east | 2 |
| Wednesday 18 | East | 1 |
| Thursday 19 | South-east | 0 |
| Friday 20 | South-west | 4 |
| **Total** | | **40** |

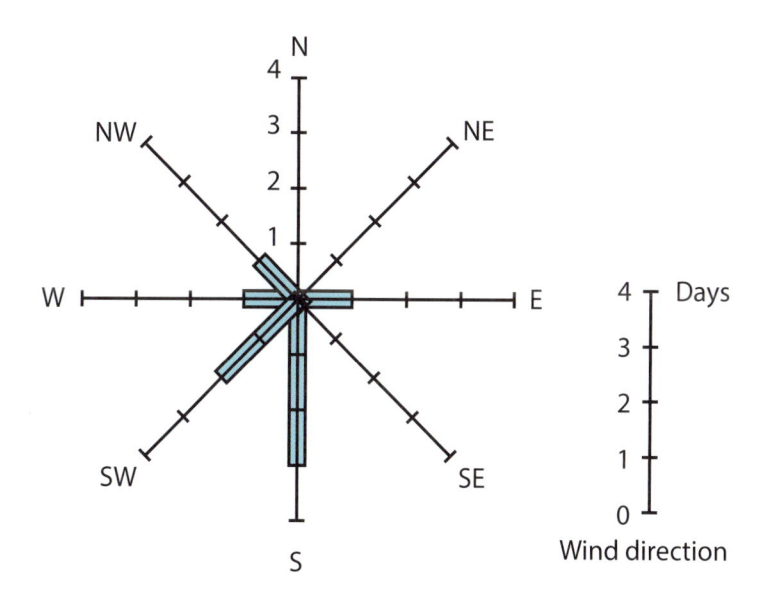

**Fig. 6**

The students plotted the wind direction data as a wind rose shown in Fig. 6 above. Complete the wind rose by plotting the wind direction data for winds from the south-east. [1]

(iii) What was the students' conclusion about *Hypothesis 2*: *'The school receives most of its rainfall when the wind blows from the south and south-west'*? Circle your choice below.

    True        Partly true        False [1]

(iv) Explain your decision in (iii) above using evidence from Fig 6. [2]

(d) After completing the fieldwork, the students discussed ways in which they could have improved their methods to make the results and conclusions more reliable. Suggest **three** improvements they could have made. [3]

[Total: 30 marks]

# Part D

# Preparing for Examinations

The next few pages will help you to prepare for examinations and to understand how the knowledge and skills that you have developed throughout this course are likely to be assessed. Example questions from previous examinations are followed by a variety of answers (written by the authors), as well as commentaries to help you realise what is good and bad practice. Studying these carefully will enable you to improve your own responses to examination questions and your overall achievement.

# Geographical Themes: Case Studies

The next four pages provide examples of student answers to case studies which are each worth 7 out of 25 marks. (These questions are from Cambridge IGCSE Geography 0460 Paper 11, Q1c, 4c and 5c, June 2012.) Note that all answers, marks and comments have been created by the authors. One question has been chosen from each theme and, for each one, three responses of different quality are provided and commented on.

Before studying each answer it is important that you understand how the mark scheme works. A 'Level of Response' mark scheme is used to mark the case studies. It is the overall quality that determines which level an answer is awarded rather than the number of correct statements contained within it. However, once assigned to a level, the mark achieved within that level is determined by the number of points made.

Levels 1 and 2 are distinguished by whether statements are simple (Level 1) or developed (Level 2). In order to achieve Level 3 a student must have already reached the top end of Level 2 – in addition the answer should have a clear example and include place-specific information as well:

**Level 1**: Simple individual points. (1–3 marks)
In order to score the full 3 marks students need to write three correct simple statements.

**Level 2**: Developed statements. (4–6 marks)
In order to score the full 6 marks students need to give an appropriate named example and write three correct developed statements.

**Level 3**: A comprehensive answer, including developed statements and place-specific detail. (7 marks)

In order to score the 7 marks, students need to give an appropriate named example and write three correct developed statements. Part of the answer should include place-specific detail and all parts of the question must be answered.

The commentary and examples below will help you to understand how the marking scheme works and your teacher will explain it in detail as you go through the answers.

**A** Theme 1: Population and Settlement

**B** Theme 2: The Natural Environment

**C** Theme 3: Economic Development

# Preparing for Examinations

## Theme 1: Population and Settlement

For an example of international migration which you have studied, name the countries between which people moved. Explain why many people made the decision to migrate. You should refer both to pull and to push factors. [7]

*Cambridge IGCSE Geography 0460 Paper 11, Q1c June 2012. Reproduced by permission of Cambridge International Examinations.*

---

**Answer 1:**

From Mexico to USA

Mexico is a very dangerous country. Since 2006 many drug deaths are occurring. USA's pull factors are that it is very secure and well policed, with less chance of being affected by crime. Also with 10 000 persons per doctor in some parts of rural Mexico that is very poor health care and in USA there is 400 people per doctor so the health care is much better. As a result the death rate in Mexico is higher and life expectancy is longer in the USA.

Also in USA there is a lot of low paid jobs that Mexicans are able to do which are not available in their country. A lot of them move to areas like California to work as gardeners and cleaners.

---

**Answer 2:**

From Poland to UK

People make decisions to migrate because of either push or pull factors. The pull factors that bring people to the UK are better paying jobs, better education and better health care. The Polish people move to UK to find a better job so that they can earn more money and afford more luxuries. They want their children to have better education so they will be able to get a better job in the future.

---

**Answer 3:**

From Somalia to France

In Somalia there has been a war and famine so they move to France where there is no war or famine. In France they also get better education and jobs. They also have equal rights when they get there.

---

**Comment**

All examples chosen are suitable and offer lots of scope for students to explain why the migration took place. Indeed all three students offer several valid ideas, though the answers vary in quality.

Answer 3 identifies five simple ideas: war, famine, education, jobs and equal rights. However none of these ideas are really developed, so the answer meets the Level 1 criteria. As there are at least three simple statements this answer has been given a mark at the top of Level 1.

Answer 2 refers to only three ideas but meets Level 2 criteria as two of these ideas are developed; the fact that better paying jobs would enable people to afford more luxuries, and (with better education) it would be possible for their children to get a good job in the future. The third idea (better health care) is only a simple statement so the answer only has two valid developed statements and has been given a mid-range mark within the Level 2 criteria.

Answer 1 is a Level 3 answer that meets all the criteria in full. The case study chosen is valid and there are place-specific references (such as 'California' and the comparative statistics for Mexico and the USA). Three clear ideas are well developed: the references to safety, health care and employment, and both the factors which pull migrants to the USA are mentioned along with those which push people away from Mexico. Therefore the answer is comprehensive, with developed statements and place-specific detail.

# Cambridge IGCSE Geography — Preparing for Examinations

## Theme 2: The Natural Environment

For a named example which you have studied, explain why people live close to a volcano. [7]

*Cambridge IGCSE Geography 0460 Paper 11, Q4c June 2012. Reproduced by permission of Cambridge International Examinations.*

---

**Answer 1:**

Vesuvius

Next to Vesuvius is the city of Naples which is visited by many tourists. People living there can make money as tourists' guides as many visitors want to see the volcano. When people were born and raised there they do not want to move because they have friends and relatives they do not want to move away from. They are willing to take a risk as they know volcanoes do not erupt often and they are confident that if Vesuvius does erupt they will get a warning so they can escape. They also live there as it is very close to the seaport at Naples where there are lots of jobs.

---

**Answer 2:**

Mt Merapi

People live close to Merapi for a number of reasons. Crops grown near a volcano can be very successful and produce high yields as near the volcano the soil is very fertile. Also people like to live close to volcanoes because they are tourist attractions so a lot of tourists visit the area which can be good for hotels, shops and services which will all benefit from the tourists. Many of the people who live near the volcano are too poor to move as they are subsistence farmers so they have no choice but to stay there.

---

**Answer 3:**

Sierra Nevada de Santa Marta

People live here because it is their home. Others because all the family live there. Some farmers grow crops near the volcano. If they wanted to move people would not be able to afford to. There are lots of opportunities because tourists go there and the people wish that the volcano stays asleep.

---

### Comment

All three answers include some valid points, explaining why people live close to a volcano.

As Answer 3 has not named a valid example of a volcano (as Sierra Nevada de Santa Marta is a mountain area in Colombia which is not volcanic) only the simple ideas shown are acceptable for credit. Without a valid example answers can still score up to five marks within Level 2, however none of the ideas in Answer 3 are developed so it remains a response at the top of Level 1.

Answer 2 referred to Mt Merapi, which is an active volcano in Indonesia. The three points made are all clear and developed so the answer has been given a mark at the top end of Level 2. It cannot be a Level 3 answer as the answer has no place-specific detail other than naming the volcano. Compare this answer with Answer 3 and you will see the difference between simple and developed statements. For example Answer 3 simply states that 'farmers grow crops near the volcano' compared with Answer 2 which develops the idea by stating that 'crops grown near a volcano can be very successful and produce high yields as near the volcano the soil is very fertile'. The only thing that this answer lacks is place-specific detail; reading through this answer, it could apply to any volcano.

Answer 1 provides place-specific detail. Note the reference to Naples which is close to Mt Vesuvius. This answer also develops several ideas: how many developed ideas can you find and what are they? With at least three ideas being developed and the Naples reference it is a Level 3 response that meets all the criteria in full.

# Preparing for Examinations

## Theme 3: Economic Development

For a named area which you have studied, explain how tourism is damaging the **natural environment**. [7]

Cambridge IGCSE Geography 0460 Paper 11, Q5c June 2012. Reproduced by permission of Cambridge International Examinations.

**Answer 1:**

Caroni Swamp, Trinidad

The Caroni Swamp, where the Caroni River meets the Gulf of Paria is the home to the national bird of Trinidad, the Scarlet Ibis, which makes it a major tourist attraction. Many tourists visit the Caroni Bird Sanctuary and some drop litter in the area and due to this some birds have died after swallowing plastic. Species of plants have been destroyed as parts of the marshes have been drained to build tourist facilities and this has resulted in the loss of habitat of creatures living there. The loss of marsh vegetation had also meant that the food chain has been disrupted and some birds which live on fish now have migrated from the area so biodiversity in the area is being reduced.

**Answer 2:**

The Bahamas

Resorts are set up near to the coast. They have to clear lots of land for them to build them so many trees are lost which destroys animal habitats. Their waste disposal pollutes the air and water. Artificial beaches and structural changes to the coastline have increased coastal erosion.

**Answer 3:**

Wasatch Mountains

Many ski resorts are located in the Wasatch Mountains and roads have been cut into the mountain. The trees are cut down to build ski runs. Wildlife is scared by noise from the skiers. The natural beauty has been spoiled because of all the buildings and the air is polluted by people driving cars to get there.

## Comment

It is very useful to use local examples as it is easier for students to include place-specific details if the case study is known personally to them. Tourism is an ideal topic to use local examples as all countries have areas which are important for tourism.

Answer 1 is the highest quality response. Notice the place-specific details included: the references to the Scarlet Ibis, The Caroni Bird Sanctuary and the Gulf of Paria. References to the impacts of litter from tourists, along with the draining of marshland and disruption to the food chain due to the construction of tourist facilities, are all well developed. The answer therefore has been given a mark in Level 3 as it meets all the criteria in full.

Answer 2 refers to the Bahamas though no place-specific information is included. It does include, however, several impacts of tourism on the natural environment, one of which is developed: the reference to the clearance of trees which leads to loss of habitat. None of the other valid ideas included, such as air and water pollution or the increase of coastal erosion, are developed. With one developed statement the answer has been given a mark at the bottom end of Level 2.

Answer 3 achieves only Level 1 as all the points made are simple points.

**Can you think of ways in which each impact on the natural environment could have been developed to move the answer into Level 2?**

As the area is known to the student, it should have been easy to include some place-specific detail, such as the name of a ski resort in the area or the number of one of the roads which has been cut into the mountain. These improvements would have changed the answer to a Level 3 answer. However, without them, it is a response at the top end of Level 1 only. **Do you understand why?**

# Geographical Skills

There are six questions in the Geographical Skills examination which is worth 60 marks. Question 1, which is always based on a 1:25 000 or 1:50 000 scale map, is worth 20 marks. Although a large map extract with a key is provided in the examination, that would be impractical to reproduce in a textbook. Instead, responses to questions that may prove difficult have been given to illustrate the different quality of possible answers. (These questions are from Cambridge IGCSE Geography 0460 Paper 21 Q2 a and Q4 b June 2012.) Note that all answers, marks and comments have been created by the authors.

A student was researching the tropical rainforests of Africa on the internet. She found two maps, Fig. 4 and Fig. 5, which showed the distribution of these rainforests.

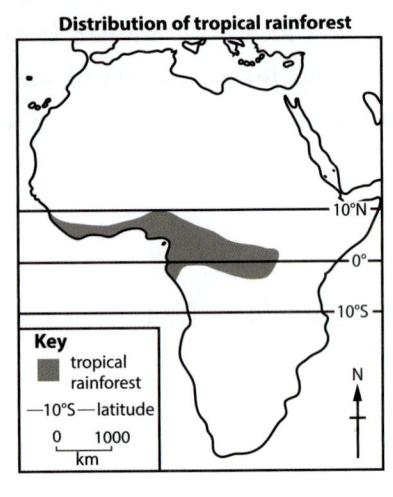

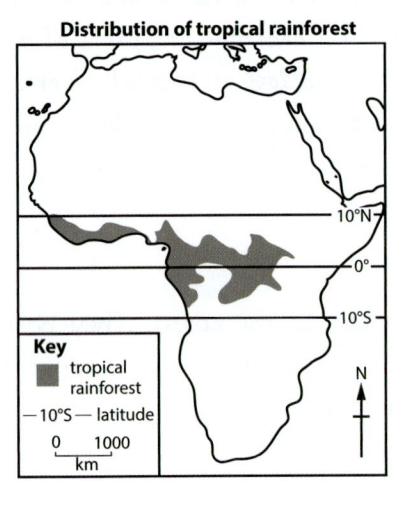

Fig. 4

Fig. 5

Describe the distribution of tropical rainforests shown on Fig. 4. [3]

Cambridge IGCSE Geography 0460 Paper 21, Q2a i June 2012. Reproduced by permission of Cambridge International Examinations.

**Answer 1:**
The rainforests shown are mainly between 10°N and 10°S parallel. They are on the west side of Africa. Much of these forests are along the coastline and then stretch inland to the middle of Africa.

**Answer 2:**
The tropical rainforests shown on Fig. 4 are located between the Tropic of Capricorn and Cancer, but more on the Tropic of Cancer between 0 and 10° N at the west side of Africa (it is concentrated at this side).

**Answer 3:**
The majority of the distribution is between 0 and 10°N. No rainforest over 10°N and none over 10°S. Majority on east coast of Africa or the middle.

**Comment**
Most of these three students have studied the correct map and made some worthwhile distribution points. Answer 1 correctly describes the rainforests' location between the 10°N and 10°S lines of latitude, notes that they are on the west side and also along the coast, and so fulfil the requirements of the question for full marks. In Answer 2 there can be no credit for references to the two Tropics as they are not marked on the map and it is a knowledge answer rather than a skill-based answer using the map. However, the student does note that the rainforests are between 0° and 10° N and they are concentrated on the west side so gains some credit for that. Answer 3 gains minimum credit for only noting where they are and does not gain any credit for noting where they are not. This answer also mistakenly refers to the east coast instead of the west coast. (Students are expected to know the 16-point compass in this syllabus so the 8-point compass should not be a problem.)

# Preparing for Examinations

*Cambridge IGCSE Geography 0460 Paper 21, Q4b June 2012. Reproduced by permission of Cambridge International Examinations.*
Fig. 6 shows settlements in a rural area.

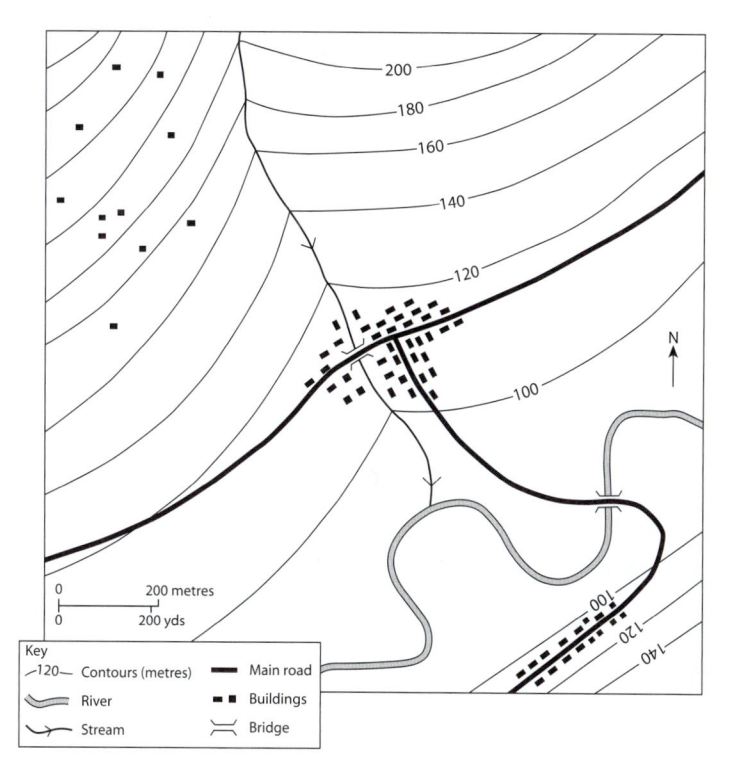

**Fig. 6**

### Comment
Part (a) of this question requires students to locate an area of Dispersed (D), Linear (L), and Nucleated (N) settlement on the map (Fig.6). This is a straightforward question to answer but the follow-up question (b) below might prove a bit tricky!

Look at the settlement in the centre of Fig. 6. Explain how the site and position of this settlement have been influenced by each of the following factors:
**transport and accessibility;** [1]

### Answer 1:
Traffic can reach this area easily and the river can provide water for the horses to drink.

### Answer 2:
There are two main roads, one going from NE to SW and the other towards the south of the town so it is easy to travel and for transport it is accessible.

### Answer 3:
It is a bridging point as many communication routes such as roads and the river cross their paths here therefore a settlement has developed here as the site is accessible.

### Comment
Reference is needed to either the bridge (bridging point) across the river or the road junction to gain the mark. Answers 2 and 3 give acceptable responses; note that Answer 3 actually covers both points though only one is required. Answer 1 does not get the mark; it does not refer to the reason why traffic can reach this point easily i.e. where two roads meet, and the reference to drinking water is more relevant to the next section (water supply) than to transport and accessibility.

**water supply;** [1]

| **Answer 1:** |
|---|
| When the settlement was first built here, the water in the stream could be used for people and animals to drink and wash. |

| **Answer 2:** |
|---|
| The river would provide water for domestic activities. |

| **Answer 3:** |
|---|
| There is a stream. |

| **Comment** |
|---|
| This is a straightforward question which requires students to use the key and link the stream and river to water supply. The first two answers cover all that is required; they have both made a point that links water supply to aspects of settlement e.g. drinking, washing and domestic activities. Answer 3 recognises the existence of a stream but needs a little more as the question is about linking settlement location to water supply. |

**relief and drainage.** [3]

| **Answer 1:** |
|---|
| The stream runs down towards a river so quick and easy drainage, plus they are on a slight hill so drainage would be easier and so would defending the town. |

| **Answer 2:** |
|---|
| The relief in this area is gradual, rising to the north at about 20 metres every 150 metres travelled. This would allow water to drain away into the valley but past the settlement. This is above the valley floor so it would not flood unless there was a monsoon which made the river fill the whole valley floor. |

| **Answer 3:** |
|---|
| It is not a high place because there is a stream flowing. Where the main road is far there are less people. There are always concentrations of people near rivers and roads, rivers for peopwle and roads to get to work or malls (CBD). |

| **Comment** |
|---|
| Relief (i.e. the shape and height of the land) and drainage are topics that students sometimes find difficult. Three points are required here but it is possible to develop one point to get 2 marks. Answer 1 recognises the gentle slope linked to easy drainage for minimum credit. Answer 3 provides a lot of irrelevant information; reference to low height is not linked to settlement growth so this is a poor response. Answer 2, however, shows good understanding with references to gradual changes in height (with data from the map), links to drainage and the settlement avoiding flooding by its location above the valley floor. The monsoon reference is of local relevance. |

# Preparing for Examinations

# The Alternative to Coursework

The Alternative to Coursework examination consists of two questions: one is usually based on physical geography and the other on human geography. The following pages are from Cambridge IGCSE Geography 0460 Paper 41 Q2 June 2012, with a variety of responses that illustrate good and bad practice and commentaries where relevant. Note that all answers, marks and comments have been created by the authors.

**A question from June 2012**

Students wanted to find out more about the conditions in two squatter settlements in a city in Bangladesh. Settlement A had grown up in the last 15 years and settlement B had grown rapidly in the last three years. They decided to investigate the following hypotheses:

**Hypothesis 1:** *Services in squatter settlement A are better than services in squatter settlement B.*
**Hypothesis 2:** *Family homes in squatter settlement A are more crowded than homes in squatter settlement B.*

> **Comment**
> When an examination starts, many students are keen to get writing but there is plenty of time to read and understand the context of a question. It is vital that students do this because they will then understand the set-up for the investigation before answering questions on it. Students who do not read the context carefully do not score well on later questions that may ask how the methods of investigation could have been improved. For example, some students will say that 'they should have worked in pairs' when the context at the start told them they were working in pairs anyway. Such careless errors can be avoided by reading the introduction to questions carefully.

(a) The students decided to investigate their hypotheses by using a questionnaire with 100 people who lived in each squatter settlement.
(i) Describe a suitable sampling method for the students to choose people to interview.
Explain why you have chosen this method.
[2]

> **Answer 1:**
> Choose every 10th person to walk past because then there is no personal preference or bias of the asker and there is a chance for any type of person. This is called systematic sampling.

> **Answer 2:**
> Systematic sampling. They hand out the questionnaire to every 10th person.

> **Answer 3:**
> The student could visit various homes along a transect line and hand out the survey to the residents in order to obtain unbiased results via the transect line and to assess the people who live in the squatter settlements.

> **Comment**
> Knowledge and understanding of three key sampling techniques—systematic, random and stratified—are often tested in this examination. There are 2 marks available here; 1 for describing or stating a sampling technique and 1 for explaining the choice. Answer 2 states what systematic sampling involves but does not say why it was chosen so cannot gain both marks. Answer 3 does not describe a technique and using a transect line is an inappropriate method to interview people anyway so gains no credit. Answer 1, however has stated a technique, described it and explained how it avoids bias and can target anybody. This meets the requirements for both marks. Stratified or random sampling would be acceptable answers here too.

(ii) Fig. 4, opposite, is the questionnaire which the students used. In the spaces provided on Fig. 4 add **two** other age groups which are appropriate for classifying the people interviewed. Two age groups have already been included. [2]

> **Comment**
> It is important, when devising a questionnaire with different ranges of age groups, that no age can fit into two groups; the groups must be 'mutually exclusive'. The ideal answers would be 15–35 then 36–60. This ensures that those interviewees under 15, 35 or 36 and over 60 could not be ticked in two groups. One mark would likely be gained for acceptable ranges; another for avoiding an overlap between categories. So why are the following answers wrong:
>
> - 16–35 then 36–59?
> - 15–35 then 35–50?
> - 15–36 then 36–60?
> - Over 15 then Under 35?

(iii) Complete the partly completed example of a questionnaire given in Fig. 4 by adding the following answers from a resident. Put ticks in the correct boxes on Fig. 4. [1]

| |
|---|
| I get my water from a tap in the street |
| I do not have a toilet in my house so my family has to use the public toilet |
| I get electricity from a cable installed by the city authority |
| I have two rooms in my home |
| There are six people in my family home |

> **Comment**
> Answers should show ticks in the correct box for each of the five questions that were asked on the questionnaire. In answering questions on the Alternative to Coursework examination, it is important to realise that there are always a lot of graphs, tables and other information in diagrammatic form and that between these there are questions to answer. Students can easily miss these questions if they do not take care.

(iv) Suggest **two** 'other' sources of water supply in a squatter settlement in addition to those listed in the questionnaire. [2]

Cambridge IGCSE Geography 0460 Paper 41, Q2a i, ii, iii, iv June 2012. Reproduced by permission of Cambridge International Examinations.

**Answer 1:**
1 From a well (either public or privately owned).
2 From a river or stream nearby.

**Answer 2:**
1 Pipes
2 –

**Answer 3:**
1 Rainwater
2 Water bottles

> **Comment**
> It was important for students to notice the word 'other' in the question. Answers that duplicated those in the questionnaire, such as standpipes or taps in the home, cannot gain credit. Most students could give a river or stream; other acceptable answers include wells, water tanks, road tankers and water bottles. Here, Answer 1 meets the requirements in full, Answer 2 only gives one answer and is too vague to credit. Answer 3 gets credit for 'water bottles' but none for 'rainwater' which, on its own, is not a source of water supply but a source of water from which a supply can be created.

**Preparing for Examinations**

## Resident Questionnaire

Squatter settlement A ✓  B ☐

Age group

Under 15 ✓  _____ ☐  _____ ☐  Over 60 ☐

Gender  Male ✓  Female ☐

**Question 1**

Where do you get your water supply?

- Standpipe (tap in the street) ☐
- Tap in the home ☐
- Other ☐

**Question 2**

What are your toilet facilities?

- Public toilet ☐
- Toilet in the home ☐

**Question 3**

How do you get your electricity supply?

- No electricity supply ☐
- From the city authority ☐
- By attaching a cable into the official supply ☐

**Question 4**

How many rooms are there in your family home?

1 ☐   2 ☐   3 ☐   4 or more ☐

**Question 5**

How many people live in your family home?

1 ☐   2 ☐   3 ☐   4 or more ☐

Fig. 4

**Cambridge IGCSE Geography** — Preparing for Examinations

(v) Suggest why some people may not give a true answer to the question 'How do you get your electricity supply?' [1]

> **Comment**
> Answers relating to people tapping illegally into the electricity supply would be credited, as would answers suggesting that people may not want to admit to this due to shame or embarrassment. Answers suggesting that by admitting to illegal activity in the questionnaire they could be found out and prosecuted would also be credited.

(b) The students produced a results table for each question.

**Table 2**

**Answers to Question 1: Where do you get your water supply?**

|  | Settlement A (%) | Settlement B (%) |
| --- | --- | --- |
| Standpipe (tap in street) | 18 | 38 |
| Tap in the home | 72 | 5 |
| Other | 10 | 57 |

(i) Use the results in Table 2 to complete the divided bar graph for settlement A on Fig. 5 below. [3]

**Where people get their water supply from**

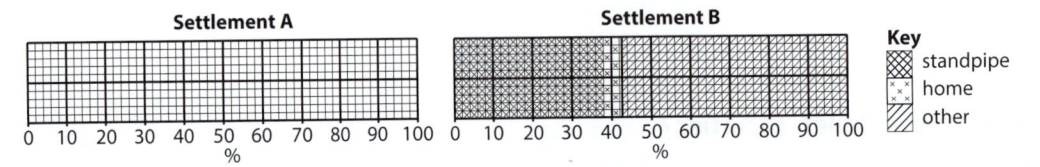

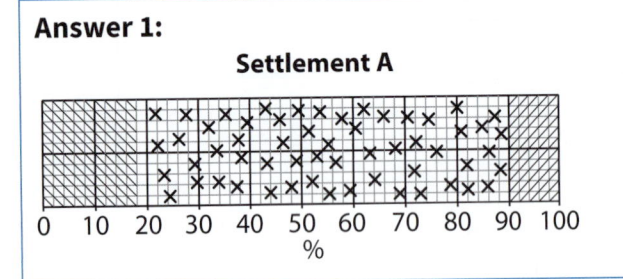

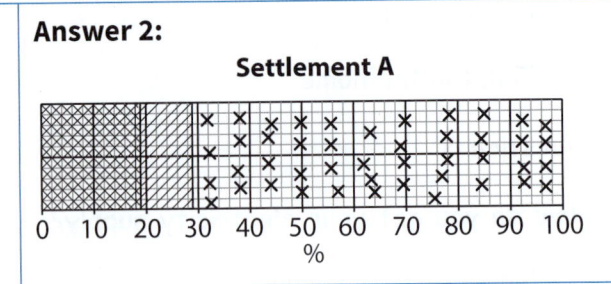

Settlement A / Settlement B

Key: standpipe, home, other

**Answer 1:** Settlement A

**Answer 2:** Settlement A

**Answer 3:** Settlement A

> **Comment**
> Here, there are two lines to plot at 18% and then along a further 72% (i.e. at 90%). The completed settlement B graph shows the order in which the different water supplies should be plotted and the key indicates the shading to be used. There is 1 mark available for each correct plot and 1 for the shading. Answer 1 is perfect; the two plots are correct and plotted from the left side of the bar and the shading is correct using the provided key. Answer 2 has the correct shading for the bars but the plotting is not in the correct order, with 72% plotted last instead of in the middle. Therefore, this has only been given marks for the correct plot at 18% and for the shading being correct in relation to the bar size. Answer 3 has not plotted the 'Other' 10% information so only gets the mark for the correct plot at 18%. Here, although the shading is correct, there are only two bars to shade.

# Preparing for Examinations

### Table 3
**Answers to Question 2: What are your toilet facilities?**

|  | Settlement A (%) | Settlement B (%) |
|---|---|---|
| Public toilet | 49 | 100 |
| Toilet in the home | 51 | 0 |

### Table 4
**Answers to Question 3: How do you get your electricity supply?**

|  | Settlement A (%) | Settlement B (%) |
|---|---|---|
| No electricity supply | 2 | 36 |
| From the city authority | 80 | 17 |
| By attaching a cable into the official supply | 18 | 47 |

(ii) Use the results in Table 4 to complete the bar graph for settlement A on Fig. 6 below. [2]

**How do people get their electricity supply?**

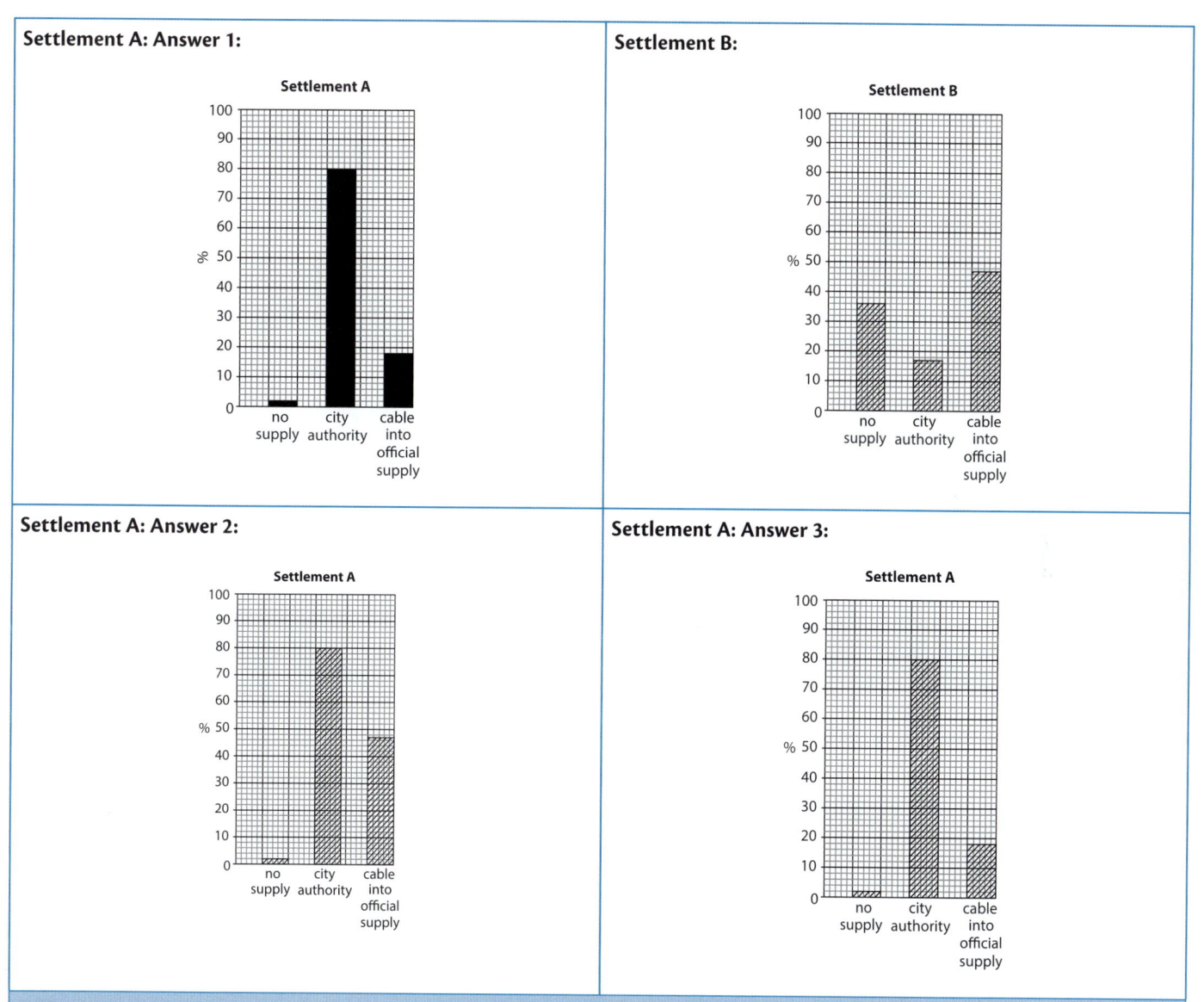

Settlement A: Answer 1:

Settlement B:

Settlement A: Answer 2:

Settlement A: Answer 3:

### Comment

Here, 1 mark is available for plotting the two bars at 80% and 18%; a second mark is for the correct shading based on B. **Answer 3 is worth full marks; can you see why?** Answer 2 makes a mistake in the third bar because they have read the wrong part of Table 4. **Check this out above.** The two plots on Answer 1 are correct for the plotting mark but the student does not use the cross-hatch style of shading on the Settlement B graph; therefore no shading mark has been credited.

(iii) Do the results in Tables 2, 3 and 4 support **Hypothesis 1**: 'Services in squatter settlement A are better than services in squatter settlement B.'? Use information from the tables to explain your answer. [4]

> **Answer 1:**
> It is correct. Settlement A is better than settlement B in each of three services. 72% of people in A get their water supply from the tap in their house much more than the 5% in B. Just under half use public toilets because 51% have private toilets in A but in B all 100% have to use public toilets which is the whole population. They have no private toilets of their own in B. Few people in A, only a 2% do not have electricity but in B much more at 36% do not have electricity. In conclusion with the data given settlement A provides better services than B.

> **Answer 2:**
> No, hypothesis is correct because of evidence in Tables 2, 3 and 4. Table 2 shows that the majority of people in settlement A have taps in their homes (72%). Table 3 shows that there are more toilets in home (51%) than public toilets (49%). Table 4 shows that settlement A has 80% of people who have city authority for electricity.

> **Answer 3:**
> Every table fits with Hypothesis 1 except for the table about electricity is debatable but for the most part Hypothesis 1 is extremely accurate and fits in with the tables that show Hypothesis 1 is accurate and living in settlement A is much better than living in settlement B.

> **Comment**
> Answer 1 is an excellent response. First the student makes a decision about the hypothesis, stating it to be correct, and then uses data from three different services – water supply, toilets, electricity – to back this decision up. The student also compares settlement A and B with data and words such as 'more than' and 'only'.
>
> Answer 2 is confused by using the word 'No' but then stating it to be correct. This is a difficult answer to credit as the decision is uncertain and, although it provides data, it is all about settlement A so does not compare any evidence with B to justify the hypothesis being correct; therefore, it has not been given any credit. Answer 3 has a lot of words that say little; it has been given 1 mark for the judgement that the hypothesis is accurate – but no evidence for this is provided.

(c) The results of questions 4 and 5 are shown in Table 5 below and in Table 6 on page 280.

Table 5

Answers to Question 4: How many rooms are there in your family home?

|  | Settlement A (%) | Settlement B (%) |
|---|---|---|
| 1 room | 39 | 64 |
| 2 rooms | 23 | 30 |
| 3 rooms | 25 | 6 |
| 4 or more rooms | 13 | 0 |

(i) Use the results in Table 5 to complete Fig. 7 below. [2]

**Settlement A: Number of rooms in the family home**

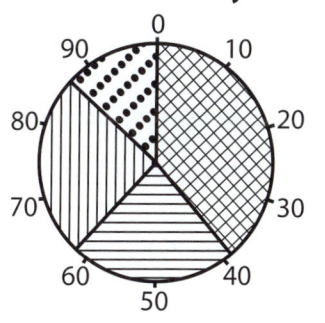

**Settlement B: Number of rooms in the family home**

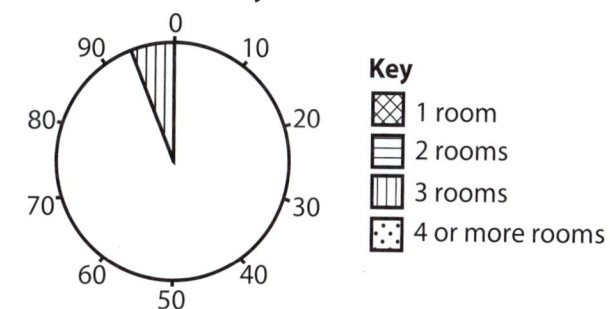

**Key**
- 1 room
- 2 rooms
- 3 rooms
- 4 or more rooms

Fig. 7

---

**Answer 1:**

Settlement B: Number of rooms in the family home

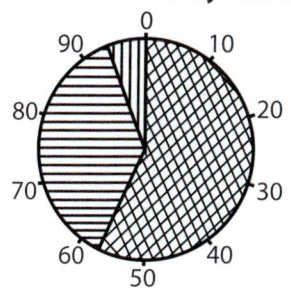

**Answer 2:**

Settlement B: Number of rooms in the family home

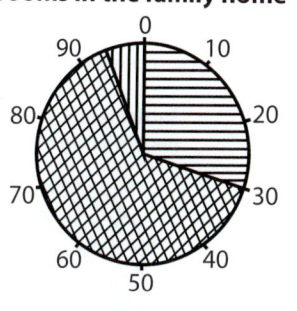

**Answer 3:**

Settlement B: Number of rooms in the family home

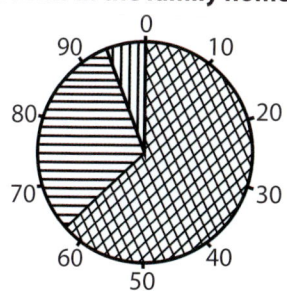

**Comment**

Here the students are required to plot the number of rooms in settlement B on the pie chart which has the 6% slice for '3 rooms' already plotted and shaded. As the '4 or more rooms' data was 0% all that is required is one line plot at 64% and the correct shading either side of it using the key provided. It is a convention that pie charts are plotted in a clockwise order and the completed chart for settlement A and the shading order dictate how B should have been completed. This would probably receive 1 mark for the plot and 1 mark for shading the two slices correctly using the key.

Which answer is correct in plotting and shading so can gain the full 2 marks?

Which answer plots the line correctly but in an anti-clockwise order?

Which answer plots the line at 56%? Why have they done this?

All three answers have been given the mark for shading as they have all shaded the slices correctly according to size and by using the provided shading key.

(ii) Use the information in Table 5 and Fig. 7 to complete the following sentences. Circle your answer.
The most common number of rooms in a family home in settlement B is **1 / 2 / 3**.
Settlement A has a **smaller / larger / same** percentage of homes with at least 3 or 4 rooms compared with settlement B. [2]

> **Comment**
> The answers are '1' and 'larger'; most students can choose the correct answers. You must look carefully at every page for questions such as this. They often come between diagrams and may be easily missed as you work your way through an examination.

**Table 6**
**Answers to Question 5: How many people live in your family home?**

|  | Settlement A (%) | Settlement B (%) |
|---|---|---|
| 1 person | 6 | 1 |
| 2 people | 12 | 3 |
| 3 people | 20 | 10 |
| 4 or more people | 62 | 86 |

(iii) The results in Table 6 are shown in Fig. 8 below. Use the results in Table 6 to complete the key. [2]

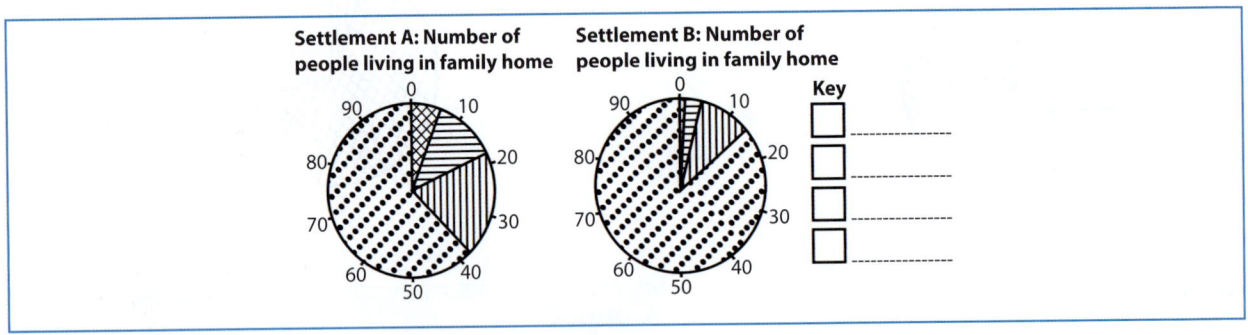

Fig. 8

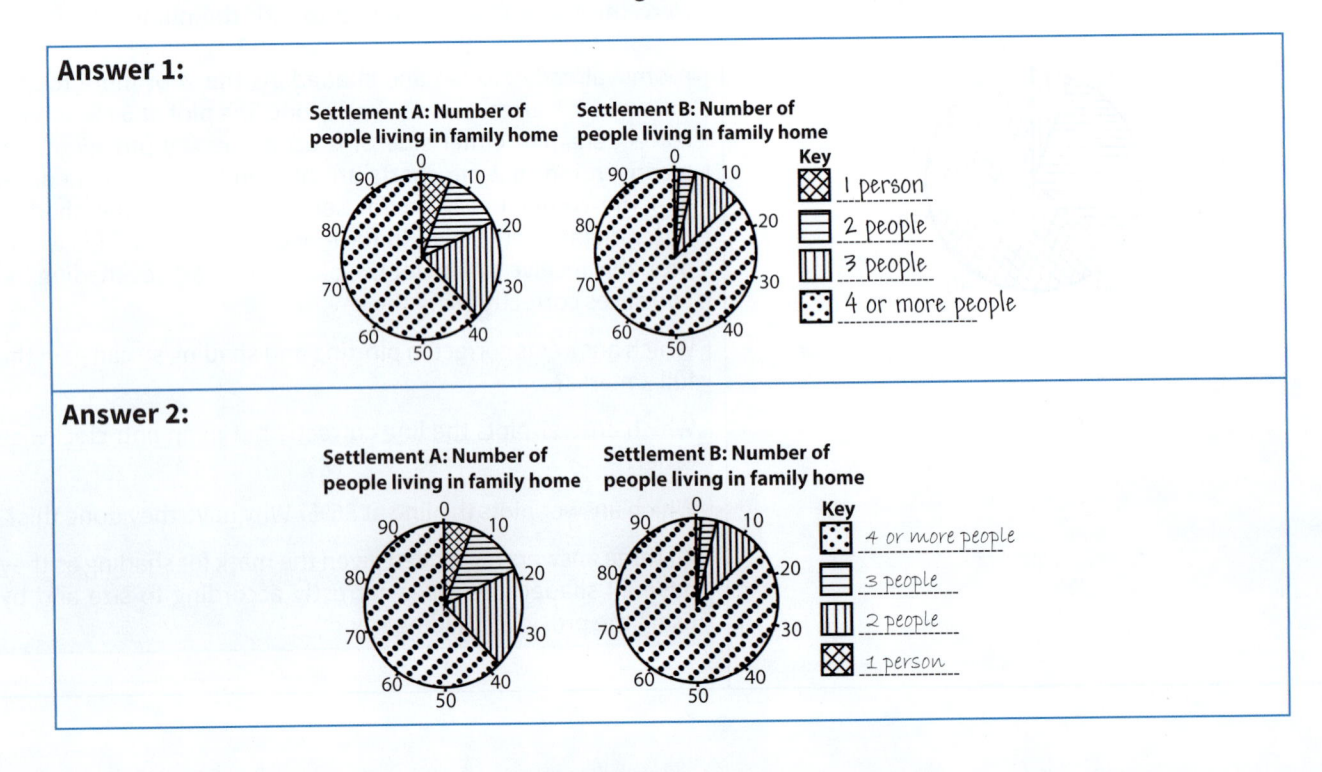

**Answer 1:**
Key:
- 1 person
- 2 people
- 3 people
- 4 or more people

**Answer 2:**
Key:
- 4 or more people
- 3 people
- 2 people
- 1 person

> **Comment**
> Here, both pie charts have been completed from the data in Table 6. Both contain 4 slices related to the different numbers of people living in rooms in Settlements A and B. This is a test to see if students knew that the key should start at '12 o clock' and go clockwise in the order of the rooms and shading provided. The previous question (c)(i) gave a clue with the lowest number at the top and the highest number as the bottom. Answer 1 does enough for both marks. Answer 2, however, gets no credit because it has the highest number at the top which does not match the order of the pie chart or data in Table 6 and it has confused the shading for 2 and 3 people.

(iv) Use the information in Table 6 and Fig. 8 to compare the number of people living in family homes in the two squatter settlements.

[2]

**Answer 1:**
In most of the homes it is usually 4 or more people living in the two settlements.

**Answer 2:**
In settlement A the majority says that 4 or more people live in their family homes as well is said in settlement B. In settlement A there are more self-living persons with 6% in A and only 1% in B.

**Answer 3:**
Both settlements have a majority of family homes containing 4+ people residing within, however settlement A has a higher percentage of 1, 2 and 3 people living in one house while also having a smaller percentage of 4+ homes with a level of 62% compared with settlement B's level at 86%.

**Answer 4:**
- In the settlement B there are usually more people living in every house, because they are more poor.
- People in settlement A live more comfortably, since there are more people living in a house with 2 or less people.

> **Comment**
> The key command word in the question is 'compare' – this means what is similar and what is different whereas the command word 'contrast' means only what is different.
>
> Although very short, Answer 1 does recognise that, in both settlements, 4 or more people is the 'most' living in homes so has been given 1 mark.
>
> Although not well expressed, Answer 2 also recognises that the majority in both settlements is 4 or more people but it also provides a difference stating that more live alone in settlement A with statistics to back this up so Answer 2 is worth both marks.
>
> Answer 3 is clearly worth both marks. It recognises the common majority of 4 or more in both settlements while also stating that A has the smaller percentage; it also recognises the difference in 1, 2 or 3 people living in the family home as it is smaller in B.
>
> Answer 4 raises some interesting issues. The data is given in percentages while the student refers to 'number of people'; as 100 were surveyed in each settlement this is acceptable but would not be if the numbers were not known or they surveyed different numbers in each settlement! The reference to 'more people living in every house' is wrong as this only applies to 86% of those surveyed in B. The comment regarding poverty is not known or needed. The student also states that in Settlement A where percentages are higher (18%) with 2 or less people living in the home, that this is more comfortable i.e. less crowded, which is true. This answer scrapes one mark for (vague) contrast with B.

**Cambridge IGCSE Geography** — Preparing for Examinations

(v) Do the results of Questions 4 and 5 support **Hypothesis 2**: 'Family homes in squatter settlement A are more crowded than homes in squatter settlement B.'? Explain your answer. [2]

> **Answer 1:**
> No – the results do not support the hypothesis. There is a larger percentage of people crowded into homes with fewer rooms in settlement B than in settlement A. 14% live in rooms with 3 people or less in B but this figure rises to 38% in A so A is less crowded than B.
>
> **Answer 2:**
> No, the hypothesis is incorrect, because thanks to the results of questions 4 and 5 we can see that population is much more bigger in squatter settlement B than in squatter settlement A.
>
> **Answer 3:**
> Yes – the hypothesis is incorrect because settlement B has a high percentage of persons living in one home when compared with the settlement A except for the first 3 responses, settlement B has 4 or more people living in one home.

**Comment**
All three answers have correctly judged the hypothesis as being incorrect despite Answer 3 initially stating Yes when they clearly mean No. Therefore, all get one mark for the hypothesis judgement. Answer 1 gets the second mark as the student has realised that, with 86% of people living in homes with 4 or more people, B is more crowded than A with 62%. They have also recognised that the higher percentage of homes with 3 or less people in A makes it less crowded. Answer 2 makes a sweeping statement about a bigger population in B than A which is not worthy of credit. Answer 3 adds nothing regarding evidence to its initial judgement; only vague statements about people living in 'one home.'

(e) Suggest three difficulties of conducting fieldwork in squatter settlements. [3]

> **Answer 1:**
> 1 It is difficult to navigate around the squatter settlements.
> 2 Some people might be unpolite when it comes to talking with the students.
> 3 Some people might be illiterate, so when they have to fill out the questionnaires, the students will have to help them.
>
> **Answer 2:**
> 1 It might be hard to find 100 people to interview in each settlement.
> 2 They could easily get lost as they might not have a map and the housing is very crowded.
> 3 There may be difficulties in language and the squatters may not want to answer questions or lie.
>
> **Answer 3:**
> 1 It is too crowded so there isn't much space.
> 2 Most likely a lot of pollution.
> 3 The soil is probably not very fertile.

**Comment**
Imagine your class was going to carry out interviews for questionnaires in squatter settlements. Look at the three answers above and decide on a rank order for which answer best suggests three difficulties you might find in carrying out your survey. The top-ranked answer should be Answer 2 which covers more than three difficulties and would get all 3 marks. Getting lost and people being rude or impolite would be acceptable answers in Answer 1 but the squatters would not be filling in the questionnaires so the third mark would not be awarded. Answer 3 makes statements that may be true of squatter settlements but none are worthy of credit as they are irrelevant to carrying out the survey.

**Did you agree with the rank order: 2, 1, and 3?**

World map

Glossary

Index

Acknowledgements

© Collins Bartholomew Ltd 2015

### Abbreviations of Country Names

**SOUTH AMERICA**
- FR.G. FRENCH GUIANA
- GUY. GUYANA
- SUR. SURINAME

**AFRICA**
- B. BURUNDI
- BE. BENIN
- BUR. BURKINA FASO
- CAM. CAMEROON
- C.D'I. CÔTE D'IVOIRE
- EQ. G. EQUATORIAL GUINEA
- GH. GHANA
- R. RWANDA
- T. TOGO

**EUROPE**
- A. ANDORRA
- ALB. ALBANIA
- AUS. AUSTRIA
- BEL. BELGIUM
- BELA. BELARUS
- B.H. BOSNIA & HERZEGOVINA
- CR. CROATIA
- CZ. CZECH REPUBLIC
- DEN. DENMARK
- EST. ESTONIA
- GER. GERMANY
- H. HUNGARY
- K. KOSOVO
- LAT. LATVIA
- LITH. LITHUANIA
- LUX. LUXEMBOURG
- M. MONTENEGRO

- MA. MACEDONIA
- MO. MOLDOVA
- NETH. NETHERLANDS
- RU. RUSSIA
- S. SLOVENIA
- SER. SERBIA
- SL. SLOVAKIA
- SW. SWITZERLAND

**ASIA**
- AR. ARMENIA
- AZ. AZERBAIJAN
- CYP. CYPRUS
- GEO. GEORGIA
- IS. ISRAEL
- JOR. JORDAN
- LEB. LEBANON
- U.A.E. UNITED ARAB EMIRATES

International boundaries in the sea shown on this map indicate ownership of islands and island groups only. They do not infer the alignments of legal maritime boundaries.

## Time Comparisons

Time varies around the world due to the earth's rotation causing different parts of the world to be in light or darkness at any one time. To account for this, the world is divided into twenty-four Standard Time Zones based on 15° intervals of longitude.

| 1:00am | 2:00am | 3:00am | 4:00am | 5:00am | 6:00am | 7:00am | 8:00am |

## Map Legend

- ■ Capital city
- ● Other town/city

**Scale 1 : 80 000 000**

0 — 1000 — 2000 — 3000 km

The table below gives examples of times observed at different parts of the world when it is 12 noon in the zone at the Greenwich Meridian (0° longitude). The time at 0° is known as Greenwich Mean Time (GMT).

| 1:00pm | 2:00pm | 3:00pm | 4:00pm | 5:00pm | 6:00pm | 7:00pm | 8:00pm | 9:00pm | 10:00pm | 11:00pm | midnight |
|---|---|---|---|---|---|---|---|---|---|---|---|
| Oslo Paris Kinshasa | Helsinki Cairo Cape Town | Moscow Riyadh Dodoma | U.A.E. Mauritius | Yekaterinburg Dushanbe Karachi | Novosibirsk Almaty Dhaka | Bangkok Jakarta | Ulan Bator Hong Kong Perth | P'yŏngyang Tōkyō Palau | Port Moresby Brisbane Canberra | Solomon Is Vanuatu New Caledonia | Marshall Is Fiji Wellington |

28

# Glossary

**Abiotic** Non-living parts of an ecosystem e.g. minerals, soil, air.

**Access** How easy it is to obtain goods or services. It can be measured in terms of cost, time or distance.

**African Union (AU)** Created in 2002, this organisation brings together the governments of 54 African states. The AU aims to develop peace, unity, and integration within the African continent.

**Aquifer** A rock structure which will hold water. Water can be abstracted from the rock by drilling wells and boreholes.

**Backwash** The retreat of a sea wave down the beach after the breaking of a wave.

**Bay** Part of the sea that fills a wide-mouthed opening in the coastline.

**Biome** A large ecosystem at the global scale where the climate and vegetation are uniform.

**Biosphere** The regions of the Earth and atmosphere where plants and animals live.

**Biotic** Living parts of an ecosystem e.g. plants and animals.

**Birth rate** The number of live births per year per 1000 population.

**Brownfield sites** Land, usually in urban areas, that was previously used for industry or commercial purpose and that has the potential for redevelopment once any derelict buildings have been removed and any contamination has been cleaned away.

**Capacity** The total amount of sediment or load that a stream or river can carry at any one time.

**Census** An official count of the population carried out by a government at regular intervals.

**Central Business District (CBD)** The CBD is the main commercial and shopping area of a town or city.

**Chain Stores** A series of shops owned by the same firm or company that sell the same goods.

**Climatologists** Scientists who specialise in the study of climate.

**Colony** A country that has been taken over and ruled by another country.

**Commercial farmer** A farmer whose main aim is to grow crops or keep livestock to sell for a profit.

**Common Agricultural Policy (CAP)** Strategies for the control and development of farming that have been adopted by all members of the European Union (EU).

**Competence** The maximum size of particle that a stream or river can carry.

**Comprehensive redevelopment** A housing policy that involves the clearing of areas of low-quality buildings and replacing them with a new higher-quality environment.

**Concordant** A concordant coastline is one where the rock layers are parallel to the coastline. The coast is often eroded at the same rate along its length so moves back evenly.

**Conservation** The care of species, resources and environments so that they will survive for future generations.

**Constructive waves** These waves are low and have a long wavelength. They are low energy waves that have a strong swash and weak backwash. They are usually associated with beach deposition.

**Continent** Any of the Earth's great expanses of continuous land e.g. North America.

**Convection currents** Differences in temperature of material beneath the plates of the Earth's crust leads to the creation of currents to transfer the heat. These currents move the plates above them. The term also applies when air is heated and rises in the atmosphere.

**Convectional rainfall** This occurs when land is heated up and the warm air above it rises, cools and condenses to give clouds and rain.

**Core area** A highly developed urban region to which people are attracted and which receives the most investment.

**Counter-urbanisation** The process by which an increasing number of people within a country live in the countryside instead of in towns and cities. This could be the result of natural increase and/or migration.

**Death rate** The number of deaths per year per 1000 population.

**Degradation** This is where human activity leads to a reduction in the quality of the natural environment e.g. deforestation, removal of topsoil, water pollution.

**Delta** A landform, often triangular in shape, which develops where a river meets a slow body of moving water such as a lake or ocean. Sediment builds up above the water level forcing the river to split into distributaries to form a delta.

**Demographer** A person who studies human populations – their size, distribution and composition.

**Dengue fever** Also known as breakbone fever, this is a tropical disease caused by mosquitoes which carry the dengue virus.

**Dependency ratio** A relationship between the number of people of working age (15–64) and the young dependents (0–14) and old dependents (65+) who depend on them for e.g. benefits, pensions.

**Deposition** The laying down of solid material such as mud or sand on the sea floor and river or lake beds.

**Desalination** The extraction of fresh water from salty sea water.

**Desert** A dry area, hot or cold, where the total annual precipitation is less than 250 mm.

**Desertification** The spread of desert conditions caused mainly by natural factors e.g. less rainfall in a region which was not previously a desert.

**Destructive waves** These waves are high and steep with a short wavelength. They are high energy waves that have a weak swash and strong backwash. They are usually associated with beach erosion.

**Direct payments** These are EU payments which are given directly to farmers who meet certain requirements of the EU for growing crops, keeping livestock or looking after the countryside.

**Discharge** The amount of water flowing across the width of a river at a given point.

It is usually measured in cubic metres per second (cumecs).

**Discordant** A discordant coastline is one where the rock layers are at 90 degrees to the coastline. Hard and soft rocks often cause headlands and bays to develop.

**Disposable income** This is money that people have to spend after taxes and insurance have been taken off their gross income. It can be referred to as 'take-home' pay.

**Distributaries** A stream or river channel resulting from the division of a larger stream channel. They are usually found in a delta.

**Division of labour** The way that a community shares the work between its members.

**Drainage basin** The area of land drained by a river and its tributaries (streams). This is also known as the catchment area.

**Drought** A long, continuous period of dry weather where any rainfall is below the average expected.

**Economic development** The progress made by a country as it develops its economy. Measurable economic indicators such as GDP per person, income per person are used to assess the economic development of a country.

**Ecosystem** A system of links between plants and animals (the living community) and the habitats where they live, including the non-living environment.

**Emigrants** People who permanently leave one country to live in another.

**Emirates** An emirate is a political territory ruled by an Arab emir. It also means principality. The United Arab Emirates is made up of seven emirates e.g. Dubai.

**Epicentre** The location at the surface of the ground above the focus or origin of an earthquake.

**Erosion** The wearing away and removal of rocks by the action of the agents of erosion – wind, water, ice, gravity.

**European Union (EU)** The EU is a group of European countries that have joined together to create an area for free trade of goods and services as well as movement of people. The common trading, economic and social policies are intended to be beneficial to all member countries of which there were 28 in 2014.

**Extensive farming** Where there are small inputs of capital and labour compared with the large amount of land used e.g. cattle-rearing. Yields per hectare are low.

**Fauna** Animals (including birds and insects) of an area.

**Fertility rate** In a country or region the average number of children a woman will have in her lifetime.

**Flood plain** An area next to a river that would be affected by flooding if the river overflowed its banks.

**Flora** Plants of an area.

**Focus** The location of the source of an earthquake below the ground; also called the origin.

**Food and Agricultural Organisation (FAO)** The FAO, based in Rome, is part of the United Nations. The organisation was created in 1945 to lead UN efforts to defeat hunger in both LEDCs and MEDCs.

**Free trade** The movement of goods and services within a country or trade group which does not require the payment of custom duties.

**Glacial** To do with ice, its movements and the features formed by it.

**Globalisation** The expansion of a company from its original country to a position where it has branches in many countries. These have an important influence on global trade.

**GNI per capita (person)** The Gross National Income divided by the population of the country to produce the Average Gross Income per person.

**Gorge** A deep, narrow valley with steep, rocky sides often with a stream or river flowing through it.

**Grants** A sum of money given to an individual or organisation for a specific purpose.

**Gross Domestic Product (GDP)** The total value of all the goods and services produced in a country in one year by all the people living in that country.

**Gross Domestic Product (GDP) per person** The total value of all the goods and services produced in a country in one year by all the people living in that country, divided by the population. It is a measure of wealth.

**Gross National Income (GNI)** The total value of goods and services produced by the people of a country in one year whether or not they are living there at the time.

**Hard engineering** These are expensive imposing structures that have a major impact on landscapes while providing flood control e.g. dams.

**Headland** A point of higher land jutting out into the sea, usually made of a resistant rock such as granite.

**High order** Goods or services that are bought infrequently and are expensive.

**High order settlements** Settlements, usually towns and cities, which provide goods and services that are bought infrequently and that are expensive so people are willing to travel a long way to buy or use them.

**HIV/AIDS** Human Immunodeficiency Virus (HIV) is a sexually transmitted infection (STI). The virus attacks the immune system and when this stops working the person has Acquired Immune Deficiency Syndrome (AIDS). This is usually fatal.

**Hot spots** A part of the Earth's crust which is thin enough to let magma through to form a volcano. Most volcanoes that are not at hot spots are at plate boundaries.

**Hydro-electric power (HEP)** Electricity generated by using moving water to turn turbines.

**Hydrograph** A graph which shows the pattern of a river's discharge. It is measured in cubic metres per second (cumecs) over a period of time.

**Impermeable** These rocks do not allow water to pass through. They are watertight e.g. clay.

**Independence** When a government takes on sole responsibility for making decisions about how to run the country it governs.

**Indigenous** The original inhabitants of a region or country before colonisation by people from other countries e.g. Aborigines in Australia.

**Industrial** To do with factories and manufacturing.

**Industrial Revolution** The period of time in a country or region's development when it changes from being mainly a rural agricultural society with small-scale cottage industries to one that is based on large-scale manufacturing industry in urban areas.

**Infrastructure** The pattern of communication and transport links, power supplies, administrative, health, education and other services necessary for economic development.

**Insolation** The amount of sun's energy reaching the Earth's surface.

**Intensive farming** Where there are large inputs of capital and labour compared with the small amount of land used e.g. battery hen farming. Yields per hectare are high.

**Internally-displaced people (IDP)** People who are forced to leave their homes but who are not refugees because they stay within the country's borders.

**Isobar** A line on a map joining places of equal pressure.

**Isohyet** A line on a map joining places of equal rainfall.

**Isotherm** A line on a map joining places of equal temperature.

**Lagoon** A bay or sea inlet that is partly enclosed by a spit or wholly enclosed by a sand bar.

**Lahars** A volcanic mudflow that contains a mixture of rocky debris, ash and water. It usually flows down a river valley from a volcano.

**Land-locked** An area or country whose borders are surrounded by land so there is no direct access to a sea or ocean.

**Lateral erosion** Where a stream or river wears away the sides and banks on each side of the channel.

**Lava** Magma that has escaped from beneath the Earth's crust and has flowed onto the surface.

**LEDCs** Less economically developed countries as defined by the Brandt report (1980).

**Leeward** The side of a hill or mountain that is sheltered from the direction the wind is coming from.

**Longshore drift** The zig-zag movement of sediment along a shore caused by waves going up the beach at an oblique angle (swash) and returning at right angles (backwash).

**Low order** Goods or services that are bought frequently and which are usually cheap.

**Low order settlements** Settlements, usually villages and hamlets, that provide goods and services that are bought frequently and are cheap so people are only willing to travel a short distance to buy or use them.

**Magma** Molten rock found beneath the Earth's crust.

**MEDCs** More economically developed countries as defined by the Brandt report (1980).

**Meteorologists** Scientists who specialise in the study of weather.

**Metropolitan** Refers to a single urban settlement of outstanding size and importance which has absorbed other urban areas. It is often the capital city of a country. The Greater Tokyo Metropolitan area is the largest with about 35 million people.

**Mudflows** A mass-movement of rocks and soil down a slope that is often triggered by heavy rain. Volcanic ash often develops into mud flows.

**Multiplier effect** This describes how one economic activity sets up a chain reaction whereby other activities develop in the area because of it. Multiplier effects can be positive or negative.

**Net migration** The difference between the number of people moving into a country (immigrants) and the number of people moving out of a country (emigrants).

**Newly Industrialising Countries (NIC)** These countries, mostly based in south-east Asia showed rapid growth in the late 20th century, largely through the creation and expansion of transnational companies based on modern technology and IT.

**Nomadic** People, usually farmers, who move from place to place seasonally to find good land or pasture.

**Origin** The location of the source of an earthquake below the ground; also called the focus.

**Orographic (relief) rainfall** This occurs when moist air is forced to rise by mountains. It then cools, condenses to give clouds and rain on the windward side. Once over the mountain the air descends, warms and is drier – this leeward side is said to be in the 'rain shadow.'

**Over-populated** When a country or region does not have enough resources to keep its people at a reasonable standard of living.

**Peninsula** A piece of land jutting into the sea and almost surrounded by it.

**Periphery** The rural surrounds of a region that people may wish to migrate from towards the core region because of low investment and low prospects.

**Permeable** These rocks allow water to pass through them e.g. limestone.

**Photosynthesise** The process whereby plants take the sun's energy with carbon dioxide and water to produce energy, oxygen and plant tissue.

**Plate boundaries** The edge of a tectonic plate where earthquakes, volcanoes and fold mountains are formed or take place.

**Population density** The average number of people in a given area e.g. per km$^2$.

**Population distribution** The way in which the population is spread out over an area, region, country, continent or the world.

**Porous** These rocks contain many small air spaces e.g. chalk. Most porous rocks are permeable.

**Precipitation** Any form of water falling on the Earth's surface from the atmosphere. The main categories are dew, fog, frost, hail, mist, rain, sleet and snow.

**Prevailing winds** The direction from which the wind blows into an area for most of the year.

**Quality of life** The happiness, well-being and satisfaction of a person. Among the many factors that influence quality of life are the person's family, income and access to services.

**Range** The distance people are prepared to travel to buy a good or service e.g. low order goods and services have a small range; high order goods and services have a large range.

**Reclamation** To use or re-use resources that are serving no worthwhile purpose at present e.g. derelict sites in inner city areas, marshy land.

**Reservoir** A structure that involves building a dam across a river to create a water body or large lake behind it. The purpose of a reservoir is usually to provide a water supply or to control flooding.

**Residential** To do with housing.

**Retail Park** A shopping development situated outside a town or city that typically contains a large number of chain stores, food outlets and car parking spaces.

**Rural** To do with villages and the countryside.

**Rural depopulation** Also known as rural-urban migration, this is the fall in population of rural areas by migration or by a fall in birth rate as young people move away.

**Rural-urban fringe** The area on the very edge of a town or city where it meets the rural area or countryside.

**Sedentary** Farmers who are settled in one particular place.

**Sedimentary rock** Material that has been deposited by the force which originally carried it from elsewhere e.g. wind, water or ice. It can also consist of the accumulated remains of dead sea animals e.g. limestone.

**Self-sufficient** Needing no outside help in providing one's basic needs especially regarding the production of food.

**Shield volcanoes** A low flat volcano, like an upturned shield, made from runny basic lava.

**Shifting cultivation** A farming system often found in rainforests in LEDCs where a patch of land is cleared, crops are grown, then a patch is deserted until it regains its fertility.

**Social development** The progress made by a country as it develops its social aspect. Measurable social indicators such as divorce rates, health statistics, and degree of obesity indicate the social development of a country.

**Soft engineering** These are environmentally-friendly, inexpensive solutions which have the least impact on the landscape while providing flood control e.g. afforestation, overflow lakes.

**Sphere of influence** The area surrounding an activity that is influenced by it e.g. a sports centre or a local park. It is also called the catchment area.

**Squatter settlements** An area of makeshift housing that usually develops in unfavourable sites in and around an LEDC city. They are also known as 'shanty' towns.

**Standard of living** The factors that affect a person's quality of life and which can be measured. Many measures to do with a person's standard of living are to do with material possessions.

**Strato-volcanoes** A high steep-sided volcano made from thick acid lava.

**Subsidies** A benefit given to an individual or organisation usually in the form of a cash contribution or a reduction in tax to offset the full cost of the activity that the subsidy was provided for.

**Subsistence agriculture** A means of supporting life by being able to meet one's own basic needs of food, water and shelter.

**Subsistence farmer** A farmer whose aim is to support himself and his family by growing crops or keeping livestock to survive and meet their basic needs for food.

**Sustainable** Capable, by careful use and management, of being maintained over time for future generations to use or enjoy whilst meeting the needs of the present.

**Swash** The advance of a sea wave up a beach after the breaking of a wave.

**Tectonic plates** Rigid segments of rock that make up the Earth's crust. They meet at plate boundaries where earthquakes, volcanoes and fold mountains are created.

**Tenement** A building that is split up into several apartments or flats.

**Thermal power** Energy generated by heating water to make steam which then turns turbines to create electricity. The heat source can be coal, oil, gas, geothermal or nuclear.

**Threshold population** The number of people needed to justify the provision of a good or service.

**Transmigration** The relocation of a large number of people as a result of a government plan.

**Tsunami** A sea or tidal wave that is triggered by an undersea earthquake or volcanic eruption that displaces the water above it setting up a series of waves that build up to form a powerful devastating wave at the coast.

**Tundra** Areas in Alaska, northern Canada, northern Europe and Asia where the ground is permanently frozen for most of the year. Only lichen, moss, grasses and dwarf shrubs and trees can grow here.

**Under-populated** When a country or region has more resources available than are being used by the people living there.

**United Nations (UN)** An organisation created in 1945 and made up of delegates from almost all countries of the world. It deals with issues of global importance including those related to global peace and development.

**Urban** To do with towns and cities.

**Urban regeneration** The renewal of a declining part of a town or city by removing existing houses and buildings as well as redeveloping the area.

**Urban sprawl** The expansion of towns and cities into the surrounding rural area or countryside.

**Urbanisation** The process by which an increasing proportion of people live in towns and cities instead of the countryside. This could be the result of natural increase and/or migration.

**Vertical erosion** Where a stream or river flowing quickly down a steep gradient in an upland area wears away the bed at a faster rate than the valley sides, leading to a narrow V-shaped valley.

**Vulcanologists** Scientists who study volcanoes.

**Watershed** The boundary of a drainage basin. It is also known as a divide.

**Windward** The side of a hill or mountain that faces the direction the wind is coming from.

# Index

abiotic 184, 286
access 32, 286
Accra 41
afforestation 89
Afghanistan 15, 28, 29, 151
Africa 61, 62, 204, 270
African Union (AU) 153
agricultural systems 36, 146–7, 289 see also farming
Airport, Montego Bay 212, 213, 214
Albania 181
alluvium 80, 85
Amazon Basin 114, 118, 119, 120, 121, 147
Antarctica 184, 185
aquifers 174, 175, 286
Arctic 184
Arusha Declaration 164
Atlanta 50–1
atolls 98
attrition 80, 92
Australia 6, 10, 11, 32, 95, 98, 124

backwash 96, 286
Barcelona 47
barometers 248, 260
barrier reef 98, 235
bays 94, 286
biofuels 169
biomes 116, 124, 286
biosphere 116, 164, 165, 286
biotic 184, 286
birth rate 12–13, 16, 18, 29, 286
Blue Hole, Belize 98
Botswana 62, 112
Brazil 114, 119, 147
brownfield sites 50, 286
Burkina Faso 183

Cairo 48, 55
caldera 70, 286
California 186–7
capacity of rivers 81, 286
carbon dioxide 181, 132
Caribbean 98, 216
catchment area 42, 78–9, 90, 259, 287
census 28, 286
Central Business District (CBD) 46, 225, 242–3, 286
chain stores 229, 286
China 20–1, 25, 32, 141, 144–5, 177
cities 42, 46, 47, 48, 225, 226
climate 106, 110, 113–15, 130, 132, 197
climatologists 113, 286
clouds 109
coastal deposition 92, 96–7, 286
coastal erosion 92-5, 102–3, 104
coastal features 92, 94, 95, 96–7, 102
coasts 92–8, 100, 102–3

colony 20, 286
commercial farmers 146, 286
Common Agricultural Policy (CAP) 148, 286
competence (rivers) 81, 286
comprehensive redevelopment 49, 286
concordant coastline 93, 94, 286
condensation 78, 79
Congo, Democratic Republic 117, 119, 136, 169
conservation issues 184–5, 286
constructive waves 92, 198, 286
consumers 117, 184
continent 184, 286
contours 207, 208, 209, 211
convection currents 66, 67, 286
convectional rainfall 115, 286
coral reefs 98, 104, 235
core area (urban regions) 137, 286
corrasion (abrasion) 80, 92
counter-urbanisation 52, 286
crust 'bins' and 'factories' 67

dams 87, 89, 174, 175, 178, 179
Darfur 152–3
data collecting 106–8, 250–1
death rate 12–13, 16, 18, 286
decomposers 117, 184
degradation of land 126, 286
deltas 84, 85, 87, 286
demographers 29, 286
Demographic Transition Model 13
dengue fever 222–3, 286
dependency ratio 30, 286
depopulation, rural 52, 289
deposition 80, 85, 92, 96–7, 286
desalination 163, 174, 286
deserts 16, 36, 122–3, 124–5, 126–7, 286
  Dubai 166, 167
  Sahara 123, 126, 127
destructive waves 92, 286
direct payments (from EU) 148, 149, 286
discharge of rivers 78, 88, 287
discordant (coastline) 93, 94, 287
disposable income 160, 287
distributaries 84, 287
division of labour 147, 287
drainage basins 42, 78–9, 90, 259, 287
drought 36, 287
Dubai 166–7

earthquakes 64, 65, 67, 69, 72–3, 74–5, 236
ecological cities 183
economic development 134, 287
ecosystems 116–21, 184, 287
ecotourism 164, 165
Ecuador 120
Elbe river 90–1

emigrants 22, 287
emirates 166, 287
employment structure 138, 140–1
energy, renewable 169, 171, 172–3
epicentre (earthquakes) 64, 287
equatorial climate 114–15, 116–21, 270
erosion, coastal 92–7, 102–3, 104, 287
erosion, rivers 80–2, 287
Ethiopia 40
Etna, Mount 65
European Union (EU) 148, 287
evapotranspiration 78, 79

farming 119, 146–7, 148–9, 183, 286
   extensive 146, 287
   intensive 146, 288
   subsistence 56, 57, 146, 147, 220–1, 289
   urban 202–3
fauna 116, 124, 126, 127, 287
fertility rates 16, 287
flood plains 80, 84, 85, 88–9, 287
flora 116–17, 127, 287
focus (earthquakes) 64, 287
fold mountains 67
Food and Agricultural Organisation (FAO) 150, 287
food shortages 150–3
food webs 117, 121, 125
fossil fuels 168
fracking 168, 186–7
France 39, 169
free trade 142, 287

Galapagos Islands 165
geographical enquiry 239–40, 241, 243
geographical skills 195, 201, 208, 209–11, 213, 214
geothermal energy 71, 171, 172–3
glacial (ice) 70, 287
global warming 181, 132
globalisation 142–3, 287
gorges 82, 83, 287
gradients 210
Grand Canyon 82
grants 148, 149, 287
Great Barrier Reef 98, 235
greenhouse gases 132, 181
Gross Domestic Product (GDP) 14, 36, 134, 205, 287
Gross National Income (GNI) 134, 188, 287

Harare 200, 202–4
hard engineering 89, 102, 287
Hawaii 68, 69, 103
headlands 94, 95, 287
high order 42, 43, 287
HIV/AIDS 18, 62, 287
hot spots (Earth's crust) 68, 69, 287
Human Development Index (HDI) 135, 136
humidity 106, 107, 109, 111
hydraulic action 80, 84, 92
hydro-electric power (HEP) 169, 171, 172, 173, 287
hydrographs 88, 287
hydrological cycle 78, 176

hygrometer 106, 107, 111
hypotheses 247, 249, 254, 260

Iceland 32, 33, 70, 172–3
impermeable 175, 287
independence 136, 287
India 12, 141, 237, 246
indigenous 147, 287
Indonesia 71, 76–7, 119, 137, 189, 218–23
industrial processing 139, 154–5, 158, 287
Industrial Revolution 47, 141, 168, 180, 287
industry, locating 40, 46, 156–7, 159
infrastructure 54, 288
insolation 114, 288
internally-displaced people (IDPs) 153, 288
Ireland 42, 230–2
isobars, isohyets, isotherms 110, 288
Italy 30–1, 161

Jakarta 6, 48, 183
Jamaica 212–17
Japan 34–5

Kenya 38, 238
Kyoto Protocol 132

lagoons 96, 98, 104, 288
lahars 70, 288
land reclamation 34, 167, 288
land use, urban 46, 47, 202, 255
land-locked 16, 288
lateral erosion 80, 288
LEDCs 14, 46, 48, 72, 132, 288
   urban areas 52, 54, 55
leeward 198, 288
Leicester 224–9
Lesotho Highlands Water Project (LHWP) 178–9
levées 84, 85, 89
Lima 56–7, 197
limestone 93, 95, 98, 122
longshore drift 96, 97, 102, 131, 288
low order 42, 288

magma 65, 66, 67, 71, 288
Malaysia 119, 140
mangrove swamps 99, 217
mantle, Earth's 66, 67
map interpretation 195, 207, 211, 225
maps 194, 284–5
marine national park 217, 235
Mauritius 104–5, 161
meanders 84
MEDCs 14, 46, 49, 52, 72, 288
Merapi, Mount 71, 76
meteorologists 112, 288
metropolitan 50, 288
Mid-Atlantic Ridge 172
migration 11, 12, 22–7, 56–7
   international 26–7, 226, 267
net 12, 288
mining 36, 71, 125

Montego Bay 212–17
Monument Valley 122, 123
mosquitoes 222, 223
mudflows 70, 288
multiplier effect 162, 288
Mumbai 48, 54

Namibia 36–7
national parks 121, 164, 165, 206–7, 217, 235
New York 60, 161, 242–3
New Zealand 64, 71, 72, 110, 140, 236
Newly Industrialised Countries (NIC) 140, 288
Niger 16–17, 30
Nigeria 8–9
Nile, river 84, 87, 152
Nokia 144–5
nomadic 16, 288
nuclear power 169, 170, 191

ocean currents 122
oil 120, 121, 168, 186–7
Optimum Population Trust 7
origin (focus) of earthquakes 64, 287
over-population 6, 7, 8, 9
oxbow lakes 78, 84, 85

Pakistan Steel 158–9
peninsula 32, 288
periphery 137, 288
permeable 175, 288
Peru 56–7, 194, 197–8
Philippines 101, 151, 192
photosynthesis 116, 117, 184, 288
plant adaptation 116, 127
plate boundaries 66, 74, 76, 288
plate tectonics 66–7
plateaus 82, 207, 209
Poland 12, 43, 97
pollution 132, 154, 177, 180, 181, 187
population 20–1, 22–7, 28–31
    change 4, 12–13, 14–15, 16–19, 29
    density 32–7, 288
    distribution 32–7, 59, 288
    pyramids 28–9, 57, 237
porous rock 175, 288
ports 40, 44, 45, 100, 159
precipitation 78, 108, 288
pressure (weather) 110, 115, 123
prevailing winds 78, 96, 111, 122, 288
producers 117, 184

Qatar 26–7
quality of life 9, 22, 48, 204–5, 288
questionnaires 247, 251, 257–9, 274, 275

rain gauge 108, 253, 262
rainfall 78, 79, 110, 115, 176, 286
rainforest, tropical 114–15, 117, 118–19
range of settlement 42, 288
recycling 117, 192
relief features 67, 68, 82, 94–7, 208, 209

reservoirs 174, 175, 288
residential zones 46, 288
retail park 229, 288
Reunion 234
rice growing 219, 220, 221
Richter scale 64
ridges (relief) 67, 209
'Ring of Fire' 68, 70, 76
rivers 78, 80–2, 83, 86, 176, 208
    deposition 80, 85, 286
    floods, managing 86, 88–91
    investigating 244–5
    landforms created by 82-5
rural 38, 40, 42, 52, 289
rural-urban fringe 228, 289
Russia 18–19

safety, fieldwork 252
Sahel 126
saltmarsh 96
sampling 246, 247
sand bars, dunes, spits 92, 96, 97, 198–9
Sangster International Airport 212, 213, 214
Sardinia 44–5
scree 82
sea, work of 92–100, 102
sedentary 16, 289
sedimentary rock 95, 289
self-sufficient 40, 289
settlements 38–40, 41, 42–3, 44, 46–51, 271–8
Seychelles 163
Shanghai 32, 33, 48
shifting cultivation 146, 147, 289
Silicon Valley 139
Singapore 7, 20, 24, 112, 114
site and situation description 213
slums (shanty towns) 9, 49, 54, 56, 61, 289
social development 134, 289
soft engineering 89, 102, 289
solar power 169, 171
solution (corrosion) 80, 92
South Africa 22, 112, 141
sphere of influence 42, 79, 259, 289
squatter settlements 9, 49, 54, 56, 61, 289
St Helens, Mount 70
standard of living 22, 289
steelworks 156, 158–9
Stevenson Screen 106, 248
subsidies 148, 149, 289
subsistence agriculture 36, 289
sunshine recorder 108
sustainability 147, 182–3, 289
swash 96, 289

Tanzania 39, 174
tectonic plates 66, 67, 68, 289
temperature, measuring 107, 109
tenement blocks 47, 289
Thames, river floods 86
thermal power 170, 289
threshold population 42, 289

tourism 40, 87, 104, 125, 160–7, 233
  damage 269
  India 246
  investigating 246–7
  Jamaica 216–17
transmigration 137, 289
transnational corporations (TNCs) 143–5, 157
trees 116–17, 127
triangulation stations 207
tribal issues 119, 121
tropical rainforest 114–15, 116–21, 270
tropical storms 100, 101, 105
Tropics of Cancer and Capricorn 100, 114, 115, 123
tsunamis 100, 289
tundra 122, 184, 289
Tunisia 28, 141, 174
Twelve Apostles 95

under-population 6, 7, 10, 11, 289
United Arab Emirates 166, 167
United Nations (UN) 182, 289
United States of America 10, 29, 122–3, 191
urban 38, 46, 48–9, 51, 289
  farming 202–3
  growth 51, 54, 61
  land use 46, 47, 202, 255
  regeneration 49, 289
  settlements 40, 41, 44, 46–51
  sprawl 51, 228–9, 289
urbanisation 52–7, 289

valleys 80, 81, 82, 83, 209
vertical erosion 80, 81, 82, 289
Vietnam 93, 145
volcanoes 65, 68–9, 70–1, 73, 76–7, 129
  shield 65, 67, 68, 289
  strato (conical) 65, 67, 70, 289
vulcanologists 73, 289

wars 57, 136, 151, 152
water cycle 78, 176
water management 174, 176–7
water table 175
waterfalls 83
watershed (divide) 79, 289
waves 92, 171
weather 106–12, 196, 248, 249
wind 108, 100, 111, 169, 171, 249, 262
windward 198, 289

Zimbabwe 58, 151, 174, 200–4

94

# Acknowledgements

The author and publishers acknowledge the following sources of copyright material and are grateful for the permissions granted. While every effort has been made, it has not always been possible to identify the sources of all the material used, or to trace all copyright holders. If any omissions are brought to our notice, we will be happy to include the appropriate acknowledgements on reprinting.

**Text Permissions**

p.5 from article October 2011, NBC News; p.7 courtesy of Population Matters, using data from the Global Footprint Network; p.8 reproduced with permission from the Lonely Planet website www.lonelyplanet.com © 2015 Lonely; p.11 adapted from article by Peter Ryan, January 2014, Reproduced by permission of the Australian Broadcasting Corporation – Library Sales © 2014 ABC; p.15 Aunohita Mojumdar for Woman's News Network; p.19 from article by Fred Weir, 2006, Christian Science Monitor; p.19 from article by Charles Clover, December 2012, Financial Times; p.21 adapted from article by Harry Davies, December 2013, The Independent; pp.22, 24, 65, 75, 86, 119, 121, 185 The Times/News Syndication; pp.25, 77 © Telegraph Media Group Limited 2014; p.34 www.diercke.com © westermann, Braunschweig; pp.39, 240, 267-273 reproduced by permission of Cambridge International Examinations; p.50 Atlanta BeltLine, Inc; p.57 Copyright Guardian News & Media Ltd 2010; p.82 excerpt from The Lost Continent: travels in small-town America by Bill Bryson. Copyright © 1989 by Bill Bryson. Reprinted by permission of The Random House Group Limited, HarperCollins Publishers, and Anchor Books, Random House Canada; p.93 ecoRI News; p.93 Inter Press Service; p.101 CNN; p.103 CBS News; p.105 AlertNet (Thompson Reuters) on AllAfrica.com; p.120 reproduced with permission from Ecuador & Galapagos Islands 9 © 2012 Lonely Planet; p.144 Nokia; p.145 Gigaom.com; p.145 Vietnam News p.145 with permission of Fonearena.com; p.145 from article by Mark Wembridge, Maija Palmer and Chris Bryant, September 2011, Financial Times; p.162 from The Final Call by Leo Hickman, published by Eden Project Books, reprinted by permission of The Random House Group Limited; p.164 Travel Daily News; p.203 with permission from Harare News; p.243 ©AA Media Limited 2015/Openstreetmap.org © OpenStreetMap contributors

**Image Permissions**

pp.1l, 3 David Ball/Alamy; p.1c Ron Ellis/Shutterstock; p.1r Tom Stoddart Archive/Getty Images; p.4 thefinalmiracle/iStock/Getty Images; p.5 TED ALJIBE/Getty Images; p.5 cartoon China Daily; p.6 frans lemmens/Alamy; p.11 Andrew Bain/Lonely Planet Images/Getty Images; p.17 Boureima/HAMA - AFP/Getty Images; p.22 ALBERTO LOWE/Reuters/Corbis; p.23 Mauro Seminara/AFP/Getty Images; p.27 Amos Chapple/Lonely Planet Images/Getty Images; p.31br David Litschel/Alamy; p.31l xPACIFICA/Alamy; p.31tr Randy Olson/National Geographic Creative/Corbis; p.35c DAJ/Getty Images; p.35t Marco Betti/Alamy; p.35b Shogoro/amana images/Getty Images; p.38l courtesy of The Clwydd-Powys Archaeological Trust (ref. 06-C-0043); p.38r Ted Spiegel/National Geographic/Getty Images; p.40 Ariadne Van Zandbergen/ Alamy; p.48 epa european pressphoto agency b.v./Alamy; p.51 Bildarchiv Monheim GmbH/Alamy; p.54l audioscience/Shutterstock; p.54r Alexander Mazurkevich/Shutterstock; p.56 Paul Stringer/Shutterstock; p.56 Christian Vinces/Shutterstock; p.62 Mike Goldwater/Alamy; p.63 Ron Ellis/Shutterstock; p.69 James L. Amos/Corbis; p.70t Vince Streano/CORBIS; p.70c Paul A. Souders/CORBIS; p.70b Jon Helgason/Alamy; p.72t Nigel Spiers/Alamy; p.72b Tim Cuff/Alamy; p.75 Pascal Deloche/Getty Images; p.76 Adek Berry/AFP/Getty Images; p.77 Ulet Ifansasti/ Getty Images; p.82l Annette Kiesow/Stockimo/Alamy; p.82r sumikophoto/ Shutterstock; p.84 David Wootton Alamy; p.89t Andrew Zarivny/Shutterstock; p.89b ImageRite/Alamy; p.91l epa european pressphoto agency b.v/Alamy; p.91tr TOBIAS SCHWARZ/Reuters/Corbis; p.91br Sara Winter/Alamy; p.93 Albanpix; p.95 Thomas Enguehard/Wikimedia; p.97 NASA; p.98l Atmotu Images/Alamy; p.98c David Ball/Alamy; p.98r Ian Bottle/Alamy; p.98l Stuart Chape; p.101 Bryan Denton/Corbis; p.103 Audrey McAvoy/AP/Press Association Images; p.106b Pablo Paul/Alamy; p.107r iStock/Getty Images; pp.108(1), 109l Dorling Kindersley Images; p.108(4) Jixin YU/Shutterstock; p.109r Eugene Shapovalov/Shutterstock; p.116 Robbie Shone/Alamy; p.119 Konrad Wothe/Getty Images; p.121 david tipling/Alamy; p.122 Alexey Stiop/Alamy; p.124tr Westend61 GmbH/Alamy; p.124l Michele Falzone/Alamy; p.125 Oleksandr Lysenko/Shutterstock; p.126 Mike P Shepherd/Alamy; p.127t blickwinkel/Alamy; p.127c Graeme Shannon/Shutterstock; p.127b Danita Delimont/Alamy; p.133 Tom Stoddart Archive/Getty Images; p.136r Images of Africa Photobank/Alamy; p.138bc RosaIreneBetancourt 4/Alamy; p.139bl MC_PP/Shutterstock; p.139br Jinx Photography/Alamy; p.139 Map used by permission of Silicon Valley Map www.siliconvalleymap.com; p.142 creator unknown; p.144 Patiwit Hungsang/Shutterstock; p.145l JOKER/Martina Hengesbach/ullstein bild via Getty Images, p.145r Raj Singh/Alamy; p.147 Hervé Collart/Sygma/Corbis; p.153 Brian Harris/Alamy; p.154tl © Frans Lemmens/Alamy; p.154tr Agencja Fotograficzna Caro/Alamy; p.154bl bibiphoto/Shutterstock; p154br Blend Images/Alamy; p.156 © Crown Copyright: Royal Commission on the Ancient & Historic Monuments of Wales: Aerofilms Collection; p.159 Horizons WWP/Alamy; p.163 Ace Stock Ltd/Alamy; p.164 Frank Herholdt/Getty Images; p.165l Tui De Roy/Minden Pictures/FLPA; p.165r Alberto Biscaro/Masterfile/Corbis; p.167 Richard Allenby-Pratt/Getty Images; p.168 Sinopix/Rex Features; p.169 travelpixs/Alamy; p.169 Aurora Photos/Alamy; p.173 Emil Thor Sigurdsson; p.174bl WaterAid/Marco Betti; p.175 Paul Glendell/Alamy; p.176 cartoon from the May 2002 calendar of the Water & Sanitation Program (World Bank) p.177t National Geographic Image Collection/Alamy; p.177b Amit Dave/Reuters/ Corbis; p.179 Walter Dhladhla, staff AFP/Getty Images; p.180tl Aflo Co. Ltd/ Alamy; p.180tr ZUMA Press, Inc./Alamy; p.180bl KHALED DESOUKI/ AFP/Getty Images; p.180br Greg Blok/Shutterstock; p.182 Natalia Bratslavsky/ Shutterstock; p.183t John Isaac/UN Photo Library; p.183b Wolfgang Kaehler/ Corbis; p.187 Christopher Halloran/Shutterstock; p.192l Frederic Soreau/Getty Images; p.197 steve estvanik/ Shutterstock; p.199tr Paul Kingsley/Alamy; p.203 Wayne Hutchinson/Alamy; p.204 Tsvangirayi Mukwazhi/AP/PAPhotos; p.213 AbbieImages/iStock/Getty Images; p.217t Ian G Dagnall/Alamy; p.217b Monetgo Bay Marine Park www.mbmp.org; p.226 ALANDAWSONPHOTOGRAPHY/Alamy; p.239 michaeljung/Shutterstock; p.240 geogphotos/Alamy; p.243 Phil Degginger/ Alamy; p.250l Riccardo Sergnese/Alamy; p.250tr Chris Willson/Alamy; p.250cr Richard G. Bingham II/Alamy; p.250br Peter Treanor/Alamy; p.252 AsiaTravelCollection/Alamy; p.265 aberCPC/Alamy; p.266l DENIS CHARLET/ AFP/Getty Images; p.266r Rainer Albiez/Getty Images

Other photographs throughout are reproduced with kind permission of the authors.

## Map permissions

p.39t extract from map 1710E Séries Bleue Guémené-sue-Scoff, (c) IGN-Paris-2015; p.39b reproduced by permission of Cambridge International Examinations; p.99 map based on Deltares, from the National Oceanic and Atmospheric Administration website; p.81 (River Usk 1:25000) , p.148 (Horncastle map 1:25000), p.206 (North York Moors 1:25000), pp.224, 225, 228 (Leicester, Coventry, Rugby 1:50000) Ordnance Survey maps © Crown copyright 2015, OS Licence Number 100001679; p.104 Mauritius 1:25000 (extract no 1220/Port Louis) map printed by Ordnance Survey 2000 © Government of Mauritius 1989; p.194 Monsferu, Peru 1:50000 (Chiclayo) prepared by Army Map Service (SX), Corps of Engineers, US Army, Washington DC, 1967; p.200 Harare, Zimbabwe 1:50000 (Lake Chivero) published by the Surveyor General, Zimbabwe 1994; p.212 National Land Agency, Survey & Mapping Division, Jamaica; p.218 BAKOSURTANAL, the Indonesian National Coordinating Agency for Surveys and Mapping; p227 ©AA Media Limited 2015 © Crown copyright and database rights 2005 Ordnance Survey. 100021153; p.230 Ordnance Survey of Ireland (OSi) from Discovery Series 6, 1:50000; p.238 Ewaso Kedong, Kenya 1:50000 (Lumuru) published for the Kenyan government by the British Government's Ministry of Overseas Surveys, copyright 1976 Kenyan Governement; p.243 ©AA Media Limited 2015/Openstreetmap.org © OpenStreetMap contributors; p284 world map © Collins Bartholomew Ltd, 2015

## Text Permissions CD

Topics 6, 17, 18 The Times/News Syndication; Topic 46 Source, Geographical skills 2: The World Factbook (Central Intelligence Agency); Topic 59 the Sunday Nation

## Image permissions CD

A.1.6 Stu Forster/Getty Images; A.1.CSl Shaun Botterill – FIFA via Getty Images; A.1.CSr Robert Harding Picture Library Ltd/Alamy; A.2.17 Wead/Shutterstock; A.2.20l Jon Helgason/Alamy; A.2.CS epa european pressphoto agency b.v./ Alamy; A.2.24 Niagara Falls map from Natural resources Canada under Open Governement Licence – Canada; A.2.24 Stuart Currie; A.2.34 Pablo Paul/ Alamy; A.2.35 Dorling Kindersley Images; A.2.39 Nick Greaves/Alamy; A.2.42 photo reproduced from World Soils by EM Bridges, Cambridge University Press, 1970; A.3.50 Peter Mah/Thinkstock/Getty Images; A.3.59 MyLoupe/UIG/Getty Images

All other photographs on CD used with kind permission of the authors

Artworks throughout by Kathy Baxendale, Mike Adams and Pete Smith (Beehive)

The publisher would like to thank the following people who assisted in reviewing this book: Graham Smith and Ernest Musa.